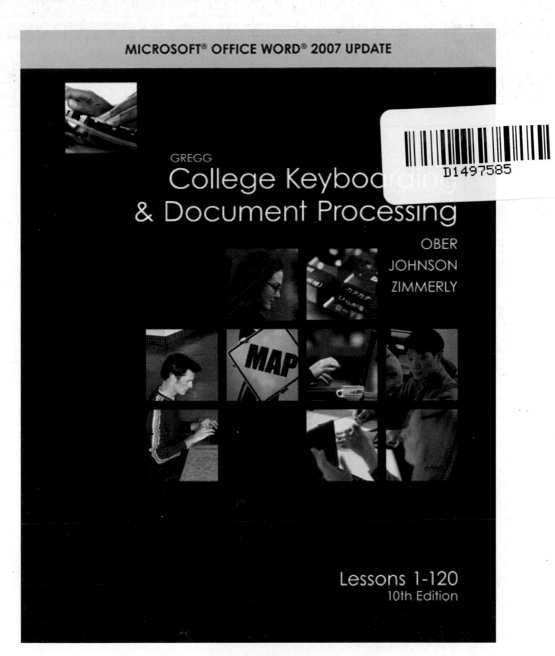

MICROSOFT® OFFICE WORD® 2007 UPDATE

GREGG

College Keyboarding & Document Processing

OBER
JOHNSON
ZIMMERLY

MAP

Lessons 1-120
10th Edition

Scot Ober
Ball State University

Jack E. Johnson
University of West Georgia

Arlene Zimmerly
Los Angeles City College

Visit the *College Keyboarding* Web site at **www.mhhe.com/gdp**

 McGraw-Hill Higher Education

Boston   Burr Ridge, IL   Dubuque, IA   New York   San Francisco   St. Louis
Bangkok   Bogotá   Caracas   Kuala Lumpur   Lisbon   London   Madrid   Mexico City
Milan   Montreal   New Delhi   Santiago   Seoul   Singapore   Sydney   Taipei   Toronto

McGraw-Hill
Higher Education

GREGG COLLEGE KEYBOARDING & DOCUMENT PROCESSING, MICROSOFT® OFFICE WORD® 2007 UPDATE, LESSONS 1-120
Published by McGraw-Hill, a business unit of The McGraw-Hill Companies, Inc., 1221 Avenue of the Americas, New York, NY, 10020. Copyright © 2008 by The McGraw-Hill Companies, Inc. All rights reserved. No part of this publication may be reproduced or distributed in any form or by any means, or stored in a database or retrieval system, without the prior written consent of The McGraw-Hill Companies, Inc., including, but not limited to, in any network or other electronic storage or transmission, or broadcast for distance learning.

Some ancillaries, including electronic and print components, may not be available to customers outside the United States.

This book is printed on acid-free paper.

4 5 6 7 8 9 0 BAN/BAN 0 9

ISBN   978-0-07-337217-4
MHID   0-07-337217-X

Vice President/Editor in Chief: *Elizabeth Haefele*
Vice President/Director of Marketing: *John E. Biernat*
Developmental editor: *Alaina Grayson*
Marketing manager: *Keari Bedford*
Marketing manager: *Megan Gates*
Lead media producer: *Damian Moshak*
Media producer: *Benjamin Curless*
Director, Editing/Design/Production: *Jess Ann Kosic*
Project manager: *Marlena Pechan*
Freelance project manager: *Rebecca Komro*
Senior production supervisor: *Janean A. Utley*
Designer: *Marianna Kinigakis*
Media project manager: *Mark Dierker*
Typeface: *11/12 Times Roman*
Compositor: *Aptara*
Printer: *45# Pub Matte, R.R.Donnelley*

Credits: The credits section for this book appears after the index and is considered an extension of the copyright page.

Library of Congress Cataloging-in-Publication Data

Ober, Scot, 1946-
    Gregg college keyboarding & document processing. Lessons 1-120 / Scot Ober, Jack E. Johnson, Arlene Zimmerly. — 10th ed.
        p. cm.
    Rev. ed. of: Gregg college keyboarding & document processing. Lessons 1-120 / Scot Ober ... [et al.].
    Includes index.
    ISBN: 0-07-296338-7 (spiral-bound : acid-free paper)
    1. Word processing—Problems, exercises, etc. 2. Keyboarding—Problems, exercises, etc.
3. Commercial correspondence—Problems, exercises, etc. 4. Report writing—Problems, exercises, etc. I. Johnson, Jack E. II. Zimmerly, Arlene. III. Title.
ZA52.3 .G74 2006
652.3'0076--dc22

                                                                    2004059728

The Internet addresses listed in the text were accurate at the time of publication.
The inclusion of a Web site does not indicate an endorsement by the authors or McGraw-Hill, and McGraw-Hill does not guarantee the accuracy of the information presented at these sites.

www.mhhe.com

CONTENTS

PART ONE: The Alphabet, Number, and Symbol Keys

PART TWO
Basic
Business
Documents

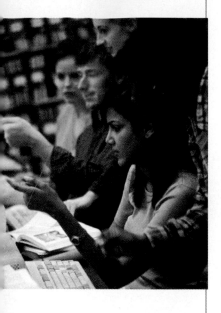

PART THREE:
Reports, Correspondence, and Employment Documents

PART FOUR: Advanced Formatting

PART FIVE:
Specialized
Applications

PART SIX:
Using and Designing Business Documents

ABOUT KEYBOARDING

Each day the world becomes more and more technologically advanced. As a result, learning new skills for the world of work is even more important.

One such skill that can prepare you for virtually any job in the world is keyboarding. From accountants to zoologists and every occupation in between, the ability to quickly and accurately type information is an essential skill that can increase your chances of being hired (or getting your dream job).

Formerly referred to as "typing," keyboarding is the act of entering data by means of designated computer keys. Today, as we rely more and more on computers to handle everyday work and leisure activities, the ability to accurately convey information is a necessity. So, whether you are e-mailing a relative, developing a class presentation, or downloading map directions, keyboarding knowledge can make the job easier.

Gregg College Keyboarding & Document Processing Lessons 1–120, 2007 Update Edition, is a multi-component instructional program designed to give the student and the instructor a high degree of flexibility and a high degree of success in meeting their respective goals. For student and instructor convenience, the core components of this instructional system are available in either a kit format or a book format. *Gregg College Keyboarding Lessons 1–20, 10th Edition,* is also available for the development of touch-typing skills for use in shorter computer keyboarding classes.

The Kit Format

Gregg College Keyboarding & Document Processing Lessons 1–120, 2007 Update Edition, provides a complete kit of materials for both courses in the keyboarding curriculum generally offered by colleges. Each kit, which is briefly described below, contains a softcover textbook and a student word processing manual.

Kit 1: Lessons 1–60. This kit provides the text and word processing manual for the first course. Since this kit is designed for the beginning student, its major objectives are to develop touch control of the keyboard and proper typing techniques, to build basic speed and accuracy, and to provide practice in applying those basic skills to the formatting of reports, letters, memos, tables, and other kinds of personal and business communications.

Kit 2: Lessons 61–120. This kit provides the text and word processing manual for the second course. This course continues developing of basic typing skills and emphasizes the formatting of various kinds of business correspondence, reports, tables, electronic forms, and desktop publishing projects from arranged, unarranged, and rough-draft sources.

The Book Format

For the convenience of those who wish to obtain the core instructional materials in separate volumes, *Gregg College Keyboarding & Document Processing Lessons 1–120, 2007 Update Edition,* offers textbooks for the first course: *Gregg College Keyboarding & Document Processing Lessons 1–60, 2007 Update Edition,* or *Gregg College Keyboarding Lessons 1–20, 10th Edition.* For the second course, *Gregg College Document Processing Lessons 61–120, 2007 Update Edition* is offered, and for the two-semester course, *Gregg College Keyboarding & Document Processing Lessons 1–120, 2007 Update Edition* is available. In each instance, the content of the textbooks is identical to that of the corresponding textbooks in kit format. Third-semester instruction is available in *Gregg College Document Processing Lessons 121–180.*

Supporting Materials

Gregg College Keyboarding & Document Processing Lessons 1–120, 2007 Update Edition, includes the following additional components:

Instructional Materials. Supporting materials are provided for instructor use with either the kits or the textbooks. The special Instructor Wraparound Edition (IWE) offers lesson plans and reduced-size student pages to enhance classroom instruction. Distance-learning tips, instructional methodology, adult learner strategies, and special needs features are also included in this wraparound edition. Solution keys for all of the formatting exercises in Lessons 1–180 are contained in separate booklets used with this program. Finally, test booklets are available with the objective tests and alternative document processing tests for each part.

Computer Software. PC-compatible computer software is available for the entire program. The computer software provides complete lesson-by-lesson instruction for the entire 120 lessons.

Structure

Gregg College Keyboarding & Document Processing, 2007 Update Edition, opens with a two-page part opener that introduces students to the focus of the instruction. Objectives are presented, and opportunities within career clusters are highlighted. The unit opener familiarizes students with the lesson content to be presented in the five lessons in the unit.

Every lesson begins with a Warmup that should be typed as soon as students are settled at the keyboard. In the New Keys Section, all alphabet, number, and symbol keys are introduced in the first 20 lessons. Drill lines in this section provide the practice necessary to achieve keyboarding skills.

An easily identifiable Skillbuilding section can be found in every lesson. Each drill presents to the student a variety of different activities designed to improve speed and accuracy. Skillbuilding exercises include Technique Timings, Diagnostic Practice, Paced Practice, Progressive Practice, MAP (Misstroke Analysis and Prescription), and Timed Writings, which progress from 1 to 5 minutes in length.

Many of the Skillbuilding sections also include a Pretest/Practice/Posttest routine. This routine is designed to build speed and accuracy skills as well as confidence. The Pretest helps identify speed and accuracy needs. The Practice activities consist of a variety of intensive enrichment drills. Finally, the Posttest measures improvement.

Part 1

The Alphabet, Number, and Symbol Keys

Keyboarding in Arts, Audio, Video Technology, and Communications Services

Occupations in this cluster deal with organizing and communicating information to the public in various forms and media. This cluster includes jobs in radio and television broadcasting, journalism, motion pictures, the recording industry, the performing arts, multimedia publishing, and the entertainment services. Book editors, computer artists, technical writers, radio announcers, news correspondents, and camera operators are just a few jobs within this cluster.

Qualifications and Skills
Strong oral and written communication skills and technical skills are necessary for anyone in communications and media. Without a doubt, competent keyboarding skill is extremely advantageous.

Working in the media requires creativity, talent, and accurate use of language. In journalism, being observant, thinking clearly, and seeing the significance of events are all of utmost importance. Announcers must have exceptional voices, excellent speaking skills, and a unique style. The ability to work under pressure is important in all areas of media.

Objectives

KEYBOARDING
• Operate by touch the letter, number, and symbol keys.
• Demonstrate proper typing technique.
• Use the correct spacing with punctuation.
• Type at least 28 words per minute on a 2-minute timed writing with no more than 5 errors.

TECHNICAL
• Answer correctly at least 90 percent of the questions on an objective test.

Goals

- Type at least 30wpm/3'/5e
- Format one-page business reports

Starting a Lesson

Each lesson begins with the goals for that lesson. Read the goals carefully so that you understand the purpose of your practice. In the example at the left (from Lesson 26), the goals for the lesson are to type 30wpm (words per minute) on a 3-minute timed writing with no more than 5 errors and to format one-page business reports.

Building Straight-Copy Skill

Warmups. Each lesson begins with a Warmup that reinforces learned alphabet, number, and/or symbol keys.

Skillbuilding. The Skillbuilding portion of each lesson includes a variety of drills to individualize your keyboarding speed and accuracy development. Instructions for completing the drills are always provided beside each activity.

Additional Skillbuilding drills are included in the back of the textbook. These drills are intended to help you meet your individual goals.

Measuring Straight-Copy Skill

Straight-copy skill is measured in wpm. All timed writings are the exact length needed to meet the speed goal for the lesson. If you finish a timed writing before time is up, you have automatically reached your speed goal for the lesson.

Counting Errors. Specific criteria are used for counting errors. Count an error when:

1. Any stroke is incorrect.
2. Any punctuation after a word is incorrect or omitted. Count the word before the punctuation as incorrect.
3. The spacing after a word or after its punctuation is incorrect. Count the word as incorrect.
4. A letter or word is omitted.
5. A letter or word is repeated.
6. A direction about spacing, indenting, and so on, is violated.
7. Words are transposed.

(**Note:** Only one error is counted for each word, no matter how many errors it may contain.)

Determining Speed. Typing speed is measured in wpm. To compute wpm, count every 5 strokes, including spaces, as 1 "word." Horizontal word scales below an activity divide lines into 5-stroke words. Vertical word scales beside an activity show the number of words in each line cumulatively totaled. For example, in the illustration below, if you complete a line, you have typed 8 words. If you complete 2 lines, you have typed 16 words. Use the bottom word scale to determine the word count of a partial line. Add that number to the cumulative total for the last complete line.

```
23  Ada lost her letter; Dee lost her card.              8
24  Dave sold some of the food to a market.             16
25  Alva asked Walt for three more matches.             24
26  Dale asked Seth to watch the last show.             32
    |  1  |  2  |  3  |  4  |  5  |  6  |  7  |  8  |
```

Correcting Errors

As you learn to type, you will probably make some errors. To correct an error, press BACKSPACE (shown as ← on some keyboards) to delete the incorrect character. Then type the correct character.

If you notice an error on a different line, use the up, down, left, or right arrows to move the insertion point immediately to the left or right of the error. Press BACKSPACE to delete a character to the left of the insertion point, or DELETE to delete a character to the right of the insertion point. Error-correction settings in the GDP software determine whether you can correct errors in timed writings and drills. Consult your instructor for error-correction guidelines.

Typing Technique

Correct position at the keyboard enables you to type with greater speed and accuracy and with less fatigue. When typing for a long period, rest your eyes occasionally by looking away from the screen. Change position, walk around, or stretch when your muscles feel tired. Making such movements and adjustments may help prevent your body from becoming too tired. In addition, long-term bodily damage, such as carpal tunnel syndrome, can be prevented.

If possible, adjust your workstation as follows:

Chair. Adjust the height so that your upper and lower legs form a 90-degree angle and your lower back is supported by the back of the chair.
Keyboard. Center your body opposite the J key, and lean forward slightly. Keep your forearms horizontal to the keyboard.
Screen. Position the monitor so that the top of the screen is just below eye level and about 18 to 26 inches away.
Text. Position your textbook or other copy on either side of the monitor as close to it as vertically and horizontally possible to minimize head and eye movement and to avoid neck strain.

Using Microsoft Windows

If you are using *Gregg College Keyboarding & Document Processing Lessons 1–120, 2007 Update Edition,* you must know how to use a mouse, and you must know some basic information about Microsoft Windows. Use the Help feature in Windows to familiarize yourself with basic Windows commands.

Starting Your Program

Once you have completed the Getting Started section in your word processing manual, you are ready to begin Lesson 1. If you are using the *Gregg College Keyboarding & Document Processing Lessons 1–120, 2007 Update Edition* software (hereafter referred to as GDP), begin by starting Windows.

Next, start GDP by locating and clicking the Keyboarding group icon in your Windows program list to open the program group. (**Note:** If you are saving data to a data disk, you should insert it now.) If you are working at your school on a network, click the GDP Classes icon, click your class and then your name for the class list. If you are a new student, follow the directions on the screen to add yourself as a new student. Then follow the directions to log on and begin using GDP.

If you see any other icons or are working on a different installation of GDP, consult your instructor for help in logging on.

Part 2

Basic Business Documents

Each **Part Opener** is a two-page spread that provides a list of the part objectives and a special feature that focuses on the use of your keyboarding skills in various career clusters.

Keyboarding in Business and Administrative Services

Opportunities in Business and Administrative Careers

Occupations in the business and administrative services cluster focus on providing management and support services for various companies. The many positions found in this cluster include receptionist, bookkeeper, administrative professional or assistant, claim examiner, accountant, word processor, office manager, and chief executive officer.

Managers and administrators are in charge of planning, organizing, and controlling businesses. Management support workers gather and analyze data to help company executives make decisions. Administrative support workers perform a variety of

tasks, such as recordkeeping, operating office equipment, managing their own projects and assignments, and developing high-level integrated software skills as well as Internet research skills. Ideally, everyone in business should be patient, detail-oriented, and cooperative. Excellent written and oral communication skills are definitely an asset as well.

Many companies have been revolutionized by advances in computer technology. As a result, keyboarding skill provides a definite advantage for those who work in business and administrative services. Now, more than ever, success in the business world is dependent upon adaptability and education.

Objectives

KEYBOARDING
- Operate the keyboard by touch.
- Type at least 36 words per minute on a 3-minute timed writing with no more than 4 errors.

LANGUAGE ARTS
- Develop proofreading skills and correctly use proofreaders' marks.
- Use capitals, commas, and apostrophes correctly.
- Develop composing and spelling skills.

WORD PROCESSING
- Use the word processing commands necessary to complete the document processing activities.

DOCUMENT PROCESSING
- Format e-mail, business and academic reports, business letters in block style, envelopes, memos, and tables.

TECHNICAL
- Answer at least 90 percent of the questions correctly on an objective test.

49

Unit 1

Keyboarding:
The Alphabet

LESSON 1
A S D F J K L ;
ENTER   SPACE BAR

LESSON 2
H E O R

LESSON 3
M T P C

LESSON 4
RIGHT SHIFT V . W

LESSON 5
Review

2   UNIT ONE   Keyb

The **Unit Opener** helps you organize your study of unit concepts. The listing of the lessons clearly previews what will be taught in the unit.

New Keys   Lesson 4

Goals

* Touch-type the RIGHT SHIFT, V, period, and W keys
* Count errors
* Type at least 13wpm/1'/3e

A. Type 2 times.

A. WARMUP

1 the farmer asked her to feed the mares;
2 the late callers came to mop the floor;

NEW KEYS

B. Type each line 2 times.

Use the Sem finger.

SHIFT

B.   THE RIGHT SHIFT KEY

To capitalize letters on the left half of the keyboard:
1. With the J finger at home, press and hold down the RIGHT SHIFT key with the Sem finger.
2. Press the letter key.
3. Release the RIGHT SHIFT key and return fingers to home position.

3 ;;; ;A; ;A; ;;; ;S; ;S; ;;; ;D; ;D; ;;;
4 Art Alf Ada Sal Sam Dee Dot Flo Ted Tom
   Carl Chet Elsa Fred Sara Todd Elda
   Amos took Sara Carter to the races

      KEY

   f fvf vfv fff fvf fvf vfv fff fvf
     Eva vet Ava vat Eve ova Vel vee
   se Vera ever vast Reva dove vest
   ted for Vassar; Val voted for me

      KEY

   1.1 .1. 111 1.1 1.1 .1. 111 1.1
   ea. ea. sr. sr. Dr. Dr. Sr. Sr.
   t. A.D. p.m. Corp. amt. Dr. Co.
   t. Dave left. Sarah came home.

UNIT 1   Lesson 4   9

Color Coding is used in the early lessons to help you differentiate which finger is used. On the keyboard chart shown at the beginning of each new-key lesson, new keys are highlighted, previously learned keys are labeled but not highlighted, and unlearned keys are blank. You will have a sense of progress as you move through the 20 new-key lessons.

Handwritten examples are used to make lessons more realistic since many letters, reports, and so on, are originally prepared with pen and paper. Including handwritten manuscript also enhances your ability to accurately read and type at the same time.

```
22  tor inventor detector debtor orator doctor factor
23  lly industrially logically legally ideally really
24  ert convert dessert expert invert diverts asserts
25  ink shrink drink think blink clink pink sink rink
```

E. PROGRESSIVE PRACTICE: ALPHABET

If you are not using the GDP software, turn to page SB-7 and follow the directions for this activity.

F. HANDWRITTEN PARAGRAPH

F. Take two 1-minute timed writings. Review your speed and errors.

In this book you have learned the reaches for all alphabetic and number keys. You have also learned a few of the symbol keys. In the remaining lessons you will learn the other symbol keys. You will also build your speed and accuracy when typing.

G. DIAGNOSTIC PRACTICE: NUMBERS

If you are not using the GDP software, turn to page SB-5 and follow the directions for this activity.

H. 2-MINUTE TIMED WRITING

H. Take two 2-minute timed writings. Review your speed and errors.

Goal: At least 25wpm/2'/5e

```
32  From the tower John s... lose six big
33  planes could crash as the...
34  treetops on their way to...
35  was scheduled to begin v...
36  is no accident and that...
37  airports safely.
```

Strategies for Career Succe...

Goodwill Messages

Would you like to strengthen your relat...
unexpected goodwill message! Your e...
relationships.

Messages of congratulations or...
goodwill. These messages can be c...
ten note on a professional note car...

A note of congratulations migh...
promotion, etc.). My very best wis...
ring me to. . . . Your confidence a...

YOUR TURN Send a goodwill messa...

40 UNIT 4 Lesson 17

D. THE ! KEY

D. Exclamation is the shift of 1. Space 1 time after an exclamation point at the end of a sentence. Type each line 2 times.

Use the A finger.

```
16  aqa aqla aq!a a!!a a!!a Where! Whose! What! When!
17  Put those down! Do not move them! Leave it there!
18  He did say that! Jake cannot take a vacation now!
19  You cannot leave at this time! Janie will go now!
```

SKILLBUILDING

E. TECHNIQUE PRACTICE: SPACE BAR

E. Type the paragraph 2 times.

```
20  We will all go to the race if I win the one
21  I am going to run today. Do you think I will be
22  able to run at the front of the pack and win it?
```

F. 12-SECOND SPEED SPRINTS

F. Take three 12-second timed writings on each line. The scale below the last line shows your wpm speed for a 12-second timed writing.

```
23  Walking can perk you up if you are feeling tired.
24  Your heart and lungs can work harder as you walk.
25  It may be that a walk is often better than a nap.
26  If you walk each day, you may have better health.
    |  5  |  10  |  15  |  20  |  25  |  30  |  35  |  40  |  45  |  50
```

G. PACED PRACTICE

If you are not using the GDP software, turn to page SB-14 and follow the directions for this activity.

H. 2-MINUTE TIMED WRITING

H. Take two 2-minute timed writings. Review your speed and errors.

Goal: At least ...wpm/2'/5e

```
27  Katie quit her zoo job seven days after she           9
28  learned that she was expected to travel to four
29  different zoos in the first month of employment.     19
30  After quitting that job, she found an excellent      28
31  position which did not require her to travel much.   38
    |  1  |  2  |  3  |  4  |  5  |  6  |  7  |  8  |  9  |  10   48
```

UNIT 4 Lesson 16

Timed Writings are used to improve both accuracy and speed. Timed Writings measure how well you are progressing in keyboarding skill development. In addition, timed writings bolster your self-confidence and ability.

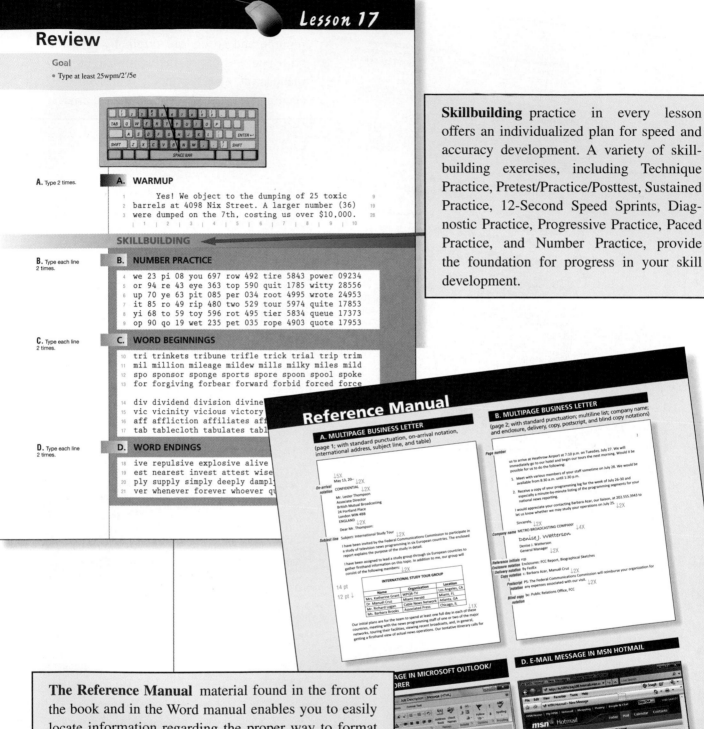

Lesson 17

Review

Goal
- Type at least 25wpm/2'/5e

A. Type 2 times.

A. WARMUP

```
1        Yes! We object to the dumping of 25 toxic        9
2  barrels at 4098 Nix Street. A larger number (36)      19
3  were dumped on the 7th, costing us over $10,000.      28
   | 1 | 2 | 3 | 4 | 5 | 6 | 7 | 8 | 9 | 10
```

SKILLBUILDING

B. Type each line 2 times.

B. NUMBER PRACTICE

```
4  we 23 pi 08 you 697 row 492 tire 5843 power 09234
5  or 94 re 43 eye 363 top 590 quit 1785 witty 28556
6  up 70 ye 63 pit 085 per 034 root 4995 wrote 24953
7  it 85 ro 49 rip 480 two 529 tour 5974 quite 17853
8  yi 68 to 59 toy 596 rot 495 tier 5834 queue 17373
9  op 90 qo 19 wet 235 pet 035 rope 4903 quote 17953
```

C. Type each line 2 times.

C. WORD BEGINNINGS

```
10 tri trinkets tribune trifle trick trial trip trim
11 mil million mileage mildew mills milky miles mild
12 spo sponsor sponge sports spore spoon spool spoke
13 for forgiving forbear forward forbid forced force

14 div dividend division divine
15 vic vicinity vicious victory
16 aff affliction affiliates aff
17 tab tablecloth tabulates tabl
```

D. Type each line 2 times.

D. WORD ENDINGS

```
18 ive repulsive explosive alive
19 est nearest invest attest wise
20 ply supply simply deeply damply
21 ver whenever forever whoever qu
```

Skillbuilding practice in every lesson offers an individualized plan for speed and accuracy development. A variety of skill-building exercises, including Technique Practice, Pretest/Practice/Posttest, Sustained Practice, 12-Second Speed Sprints, Diagnostic Practice, Progressive Practice, Paced Practice, and Number Practice, provide the foundation for progress in your skill development.

The Reference Manual material found in the front of the book and in the Word manual enables you to easily locate information regarding the proper way to format business letters, reports, e-mail messages, memoranda, and other forms of written communication. Elements such as line spacing and the placement of letterhead and body text are all illustrated in detail for your instructional support. In addition, 50 "must-know" rules for language arts in business contexts are included with examples in the Reference Manual to help improve writing skills.

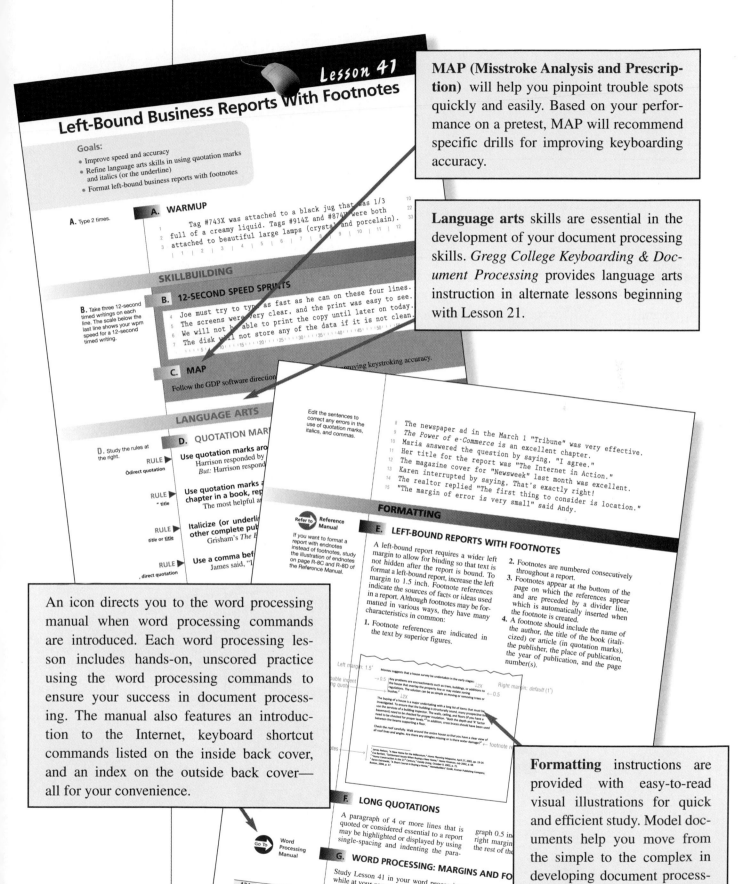

MAP (Misstroke Analysis and Prescription) will help you pinpoint trouble spots quickly and easily. Based on your performance on a pretest, MAP will recommend specific drills for improving keyboarding accuracy.

Language arts skills are essential in the development of your document processing skills. *Gregg College Keyboarding & Document Processing* provides language arts instruction in alternate lessons beginning with Lesson 21.

An icon directs you to the word processing manual when word processing commands are introduced. Each word processing lesson includes hands-on, unscored practice using the word processing commands to ensure your success in document processing. The manual also features an introduction to the Internet, keyboard shortcut commands listed on the inside back cover, and an index on the outside back cover—all for your convenience.

Formatting instructions are provided with easy-to-read visual illustrations for quick and efficient study. Model documents help you move from the simple to the complex in developing document processing skills.

Lesson 41

Left-Bound Business Reports With Footnotes

Goals:
- Improve speed and accuracy
- Refine language arts skills in using quotation marks and italics (or the underline)
- Format left-bound business reports with footnotes

A. Type 2 times.

A. WARMUP

Tag #743X was attached to a black jug that was 1/3
full of a creamy liquid. Tags #914Z and #874W were both
attached to beautiful large lamps (crystal and porcelain).

SKILLBUILDING

B. Take three 12-second timed writings on each line. The scale below the last line shows your wpm speed for a 12-second timed writing.

B. 12-SECOND SPEED SPRINTS

Joe must try to type as fast as he can on these four lines.
The screens were very clear, and the print was easy to see.
We will not be able to print the copy until later on today.
The disk will not store any of the data if it is not clean.

C. MAP

Follow the GDP software directions ... improving keystroking accuracy.

LANGUAGE ARTS

D. Study the rules at the right.

D. QUOTATION MARKS

RULE ▶ direct quotation

Use quotation marks aro...
Harrison responded by...
But: Harrison respond...

RULE ▶ " title

Use quotation marks a...
chapter in a book, rep...
The most helpful a...

RULE ▶ title or title

Italicize (or underli...
other complete pub...
Grisham's *The B...

RULE ▶ , direct quotation

Use a comma bef...
James said, "...

Edit the sentences to correct any errors in the use of quotation marks, italics, and commas.

8 The newspaper ad in the March 1 "Tribune" was very effective.
9 *The Power of e-Commerce* is an excellent chapter.
10 Maria answered the question by saying, "I agree."
11 Her title for the report was "The Internet in Action."
12 The magazine cover for "Newsweek" last month was excellent.
13 Karen interrupted by saying, That's exactly right!
14 The realtor replied "The first thing to consider is location."
15 "The margin of error is very small" said Andy.

Refer to Reference Manual

If you want to format a report with endnotes instead of footnotes, study the illustration of endnotes on page R-8C and R-8D of the Reference Manual.

FORMATTING

E. LEFT-BOUND REPORTS WITH FOOTNOTES

A left-bound report requires a wider left margin to allow for binding so that text is not hidden after the report is bound. To format a left-bound report, increase the left margin to 1.5 inch. Footnote references indicate the sources of facts or ideas used in a report. Although footnotes may be formatted in various ways, they have many characteristics in common:

1. Footnote references are indicated in the text by superior figures.

2. Footnotes are numbered consecutively throughout a report.

3. Footnotes appear at the bottom of the page on which the references appear and are preceded by a divider line, which is automatically inserted when the footnote is created.

4. A footnote should include the name of the author, the title of the book (italicized) or article (in quotation marks), the publisher, the place of publication, the year of publication, and the page number(s).

F. LONG QUOTATIONS

A paragraph of 4 or more lines that is quoted or considered essential to a report may be highlighted or displayed by using single-spacing and indenting the paragraph 0.5 in...
right margin...
the rest of the...

Go To Word Processing Manual

G. WORD PROCESSING: MARGINS AND FO...

Study Lesson 41 in your word processing manual. Comple...
while at your computer. Then format the jobs that follow.

124   UNIT 9   Lesson 41

The last document processing exercise in most units is designated as a Progress Check/Proofreading Check. Make it your goal is to have zero typographical errors when the GDP software first scores the document.

Special features are designed to enhance your study of keyboarding. The *Keyboarding Connection* features illustrate the importance of keyboarding skills outside of the classroom. The *Strategies for Career Success* features offer an employment-related narrative, including useful hints for succeeding in any career.

Correspondence
55-44

Personal-Business
Letter in Modified-
Block Style

Progress and Proofreading Check

Documents designated as Proofreading Checks serve as a check of your proofreading skill. Your goal is to have zero typographical errors when the GDP software first scores the document.

Assume that you have interviewed for the position mentioned in the previous letter and that you would now like to send a follow-up letter dated June 15, 20--, to Mr. Blair N. Scarborough, thanking him for the interview. Use the inside address, salutation, and closing lines shown in Correspondence 55-43 to create the follow-up letter below:

¶ Thank you for the time you spent with me, telling me about the Computer Specialist position with Wyatt. My interview with you reaffirmed my interest in working for Wyatt.

¶ I was very impressed with work done in your Information Processing department. The hardware and software you use for writing computer code and the people working in that department are very appealing to me.

¶ I believe my particular background and skills blend perfectly with this position. I hope to hear from you by the end of next week for a positive decision on my employment. Thank you for bringing me in for the interview.

Strategies for Career Success

Looking for a Job

... time! Start your job search early. Scan the Help Wanted section in major Sunday ... for job descriptions and salaries. The Internet provides electronic access to ... listings. If you are interested in a particular company, access its home page. ... ence librarian for handbooks (for example, *Occupational Outlook Handbook*), ... ications (for example, *Federal Career Opportunities*), and journals or ... field. Visit your college placement office. Sign up for interviews with ... in your field to get advice. Look for an internship or join a professional ... eld. Attend local chapter meetings to network with people in your

... n your job search will pay off!

... te for the *National Business Employment Weekly* at ... mentguide.com, which provides more than 45,000 national and

Ten-Key Numeric Keypad

Goal
• To control the ten-key numeric keypad keys.

Some computer keyboards have a separate ten-key numeric keypad located to the right of the alphanumeric keyboard. The arrangement of the keypad enables you to type numbers more rapidly than you can when using the top row of the alphanumeric keyboard.

To input numbers using the ten-key numeric keypad, you must activate the Num Lock (Numeric Lock) key. Usually, an indicator light signals that the Num Lock is activated.

On the keypad, 4, 5, and 6 are the home keys. Place your fingers on the keypad home row as follows:

• First finger (J finger) on 4
• Second finger (K finger) on 5
• Third finger (L finger) on 6

The keypad keys are controlled as follows:

• First finger controls 1, 4, and 7
• Second finger controls 2, 5, and 8
• Third finger controls 3, 6, 9, and decimal point

• Right thumb controls 0
• Fourth finger controls ENTER

Since different computers have different arrangements of ten-key numeric keypads, study the arrangement of your keypad. The illustration shows the most common arrangement. If your keypad is arranged differently from the one shown in the illustration, check with your instructor for the correct placement of your fingers on the keypad.

The Appendix contains instructions for the Ten-Key Numeric Keypad. Students practice entering numerical data using touch-typing techniques.

NEW KEYS

A. THE 4, 5, AND 6 KEYS

A. Use the first finger to control the 4 key, the second finger to control the 5 key, and the third finger to control the 6 key.

Keep your eyes on the copy.

Before beginning, check to be sure the Num Lock key is activated.

Type the first column from top to bottom. Next, type the second column, then type the third column. Press ENTER after typing the final digit of each number.

		454
	456	464
444	654	546
555	445	564
666	446	654
455	554	645
466	556	666
544	664	555
566	665	444
644	456	456
655	654	
456		

APPENDIX   Ten-Key Numeric Keypad

A-1

SKILLBUILDING

70wpm

Indexing is the ability of a word processor to accumulate a list of words that appear in a document, including page numbers, and then print a revised list in alphabetic order.

72wpm

When a program needs information from you, a dialog box will appear on the desktop. Once the dialog box appears, you must identify the option you desire and then choose that option.

74wpm

A facsimile is an exact copy of a document, and it is also a process by which images, such as typed letters, graphs, and signatures, are scanned, transmitted, and then printed on paper.

76wpm

Compatibility refers to the ability of a computer to share information with another computer or to communicate with some other apparatus. It can be accomplished by using hardware or software.

78wpm

Some operators like to personalize their desktops when they use Windows by making various changes. For example, they can change their screen colors and the pointer so that they will have more fun.

80wpm

Wraparound is the ability of a word processor to move words from one line to another line and from one page to the next page as a result of inserting and deleting text or changing the size of margins.

82wpm

It is possible when using Windows to evaluate the contents of different directories o___ ___reen at the very same time. You can then choose to ___ ___rticular file from one directory to anoth___

84wpm

List processing is a___ lists of data that c___ numeric order. A li___ is stored in one's s___

86wpm

A computer is a wo___ input and then pr___ computer performs___ programs, which ___

88wpm

The configurati___ processing sys___ used for enter___ one disk driv___

The back-of-the book skillbuilding routines are designed with YOU in mind. The Paced Practice skillbuilding paragraphs use an upbeat, motivational storyline with guidance in career choices. The Supplementary Timed Writings relate critical-thinking skills to careers.

SKILLBUILDING

Supplementary Timed Writing 3

Office employees perform a variety of tasks during their workday. These tasks vary from handling telephone calls to forwarding personal messages, from sending short e-mail messages to compiling complex office reports, and from writing simple letters to assembling detailed letters with tables, graphics, and imported data. Office workers are a fundamental part of a company's structure.

The office worker uses critical thinking in order to accomplish a wide array of daily tasks. Some of the tasks are more urgent than other tasks and should be completed first. Some tasks take only a short time, while others take a lot more time. Some tasks demand a quick response, while others may be taken up as time permits or even postponed until the future. Some of the tasks require input from coworkers or managers. Whether a job is simple or complex, big or small, the office worker must decide what is to be tackled first by determining the priority of each task.

When setting priorities, critical thinking skills are essential. The office worker evaluates each aspect of the task. It is a good idea to identify the size of the task, determine its complexity, estimate its effort, judge its importance, and set its deadline. Once the office worker assesses each task that is to be finished within a certain period of time, then the priority for completing all tasks can be set. Critical thinking skills, if applied well, can save the employer money or, if executed poorly, can cost the employer.

| 10
| 21
| 33
| 44
| 56
| 67
| 77
| 88
| 100
| 111
| 123
| 135
| 147
| 158
| 170
| 182
| 193
| 204
| 216
| 228
| 239
| 250
| 262
| 274
| 285
| 296
| 300

| 1 | 2 | 3 | 4 | 5 | 6 | 7 | 8 | 9 | 10 | 11 | 12

Reference Manual

Reference Manual

A. MAJOR PARTS OF A MICROCOMPUTER SYSTEM

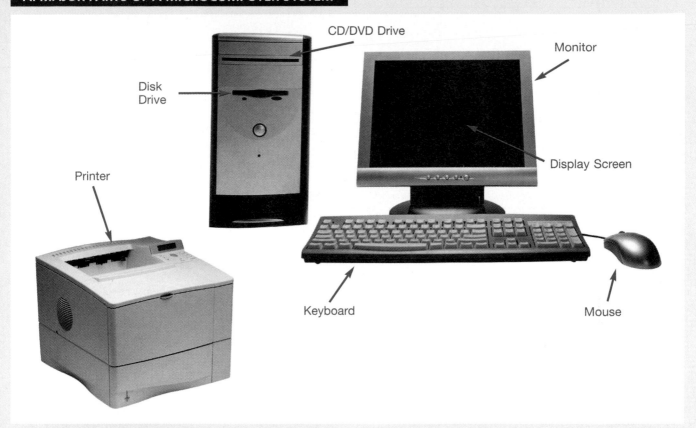

CD/DVD Drive

Monitor

Disk Drive

Display Screen

Printer

Keyboard

Mouse

B. THE COMPUTER KEYBOARD

Escape Key

Function Keys

Backspace Key

Tab Key

Caps Lock Key

Shift Key

Alternate Keys

Windows Keys

Control Keys

Enter Key

Arrow Keys

Numeric Keypad

Reference Manual

A. BUSINESS LETTER IN BLOCK STYLE
(with standard punctuation)

	↓5X
Date line	September 5, 20-- ↓4X
Inside address	Ms. Joan R. Hunter Bolwater Associates One Parklands Drive Darien, CT 06820 ↓2X
Salutation	Dear Ms. Hunter: ↓2X
Body	You will soon receive the signed contract to have your organization conduct a one-day workshop for our employees on eliminating repetitive-motion injuries in the workplace. As we agreed, this workshop will apply to both our office and factory workers and you will conduct separate sessions for each group. We revised Paragraph 4-b to require the instructor of this workshop to be a full-time employee of Bolwater Associates. In addition, we made changes to Paragraph 10-c to require our prior approval of the agenda for the workshop. If these revisions are satisfactory, please sign and return one copy of the contract for our files. We look forward to this opportunity to enhance the health of our employees. I know that all of us will enjoy this workshop. ↓2X
Complimentary closing	Sincerely, ↓4X
Writer's identification	Jeffrey Olszewski Jeffrey Olszewski, Director ↓2X
Reference initials	fej

B. BUSINESS LETTER IN MODIFIED-BLOCK STYLE
(with open punctuation, multiline list, and enclosure notation)

Left tab: 3.25"
↓5X
→tab to centerpoint   May 15, 20-- ↓4X

Mr. Ichiro Xie
Bolwater Associates
One Parklands Drive
Darien, CT 06820 ↓2X

Dear Mr. Xie ↓2X

I am returning a signed contract to have your organization conduct a one-day workshop for our employees on eliminating repetitive-motion injuries in the workplace. We have made the following changes to the contract:

Multiline list	1. We revised Paragraph 4-b to require the instructor of this workshop to be a full-time employee of Bolwater Associates. 2. We made changes to Paragraph 10-c to require our prior approval of the agenda for the workshop.

If these revisions are satisfactory, please sign and return one copy of the contract for our files. We look forward to this opportunity to enhance the health of our employees. I know that all of us will enjoy this workshop. ↓2X

→tab to centerpoint   Sincerely ↓4X

Chalita Dudley
Chalita Dudley, Director ↓2X

Enclosure notation	pec Enclosure

C. BUSINESS LETTER IN SIMPLIFIED STYLE
(with single-line list, enclosure notation, and copy notation)

↓5X
October 5, 20-- ↓4X

Mr. Dale P. Griffin
Bolwater Associates
One Parklands Drive
Darien, CT 06820 ↓3X

Subject line	WORKSHOP CONTRACT ↓3X

I am returning the signed contract, Mr. Griffin, to have your organization conduct a one-day workshop for our employees on eliminating repetitive-motion injuries in the workplace. We have amended the following sections of the contract:

Single-line list	• Paragraph 4-b • Table 3 • Attachment 2

If these revisions are satisfactory, please sign and return one copy of the contract for our files. We look forward to this opportunity to enhance the health of our employees. I know that all of us will enjoy this workshop. ↓4X

Rogena Kyles
ROGENA KYLES, DIRECTOR ↓2X

iww
Enclosure

Copy notation	c: Legal Department

D. PERSONAL-BUSINESS LETTER IN MODIFIED-BLOCK STYLE
(with standard punctuation and international address)

Left tab: 3.25"
↓5X
→tab to centerpoint   July 15, 20-- ↓4X

Mr. Luis Fernandez
Vice President
Arvon Industries, Inc.
21 St. Claire Avenue East

International Address	Toronto, ON M4T IL9 CANADA ↓2X

Dear Mr. Fernandez: ↓2X

As a former employee and present stockholder of Arvon Industries, I wish to protest the planned sale of the Consumer Products Division.

According to published reports, consumer products accounted for 19 percent of last year's corporate profits, and they are expected to account for even more this year. In addition, Dun & Bradstreet predicts that consumer products nationwide will outpace the general economy for the next five years.

I am concerned about the effect that this planned sale might have on overall corporate profits, on our cash dividends for investors, and on the economy of Melbourne, where the two consumer-products plants are located. Please ask your board of directors to reconsider this matter. ↓2X

→tab to centerpoint   Sincerely, ↓4X

Jeanine Ford

Return address	Jeanine Ford 901 East Benson, Apt. 3 Fort Lauderdale, FL 33301

A. BUSINESS LETTER ON EXECUTIVE STATIONERY

(7.25" x 10.5"; 1" side margins; with standard punctuation and delivery notation)

↓5X

July 18, 20--
↓4X

Mr. Rodney Eastwood
BBL Resources
52A Northern Ridge
Fayetteville, PA 17222
↓2X

Dear Rodney: ↓2X

I see no reason why we should continue to consider the locality around Geraldton for our new plant. Even though the desirability of this site from an economic view is undeniable, there is not sufficient housing readily available for our workers.

In trying to control urban growth, the city has been turning down the building permits for much new housing or placing so many restrictions on foreign investment as to make it too expensive.

Please continue to seek out other areas of exploration where we might form a joint partnership.
↓2X

Sincerely, ↓4X

Jennifer Gwatkin

Jennifer Gwatkin
Vice President for Operations ↓2X

mme
Delivery notation By Fax

B. BUSINESS LETTER ON HALF-PAGE STATIONERY

(5.5" x 8.5"; 0.75" side margins; with standard punctuation)

↓4X

July 18, 20--
↓4X

Mr. Aristeo Olivas
BBL Resources
52A Northern Ridge
Fayetteville, PA 17222
↓2X

Dear Aristeo: ↓2X

We should discontinue considering Geraldton for our new plant. Even though the desirability of this site from an economic view is undeniable, there is insufficient housing readily available.

Please continue to search out other areas of new exploration where we might someday form a joint partnership. ↓2X

Sincerely, ↓4X

Chimere Jones

Chimere Jones
Vice President for Operations ↓2X

adk

C. BUSINESS LETTER FORMATTED FOR A WINDOW ENVELOPE

(with standard punctuation)

↓5X

July 18, 20--
↓3X

Ms. Reinalda Guerrero
BBL Resources
52A Northern Ridge
Fayetteville, PA 17222
↓3X

Dear Ms. Guerrero: ↓2X

I see no reason why we should even continue to consider the locality around Geraldton for our new plant. Even though the desirability of this site from an economic view is undeniable, there is insufficient housing readily available for our workers.

In trying to control urban growth, the city has been turning down the building permits for new housing or placing so many restrictions on foreign investment as to make it too expensive.

Please continue to seek out other areas of exploration where we might form a joint partnership. ↓2X

Sincerely, ↓4X

Augustus Mays

Augustus Mays
Vice President for Operations ↓2X

woc

D. MEMO

(with table and attachment notation)

↓5X →tab

MEMO TO: Nancy Price, Executive Vice President ↓2X

FROM: Arlyn J. Bunch, Operations *ajb* ↓2X

DATE: July 18, 20-- ↓2X

SUBJECT: New Plant Site ↓2X

As you can see from the attached letter, I've informed BBL Resources that I see no reason why we should continue to consider the locality around Geraldton for our new plant. Even though the desirability of this site from an economic standpoint is undeniable, there is insufficient housing available. In fact, as of June 25, the number of appropriate single-family houses listed for sale within a 25-mile radius of Geraldton was as follows: ↓2X

Agent	Units
Belle Real Estate	123
Castleton Homes	11
Red Carpet	9
Geraldton Homes	5

↓1X
In addition, in trying to control urban growth, Geraldton has been either turning down building permits for new housing or placing excessive restrictions on them.

Because of this deficiency of housing for our employees, we have no choice but to look elsewhere. ↓2X

woc
Attachment notation Attachment

A. MULTIPAGE BUSINESS LETTER

(page 1; with standard punctuation, on-arrival notation, international address, subject line, and table)

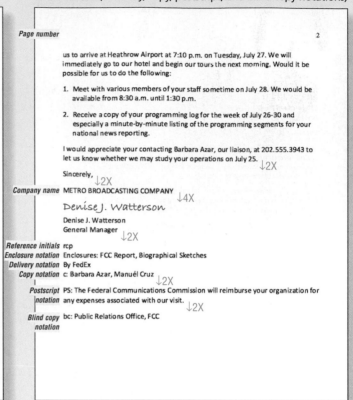

B. MULTIPAGE BUSINESS LETTER

(page 2; with standard punctuation; multiline list; company name; and enclosure, delivery, copy, postscript, and blind copy notations)

C. E-MAIL MESSAGE IN MICROSOFT OUTLOOK/ INTERNET EXPLORER

D. E-MAIL MESSAGE IN MSN HOTMAIL

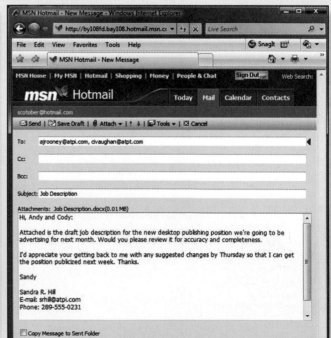

Reference Manual

A. FORMATTING ENVELOPES

A standard large (No. 10) envelope is 9.5 by 4.125 inches. A standard small (No. 6¾) envelope is 6.5 by 3.625 inches. Although either address format shown below is acceptable, the format shown for the large envelope (all caps and no punctuation) is recommended by the U.S. Postal Service for mail that will be sorted by an electronic scanning device.

Window envelopes are often used in a word processing environment because of the difficulty of aligning envelopes correctly in some printers. A window envelope requires no formatting, since the letter is formatted and folded so that the inside address is visible through the window.

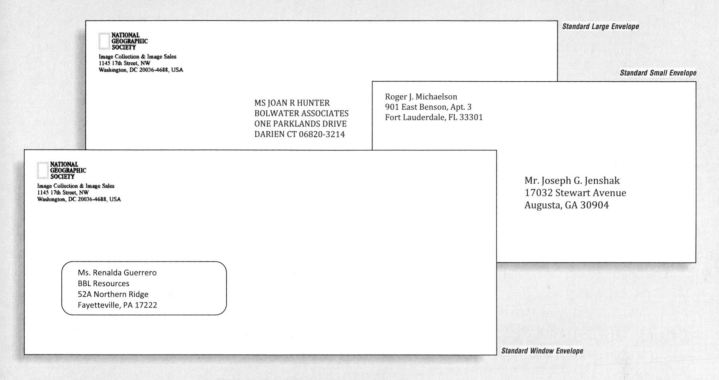

Standard Large Envelope

Standard Small Envelope

Standard Window Envelope

B. FOLDING LETTERS

To fold a letter for a large envelope:

1. Place the letter *face up* and fold up the bottom third.
2. Fold the top third down to 0.5 inch from the bottom edge.
3. Insert the last crease into the envelope first, with the flap facing up.

To fold a letter for a small envelope:

1. Place the letter *face up* and fold up the bottom half to 0.5 inch from the top.
2. Fold the right third over to the left.
3. Fold the left third over to 0.5 inch from the right edge.
4. Insert the last crease into the envelope first, with the flap facing up.

To fold a letter for a window envelope:

1. Place the letter *face down* with the letterhead at the top and fold the bottom third of the letter up.
2. Fold the top third down so that the address shows.
3. Insert the letter into the envelope so that the address shows through the window.

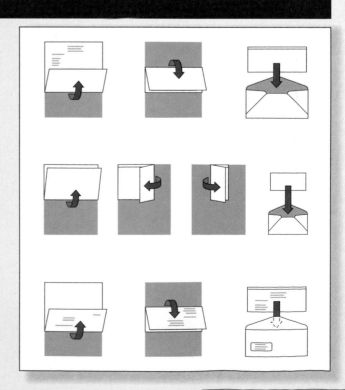

Reference Manual

A. OUTLINE

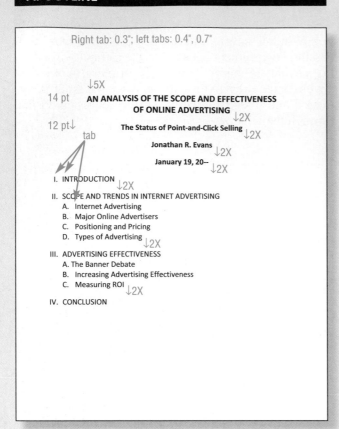

Right tab: 0.3"; left tabs: 0.4", 0.7"

↓5X

14 pt **AN ANALYSIS OF THE SCOPE AND EFFECTIVENESS**
OF ONLINE ADVERTISING ↓2X

12 pt↓ **The Status of Point-and-Click Selling** ↓2X

→ tab **Jonathan R. Evans** ↓2X

January 19, 20-- ↓2X

I. INTRODUCTION ↓2X

II. SCOPE AND TRENDS IN INTERNET ADVERTISING
   A. Internet Advertising
   B. Major Online Advertisers
   C. Positioning and Pricing
   D. Types of Advertising ↓2X

III. ADVERTISING EFFECTIVENESS
   A. The Banner Debate
   B. Increasing Advertising Effectiveness
   C. Measuring ROI ↓2X

IV. CONCLUSION

B. TITLE PAGE

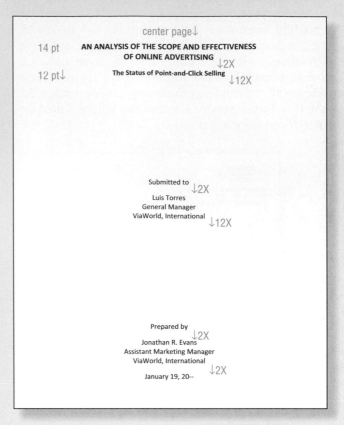

center page↓

14 pt **AN ANALYSIS OF THE SCOPE AND EFFECTIVENESS**
OF ONLINE ADVERTISING ↓2X

12 pt↓ **The Status of Point-and-Click Selling** ↓12X

Submitted to ↓2X

Luis Torres
General Manager
ViaWorld, International ↓12X

Prepared by ↓2X

Jonathan R. Evans
Assistant Marketing Manager
ViaWorld, International ↓2X

January 19, 20-- ↓2X

C. TRANSMITTAL MEMO

(with 2-line subject line and attachment notation)

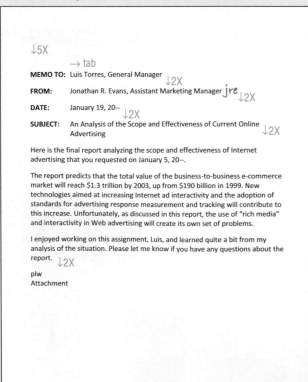

↓5X

→ tab

MEMO TO: Luis Torres, General Manager ↓2X

FROM: Jonathan R. Evans, Assistant Marketing Manager *jre* ↓2X

DATE: January 19, 20-- ↓2X

SUBJECT: An Analysis of the Scope and Effectiveness of Current Online
Advertising ↓2X

Here is the final report analyzing the scope and effectiveness of Internet
advertising that you requested on January 5, 20--.

The report predicts that the total value of the business-to-business e-commerce
market will reach $1.3 trillion by 2003, up from $190 billion in 1999. New
technologies aimed at increasing Internet ad interactivity and the adoption of
standards for advertising response measurement and tracking will contribute to
this increase. Unfortunately, as discussed in this report, the use of "rich media"
and interactivity in Web advertising will create its own set of problems.

I enjoyed working on this assignment, Luis, and learned quite a bit from my
analysis of the situation. Please let me know if you have any questions about the
report. ↓2X

plw
Attachment

D. TABLE OF CONTENTS

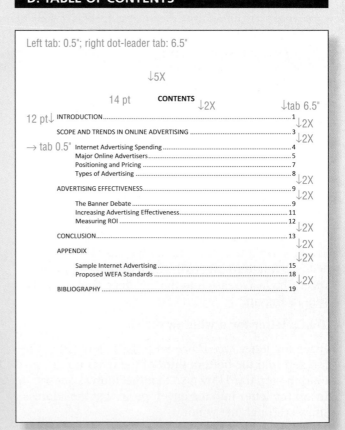

Left tab: 0.5"; right dot-leader tab: 6.5"

↓5X

14 pt **CONTENTS** ↓2X ↓tab 6.5"

Reference Manual

A. BUSINESS REPORT

(page 1; with multiline list and footnotes)

↓5X

Title 14 pt **AN ANALYSIS OF THE SCOPE AND EFFECTIVENESS OF ONLINE ADVERTISING** ↓2X

Subtitle 12 pt↓ **The Status of Point-and-Click Selling** ↓2X

Byline Jonathan R. Evans ↓2X

Date January 19, 20-- ↓2X

Over the past three years, the number of American households online has tripled, from an estimated 30 million in 2001 to 95 million in 2004. Juniper Online Communications predicts that by the year 2010, 120 million households, representing about 82 percent of all U.S. households, will be online.[1] ↓2X

Side head **GROWTH FACTORS** ↓2X

Online business has grown in tandem with the expanding number of Internet users. Juniper predicts that the total value of business-to-business e-commerce will reach $159 billion in 2005 and is likely to reach $2.3 trillion by 2008. ↓2X

Paragraph head **Uncertainty.** The uncertainties surrounding advertising on the Internet remain one of the major impediments to the expansion. All of the Internet advertising industry is today in a state of flux. ↓2X

Reasons for Not Advertising Online. A recent Association of National Online Advertisers survey found two main reasons cited for not advertising online:[2] ↓2X

1. The difficulty of determining return on investment, especially in terms of repeat business and first-time shoppers

2. The lack of reliable tracking and measurement data.

Footnotes
[1] George Anders, "Buying Frenzy," *The Wall Street Daily,* July 12, 2006, p. R6.
[2] "eStats: Advertising Revenues and Trends in the United States," *eMarketing Home page,* August 11, 2004, <http://www.emarketing.com/estats/ad>, accessed on January 7, 2007.

B. BUSINESS REPORT

(page 3; with long quotation and table)

3

who argue that banners have a strong potential for advertising effectiveness point out that it is not the banner format itself which presents a problem to advertising effectiveness, but rather the quality of the banner and the attention to its placement. According to Mike Windsor, president of Online Interactive: ↓2X

indent 0.5"→ Long quotation
It is more a case of bad banner ads, just like there are bad TV ads. The space itself has huge potential. Unlike broadcast media, the Web offers advertisers the opportunity to reach a specific audience based on data gathered about who is surfing at a site and what their interests are.[1] ↓2X
←indent 0.5"

Thus, while some analysts continue to argue that the banner advertisement is passé, there is little evidence of its abandonment. Instead, ad agencies are focusing on increasing the banner's effectiveness. ↓2X

SCOPE AND TRENDS IN ONLINE ADVERTISING ↓2X

Starting from zero in 1994, analysts agree that the volume of Internet advertising spending has risen rapidly. However, as indicated in Table 3, analysts provide a wide range of the exact amount of such advertising. ↓2X

14 pt
12 pt ↓

TABLE 3. INTERNET ADVERTISING 2005 Estimates	
Source	**Estimate**
Internet Advertising Conference	$3.92 billion
Forecaster	$3.30 billion
IPC International	$3.20 billion
Brown Media	$980 million

Table source
Source: "eMarketing Research Report," *Advertising Daily,* May 3, 2006, p. 24. ↓1X

The differences in estimates of total Web advertising spending is generally attributed to the different methodologies used by the research agencies to gather

[1] Lisa Napoliano, "Banner Ads Are Under the Gun—And On the Move," *The New York Financial Times,* June 17, 2005, p. D1.

C. ACADEMIC REPORT

(page 1; with indented multiline list and endnote references)

↓5SS

14 pt **AN ANALYSIS OF THE SCOPE AND EFFECTIVENESS** ↓1DS
OF ONLINE ADVERTISING ↓1DS

12 pt↓ **The Status of Point-and-Click Selling** ↓1DS

Jonathan R. Evans ↓1DS

January 19, 20-- ↓1DS

Over the past three years, the number of American households online has tripled, from an estimated 30 million in 2001 to more than 95 million in 2004.[i] ↓1DS

GROWTH FACTORS ↓1DS

Online business has grown in tandem with the expanding number of Internet users. Juniper predicts that the total value of business-to-business e-commerce will reach $159 billion in 2005 and will reach $2.3 trillion by 2008.

Reasons for Not Advertising Online. An Association of National Online Advertisers survey found two main reasons cited for not advertising online:[ii]

1. The difficulty of determining return on investment, especially in terms of repeat business.

2. The lack of reliable tracking and measurement data

The uncertainties surrounding advertising on the Internet remain one of the major impediments to the expansion. All of the Internet advertising industry is today in a state of flux. Some analysts argue that advertising on the Internet can

D. ACADEMIC REPORT

(last page; with long quotation and endnotes)

14

advertising effectiveness, but rather the quality of the banner and the attention to its placement. According to Mike Windsor, president of Ogilvy Interactive:[vi]

indent 0.5"→ Long quotation
It's more a case of bad banner ads, just like there are bad TV ads. The space itself has huge potential. As important as using the space within the banner creatively is to aim it effectively. Unlike broadcast media, the Web offers advertisers the opportunity to reach a specific audience based on data gathered about who is surfing at a site and what their interests are.
←indent 0.5"

From the advertiser's perspective, the most effective Internet ads do more than just deliver information to the consumer and grab the consumer's attention—they also gather information about consumers (e.g., through "cookies" and other methodologies). From the consumer's perspective, this type of interactivity may represent an intrusion and an invasion of privacy. There appears to be a shift away from the ad-supported model and toward the transaction model, wherein users pay for the content they want and the specific transactions they perform.

Endnotes
[i] Greg Anderson, "Online Buying Frenzy," *The Wall Street Financial Journal,* July 12, 2008, p. R6.
[ii] "eStats: Advertising Revenues and Expenses," *eMarketing Home page,* August 11, 2005, <http://www.emarketer.com/estats/ad>, accessed on January 7, 2007.
[iii] Bradley Jenson, Net Ratings Index Shows 14% Rise in Web Ads," *Advertising Age,* July 19, 2006, p. 18.
[iv] Tom Highland, "Web Advertising: A Decade of Growth," *Internet Advertising Conference Home page,* November 13, 2005, <http://www.iab.net/advertise>, accessed on January 8, 2007.
[v] Adrian Mandlay, "Click Here: Free Ride Doles Out Freebies to Ad Surfers," *Brand Age,* March 8, 2006, p. 30.
[vi] Andrea Peters, "High Price of Banner Ads Slips Amid Increase in Web Sites," *The Wall Street Journal,* March 2, 2007, p. B20.
[vii] Lisa Napoliano, "Banner Ads Are On the Move," *The New York Financial Times,* June 17, 2006, p. D1.

Reference Manual

A. LEFT-BOUND BUSINESS REPORT

(page 1; with endnote references and single-line list)

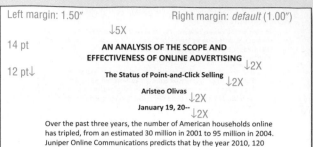

Left margin: 1.50" Right margin: *default* (1.00")

↓5X

14 pt **AN ANALYSIS OF THE SCOPE AND
EFFECTIVENESS OF ONLINE ADVERTISING** ↓2X

12 pt↓ **The Status of Point-and-Click Selling** ↓2X

Aristeo Olivas ↓2X

January 19, 20-- ↓2X

Over the past three years, the number of American households online has tripled, from an estimated 30 million in 2001 to 95 million in 2004. Juniper Online Communications predicts that by the year 2010, 120 million households, representing about 82 percent of all U.S. households, will be online.[i] ↓2X

GROWTH FACTORS ↓2X

Online business has grown in tandem with the expanding number of Internet users. Juniper online predicts that the total value of business-to-business e-commerce will reach $159 billion in 2005 and is likely to reach $2.3 trillion by 2008. ↓2X

Uncertainty. The uncertainties surrounding advertising on the Internet remain one of the major impediments to the expansion. Dating from just 1994, when the first banner ads appeared on the Hotwired home page, the Internet advertising industry is today in a state of flux. ↓2X

Some analysts argue that advertising on the Internet can and should follow the same principles as advertising on television and other visual media. Others contend that advertising on the Internet should reflect the unique characteristics of this new medium. ↓2X

Reasons for Not Advertising Online. A recent Association of National Online Advertisers survey found two reasons cited for not advertising:[ii] ↓2X

1. The difficulty of determining return on investment
2. The lack of reliable tracking and measurement data

B. BIBLIOGRAPHY

(for business or academic style using either endnotes or footnotes)

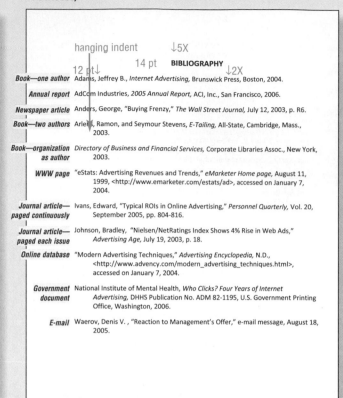

hanging indent ↓5X

12 pt↓ 14 pt **BIBLIOGRAPHY** ↓2X

Book—one author Adams, Jeffrey B., *Internet Advertising*, Brunswick Press, Boston, 2004.

Annual report AdCom Industries, *2005 Annual Report*, ACI, Inc., San Francisco, 2006.

Newspaper article Anders, George, "Buying Frenzy," *The Wall Street Journal*, July 12, 2003, p. R6.

Book—two authors Arlen, Ramon, and Seymour Stevens, *E-Tailing*, All-State, Cambridge, Mass., 2003.

Book—organization as author *Directory of Business and Financial Services*, Corporate Libraries Assoc., New York, 2003.

WWW page "eStats: Advertising Revenues and Trends," *eMarketer Home page*, August 11, 1999, <http://www.emarketer.com/estats/ad>, accessed on January 7, 2004.

Journal article— paged continuously Ivans, Edward, "Typical ROIs in Online Advertising," *Personnel Quarterly*, Vol. 20, September 2005, pp. 804-816.

Journal article— paged each issue Johnson, Bradley, "Nielsen/NetRatings Index Shows 4% Rise in Web Ads," *Advertising Age*, July 19, 2003, p. 18.

Online database "Modern Advertising Techniques," *Advertising Encyclopedia*, N.D., <http://www.advency.com/modern_advertising_techniques.html>, accessed on January 7, 2004.

Government document National Institute of Mental Health, *Who Clicks? Four Years of Internet Advertising*, DHHS Publication No. ADM 82-1195, U.S. Government Printing Office, Washington, D.C.

E-mail Waerov, Denis V. , "Reaction to Management's Offer," e-mail message, August 18, 2005.

C. MEMO REPORT

(page 1, with single-line list)

↓5X →tab

MEMO TO: Luis Torres, General Manager ↓2X

FROM: Jonathan R. Evans, Assistant Marketing Manager *jre* ↓2X

DATE: January 19, 20-- ↓2X

SUBJECT: An Analysis of the Scope and Effectiveness of Online Advertising ↓2X

Over the past three years, the number of American households online has tripled, from an estimated 30 million in 2001 to 95 million in 2004. Juniper Online Communications predicts that by the year 2010, 120 million households, representing about 82 percent of all U.S. households, will be online.[i] ↓2X

Online business has grown in tandem with the expanding number of Internet users. Juniper predicts that the total value of business-to-business e-commerce will reach $159 billion in 2005 and is likely to reach $2.3 trillion by 2008. Some experts predict an even larger volume.[ii] ↓2X

UNCERTAINTY ↓2X

The uncertainties surrounding advertising on the Internet remain one of the major impediments to the expansion. Dating from just 1994, when the first banner ads appeared on the Hotwired home page, the Internet advertising industry is today in a state of flux. Dramatic changes are frequent, and so are the repercussions of these many changes.

Some analysts argue that advertising on the Internet can and should follow the same principles as advertising on television and other visual media. Others contend that all of the advertising on the Internet should reflect the unique characteristics of this new medium.

A recent Association of National Online Advertisers survey found two main reasons cited for not advertising online:

1. The difficulty of determining return on investment
2. The lack of reliable tracking and measurement data

D. REPORTS: SPECIAL FEATURES

Margins and Spacing. Use a 2-inch top margin for the first page of each section of a report (for example, the table of contents, first page of the body, and bibliography page) and a 1-inch top margin for other pages. Use default side and bottom margins (1 inch) for all pages. If the report is going to be bound on the left, add 0.5 inch to the left margin. Single-space business reports and double-space academic reports.

Headings. Center the report title in 14-point font (press ENTER to space down before switching to 12-point font). Single-space multiline report titles in a single-spaced report and double-space multiline titles in a double-spaced report. Insert 1 blank line before and after all parts of a heading block (consisting of the title, subtitle, author, and/or date) and format all lines in bold.

Insert 1 blank line before and after side headings and format in bold, beginning at the left margin. Format paragraph headings in bold; begin at the left margin for single-spaced reports and indent for double-spaced reports. The text follows on the same line, preceded by a period and 1 space.

Citations. For business and academic reports, format citations using your word processor's footnote (or endnote) feature. For reports formatted in APA or MLA style, use the format shown on page R-10.

Reference Manual

A. REPORT IN APA STYLE

(page 1; with author/year citations)

Top, bottom, and side margins: 1"

Online Advertising 3 *header*

An Analysis of the Scope and Effectiveness

of Online Advertising

Jonathan R. Evans

Over the past three years, the number of American households online has

tripled, from an estimated 30 million in 2001 to 95 million in 2004. Juniper Online

Communications predicts that by the year 2010, 120 million households will be

online (Napoli, 2006).

main head Growth Factors

Online business has grown in tandem with the expanding number of

Internet users. Juniper predicts that the total value of business-to-business e-

commerce will reach $159 billion in 2005 and is likely to reach $2.3 trillion by

2008 (Arlens & Stevens, 2005).

subhead *Uncertainty*

The uncertainties surrounding advertising on the Internet remain one of

the major impediments to the expansion. Dating from just 1994, when the first

banner ads appeared on the Hotwired home page, the Internet advertising

industry is today in a state of flux.

Some analysts argue that advertising on the Internet can and should follow

the same principles as advertising on television and other visual media ("eStats,"

2007). Others contend that advertising on the Internet should reflect the unique

characteristics of this new medium.

B. REFERENCES IN APA STYLE

Top, bottom, and side margins: 1"; double-space throughout.

Online Advertising 14 *header*

References

hanging indent

Book—one author Adams, J. B. (2004). *Internet advertising and the upcoming electronic upheaval.*

Boston: Brunswick Press.

Annual report AdCom Industries. (2006). *2005 annual report.* San Francisco: ACI, Inc.

Newspaper article Anders, G. (2003, July 12). Buying frenzy. *The Wall Street Journal,* p. R6.

Book—two authors Arlens, R., & Stevens, S. (2003). *E-tailing.* Cambridge, MA: All-State.

Book—organization as author *Directory of business and financial services.* (2003). New York: Corporate Libraries

Association.

WWW page eStats: Advertising revenues and trends. (n.d.). New York: eMarketer. Retrieved

August 11, 2004, from the World Wide Web:

http://www.emarketer.com/estats/2507manu.ad

Journal article— paged continuously Ivans, E. (2005). Typical ROIs in online advertising. *Personnel Quarterly, 20,* 804-

816.

Journal article— paged each issue Johnson, B. (2003, July 19). Nielsen/NetRatings Index shows 4% rise in Web ads.

Advertising Age, 39, 18.

Online database *Modern advertising techniques.* (1998, January). *Advertising Encyclopedia.*

Retrieved January 7, 2004, from http://www.advency.com/ads.html

Government document National Institute of Mental Health (2006). *Who clicks? Four years of Internet*

advertising (DHHS Publication No. ADM 82-1195). Washington, DC.

C. REPORT IN MLA STYLE

(page 1; with author/page citations)

Top, bottom, and side margins: 1"

Double-space throughout.

Evans 1 *header*

Jonathan R. Evans

Professor Inman

Management 302

19 January 20--

An Analysis of the Scope and Effectiveness

of Online Advertising

Over the past three years, the number of American households online has

tripled, from an estimated 30 million in 2001 to 95 million in 2004. Juniper Online

Communications predicts that by the year 2010, 120 million households,

representing 62 percent of all U.S. households, will be online (Napoli D1). Online

business has grown in tandem with the expanding number of Internet users.

Juniper predicts that the total value of business-to-business e-commerce will

reach $159 billion in 2005 (Arlens & Stevens 376-379).

The uncertainties surrounding advertising on the Internet remain one of

the major impediments to the expansion. Dating from just 1994, when the first

banner ads appeared on the Hotwired home page, the Internet advertising

industry is today in a state of flux.

Some analysts argue that advertising on the Internet can and should follow

the same principles as advertising on television and other visual media ("eStats,"

D. WORKS CITED IN MLA STYLE

Top, bottom, and side margins: 1"; double-space throughout.

Evans 13 *header*

hanging indent

Works Cited

Book—one author Adams, Jeffrey B. *Internet Advertising and the Coming Electronic Frenzy.* Boston:

Brunswick Press, 2004.

Annual report AdCom Industries. *2005 Annual Report.* San Francisco: ACI, Inc., 2006.

Newspaper article Anders, George. "Buying Frenzy." *The Wall Street Journal* 12 July 2003: R6.

Book—two authors Arlens, Ramon, and Seymour Stevens. *E-tailing.* Cambridge, MA: All-State, 2003.

Book—organization as author Corporate Libraries Association. *Directory of Business and Financial Services.* New

York: Corporate Libraries Association, 2003.

WWW page "eStats: Advertising Revenues and Trends." *eMarketer home page.* 11 Aug. 1999.

7 Jan. 2004 <http://www.emarketer.com/estats/ad>.

Journal article— paged continuously Ivans, Edward. "Typical ROIs in Online Advertising." *Personnel Quarterly* Sept.

2005: 804-816.

Journal article— paged each issue Johnson, Bradley. "Nielsen/NetRatings Index Shows 4% Rise in Web Ads."

Advertising Age 19 July 2003: 18.

Online database *Modern Advertising Techniques.* 1998. Advertising Encyclopedia. 7 Jan. 2004

<http://www.advency.com/modern_advertising_techniques.html>.

Government document National Institute of Mental Health. *Four Years of Internet Advertising.* DHHS

Publication No. ADM 82-1195. Washington, DC: GPO, 2006.

E-mail Richards, Denis V. "Online Advertising." E-mail to the author. 18 Dec. 2005.

Reference Manual

A. MEETING AGENDA

↓5X

14 pt

MILES HARDWARE EXECUTIVE COMMITTEE ↓2X

12 pt↓

Meeting Agenda ↓2X

June 7, 20--, 3 p.m. ↓2X

1. Call to order ↓2X

2. Approval of minutes of May 5 meeting

3. Progress report on building addition and parking lot restrictions (Norman Hodges and Anthony Pascarelli)

4. May 15 draft of Five-Year Plan

5. Review of National Hardware Association annual convention

6. Employee grievance filed by Ellen Burrows (John Landstrom)

7. New expense-report forms (Anne Richards)

8. Announcements

9. Adjournment

B. MINUTES OF A MEETING

↓5X

14 pt **RESOURCE COMMITTEE** ↓2X

12 pt↓ **Minutes of the Meeting** ↓2X

March 13, 20-- ↓1X

ATTENDANCE	The Resource Committee met on March 13, 20--, at the Airport Sheraton in Portland, Oregon, with all members present. Michael Davis, chairperson, called the meeting to order at 2:30 p.m. ↓1X
APPROVAL OF MINUTES	The minutes of the January 27 meeting were read and approved. ↓1X
OLD BUSINESS	The members of the committee reviewed the sales brochure on electronic copyboards and agreed to purchase one for the conference room. Cynthia Giovanni will secure quotations from at least two suppliers. ↓1X
NEW BUSINESS	The committee reviewed a request from the Purchasing Department for three new computers. After extensive discussion regarding the appropriate use of the computers and software to be purchased, the committee approved the request. ↓1X
ADJOURNMENT	The meeting was adjourned at 4:45 p.m. ↓2X Respectfully submitted, ↓4X *D. S. Madsen* D. S. Madsen, Secretary

(Note: Table shown with "View Gridlines" active.)

C. ITINERARY

↓5X

14 pt **ITINERARY** ↓2X

12 pt↓ **For Arlene Gilsdorf** ↓2X

March 12-15, 20-- ↓1X

THURSDAY, MARCH 12	↓1X
5:10 p.m.-7:06 p.m.	Flight from Detroit to Portland; Northwest 83 (Phone: 800-555-1212); e-ticket; Seat 8D; nonstop; dinner ↓2X Jack Weatherford (Home: 503-555-8029; Office: 503-555-7631) will meet your flight on Thursday, provide transportation during your visit, and return you to the airport on Saturday morning. ↓2X Airport Sheraton (503-555-4032) King-sized bed, nonsmoking room; late arrival guaranteed (Reservation No. 30ZM6-02) ↓1X
FRIDAY, MARCH 13	
9 a.m.-5:30 p.m.	Portland Sales Meeting 1931 Executive Way, Suite 10 Portland (503-555-7631)
Evening	On your own
SATURDAY, MARCH 14	
7:30 a.m.-2:47 p.m.	Flight from Portland to Detroit; Northwest 360; e-ticket; Seat 9a; nonstop; breakfast

(Note: Table shown with "View Gridlines" active.)

D. LEGAL DOCUMENT

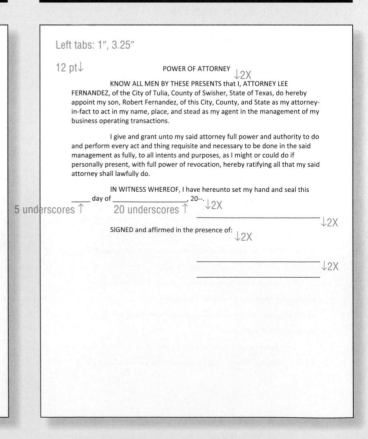

Left tabs: 1", 3.25"

12 pt↓

POWER OF ATTORNEY ↓2X

KNOW ALL MEN BY THESE PRESENTS that I, ATTORNEY LEE FERNANDEZ, of the City of Tulia, County of Swisher, State of Texas, do hereby appoint my son, Robert Fernandez, of this City, County, and State as my attorney-in-fact to act in my name, place, and stead as my agent in the management of my business operating transactions.

I give and grant unto my said attorney full power and authority to do and perform every act and thing requisite and necessary to be done in the said management as fully, to all intents and purposes, as I might or could do if personally present, with full power of revocation, hereby ratifying all that my said attorney shall lawfully do.

IN WITNESS WHEREOF, I have hereunto set my hand and seal this _____ day of _____, 20--. ↓2X

5 underscores ↑   20 underscores ↑

_____ ↓2X

SIGNED and affirmed in the presence of: ↓2X

_____ ↓2X

_____ ↓2X

Reference Manual

A. RESUME

↓5X

Cambria Bold 14 pt **TERRY M. MARTINA**
↓2X
Cambria Bold 12 pt ↓ **250 Maxwell Avenue, Boulder, CO 80305**
↓1X **Phone: 303-555-9311; e-mail: tmartina@ecc.edu**
↓1X

Calibri 12 pt

Calibri Bold 12 pt	
OBJECTIVE	Position in resort management anywhere in Colorado or the Southwest. ↓1X
EDUCATION	A. A. in hotel management to be awarded May 2007 Edgewood Community College, Boulder, Colorado Achieved grade point average of 3.1 (on 4.0 scale). Received Board of Regents tuition scholarship. Financed all college expenses. ↓1X
EXPERIENCE	*Assistant Manager, Burger King Restaurant* Boulder, Colorado: 2005-Present Was in charge of balancing the cash register, closing the restaurant, and making night deposits. ↓2X *Student Intern, Ski Valley Haven* Aspen, Colorado: September-December 2006 Worked as an assistant to the night manager. Gained experience in operating First-Guest software. Was in charge of producing daily occupancy reports. Received Employee-of-the-Month award. ↓1X
PERSONAL	• Speak and write fluent Spanish. • Competent in Microsoft Office 2007. • Secretary of ECC Hospitality Services Association. • Special Olympics volunteer: Summer 2006. ↓1X
REFERENCES	Available upon request

(Note: Table shown with "View Gridlines" active.)

B. APPLICATION LETTER IN BLOCK STYLE

(with standard punctuation)

↓5X

March 1, 20-- ↓4X

Mr. Lou Mansfield, Director
Human Resources Department
Rocky Resorts International
P.O. Box 1412
Denver, CO 80214 ↓2X

Dear Mr. Mansfield: ↓2X

Please consider me an applicant for the position of concierge for Suite Retreat, as advertised in last Sunday's *Denver Times*.

I will receive my A.A. degree in hotel administration from Edgewood Community College in May and will be available for full-time employment immediately. In addition to my extensive coursework in hospitality services and business, I've had experience in working for a ski lodge similar to Suite Retreats in Aspen. As a lifelong resident of Colorado and an avid skier, I would be able to provide your guests with any information they request.

After you've reviewed my enclosed resume, I would appreciate having an opportunity to discuss with you why I believe I have the right qualifications and personality to serve as your concierge. I can be reached at 303-555-9311. ↓2X

Sincerely, ↓4X

Terry M. Martina

Terry M. Martina
250 Maxwell Avenue, Apt. 8
Boulder, CO 80305 ↓2X

Enclosure

C. FORMATTING LISTS

Numbers or bullets may be used in letters, memos, and reports to call attention to items in a list. If the sequence of the items is important, use numbers rather than bullets.

❑ Begin the number or bullet at the paragraph point, that is, at the left margin for blocked paragraphs and indented 0.5 inch for indented paragraphs.
❑ Insert 1 blank line before and after the list.
❑ Within the list, use the same spacing (single or double) as is used in the rest of the document.
❑ For single-spaced documents, if all items require no more than 1 line, single-space the items in the list. If any item requires more than 1 line, single-space each item and insert 1 blank line between each item.

To format a list:

1. Type the list unformatted and press ENTER 1 time.
2. Select the items in the list (but not any blank lines).
3. Apply the number or bullet feature.
4. Decrease or increase the indent as needed to adjust the position of the list.

The three bulleted and numbered lists shown at the right are all formatted correctly.

D. EXAMPLES OF DIFFERENT TYPES OF LISTS

According to PricewaterhouseCoopers and the Internet Advertising Bureau, the following are the most common types of advertising on the Internet:

• Banner ads that feature some type of appropriate animation to attract the viewer's attention and interest.

• Sponsorship, in which an advertiser sponsors a content-based Web site.

• Interstitials, ads that flash up while a page downloads.

There is now considerable controversy about the effectiveness of banner ads. As previously noted, a central goal of banner advertisements is to increase the amount of

*****

According to PricewaterhouseCoopers, the following are the most common types of advertising on the Internet, shown in order of popularity:

1. Banner ads
2. Sponsorship
3. Interstitials

There is now considerable controversy about the effectiveness of banner ads. As previously noted, a central goal of banner advertisements is to increase the amount of

*****

According to PricewaterhouseCoopers, the following are the most common

types of advertising on the Internet:

• Banner ads that feature animation to attract the viewer's attention.

• Sponsorship, in which an advertiser sponsors a Web site.

• Interstitials, ads that flash up while a page downloads.

There is now considerable controversy about the effectiveness of banner

advertising. As previously noted, a central goal of banner advertisements is to

Reference Manual

A. BOXED TABLE (DEFAULT STYLE)

(with subtitle, braced headings, total line, and table note)

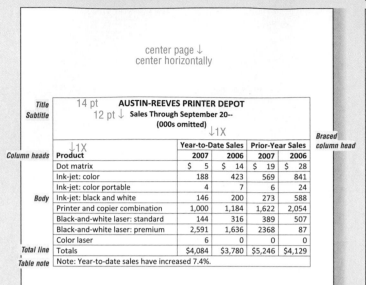

center page ↓
center horizontally

		14 pt	**AUSTIN-REEVES PRINTER DEPOT**			
Title						
Subtitle		12 pt ↓	Sales Through September 20--			
			(000s omitted)			
			↓1X			

	Year-to-Date Sales		Prior-Year Sales	
↓1X Product	2007	2006	2007	2006
Dot matrix	$ 5	$ 14	$ 19	$ 28
Ink-jet: color	188	423	569	841
Ink-jet: color portable	4	7	6	24
Ink-jet: black and white	146	200	273	588
Printer and copier combination	1,000	1,184	1,622	2,054
Black-and-white laser: standard	144	316	389	507
Black-and-white laser: premium	2,591	1,636	2368	87
Color laser	6	0	0	0
Totals	$4,084	$3,780	$5,246	$4,129
Note: Year-to-date sales have increased 7.4%.				

Column heads / *Body* / *Total line* / *Table note*

Braced column head

B. OPEN TABLE

(with subtitle, left- and right-aligned column headings, and 2-line headings)

center page ↓
center horizontally

14 pt **SUITE RETREAT**
12 pt ↓ **New Lodging Rates** ↓1X

Location	Rack Rate	Discount Rate	Saving
Bozeman, Montana	$ 95.75	$ 91.50	4.4%
Chicago, Illinois	159.00	139.50	12.3%
Dallas, Texas	249.50	219.00	12.2%
Las Vegas, Nevada	98.50	89.95	8.7%
Los Angeles, California	179.00	139.00	22.3%
Minneapolis, Minnesota	115.00	95.00	17.4%
New York, New York	227.50	175.00	23.1%
Orlando, Florida	105.75	98.50	6.3%
Portland, Maine	93.50	93.50	0.0%
Seattle, Washington	143.75	125.75	12.5%

C. RULED TABLE

(with table number and centered column headings)

2

an effort to reduce errors and provide increased customer support, we have recently added numerous additional telephone support services, some of which are available 24 hours a day and others available during the workday. These are shown in Table 2.
↓2X

14 pt **Table 2. WINTERLAND SKI SHOP COMPUTER AND TECHNICAL SUPPORT SERVICES** ↓1X

12 pt↓

Support Service	Telephone	Hours
Product literature	800-555-3867	6 a.m. to 5 p.m.
Replacement parts	303-555-3388	24 hours a day
Technical documentation	408-555-3309	24 hours a day
Troubleshooting	800-555-8277	10 a.m. to 5 p.m.
Printer drivers	800-555-2377	6 a.m. to 5 p.m.
Software notes	800-555-3496	24 hours a day
Technical support	800-555-1205	24 hours a day
Hardware information	303-555-4289	6 a.m. to 5 p.m.

↓1X
We hope you will take advantage of these additional services to ensure that the computer hardware and software you purchase from Computer Supplies continues to provide you the quality and service you have come to expect from our company.

Sincerely,

Douglas Pullis

Douglas Pullis
General Manager

cds

D. TABLES: SPECIAL FEATURES

Vertical Placement. Vertically center a table that appears on a page by itself. Insert 1 blank line before and after a table appearing with other text.

Heading Block. Center and bold all lines of the heading, typing the title in all caps and 14-point font and the subtitle in upper- and lowercase and in 12-point font. If a table has a number, type the word *Table* in upper- and lowercase. Follow the table number with a period and 1 space.

Column Headings. If *all* columns in the table consist of text (such as words, phone numbers, or years), center all column headings and left-align all column entries. In all other situations, left-align all text column headings and text column entries and right-align all quantity column headings and quantity column entries. Regardless of the type of column, center braced headings. Use bold upper- and lowercase.

Column Capitalization. Capitalize only the first word and proper nouns in column entries.

Percentages and Dollars. Repeat the % sign for each number in a column (unless the heading identifies the data as percentages). Insert the $ sign only before the first amount and before a total amount. Align the $ sign with the longest amount in the column, inserting spaces after the $ sign as needed (leaving 2 spaces for each digit and 1 space for each comma).

Total Line. Add a border above a total line. Use the word *Total* or *Totals* as appropriate.

Reference Manual

A. FORMATTING BUSINESS FORMS

Many business forms can be created and filled in by using templates that are provided within commercial word processing software. Template forms can be used "as is" or they can be edited. Templates can also be used to create customized forms for any business.

When a template is opened, the form is displayed on screen. The user can then fill in the necessary information, including personalized company information. Data are entered into cells or fields, and you can move quickly from field to field with a single keystroke—usually by pressing TAB or ENTER.

B. U.S. POSTAL SERVICE ABBREVIATIONS

(for States, Territories, and Canadian Provinces)

States and Territories

Alabama	AL
Alaska	AK
Arizona	AZ
Arkansas	AR
California	CA
Colorado	CO
Connecticut	CT
Delaware	DE
District of Columbia	DC
Florida	FL
Georgia	GA
Guam	GU
Hawaii	HI
Idaho	ID
Illinois	IL
Indiana	IN
Iowa	IA
Kansas	KS
Kentucky	KY
Louisiana	LA
Maine	ME
Maryland	MD
Massachusetts	MA
Michigan	MI
Minnesota	MN
Mississippi	MS
Missouri	MO
Montana	MT
Nebraska	NE
Nevada	NV
New Hampshire	NH
New Jersey	NJ
New Mexico	NM
New York	NY
North Carolina	NC
North Dakota	ND
Ohio	OH
Oklahoma	OK
Oregon	OR
Pennsylvania	PA
Puerto Rico	PR
Rhode Island	RI
South Carolina	SC
South Dakota	SD
Tennessee	TN
Texas	TX
Utah	UT
Vermont	VT
Virgin Islands	VI
Virginia	VA
Washington	WA
West Virginia	WV
Wisconsin	WI
Wyoming	WY

Canadian Provinces

Alberta	AB
British Columbia	BC
Labrador	LB
Manitoba	MB
New Brunswick	NB
Newfoundland	NF
Northwest Territories	NT
Nova Scotia	NS
Ontario	ON
Prince Edward Island	PE
Quebec	PQ
Saskatchewan	SK
Yukon Territory	YT

C. PROOFREADERS' MARKS

Proofreaders' Marks		Draft	Final Copy
⌒	Omit space	data base	database
∨ or ∧	Insert	if he's going	if he's not going,
☰	Capitalize	Maple street	Maple Street
✗	Delete	a final draft	a draft
#	Insert space	allready to	all ready to
when / if	Change word	and if you	and when you
/	Use lowercase letter	our President	our president
¶	Paragraph	… to use it. We can	… to use it. We can
•••	Don't delete	a true story	a true story
○	Spell out	the only 1	the only one
∽	Transpose	they all see	they see all

Proofreaders' Marks		Draft	Final Copy
SS	Single-space	first line / second line	first line / second line
ds	Double-space	first line / second line	first line / second line
⌐	Move right	Please send	Please send
⌐	Move left	May I	May I
∿	Bold	Column Heading	**Column Heading**
ital	Italic	Time magazine	*Time* magazine
u/l	Underline	Time magazine	Time magazine readers
♂	Move as shown	readers will see	will see

Language Arts for Business

(50 "must-know" rules)

PUNCTUATION

COMMAS

RULE 1
, direct address
(L. 21)

Use commas before and after a name used in direct address.
Thank you, John, for responding to my e-mail so quickly.
Ladies and gentlemen, the program has been canceled.

RULE 2
, independent clause
(L. 27)

Use a comma between independent clauses joined by a coordinate conjunction (unless both clauses are short).
Ellen left her job with IBM, and she and her sister went to Paris.
But: Ellen left her job with IBM and went to Paris with her sister.
But: John drove and I navigated.
Note: An independent clause is one that can stand alone as a complete sentence. The most common coordinate conjunctions are *and, but, or,* and *nor.*

RULE 3
, introductory expression
(L. 27)

Use a comma after an introductory expression (unless it is a short prepositional phrase).
Before we can make a decision, we must have all the facts.
But: In 2004 our nation elected a new president.
Note: An introductory expression is a group of words that come before the subject and verb of the independent clause. Common prepositions are *to, in, on, of, at, by, for,* and *with.*

RULE 4
, direct quotation
(L. 41)

Use a comma before and after a direct quotation.
James said, "I shall return," and then left.

RULE 5
, date
(L. 51)

Use a comma before and after the year in a complete date.
We will arrive on June 2, 2006, for the conference.
But: We will arrive on June 2 for the conference.

RULE 6
, place
(L. 51)

Use a comma before and after a state or country that follows a city (but not before a ZIP Code).
Joan moved to Vancouver, British Columbia, in May.
Send the package to Douglasville, GA 30135, by Express Mail.
But: Send the package to Georgia by Express Mail.

Reference Manual

RULE 7 ▶
, series
(L. 61)

Use a comma between each item in a series of three or more.

We need to order paper, toner, and font cartridges for the printer.

They saved their work, exited their program, and turned off their computers when they finished.

Note: Do not use a comma after the last item in a series.

RULE 8 ▶
, transitional expression
(L. 61)

Use a comma before and after a transitional expression or independent comment.

It is critical, therefore, that we finish the project on time.

Our present projections, you must admit, are inadequate.

But: You must admit our present projections are inadequate.

Note: Examples of transitional expressions and independent comments are *in addition to, therefore, however, on the other hand, as a matter of fact,* and *unfortunately.*

RULE 9 ▶
, nonessential expression
(L. 71)

Use a comma before and after a nonessential expression.

Andre, who was there, can verify the statement.

But: Anyone who was there can verify the statement.

Van's first book, *Crisis of Management,* was not discussed.

Van's book *Crisis of Management* was not discussed.

Note: A nonessential expression is a group of words that may be omitted without changing the basic meaning of the sentence. Always examine the noun or pronoun that comes before the expression to determine whether the noun needs the expression to complete its meaning. If it does, the expression is *essential* and does *not* take a comma.

RULE 10 ▶
, adjacent adjectives
(L. 71)

Use a comma between two adjacent adjectives that modify the same noun.

We need an intelligent, enthusiastic individual for this job.

But: Please order a new bulletin board for our main conference room.

Note: Do not use a comma after the second adjective. Also, do not use a comma if the first adjective modifies the combined idea of the second adjective and the noun (for example, *bulletin board* and *conference room* in the second example above).

SEMICOLONS

RULE 11 ▶
; no conjunction
(L. 97)

Use a semicolon to separate two closely related independent clauses that are *not* joined by a conjunction (such as *and, but, or,* or *nor*).

Management favored the vote; stockholders did not.

But: Management favored the vote, but stockholders did not.

RULE 12 ▶
; series
(L. 97)

Use a semicolon to separate three or more items in a series if any of the items already contain commas.

Staff meetings were held on Thursday, May 7; Monday, June 7; and Friday, June 12.

Note: Be sure to insert the semicolon *between* (not within) the items in a series.

Reference Manual

RULE 13 ▶
- number
(L. 57)

Hyphenate compound numbers between twenty-one and ninety-nine and fractions that are expressed as words.

Twenty-nine recommendations were approved by at least three-fourths of the members.

RULE 14 ▶
- compound adjective
(L. 67)

Hyphenate compound adjectives that come before a noun (unless the first word is an adverb ending in -*ly*).

We reviewed an up-to-date report on Wednesday.

But: The report was up to date.

But: We reviewed the highly rated report.

Note: A compound adjective is two or more words that function as a unit to describe a noun.

APOSTROPHES

RULE 15 ▶
' singular noun
(L. 37)

Use '*s* to form the possessive of singular nouns.

The hurricane's force caused major damage to North Carolina's coastline.

RULE 16 ▶
' plural noun
(L. 37)

Use only an apostrophe to form the possessive of plural nouns that end in *s*.

The investors' goals were outlined in the stockholders' report.

But: The investors outlined their goals in the report to the stockholders.

But: The women's and children's clothing was on sale.

RULE 17 ▶
' pronoun
(L. 37)

Use '*s* to form the possessive of indefinite pronouns (such as *someone's* or *anybody's*); do not use an apostrophe with personal pronouns (such as *hers, his, its, ours, theirs,* and *yours*).

She could select anybody's paper for a sample.

It's time to put the file back into its cabinet.

Reference Manual

RULE 18 ▶
: explanatory material
(L. 91)

Use a colon to introduce explanatory material that follows an independent clause.

The computer satisfies three criteria: speed, cost, and power.

But: The computer satisfies the three criteria of speed, cost, and power.

Remember this: only one coupon is allowed per customer.

Note: An independent clause can stand alone as a complete sentence. Do not capitalize the word following the colon.

PERIODS

RULE 19 ▶
. polite request
(L. 91)

Use a period to end a sentence that is a polite request.

Will you please call me if I can be of further assistance.

Note: Consider a sentence a polite request if you expect the reader to respond by doing as you ask rather than by giving a yes-or-no answer.

QUOTATION MARKS

RULE 20 ▶
" direct quotation
(L. 41)

Use quotation marks around a direct quotation.

Harrison responded by saying, "Their decision does not affect us."

But: Harrison responded by saying that their decision does not affect us.

RULE 21 ▶
" title
(L. 41)

Use quotation marks around the title of a newspaper or magazine article, chapter in a book, report, and similar terms.

The most helpful article I found was "Multimedia for All."

ITALICS (OR UNDERLINE)

RULE 22 ▶
title or title
(L. 41)

Italicize (or underline) the titles of books, magazines, newspapers, and other complete published works.

Grisham's *The Brethren* was reviewed in a recent *USA Today* article.

Reference Manual

GRAMMAR

SENTENCES

RULE 23 ▶
fragment
(L. 21)

Avoid sentence fragments.

Not: She had always wanted to be a financial manager. But had not had the needed education.

But: She had always wanted to be a financial manager but had not had the needed education.

Note: A fragment is a part of a sentence that is incorrectly punctuated as a complete sentence. In the first example above, "but had not had the needed education" is not a complete sentence because it does not contain a subject.

RULE 24 ▶
run-on
(L. 21)

Avoid run-on sentences.

Not: Mohamed is a competent worker he has even passed the MOS exam.

Not: Mohamed is a competent worker, he has even passed the MOS exam.

But: Mohamed is a competent worker; he has even passed the MOS exam.

Or: Mohamed is a competent worker. He has even passed the MOS exam.

Note: A run-on sentence is two independent clauses that run together without any punctuation between them or with only a comma between them.

AGREEMENT

RULE 25 ▶
agreement singular
agreement plural
(L. 67)

Use singular verbs and pronouns with singular subjects; use plural verbs and pronouns with plural subjects.

I <u>was</u> happy with <u>my</u> performance.

<u>Janet and Phoenix</u> <u>were</u> happy with <u>their</u> performance.

Among the items discussed <u>were</u> our <u>raises and benefits</u>.

RULE 26 ▶
agreement pronoun
(L. 81)

Some pronouns *(anybody, each, either, everybody, everyone, much, neither, no one, nobody,* and *one)* are always singular and take a singular verb. Other pronouns *(all, any, more, most, none,* and *some)* may be singular or plural, depending on the noun to which they refer.

<u>Each</u> of the employees <u>has</u> finished <u>his or her</u> task.

<u>Much</u> <u>remains</u> to be done.

<u>Most</u> of the pie <u>was</u> eaten, but <u>most</u> of the cookies <u>were</u> left.

RULE 27 ▶
agreement intervening
words
(L. 81)

Disregard any intervening words that come between the subject and verb when establishing agreement.

The <u>box</u> containing the books and pencils <u>has</u> not been found.

<u>Alex</u>, accompanied by Tricia, <u>is</u> attending the conference and taking <u>his</u> computer.

RULE 28 ▶
agreement nearer noun
(L. 101)

If two subjects are joined by *or, either/or, neither/nor,* or *not only/but also,* make the verb agree with the subject nearer to the verb.

Neither the coach nor the <u>players</u> <u>are</u> at home.

Not only the coach but also the <u>referee</u> <u>is</u> at home.

But: <u>Both</u> the coach and the referee <u>are</u> at home.

Reference Manual

PRONOUNS

RULE 29 ▶
nominative pronoun
(L. 107)

Use nominative pronouns (such as *I, he, she, we, they,* and *who*) as subjects of a sentence or clause.

The programmer and <u>he</u> are reviewing the code.

Barb is a person <u>who</u> can do the job.

RULE 30 ▶
objective pronoun
(L. 107)

Use objective pronouns (such as *me, him, her, us, them,* and *whom*) as objects of a verb, preposition, or infinitive.

The code was reviewed by the programmer and <u>him</u>.

Barb is the type of person <u>whom</u> we can trust.

ADJECTIVES AND ADVERBS

RULE 31 ▶
adjective/adverb
(L. 101)

Use comparative adjectives and adverbs (*-er, more,* and *less*) when referring to two nouns or pronouns; use superlative adjectives and adverbs *(-est, most,* and *least*) when referring to more than two.

The <u>shorter</u> of the <u>two</u> training sessions is the <u>more</u> helpful one.

The <u>longest</u> of the <u>three</u> training sessions is the <u>least</u> helpful one.

WORD USAGE

RULE 32 ▶
accept/except
(L. 117)

***Accept* means "to agree to"; *except* means "to leave out."**

All employees <u>except</u> the maintenance staff should <u>accept</u> the agreement.

RULE 33 ▶
affect/effect
(L. 117)

***Affect* is most often used as a verb meaning "to influence"; *effect* is most often used as a noun meaning "result."**

The ruling will <u>affect</u> our domestic operations but will have no <u>effect</u> on our Asian operations.

RULE 34 ▶
farther/further
(L. 117)

***Farther* refers to distance; *further* refers to extent or degree.**

The <u>farther</u> we drove, the <u>further</u> agitated he became.

RULE 35 ▶
personal/personnel
(L. 117)

***Personal* means "private"; *personnel* means "employees."**

All <u>personnel</u> agreed not to use e-mail for <u>personal</u> business.

RULE 36 ▶
principal/principle
(L. 117)

***Principal* means "primary"; *principle* means "rule."**

The <u>principle</u> of fairness is our <u>principal</u> means of dealing with customers.

Reference Manual

MECHANICS

CAPITALIZATION

RULE 37 ▶
≡ sentence
(L. 31)

Capitalize the first word of a sentence.
> Please prepare a summary of your activities.

RULE 38 ▶
≡ proper noun
(L. 31)

Capitalize proper nouns and adjectives derived from proper nouns.
> Judy Hendrix drove to Albuquerque in her new Pontiac convertible.

Note: A proper noun is the official name of a particular person, place, or thing.

RULE 39 ▶
≡ time
(L. 31)

Capitalize the names of the days of the week, months, holidays, and religious days (but do not capitalize the names of the seasons).
> On Thursday, November 25, we will celebrate Thanksgiving, the most popular holiday in the fall.

RULE 40 ▶
≡ noun #
(L. 77)

Capitalize nouns followed by a number or letter (except for the nouns *line*, *note*, *page*, *paragraph*, and *size*).
> Please read Chapter 5, which begins on page 94.

RULE 41 ▶
≡ compass point
(L. 77)

Capitalize compass points (such as *north*, *south*, or *northeast*) only when they designate definite regions.
> From Montana we drove south to reach the Southwest.

RULE 42 ▶
≡ organization
(L. 112)

Capitalize common organizational terms (such as *advertising department* and *finance committee*) only when they are the actual names of the units in the writer's own organization and when they are preceded by the word *the*.
> The report from the Advertising Department is due today.

> *But:* Our advertising department will submit its report today.

RULE 43 ▶
≡ course
(L. 112)

Capitalize the names of specific course titles but not the names of subjects or areas of study.
> I have enrolled in Accounting 201 and will also take a marketing course.

NUMBER EXPRESSION

RULE 44 ▶
general
(L. 47)

In general, spell out numbers zero through ten, and use figures for numbers above ten.
> We rented two movies for tonight.

> The decision was reached after 27 precincts sent in their results.

Reference Manual

RULE 45
 # figure
(L. 47)

Use figures for

❑ **Dates. (Use *st, d,* or *th* only if the day comes before the month.)**
The tax report is due on April 15 (*not* April 15<u>th</u>)
We will drive to the camp on the 23d (or *23rd* or *23rd*) of May.

❑ **All numbers if two or more *related* numbers both above and below ten are used in the same sentence.**
Mr. Carter sent in 7 receipts, and Ms. Cantrell sent in 22.
But: The 13 accountants owned three computers each.

❑ **Measurements (time, money, distance, weight, and percent).**
The $500 statue we delivered at 7 a.m. weighed 6 pounds.

❑ **Mixed numbers.**
Our sales are up 9½ (or *9 1/2*) percent over last year.

RULE 46
 # word
(L. 57)

Spell out

❑ **A number used as the first word of a sentence.**
Seventy-five people attended the conference in San Diego.

❑ **The shorter of two adjacent numbers.**
We have ordered 3 two-pound cakes and one 5-pound cake for the reception.

❑ **The words *million* and *billion* in even amounts (do not use decimals with even amounts).**
Not: A $5.00 ticket can win $28,000,000 in this month's lottery.
But: A $5 ticket can win $28 million in this month's lottery.

❑ **Fractions.**
Almost one-half of the audience responded to the question.
Note: When fractions and the numbers twenty-one through ninety-nine are spelled out, they should be hyphenated.

ABBREVIATIONS

RULE 47
abbreviate none
(L. 67)

In general business writing, do not abbreviate common words (such as *dept.* or *pkg.*), compass points, units of measure, or the names of months, days of the week, cities, or states (except in addresses).
Almost one-half of the audience indicated they were at least 5 feet 8 inches tall.
Note: Do not insert a comma between the parts of a single measurement.

RULE 48
abbreviate measure
(L. 87)

In technical writing, on forms, and in tables, abbreviate units of measure when they occur frequently. Do not use periods.
14 oz   5 ft 10 in   50 mph   2 yrs 10 mo

RULE 49
abbreviate lowercase
(L. 87)

In most lowercase abbreviations made up of single initials, use a period after each initial but no internal spaces.
a.m.   p.m.   i.e.   e.g.   e.o.m.
Exceptions: mph   mpg   wpm

RULE 50
abbreviate ≡
(L. 87)

In most all-capital abbreviations made up of single initials, do not use periods or internal spaces.
OSHA   PBS   NBEA   WWW   VCR   MBA
Exceptions: U.S.A.   A.A.   B.S.   Ph.D.   P.O.   B.C.   A.D.

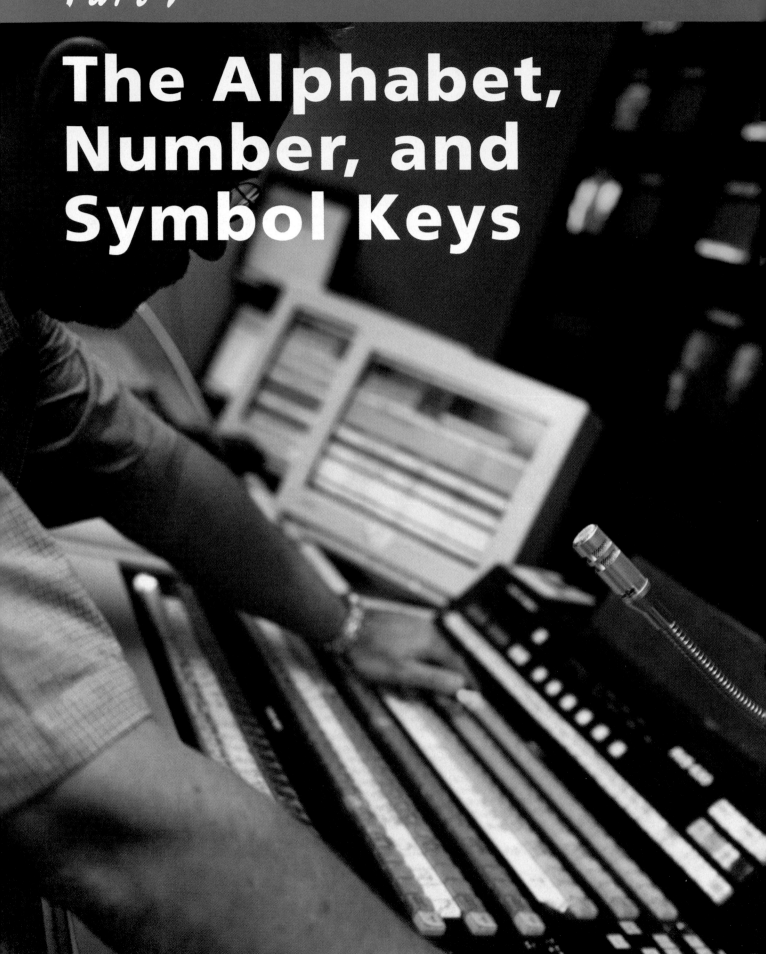

Part 1

The Alphabet, Number, and Symbol Keys

Keyboarding in Arts, Audio, Video Technology, and Communications Services

Occupations in this cluster deal with organizing and communicating information to the public in various forms and media. This cluster includes jobs in radio and television broadcasting, journalism, motion pictures, the recording industry, the performing arts, multimedia publishing, and the entertainment services. Book editors, computer artists, technical writers, radio announcers, news correspondents, and camera operators are just a few jobs within this cluster.

Qualifications and Skills

Strong oral and written communication skills and technical skills are necessary for anyone in communications and media. Without a doubt, competent keyboarding skill is extremely advantageous.

Working in the media requires creativity, talent, and accurate use of language. In journalism, being observant, thinking clearly, and seeing the significance of events are all of utmost importance. Announcers must have exceptional voices, excellent speaking skills, and a unique style. The ability to work under pressure is important in all areas of media.

Objectives

KEYBOARDING

- Operate by touch the letter, number, and symbol keys.

- Demonstrate proper typing technique.

- Use the correct spacing with punctuation.

- Type at least 28 words per minute on a 2-minute timed writing with no more than 5 errors.

TECHNICAL

- Answer correctly at least 90 percent of the questions on an objective test.

Unit 1

Keyboarding: The Alphabet

Home Keys

Goals

- Touch-type the home keys (A S D F J K L ;)
- Touch-type the SPACE BAR
- Touch-type the ENTER key
- Type at least 10wpm/1'/3e

LEFT HAND

First Finger	F
Second Finger	D
Third Finger	S
Fourth Finger	A

RIGHT HAND

J	First Finger
K	Second Finger
L	Third Finger
;	Fourth Finger
SPACE BAR	Thumb

NEW KEYS

A. Follow the directions to become familiar with the home keys.

The semicolon (;) is commonly called the sem key.

A. THE HOME KEYS

The **A S D F J K L ;** keys are known as the home keys.

1. Place the fingers of your left hand on the home keys as follows: first finger on **F**; second finger on **D**; third finger on **S**; fourth finger on **A**.
2. Place the fingers of your right hand on the home keys as follows: first finger on **J**; second finger on **K**; third finger on **L**; and fourth finger on **;**.
3. Curve your fingers.
4. Using the correct fingers, type each character as you say it to yourself: a s d f j k l ;.
5. Remove your fingers from the keyboard and replace them on the home keys.
6. Press each home key again as you say each character: a s d f j k l ;.

B. THE **SPACE** BAR

The SPACE BAR, located beneath the letter keys, is used to space between words and after marks of punctuation.

1. With fingers held motionless on the home keys, poise your right thumb about a half inch above the SPACE BAR.
2. Type the characters and then press the SPACE BAR 1 time. Bounce your thumb off.

C. Type each line 1 time, pressing the SPACE BAR where you see a space and pressing the ENTER key at the end of a line.

C. THE **ENTER↵** KEY

The ENTER key moves the insertion point to the beginning of a new line. Reach to the ENTER key with the fourth finger of your right hand. Keep your J finger at home. Lightly press the ENTER key. Practice using the ENTER key until you can do so with confidence and without looking at your hands.

```
asdf jkl; asdf jkl; ↵
asdf jkl; asdf jkl; ↵
```

LEFT HAND
First Finger   F
Second Finger   D
Third Finger   S
Fourth Finger   A

RIGHT HAND
J   First Finger
K   Second Finger
L   Third Finger
;   Fourth Finger
SPACE BAR   Thumb

D. Press the SPACE BAR with your right thumb. Type each line 2 times.

D. THE F AND J KEYS

```
1  fff fff jjj jjj fff jjj ff jj ff jj f j
2  fff fff jjj jjj fff jjj ff jj ff jj f j
```

E. The A and Sem fingers remain on the home keys. Type each line 2 times.

E. THE D AND K KEYS

```
3  ddd ddd kkk kkk ddd kkk dd kk dd kk d k
4  ddd ddd kkk kkk ddd kkk dd kk dd kk d k
```

F. The A and Sem fingers remain on the home keys. Type each line 2 times.

F. THE S AND L KEYS

```
5  sss sss lll lll sss lll ss ll ss ll s l
6  sss sss lll lll sss lll ss ll ss ll s l
```

G. The F and J fingers remain on the home keys. Type each line 2 times.

G. THE A AND ; KEYS

```
7  aaa aaa ;;; ;;; aaa ;;; aa ;; aa ;; a ;
8  aaa aaa ;;; ;;; aaa ;;; aa ;; aa ;; a ;
```

SKILLBUILDING

H. Type lines 9–15 two times. Press ENTER 2 times to leave a blank line after each pair. Note the word patterns.

H. WORD BUILDING

```
9   aaa ddd ddd add aaa lll lll all add all
10  aaa sss kkk ask ddd aaa ddd dad ask dad
11  lll aaa ddd lad fff aaa ddd fad lad fad
12  aaa ddd ;;; ad; aaa sss ;;; as; ad; as;
13  f fa fad fads; a as ask asks; d da dad;
14  l la las lass; f fa fal fall; s sa sad;
15  a ad add adds; l la lad lads; a ad ads;
```

I. Type lines 16–17 two times. Space 1 time after a semicolon. Leave a blank line after each pair. Note the phrase patterns.

I. PHRASES

```
16  dad ask; ask a lad; dad ask a lad; as a
17  a fall; a lass; ask a lass; a lad asks;
```

J. Take two 1-minute timed writings. Try to complete both lines each time.

Goal: At least 10wpm/1'/3e

J. 1-MINUTE TIMED WRITING

```
18  ask a sad lad; a fall fad; add a salad;
19  ask a dad;
    | 1 | 2 | 3 | 4 | 5 | 6 | 7 | 8 |
```

New Keys

Goals

- Touch-type the H, E, O, and R keys
- Type at least 11wpm/1'/3e

Fingers are named for
home keys. (Example:
The middle finger of the
left hand is the D finger.)

A. Type 2 times.

A. WARMUP

```
1  fff jjj ddd kkk sss lll aaa ;;; fff jjj
2  a salad; a lad; alas a fad; ask a lass;
```

NEW KEYS

B. Type each line 2
times. Space 1 time
after a semicolon.

Use the J
finger.

B. THE H KEY

```
3  jjj jhj jhj hjh jjj jhj jhj hjh jjj jhj
4  has has hah hah had had aha aha ash ash
5  hash half sash lash dash hall shad shah
6  as dad had; a lass has half; add a dash
```

C. Type each line 2
times. Keep your eyes
on the copy as you type.

Use the D
finger.

C. THE E KEY

```
7  ddd ded ded ede ddd ded ded ede ddd ded
8  lea led he; he see; eke fed sea lee fee
9  feed keel ease heal held seal lead fake
10 he fed a seal; she held a lease; a keel
```

D. Type each line
2 times. Keep fingers
curved.

Use the L
finger.

D. THE O KEY

```
11 lll lol lol olo lll lol lol olo lll lol
12 doe off foe hod oh; oak odd ode old sod
13 shoe look kook joke odes does solo oleo
14 he held a hook; a lass solos; old foes;
```

E. Type each line 2 times. Keep the A finger at home.

Use the F finger.

E. THE [R] KEY

```
15  fff frf frf rfr fff frf frf rfr fff frf
16  red ark ore err rah era rod oar her are
17  oars soar dear fare read role rare door
18  a dark red door; he read a rare reader;
```

SKILLBUILDING

F. Type each line 2 times. Do not type the red vertical lines.

F. WORD PATTERNS

```
19  dale kale sale hale|fold sold hold old;
20  feed deed heed seed|dash sash lash ash;
21  lake rake sake fake|dear sear rear ear;
```

G. Take two 1-minute timed writings. Try to complete both lines each time. Press ENTER only at the end of line 23.

Goal: At least 11wpm/1′/3e

G. 1-MINUTE TIMED WRITING

```
22  she asked for a rare old deed; he held
23  a red door ajar;
    |  1  |  2  |  3  |  4  |  5  |  6  |  7  |  8  |
```

Keyboarding Connection

What Is the Internet?

What is the easiest way to go to the library? Try using your fingertips! The Internet creates a "virtual library"—a library with no walls. Nothing can match the Internet as a research device. It is not just one computer but an immense connection of computers talking to one another and organizing and exchanging information.

The Internet is synonymous with cyberspace, a word describing the power and control of information. The Internet has been called "a network of networks" linked together to deliver information to users. The Internet connects more than 200 million people to over 3 million computer networks.

The Internet is considered a wide area network (WAN) because the computers on it span the entire world. Each day the Net increases at about 1000 new users every hour.

YOUR TURN   List some ways the Internet, as a virtual library, enhances your research activities.

New Keys

Goals

- Touch-type the M, T, P, and C keys
- Type at least 12wpm/1'/3e

A. Type 2 times.

A. WARMUP

```
1  aa ;; ss ll dd kk ff jj hh ee oo rr aa;
2  he held a sale for her as she had asked
```

NEW KEYS

B. Type each line 2 times.

Use the J finger.

B. THE M KEY

```
3  jjj jmj jmj mjm jjj jmj jmj mjm jjj jmj
4  mad mom me; am jam; ram dam ham mar ma;
5  arms loam lame roam make fame room same
6  she made more room for some of her ham;
```

C. Type each line 2 times.

Use the F finger.

C. THE T KEY

```
7  fff ftf ftf tft fff ftf ftf tft fff ftf
8  tar tam mat hot jot rat eat lot art sat
9  told take date late mart mate tool fate
10 he told her to set a later date to eat;
```

D. Type each line 2 times.

Use the Sem finger.

D. THE P KEY

```
11 ;;; ;p; ;p; p;p ;;; ;p; ;p; p;p ;;; ;p;
12 pat pal sap rap pet par spa lap pad mop
13 pale palm stop drop pelt plea slap trap
14 please park the red jeep past the pool;
```

E. Type each line 2 times.

Use the D finger.

E. THE C KEY

```
15  ddd dcd dcd cdc ddd dcd dcd cdc ddd dcd
16  cot cod sac act car coo arc ace cop cat
17  pack tack chat coat face aces deck cost
18  call her to race cool cars at the track
```

SKILLBUILDING

F. Sit in the correct position as you type these drills. Refer to the illustration in the Introduction. Type each line 2 times. Do not type the red vertical lines.

F. SHORT PHRASES

```
19  as so|she had|has met|let her|fast pace
20  to do|ask her|for the|had pop|look past
21  do as|lap top|her pad|let pat|halt them
22  as he|had for|red cap|she let|fast plot
```

G. Take two 1-minute timed writings. Try to complete both lines each time. Use word wrap. Press ENTER only at the end of line 24.

Goal: At least 12wpm/1'/3e

G. 1-MINUTE TIMED WRITING

```
23  the old store at home had lots of cheap
24  stools for the sale;
     |  1  |  2  |  3  |  4  |  5  |  6  |  7  |  8  |
```

Strategies for Career Success

Being a Good Listener

Silence is golden! Listening is essential for learning, getting along, and forming relationships.

Do you tend to forget people's names after being introduced? Do you look away from the speaker instead of making eye contact? Do you interrupt the speaker before he or she finishes talking? Do you misunderstand people? Answering yes can indicate poor listening skills.

To improve your listening skills, follow these steps. *Hear the speaker clearly.* Do not interrupt; let the speaker develop his or her ideas before you speak. *Focus on the message.* At the end of a conversation, identify major items discussed. Mentally ask questions to help you assess the points the speaker is making. *Keep an open mind.* Do not judge. Developing your listening skills benefits everyone.

YOUR TURN Assess your listening behavior. What techniques can you use to improve your listening skills? Practice them the next time you have a conversation with someone.

New Keys

Goals

- Touch-type the RIGHT SHIFT, V, period, and W keys
- Count errors
- Type at least 13wpm/1'/3e

A. Type 2 times.

A. WARMUP

1 the farmer asked her to feed the mares;
2 the late callers came to mop the floor;

NEW KEYS

B. Type each line 2 times.

Use the Sem finger.

SHIFT

B. THE RIGHT **SHIFT** KEY

To capitalize letters on the left half of the keyboard:

1. With the J finger at home, press and hold down the RIGHT SHIFT key with the Sem finger.

2. Press the letter key.
3. Release the RIGHT SHIFT key and return fingers to home position.

3 ;;; ;A; ;A; ;;; ;S; ;S; ;;; ;D; ;D; ;;;
4 Art Alf Ada Sal Sam Dee Dot Flo Ted Tom
5 Amos Carl Chet Elsa Fred Sara Todd Elda
6 Carl Amos took Sara Carter to the races

C. Type each line 2 times.

Use the F finger.

C. THE **V** KEY

7 fff fvf fvf vfv fff fvf fvf vfv fff fvf
8 Val eve Eva vet Ava vat Eve ova Vel vee
9 have vase Vera ever vast Reva dove vest
10 Dave voted for Vassar; Val voted for me

D. Type each line 2 times. Space 1 time after a period following an abbreviation; do not space after a period within an abbreviation; space 1 time after a period ending a sentence.

Use the L finger.

D. THE **.** KEY

11 111 1.1 1.1 .1. 111 1.1 1.1 .1. 111 1.1
12 dr. dr. ea. ea. sr. sr. Dr. Dr. Sr. Sr.
13 a.m. acct. A.D. p.m. Corp. amt. Dr. Co.
14 Selma left. Dave left. Sarah came home.

E. Type each line 2 times.

Use the S finger.

E. THE W KEY

```
15  sss sws sws wsw sss sws sws wsw sss sws
16  wow sow war owe was mow woe few wee row
17  wake ward wart wave wham whom walk what
18  Wade watched Walt Shaw walk for a week.
```

SKILLBUILDING

F. Type each line 2 times.

F. BUILD SKILL ON SENTENCES

```
19  Amos Ford saw Emma Dale feed the mares.
20  Dr. Drake called Sam; he asked for Ted.
21  Vera told a tale to her old classmates.
22  Todd asked Cale to move some old rakes.
```

G. Type each line 1 time. After typing all the lines, count your errors. Refer to the Introduction if you need help.

G. COUNTING ERRORS IN SENTENCES

```
23  Ada lost her letter; Dee lost her card.
24  Dave sold some of the food to a market.
25  Alva asked Walt for three more matches.
26  Dale asked Seth to watch the last show.
```

H. Take two 1-minute timed writings. Try to complete both lines each time.

Goal: At least 13wpm/1'/3e

H. 1-MINUTE TIMED WRITING

```
27  Val asked them to tell the major to see
28  Carla at that local farm.
```
| 1 | 2 | 3 | 4 | 5 | 6 | 7 | 8 |

Review

Goals

- Reinforce new-key reaches
- Type at least 14wpm/1'/3e

A. Type 2 times.

A. WARMUP

1 Dave called Drew to ask for a road map.
2 Elsa took three old jars to her mother.

SKILLBUILDING

B. Type each line 2 times. Do not type the red vertical lines.

B. WORD PATTERNS

3 feed seed deed heed|fold cold mold told
4 fame tame lame same|mate late date fate
5 lace face mace race|vast last cast fast
6 park dark hark mark|rare dare fare ware

C. Type each line 2 times.

C. PHRASES

7 at the|he has|her hat|for the|come home
8 or the|he had|her top|ask the|late date
9 to the|he met|her mop|ask her|made more
10 of the|he was|her pop|ask too|fast pace

D. Type each line 2 times.

D. BUILD SKILL ON SENTENCES

11 She asked Dale to share the jar of jam.
12 Cal took the tools from store to store.
13 Darel held a sale to sell some clothes.
14 Seth watched the old cat chase the car.

E. Take a 1-minute timed writing on each line. Review your speed and errors.

E. SENTENCES

```
15  Carl loved to talk to the tall teacher.
16  She dashed to take the jet to her home.
17  Walt asked her to deed the farm to Ted.
    | 1 | 2 | 3 | 4 | 5 | 6 | 7 | 8 |  = Number of 5-stroke words
```

F. Take two 1-minute timed writings on the paragraph. Press ENTER only at the end of the paragraph. Review your speed and errors.

F. PARAGRAPH

CUMULATIVE WORDS

```
18  Rachael asked Sal to take her to school          8
19  for two weeks. She had to meet Freda or         16
20  Walt at the school to work on the maps.         24
    | 1 | 2 | 3 | 4 | 5 | 6 | 7 | 8 |
```

G. Take two 1-minute timed writings. Review your speed and errors.

Goal: At least 14wpm/1'/3e

G. 1-MINUTE TIMED WRITINGS

```
21  Dot Crews asked Al Roper to meet her at          8
22  the tree to look for a jacket.                  14
    | 1 | 2 | 3 | 4 | 5 | 6 | 7 | 8 |
```

Keyboarding Connection

Using Search Engines

How can you most efficiently find information on the Web? Use a search engine! A search engine guides you to the Web's resources. It analyzes the information you request, navigates the Web's many networks, and retrieves a list of relevant documents. Popular search engines include Google, Excite, Alta Vista, and Yahoo.

A search engine examines electronic databases, wire services, journals, article summaries, articles, home pages, and user group lists. It can access material found in millions of Web sites. When you request a specific keyword search, a search engine scans its large database and searches the introductory lines of text, as well as the title, headings, and subheadings of a Web page. The search engine displays the information that most closely matches your request.

YOUR TURN Try different search engines and see which ones you like best. Choose three of your favorite search engines. Then conduct a search using the keywords "touch typing." (Don't forget the quotation marks.) Compare the results for each search engine.

Unit 2

Keyboarding:
The Alphabet

New Keys

Goals

- Touch-type the I, LEFT SHIFT, hyphen, and G keys
- Type at least 15wpm/1'/3e

A. Type 2 times.

A. WARMUP

1 The major sold three wool hats at cost.
2 Dale took her cats to the vet at three.

NEW KEYS

B. Type each line 2 times.

Use the K finger.

B. THE I KEY

3 kkk kik kik iki kkk kik kik iki kkk kik
4 aid did fir him kid lid mid pit sip tip
5 chip dice itch film hide iris kite milk
6 This time he left his tie at the store.

C. Type each line 2 times.

Use the A finger.

C. THE LEFT SHIFT KEY

To capitalize letters on the right half of the keyboard:

1. With the F finger at home, press and hold down the LEFT SHIFT key with the A finger.
2. Press the letter key.
3. Release the LEFT SHIFT key and return fingers to the home position.

7 aaa Jaa Jaa aaa Kaa Kaa aaa Laa Laa aaa
8 Joe Kip Lee Hal Mat Pat Jim Kim Les Pam
9 Jake Karl Lake Hope Mark Jack Kate Hale
10 Les Lee rode with Pat Mace to the park.

D. Type each line 2 times. Do not space before or after a hyphen; keep the J finger in home position.

Use the Sem finger.

D. THE - KEY

11 ;;; ;p; ;-; ;-; -;- ;;; ;-; -;- ;;; ;-;
12 two-thirds two-fifths trade-off tip-off
13 look-alike jack-of-all-trades free-fall
14 I heard that Ms. Lee-Som is well-to-do.

E. Type each line 2 times. Keep wrists low but not resting on the keyboard.

Use the F finger. F → G

E. THE G KEY

```
15  fff fgf fgf gfg fff fgf fgf gfg fff fgf
16  age cog dig fig hog jog lag peg rag sag
17  gold rage sage grow page cage gate wage
18  Gail G. Grove greeted the great golfer.
```

SKILLBUILDING

F. Type each line 2 times.

F. TECHNIQUE PRACTICE: SPACE BAR

```
19  Vic will meet. Ed is here. Ava is here.
20  See them. Do it. Make these. Hold this.
21  See Lester. See Kate. See Dad. See Mom.
22  Take this car. Make the cakes. Hide it.
```

G. Type each line 2 times.

G. TECHNIQUE PRACTICE: HYPHEN KEY

```
23  Two-thirds were well-to-do look-alikes.
24  Jo Hames-Smith is a jack-of-all-trades.
25  Phil saw the trade-offs at the tip-off.
26  Two-fifths are packed for Jo Mill-Ross.
```

H. Take two 1-minute timed writings. Review your speed and errors.

Goal: At least 15wpm/1'/3e

H. 1-MINUTE TIMED WRITING

WORDS
```
27  Al Hall left the firm two weeks ago. I      8
28  will see him at the office at three.        15
    |  1  |  2  |  3  |  4  |  5  |  6  |  7  |  8  |
```

New Keys

Goals

- Touch-type the U, B, colon, and X keys
- Type at least 16wpm/1′/3e

A. Type 2 times.

A. WARMUP

1 Evette jogged eight miles with Christi.
2 Philip gave Shari the award for spirit.

NEW KEYS

B. Type each line 2 times. Keep your other fingers at home as you reach to U.

Use the J finger.

B. THE U KEY

3 jjj juj juj uju jjj juj juj uju jjj juj
4 cue due hue put rut cut dug hut pup rum
5 cult duet fuel hulk just lump mule pull
6 Hugh urged us to put out the hot fires.

C. Type each line 2 times.

Use the F finger.

C. THE B KEY

7 fff fbf fbf bfb fff fbf fbf bfb fff fbf
8 bag cab bad lab bat rib bar tab beg web
9 bake back bead beef bath bail beam both
10 Bart backed Bill for a big blue bumper.

D. The colon is the shift of the semicolon key. Type each line 2 times. Space 1 time after a period following an abbreviation and 1 time after a colon.

Use the Sem finger.

D. THE : KEY

11 ;:; ;:; ;:; :;: ;:; ;:; ;:; :;: ;:; ;:;
12 Dr. Poole: Ms. Shu: Mr. Rose: Mrs. Tam:
13 Dear Ed: Dear Flo: Dear James: Dear Di:
14 Date: To: From: Subject: for the dates:

E. Type each line 2 times.

Use the S finger.

E. THE X KEY

15 sss sxs sxs xsx sss sxs sxs xsx sss sxs
16 box fox hex lax lux mix six tax vex wax
17 apex axle exam flax flex flux taxi text
18 Max asked six pals to fix a sixth taxi.

SKILLBUILDING

F. Type each line 2 times.

F. TECHNIQUE PRACTICE: COLON KEY

19 as follows: these people: this example:
20 Dear Sirs: Dear Madam: Dear Mrs. Smith:
21 Dear Di: Dear Bo: Dear Peter: Dear Mom:
22 for this part: as listed: the projects:

G. Type each line 2 times.

G. WORD PRACTICE

Top row

23 We were told to take our truck to Hugo.
24 There were two tired people at the hut.
25 Please write to their home to tell Tom.

Home row

26 Jake asked his dad for small red flags.
27 Sara added a dash of salt to the salad.
28 Dale said she had a fall sale at Drake.

Bottom row

29 He came to the mall at five to meet me.
30 Victoria came to vote with ample vigor.
31 Mable Baxter visited via the Marta bus.

H. Take two 1-minute timed writings. Review your speed and errors.

Goal: At least 16wpm/1'/3e

H. 1-MINUTE TIMED WRITING

WORDS

32 Dear Jack: Fred would like to take Jill   8
33 Wells to the home game at five tomorrow.   16

     | 1 | 2 | 3 | 4 | 5 | 6 | 7 | 8 |

New Keys

Goals

- Touch-type the Y, comma, Q, and slash keys
- Type at least 17wpm/1'/3e

A. Type 2 times.

A. WARMUP

1 Jack asked Philip if Charlie came home.
2 Kim had a short meal with Victor Baker.

NEW KEYS

B. Type each line 2 times.

Use the J finger.

B. THE Y KEY

3 jjj jyj jyj yjy jjj jyj jyj yjy jjj jyj
4 boy cry day eye fly guy hay joy key may
5 yard year yelp yoke yolk your yule play
6 Peggy told me that she may try to stay.

C. Type each line 2 times.

Use the K finger.

C. THE , KEY

7 kkk k,k k,k ,k, kkk k,k k,k ,k, kkk k,k
8 as, at, do, if, is, it, of, oh, or, so,
9 if so, if it is, what if, what of, too,
10 Dale, Barbra, Sadie, or Edith left too.

D. Type each line 2 times.

Use the A finger.

D. THE Q KEY

11 aaa aqa aqa qaq aaa aqa aqa qaq aaa aqa
12 quip quit quack quail quake quart quash
13 quest quick quilts quotes quaver queasy
14 Four quiet squires quilted aqua quilts.

E. Type each line
2 times. Do not space
before or after a slash.

Use the
Sem finger.

E. THE / KEY

15 ;;; ;/; ;/; /;/ ;;; ;/; ;/; /;/ ;;; ;/;
16 his/her him/her he/she either/or ad/add
17 do/due/dew hale/hail fir/fur heard/herd
18 Ask him/her if he/she chose true/false.

SKILLBUILDING

F. Type each line
2 times.

F. PHRASES

19 if it is|she will do|will he come|he is
20 he said so|who left them|will she drive
21 after all|he voted|just wait|to ask her
22 some said it|for that firm|did she seem

G. Type each line
2 times.

G. TECHNIQUE PRACTICE: SHIFT KEY

23 Ada, Idaho; Kodiak, Alaska; Lima, Ohio;
24 Lula, Georgia; Sully, Iowa; Alta, Utah;
25 Mr. Ray Tims; Mr. Ed Chu; Mr. Cal York;
26 Ms. Vi Close; Ms. Di Ray; Ms. Sue Ames;

H. Take two 1-minute
timed writings. Review
your speed and errors.

Goal: At least
17wpm/1'/3e

H. 1-MINUTE TIMED WRITING

27 George predicted that Lu will have five   8
28 boxed quilts. David Quayle was to pack   16
29 a mug.   17
   | 1 | 2 | 3 | 4 | 5 | 6 | 7 | 8 |

New Keys

Goals

- Touch-type the N, Z, question mark, and TAB keys
- Type at least 18wpm/1'/3e

A. Type 2 times.

A. WARMUP

1 I quit the sales job at Huber, Georgia.
2 Alice packed two boxes of silver disks.

NEW KEYS

B. Type each line 2 times.

Use the J finger.

B. THE N KEY

3 jjj jnj jnj njn jjj jnj jnj njn jjj jnj
4 and ban can den end fan nag one pan ran
5 aunt band chin dent find gain hang lawn
6 Al and Dan can enter the main entrance.

C. Type each line 2 times. Keep the F finger at home as you reach to the Z.

Use the A finger.

C. THE Z KEY

7 aaa aza aza zaz aaa aza aza zaz aaa aza
8 zap zig buzz gaze haze jazz mazes oozes
9 zip zoo zinc zing zone zoom blaze craze
10 The size of the prized pizza amazed us.

D. The question mark is the shift of the slash. Space 1 time after a question mark at the end of a sentence. Type each line 2 times.

Use the Sem finger.

D. THE ? KEY

11 ;;; ;?; ;?; ?;? ;;; ;?; ;?; ?;? ;;; ;?;
12 Can John go? If not Jane, who? Can Ken?
13 Who will see? Can this be? Is that you?
14 Why not quilt? Can they go? Did he ask?

E. The word counts in this book credit you with 1 stroke for each paragraph indention in a timed writing. Press the TAB key after the timing starts.

Use the A finger.

E. THE **TAB** KEY

The TAB key is used to indent paragraphs. Reach to the TAB key with the A finger. Keep your other fingers on the home keys as you quickly press the TAB key. Pressing the TAB key moves the insertion point 0.5 inch (the default setting) to the right.

F. Type each paragraph 2 times. Press ENTER only at the end of the paragraph.

F. PRACTICE THE **TAB** KEY

```
15  Each  Tab→  day   Tab→  set   Tab→  your  Tab→  goal
16  to          type        with        more        speed.

17  You         will        soon        reach       your
18  goal        if          you         work        hard.
```

SKILLBUILDING

G. Type each line 2 times.

G. TECHNIQUE PRACTICE: QUESTION MARK

```
19  Who? Why? How? When? What? True? False?
20  Is it Mo? Why not? What for? Which one?
21  Did Mary go? Is Clinton ready? Why not?
22  Who competed with me? Dana? James? Kay?
```

H. Type each line 2 times.

H. PHRASES

```
23  and the|for the|she is able|can they go
24  for him|ask him|they still|did they fly
25  of them|with us|can he send|ought to be
26  has been able|they need it|he will call
```

I. Type each paragraph 2 times.

I. TECHNIQUE PRACTICE: HYPHEN

Hyphens are used:

- To show that a word is divided (lines 27 and 31).
- To make a dash using two hyphens with no space before or after (lines 28 and 31).
- To join words in a compound word (lines 29, 30, and 32).

```
27        Can Larry go to the next tennis tourna-
28  ment? I am positive he--like Lane--will find
29  the event to be a first-class sports event.
30  If he can go, I will get first-rate seats.
31        Larry--like Ella--enjoys going to tourna-
32  ments that are always first-rate, first-class
33  sporting events.
```

J. Space 1 time after a semicolon, colon, and comma and 1 time after a period and question mark at the end of a sentence. Type each line 2 times.

J. PUNCTUATION PRACTICE

```
34  Kate writes; John sings. Are they good?
35  Send these items: pens, pencils, clips.
36  Hal left; she stayed. Will they attend?
37  Wes made these stops: Rome, Bern, Kiev.
```

K. Take two 1-minute timed writings. Review your speed and errors.

Goal: At least 18wpm/1'/3e

K. 1-MINUTE TIMED WRITING

```
38        Zelda judged six typing contests          7
39  that a local firm held in Piqua. Vick         14
40  Bass was a winner.                            18
    | 1  | 2  | 3  | 4  | 5  | 6  | 7  | 8  |
```

Strategies for Career Success

Preparing a Job Interview Portfolio

Don't go empty-handed to that job interview! Take a portfolio of items with you. Definitely include copies of your resume and your list of references, with at least three professional references. Your academic transcript is useful, especially if you are asked to complete a company application form. Appropriate work samples and copies of certificates and licenses are also helpful portfolio items.

The interview process provides you the opportunity to interview the organization. Include a list of questions you want to ask during the interview.

A comprehensive portfolio of materials will benefit you by giving you a measure of control during the interview process.

YOUR TURN Start today to compile items for your interview portfolio. Include copies of your resume, your reference list, and copies of certificates and licenses. Begin developing a list of interview questions. Think about appropriate work samples to include in your portfolio.

Review

Goals

- Reinforce new key reaches
- Type at least 19wpm/1'/3e

A. Type 2 times.

A. WARMUP

```
1       She expects to work hard at her job.
2   Keith had a very quiet, lazy afternoon.
```

SKILLBUILDING

B. Take a 1-minute timed writing on each paragraph. Review your speed and errors.

B. SHORT PARAGRAPHS

```
3       You can utilize your office skills      7
4   to complete tasks. Some types of jobs      15
5   require more skills.                        19

6       You will be amazed at how easily        7
7   and quickly you complete your task when     15
8   you can concentrate.                        19
    |  1  |  2  |  3  |  4  |  5  |  6  |  7  |  8  |
```

C. Type each line 2 times.

C. WORD PATTERNS

```
9   banister minister adapter filter master
10  disable disband discern discord discuss
11  embargo emerge embody empty employ emit
12  enforce endure energy engage engine end
13  precept precise predict preside premier
14  subtract subject subsist sublime subdue
15  teamster tearful teaches teak team tear
16  theater theirs theory thefts therm them
17  treason crimson season prison bison son
18  tribune tribute tripod trial tribe trim
```

D. Type each line 2 times. Keep fingers curved and wrists low but not resting on the keyboard as you practice these lines.

D. ALPHABET REVIEW

19 Alda asked Alma Adams to fly to Alaska.
20 Both Barbara and Bill liked basketball.
21 Carl can accept a classic car in Cairo.
22 David dined in a dark diner in Detroit.
23 Elmo said Eddie edited the entire text.
24 Five friars focused on the four fables.
25 Guy gave a bag of green grapes to Gina.
26 Haughty Hugh hoped Hal had helped Seth.
27 Irene liked to pickle pickles in brine.
28 Jon Jones joined a junior jogging team.
29 Kenny kept a kayak for a trek to Akron.
30 Lowell played a well-planned ball game.
31 Monica made more money on many markups.
32 Ned knew ten men in a main dining room.
33 Opal Orem opened four boxes of oranges.
34 Pat paid to park the plane at the pump.
35 Quincy quickly quit his quarterly quiz.
36 Robin read rare books in their library.
37 Sam signed, sealed, and sent the lease.
38 Todd caught trout in the little stream.
39 Uncle Rubin urged Julie to go to Utica.
40 Viva Vista vetoed the five voice votes.
41 Walt waited while Wilma went to Weston.
42 Xu mixed extra extract exactly as told.
43 Yes, your young sister played a cymbal.
44 Zesty zebras zigzagged in the Ohio zoo.

E. Take two 1-minute timed writings. Review your speed and errors.

Goal: At least 19wpm/1'/3e

E. 1-MINUTE TIMED WRITING

45   Zoe expected a quiet morning to do   7
46 all of her work. Jean Day was to bring   15
47 five of the tablets.   19
     | 1 | 2 | 3 | 4 | 5 | 6 | 7 | 8 |

Unit 3

Keyboarding: The Numbers

Number Keys

Goals

- Touch-type the 5, 7, 3, and 9 keys
- Type at least 19wpm/2'/5e

A. Type 2 times.

A. WARMUP

```
1        The law firm of Quayle, Buster, Given, and      9
2   Rizzo processed all the cases last June and July;    19
3   however, we will seek a new law firm next summer.    29
    | 1 | 2 | 3 | 4 | 5 | 6 | 7 | 8 | 9 | 10 |
```

NEW KEYS

B. Type each line 2 times.

Use the F finger.

B. THE 5 KEY

```
4   fr5f fr5f f55f f55f f5f5 f5f5 5 55 555 5,555 5:55
5   55 fibs 55 foes 55 fibs 55 fads 55 furs 55 favors
6   The 55 students read the 555 pages in 55 minutes.
7   He found Item 55 that weighed 55 pounds 5 ounces.
```

C. Type each line 2 times.

Use the J finger.

C. THE 7 KEY

```
8   ju7j ju7j j77j j77j j7j7 j7j7 7 77 777 7,777 7:77
9   77 jigs 77 jobs 77 jugs 77 jets 77 jars 77 jewels
10  The 77 men bought Items 77 and 777 for their job.
11  Joe had 57 books and 77 tablets for a 7:57 class.
```

D. Type each line 2 times.

Use the D finger.

D. THE 3 KEY

```
12  de3d de3d d33d d33d d3d3 d3d3 3 33 333 3,333 3:33
13  33 dots 33 dies 33 dips 33 days 33 dogs 33 drains
14  The 33 vans moved 73 cases in less than 33 hours.
15  Add 55 to 753; subtract 73 to get a total of 735.
```

E. Type each line 2 times.

Use the L finger.

E. THE 9 KEY

16 lo9l lo9l 1991 1991 1919 1919 9 99 999 9,999 9:99
17 99 lads 99 lights 99 labs 99 legs 99 lips 99 logs
18 Their 99 cans of No. 99 were sold to 99 managers.
19 He had 39 pens, 59 pads, 97 pencils, and 9 clips.

SKILLBUILDING

F. Type each line 2 times.

F. NUMBER PRACTICE: 5, 7, 3, AND 9

20 The 57 tickets were for the April 3 show at 9:59.
21 Mary was to read pages 33, 57, 95, and 97 to him.
22 Kate planted 53 tulips, 39 mums, and 97 petunias.
23 Only 397 of the 573 coeds could register at 5:39.

G. Type each line 2 times. Keep other fingers at home as you reach to the SHIFT keys.

G. TECHNIQUE PRACTICE: SHIFT KEY

24 Vera Rosa Tao Fay Jae Tab Pat Yuk Sue Ann Sal Joe
25 Andre Fidel Pedro Chong Alice Mike Juan Fern Dick
26 Carlos Caesar Karen Ojars Julie Marta Scott Maria
27 Marge Jerry Joan Mary Bill Ken Bob Ray Ted Mel Al

H. PROGRESSIVE PRACTICE: ALPHABET

If you are not using the GDP software, turn to page SB-7 and follow the directions for this activity.

I. Take two 2-minute timed writings. Review your speed and errors.

Goal: At least 19wpm/2'/5e

I. 2-MINUTE TIMED WRITING

28   Zach paid for six seats and quit because he   9
29 could not get the views he wanted near the middle   19
30 of the field. In August he is thinking of going   29
31 to the ticket office early to purchase tickets.   38
   | 1 | 2 | 3 | 4 | 5 | 6 | 7 | 8 | 9 | 10

Review

Goal

- Type at least 20wpm/2'/5e

A. Type 2 times.

A. WARMUP

1   Rex played a very quiet game of bridge with   9
2   Zeke. In March they played in competition with   18
3   39 players; in January they played with 57 more. 28

| 1 | 2 | 3 | 4 | 5 | 6 | 7 | 8 | 9 | 10

SKILLBUILDING

B. Take three 12-second timed writings on each line. The scale below the last line shows your wpm speed for a 12-second timed writing.

B. 12-SECOND SPEED SPRINTS

4   A good neighbor paid for these ancient ornaments.
5   Today I sit by the big lake and count huge rocks.
6   The four chapels sit by the end of the old field.
7   The signal means help is on its way to the child.

| | | | 5 | | | | 10 | | | | 15 | | | | 20 | | | | 25 | | | | 30 | | | | 35 | | | | 40 | | | | 45 | | | | 50

C. Take a 1-minute timed writing on the first paragraph to establish your base speed. Then take four 1-minute timed writings on the remaining paragraphs. As soon as you equal or exceed your base speed on one paragraph, advance to the next, more difficult paragraph.

C. SUSTAINED PRACTICE: SYLLABIC INTENSITY

8   People continue to rent autos for personal   9
9   use and for their work, and car rental businesses 19
10 just keep growing. You may want to try one soon. 29

11   It is likely that a great deal of insurance   9
12 protection is part of the standard rental cost to 19
13 you. You may, however, make many other choices.   28

14   Perhaps this is not necessary, as you might   9
15 already have the kind of protection you want in a 19
16 policy that you currently have on the automobile. 29

17   Paying separate mileage charges could evolve   9
18 into a very large bill. This will undoubtedly be 19
19 true if your trip involves distant destinations. 29

D. Type each line 2 times.

D. ALPHABET PRACTICE

20 Packing jam for the dozen boxes was quite lively.
21 Fay quickly jumped over the two dozen huge boxes.
22 We vexed Jack by quietly helping a dozen farmers.
23 The quick lynx from the zoo just waved a big paw.
24 Lazy brown dogs do not jump over the quick foxes.

E. Type each line 2 times.

E. NUMBER PRACTICE

25 Mary was to read pages 37, 59, 75, and 93 to Zoe.
26 He invited 53 boys and 59 girls to the 7:35 show.
27 The 9:37 bus did not come to our stop until 9:55.
28 Purchase Order 53 listed Items 35, 77, 93, and 9.
29 Flight 375 will be departing Gate 37 at 9:59 p.m.

F. Type each sentence on a separate line. Type 2 times.

F. TECHNIQUE PRACTICE: ENTER KEY

30 Can he go? If so, what? We are lost. Jose is ill.
31 Did she type the memos? Tina is going. Jane lost.
32 Max will drive. Xenia is in Ohio. She is tallest.
33 Nate is fine. Ty is not. Who won? Where is Nancy?
34 No, she cannot go. Was he here? Where is Roberta?

G. Type each line 2 times. Space without pausing.

G. TECHNIQUE PRACTICE: SPACE BAR

35 a b c d e f g h i j k l m n o p q r s t u v w x y
36 an as be by go in is it me no of or to we but for
37 Do you go to Ada or Ida for work every day or so?
38 I am sure he can go with you if he has some time.
39 He is to be at the car by the time you get there.

H. Take two 2-minute timed writings. Review your speed and errors.

Goal: At least 20wpm/2'/5e

H. 2-MINUTE TIMED WRITING

40   Jack and Alex ordered six pizzas at a price   9
41 that was quite a bit lower than was the one they   19
42 ordered yesterday. They will order from the same   29
43 place tomorrow for the parties they are planning   38
44 to have.   40

| | 1 | 2 | 3 | 4 | 5 | 6 | 7 | 8 | 9 | 10 |

Number Keys

Goals

- Touch-type the 8, 2, and 0 keys
- Type at least 21wpm/2'/5e

A. Type 2 times.

A. WARMUP

1   Mary, Jenny, and Quinn packed 79 prizes in   9
2   53 large boxes for the party. They will take all   19
3   of the boxes to 3579 North Capitol Avenue today.   29
  | 1 | 2 | 3 | 4 | 5 | 6 | 7 | 8 | 9 | 10

NEW KEYS

B. Type each line 2 times.

Use the K finger.

B. THE 8 KEY

4   ki8k ki8k k88k k88k k8k8 k8k8 8 88 888 8,888 8:88
5   88 inks 88 inns 88 keys 88 kits 88 kids 88 knives
6   Bus 38 left at 3:38 and arrived here at 8:37 p.m.
7   Kenny called Joe at 8:38 at 883-7878 or 585-3878.

C. Type each line 2 times.

Use the S finger.

C. THE 2 KEY

8   sw2s sw2s s22s s22s s2s2 s2s2 2 22 222 2,222 2:22
9   22 seas 22 sets 22 sons 22 subs 22 suns 22 sports
10   The 22 seats sold at 2:22 to 22 coeds in Room 22.
11   He added Items 22, 23, 25, 27, and 28 on Order 2.

D. Type each line 2 times.

Use the Sem finger.

D. THE 0 KEY

12   ;p0; ;p0; ;00; ;00; ;0;0 ;0;0 0 00 000 0,000 0:00
13   20 pads 30 pegs 50 pens 70 pins 80 pits 900 parks
14   You will get 230 when you add 30, 50, 70, and 80.
15   The 80 men met at 3:05 with 20 agents in Room 90.

SKILLBUILDING

E. Type each line 2 times.

E. NUMBER PRACTICE

16 Jill bought 55 tickets for the 5:50 or 7:50 show.
17 Maxine called from 777-7370 or 777-7570 for Mary.
18 Sally had 23 cats, 23 dogs, and 22 birds at home.
19 Items 35, 37, 38, and 39 were sent on October 30.
20 Did Flight 2992 leave from Gate 39 at 9:39 today?
21 Sue went from 852 28th Street to 858 28th Street.
22 He sold 20 tires, 30 air filters, and 200 wipers.

F. Type each sentence on a separate line. For each sentence, press TAB, type the sentence, and then press ENTER. After you have typed all 11 sentences, insert a blank line and type them all a second time.

F. TECHNIQUE PRACTICE: TAB KEY

23   Casey left to go home. Where is John? Did
24 Susan go home with them?

25   Isaiah drove my car to work. Sandy parked
26 the car in the lot. They rode together.

27   Pat sold new cars for a new dealer. Dana
28 sold vans for the same dealer.

29   Nick bought the nails to finish the job.
30 Chris has the bolts. Dave has the wood.

G. PACED PRACTICE

If you are not using the GDP software, turn to page SB-14 and follow the directions for this activity.

H. PROGRESSIVE PRACTICE: ALPHABET

If you are not using the GDP software, turn to page SB-7 and follow the directions for this activity.

I. Take two 2-minute timed writings. Review your speed and errors.

Goal: At least 21wpm/2'/5e

I. 2-MINUTE TIMED WRITING

31 Jim told Bev that they must keep the liquid	9
32 oxygen frozen so that it could be used by the new	19
33 plant managers tomorrow. The oxygen will then be	29
34 moved quickly to its new location by transport or	39
35 rail on Tuesday.	42

| 1 | 2 | 3 | 4 | 5 | 6 | 7 | 8 | 9 | 10

Number Keys

Goals

- Touch-type the 4, 6, and 1 keys
- Type at least 22wpm/2'/5e

A. Type 2 times.

A. WARMUP

```
1        We quickly made 30 jars of jam and won a big      9
2   prize for our efforts on March 29. Six of the jam     19
3   jars were taken to 578 Culver Drive on April 28.      29
    |  1  |  2  |  3  |  4  |  5  |  6  |  7  |  8  |  9  |  10
```

NEW KEYS

B. Type each line 2 times.

Use the F finger.

B. THE 4 KEY

```
4   fr4f fr4f f44f f44f f4f4 f4f4 4 44 444 4,444 4:44
5   44 fans 44 feet 44 figs 44 fins 44 fish 44 flakes
6   The 44 boys had 44 tickets for the games at 4:44.
7   Matthew read 4 books, 54 articles, and 434 lines.
```

C. Type each line 2 times.

Use the J finger.

C. THE 6 KEY

```
8    jy6j jy6j j66j j66j j6j6 j6j6 6 66 666 6,666 6:66
9    66 jabs 66 jams 66 jobs 66 jars 66 jots 66 jewels
10   Tom Lux left at 6:26 on Train 66 to go 600 miles.
11   There were 56,640 people in Bath; 26,269 in Hale.
```

D. Type each line 2 times.

Use the A finger.

D. THE 1 KEY

```
12   aq1a aq1a a11a a11a a1a1 a1a1 1 11 111 1,111 1:11
13   11 aces 11 arms 11 aims 11 arts 11 axes 11 arenas
14   Sam left here at 1:11, Sue at 6:11, Don at 11:11.
15   Eric moved from 1661 Main Street to 1116 in 1995.
```

E. NUMBER PRACTICE

E. Type each line 2 times. Focus on accuracy rather than speed as you practice the number drills.

16 Adding 10 and 20 and 30 and 40 and 70 totals 170.
17 Al selected Nos. 15, 16, 17, 18, and 19 to study.
18 The test took Sam 10 hours, 8 minutes, 3 seconds.
19 Did the 39 men drive 567 miles on Route 23 or 27?
20 The 18 shows were sold out by 8:37 on October 18.
21 On April 29-30 we will be open from 7:45 to 9:30.

F. PROGRESSIVE PRACTICE: NUMBERS

If you are not using the GDP software, turn to page SB-11 and follow the directions for this activity.

G. HANDWRITTEN PARAGRAPH

G. Take two 1-minute timed writings. Review your speed and errors.

22 *Good writing skills are critical for success* 9
23 *in business. Numerous studies have shown* 18
24 *that these skills are essential for job advancement.* 27

| 1 | 2 | 3 | 4 | 5 | 6 | 7 | 8 | 9 | 10

H. PACED PRACTICE

If you are not using the GDP software, turn to page SB-14 and follow the directions for this activity.

I. 2-MINUTE TIMED WRITING

I. Take two 2-minute timed writings. Review your speed and errors.

Goal: At least 22wpm/2'/5e

25   James scheduled a science quiz next week for   9
26 George, but he did not let him know what time the 19
27 exam was to be taken. George must score well on   29
28 this exam in order to be admitted to the class   38
29 at the Mount Garland Academy.   44

| 1 | 2 | 3 | 4 | 5 | 6 | 7 | 8 | 9 | 10

Review

Goal

- Type at least 23wpm/2'/5e

A. Type 2 times.

A. WARMUP

```
 1        Jeffrey Mendoza quickly plowed six fields so     9
 2   that he could plant 19 rows of beets, 28 rows of     19
 3   corn, 37 rows of grapes, and 45 rows of olives.      28
     |  1  |  2  |  3  |  4  |  5  |  6  |  7  |  8  |  9  |  10
```

SKILLBUILDING

B. Take three 12-second timed writings on each line. The scale below the last line shows your wpm speed for a 12-second timed writing.

B. 12-SECOND SPEED SPRINTS

```
 4   The lane to the lake might make the auto go away.
 5   They go to the lake by bus when they work for me.
 6   He just won and lost, won and lost, won and lost.
 7   The man and the girl rush down the paths to town.
     I I I 5 I I I 10 I I I 15 I I I 20 I I I 25 I I I 30 I I I 35 I I I 40 I I I 45 I I I 50
```

C. Press TAB 1 time between columns. Type 2 times.

C. TECHNIQUE PRACTICE: TAB KEY

```
 8   aisle   Tab→ break   Tab→ crank   Tab→ draft   Tab→ earth
 9   Frank        Guinn        Henry        Ivan         Jacob
10   knack        learn        mason        night        ocean
11   print        quest        rinse        slide        title
12   Umberto      Victor       Wally        Xavier       Zenger
```

D. Type each line 2 times. Try not to slow down for the capital letters.

D. TECHNIQUE PRACTICE: SHIFT KEY

```
13   Sue, Pat, Ann, and Gail left for Rome on June 10.
14   The St. Louis Cardinals and New York Mets played.
15   Dave Herr took Flight 481 for Memphis and Toledo.
16   An address for Karen Cook is 5 Bar Street, Provo.
17   Harry Truman was born in Missouri on May 8, 1884.
```

E. Type each line 2 times.

E. PUNCTUATION PRACTICE: HYPHEN

18 Jan Brooks-Smith was a go-between for the author.
19 The off-the-record comment led to a free-for-all.
20 Louis was a jack-of-all-trades as a clerk-typist.
21 Ask Barbara--who is in Central Data--to find out.
22 Joanne is too old-fashioned to be that outspoken.

PPP   PRETEST → PRACTICE → POSTTEST

PRETEST
Take a 1-minute timed writing. Review your speed and errors.

F. PRETEST: Vertical Reaches

23   A few of our business managers attribute the   9
24 success of the bank to a judicious and scientific   19
25 reserve program. The bank cannot drop its guard.   29
     | 1 | 2 | 3 | 4 | 5 | 6 | 7 | 8 | 9 | 10

PRACTICE
Speed Emphasis:
If you made 2 or fewer errors on the Pretest, type each *individual line* 2 times.
Accuracy Emphasis:
If you made 3 or more errors, type each *group* of lines (as though it were a paragraph) 2 times.

G. PRACTICE: Up Reaches

26 at atlas plate water later batch fatal match late
27 dr draft drift drums drawn drain drama dress drab
28 ju jumpy juror junky jumbo julep judge juice just

H. PRACTICE: Down Reaches

29 ca cable cabin cadet camel cameo candy carve cash
30 nk trunk drink prank rinks brink drank crank sink
31 ba batch badge bagel baked banjo barge basis bank

POSTTEST
Repeat the Pretest timed writing and compare performance.

I. POSTTEST: Vertical Reaches

J. PROGRESSIVE PRACTICE: ALPHABET

If you are not using the GDP software, turn to page SB-7 and follow the directions for this activity.

K. Take two 2-minute timed writings. Review your speed and errors.

Goal: At least 23wpm/2'/5e

K. 2-MINUTE TIMED WRITING

32   Jeff Malvey was quite busy fixing all of the   9
33 frozen pipes so that his water supply would not   19
34 be stopped. Last winter Jeff kept the pipes from   29
35 freezing by wrapping them with an insulated tape   38
36 that protected them from snow and ice.   46
     | 1 | 2 | 3 | 4 | 5 | 6 | 7 | 8 | 9 | 10

Unit 4

Keyboarding: The Symbols

Symbol Keys

Goals

- Touch-type the $ ( ) and ! keys
- Type at least 24wpm/2′/5e

A. Type 2 times.

A. WARMUP

```
1        Gill was quite vexed by that musician who        9
2   played 5 jazz songs and 13 country songs at the      18
3   fair. He wanted 8 rock songs and 4 blues songs.      28
    |  1  |  2  |  3  |  4  |  5  |  6  |  7  |  8  |  9  |  10
```

NEW KEYS

B. DOLLAR is the shift of 4. Do not space between the dollar sign and the number. Type each line 2 times.

Use the F finger.

B. THE $ KEY

```
4   frf fr4f f4f f4$f f$$f f$$f $44 $444 $4,444 $4.44
5   I quoted $48, $64, and $94 for the set of chairs.
6   Her insurance paid $150; our insurance paid $175.
7   Season concert seats were $25, $30, $55, and $75.
```

C. PARENTHESES are the shifts of 9 and 0. Do not space between the parentheses and the text within them. Type each line 2 times.

Use the L finger on (. Use the Sem finger on).

C. THE (AND) KEYS

```
8    lo9l lo9l lo(l lo(l l((l ;p0; ;p0; ;p); ;p); ;));
9    Please ask (1) Al, (2) Pat, (3) Ted, and (4) Dee.
10   Sue has some (1) skis, (2) sleds, and (3) skates.
11   Mary is (1) prompt, (2) speedy, and (3) accurate.

12   Our workers (Lewis, Jerry, and Ty) were rewarded.
13   The owner (Ms. Parks) went on Friday (August 18).
14   The Roxie (a cafe) had fish (salmon) on the menu.
15   The clerk (Ms. Fay Green) will vote yes (not no).
```

D. THE ! KEY

D. EXCLAMATION is the shift of 1. Space 1 time after an exclamation point at the end of a sentence. Type each line 2 times.

Use the A finger.

16 aqa aqla aq!a a!!a a!!a Where! Whose! What! When!
17 Put those down! Do not move them! Leave it there!
18 He did say that! Jake cannot take a vacation now!
19 You cannot leave at this time! Janie will go now!

SKILLBUILDING

E. Type the paragraph 2 times.

E. TECHNIQUE PRACTICE: SPACE BAR

20   We will all go to the race if I win the one
21 I am going to run today. Do you think I will be
22 able to run at the front of the pack and win it?

F. Take three 12-second timed writings on each line. The scale below the last line shows your wpm speed for a 12-second timed writing.

F. 12-SECOND SPEED SPRINTS

23 Walking can perk you up if you are feeling tired.
24 Your heart and lungs can work harder as you walk.
25 It may be that a walk is often better than a nap.
26 If you walk each day, you may have better health.
     | | | | 5 | | | | 10 | | | | 15 | | | | 20 | | | | 25 | | | | 30 | | | | 35 | | | | 40 | | | | 45 | | | | 50

G. PACED PRACTICE

If you are not using the GDP software, turn to page SB-14 and follow the directions for this activity.

H. Take two 2-minute timed writings. Review your speed and errors.

Goal: At least 24wpm/2'/5e

H. 2-MINUTE TIMED WRITING

27   Katie quit her zoo job seven days after she   9
28 learned that she was expected to travel to four   19
29 different zoos in the first month of employment.   28
30 After quitting that job, she found an excellent   38
31 position which did not require her to travel much.   48
     | 1 | 2 | 3 | 4 | 5 | 6 | 7 | 8 | 9 | 10

Review

Goal

- Type at least 25wpm/2'/5e

A. Type 2 times.

A. WARMUP

```
1        Yes! We object to the dumping of 25 toxic       9
2   barrels at 4098 Nix Street. A larger number (36)    19
3   were dumped on the 7th, costing us over $10,000.    28
      |  1  |  2  |  3  |  4  |  5  |  6  |  7  |  8  |  9  |  10
```

SKILLBUILDING

B. Type each line 2 times.

B. NUMBER PRACTICE

```
4   we 23 pi 08 you 697 row 492 tire 5843 power 09234
5   or 94 re 43 eye 363 top 590 quit 1785 witty 28556
6   up 70 ye 63 pit 085 per 034 root 4995 wrote 24953
7   it 85 ro 49 rip 480 two 529 tour 5974 quite 17853
8   yi 68 to 59 toy 596 rot 495 tier 5834 queue 17373
9   op 90 qo 19 wet 235 pet 035 rope 4903 quote 17953
```

C. Type each line 2 times.

C. WORD BEGINNINGS

```
10   tri trinkets tribune trifle trick trial trip trim
11   mil million mileage mildew mills milky miles mild
12   spo sponsor sponge sports spore spoon spool spoke
13   for forgiving forbear forward forbid forced force

14   div dividend division divine divide diving divers
15   vic vicinity vicious victory victims victor vices
16   aff affliction affiliates affirms affords affairs
17   tab tablecloth tabulates tableau tabloids tablets
```

D. Type each line 2 times.

D. WORD ENDINGS

```
18   ive repulsive explosive alive drive active strive
19   est nearest invest attest wisest nicest jest test
20   ply supply simply deeply damply apply imply reply
21   ver whenever forever whoever quiver waiver driver
```

```
22  tor inventor detector debtor orator doctor factor
23  lly industrially logically legally ideally really
24  ert convert dessert expert invert diverts asserts
25  ink shrink drink think blink clink pink sink rink
```

E. PROGRESSIVE PRACTICE: ALPHABET

If you are not using the GDP software, turn to page SB-7 and follow the directions for this activity.

F. Take two 1-minute timed writings. Review your speed and errors.

F. HANDWRITTEN PARAGRAPH

```
26   In this book you have learned the reaches     9
27   for all alphabetic and number keys. You have  18
28   also learned a few of the symbol keys. In the  27
29   remaining lessons you will learn the other     36
30   symbol keys. You will also build your speed    45
31   and accuracy when typing.                      50
     |  1  |  2  |  3  |  4  |  5  |  6  |  7  |  8  |  9  |  10
```

G. DIAGNOSTIC PRACTICE: NUMBERS

If you are not using the GDP software, turn to page SB-5 and follow the directions for this activity.

H. Take two 2-minute timed writings. Review your speed and errors.

Goal: At least 25wpm/2'/5e

H. 2-MINUTE TIMED WRITING

```
32      From the tower John saw that those six big    9
33   planes could crash as they zoomed quickly over  18
34   treetops on their way to the demonstration that 28
35   was scheduled to begin very soon. We hope there 37
36   is no accident and that the pilots reach their   47
37   airports safely.                                 50
     |  1  |  2  |  3  |  4  |  5  |  6  |  7  |  8  |  9  |  10
```

Strategies for Career Success

Goodwill Messages

Would you like to strengthen your relationship with a customer, coworker, or boss? Send an unexpected goodwill message! Your expression of goodwill has a positive effect on business relationships.

Messages of congratulations or appreciation provide special opportunities to express goodwill. These messages can be quite brief. If your handwriting is good, send a handwritten note on a professional note card. Otherwise, send a letter or e-mail.

A note of congratulations might be "I just heard the news about your (award, promotion, etc.). My very best wishes." An appreciation note could be "Thank you for referring me to . . . Your confidence and trust are sincerely appreciated."

YOUR TURN Send a goodwill message to someone to express congratulations or appreciation.

Symbol Keys

Lesson 18

Goals

- Touch-type * # and ' keys
- Type at least 26wpm/2'/5e

A. Type 2 times.

A. WARMUP

```
1      Bill Waxmann quickly moved all 35 packs of      9
2  gear for the Amazon trip (worth $987) 26 miles      18
3  into the jungle. The move took 14 days in all.      27
   |  1  |  2  |  3  |  4  |  5  |  6  |  7  |  8  |  9  |  10
```

NEW KEYS

B. Asterisk is the shift of 8. Type each line 2 times.

Use the K finger.

B. THE * KEY

```
4  kik ki8k k8*k k8*k k**k k**k This book* is great.
5  Use an * to show that a table source is included.
6  Asterisks keyed in a row (*******) make a border.
7  The article quoted Hanson,* Pyle,* and Peterson.*
```

C. Number (if before a figure) or Pounds (if after a figure) is the shift of 3. Type each line 2 times.

Use the D finger.

C. THE # KEY

```
8  de3d de3#d d3#d d3#d d##d d##d #3 #33 #333 #3,333
9  Al wants 33# of #200 and 38# of #400 by Saturday.
10 My favorite seats are #2, #34, #56, #65, and #66.
11 Please order 45# of #245 and 13# of #24 tomorrow.
```

UNIT 4   Lesson 18   41

D. APOSTROPHE is to the right of the semicolon. Type each line 2 times.

Use the
Sem finger.

D. THE ' KEY

12 ;'; ';' ;'; ';' Can't we go in Sue's or Al's car?
13 It's Bob's job to cover Ted's work when he's out.
14 What's in Joann's lunch box for Sandra's dessert?
15 He's gone to Ty's banquet, which is held at Al's.

SKILLBUILDING

E. PACED PRACTICE

If you are not using the GDP software, turn to page SB-14 and follow the directions for this activity.

F. PROGRESSIVE PRACTICE: NUMBERS

If you are not using the GDP software, turn to page SB-11 and follow the directions for this activity.

G. Take two 1-minute timed writings. Review your speed and errors.

G. HANDWRITTEN PARAGRAPH

16 *You have completed the first segment of* 8
17 *your class. You have learned to type all of* 17
18 *the alphabetic keys, the number keys, and some* 26
19 *of the symbol keys. Next you will learn the* 35
20 *remaining symbol keys on the top row.* 42

| 1 | 2 | 3 | 4 | 5 | 6 | 7 | 8 | 9 | 10

H. Take two 2-minute timed writings. Review your speed and errors.

Goal: At least 26wpm/2'/5e

H. 2-MINUTE TIMED WRITING

21   Max had to make one quick adjustment to his   9
22 television set before the football game began.   18
23 The picture during the last game was fuzzy and   28
24 hard to see. If he cannot fix the picture, he may   38
25 have to purchase a new television set; and that   47
26 may be difficult to do.   52

| 1 | 2 | 3 | 4 | 5 | 6 | 7 | 8 | 9 | 10

Symbol Keys

Goals

- Touch-type & % " and @ keys
- Type at least 27wpm/2'/5e

A. Type 2 times.

A. WARMUP

```
1       The teacher (James Quayle) gave us some work    9
2   to do for homework for 11-28-05. Chapters 3 and 4   19
3   from our text* are to be read for a hard quiz.      28
    |  1  |  2  |  3  |  4  |  5  |  6  |  7  |  8  |  9  |  10
```

NEW KEYS

B. AMPERSAND (sign for *and*) is the shift of 7. Space before and after the ampersand. Type each line 2 times.

Use the J finger.

B. THE & KEY

```
4   juj ju7j j7j j7&j j&&j j&&j Max & Dee & Sue & Ken
5   Brown & Sons shipped goods to Crum & Lee Company.
6   Johnson & Loo brought a case against May & Green.
7   Ball & Trump vs. Vens & See is being decided now.
```

C. PERCENT is the shift of 5. Do not space between the number and the percent sign. Type each line 2 times.

Use the F finger.

C. THE % KEY

```
8   ft5f ft5%f f5%f f5%f f%%f f%%f 5% 55% 555% 5,555%
9   Robert quoted rates of 8%, 9%, 10%, 11%, and 12%.
10  Pat scored 82%, Jan 89%, and Ken 90% on the test.
11  Only 55% of the students passed 75% of the exams.
```

D. QUOTATION is the shift of the apostrophe. Do not space between quotation marks and the text they enclose. Type each line 2 times.

Use the Sem finger.

D. THE " KEY

12   ;'; ";" ;"; ";" "That's a super job," said Mabel.
13   The theme of the meeting is "Improving Your Job."
14   John said, "Those were good." Sharon said, "Yes."
15   Allison said, "I'll take Janice and Ed to Flint."

E. AT is the shift of 2. Space before and after @ except when used in an e-mail address. Type each line 2 times.

Use the S finger.

E. THE @ KEY

16   sws sw2s s2@s s2@s s@@s s@@s Buy 15 @ $5 in June.
17   He can e-mail us at this address: projec@edu.com.
18   Order 12 items @ $14 and another 185 items @ $16.
19   Lee said, "I'll buy 8 shares @ $6 and 5 @ $7.55."

FORMATTING

F. Read these rules about the placement of quotation marks. Then type lines 20-23 two times.

F. PLACEMENT OF QUOTATION MARKS

1. The closing quotation mark is always typed *after* a period or comma but *before* a colon or semicolon.
2. The closing quotation mark is typed *after* a question mark or exclamation point if the quoted material itself is a question or an exclamation; otherwise, the quotation mark is typed *before* the question mark or exclamation point.

20   "Hello," I said. "My name is Hal; I am new here."
21   Zack read the article "Can She Succeed Tomorrow?"
22   James said, "I'll mail the check"; but he didn't.
23   Did Amy say, "We lost"? She said, "I don't know."

SKILLBUILDING

G. Type each line 2 times.

G. ALPHABET AND SYMBOL PRACTICE

24 Gaze at views of my jonquil or red phlox in back.
25 Jan quickly moved the six dozen big pink flowers.
26 Joe quietly picked six razors from the woven bag.
27 Packing jam for the dozen boxes was quite lively.

28 Mail these "Rush": #38, #45, and #67 (software).
29 No! Joe's note did not carry a rate of under 9%.
30 Lee read "The Computer Today." It's here Monday.
31 The book* cost us $48.10, 12% higher than yours.

H. Take a 1-minute timed writing on the first paragraph to establish your base speed. Then take four 1-minute timed writings on the remaining paragraphs. As soon as you equal or exceed your base speed on one paragraph, advance to the next, more difficult paragraph.

H. SUSTAINED PRACTICE: NUMBERS AND SYMBOLS

32   We purchased several pieces of new computer   9
33 equipment for our new store in Boston. We were   19
34 amazed at all the extra work we could get done.   28

35   For our department, we received 5 printers,   9
36 12 computers, and 3 fax machines. We heard that   19
37 the equipment cost us several thousand dollars.   28

38   Next week 6 computers (Model ZS86), 4 old   9
39 copiers (drums are broken), and 9 shredders will   18
40 need to be replaced. Total cost will be high.   28

41   Last year $150,890 was spent on equipment   9
42 for Iowa's offices. Breaman & Sims predicted a   18
43 17% to 20% increase (*over '99); that's amazing.   28

| 1 | 2 | 3 | 4 | 5 | 6 | 7 | 8 | 9 | 10 |

I. Take two 2-minute timed writings. Review your speed and errors.

Goal: At least 27wpm/2'/5e

I. 2-MINUTE TIMED WRITING

44   Topaz and onyx rings were for sale at a very   9
45 reasonable price last week. When Jeanette saw the   19
46 rings with these stones, she quickly bought them   29
47 both for her sons. These jewels were difficult to   39
48 find, and Jeanette was pleased she could purchase   49
49 those rings when she did.   54

| 1 | 2 | 3 | 4 | 5 | 6 | 7 | 8 | 9 | 10 |

Review

Goal

- Type at least 28wpm/2′/5e

A. Type 2 times.

A. WARMUP

```
1        Vin went to see Exhibits #794 and #860. He        9
2   had quickly judged these zany projects that cost       19
3   $321 (parts & labor)--a 5% markup from last year.      29
    |  1  |  2  |  3  |  4  |  5  |  6  |  7  |  8  |  9  | 10
```

SKILLBUILDING

B. Type each line 2 times.

B. PUNCTUATION PRACTICE

period
comma
semicolon
colon, hyphen
exclamation point

question mark
colon, apostrophe
dash
quotation marks
parentheses

```
4   Go to Reno. Drive to Yuma. Call Mary. Get Samuel.
5   We saw Nice, Paris, Bern, Rome, Munich, and Bonn.
6   Type the memo; read reports. Get pens; get paper.
7   Read the following pages: 1-10, 12-22, and 34-58.
8   No! Stop! Don't look! Watch out! Move over! Jump!

9   Can you wait? Why not? Can he drive? Where is it?
10  I have these reports: Susan's, Bill's, and Lou's.
11  It's the best--and cheapest! Don't lose it--ever.
12  "I can," she said, "right now." Val said, "Wait!"
13  Quint called Rome (GA), Rome (NY), and Rome (WI).
```

PPP PRETEST → PRACTICE → POSTTEST

PRETEST
Take a 1-minute timed writing. Review your speed and errors.

C. PRETEST: Alternate- and One-Hand Words

```
14        The chairman should handle the tax problem       9
15  downtown. If they are reversed, pressure tactics       19
16  might have changed the case as it was discussed.       28
    |  1  |  2  |  3  |  4  |  5  |  6  |  7  |  8  |  9  | 10
```

PRACTICE
Speed Emphasis:
If you made 2 or fewer errors on the Pretest, type each *individual* line 2 times.
Accuracy Emphasis:
If you made 3 or fewer errors, type each *group* of lines (as though it were a paragraph) 2 times.

D. PRACTICE: Alternate-Hand Words

```
17  the with girl right blame handle antique chairman
18  for wish town their panel formal problem downtown
19  pan busy they flair signs thrown signals problems
```

E. PRACTICE: One-Hand Words

```
20  lip fact yolk poplin yummy affect reverse pumpkin
21  you cast kill uphill jumpy grease wagered opinion
22  tea cage lump limply hilly served bravest minimum
```

POSTTEST
Repeat the Pretest timed writing and compare performance.

F. POSTTEST: Alternate- and One-Hand Words

G. Take three 12-second timed writings on each line. The scale below the last line shows your wpm speed for a 12-second timed writing.

G. 12-SECOND SPEED SPRINTS

```
23  Paul likes to work for the bank while in college.
24  They will make a nice profit if the work is done.
25  The group of friends went to a movie at the mall.
26  The man sent the forms after she called for them.
      |  |  |  5  |  |  |  10  |  |  |  15  |  |  |  20  |  |  |  25  |  |  |  30  |  |  |  35  |  |  |  40  |  |  |  45  |  |  |  50
```

H. Take two 1-minute timed writings. Review your speed and errors.

H. HANDWRITTEN PARAGRAPH

```
27  In your career, you will use the          7
28  skills you are learning in this course.   15
29  However, you will soon discover that you  23
30  must also possess human relations skills. 31
```

I. MAP

Follow the GDP software directions for this exercise in improving keystroking accuracy.

J. DIAGNOSTIC PRACTICE: NUMBERS

If you are not using the GDP software, turn to page SB-5 and follow the directions for this activity.

K. Take two 2-minute timed writings. Review your speed and errors.

Goal: At least 28wpm/2'/5e

K. 2-MINUTE TIMED WRITING

```
31      Jake or Peggy Zale must quickly fix the fax    9
32  machine so that we can have access to regional    18
33  reports that we think might be sent within the    28
34  next few days. Without the fax, we will not be    37
35  able to complete all our monthly reports by the   47
36  deadlines. Please let me know of any problems.    56
      |  1  |  2  |  3  |  4  |  5  |  6  |  7  |  8  |  9  |  10
```

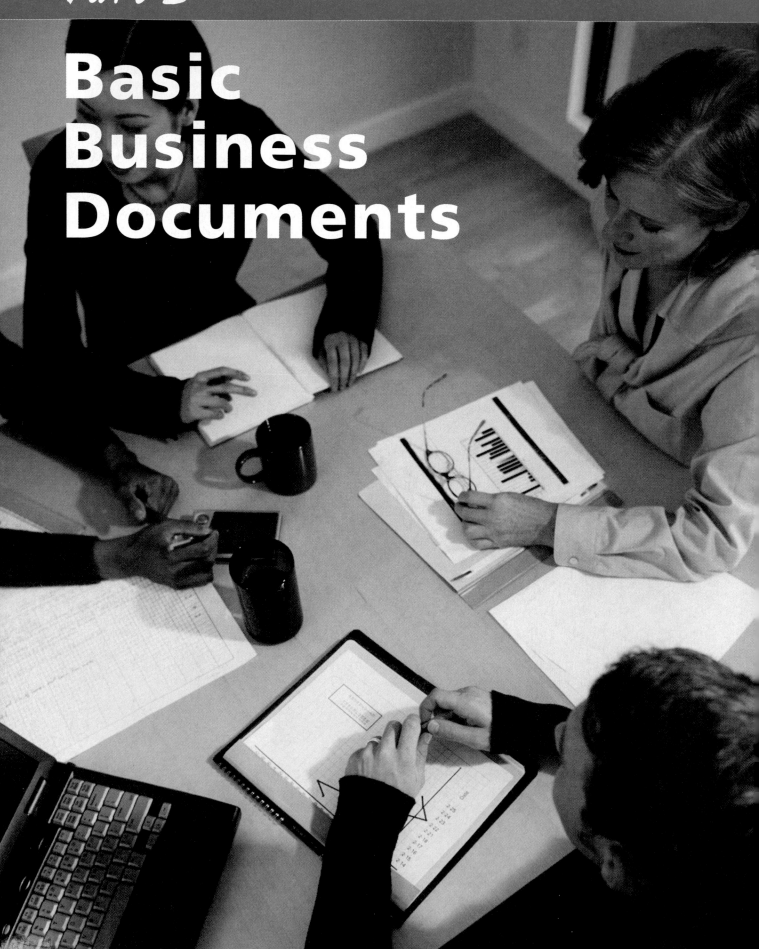

Part 2

Basic Business Documents

Keyboarding in Business and Administrative Services

Opportunities in Business and Administrative Careers

Occupations in the business and administrative services cluster focus on providing management and support services for various companies. The many positions found in this cluster include receptionist, bookkeeper, administrative professional or assistant, claim examiner, accountant, word processor, office manager, and chief executive officer.

Managers and administrators are in charge of planning, organizing, and controlling businesses. Management support workers gather and analyze data to help company executives make decisions. Administrative support workers perform a variety of tasks, such as recordkeeping, operating office equipment, managing their own projects and assignments, and developing high-level integrated software skills as well as Internet research skills. Ideally, everyone in business should be patient, detail-oriented, and cooperative. Excellent written and oral communication skills are definitely an asset as well.

Many companies have been revolutionized by advances in computer technology. As a result, keyboarding skill provides a definite advantage for those who work in business and administrative services. Now, more than ever, success in the business world is dependent upon adaptability and education.

Objectives

KEYBOARDING

- Operate the keyboard by touch.
- Type at least 36 words per minute on a 3-minute timed writing with no more than 4 errors.

LANGUAGE ARTS

- Develop proofreading skills and correctly use proofreaders' marks.
- Use capitals, commas, and apostrophes correctly.
- Develop composing and spelling skills.

WORD PROCESSING

- Use the word processing commands necessary to complete the document processing activities.

DOCUMENT PROCESSING

- Format e-mail, business and academic reports, business letters in block style, envelopes, memos, and tables.

TECHNICAL

- Answer at least 90 percent of the questions correctly on an objective test.

Unit 5

E-Mail and Word Processing

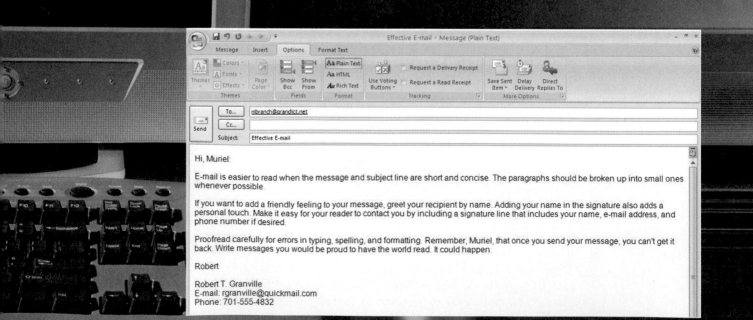

Orientation to Word Processing: A

Goals

- Improve speed and accuracy
- Refine language arts skills in punctuation and grammar
- Practice basic word processing commands

A. Type 2 times.

A. WARMUP

```
1        Juan Valdez will lead 10 managers during this sales     10
2    period; his expert input has always been valuable. Will     22
3    Quentin earn 8% commission ($534) after order #K76 arrives?  34
     |  1  |  2  |  3  |  4  |  5  |  6  |  7  |  8  |  9  |  10  |  11  |  12
```

SKILLBUILDING

B. PROGRESSIVE PRACTICE: NUMBERS

If you are not using the GDP software, turn to page SB-11 and follow the directions for this activity.

C. PACED PRACTICE

If you are not using the GDP software, turn to page SB-14 and follow the directions for this activity.

LANGUAGE ARTS

D. Study the rules at the right.

D. COMMAS AND SENTENCES

Note: The callout signals in the left margin indicate which language arts rule from this lesson has been applied.

RULE ▶
, direct address

Use commas before and after a name used in direct address.

Thank you, John, for responding to my e-mail so quickly.

Ladies and gentlemen, the program has been canceled.

RULE ▶
fragment

Avoid sentence fragments.

Not: She had always wanted to be a financial manager. But had not had the needed education.

But: She had always wanted to be a financial manager but had not had the needed education.

Note: A fragment is a part of a sentence that is incorrectly punctuated as a complete sentence. In the first sentence above, "but had not had the needed education" is not a complete sentence because it does not contain a subject.

RULE ▶
run-on

Avoid run-on sentences.

Not: Mohamed is a competent worker he has even passed the MCSE exam.

Not: Mohamed is a competent worker, he has even passed the MCSE exam.

But: Mohamed is a competent worker; he has even passed the MCSE exam.

Or: Mohamed is a competent worker. He has even passed the MCSE exam.

Note: A run-on sentence is two independent clauses that run together without any punctuation between them or with only a comma between them.

Edit the paragraph to insert any needed punctuation and to correct any errors in grammar.

4   You must be certain, Sean that every e-mail message is
5 concise. And also complete. In addition, Sean, use a clear
6 subject line the subject line describes briefly the principal
7 content of the e-mail message. You should use a direct style
8 of writing, use short lines and paragraphs. The recipient of
9 your e-mail message will be more likely to read and respond to
10 a short message. Than a long one. Your reader will be grateful
11 for any writing techniques. That save time. Another thing you
12 should do Sean is to include an appropriate closing, your
13 reader should know immediately who wrote the message.

FORMATTING

Word Processing Manual

E. WORD PROCESSING

Study Lesson 21 in your word processing manual. Complete all of the shaded steps while at your computer.

Keyboarding Connection

Defining the E-Mail Address

With most e-mail software, a header at the top of each e-mail message contains the sender's address. What is the meaning of the strange configuration of an e-mail address?

An e-mail address contains three parts: anyname@server.com. First is the e-mail user's name (before the @ symbol). Next is the name of the host computer the person uses (before the period). The third part is the zone, or domain, for the type of organization or institution to which the host belongs (e.g., *edu* = education; *gov* = government; *com* = company).

Be careful to include each part of an e-mail address and punctuate the address completely and correctly. Even a small error will prevent your message from reaching the recipient.

YOUR TURN Have you ever sent an e-mail that did not reach its recipient because of an address error? What type of error did you make?

Orientation to Word Processing: B

Goals

- Practice hyphenation
- Type at least 28wpm/3′/5e
- Practice basic word processing commands

A. Type 2 times.

A. WARMUP

```
1        Zenobia bought 987 reams of 16# bond paper from V & J    11
2   Co. @ $5/ream. Part of this week's order is usable. About     23
3   24 percent is excellent quality; the rest cannot be used.     34
      |  1  |  2  |  3  |  4  |  5  |  6  |  7  |  8  |  9  |  10  |  11  |  12
```

SKILLBUILDING

B. Type each line 2 times.

B. HYPHEN PRACTICE

Hyphens are used:

1. To show that a word is divided (lines 4 and 8).
2. To make a dash by typing two hyphens with no space before or after (lines 5 and 8).
3. To join words in a compound (lines 6, 7, and 9).

```
4   Can Larry possibly go with us next week to the golf tourna-
5   ment? I am positive that he--like you--would enjoy the game
6   and realize that it is a first-class sporting event. If you
7   think he can go, I will get first-class reservations on the
8   next plane. Larry--just like Tom and me--always likes every-
9   thing to be first-class and first-rate. Money is no object.
```

Note: In your word processing program, when you type text followed by two hyphens (--) followed by more text and then a space, an em dash (—) will automatically be inserted.

C. PROGRESSIVE PRACTICE: ALPHABET

If you are not using the GDP software, turn to page SB-7 and follow the directions for this activity.

D. Take two 3-minute timed writings. Review your speed and errors.

Goal: At least 28wpm/3′/5e

D. 3-MINUTE TIMED WRITING

```
10      Once you learn to use a variety of software programs,    11
11  you will feel confident and comfortable as you are using a   23
12  computer. All you have to do is take that first step and     34
13  decide to strive for excellence.                             41
14      Initially, you might have several questions as you       52
15  gaze up at a screen that is filled with icons. If you try    62
16  to learn to use just one or two commands each day, you may   75
17  soon find that using software is very exciting.              84
    |  1  |  2  |  3  |  4  |  5  |  6  |  7  |  8  |  9  |  10  |  11  |  12
```

FORMATTING

Word Processing Manual

E. WORD PROCESSING

Study Lesson 22 in your word processing manual. Complete all of the shaded steps while at your computer.

Strategies for Career Success

Preparing to Conduct a Meeting

Do you want to conduct a successful meeting? Meetings tend to fail because they last too long and attendees do not stay focused. First, determine the meeting's purpose (e.g., to make a decision or obtain/provide information).

Decide who needs to attend the meeting. Include those who can significantly contribute, as well as decision makers. Prepare an agenda, that is, a list of items to be discussed. Distribute it to attendees a few days before the meeting.

Choose where you will conduct the meeting and schedule the room. Determine if you will be teleconferencing, videoconferencing, or needing audiovisual equipment. If appropriate, arrange for refreshments. Check the room temperature, acoustics, and lighting. Attention to these details will increase your chances for a successful outcome.

YOUR TURN Think about a meeting you attended that was a failure. What could the meeting leader have done to better prepare for the meeting?

Orientation to Word Processing: C

Goals

- Improve speed and accuracy
- Refine language arts skills in composing
- Practice basic word processing commands

A. Type 2 times.

A. WARMUP

```
1        We expect the following sizes to be mailed promptly     11
2   on January 8: 5, 7, and 9. Send your payment quickly so      22
3   that the items will be sure to arrive before 2:35* (*p.m.)!   33
    |  1  |  2  |  3  |  4  |  5  |  6  |  7  |  8  |  9  |  10  |  11  |  12
```

SKILLBUILDING

B. Take a 1-minute timed writing on the first paragraph to establish your base speed. Then take four 1-minute timed writings on the remaining paragraphs. As soon as you equal or exceed your base speed on one paragraph, advance to the next, more difficult paragraph.

B. SUSTAINED PRACTICE: CAPITALS

```
4         The insurance industry will see some changes because   11
5    of the many natural disasters the United States has seen in  23
6    the last few years in places like California and Florida.    34

7         The major earthquakes in San Francisco, Northridge,     11
8    and Loma Prieta cost thousands of dollars. Faults like       22
9    the San Andreas are being watched carefully for activity.    33

10        Some tropical storms are spawned in the West Indies     11
11   and move from the Caribbean Sea into the Atlantic Ocean.     22
12   They could affect Georgia, Florida, Alabama, and Texas.      33

13        Some U.S. cities have VHF-FM radio weather stations.    11
14   NASA and NOAA are agencies that launch weather satellites    23
15   to predict the locations, times, and severity of storms.     34
```

C. DIAGNOSTIC PRACTICE: SYMBOLS AND PUNCTUATION

If you are not using the GDP software, turn to page SB-2 and follow the directions for this activity.

D. Answer each question with a complete sentence.

D. COMPOSING SENTENCES

16   Do you prefer Word as a word processing software, or do you prefer something else?
17   What search engine do you prefer when you search for information on the Web?
18   Do you like Internet Explorer, or do you prefer Netscape Navigator as a Web browser?
19   What class are you now taking that is best preparing you for the workplace?
20   If you could work in any foreign country, which one would you choose?
21   What documents do you type most frequently as a student: letters, reports, or tables?

FORMATTING

Go To Word Processing Manual

E. WORD PROCESSING

Study Lesson 23 in your word processing manual. Complete all of the shaded steps while at your computer.

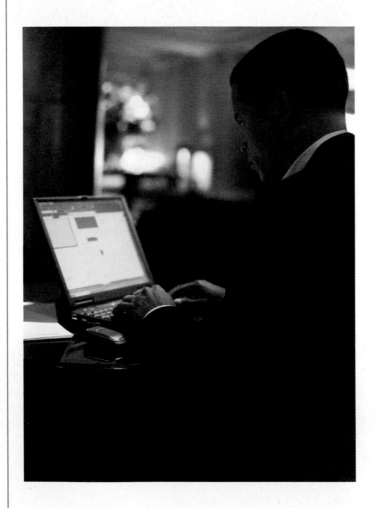

Orientation to Word Processing: D

Goals

- Type at least 29wpm/3'/5e
- Practice basic word processing commands

A. Type 2 times.

A. WARMUP

```
1        The experts quickly realized that repairs could cost     11
2   "$985 million" and might exceed 60% of their budget. Will     22
3   Valdez & Co. begin work before 12 or just wait until 4:30?    34
    | 1 | 2 | 3 | 4 | 5 | 6 | 7 | 8 | 9 | 10 | 11 | 12
```

SKILLBUILDING

B. Take three 12-second timed writings on each line. The scale below the last line shows your wpm speed for a 12-second timed writing.

B. 12-SECOND SPEED SPRINTS

```
4   Mary will be able to go home when she can run fast and far.
5   Sam can come to the store if he is able to stop for a soda.
6   Suzy knows that she must send the mail out by noon or else.
7   Only a few good desks will be made by the end of this week.
    | | | |5| | | |10| | | 15| | | 20| | | 25| | | 30| | | 35| | | 40| | | 45| | | 50| | | 55| | | 60
```

PPP PRETEST → PRACTICE → POSTTEST

PRETEST
Take a 1-minute timed writing. Review your speed and errors.

C. PRETEST: Common Letter Combinations

```
8         He tried to explain the delay in a logical way. The    11
9   man finally agreed to insure the package and demanded to     22
10  know why the postal worker did not record the total amount.   34
    | 1 | 2 | 3 | 4 | 5 | 6 | 7 | 8 | 9 | 10 | 11 | 12
```

PRACTICE
Speed Emphasis:
If you made 2 or fewer errors on the Pretest, type each *individual* line 2 times.
Accuracy Emphasis:
If you made 3 or more errors, type each *group* of lines (as though it were a paragraph) 2 times.

D. PRACTICE: Word Beginnings

```
11  re reuse react relay reply return reason record results red
12  in inset inept incur index indeed intend inning insured ink
13  de dents dealt death delay detest devote derive depicts den
```

E. PRACTICE: Word Endings

```
14  ly lowly dimly apply daily barely unruly deeply finally sly
15  ed cured tamed tried moved amused tasted billed creamed fed
16  al canal total equal local postal plural rental logical pal
```

POSTTEST
Repeat the Pretest timed writing and compare performance.

F. POSTTEST: Common Letter Combinations

G. Take two 3-minute timed writings. Review your speed and errors.

Goal: At least 29wpm/3′/5e

G. 3-MINUTE TIMED WRITING

```
17        If you ever feel tired as you are typing, you should    11
18   take a rest. Question what you are doing that is causing      22
19   your muscles to be fatigued. You will realize that you        33
20   can change the fundamental source of your anxiety.            43
21        Take a deep breath and enjoy the relaxing feeling as     54
22   you exhale slowly. Check your posture to be sure that         65
23   you are sitting up straight with your back against the        76
24   chair. Stretch your neck and back for total relaxation.       87
   |  1  |  2  |  3  |  4  |  5  |  6  |  7  |  8  |  9  |  10 |  11 |  12
```

FORMATTING

Word Processing Manual

H. WORD PROCESSING

Study Lesson 24 in your word processing manual. Complete all of the shaded steps while at your computer.

Keyboarding Connection

Business E-Mail Style Guide

Watch those e-mail p's and q's! Even though e-mail is relatively informal, you need to be succinct and clear. Greet your reader with a formal "Dear . . . ," or an informal "Hi . . . ," etc. Put the most important part of your message first. Watch the length of your paragraphs; four to five lines per paragraph won't put off your reader.

Use asterisks, caps, dashes, etc., for emphasis. Avoid unfamiliar abbreviations, slang, or jargon. Not everyone who receives your business e-mail may know a particular catchword or phrase. Proofread your e-mail. Be concerned about grammar, punctuation, and word choice. Use your e-mail's spell checker.

End your business e-mail politely. Expressions of appreciation (e.g., "Thanks") or goodwill (e.g., "Best wishes") let your reader know you are finishing your message.

YOUR TURN In Lesson 25 you will learn how to format and compose e-mail messages. Create an e-mail message to send to a coworker, colleague, or friend. Review the e-mail for adherence to the guidelines listed above.

E-Mail Basics

Goals

- Improve speed and accuracy
- Refine language arts skills in proofreading
- Format and compose a basic e-mail message

A. Type 2 times.

A. WARMUP

```
1       Exactly 610 employees have quit smoking! About half    11
2  of them just quit recently. They realized why they can't    22
3  continue to smoke inside the buildings and decided to stop.  34
   | 1 | 2 | 3 | 4 | 5 | 6 | 7 | 8 | 9 | 10 | 11 | 12
```

SKILLBUILDING

B. Tab 1 time between columns. Type 2 times.

B. TECHNIQUE PRACTICE: TAB KEY

```
4  A. Uyeki    B. Vorton    C. Wetzel   D. Xenios    E. Young
5  F. Zeller   G. Ambrose   H. Brown    I. Carter    J. Denney
6  K. Elmer    L. Fraser    M. Greene   N. Hawkins   O. Irvin
7  P. Jarvis   Q. Krueger   R. Larkin   S. Majors    T. Norris
8  U. Vassar   V. Hagelin   W. Wesley   X. Bernet    Y. Robins
```

C. MAP

Follow the GDP software directions for this exercise in improving keystroking accuracy.

LANGUAGE ARTS

D. Study the proofreading techniques at the right.

D. PROOFREADING YOUR DOCUMENTS

Proofreading and correcting errors are essential parts of document processing. To become an expert proofreader:

1. Use the spelling feature of your word processing software to check for spelling errors; then read the copy aloud to see if it makes sense.

2. Proofread for all kinds of errors, especially repeated, missing, or transposed words; grammar and punctuation; and numbers and names.

3. Check for formatting errors such as line spacing, tabs, margins, and use of bold.

E. Compare these lines with lines 4–7 in the 12-second speed sprints on page 57. Edit the lines to correct any errors.

E. PROOFREADING

```
9   Mary will be able to go when she can run fast and far.
10  Sam can come to the store if she is able to stop for soda.
11  Suzy know that she must send the mail out by noon or else.
12  Only a few good disks will be made by the end of this week.
```

F. BASIC PARTS OF AN E-MAIL MESSAGE

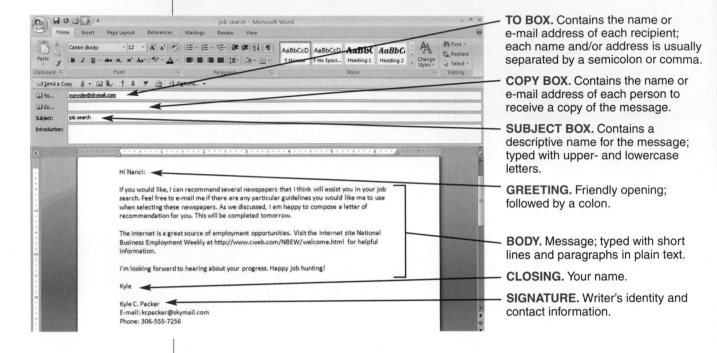

TO BOX. Contains the name or e-mail address of each recipient; each name and/or address is usually separated by a semicolon or comma.

COPY BOX. Contains the name or e-mail address of each person to receive a copy of the message.

SUBJECT BOX. Contains a descriptive name for the message; typed with upper- and lowercase letters.

GREETING. Friendly opening; followed by a colon.

BODY. Message; typed with short lines and paragraphs in plain text.

CLOSING. Your name.

SIGNATURE. Writer's identity and contact information.

G. FORMATTING AND COMPOSING AN E-MAIL MESSAGE

E-mail formats will vary, depending on your e-mail provider. Most e-mail message screens will allow space for the *To*, *Cc*, and *Subject* entries as well as a separate area for the e-mail message. The attachment feature is often displayed on the toolbar as a paper clip icon.

1. Use the address book feature or type the e-mail address of each recipient in the *To, Cc,* or *Bcc* boxes. A semicolon or comma is usually automatically inserted to separate several names.

2. If you use the reply feature, include the original message if it helps the reader remember the topic(s) more easily.

3. Use a descriptive, concise subject line with upper- and lowercase letters.

   Example: Items for Meeting Agenda

4. Use the attachment feature if you need to attach a file or document.

5. Use a friendly greeting. Follow the greeting with a colon. Use the recipient's first name or a courtesy title and last name for a more businesslike greeting.

   Example: Hi, Jim: or Dear Jim:

   Example: Jim: or Mr. Andrews:

6. Use short lines (about 60 characters) with plain text, or let the lines word wrap if your e-mail program supports word wrap.

7. Keep paragraphs short and type them with normal capitalization and punctuation in plain text. Typing in all-caps is considered shouting.

8. Type paragraphs single-spaced and blocked at the left with 1 blank line between them.

9. A closing is optional. Type your name in the closing, and leave 1 blank line above and below the closing.

   Example: Sandy Hill or Sandy

10. Use a signature line so the recipient clearly knows your identity and contact information.

    Example:
    Sandra R. Hill
    E-mail: srhill@server.com
    Phone: 661-555-1223

11. Revise and proofread your message carefully before sending it. You can't get it back!

H. WORD PROCESSING: E-MAIL A DOCUMENT

Study Lesson 25 in your word processing manual. Complete all of the shaded steps while at your computer. Then format the jobs that follow.

DOCUMENT PROCESSING

Correspondence 25-1

E-Mail Message

1. Type the greeting and body for the e-mail message below.
2. Type the sender's name 1 blank line below the final line of the e-mail message.
3. Type the sender's signature line, including the e-mail address, 1 blank line below the sender's name
4. Type the phone number below the signature line.

5. Proofread your e-mail message for typing, spelling, and formatting errors.
6. Because the functionality of your word processor's e-mail features depends upon what software you use for e-mail, what browser you use, and other factors that are beyond the scope of this textbook, you will not actually send this e-mail message.

Hi, Muriel: ↓2X

E-mail is easier to read when the message and subject line are short and concise. The paragraphs should be broken up into small ones whenever possible. ↓2X

If you want to add a friendly feeling to your message, greet your recipient by name. Adding your name in the signature also adds a personal touch. Make it easy for your reader to contact you by including a signature line that includes your name, e-mail address, and phone number if desired. ↓2X

Proofread carefully for errors in typing, spelling, and formatting. Remember, Muriel, that once you send your message, you can't get it back. Write messages you would be proud to have the world read. It could happen. ↓2X

Robert ↓2X

Robert T. Granville
E-mail: rgranville@quickmail.com
Phone: 701-555-4832

Correspondence 25-2

E-Mail Message

1. Type an e-mail message to Ernesto Sanchez.
2. Type the greeting as: Hi, Ernesto:
3. Type the following message: I now have e-mail access using my new cable modem. You can now send me the photos you took at our annual meeting, because I will be able to access them at a much faster rate. Thank you, Ernesto, for bringing your digital camera to the meeting so that we could all enjoy the photos you took.

4. Type the closing as Karen and the signature line as Karen Drake.
5. Type Karen Drake's e-mail address as kdrake@brightway.net and her phone number as 404-555-6823.
6. Proofread your e-mail message for typing, spelling, and formatting errors.
7. Because the functionality of your word processor's e-mail features depends upon what software you use for e-mail, what browser you use, and other factors that are beyond the scope of this textbook, you will not actually send this e-mail message.

Unit 6

Reports

AN ANALYSIS OF CORPORATE
SICK-LEAVE POLICIES

Recent Trends in the Business World

Linda C. Motonaga

April 5, 20--

Corporate sick-leave policies must be studied carefully in order to maximize employee productivity and minimize excessive absenteeism. The reasons for absences and the responsiveness of employers to the needs of the employees must be examined in order to determine some practical alternatives to current policies.

REASONS FOR ABSENCE

There are many reasons employees are absent from work. Illness and personal emergency are common reasons for absenteeism. However, recent surveys have shown that about 28 percent of reported sick time isn't due to illness. This percentage is on the rise. Recent studies have also shown that absences due to personal needs are increasing. Also, many workers believe that they are "entitled" to a day off now and then. Perhaps it is time for employers to revamp their sick-leave policies and make these policies more responsive to the needs of the employees.

RESPONSIVENESS OF EMPLOYERS

If employees are finding it necessary to take sick days when they are not ill, it makes sense to conclude that possibly employers either are not aware of why absenteeism exists or have chosen not to respond to their employees' needs. One thing is certain—ignoring the problem will not make it go away.

POSSIBLE SOLUTIONS

Flexible scheduling is one creative way in which employers can respond to the needs of employees. If workers are given the opportunity for a flexible working schedule, stress levels should go down and personal needs can be handled during the time they are off. Another solution might be to give employees a fixed number of days off each year for reasons other than illness. This gives workers a legitimate reason for a planned absence and gives employers some advance notice so that absences do not hurt productivity.

ENDING PROCRASTINATION

Judy Baca

Everyone at one time or another has put off some task, goal, or important plan at work for any number of reasons. Perhaps you think time is too short or the task isn't really that important. Either way, procrastination can lead to a stalled life and career.

EVALUATE YOUR SITUATION

Joyce Winfrey, of Time Management Incorporated, has some very good advice that will help you begin to move forward. She says that you should ask yourself two very basic questions about why you are procrastinating:

1. Am I procrastinating because the task at hand is not really what I want?

2. Is there a valid reason for my procrastination?

After you have asked yourself these questions, Ms. Winfrey suggests that you do the following:

Look deep within yourself. If you are looking for excuses, then the process of asking these questions will be a waste of your time. However, if you answer these questions honestly, you might find answers that surprise you and that will help clarify your situation.

She also recommends several techniques that can help you get back on task.

PRACTICE NEW TECHNIQUES

Identifying and understanding the techniques that follow is the first step. Once you know what to do, you can begin to practice these steps daily.

2

Take Baby Steps. Don't make any task bigger than it really is by looking at the whole thing at once. Break it down into baby steps that are manageable.

Don't Strive for Perfectionism. If you are waiting for the perfect solution or the perfect opportunity, you will be immobilized. Accept the fact that no one and nothing is perfect. Then accept your mistakes and move on.

Enjoy the Task. Enjoy the task at hand and find something in it that is positive and rewarding. Confront your fears with a plan of action.

Remind yourself of all these techniques daily. Post them by your telephone, by your desk, or in your car. You will find that your personal life and career will gain momentum, and success will soon be yours.

One-Page Business Reports

Goals

- Type at least 30wpm/3'/5e
- Format one-page business reports

A. Type 2 times.

A. WARMUP

```
1      Mr. G. Yoneji ordered scanners* (*800 dots per inch)     11
2  in vibrant 24-bit color! He quickly realized that exactly    22
3  31% of the work could be scanned in order to save money.     34
   |  1  |  2  |  3  |  4  |  5  |  6  |  7  |  8  |  9  |  10  |  11  |  12
```

SKILLBUILDING

B. Take three 12-second timed writings on each line. The scale below the last line shows your wpm speed for a 12-second timed writing.

B. 12-SECOND SPEED SPRINTS

```
4  She went to the same store to find some good books to read.
5  Frank will coach eight games for his team when he has time.
6  Laura sent all the mail out today when she left to go home.
7  These pages can be very hard to read when the light is dim.
   | | | | 5 | | | | 10 | | | | 15 | | | | 20 | | | | 25 | | | | 30 | | | | 35 | | | | 40 | | | | 45 | | | | 50 | | | | 55 | | | | 60
```

C. DIAGNOSTIC PRACTICE: SYMBOLS AND PUNCTUATION

If you are not using the GDP software, turn to page SB-2 and follow the directions for this activity.

D. Take two 3-minute timed writings. Review your speed and errors.

Goal: At least 30wpm/3'/5e

D. 3-MINUTE TIMED WRITING

```
8       Holding a good business meeting may require a great      11
9   deal of thought and planning. The meeting must be well       22
10  organized, and an agenda must be prepared. It may be hard     33
11  to judge how long a meeting will take or how many people      45
12  will discuss important issues.                                51
13      A good leader is required to execute the agenda. He or    62
14  she must know when to move on to the next topic or when to    73
15  continue debate on a topic. After a productive meeting, a     85
16  leader should be pleased.                                     90
    |  1  |  2  |  3  |  4  |  5  |  6  |  7  |  8  |  9  |  10  |  11  |  12
```

Reference Manual

Refer to page R-8C of the Reference Manual for an illustration of a report in academic style.

E. BASIC PARTS OF A REPORT

There are two basic styles of reports: business and academic. The illustration that follows is for a business report.

↓5X

14 pt   **AN ANALYSIS OF CORPORATE
SICK-LEAVE POLICIES** ↓2X

12 pt↓   **Recent Trends in the Business World**

Linda C. Motonaga ↓2X

April 5, 20-- ↓2X

Corporate sick-leave policies must be studied carefully in order to maximize employee productivity and minimize excessive absenteeism. The reasons for absences and the responsiveness of employers to the needs of the employees must be examined in order to determine some practical alternatives to current policies. ↓2X

REASONS FOR ABSENCE ↓2X

There are many reasons employees are absent from work. Illness and personal emergency are common reasons for absenteeism. ↓2X

Illness. Illness is often caused by all the stress in the workplace. Employees may have to care for parents and children. ↓2X

Personal Needs. Recent studies have also shown that absences due to personal needs are increasing. Two important questions must be addressed. ↓2X

1. Should employers rethink their sick-leave policies? ↓2X

2. How can a newly instituted sick-leave policy be more responsive to the needs of the employee? ↓2X

POSSIBLE SOLUTIONS ↓2X

Flexible scheduling is one creative way in which employers can respond to the needs of employees. If workers are given the opportunity for a flexible working schedule, stress levels should go down and personal needs can be handled during the time they are off. Another solution might be to give employees a fixed number of days off each year for reasons other than illness. This gives workers a legitimate reason for a planned absence and gives employers some advance notice so that absences do not hurt productivity.

TITLE. Subject of the report; centered; typed 2 inches from the top of the page in bold and all-caps, with a 14-point font size; 2-line titles are single-spaced.

SUBTITLE. Secondary or explanatory title; centered; typed 1 blank line below the title, in bold, with upper- and lowercase letters.

BYLINE. Name of the writer; centered; typed 1 blank line below the previous line, in bold.

DATE. Date of the report; centered; typed 1 blank line below the previous line, in bold.

BODY. Text of the report; typed 1 blank line below the previous line, single-spaced and positioned at the left margin, with 1 blank line between paragraphs.

SIDE HEADING. Major subdivision of the report; typed 1 blank line below the previous line and beginning at the left margin, in bold and all-caps.

PARAGRAPH HEADING. Minor subdivision of the report; typed 1 blank line below the previous line at the left margin, in bold, with upper- and lowercase letters; followed by a period (also in bold).

LIST. Numbered or bulleted items in a report; typed at the left margin, single-spaced, with 1 blank line above and below the list. If the list includes multiline items, insert 1 blank line between the individual items.

F. BUSINESS REPORTS

To format a business report:

- Single-space business reports.
- Press ENTER 5 times to begin the first line of the report 2 inches from the top of the page.
- Change the font size to 14 point, and type the title in all-caps, centered, in bold. Single-space a 2-line title.
- Press ENTER 2 times and change the font size to 12 point.

- If the report includes a subtitle, byline, or date, type each item centered and in bold upper- and lowercase letters.
- Press ENTER 2 times after each line in the heading block.
- Insert 1 blank line after all paragraphs.
- Do not number the first page of a report.

G. REPORTS WITH SIDE HEADINGS

To format side headings:

- Insert 1 blank line before and after side headings.

- Type side headings at the left margin, in bold, and in all-caps.

Word
Processing
Manual

H. WORD PROCESSING: ALIGNMENT AND FONT SIZE

Study Lesson 26 in your word processing manual. Complete all of the shaded steps while at your computer. Then format the jobs that follow.

DOCUMENT PROCESSING

Report 26-1

Business Report

Type this report in standard format for a business report with side headings.

Type the actual current year in place of 20--.

In your word processor, when you type text followed by two hyphens (--), followed by more text and then a space, an em dash (—) will automatically be inserted.

↓5X

14 pt **AN ANALYSIS OF CORPORATE** ↓1X
SICK-LEAVE POLICIES ↓2X

12 pt↓ **Recent Trends in the Business World** ↓2X

Linda C. Motonaga ↓2X

April 5, 20-- ↓2X

Corporate sick-leave policies must be studied carefully in order to maximize employee productivity and minimize excessive absenteeism. The reasons for absences and the responsiveness of employers to the needs of the employees must be examined in order to determine some practical alternatives to current policies. ↓2X

REASONS FOR ABSENCE ↓2X

There are many reasons employees are absent from work. Illness and personal emergency are common reasons for absenteeism. However, recent surveys have shown that about 28 percent of reported sick time isn't due to illness. This percentage is on the rise. Recent studies have also shown that absences due to personal needs are increasing. Also, many workers believe that they are "entitled" to a day off now and then. Perhaps it is time for employers to revamp their sick-leave policies and make these policies more responsive to the needs of the employees. ↓2X

RESPONSIVENESS OF EMPLOYERS ↓2X

If employees are finding it necessary to take sick days when they are not ill, it makes sense to conclude that possibly employers either are not aware of why absenteeism exists or have chosen not to respond to their employees' needs. One thing is certain—ignoring the problem will not make it go away. ↓2X

(Continued on next page)

POSSIBLE SOLUTIONS ↓2X

Flexible scheduling is one creative way in which employers can respond to the needs of employees. If workers are given the opportunity for a flexible working schedule, stress levels should go down and personal needs can be handled during the time they are off. Another solution might be to give employees a fixed number of days off each year for reasons other than illness. This gives workers a legitimate reason for a planned absence and gives employers some advance notice so that absences do not hurt productivity.

Report 26-2

Business Report

Open the file for Report 26-1 and make the following changes:

1. Delete the subtitle, and change the byline to Amy Ho.
2. Change the date to October 23.
3. Change the second side heading to EMPLOYER RESPONSIVENESS.
4. Delete the last two sentences in the last paragraph at the end of the report. Add the following sentences to the end of the last paragraph:

Employees will not feel the need to invent elaborate reasons for their absences. They will feel as if they are in control of their schedule outside of work so that they can determine the best way to schedule their time off. When they return to work, they will feel relaxed and ready to work.

Multipage Rough-Draft Business Reports

Goals

- Improve speed and accuracy
- Refine language arts skills in punctuation
- Identify and apply basic proofreaders' marks
- Format multipage rough-draft business reports

A. Type 2 times.

A. WARMUP

```
1       On 7/23 the office will convert to a new phone system.   11
2   A freeze on all toll calls is requested for July. Account    23
3   #GK95 has a balance of $68 and isn't expected to "pay up."    35
    | 1 | 2 | 3 | 4 | 5 | 6 | 7 | 8 | 9 | 10 | 11 | 12
```

SKILLBUILDING

B. Take a 1-minute timed writing on the first paragraph to establish your base speed. Then take four 1-minute timed writings on the remaining paragraphs. As soon as you equal or exceed your base speed on one paragraph, advance to the next, more difficult paragraph.

B. SUSTAINED PRACTICE: PUNCTUATION

```
4        Anyone who is successful in business realizes that the   11
5   needs of the customer must always come first. A satisfied     23
6   consumer is one who will come back to buy again and again.    34

7        Consumers must learn to lodge a complaint in a manner    11
8   that is fair, effective, and efficient. Don't waste time      22
9   talking to the wrong person. Go to the person in charge.      34

10       State your case clearly; be prepared with facts and      11
11  figures to back up any claim--warranties, receipts, bills,    22
12  and checks are all very effective. Don't be intimidated.      34

13       If the company agrees to work with you, you're on the    11
14  right track. Be specific: "I'll expect a check Tuesday,"      22
15  or "I'll expect a replacement in the mail by Saturday."       33
```

C. PROGRESSIVE PRACTICE: ALPHABET

If you are not using the GDP software, turn to page SB-7 and follow the directions for this activity.

D. COMMAS AND SENTENCES

Note: The callout signals in the left margin indicate which language arts rule from this lesson has been applied.

RULE ▶

, independent

The underline calls attention to a point in the sentence where a comma might mistakenly be inserted.

Use a comma between independent clauses joined by a coordinate conjunction (unless both clauses are short).

Ellen left her job with IBM, and she and her sister went to Paris.

But: Ellen left her job with IB<u>M</u> and went to Paris with her sister.

But: John drove_and I navigated.

Note: An independent clause is one that can stand alone as a complete sentence. The most common coordinate conjunctions are *and, but, or,* and *nor.*

RULE ▶

, introductory

Use a comma after an introductory expression (unless it is a short prepositional phrase).

Before we can make a decision, we must have all the facts.

But: In 200<u>0</u> our nation elected a new president.

Note: An introductory expression is a group of words that come before the subject and verb of the independent clause. Common prepositions are *to, in, on, of, at, by, for,* and *with.*

Edit the paragraph to insert any needed punctuation and to correct any errors in grammar.

```
16     Business reports should be single-spaced and all lines in
17  the heading block should be typed in bold. If the report title
18  has two lines it should be single-spaced and in all caps.
19  Include a subtitle below the title. You should type the
20  subtitle 1 blank line below the title and it should be typed
21  in both upper- and lowercase letters. Most reports include a
22  byline and a date. After the date begin typing the report
23  body. If there is a side heading type it in all caps and bold.
```

FORMATTING

E. BASIC PROOFREADERS' MARKS

Proofreaders' marks are used to indicate changes or corrections to be made in a document (called a *rough draft*) that is being revised for final copy. Study the chart to learn what each proofreaders' mark means.

Proofreaders' Marks	Draft	Final copy
⌒ Omit space	data base	database
˅ or ∧ Insert	if he's going,	if he's not going,
≡ Capitalize	Maple street	Maple Street
⟋ Delete	a final draft	a draft
# ∧ Insert space	allready to	all ready to

(Continued on next page)

Proofreaders' Marks	Draft	Final Copy
when ~~if~~ ∧ Change word	*when* and ~~if~~ ∧ you	and when you
/ Use lowercase letter	our /President	our president
∿ Transpose	they ⌣all⌣see	they see all
SS Single-space	SS ⌈first line ⌊second line	first line second line
¶ New paragraph	. . . to use it. ¶ We can	. . . to use it. We can

F. MULTIPAGE BUSINESS REPORTS

To format a multipage report:

- Press ENTER 5 times to begin the first line of the report 2 inches from the top of the page.
- Do not number the first page. Insert a page number in the top right-hand corner of the page header of all continuing pages, and remove the page number from the first page.

Note: When you reach the bottom of a page, your word processing software will automatically end the page. If you see a single line (one line of a heading or one line of a new paragraph) as the last line of a page, insert a manual page break above the heading or the one-line paragraph. Likewise, when you move to the top of the next page, it should not begin with a single line of a paragraph. See Lesson 27 in your word processing manual for detailed steps.

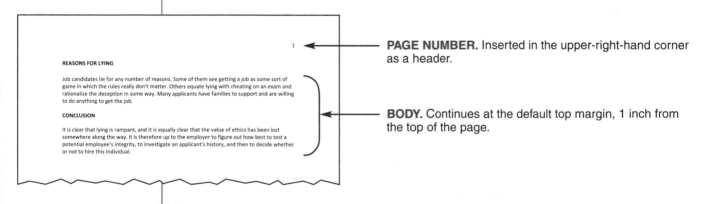

PAGE NUMBER. Inserted in the upper-right-hand corner as a header.

BODY. Continues at the default top margin, 1 inch from the top of the page.

REASONS FOR LYING

Job candidates lie for any number of reasons. Some of them see getting a job as some sort of game in which the rules really don't matter. Others equate lying with cheating on an exam and rationalize the deception in some way. Many applicants have families to support and are willing to do anything to get the job.

CONCLUSION

It is clear that lying is rampant, and it is equally clear that the value of ethics has been lost somewhere along the way. It is therefore up to the employer to figure out how best to test a potential employee's integrity, to investigate an applicant's history, and then to decide whether or not to hire this individual.

G. BUSINESS REPORTS WITH PARAGRAPH HEADINGS

To format paragraph headings:

- Type paragraph headings at the left margin in bold and in upper- and lower-case letters.
- Follow the paragraph heading by a bold period and 1 space.

Word Processing Manual

Go To

H. WORD PROCESSING: PAGE NUMBERING AND PAGE BREAK

Study Lesson 27 in your word processing manual. Complete all of the shaded steps while at your computer. Then format the jobs that follow.

Note: The report lines are shown with extra spacing to accommodate the proofreaders' marks. Use standard business report spacing when you type the report.

1. Type the report using standard business report format.
2. Type side headings at the left margin in bold and all-caps.
3. Type any paragraph headings at the left margin in bold and in upper- and lowercase letters, followed by a bold period and 1 space.
4. Insert a page number at the top right, and suppress the page number on the first page.
5. Spell-check, preview, and proofread your document for spelling and formatting errors before printing it.

The ¶ symbol indicates the start of a new paragraph. In a business report, paragraphs are blocked (not indented).

THE INTEGRITY AND ~~MORALS~~ ETHICS OF JOB APPLICANTS

By Elizabeth Reddix

April 5, 20--

INTRODUCTION

¶ Some studies have found that about ~~9 out of 10~~ 90 percent of job applicants have lied in some way in order to land a job. The lies range from small exaggerations to blatant and completely fraudulent information such as lying about a degree or perhaps about ones history of earnings. After tallying the results of a survey of a large group of college students, one psychologist found that ~~approximately~~ about 90 out of 100 of them were willing to lie ~~in order~~ to land a job that they really wanted.

, introductory

¶ One way to help screen out the deceptions from the truth is to identify the most common deceptions. Another way is to try to understand why applicants feel the need to lie. After these factors are identified and understood, it will be easier to make some judgment calls on the ethical integrity of an applicant.

, introductory

COMMON DECEPTIONS

¶ There are ~~a great~~ many areas in which job applicants are willing to make false statements in order to get a job. These could include verbal statements or written ones.

School activities. Many ~~job~~ applicants are willing to exaggerate or totally falsify ~~totally~~ their participation in school activities. In order to prove leadership ability, an applicant might be willing to say that he or she was president of a nonexistent club or perhaps organized some type of fictional fund-raising activity.

, introductory

(Continued on next page)

, introductory

Former Job titles. Another area rampant with deception is the list of previous Job Titles. In order to make a ~~previous~~ *former* job sound more impressive, a job contender might add a word or two to the title or perhaps rename the title al together.

, introductory

Computer Experience. Since we live in an age of computer technology, most employers are looking for people with computer experience. Usually, the more *computer* experience a ~~person~~ *candidate* has, the better off he or she willbe in terms of competing with others for the same position.

REASONS FOR LYING

¶ Job Candidates lie for any number of reasons. Some of them see getting a job as some sort of game in which the rules don't really matter. Others equate lying with cheating on an exam and rationalize the deception in some way. Many applicants have families to support and are willing to do any thing to get the job.

Conclusion

, independent

¶ It is clear that lying is ~~quite~~ rampant, and it is equally clear that the value of ethics has been lost some where along the way. It is therefore up to the employer to figure out how best to test a potential employee's integrity, to investigate an applicant's history, and then to decide whether *or not* to hire this individual.

Report 27-4

Business Report

Open the file for Report 27-3 and make the following changes:

1. Change the byline to Diane Jackson.
2. Change the date to July 7.
3. Change the third side heading to COMMON REASONS FOR LYING.

4. Add this sentence to the end of the last paragraph:

   The importance of ethics in a future employee should never be underestimated.

Business Reports With Lists

Goals

- Type at least 31wpm/3'/5e
- Format business reports with bulleted and numbered lists

A. Type 2 times.

A. WARMUP

```
1     At 8:30, Horowitz & Co. will fax Order #V546 to us for   11
2   immediate processing! Just how many additional orders they  23
3   will request isn't known. About 7% of the orders are here.  35
    | 1 | 2 | 3 | 4 | 5 | 6 | 7 | 8 | 9 | 10 | 11 | 12
```

SKILLBUILDING

B. Take three 12-second timed writings on each line. The scale below the last line shows your wpm speed for a 12-second timed writing.

B. 12-SECOND SPEED SPRINTS

```
4   Mary will not be able to meet them at the game later today.
5   The class is not going to be able to meet if they are gone.
6   They could not open that old door when the chair fell over.
7   This very nice piece of paper may be used to print the job.
    5    10    15    20    25    30    35    40    45    50    55    60
```

PPP   PRETEST → PRACTICE → POSTTEST

PRETEST
Take a 1-minute timed writing. Review your speed and errors.

C. PRETEST: Close Reaches

```
8      The growth in the volume of company assets is due to    11
9   the astute group of twenty older employees. Their answers   23
10  were undoubtedly the reason for the increase in net worth.  35
    | 1 | 2 | 3 | 4 | 5 | 6 | 7 | 8 | 9 | 10 | 11 | 12
```

PRACTICE
Speed Emphasis:
If you made 2 or fewer errors on the Pretest, type each *individual* line 2 times.
Accuracy Emphasis:
If you made 3 or more errors, type each *group* of lines (as though it were a paragraph) 2 times.

D. PRACTICE: Adjacent Keys

```
11  as ashes cases class asset astute passes chased creased ask
12  we weave tweed towed weigh wealth twenty fewest answers wet
13  rt worth alert party smart artist sorted charts turtles art
```

E. PRACTICE: Consecutive Fingers

```
14  un undue bunch stung begun united punish outrun untie funny
15  gr grand agree angry grade growth egress hungry group graph
16  ol older solid tools spool volume evolve uphold olive scold
```

POSTTEST
Repeat the Pretest timed writing and compare performance.

F. POSTTEST: Close Reaches

G. Take two 3-minute timed writings. Review your speed and errors.

Goal: At least 31wpm/3'/5e

G. 3-MINUTE TIMED WRITING

17	Credit cards can make shopping very convenient, and	11
18	they frequently help you record and track your spending.	22
19	However, many card companies charge high fees for using	33
20	their credit cards.	37
21	You must realize that it may be better to pay in cash	48
22	and not use a credit card. Look at all your options. Some	60
23	card companies do not charge yearly fees. Some may give	71
24	you extended warranties on goods you buy with their credit	83
25	cards. Judge all the details; you may be surprised.	93

| 1 | 2 | 3 | 4 | 5 | 6 | 7 | 8 | 9 | 10 | 11 | 12

FORMATTING

H. BULLETED AND NUMBERED LISTS

- Numbers or bullets call attention to items in a list. If the sequence of the items is important, use numbers rather than bullets.
- Numbers or bullets should be positioned either at the left margin in blocked documents like business reports or letters, or they should be positioned at the same point as the indented paragraphs in a document such as an academic report.
- The text in carryover lines in lists will be indented automatically to align with the text in the previous line.

I. BUSINESS REPORTS WITH LISTS

To format a list in a business report:

- Press ENTER 2 times to insert 1 blank line above the list.
- Type the list *unformatted* (without the bullets or numbers) at the left margin.
- If all the items in the list are 1 line long, single-space the entire list.
- If any items in the list are multiline, single-space each item in the list but insert a blank line between the items for readability.
- Press ENTER 2 times to insert 1 blank line below the list.
- Select all lines of the list and apply the number or bullet feature to the selected lines of the list only.
- Decrease the indent to position the list at the left margin.

 Word Processing Manual

J. WORD PROCESSING: BULLETS AND NUMBERING

Study Lesson 28 in your word processing manual. Complete all of the shaded steps while at your computer. Then format the jobs that follow.

Report 28-5

Business Report

1. Type the report using standard business report format.
2. Use the bullet and numbering feature to add bullets or numbers to the lists after typing the lists unformatted.
3. Decrease the indent on both lists to position them at the left margin.

INCREASING YOUR ENERGY
Shannon Wahlberg
August 21, 20--

When your energy level is running high, you are more creative, happier, and more relaxed. Some people believe that we are born with a personality that is innately energetic, lethargic, or somewhere in between. However, we are all capable of generating more energy in our lives at home or at work.

CREATING MORE ENERGY

There are many ways in which you can generate more energy before you leave for work. These two methods are simple and can be practiced without a great deal of planning:

1. Wake up to natural light by opening your curtains before you go to bed. The light coming in signals your body to stop releasing melatonin, a hormone that tells your body to continue sleeping.
2. Play music that is lively and upbeat. This will set the tone for the day.

MAINTAINING MORE ENERGY

Once you have raised your energy level at home, you can also learn to maintain your energy level at work.

• Remain positive throughout the day.
• Avoid people who are negative and have low energy. Instead, seek out those who are cheerful and positive. They will boost your energy level.
• Avoid high-fat foods, sweets, and heavy meals during the working day.
• Accept your periods of low energy as natural rhythms, knowing that they will pass. This will help you relax.

If you practice these methods to create and maintain your energy levels, you will find that these techniques will become a natural part of your daily life. Enjoy the change and experiment with your own techniques!

Report 28-6

Business Report

Open the file for Report 28-5 and make the following changes:

1. Change the first side heading to HOW TO CREATE MORE ENERGY.
2. Change the second side heading to HOW TO MAINTAIN MORE ENERGY.
3. Change the third bulleted item to this: Avoid foods with caffeine, such as sodas and coffee.
4. Change the fourth bulleted item to this: Monitor your sleeping habits. Sleeping too long can make you just as tired as sleeping too little.

Academic Reports

Goals

- Improve speed and accuracy
- Refine language arts skills in proofreading
- Format academic reports

A. Type 2 times.

A. WARMUP

```
1      Will the package arrive at 9:45 or 11:29? The exact      11
2   answer to this question could mean the difference between    23
3   losing or saving their account; Joyce also realizes this.   34
    |  1  |  2  |  3  |  4  |  5  |  6  |  7  |  8  |  9  |  10  |  11  |  12
```

SKILLBUILDING

B. Type each paragraph 1 time. Change every masculine pronoun to a feminine pronoun. Change every feminine pronoun to a masculine pronoun.

B. TECHNIQUE PRACTICE: CONCENTRATION

```
4      She will finish composing the report as soon as he has
5   given her all the research. Her final draft will be turned in
6   to her boss; he will submit it to the company president.
7      His new job with her company was fascinating. When the
8   chance to join her firm came up, he jumped at it immediately.
9   I wonder if she will give him a promotion anytime soon.
```

C. PACED PRACTICE

If you are not using the GDP software, turn to page SB-14 and follow the directions for this activity.

Strategies for Career Success

Turning Negative Messages Positive

Accentuate the positive. When communicating bad news (e.g., layoffs, product recalls, price increases, personnel problems), find the positive.

People respond better to positive rather than negative language, and they are more likely to cooperate if treated fairly and with respect. Avoid insults, accusations, criticism, or words with negative connotations (e.g., *failed*, *delinquent*, *bad*). Focus on what the reader can do rather than on what you won't or can't let the reader do. Instead of "You will not qualify unless . . . ," state "You will qualify if you are . . . ."

Assuage your audience's response by providing an explanation to support your decision and examples of how they might benefit. Analyze your audience and decide whether to give the negative news in the beginning, middle, or end of your message. Regardless of your approach, always maintain goodwill.

YOUR TURN   Review some of your written documents and observe if they have a positive tone.

D. Type these frequently misspelled words, paying special attention to any spelling problems in each word.

D. SPELLING

```
10  personnel information its procedures their committee system
11  receive employees which education services opportunity area
12  financial appropriate interest received production contract
13  important through necessary customer employee further there
14  property account approximately general control division our
```

Edit the sentences to correct any misspellings.

```
15  All company personel will receive important information.
16  Are division has some control over there financial account.
17  There comittee has received approximately three contracts.
18  The employe and the customer have an oportunity to attend.
19  We have no farther interest in the property or it's owner.
20  When it is necessary, apropriate proceedures are followed.
```

FORMATTING

E. MORE PROOFREADERS' MARKS

1. Review the most frequently used proofreaders' marks introduced in Lesson 27.

2. Study the additional proofreaders' marks presented here.

Proofreaders' Marks		Draft	Final Copy
ds	Double-space	ds [first line / second line	first line / second line
......	Don't delete	a ~~true~~ story	a true story
◯	Spell out	the only ①	the only one
⊐	Move right	Please send	Please send
⊏	Move left	May 1	May 1
∼∼∼	Bold	Column Heading	**Column Heading**
ital	Italic	ital Time magazine	*Time* magazine
u/l	Underline	u/l Time magazine	Time magazine readers
♂	Move as shown	readers will see	will see

Note that a new paragraph may be formatted either by inserting a blank line before it in a single-spaced document or by indenting the first line 0.5 inch (☐) in a double-spaced document.

F. ACADEMIC REPORTS

To format an academic report:

1. Press ENTER 5 times to begin the first line of the academic report 2 inches from the top of the page.
2. Change line spacing to double–academic reports are double-spaced.
3. Type the title in all-caps, centered, in bold, and change the font size to 14 point. Double-space a 2-line title.
4. Press ENTER 1 time and change the font size to 12 point.
5. If the report includes a subtitle, byline, or date, type each item centered, in bold and upper- and lowercase letters; press ENTER 1 time after each line in the heading block.
6. Type side headings at the left margin, in bold and all-caps.
7. Press TAB 1 time at the start of paragraphs and paragraph headings to indent them 0.5 inch.
8. Type paragraph headings in bold and in upper- and lowercase letters, and follow the paragraph heading with a bold period and 1 space.
9. Insert a page number in the top right-hand corner of the second page, and remove the page number from the first page.

Word Processing Manual

G. WORD PROCESSING: LINE SPACING

Study Lesson 29 in your word processing manual. Complete all of the shaded steps while at your computer. Then format the jobs that follow.

DOCUMENT PROCESSING

Report 29-7

Academic Report

1. Type this report in standard format for an academic report.
2. Type the 2-line title double-spaced, and use standard format for the rest of the heading block.
3. Insert a page number in the top right-hand corner of the second page, and remove the page number from the first page.

Reference Manual

See pages R-8C and R-8D of the Reference Manual for an illustration of a multipage report in academic style.

 Indent paragraphs in an academic report.

 Highlighted words are spelling words from the language arts activities.

ELECTRONIC SAFEGUARDS IN THE DIGITAL WORLD

Trends in Technology

Kevin Nguyen

July 13, 20--

More and more people are using computers and the Internet for a wide variety of reasons, both personal and professional. Most of the technology requires the use of passwords, user names, pin numbers, and miscellaneous other important codes to access their accounts. *for users* Unfortunately, at times it seems as if the number of codes that *are* necessary is increasing in geometric proportions. The problem is how to maintain accurate records of these various security codes and still preserve a secure environment, technologically speaking.

(Continued on next page)

SECURITY CODE OVERLOAD

People need ① or sometimes ② security codes just to log on to their computers. Several more are needed to access web sites, trade stocks, and shop and bank online, just to name a few activities. In addition, most people need to remember codes for their home phones, work phones, cell phones, and voice mail. Banks require codes to withdraw money and use credit cards and ATMs. With so many security codes proliferating on a daily basis, its no wonder that we are often frustrated and frazzled as we move through our daily lives going about our personal and professional business. To add insult to injury we are often being asked to change our passwords and codes on a regular basis.

MANAGING SECURITY CODES

Several things can be done to help manage this ever-growing list of security codes. Try to choose passwords that are in some way meaningful to you but that cannot be guessed at by an intruder. Use a combination of letters and numbers. An article in the magazine Technology Bytes suggests using using street addresses or names of pets that can be easily remembered but that have no logical association with anything else.

If you decide to keep a list of security codes, make sure to protect the file in an appropriate way. If you must write down your passwords, physically lock them up. You must control and manage these important and necessary security codes to protect your personal and financial information.

Report 29-8 ▶

Academic Report

Open the file for Report 29-7 and make the following changes:

1. Change the byline to Nancy Dodson.
2. Add this paragraph at the end of the report:

   A number of Web sites are available to help you remember your passwords and user names. However, these sites can help you do much more than simply manage your security codes. Some sites can provide instant registration at new sites with just one click. They also offer price comparisons while you shop anywhere on the Web, and they bring together the best search engines all in one place for easier searching. They can also filter e-mail to help you eliminate cluttered e-mail boxes full of junk.

Academic Reports With Displays

Goals

- Type at least 32wpm/3′/5e
- Format rough-draft academic reports with indented lists and displays

A. Type 2 times.

A. WARMUP

```
1       Did Zagorsky & Sons charge $876 for the renovation?    11
2  An invoice wasn't quite right; the exact amount charged in  22
3  July can be found in an e-mail message to zagsons@post.com. 34
   | 1 | 2 | 3 | 4 | 5 | 6 | 7 | 8 | 9 | 10 | 11 | 12
```

SKILLBUILDING

B. MAP

Follow the GDP software directions for this exercise in improving keystroking accuracy.

C. DIAGNOSTIC PRACTICE: NUMBERS

If you are not using the GDP software, turn to page SB-5 and follow the directions for this activity.

D. Take two 3-minute timed writings. Review your speed and errors.

Goal: At least 32wpm/3′/5e

D. 3-MINUTE TIMED WRITING

```
4       If you want to work in information processing, you    10
5  may realize that there are steps that you must take to     21
6  plan for such an exciting career. First, you must decide   33
7  whether or not you have the right personality traits.      44
8       Then you must be trained in the technical skills you  54
9  need in such an important field. The technology is changing 66
10 each day. You must stay focused on keeping up with these   78
11 changes. Also, you must never quit wanting to learn new    89
12 skills each day you are on the job.                        96
   | 1 | 2 | 3 | 4 | 5 | 6 | 7 | 8 | 9 | 10 | 11 | 12
```

E. ACADEMIC REPORTS WITH LISTS

To format a list in an academic report:

- Press ENTER 1 time to begin the list.
- Type the list *unformatted* at the left margin, double-spaced.
- Press ENTER 1 time after the last line in the list.
- Select all lines of the list and apply the number or bullet feature to the selected lines of the list only. Do not include the blank lines above and below the list in your selection.
- Set the indent of the list as needed so that the list begins at the same point of indention as the paragraphs in the report.

F. ACADEMIC REPORTS WITH INDENTED DISPLAYS

A paragraph having 4 lines or more that are quoted or having lines that need special emphasis should be formatted so that the paragraph stands out from the rest of the report. To format academic reports with indented displays:

- Type the paragraph single-spaced and indented 0.5 inch from both the left and the right margins (instead of enclosing it in quotation marks).
- Use the indent command in your word processing software to format a displayed paragraph.

Word Processing Manual

G. WORD PROCESSING: INCREASE INDENT AND CUT, COPY, AND PASTE

Study Lesson 30 in your word processing manual. Complete all of the shaded steps while at your computer. Then format the jobs that follow.

Report 30-9 ▶

Academic Report

Refer to | **Reference Manual**

See page R-8D of the Reference Manual for an illustration of a multipage report in academic style with a displayed paragraph.

1. Type the report using standard academic report format.
2. Type the list using standard format for lists in an academic report. Use the number feature to add numbers to the list after you have typed the list unformatted. Use the cut-and-paste feature to move the second numbered item.
3. Type the display using standard format for indented displays in an academic report.

Note: It is very important to review Lesson 30 in your word processing manual for detailed steps to arrange the displayed paragraph so that it will appear single-spaced, indented 0.5 inch from both margins, with 1 blank line above and below it. Remember to type both the displayed paragraph *and* the paragraph that follows it *before* changing line spacing.

4. Type paragraph headings indented 0.5 inch, in bold, and in upper- and lower-case letters, and follow the paragraph heading with a bold period and 1 space.
5. Insert a page number in the top right-hand corner of the second page, and remove the page number from the first page.

ENDING PROCRASTINATION

Judy Baca

Every one at one time or another has put of some task, goal or

important plan at work for any number of reasons. perhaps you think time is

(Continued on next page)

too short or the task isn't really that important. Either way, procrastination can lead to a stalled life and career.

EVALUATE YOUR SITUATION

Joyce Winfrey, of Time Management Incorporated, has some very good advice that will help you to begin to move forward. She says that you should ask yourself 2 very basic questions about why you are procrastinating:

2. 1. Is there a valid reason for my procrastination?

1. 2. Am I procrastinating because the task at hand is not really what I want?

After you have asked yourself these questions, ms. Winfrey suggests that you do the following:

Look deep within yourself. If you are looking for excuses, then the process of asking these questions will be a waste of your time. However, if you answer these questions honestly, you might find answers that surprise you and that will help clarify your situation.

She also recommends several techniques that can help you get back on task.

PRACTICE NEW TECHNIQUES

Identifying and understanding the techniques that follow is the first step. Once you know what to do, you can begin to practice these steps daily.

Take Baby Steps. Don't make any task bigger than it really is by looking at the whole thing at once. Break it down into baby steps that are manageable.

Don't Strive for Perfectionism. If you are waiting for the perfect solution or the perfect opportunity, you will be immobilized. Accept the fact that no one and nothing is perfect. Then accept your mistakes and move on.

Enjoy the Task. Enjoy the task at hand and find something in it that is positive and rewarding. Confront your fears with a plan of action.

Remind yourself of all these techniques daily. Post them by your telephone, by your desk, or in your car. You will find that your personal life and career will gain momentum, and success will soon be yours.

1. Type the report using standard academic report format for a multipage academic report with a list.

2. Make all changes as indicated by the proofreaders' marks.

TIPS FOR HELPING YOU
PREPARE FOR YOUR EXAM
Betty Goldberg
June 8, 20--

In school you have taken many exams. Whether you are an excellent exam taker or a novice at the task, you probably have experienced a degree of stress related to your performance on an exam. There are some steps you can take to reduce the stress of taking an exam, and these suggestions will likely help you throughout your life.

PREPARING FOR THE EXAM

Of course, it's always easier to take an exam from an Instructor whom you have had in previous classes, because you know what to expect. From past experience, you know whether the Instructor likes to use objective questions or subjective questions, whether the Instructor focuses on the textbook or on class notes, and the difficulty of the questions the Instructor asks.

If you don't know what to expect, however, you need to prepare for all possibilities. Be sure that you review all pertinent materials for the exam—whether they come from class notes, the textbook, field trips, or class room presentations.

SURVIVING THE DAY BEFORE THE EXAM

Be sure you know where and at what time the exam will be administered. Organize the materials you need to bring with you to the exam. You may need pencils, pens, calculators, disks, or paper. Try to get a good night's sleep the night before the exam, and don't upset your usual routine.

Taking The Exam

Now that the day of the exam has arrived, there are several actions you should take to ensure that you perform well:

ds

1. Arrive at the test site early so that you are ready to take the exam when the instructor announces the beginning time. That means that before you have to be sure to get up early enough to have a light breakfast leaving for the exam.

2. Read very carefully the instructions provided on the exam to be sure you answer the questions correctly.

3. Keep track of time so that you don't get stuck and spend too much of your time on any one part of the exam.

4. Try to keep a positive attitude.

5. Relax as best you can—a relaxed performance is much more productive than a stressed performance.

Unit 7

Correspondence

LESSON 31
Business Letters

LESSON 34
Memos

LESSON 32
Business Letters With Enclosure Notations

LESSON 35
Correspondence Review

LESSON 33
Envelopes and Labels

MEMO TO: All Salaried Employees

FROM: Amy Vigil, Human Resources

DATE: November 2, 20--

SUBJECT: Health Care Benefit Plan

Effective January 1, Allied Aerospace Industries will contract with MedNet to begin a new health benefits program for all eligible salaried personnel. A brochure outlining important program information will be mailed to you soon.

An open enrollment period will be in effect during the entire month of January. If you and your family are interested in one of the MedNet health plan options, you may transfer yourself and your dependents into any appropriate plan. All applications must be received no later than midnight, January 31. You may also access your plan over the Internet at www.mednet.com if it is more convenient.

If you have any questions or need any help understanding your options, please call me at Ext. 134. I will be happy to help you select the plan that is best for you.

urs

January 27, 20--

Ms. Linda Lopez
Account Manager
The Internet Connection
7625 Maple Avenue
Pomona, CA 91765

Dear Ms. Lopez:

Our company is interested in hosting an educational seminar this spring that will focus on meeting the growing need for information industry professionals to keep abreast of emerging new technologies and trends. We are specifically interested in information on high-speed Internet connections.

I understand that The Internet Connection specializes in these seminars and will also help businesses analyze their needs and choose an appropriate solution. I am in the process of contacting several companies similar to yours who might be interested in conducting these seminars. Please contact me by Thursday or Friday at the latest so that we can discuss this further.

I appreciate the fine service we have always received from you in the past, Ms. Lopez, and look forward to hearing from you.

Sincerely,

Ruzanna Petroska
Technology Specialist

urs

Shannon Stone
Data Systems, Inc.
2201 South Street
Racine, WI 53404

Mr. Charles Goldstein
Software Solutions
2981 Canwood Street
Roselle, IL 60172

Business Letters

Goals

- Improve speed and accuracy
- Refine language arts skills in capitalization
- Format a business letter in block style

A. Type 2 times.

A. WARMUP

```
1      You can save $1,698 when you buy the 20-part video       10
2   series! Just ask for Series #MX5265 in the next 7 days;      22
3   ordering early qualifies you for a sizable discount of 5%.    33
   | 1 | 2 | 3 | 4 | 5 | 6 | 7 | 8 | 9 | 10 | 11 | 12
```

SKILLBUILDING

B. Take three 12-second timed writings on each line. The scale below the last line shows your wpm speed for a 12-second timed writing.

B. 12-SECOND SPEED SPRINTS

```
4   Mary will be able to go home when she can run fast and far.
5   Sam can come to the store if he is able to stop for a soda.
6   Suzy knows that she must send the mail out by noon or else.
7   Only a few good desks will be made by the end of this week.
   I I I I 5 I I I 10 I I I 15 I I I 20 I I I 25 I I I 30 I I I 35 I I I 40 I I I 45 I I I 50 I I I 55 I I I 60
```

C. PROGRESSIVE PRACTICE: ALPHABET

If you are not using the GDP software, turn to page SB-7 and follow the directions for this activity.

D. PROGRESSIVE PRACTICE: NUMBERS

If you are not using the GDP software, turn to page SB-11 and follow the directions for this activity.

LANGUAGE ARTS

E. Study the rules at the right.

E. CAPITALIZATION

Note: The callout signals in the left margin indicate which language arts rule from this lesson has been applied.

RULE ▶
≡ sentence

Capitalize the first word of a sentence.
Please prepare a summary of your activities.

RULE ▶
≡ proper

Capitalize proper nouns and adjectives derived from proper nouns.
Judy Hendrix drove to Albuquerque in her new Pontiac convertible.

Note: A proper noun is the official name of a particular person, place, or thing.

(Continued on next page)

RULE ▶

≡ time

Capitalize the names of the days of the week, months, holidays, and religious days (but do not capitalize the names of the seasons).

On Thursday, November 25, we will celebrate Thanksgiving, the most popular holiday in the <u>f</u>all.

Edit the paragraph to insert or delete capitalization.

8　　　The american flag can be seen flying over the White
9　House in Washington. Our Country's flag is often seen
10　flying over Government buildings on holidays like July 4,
11　independence day. Memorial Day signals the end of spring
12　and the start of Summer. Most Americans consider Labor day
13　the beginning of the fall season. In december many people
14　observe christmas and Hanukkah. most government holidays are
15　scheduled to fall on either a Monday or a friday. Sometimes
16　the birthdays of Historical figures are also celebrated.

FORMATTING

F.　BASIC PARTS OF A BUSINESS LETTER

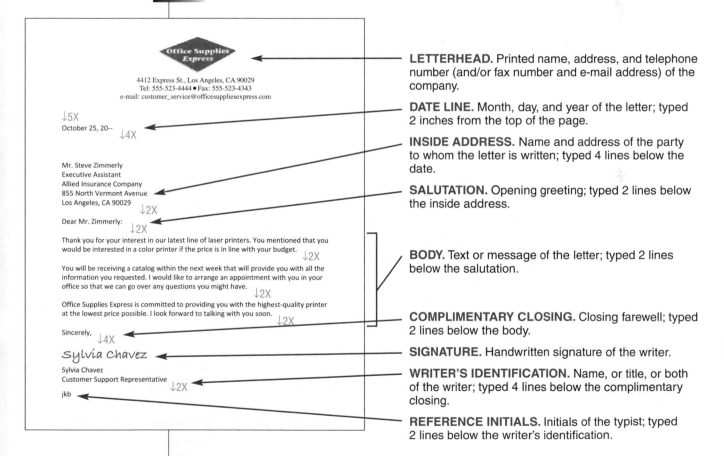

LETTERHEAD. Printed name, address, and telephone number (and/or fax number and e-mail address) of the company.

DATE LINE. Month, day, and year of the letter; typed 2 inches from the top of the page.

INSIDE ADDRESS. Name and address of the party to whom the letter is written; typed 4 lines below the date.

SALUTATION. Opening greeting; typed 2 lines below the inside address.

BODY. Text or message of the letter; typed 2 lines below the salutation.

COMPLIMENTARY CLOSING. Closing farewell; typed 2 lines below the body.

SIGNATURE. Handwritten signature of the writer.

WRITER'S IDENTIFICATION. Name, or title, or both of the writer; typed 4 lines below the complimentary closing.

REFERENCE INITIALS. Initials of the typist; typed 2 lines below the writer's identification.

G.　BUSINESS LETTERS IN BLOCK STYLE

1. Type all lines beginning at the left margin.
2. Press ENTER 5 times to begin the first line of the letter 2 inches from the top of the page, and then type the date.

3. After the date, press ENTER 4 times and type the inside address. Insert 1 space between the state and the ZIP Code.

(Continued on next page)

4. After the inside address, press ENTER 2 times and type the salutation. For standard punctuation, type a colon after the salutation. Press ENTER 2 times after the salutation.
5. Single-space the body of the letter, but press ENTER 2 times between paragraphs. Do not indent paragraphs.
6. Press ENTER 2 times after the last paragraph and type the complimentary clos-ing. For standard punctuation, type a comma after the complimentary closing.
7. Press ENTER 4 times after the complimentary closing and type the writer's identification.
8. Press ENTER 2 times after the writer's identification and type your reference initials in lowercase letters with no periods or spaces.

Word Processing Manual

H. WORD PROCESSING: INSERT DATE

Study Lesson 31 in your word processing manual. Complete all of the shaded steps while at your computer. Then format the jobs that follow.

DOCUMENT PROCESSING

Correspondence 31-3

Business Letter in Block Style

1. Type the letter using standard block style.
2. Use standard punctuation: a colon after the salutation and a comma after the complimentary closing.
3. Use word wrap for the paragraphs. Press ENTER only at the end of each paragraph. Your lines may end differ-ently from those shown in the illustration.
4. Type your initials for the reference initials.
5. Spell-check, preview, and proofread your letter for typing, spelling, and formatting errors.

↓5X

January 27, 20-- ↓4X

≡ proper

Ms. Linda Lopez
Account Manager
The Internet Connection
7625 Maple Avenue
Pomona, CA 91765 ↓2X

≡ proper

Dear Ms. Lopez: ↓2X

≡ sentence, ≡ time

Our company is interested in hosting an educational seminar this spring that will focus on meeting the growing need for information industry professionals to keep abreast of emerging new technologies and trends. We are specifically

≡ proper

interested in information on high-speed Internet connections. ↓2X

I understand that The Internet Connection specializes in these seminars and will also help businesses analyze their needs and choose an appropriate solution. I am in the process of contacting several companies similar to yours

≡ sentence

who might be interested in conducting these seminars. Please contact me by

≡ time

Thursday or Friday at the latest so that we can discuss this further. ↓2X

(Continued on next page)

≡ sentence

≡ proper

I appreciate the fine service we have always received from you in the past, Ms. Lopez, and look forward to hearing from you. ↓2X

Sincerely, ↓4X

≡ proper

≡ proper

Ruzanna Petroska
Technology Specialist ↓2X

(!) Remember to type your initials in place of urs.

urs

Correspondence 31-4 ▶

Business Letter in Block Style

Open the file for Correspondence 31-3 and make the following changes:

1. Change the date to February 8.

2. Change the writer's identification to: Gail Madison and her job title to Technology Engineer.

Correspondence 31-5 ▶

Business Letter in Block Style

Note: The | symbol indicates the end of a line. The ¶ symbol indicates the start of a new paragraph.

1. Type the letter using standard block style.

2. Spell-check, preview, and proofread your letter for typing, spelling, and formatting errors.

≡ time

≡ proper

≡ time

≡ proper

(!) The ¶ symbol indicates the start of a new paragraph. In a business letter, paragraphs are blocked (not indented).

≡ time

May 25, 20-- | Ms. Linda Lopez | Account Manager | The Internet Connection | 7625 Maple Avenue | Pomona, CA 91765 | Dear Ms. Lopez:

¶ Thank you so much for hosting the educational seminar last Tuesday that focused on the topic of high-speed Internet connections. Our company and our employees are now well prepared to make a decision about the best type of Internet connection for their particular needs.

¶ Because this seminar was so successful, I have been authorized to contract with The Internet Connection for a continuing series of seminars on any topics related to emerging new technologies and trends as they apply to the needs of our company and our employees. I will call you on Monday so that we can arrange for a meeting to finalize some contractual issues.

¶ Once again, thank you for a very successful and productive seminar!

Sincerely, | Ruzanna Petroska | Technology Specialist |

urs

Business Letters With Enclosure Notations

Goals

- Type at least 33wpm/3'/5e
- Format a business letter with an enclosure notation

A. Type 2 times.

A. WARMUP

```
1       Sales by two travel agencies (Quill, Virgil, & Johnson   11
2   and Keef & Zane) exceeded all prior amounts. Total sales     23
3   for that year were as follows: $1,540,830 and $976,233.      34
    |  1  |  2  |  3  |  4  |  5  |  6  |  7  |  8  |  9  |  10  |  11  |  12
```

SKILLBUILDING

B. Type each line 2 times.

Technique Tip:
Press the BACKSPACE key with the Sem finger without looking at your keyboard.

B. TECHNIQUE PRACTICE: BACKSPACE KEY

1. Type each letter (or group of letters) as shown.
2. When you reach the backspace sign (←), backspace 1 time to delete the last keystroke.
3. Type the next group of letters. The result will be a new word. For example, if you see "hi← at," you would type "hi," backspace 1 time, and then type "at," resulting in the new word "hat" instead of the original word "hit."

```
4   p←cat c←tab b←peg p←but p←tie t←pop m←pat f←sit m←but t←cub
5   t←mop b←fib r←fat w←fin p←tin c←top p←ban f←can y←get m←let
6   di←ye be←ag ge←um ri←ob mu←ad la←id fi←an bi←ad to←ip ro←id
7   pa←it ti←on fi←un ra←un pi←an ge←ot ba←it fa←it ma←it sa←it
8   bin←t any←t new←t was←r sea←t tap←n fan←t lap←d for←x fin←x
9   pin←t ham←d sod←n rid←p rap←n tap←n dip←n sin←p lip←d put←n
```

PPP PRETEST → PRACTICE → POSTTEST

PRETEST
Take a 1-minute timed writing. Review your speed and errors.

PRACTICE
Speed Emphasis:
If you made 2 or fewer errors on the Pretest, type each *individual* line 2 times.
Accuracy Emphasis:
If you made 3 or more errors, type each *group* of lines (as though it were a paragraph) 2 times.

C. PRETEST: Discrimination Practice

```
10      Steven saw the younger, unruly boy take flight as he    11
11  threw the coin at the jury. The brave judge stopped the      22
12  fight. He called out to the youth, who recoiled in fear.     33
    |  1  |  2  |  3  |  4  |  5  |  6  |  7  |  8  |  9  |  10  |  11  |  12
```

D. PRACTICE: Left Hand

```
13  vbv verb bevy vibes bevel brave above verbal bovine behaves
14  wew west weep threw wedge weave fewer weight sewing dewdrop
15  fgf gulf gift fight fudge fugue flags flight golfer feigned
```

E. PRACTICE: Right Hand

```
16   uyu buys your usury unity youth buoys unruly untidy younger
17   oio coin lion oiled foils foist prior recoil iodine rejoice
18   jhj jury huge enjoy three judge habit adjust slight jasmine
```

F. POSTTEST: Discrimination Practice

POSTTEST
Repeat the Pretest timed writing and compare performance.

G. Take two 3-minute timed writings. Review your speed and errors.

Goal: At least 33wpm/3'/5e

G. 3-MINUTE TIMED WRITING

```
19        Be zealous in your efforts when you write business      10
20   letters. Your business writing must convey clearly what      22
21   it is you want people to read. All of your letters should    33
22   be formatted neatly in proper business letter format.        44
23        Before sending your letters, read them quickly just to  55
24   make sure that they explain clearly what you want to say.    67
25   Proofread the letters you write for correct grammar and      78
26   spelling. Use all of your writing skills to display the      89
27   best image. Your readers will welcome the effort.            99
```
```
| 1 | 2 | 3 | 4 | 5 | 6 | 7 | 8 | 9 | 10 | 11 | 12
```

FORMATTING

H. ENCLOSURE NOTATION

- To indicate that an item is enclosed with a letter, type the word *Enclosure* on the line below the reference initials.

Example: urs
Enclosure

- If more than one item is being enclosed, type the word *Enclosures*.

DOCUMENT PROCESSING

Correspondence 32-6

Business Letter in Block Style

 Refer to Reference Manual

See page R-3B and R-3C of the Reference Manual for an illustration of a business letter with an enclosure notation.

The I symbol indicates the end of a line.

1. Type the letter using standard business letter format.

2. Spell-check, preview, and proofread your document for spelling and formatting errors.

October 10, 20-- I Ms. Denise Bradford I Worldwide Travel, Inc. I 1180 Alvarado, SE I Albuquerque, NM 87108 I Dear Ms. Bradford:
¶ Our company has decided to hold its regional sales meeting in Scottsdale, Arizona, during the second week of January. I need information on a suitable conference site.

(Continued on next page)

The ¶ symbol indicates the start of a new paragraph.

¶ We will need a meeting room with the following items: 30 computer workstations with an Internet connection, copy stands, mouse pads, and adjustable chairs; an LCD projector with a large screen; and a microphone and podium. The hotel should have a fax machine and on-site secretarial services. We might also need a messenger service.

¶ A final decision on the conference site must be made within the next two weeks. Please send me any information you have available for a suitable location in Scottsdale immediately. I have enclosed a list of conference attendees and their room preferences. Thank you for your help.

Sincerely yours, | Bill McKay | Marketing Manager | urs | Enclosure

Correspondence ▶ 32-7

Business Letter in Block Style

1. Open the file for Correspondence 32-6.
2. Change the inside address to 1032 San Pedro, SE.
3. Change the first sentence as follows:

   Our company has decided to hold its annual national sales meeting during the first week of February in Scottsdale, Arizona.

4. In the first sentence of the second paragraph, change the information after the colon as follows:

   30 computer workstations, an LCD projector with a large screen, and a microphone and podium.

Correspondence ▶ 32-8

Business Letter in Block Style

October 20, 20-- | Mr. Bill McKay | Marketing Manager | Viatech Communications | 9835 Osuna Road, NE | Albuquerque, NM 87111 | Dear Mr. McKay:

¶ Thank you for your inquiry regarding a conference site in Scottsdale, Arizona, for 35 people during the second week of January.

¶ I have enclosed the following brochures with detailed information on some properties in Scottsdale that provide exclusive service to businesses like yours: Camelback Resorts, Shadow Pines Suites, and Desert Inn Resorts and Golf Club. All these properties have meeting rooms that will accommodate your needs and also offer additional services you might be interested in using.

(Continued on next page)

¶ Please call me when you have reached a decision. I will be happy to make the final arrangements as well as issue any airline tickets you may need. Yours truly, | Ms. Denise Bradford | Travel Agent | urs | Enclosures

Envelopes and Labels

Goals

- Improve speed and accuracy
- Refine language arts skills in composing sentences
- Format envelopes and labels and fold letters

A. Type 2 times.

A. WARMUP

```
 1      Does Quentin know if half of the January order will be   11
 2  ready on 1/7/05? At 4:20 only 36% of the orders had been    23
 3  mailed! Mr. Gray expects a very sizable loss this month.    34
    | 1 | 2 | 3 | 4 | 5 | 6 | 7 | 8 | 9 | 10 | 11 | 12
```

SKILLBUILDING

B. Take three 12-second timed writings on each line. The scale below the last line shows your wpm speed for a 12-second timed writing.

B. 12-SECOND SPEED SPRINTS

```
 4  Today we want to find out if our work will be done on time.
 5  Doug will be able to drive to the store if the car is here.
 6  Jan will sign this paper when she has done all of the work.
 7  This time she will be sure to spend two days with her sons.
    I I I I 5 I I I I 10 I I I I 15 I I I I 20 I I I 25 I I I I 30 I I I 35 I I I 40 I I I I 45 I I I 50 I I I 55 I I I 60
```

C. PACED PRACTICE

If you are not using the GDP software, turn to page SB-14 and follow the directions for this activity.

LANGUAGE ARTS

D. Answer each question with a complete sentence.

D. COMPOSING: SENTENCES

8 What are your best traits that you will bring to your job when you graduate?
9 What are the best traits that you will want to see in your new boss?
10 Would you rather work for a large or a small company?
11 How much money do you expect to earn on your first job?
12 Would you like your first job to be in a small town or a large city?
13 What do you see yourself doing in ten years?
14 What types of benefits do you think you would like to have?

E. ENVELOPES

The envelope feature of your word processor simplifies your task of addressing a No. 10 envelope. The standard size for business envelopes is 9½ by 4⅛ inches. A business envelope should include the following:

- **Return Address**. If necessary, type the sender's name and address in upper- and lowercase style in the upper left corner. Business stationery usually has a printed return address. Use the default placement and the default font of your word processor for the return address.

- **Mailing Address**. Type the recipient's name and address in upper- and lower-case style (or in all-capital letters without any punctuation) toward the center of the envelope. Use the default placement and the default font of your word processor for the mailing address.

Note: Postal scanners read addresses more efficiently if they are typed in all-capital letters without any punctuation.

Trend Electronics
2206 31st Street
Minneapolis, MN 55407-1911

Mr. Charles R. Harrison
Reliable Software, Inc.
5613 Brunswick Avenue
Minneapolis, MN 55406

Standard large envelope, No. 10, is 9½ × 4⅛ inches.

F. FOLDING LETTERS

To fold a letter for a No. 10 envelope:

1. Place the letter face up, and fold up the bottom third of the page.
2. Fold the top third of the page down to about 0.5 inch from the bottom edge of the page.

3. Insert the last crease into the envelope first with the flap facing up.

G. LABELS

The label feature of your word processor simplifies the task of preparing various labels. You can use different label settings to print a full sheet of labels or to print a single label. You may want to use a mailing label as an alternative to printing an envelope.

When preparing labels, test the label settings by printing your labels on a blank page before you print them on the actual label form.

Word Processing Manual

H. WORD PROCESSING: ENVELOPES AND LABELS

Study Lesson 33 in your word processing manual. Complete all of the shaded steps while at your computer. Then format the jobs that follow.

DOCUMENT PROCESSING

Correspondence 33-9

Envelope

1. Prepare an envelope with the following mailing address:

   Mr. Charles Goldstein|
   Software Solutions|2981
   Canwood Street|Roselle, IL
   60172

2. Insert the following return address.

   Shannon Stone|Data Systems,
   Inc.|2201 South Street|
   Racine, WI 53404

3. Add the envelope to a blank document.

Correspondence 33-10

Envelope

1. Open the file for Correspondence 32-8 and prepare an envelope for the letter.

2. Do not insert a return address.
3. Add the envelope to the letter.

Correspondence 33-11

Mailing Labels

1. Select an address label product about 1 inch deep, large enough to fit a 4-line address. Label choices will vary; however, Avery standard, 5160, Address is a good choice for laser and ink jet printers.

2. Prepare address labels for the names and addresses that follow.
3. Type the addresses in order from left to right as you see them displayed below in the first row of labels.
4. Move to the second row of labels and type them again from left to right.

Purchasing Dept.
Abbott Laboratories
Abbott Park
Chicago, IL 60064

Frank Zimmerly
Cartridges, Etc.
1220 Charleston Road
Oso Park, CA 90621

John Sanchez
Adobe Systems
1585 Charleston Road
Los Angeles, CA 90029

Mike Rashid
Internet Services
901 Thompson Place
Sunnyvale, CA 94088

Jennifer Reagan
Aetna Life
151 Farmington Avenue
Hartford, CT 06156

Bob Patterson
Affiliated Publishing
135 Morrisey Boulevard
Boston, MA 02107

Correspondence 33-12 ▶

Mailing Labels

1. Select an address label product about 1 inch deep, large enough to fit a 4-line address. Label choices will vary; however, Avery standard, 5160, Address is a good choice for laser and ink jet printers.

2. Prepare a full page of the same label with the following address:

```
Shipping and Receiving|
E-Office Outlet|1122 North
Highland Street|Arlington,
VA 22201
```

Correspondence 33-13 ▶

Envelope

1. Open the file for Correspondence 32-6 and prepare an envelope for the letter.
2. Insert the following return address:

```
Bill McKay|Viatech
Communications|9835 Osana
Road, NE|Albuquerque, NM
87111
```

3. Add the envelope to the letter.

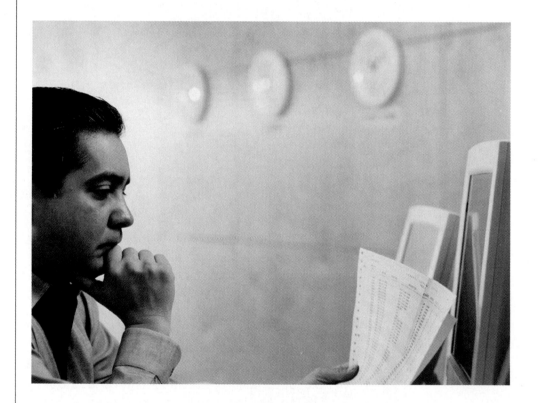

Memos

Goals

- Type at least 34wpm/3'/5e
- Format interoffice memos

A. Type 2 times.

A. WARMUP

```
1       The series* (*6 films, 28 minutes) by J. Zeller goes    11
2  beyond the "basics" of computers. Viewers keep requesting    22
3  an extension on the following due dates: 3/2, 5/5, and 8/9.  34
   | 1 | 2 | 3 | 4 | 5 | 6 | 7 | 8 | 9 | 10 | 11 | 12
```

SKILLBUILDING

B. DIAGNOSTIC PRACTICE: SYMBOLS AND PUNCTUATION

If you are not using the GDP software, turn to page SB-2 and follow the directions for this activity.

C. PROGRESSIVE PRACTICE: ALPHABET

If you are not using the GDP software, turn to page SB-7 and follow the directions for this activity.

D. Take two 3-minute timed writings. Review your speed and errors.

Goal: At least 34wpm/3'/5e

D. 3-MINUTE TIMED WRITING

```
4        Companies that place their ads on the Internet use a    11
5   process called data mining. They look for patterns in the   22
6   quantities of data they get from those who visit Web sites. 34
7        Data mining tracks buying habits of customers and then 46
8   decides to send ads to them based on their current and past 58
9   buying patterns. Data mining can also be used to explain    69
10  buyer behavior and to look at trends. First, a survey is    80
11  filled out, and then the results are gathered and stored in 92
12  a file to be analyzed in detail at a later time.            102
    | 1 | 2 | 3 | 4 | 5 | 6 | 7 | 8 | 9 | 10 | 11 | 12
```

E. MEMOS

A memo is usually sent from one person to another in the same organization. E-mail in recent years has replaced memos as an efficient means of interoffice communication in many offices. However, memos are better suited for detailed messages of a more formal nature. To format a memo on plain paper or on letterhead stationery:

1. Press ENTER 5 times for a top margin of 2 inches.
2. Type the headings (including the colons) in all-caps and bold: MEMO TO:, FROM:, DATE:, and SUBJECT:.
3. Press TAB 1 time after typing the colon to reach the point where the heading entries begin.
4. Insert 1 blank line between the heading lines and between the heading lines and the memo body.
5. Insert 1 blank line between paragraphs. Most memos are typed with blocked paragraphs (no indentions).
6. Insert 1 blank line between the body and the reference initials.

DOCUMENT PROCESSING

Correspondence 34-14

Memo

Refer to Reference Manual

Refer to page R-7C of the Reference Manual for an illustration of a memo.

1. Type the memo using standard memo format.
2. Spell-check, preview, and proofread your document for spelling and formatting errors before printing it.

↓5X

MEMO TO: All Salaried Employees ↓2X

FROM: Amy Vigil, Human Resources ↓2X

DATE: November 2, 20-- ↓2X

SUBJECT: Health Care Benefit Plan ↓2X

Effective January 1, Allied Aerospace Industries will contract with MedNet to begin a new health benefits program for all eligible salaried personnel. A brochure outlining important program information will be mailed to you soon. ↓2X

An open enrollment period will be in effect during the entire month of January. If you and your family are interested in one of the MedNet health plan options, you may transfer yourself and your dependents into any appropriate plan. All applications must be received no later than midnight, January 31. You may also access your plan over the Internet at www.mednet.com if it is more convenient. ↓2X

If you have any questions or need any help understanding your options, please call me at Ext. 134. I will be happy to help you select the plan that is best for you. ↓2X

urs

Correspondence 34-15 ▶

Memo

> The ¶ symbol indicates the start of a new paragraph. In a memo, paragraphs are blocked (not indented).

MEMO TO: Amy Vigil, Human Resources | **FROM:** Dan Westphal | **DATE:** November 23, 20-- | **SUBJECT:** MedNet Benefit Plan

¶ Thank you for the brochure detailing the various options for employees under the MedNet plan. I would like clarification on some of the services included in the plan.

¶ Because both my wife and I are employees of Allied Aerospace Industries, do we have the choice of enrolling separately under different options? In our present plan, I know that this is possible.

¶ We have two dependents. Is it possible to enroll both dependents under different options of the plan, or do they both fall under either one option or the other? I know that in the past you have asked for evidence of dependent status and dates of birth.

¶ If you need any further information, please let me know. Thank you very much for your help.

urs

Correspondence 34-16 ▶

Memo

Open the file for Correspondence 34-14 and make the following changes:

1. Send the memo to All Allied Aerospace Industries Employees.

2. Change the date to December 2.

3. Change the subject line to Health Care Open Enrollment Period.

Keyboarding Connection

Searching the Web

Research projects on the World Wide Web! Access up-to-date information from all over the world.

To conduct a search, specify keywords and certain relationships among them. Many search engines use arithmetic operators to symbolize Boolean relationships. A plus sign (+) is used instead of AND, a minus sign (−) instead of NOT, and no sign instead of OR.

Simple document searches match a single keyword (e.g., *cherry*). Advanced searches might match any of the words (e.g., *cherry pie*); all words (e.g., *+cherry +pie*); a phrase (e.g., "*cherry pie*"); or some words and not others (e.g., *+cherry +pie −tree*). There is no space between the plus or minus sign and its word.

YOUR TURN From your Web browser, open a Web search engine site. Type various searches in the entry box of the search engine and start the search. Compare the results.

Correspondence Review

Goals

- Improve speed and accuracy
- Refine language arts skills in proofreading
- Format various types of correspondence with an attachment notation
- Practice italicizing and underlining

A. Type 2 times.

A. WARMUP

```
 1      Item #876 won't be ordered until 9/10. Did you gather    11
 2  all requests and input them exactly as they appeared? Zack   23
 3  will never be satisfied until he contacts jack@orders.com.    34
    | 1 | 2 | 3 | 4 | 5 | 6 | 7 | 8 | 9 | 10 | 11 | 12
```

SKILLBUILDING

B. MAP

Follow the GDP software directions for this exercise in improving keystroking accuracy.

C. Take a 1-minute timed writing on the first paragraph to establish your base speed. Then take four 1-minute timed writings on the remaining paragraphs. As soon as you equal or exceed your base speed on one paragraph, advance to the next, more difficult paragraph.

C. SUSTAINED PRACTICE: ALTERNATE-HAND WORDS

```
 4      When eight of them began a formal discussion on some     11
 5  of the major issues, the need for a chair was very evident.  23
 6  A chair would be sure to handle the usual work with ease.     35

 7      The eight people in that group decided that the work     11
 8  would be done only if they selected one person to be chair   23
 9  of their group. They began to debate all the major issues.   35

10      One issue that needed to be settled right up front was   11
11  the question of how to handle proxy votes. It seemed for a   23
12  short time that a fight over this very issue would result.   35

13      The group worked diligently in attempting to solve the   11
14  issues that were being discussed. All of the concerns that   23
15  were brought to the group were reviewed in depth by them.    34
    | 1 | 2 | 3 | 4 | 5 | 6 | 7 | 8 | 9 | 10 | 11 | 12
```

D. Edit this paragraph to correct any typing or formatting errors.

D. PROOFREADING

```
16        It doesnt matter how fast you can  type or how well
17   you now a software program if you produce documents taht
18   are filled with errors. You must learn to watch for errors
19   in spelling punctuation, and formatting. Look carefully
20   between words and sentences.Make sure that after a period
21   at the end of a sentence, you see one space. Sometime it
22   helps to look at the characters in the sentence justabove
23   the one you are proofreading to ensure accuracy.
```

FORMATTING

E. ATTACHMENT NOTATION

The word *Attachment* (rather than *Enclosure*) is typed below the reference initials when material is physically attached (stapled or clipped) to a memo.

Example: urs
       Attachment

Word Processing Manual

F. WORD PROCESSING: ITALIC AND UNDERLINE

Study Lesson 35 in your word processing manual. Complete all of the shaded steps while at your computer. Then format the jobs that follow.

DOCUMENT PROCESSING

Correspondence 35-17

Memo

MEMO TO: All Executive Assistants I **FROM:** Barbara Azar, Staff Development Coordinator I **DATE:** March 25, 20-- I **SUBJECT:** Standardizing Document Formats

¶ Last month we received our final shipment of new laser printers. The installation of these printers in your offices marked the final phase-out of all ink-jet printers.

¶ Because all of us can now use a variety of standardized fonts in our correspondence, please note the following change: <u>From now on, all book and journal titles should be set in Arial Narrow</u>. This new formatting change will help us to standardize our correspondence.

¶ The latest edition of the book *Quick Reference for the Automated Office* has two pages of helpful information on laser printers, which I have attached. Please read these pages carefully, and we will discuss them at our next meeting.

urs I Attachment

MEMO TO: Barbara Azar, Staff Development Coordinator I **FROM:** Sharon Hearshen, Executive Assistant I **DATE:** April 3, 20-- I **SUBJECT:** Laser Printer Workshop

¶ The new laser printers we received are <u>fabulous</u>! I know that you worked very hard to get these printers for us, and all of us in the Sales and Marketing Department certainly appreciate your effort.

¶ Several of us would be very interested in seeing the printers demonstrated. Would it be possible to have a workshop with some hands-on training? We are particularly interested in learning about font selection, paper selection, and envelopes and labels.

¶ I have attached an article on laser printers from the latest issue of *Office Technology*. It is very informative, and you might like to include it as a part of the workshop. Please let me know if I can help you in any way.

urs I Attachment

Progress and Proofreading Check

Documents designated as Proofreading Checks serve as a check of your proofreading skill. Your goal is to have zero typographical errors when the GDP software first scores the document.

1. Type the following business letter, and then prepare an envelope for the document.

2. Do not include a return address.
3. Add the envelope to the letter.

October 1, 20-- I Mrs. Elizabeth McGraw I 844 Lincoln Boulevard I Santa Monica, CA 90403 I Dear Mrs. McGraw:

¶ The League of Women Voters is looking for volunteers to work at the various polling places during the upcoming elections. If you think you will be able to volunteer your time, please fill out and mail the following enclosed items: registration form, schedule of availability, and insurance waiver form.

¶ After I receive these items, I will contact you to confirm a location, time, and date.

¶ Your efforts are greatly appreciated, Mrs. McGraw. Concerned citizens like you make it possible for the public to have a convenient place to vote. Thank you for your interest in this very worthy cause!

Sincerely yours, I Ashley Abbott I Public Relations Volunteer I urs I Enclosures

Unit 8

Tables

LESSON 36
Boxed Tables

LESSON 37
Open Tables With Titles

LESSON 38
Open Tables With Column Headings

LESSON 39
Ruled Tables With Number Columns

LESSON 40
Formatting Review

GENERAL EQUITY MUTUAL FUNDS

Fund	Current Year
Duncan Insurance	16.3%
Strident Nova	9.3%
First Value	10.7%
Safeguard Policy	11.1%
Vanguard Life	8.5%

PERSONAL ASSET ACCOUNTS
Wanda Nelson

Account	Amount	Interest Rate
Interest Checking	$ 972.55	3.10%
Money Market	4,500.35	4.90%
	3,250.76	5.07%
sit	550.00	7.41%

CABLE SERVICES AVAILABILITY

Type of Service	Currently Available
Basic	Phoenix
Lifeline	Scottsdale
Expanded	Glendale
Expanded (per channel)	Camelback City

Boxed Tables

Goals

- Type at least 35wpm/3'/4e
- Format boxed tables

A. Type 2 times.

A. WARMUP

```
1        A plain paper reader/printer must be ordered; it must    11
2   accept jackets and have a footprint of 15 x 27* (*inches).    23
3   Please ask Gary to request Model Z-340 whenever he arrives.   35
    |  1  |  2  |  3  |  4  |  5  |  6  |  7  |  8  |  9  |  10  |  11  |  12
```

SKILLBUILDING

B. Take three 12-second timed writings on each line. The scale below the last line shows your wpm speed for a 12-second timed writing.

B. 12-SECOND SPEED SPRINTS

```
4   The book that is on top of the big desk will be given away.
5   Bill must pay for the tape or he will have to give it back.
6   They left the meeting after all of the group had gone away.
7   The third person to finish all of the work today may leave.
    | | | | 5 | | | 10 | | | 15 | | | 20 | | | 25 | | | 30 | | | 35 | | | 40 | | | 45 | | | 50 | | | 55 | | | 60
```

C. DIAGNOSTIC PRACTICE: SYMBOLS AND PUNCTUATION

If you are not using the GDP software, turn to page SB-2 and follow the directions for this activity.

D. Take two 3-minute timed writings. Review your speed and errors.

Goal: At least 35wpm/3'/4e

D. 3-MINUTE TIMED WRITING

```
8         Technology that tracks eye movements is used by Web     11
9    designers to judge how people interact with Web pages. It    22
10   must find out which zone of the page is viewed first, which  34
11   feature is viewed most often, and how quickly a page comes   46
12   to the screen.                                               49
13         Eye movements are tracked by use of hardware and data  60
14   analysis software. A camera is employed to find out the eye  72
15   movements of people who watch a screen. Pupil dilations and  84
16   scanning patterns of the eyes are measured to document the   96
17   amount of mental strain that has been exerted.               105
     |  1  |  2  |  3  |  4  |  5  |  6  |  7  |  8  |  9  |  10  |  11  |  12
```

E. BASIC PARTS OF A TABLE

- Tables have vertical columns (identified by a letter in the illustration) and horizontal rows (identified by a number in the illustration).
- A cell, or "box," is created where a column and a row intersect.
- Tables formatted with borders all around (as shown in the illustration) are called boxed tables.
- Tables formatted with no borders are called open tables.

- Center a table vertically when it appears alone on the page.
- Center a table horizontally if the cell widths have been adjusted automatically to fit the contents.

Note: You will learn to center tables vertically and horizontally in Lesson 38.

↓center page

14 pt **ALASKAN VACATIONS**			
12 pt↓ **Sailing Dates and Prices** ↓1X			
↓1X **Northern Departures**	**Interior Stateroom**	**Ocean View Stateroom**	↓1X **Guest**
January 12	$599	$699	$ 99
February 14	599	699	99
March 11	699	799	199
April 2	699	799	199
May 11	699	799	299
June 6	799	899	399
July 1	799	899	399
August 21	799	899	399
Column A	Column B	Column C	Column D

Row 1
Row 2
Row 3
Row 4
Row 5
Row 6
Row 7
Row 8
Row 9
Row 10

TITLE. Center and type in all-caps and bold, with a 14-point font. If there is no subtitle, insert 1 blank line after the title.

SUBTITLE. Center on the line below the title, and type in upper- and lowercase letters and bold. Press ENTER 1 time to insert a blank line below the subtitle.

HEADING BLOCK. Title and subtitle.

COLUMN HEADINGS. Center or left-align (for text) or right-align (for numbers). Press ENTER to split a 2-line column heading or to move a 1-line column heading down 1 line.

COLUMN ENTRIES. Align text entries at the left; align number entries at the right. Capitalize only the first word and proper nouns. Add spaces after the dollar sign to align with the widest column entry below (add 2 spaces for each digit and 1 space for each comma).

Word Processing Manual

F. WORD PROCESSING: TABLE—INSERT AND AUTOFIT TO CONTENTS

Study Lesson 36 in your word processing manual. Complete all of the shaded steps while at your computer. Then format the jobs that follow.

DOCUMENT PROCESSING

Table 36-1

Boxed Table

Simple tables often do not have titles, subtitles, or column headings.

1. Insert a boxed table with 3 columns and 3 rows.
2. Left-align all column entries.
3. Automatically adjust the column widths for all columns.

Mary Spangler	President	Administration
Joyce Moore	Dean	Jefferson Hall
Thelma Day	Chairperson	Da Vinci Hall

Table 36-2

Boxed Table

1. Insert a boxed table with 2 columns and 4 rows.
2. Left-align all column entries.
3. Automatically adjust the column widths for all columns.

Marie Covey, Executive Editor	Santa Clarita, California
Albert Russell, Associate Editor	Newport, Rhode Island
Bob Harris, Contributing Writer	St. Louis, Missouri
Sylvestra Zimmerly, Art Director	Albuquerque, New Mexico

Table 36-3

Boxed Table

1. Open the file for Table 36-2.
2. Change the name and title in Row 4, Column A, to Theodore Easton, Film Editor.
3. Change the city in Row 4, Column B, to Socorro.

Table 36-4

Boxed Table

Barbara Azar	Professor	Computer Technologies
Ken Kennedy	Professor	Foreign Languages
Bonnie Marquette	Instructor	Computer Technologies
Kevin Nguyen	Assistant	Social Sciences

Strategies for Career Success

Nonverbal Communication

"It's not what he said, but how he said it." More than 90 percent of your spoken message contains nonverbal communication that expresses your feelings and desires. People respond to this nonverbal language.

Posture can convey your mood. For example, leaning toward a speaker indicates interest. Leaning backward suggests dislike or indifference. Your handshake, an important nonverbal communicator, should be firm but not overpowering.

Your head position provides many nonverbal signals. A lowered head usually expresses shyness or withdrawal. An upright head conveys confidence and interest. A tilted head signifies curiosity or suspicion. Nodding your head shows positive feeling, while left-right head shakes signify negative feeling. Your face strongly expresses your emotions. Narrow, squinting eyes signify caution, reflection, or uncertainty. Wide-open eyes convey interest and attention.

YOUR TURN Turn off the sound on a television program. How much of the plot can you understand just from the nonverbal communication signals?

Open Tables With Titles

Goals

- Improve speed and accuracy
- Refine language arts skills in punctuation
- Format open tables with titles

A. Type 2 times.

A. WARMUP

```
1     The check for $432.65 wasn't mailed on time! Late       10
2  charges of up to 10% can be expected. To avoid a sizable    22
3  penalty, just send an e-mail message to quickpay@epay.com.   33
   |  1  |  2  |  3  |  4  |  5  |  6  |  7  |  8  |  9  |  10  |  11  |  12
```

SKILLBUILDING

B. Take a 1-minute timed writing on the first paragraph to establish your base speed. Then take four 1-minute timed writings on the remaining paragraphs. As soon as you equal or exceed your base speed on one paragraph, advance to the next, more difficult paragraph.

B. SUSTAINED PRACTICE: ROUGH DRAFT

```
4      Various human responses are asymmetrical. This means     11
5  that we ask more from one side of the body than the other    23
6  each time we wave, wink, clap our hands, or cross our legs.  35

7      Each one of these actions demands a clear decision,      11
8  usually unconscious and instantaneous, to start the course   23
                                          begin
9  of moving two parts of the body in different directions.     34

10 All children kids go though remarkably involved steps as they  12
                  r
11 develop their preferried. As children a child grows she or he may  23
                    ence
12 favor the right hand, the left, or both the same at times.   35

13 When most kids are eihgt or seven, stability ocurrs,         11
14 and one hand is permanently dominent over the other. For     22
                              a
15 some unknown reason, nine out of ten choose the right hand.   34
             k
   |  1  |  2  |  3  |  4  |  5  |  6  |  7  |  8  |  9  |  10  |  11  |  12
```

C. PACED PRACTICE

If you are not using the GDP software, turn to page SB-14 and follow the directions for this activity.

D. Study the rules at the right.

D. APOSTROPHE

Note: The callout signals in the left margin indicate which language arts rule from this lesson has been applied.

RULE ▶
' singular

Use 's to form the possessive of singular nouns.

The hurricane's force caused major damage to North Carolina's coastline.

RULE ▶
' plural

Use only an apostrophe to form the possessive of plural nouns that end in *s*.

The investors' goals were outlined in the stockholders' report.

But: The investors outlined their goals in the report to the stockholders.

But: The women's and children's clothing was on sale.

RULE ▶
' pronoun

Use 's to form the possessive of indefinite pronouns (such as *someone's* or *anybody's*); do not use an apostrophe with personal pronouns (such as *hers, his, its, ours, their,* and *yours*).

She could select anybody's paper for a sample.

It's time to put the file back into its cabinet.

Edit the sentences to insert any needed punctuation.

16 The womans purse was stolen as she held her childs hand.
17 If the book is yours, please return it to the library now.
18 The girls decided to send both parents donations to school.
19 The childs toy was forgotten by his mothers good friend.
20 The universities presidents submitted the joint statement.
21 The four secretaries salaries were raised just like yours.
22 One boys presents were forgotten when he left the party.
23 If these blue notebooks are not ours, they must be theirs.
24 The plant was designed to recycle its own waste products.

FORMATTING

E. TABLE HEADING BLOCK

Note: The title and subtitle (if any) make up the table heading block.

To format a table heading block:

- Type the title centered in all-caps and bold, with a 14-point font in Row 1 of the table. If the table does not have a subtitle, insert 1 blank line after the title.

- Type the subtitle (if any) with a 12-point font centered on the line below the title in upper- and lowercase letters in bold.
- Insert 1 blank line after the subtitle.

Word Processing Manual

F. WORD PROCESSING: TABLE—MERGE CELLS AND BORDERS

Study Lesson 37 in your word processing manual. Complete all of the shaded steps while at your computer. Then format the jobs that follow.

Table 37-5 ▶

Open Table

1. Insert a table with 2 columns and 5 rows.
2. Merge the cells in Row 1; then center and type the title in bold and all-caps, with a 14-point font.
3. Press ENTER once to insert 1 blank line after the title.
4. Left-align all column entries.
5. Automatically adjust the column widths for all columns.
6. Remove the table borders.

' singular

PC CONNECTION'S LOCATIONS

Valencia Mall	Santa Clarita, California
Town Center Square	Stevenson Ranch, California
Northridge Mall	Northridge, California
Granary Square	Valencia, California

Table 37-6 ▶

Open Table

1. Insert a table with 3 columns and 5 rows.
2. Merge the cells in Row 1; then center and type the title in bold and all-caps, with a 14-point font.
3. Press ENTER 1 time, change to a 12-point font, and type the subtitle centered in bold.
4. Press ENTER 1 time to insert 1 blank line after the subtitle.
5. Left-align all column entries.
6. Automatically adjust the column widths for all columns.
7. Remove the table borders.

' singular
' plural

NEWHALL DISTRICT'S REGISTRATION
Seniors' Schedule

Meadows	Monday, February 14	11 a.m.
Stevenson Ranch	Monday, February 21	10 a.m.
Old Orchard	Monday, February 28	11 a.m.
Wiley Canyon	Monday, March 7	10 a.m.

Table 37-7 ▶

Open Table

' singular

1. Insert a table with 2 columns and 6 rows.
2. Use standard table format for an open table with a title and subtitle.

MAR VISTA REALTY'S TOP SELLERS
First Quarter

James Kinkaid	Santa Clarita
Deborah Springer	Northbridge
Patricia Morelli	Woodland Hills
Jan McKay	Malibu
Daniel Aboud	San Luis Obispo

Open Tables With Column Headings

Goals

- Type at least 35wpm/3'/4e
- Format open tables with column headings

A. Type 2 times.

A. WARMUP

```
1      Jerry wrote a great article entitled "Interviewing      10
2  Techniques" on pp. 23 and 78! A&B@bookstore.com expected a  22
3  sizable number of requests; thus far, 65% have been sold.   33
   |  1  |  2  |  3  |  4  |  5  |  6  |  7  |  8  |  9  |  10  |  11  |  12
```

SKILLBUILDING

B. Take three 12-second timed writings on each line. The scale below the last line shows your wpm speed for a 12-second timed writing.

B. 12-SECOND SPEED SPRINTS

```
4  Blake was paid to fix the handle on the bowls that he made.
5  Alan led the panel of four men until the work was all done.
6  Jan will sign this paper when she has done all of the work.
7  They will focus on their main theme for the last six weeks.
   I I I I 5 I I I 10 I I I 15 I I I 20 I I I 25 I I I 30 I I I 35 I I I 40 I I I 45 I I I 50 I I I 55 I I I 60
```

C. PROGRESSIVE PRACTICE: ALPHABET

If you are not using the GDP software, turn to page SB-7 and follow the directions for this activity.

D. Take two 3-minute timed writings. Review your speed and errors.

Goal: At least 35wpm/3'/4e

D. 3-MINUTE TIMED WRITING

```
8       Telecommuting is a word you may have heard before but   11
9   do not quite understand. Very simply, it means working at   23
10  home instead of driving in to work. Many people like the    34
11  convenience of working at home. They realize they can save  46
12  money on expenses like gas, food, and child care.           56
13      Most home office workers use a computer in their job.    67
14  When their work is done, they can just fax or e-mail it to   79
15  the office. If they must communicate with other workers,    90
16  they can use a phone, fax, or computer and never have to   102
17  leave their home.                                          105
    |  1  |  2  |  3  |  4  |  5  |  6  |  7  |  8  |  9  |  10  |  11  |  12
```

Reference Manual

E. COLUMN HEADINGS

Column headings describe the information contained in the column entries. Refer to page R-13A in the Reference Manual for an illustration of column headings.

To format column headings:

- Type the column headings in upper- and lowercase letters and bold.
- If a table has a combination of 1- and 2-line column headings, press ENTER 1 time before typing the 1-line column heading to push the heading down so that it aligns vertically at the bottom of the cell.
- Center column headings in tables with all-text columns.
- Left-align column headings in a column with all text.
- Right-align column headings in a column with all numbers.

Word Processing Manual

F. WORD PROCESSING: TABLE—CENTER HORIZONTALLY AND CENTER PAGE

Study Lesson 38 in your word processing manual. Complete all of the shaded steps while at your computer. Then format the jobs that follow.

DOCUMENT PROCESSING

Table 38-8 ▶

Open Table

> Note: Center all tables horizontally and vertically from now on.

1. Insert a table with 2 columns and 6 rows.
2. Type the title block in standard table title block format.
3. Type the column headings centered in upper- and lowercase letters and bold.
4. Left-align the column entries.
5. Automatically adjust the column widths for all columns.
6. Remove all table borders.

↓center page

VENDOR LIST
July 1, 20-- ↓1X

Product	Vendor
Laser printers	Office Supplies Unlimited
Workstations	PC Junction, Inc.
Cell phones	Satellite Communications
Scanners	Atlantic-Pacific Digital

Table 38-9 ►

Open Table

1. Insert a table with 2 columns and 6 rows.
2. Type the title block in standard table title block format.
3. Type the column headings centered in upper- and lowercase letters and bold.
4. In Column A, press ENTER 1 time to split the column heading into two lines as shown.
5. In Column B, press ENTER 1 time before typing the 1-line column heading to push the heading down so that it aligns vertically at the bottom of the cell.
6. Left-align the column entries.
7. Automatically adjust the column widths for all columns.
8. Remove all table borders.

(!) Press ENTER to create a column heading of 2 lines or to move a single-line heading down 1 line.

COMMITTEE ASSIGNMENTS

Academic Committee Assignments	Professor
Institutional Integrity	Anne McCarthy
Educational Programs	Bill Zimmerman
Student Services	John Yeh
Financial Resources	Steve Williams

Table 38-10 ►

Open Table

1. Open the file for Table 38-8.
2. Change the date to September 30.
3. Change the 4 products in Column A as follows:

Copiers
Processors
Controller cards
Modems

Table 38-11 ►

Open Table

CABLE SERVICES AVAILABILITY

Type of Service	Currently Available
Basic	Phoenix
Lifeline	Scottsdale
Expanded	Glendale
Expanded (per channel)	Camelback City

Ruled Tables With Number Columns

Goals

- Improve speed and accuracy
- Refine language arts skills in spelling
- Format ruled tables with number columns

A. Type 2 times.

A. WARMUP

```
1        Does Xavier know that around 8:04 a.m. his July sales    11
2    quota was realized? Invoice #671 indicates a 9% increase!    23
3    Several of the employees weren't able to regain their lead.  34
     | 1 | 2 | 3 | 4 | 5 | 6 | 7 | 8 | 9 | 10 | 11 | 12
```

SKILLBUILDING

B. Type the paragraph 2 times. Use the CAPS LOCK key to type a word or series of words in all-caps. Tap the CAPS LOCK key with the A finger.

B. TECHNIQUE PRACTICE: SHIFT KEY AND CAPS LOCK

```
4        The new computer has CD-ROM, PCI IDE HDD controller,
5    and an SVGA card. Mr. J. L. Jones will order one from PC
6    EXPRESS out of Orem, Utah. IT ARRIVES NO LATER THAN JULY.
```

PPP PRETEST → PRACTICE → POSTTEST

PRETEST
Take a 1-minute timed writing. Review your speed and errors.

C. PRETEST: Horizontal Reaches

```
7        The chief thinks the alarm was a decoy for the armed    11
8    agent who coyly dashed away. She was dazed as she dodged    22
9    a blue sedan. He lured her to the edge of the high bluff.   33
     | 1 | 2 | 3 | 4 | 5 | 6 | 7 | 8 | 9 | 10 | 11 | 12
```

PRACTICE
Speed Emphasis:
If you made 2 or fewer errors on the Pretest, type each *individual* line 2 times.
Accuracy Emphasis:
If you made 3 or more errors, type each *group* of lines (as though it were a paragraph) 2 times.

D. PRACTICE: In Reaches

```
10   oy foyer loyal buoys enjoy decoy coyly royal cloy ploy toys
11   ar argue armed cared alarm cedar sugar radar area earn hear
12   lu lucid lunch lured bluff value blunt fluid luck lush blue
```

E. PRACTICE: Out Reaches

```
13   ge geese genes germs agent edges dodge hinge gear ages page
14   da daily dazed dance adapt sedan adage panda dash date soda
15   hi hints hiked hired chief think ethic aphid high ship chip
```

POSTTEST
Repeat the Pretest timed writing and compare performance.

F. POSTTEST: Horizontal Reaches

G. Type these frequently misspelled words, paying special attention to any spelling problems in each word.

G. SPELLING

16 prior activities additional than faculty whether first with
17 subject material equipment receiving completed during basis
18 available please required decision established policy audit
19 section schedule installation insurance possible appreciate
20 benefits requirements business scheduled office immediately

Edit the sentences to correct any misspellings.

21 We requierd the office to schedule all prior activities.
22 The business scheduled the instalation of the equipment.
23 The decision established the basis of the insurance policy.
24 Please audit any additionl material available to faculty.
25 If possible, they would appreciate recieving them soon.
26 Section requirements to receive benefits were completed.

FORMATTING

H. RULED TABLES WITH NUMBER COLUMNS

Review the use of borders in Lesson 37 or in your word processing manual as needed.

To format a ruled table with number columns:

1. Remove all table borders.
2. Apply borders to the top and bottom of Row 2 and to the bottom of the last row.
3. Right-align column headings and column entries with numbers.
4. If the column entry includes a dollar sign, add spaces after the dollar sign to align the dollar sign just to the left of the widest column entry below it as follows: add 2 spaces for each number and 1 space for each comma. In the example below, 3 spaces were added after the dollar sign.

Example:

$ 375
2,150
49

Word Processing Manual

I. WORD PROCESSING: TABLE—ALIGN TEXT IN A COLUMN

Study Lesson 39 in your word processing manual. Complete all of the shaded steps while at your computer. Then format the jobs that follow.

Table 39-12 ▶

Ruled Table

1. Insert a ruled table with 3 columns and 5 rows.
2. Type the heading block and table in standard table format.
3. Add spaces after the dollar sign as needed to align the dollar sign just to the left of the widest column entry below it.

4. Remove all table borders and apply borders to the top and bottom of Row 2 and to the bottom of the last row.

⚠ Highlighted words are spelling words from the language arts activity.

↓center page

NORTHERN BELL PHONES
Inside Wire Repair Service ↓1X

Per-Month Plan	Today's Rates	1995 Rates
Residence	$ .60	$1.00
Business	1.30	1.30
Private Line	3.50	4.50

Table 39-13 ▶

Ruled Table

1. Insert a ruled table with 4 columns and 7 rows.
2. Type the heading block and table in standard table format.
3. Add spaces after the dollar sign to align the dollar sign just to the left of the widest column entry below it.

4. Remove all table borders; then apply borders to the top and bottom of Row 2 and to the bottom of the last row.

⚠ To align the dollar sign correctly, add 2 spaces for each digit.

↓center page

HOLIDAY RESORT SUITES
Available Rates ↓1X

Hotel	Rack Rate	Club Rate	3-Night Savings
Porter Ranch Inn	$ 92.00	$36.00	$ 68.00
Jamaican Inn	119.00	59.50	178.50
Casitas Suites	120.00	60.00	180.00
The Desert Inn Resort	135.00	75.50	178.50
Sannibel Courtyard	150.00	75.00	225.00

Table 39-14 ▶

Ruled Table

GENERAL EQUITY MUTUAL FUNDS

Fund	Current Year	Previous Year
Duncan Insurance	16.3%	2.0%
Strident Nova	9.3%	3.5%
First Value	10.7%	12.1%
Safeguard Policy	11.1%	9.7%
Vanguard Life	8.5%	10.1%

Formatting Review

Goals

- Type at least 36wpm/3'/4e
- Format tables with a variety of features
- Format documents with a variety of features

A. Type 2 times.

A. WARMUP

```
1        On July 15, a check for exactly $329.86 was mailed to   11
2  Zak & Quinn, Inc.; they never received Check #104. Does     22
3  Gary know if the check cleared the company's bank account?   34
   | 1 | 2 | 3 | 4 | 5 | 6 | 7 | 8 | 9 | 10 | 11 | 12
```

SKILLBUILDING

B. MAP

Follow the GDP software directions for this exercise in improving keystroking accuracy.

C. DIAGNOSTIC PRACTICE: NUMBERS

If you are not using the GDP software, turn to page SB-5 and follow the directions for this activity.

D. Take two 3-minute timed writings. Review your speed and errors.

Goal: At least 36wpm/3'/4e

D. 3-MINUTE TIMED WRITING

```
4         Employee complaints are often viewed as a negative    10
5   force in a workplace. In fact, these complaints should be   22
6   viewed as a chance to communicate with the employee and to  34
7   improve morale. To ignore the complaint does not make it go 46
8   away. If you just listen to complaints, you may help to     57
9   solve small problems before they turn into bigger ones.     68
10        Often workers expect a chance to be heard by a person 79
11  who is willing to listen to them quite openly. That person  90
12  should recognize that the employee has concerns that need   102
13  to be addressed at this time.                               108
    | 1 | 2 | 3 | 4 | 5 | 6 | 7 | 8 | 9 | 10 | 11 | 12
```

Report 40-11 ▶

Academic Report

RELATIONSHIPS AT WORK
Jensen Zhao

¶ Do you believe that as long as you get your work done at the end of the day, you have had a successful day on the job? If so, you are badly mistaken. Doing the work is only half the job. The other half is relating to and working with the people around you.

TAKE A TEAM APPROACH

¶ Everything you do and every action you take affects those around you in a close working relationship. Operating as a team means thinking about others and taking actions that will help them reach their goals and achieve the goals of the company.

MAINTAIN A SPIRIT OF COOPERATION

¶ When you work in a spirit of cooperation, those around you will reflect that spirit. Your job will be easier because you will minimize resistance. It takes much more energy to resist one another than it does to cooperate and work together.

VALIDATE THE OPINIONS OF OTHERS

¶ You will find that this simple act of validation will go a long way in helping the spirit of your coworkers. Here are two simple ways to validate the opinions of others:
1. Take time to listen to the issues and accomplishments of those around you.
2. Reflect their opinions in your own words in a spirit of genuine interest.
There is a saying that states, "Your success is my success." Adopt this as your motto, and you will find a great deal of satisfaction at the end of each day.

Correspondence 40-20 ▶

Business Letter in Block Style

Prepare an envelope, but omit the return address. Review page 93 for formatting envelopes.

December 1, 20-- | Mrs. Yvonne Spillotro | 105 North Field Avenue | Edison, NJ 08837 | Dear mrs. Spillotro:

Thank you for choosing Insurance Alliance of America. Open enrollment for your insurance medical plan is scheduled to begin the first day of January. I hope it was possible for you to review the materials you received last week. Selecting the right benefit plan for you and your family can be an overwhelming task. To make your decision a little easier, I have enclosed a brochure that summarizes the key features of each policy.

(Continued on next page)

Please call me if I can help in any way. ⟩

‖You might want to browse through our website at www.IAA.com for further details.↗

Sincerely, | Denise Broers | Customer Support | urs | enclosure

Table
40-15 ▶

Boxed Table

PERSONAL ASSET ACCOUNTS Wanda Nelson		
Account	**Amount**	**Interest Rate**
Interest Checking	$ 972.55	3.10%
Money Market	4,500.35	4.90%
Smart Saver	3,250.76	5.07%
Certificate of Deposit	550.00	7.41%

Progress and Proofreading Check

Documents designated as Proofreading Checks serve as a check of your proofreading skill. Your goal is to have zero typographical errors when the GDP software first scores the document.

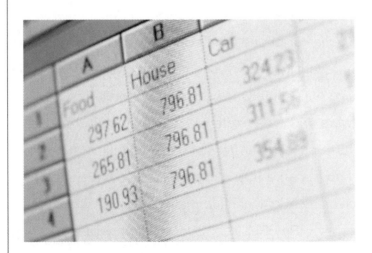

Skills Assessment on Part 2

1	From the first day of class, you have continuously	10
2	worked to improve your typing skill. You have worked hard	22
3	to increase your typing speed and accuracy. You have also	34
4	learned to format letters, memos, reports, and tables. All	46
5	of this work is quite an amazing accomplishment.	56
6	In your lessons, you have worked on learning a wide	66
7	range of word processing skills. You can expect to make	78
8	even more progress if you practice your skills regularly.	90
9	Learn as much as you can each day. Ask questions, and then	102
10	move toward a new goal each day.	108

| 1 | 2 | 3 | 4 | 5 | 6 | 7 | 8 | 9 | 10 | 11 | 12 |

Correspondence Test 2-21

Business Letter in Block Style

Note: Add an envelope to the letter. Omit the return address on the envelope.

March 17 , 20-- | Ms. ~~Arlene~~ Dorothy Turner | Global Moving and Storage | 6830 Via Del Monte | San Jose, CA 95119 | Dear Ms. Turner:

¶ Thank you ~~you~~ for registering your pc Graphics software so promptly. As a registered user, you are entitled to free technical support 24 hours a day. The (brochure enclosed) will explain in detail how you can reach us ~~either~~ by fax, e-mail or phone whenever you need help. Also, help is always (u/l) available on our website at www.pcgraphics.com. All our PC Graphics users will receive our monthly newsletter, which is filled with tips on using your new software and other material we know you will be interested in ~~seeing~~ reading. You can also access our newest graphics online at our Web site. Please call me or send me an e-mail message if you have any questions or would like to receive any additional information. Your satisfaction is our number (1) priority. Sincerely | Roy Phillips | Support Technician | urs | enclosure

Report Test 2-12

Academic Report

TELECOMMUTERS
Visibility at Work
Roy Phillips

¶ Have you ever wondered how to remain "visible" at work when you aren't there for most of the work week? This is a problem many telecommuters are struggling to overcome as

(Continued on next page)

more and more people do their work from home. We all know the advantages of working at home, but it may come with a heavy price unless you work smart. Here are some ways for telecommuters to increase visibility at work.

ATTEND KEY MEETINGS

¶ Make sure that you are notified by e-mail of all key meetings so that you can be sure to be there and make your opinions and your presence known. If meeting agendas or schedules normally are distributed through office mail, make sure there is a procedure in place that distributes these important documents electronically.

COMMUNICATE WITH YOUR SUPERVISOR

¶ Don't think that there is any virtue in keeping quiet about your accomplishments. Make your accomplishments known in an assertive, regular manner. This can be done easily in several different ways.

¶ E-Mail. Use e-mail messages or attachments to e-mail messages to summarize your accomplishments on a project. It would also be a good idea to send your list of work objectives for the week to your supervisor. When a project is finished, send the final documents related to the project. If a picture could help, invest in a digital camera or a scanner and attach a picture.

¶ Answering Machines and Pagers. Make it easy for your boss to contact you. Check your pager and answering machine frequently and return calls promptly. All of these techniques will help ensure your visibility when you aren't there.

Table Test 2-16►
Boxed Table

SIENNA VILLA CONDOMINIUMS Association Fees		
Category	Average Monthly Bill	Proposed Increase
Insurance	$150	$25
Earthquake rider	75	32
Water	65	20
Landscaping	30	5

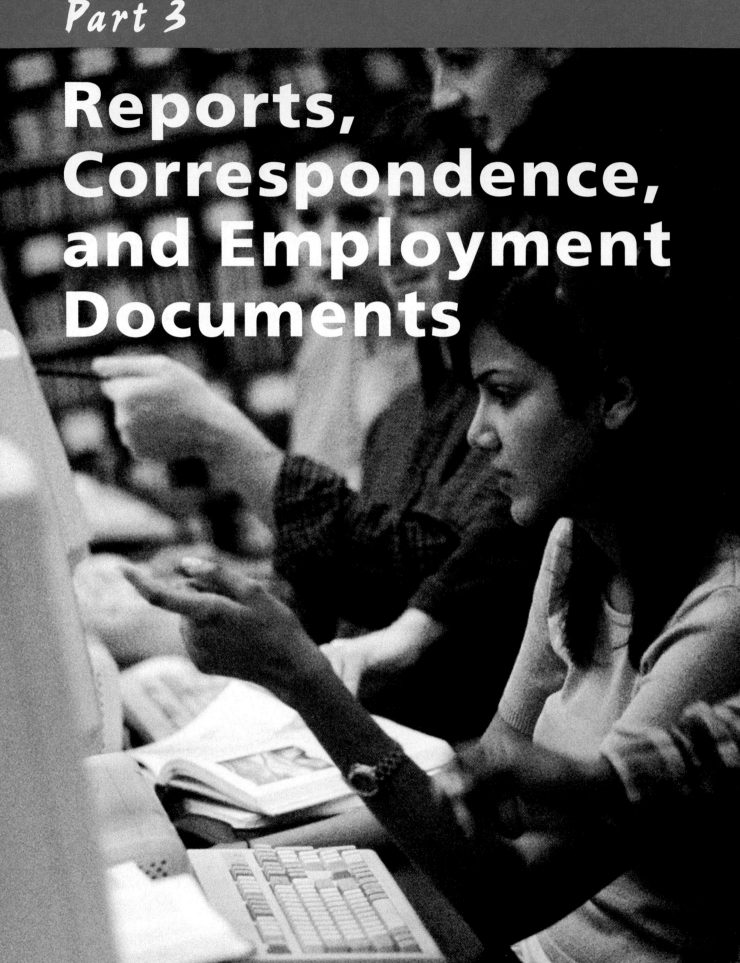

Part 3

Reports, Correspondence, and Employment Documents

Keyboarding in Education Careers

The education field has many career opportunities, including positions such as teacher, counselor, teacher assistant, administrator, and curriculum designer. Although two of three workers in educational services have professional and related occupations, the education field employs many administrative support, managerial, and service workers.

Teacher assistants provide support for classroom teachers in many ways, allowing instructors more time for lesson planning and actual teaching. Teacher assistants also grade assignments and tests, check homework, keep attendance records, and perform typing, data entry, and filing. Office administration staff perform similar functions for the heads of departments in colleges and universities and for the principals and education boards of elementary and secondary schools.

The use of computer technology in the educational setting is constantly growing. Being proficient with a computer, including keyboarding and formatting skills, is essential for success in the field. The use of the Internet in classrooms has expanded greatly, helping instructors and students to communicate with each other, as well as to perform research for class assignments. Distance learning is growing, too. Increasing numbers of higher education institutions use Internet-based technology to post lessons and coursework electronically. *The Gregg College Keyboarding & Document Processing* text and software are good examples of this development.

Objectives

KEYBOARDING

- Type at least 40 words per minute on a 5-minute timed writing with no more than 5 errors.

LANGUAGE ARTS

- Refine proofreading skills and correctly use proofreaders' marks.
- Use punctuation and grammar correctly.
- Improve composing and spelling skills.

WORD PROCESSING

- Use the word processing commands necessary to complete the document processing activities.

DOCUMENT PROCESSING

- Format business and academic reports, personal-business letters, memos, business letters in modified-block style, and resumes.

TECHNICAL

- Answer at least 90 percent of the questions correctly on an objective test.

Unit 9

Reports

LESSON 41
Left-Bound Business Reports With Footnotes

LESSON 42
Reports in APA Style

LESSON 43
Reports in MLA Style

LESSON 44
Report Citations

LESSON 45
Preliminary Report Pages

Computer Generations 4

Fourth-Generation Computers

This generation is placed in the 1971 to 1999 time category. Again, computers became smaller and faster, and the Intel chip was responsible for most of the changes taking place in this 29-year period.

Enhancements in Speed

Because of the rapid miniaturization that took place with the chip, the CPU, memory, and input/output controls could now be placed on a single chip. Computers were becoming faster and faster; and they were being used in everyday items such as microwave ovens, televisions, and automobiles.

Commercial Applications

Word processing and spreadsheet applications made their debut in this generation, as did home and video game systems. Names such as Pac-Man and Atari were very popular with computer users.

Fifth-Generation Computers

e century marks this generation, and it will be
oken word instructions, and superconductor
ow with little or no resistance (2005, p. 130).

SHOPPING FOR A HOME

Luisa Rodriguez

Buying a home is a process that many of us will go thr
many other prospective buyers, we will experience th
times in our working years. A home is typically the lar
therefore deserves our careful attention.

"Most people think that the most important criterion
The site should be on land that is well drained and fre
city zoning plan to determine if you have chosen a sit
high water levels. You should also check to see if the
considerably can cause cracks in foundations and wall

Moreau suggests that a house survey be undertaken

Key problems are encroachments such as tree
the house that overlap the property line or ma
regulations. The solution can be as simple as
bushes.[2]

The buying of a house is a major undertaking with a
investigated. To ensure that the building is structurall
use the services of a building inspector. The walls, cei
basement) need to be checked for proper insulation.
need to be checked for proper levels."[3] In addition, cr
between the beams supporting a floor.

Check the roof carefully. Walk around the entire hous
all roof lines and angles. Are there any shingles missi

---

[1] James Nelson, "A New Home for the Millennium," *Home Plann*
[2] Eva Bartlett, "Settlement Issues When Buying a New Home," *Ho*
[3] "Home Construction in the 21st Century," *Family Living*, Octob
[4] Karen Ostrowski, "A Short Course in Buying a Home," *Homebu*
Boston, 2004, p. 37.

Computer Generations 3

A Brief History of Computer Generations

Joshua T. Reynolds

The first computer was probably the abacus, which was used about 5,000 years ago in Asia Minor. As we know them today, computers were first used just after the Second World War, around 1945. Since then, several computer advancements have occurred that make it possible to classify computer power by one of the significant advancements that can be associated with particular time periods or generations. The following paragraphs summarize the major developments that occurred in each of these generations.

First-Generation Computers

The first generation of computers generally runs from 1945 to 1956. During this time, the first vacuum tube computer, the ENIAC, was invented. The first commercial computer was called the UNIVAC, and it was used by the U.S. Census Bureau. It was also used to predict President Eisenhower's victory in the 1952 presidential election (Baker, 2003).

Second-Generation Computers

During this period, 1956 to 1963, computers were run by transistors. These computers were known for their ability to accept instructions for a specific function that could be stored within the computer's memory. This is also the period when COBOL and FORTRAN were used for computer operations. The entire software industry began in this generation.

Third-Generation Computers

This computer generation ran from 1964 to 1971, and it is characterized by the use of integrated circuits to replace the transistors from the previous generation. As a result of this invention, computers became smaller, faster, and more powerful (Diaz & Moore, 2004).

Left-Bound Business Reports With Footnotes

Goals:

- Improve speed and accuracy
- Refine language arts skills in using quotation marks and italics (or the underline)
- Format left-bound business reports with footnotes

A. Type 2 times.

A. WARMUP

```
1        Tag #743X was attached to a black jug that was 1/3      10
2   full of a creamy liquid. Tags #914Z and #874V were both     22
3   attached to beautiful large lamps (crystal and porcelain).  33
    |  1  |  2  |  3  |  4  |  5  |  6  |  7  |  8  |  9  | 10  | 11  | 12
```

SKILLBUILDING

B. Take three 12-second timed writings on each line. The scale below the last line shows your wpm speed for a 12-second timed writing.

B. 12-SECOND SPEED SPRINTS

```
4   Joe must try to type as fast as he can on these four lines.
5   The screens were very clear, and the print was easy to see.
6   We will not be able to print the copy until later on today.
7   The disk will not store any of the data if it is not clean.
    | | | | 5 | | | 10 | | | 15 | | | 20 | | | 25 | | | 30 | | | 35 | | | 40 | | | 45 | | | 50 | | | 55 | | | 60
```

C. MAP

Follow the GDP software directions for this exercise in improving keystroking accuracy.

LANGUAGE ARTS

D. Study the rules at the right.

D. QUOTATION MARKS AND ITALICS (OR UNDERLINE)

RULE ▶
" direct quotation

Use quotation marks around a direct quotation.
> Harrison responded by saying, "Their decision does not affect us."
> *But:* Harrison responded by saying that their decision does not affect us.

RULE ▶
" title

Use quotation marks around the title of a newspaper or magazine article, chapter in a book, report, and similar terms.
> The most helpful article I found was "Multimedia for All."

RULE ▶
title or title

Italicize (or underline) the titles of books, magazines, newspapers, and other complete published works.
> Grisham's *The Brethren* was reviewed in a recent *USA Today* article.

RULE ▶
, direct quotation

Use a comma before and after a direct quotation.
> James said, "I shall return," and then left.

(Continued on next page)

8 The newspaper ad in the March 1 "Tribune" was very effective.
9 *The Power of e-Commerce* is an excellent chapter.
10 Maria answered the question by saying, "I agree."
11 Her title for the report was "The Internet in Action."
12 The magazine cover for "Newsweek" last month was excellent.
13 Karen interrupted by saying, That's exactly right!
14 The realtor replied "The first thing to consider is location."
15 "The margin of error is very small" said Andy.

FORMATTING

Refer to **Reference Manual**

If you want to format a report with endnotes instead of footnotes, study the illustration of endnotes on page R-8C and R-8D of the Reference Manual.

E. LEFT-BOUND REPORTS WITH FOOTNOTES

A left-bound report requires a wider left margin to allow for binding so that text is not hidden after the report is bound. To format a left-bound report, increase the left margin to 1.5 inches. Footnote references indicate the sources of facts or ideas used in a report. Although footnotes may be formatted in various ways, they have many characteristics in common:

1. Footnote references are indicated in the text by superior figures.

2. Footnotes are numbered consecutively throughout a report.

3. Footnotes appear at the bottom of the page on which the references appear and are preceded by a divider line, which is automatically inserted when the footnote is created.

4. A footnote should include the name of the author, the title of the book (italicized) or article (in quotation marks), the publisher, the place of publication, the year of publication, and the page number(s).

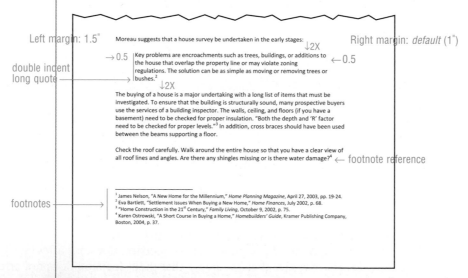

F. LONG QUOTATIONS

A paragraph of 4 or more lines that is quoted or considered essential to a report may be highlighted or displayed by using single-spacing and indenting the paragraph 0.5 inch from both the left and the right margins to make it stand out from the rest of the report.

Go To **Word Processing Manual**

G. WORD PROCESSING: MARGINS AND FOOTNOTES

Study Lesson 41 in your word processing manual. Complete all of the shaded steps while at your computer. Then format the jobs that follow.

Report 41-13 ▶

Left-Bound Business Report

1. Change the left margin to 1.5 inches.
2. Insert footnotes where you see the footnote reference marks in the copy.
3. Type the information within the footnote itself as shown on page 126 at the end of this report.
4. Indent the long quotation 0.5 inch from both the left and the right margins.

SHOPPING FOR A HOME

Luisa Rodriguez

¶ Buying a home is a process that many of us will go through in our life time. If we are like many other prospective buyers, we will experience this decision three or four major times in our working years. A home is typically the largest purchase we will make, and it deserves therefore our careful attention. ~~We must be certain to look carefully at all the information available to us.~~

" direct quotation

¶ "Most people think that the most important criteria on in shopping for a home is its site,"[1] ~~says John Calendar.~~ The site should be on land that is well drained and free from ~~from~~ flooding, ~~that can cause extensive damage.~~ Check the ~~local area~~ city zoning plan to determine if you have chosen a site that is free from flooding and high water levels, ~~that can cause extensive damage.~~ You should also check to see if the ground is stable. Ground that shifts considerably can cause cracks in foundations and walls.

¶ Moreau suggests that a ~~home~~ house survey be undertaken in the early stages:

Key problems are encroachments such as trees, buildings, or additions to the house that overlap the property line or may violate zoning regulations. The solution can be as simple as moving or removing trees or bushes ~~from the front or back of your house.~~[2]

¶ The buying of a house is a major under taking with a long list of items that must be investigated. To ensure that the building is structurally sound, many prospective buyers use the services of a building inspector. The walls, ceiling, and floors (if you have a basement) need to be checked for proper insulation. "Both the depth and 'r' factor need to be checked for proper levels."[3] In addition, crossbraces should have been used between the beams supporting a floor.

(Continued on next page)

¶ (Carefully) check the roof. Walk around the ^entire house so that you have a clear view of all roof lines and angles. Are there any shingles missing or is there water damage?[4]

" title

[1] James Nelson, "A New Home for the Millennium," *home planning magazine*, April 27, 2003, pp. 19-24.

title

[2] Eva Bartlett, "Settlement Issues when Buying a New Home," *Home Finances,* 2002 July, p. 68.

" title

[3] "Home Construction in the 21st Century," *Family Living*, October 9, 2002 ^, p. 75

title

[4] Karen Ostrowski, "A Short Course in Buying a Home," *Homebuilders' Guide*, Kramer Publishing Company, Boston, 2004, p. 37.

Report 41-14 ▶

Left-Bound Business Report

Open the file for Report 41-13 and make the following changes:

1. Add these lines to the end of the final paragraph in the report:

        Finally, a thorough check
        should be made of the
        heating, cooling, and
        electrical systems in the
        home. "These features are

as critical as any others
to be examined."[5]

---

[5] Maria Gonzalez, *Home Facilities Planning*, Bradshaw Publishing, Salt Lake City, Utah, 2003, p. 64.

2. Insert the footnote as indicated.
3. Remember to italicize book and magazine titles.

Keyboarding Connection

Inedible Cookies

Is that cookie good for you? A cookie is a short text entry stored on your computer that identifies your preferences to the server of the Web site you are viewing.

Certain Web sites use cookies to customize pages for return visitors. Only the information you provide or the selections you make while visiting a Web site are stored in a cookie. You can control how your browser uses cookies.

Use the Help feature in your browser to find out how to control cookies. Try using the keywords "cookie" or "security" when you search the Help index. You will probably find some great tips on how to increase security when working on the Internet.

YOUR TURN   Access your browser's cookie policy defaults. Decide if you want to change them.

Reports in APA Style

Goals

- Type at least 36wpm/3'/3e
- Format reports in APA style
- Format author/year citations

A. Type 2 times.

A. WARMUP

```
1        The giant-size trucks, all carrying over 600 bushels,    11
2   were operating "around the clock"; quite a few of them had    23
3   dumped their boxes at Joe's during the last 18 to 20 hours.   35
    |  1  |  2  |  3  |  4  |  5  |  6  |  7  |  8  |  9  |  10  |  11  |  12
```

SKILLBUILDING

B. PROGRESSIVE PRACTICE: ALPHABET

If you are not using the GDP software, turn to page SB-7 and follow the directions for this activity.

C. Type the paragraph 2 times, using your right thumb to press the SPACE BAR in the center.

C. TECHNIQUE PRACTICE: SPACE BAR

```
4        Dale is it. Adam is there. Mark is home. Eve was lost.
5   Helen can see. Faith can knit. Gayle can fly. Hal can type.
6   Fly the kite. Swim a mile. Close the door. Lift the weight.
```

D. Take two 3-minute timed writings. Review your speed and errors.

Goal: At least 36wpm/3'/3e

D. 3-MINUTE TIMED WRITING

```
7        The size of their first paycheck after they finish     10
8   college seems quite high to a few young men and women. They   22
9   rent a place to live that is just too much to pay, or they   34
10  may buy a car with a huge monthly payment. For some, it      45
11  takes a while to learn that there are other items in the     57
12  monthly budget.                                              60
13       Some other budget items are food, student loans, car    71
14  insurance, renters' insurance, credit card debt, health      82
15  insurance, utilities, and miscellaneous expenses. A good     93
16  goal is to put a regular amount from each paycheck into a    105
17  savings account.                                            108
    |  1  |  2  |  3  |  4  |  5  |  6  |  7  |  8  |  9  |  10  |  11  |  12
```

Reference Manual

Refer to page R-10A of the Reference Manual for additional guidance.

E. REPORTS FORMATTED IN APA STYLE

In addition to the traditional academic style, academic reports may also be formatted in APA (American Psychological Association) style. In the APA style, format the report as follows:

1. Use the default 1-inch margins.
2. Double-space the entire report.
3. Insert a header for all pages; type a shortened title and insert an automatic page number that continues the page-numbering sequence from the previous page right-aligned inside the header.
4. Type the title 1 inch from the top of the page centered using upper- and lowercase letters. Press ENTER 1 time and type the byline centered using upper- and lowercase letters. (Do not bold either the title or the byline.)
5. Indent all paragraphs 0.5 inch.
6. Type main headings centered, using upper- and lowercase letters. Press ENTER 1 time before and after the main heading.
7. Type subheadings at the left margin in italics using upper- and lowercase letters. Press ENTER 1 time before and after the subheading.

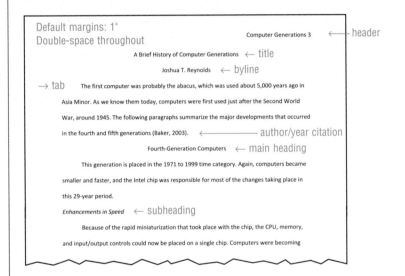

F. AUTHOR/YEAR CITATIONS

Any information based on other sources and used in a report must be documented or cited. The author/year method of citation includes the source information in parentheses at the appropriate point within the text. For more detailed information on APA citations, refer to the illustrations in this book or consult the current APA style guide.

G. WORD PROCESSING: HEADERS AND FOOTERS

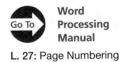
Word Processing Manual

L. 27: Page Numbering

Study Lesson 42 in your word processing manual. Complete all of the shaded steps while at your computer. Then format the jobs that follow.

Report in APA Style

⚠ Remember to add a short title and page number right-aligned in a header.

Computer Generations 3

A Brief History of Computer Generations

Joshua T. Reynolds

¶ The first computer was probably the abacus, which was used about 5,000 years ago in Asia Minor. As we know them today, computers were first used just after the Second World War, around 1945. Since then, several computer advancements have occurred that make it possible to classify computer power by one of the significant advancements that can be associated with particular time periods or generations. The following paragraphs summarize the major developments that occurred in each of these generations.

First-Generation Computers

¶ The first generation of computers generally runs from 1945 to 1956. During this time, the first vacuum tube computer, the ENIAC, was invented. The first commercial computer was called the UNIVAC, and it was used by the U.S. Census Bureau. It was also used to predict President Eisenhower's victory in the 1952 presidential election (Baker, 2003).

Second-Generation Computers

¶ During this period, 1956 to 1963, computers were run by transistors. These computers were known for their ability to accept instructions for a specific function that could be stored within the computer's memory. This is also the period when COBOL and FORTRAN were used for computer operations. The entire software industry began in this generation.

Third-Generation Computers

¶ This computer generation ran from 1964 to 1971, and it is characterized by the use of integrated circuits to replace the transistors from the previous generation. As a result of this invention, computers became smaller, faster, and more powerful (Diaz & Moore, 2004).

(Continued on next page)

Fourth-Generation Computers

¶ This generation is placed in the 1971 to 1999 time category. Again, computers became smaller and faster, and the Intel chip was responsible for most of the changes taking place in this 29-year period. Because of the rapid miniaturization that took place with the chip, the CPU, memory, and input/output controls could now be placed on a single chip. Computers were becoming faster and faster; and they were being used in everyday items such as microwave ovens, televisions, and automobiles.

Fifth-Generation Computers

¶ According to Allen, the turn of the century marks this generation, and it will be associated with artificial intelligence, spoken word instructions, and superconductor technology, which allows electricity to flow with little or no resistance (2005, p. 130).

Report 42-16

Report in APA Style

Open the file for Report 42-15 and make the following changes:

1. Place the insertion point at the end of the second sentence in the Fourth-Generation Computers paragraph, and press ENTER 1 time.
2. Type the subheading Enhancements in Speed in italics at the left margin; press ENTER 1 time.
3. Press TAB to indent the paragraph.
4. Move the insertion point to the end of the last sentence just above the Fifth-Generation Computers heading; press ENTER 1 time.
5. Type the subheading Commercial Applications in italics at the left margin; press ENTER 1 time.
6. Press TAB and type the following text as a paragraph under the new subheading:

> Word processing and spreadsheet applications made their debut in this generation, as did home and video game systems. Names such as Pac-Man and Atari were very popular with computer users.

Reports in MLA Style

Goals

- Improve speed and accuracy
- Refine language arts skills in composing sentences
- Format reports in MLA style

A. Type 2 times.

A. WARMUP

```
1      "Baxter & Heimark, Inc., sold 82 new vehicles (47 cars   11
2  and 35 trucks) during June," the sales manager reported.      23
3  This is 16.9% of quarterly sales, an amazing achievement!     34
    |  1  |  2  |  3  |  4  |  5  |  6  |  7  |  8  |  9  |  10  |  11  |  12
```

SKILLBUILDING

B. PROGRESSIVE PRACTICE: NUMBERS

If you are not using the GDP software, turn to page SB-11 and follow the directions for this activity.

C. Take a 1-minute timed writing on the first paragraph to establish your base speed. Then take four 1-minute timed writings on the remaining paragraphs. As soon as you equal or exceed your base speed on one paragraph, advance to the next, more difficult paragraph.

C. SUSTAINED PRACTICE: SYLLABIC INTENSITY

```
4      Taking care of aging parents is not a new trend. This    11
5  issue has arisen more and more, since we are now living       22
6  longer. Companies are now trying to help out in many ways.    34
7      Help may come in many ways, ranging from financial aid    12
8  to sponsoring hospice or in-home respite care. Workers may    24
9  find it difficult to work and care for aging parents.         35
10     Why are employers so interested in elder care? Rising     11
11 interest is the result of a combination of several things.    23
12 The most notable is a marked increase in life expectancy.     34
13     Another trend is the increased participation of women,    11
14 the primary caregivers, in the workforce. Businesses are      22
15 recognizing that work and family life are intertwined.        33
    |  1  |  2  |  3  |  4  |  5  |  6  |  7  |  8  |  9  |  10  |  11  |  12
```

D. Answer each question with a complete sentence.

D. COMPOSING SENTENCES

16 What margins are used in an MLA report?
17 What spacing is used in an MLA report?
18 How are titles typed in an MLA report?
19 What is the purpose of a header in a report?
20 What does "MLA" stand for?

FORMATTING

Reference Manual

Refer to page R-10C of the Reference Manual for additional guidance.

E. REPORTS FORMATTED IN MLA STYLE

In addition to the traditional academic style and APA style, academic reports may also be formatted in MLA (Modern Language Association) style. If citations are used, usually the author's last name and page number are cited inside parentheses. For more detailed information on MLA style, refer to the illustrations in this book or consult the current MLA style guide.

In the MLA style, format the report as follows:

1. Use the default 1-inch margins.
2. Double-space the entire report.

3. Insert a header for all pages; type the author's last name and the page number right-aligned inside the header.
4. Type each element of the heading information (your name, your instructor's name, the class name, and the date) on a separate line at the left margin.
5. Type the date day-month-year style (15 April 20--).
6. Center and type the title using upper- and lowercase letters.
7. Indent all paragraphs 0.5 inch.

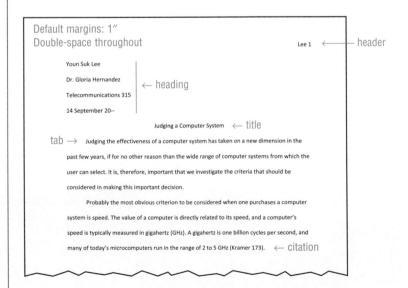

Report 43-17

Report in MLA Style

Remember to type the author's last name and page number right-aligned in the header. Remember to double-space the entire report.

Lee 1

Youn Suk Lee
Dr. Gloria Hernandez
Telecommunications 315
14 September 20--

Judging a Computer System

¶ Judging the effectiveness of a computer system has taken on a new dimension in the past few years, if for no other reason than the wide range of computer systems from which the user can select. It is, therefore, important that we investigate the criteria that should be considered in making this important decision.

¶ Probably the most obvious criterion to be considered when one purchases a computer system is speed. The value of a computer is directly related to its speed, and a computer's speed is typically measured in gigahertz (GHz). A gigahertz is one billion cycles per second, and many of today's microcomputers run in the range of 2 to 5 GHz (Kramer 173).

¶ Flexibility is especially important because of the rapid turnover of hardware and software in the computer industry. The flexibility of a computer system is important for two general reasons: to accommodate a variety of programs and to permit expandability. Hundreds and possibly thousands of software packages are available today to meet the needs of computer users. The computer you purchase must be able to accommodate this variety of software and be flexible enough to change with the increasing sophistication of software packages. Because of the substantial investment you make in a computer, you do not want to commit your resources to a computer that cannot be expanded to handle (1) newer, more powerful operating systems; (2) "memory-hungry" software packages; (3) network interfaces; and (4) additional users (Hartung and Kallock 239).

¶ A third consideration is convenience. Is it easy to learn how to operate your computer? Does the manufacturer stand by its warranty, and is it difficult to obtain repairs? How convenient is it to buy parts for your computer (such as memory boards and drives) if you want to expand your system? These questions need to be answered, and the answers should be weighed carefully before you purchase a new computer system.

Christina Espinoza
Professor Sakata
Introduction to E-commerce
9 April 20--

Internet Shopping Guidelines

¶ The Internet is dramatically changing the way we shop. In years past, our shopping practices consisted of driving to a local mall or department store, walking through the aisles until we found an item we wished to purchase, and then making the purchase and driving home. Today, it is becoming more common to find shoppers doing their shopping via the Internet. Shopping on the Internet brings with it some cautions that we should observe when we shop. Here are some basic rules to follow when shopping on the Internet.

¶ When you are asked to enter information on your order, do not disclose personal information unless it is needed for shipping your order to you. Be sure you know who is collecting this information, why it is needed, and how it is going to be used. Be certain that the information asked for is actually necessary for the purchase. For example, there are few instances when your password should be disclosed.

¶ You should always verify that the company from whom you are purchasing has secured the purchasing procedures. You will often be asked to enter your credit card number to complete the purchase. Be certain that the transfer of this information is made in a secure environment. Also, be certain that you know the exact cost of the item for which you are being charged. The company from which you are purchasing the item should have a built-in calculator so that you know at all times how much your purchase will cost you, including all necessary shipping and handling charges.

¶ Understand exactly what you should do if you encounter a problem with your purchase online. Is there an easy way to contact the company? Does the company have an e-mail address you can use to contact a customer relations representative? Does the company's order page include a telephone number that you can call if you have questions about your order?

Report Citations

Goals

- Type at least 37wpm/3'/3e
- Format bibliographies, references, and works-cited pages

A. Type 2 times.

A. WARMUP

```
1        The prize troops received the following extra gifts:    11
2   $20 from Larson's Bakery; $19 from Calsun, Ltd.;* $50 from   23
3   some judges; and quite a number of $5 gift certificates.     34
    | 1 | 2 | 3 | 4 | 5 | 6 | 7 | 8 | 9 | 10 | 11 | 12
```

SKILLBUILDING

PPP   PRETEST → PRACTICE → POSTTEST

PRETEST
Take a 1-minute timed writing. Review your speed and errors.

B. PRETEST: Vertical Reaches

```
4        Kim knew that her skills at the keyboard made her a     11
5   top rival for that job. About six persons had seen her race  23
6   home to see if the mail showed the company was aware of it.  34
    | 1 | 2 | 3 | 4 | 5 | 6 | 7 | 8 | 9 | 10 | 11 | 12
```

PRACTICE
Speed Emphasis:
If you made 2 or fewer errors on the Pretest, type each *individual* line 2 times.
Accuracy Emphasis:
If you made 3 or more errors, type each *group* of lines (as though it were a paragraph) 2 times.

C. PRACTICE: Up Reaches

```
7   se seven reset seams sedan loses eases serve used seed dose
8   ki skids kings kinks skill kitty kites kilts kite kids kick
9   rd board horde wards sword award beard third cord hard lard
```

D. PRACTICE: Down Reaches

```
10  ac races pacer backs ached acute laced facts each acre lace
11  kn knave knack knife knows knoll knots knelt knew knee knit
12  ab about abide label above abode sable abbey drab able cabs
```

POSTTEST
Repeat the Pretest timed writing and compare performance.

E. POSTTEST: Vertical Reaches

F. Take two 3-minute timed writings. Review your speed and errors.

Goal: At least 37wpm/3′/3e

F. 3-MINUTE TIMED WRITING

```
13        Every business should have its code of ethics. A code    11
14    contains rules of conduct and moral guidelines that serve    23
15    the company and its employees. Some general ethics that may   35
16    be recognized in the code are equal and fair treatment,       46
17    truth, and zeal on the job.                                   51
18        Companies may include a few rules in the code that        62
19    relate to their type of work. For example, if some laws       73
20    govern how they conduct business, an owner just might ask     85
21    employees to conduct all activities in a just and lawful      96
22    process. The code of business ethics should be equal for     107
23    all these workers.                                           111
```
| 1 | 2 | 3 | 4 | 5 | 6 | 7 | 8 | 9 | 10 | 11 | 12

FORMATTING

Reference Manual

Refer to page R-9B of the Reference Manual for additional guidance.

G. BIBLIOGRAPHIES

A bibliography is an alphabetic listing of all sources of facts or ideas used or cited in a report. The bibliography is typed on a separate page at the end of a report. In general, titles of major works like books or magazine titles are italicized, and titles of minor works like articles from magazines are typed in quotation marks. For more detailed information on entries in a bibliography, refer to the illustrations in this book or consult a current style guide.

To format a bibliography:

1. Press ENTER 5 times to begin the first line 2 inches from the top of the page.

2. Center and type BIBLIOGRAPHY in all-caps, 14-point font, and bold; then press ENTER 2 times.

3. Apply a hanging indent and type the first line. Each entry will begin at the left margin, and the carryover lines will automatically be indented 0.5 inch by the hanging indent.

4. Single-space each entry in the bibliography, and press ENTER 2 times between each entry.

↓5X

14 pt   **BIBLIOGRAPHY**

↓2X

12 pt   Ferguson, Mary, *Voice Recognition Systems*, Garden Printers, Boston, 2004.   ←—— book—one author

↓2X

Miller, Jeffrey R., Allen T. Yeung, and Mary M. Sanchez, "Perfecting Your Computer Speaking   ←—— journal article—three authors

hanging → Voice," *PC News*, November 30, 2003, pp. 32-35.

indent

Phillips, Roy, "Talking to Your Computer," *Boston News*, February 9, 2002, p. H10.   ←—— newspaper article

Thomas, Anita R., "Supporting Voice Systems," e-mail message, January 18, 2004.   ←—— e-mail

"Voice Recognition Systems Leading the Industry," *VoiceSystems Home page*, April 17, 2003,
    <http://www.voicesystems.com/trends.html>, accessed on May 15, 2000.   ←—— WWW page

Reference Manual

Refer to page R-10B of the Reference Manual for additional guidance.

H.   REFERENCE LIST PAGES IN APA STYLE

A reference list is an alphabetic listing of all sources of facts or ideas used or cited in a report formatted in APA style. The reference list is typed on a separate page at the end of a report. For more detailed information on reference list entries, refer to the illustrations in this book or consult a current APA style guide.

To format an APA reference list page:

1. Use the default margins.
2. Double-space the entire page.
3. Insert a header, type a shortened title, and insert an automatic page number that continues the page-numbering sequence from the previous page right-aligned inside the header.
4. Center and type References at the top of the page; then press ENTER 1 time.
5. Apply a hanging indent and type the first line. Each reference will begin at the left margin, and the carryover lines will automatically be indented 0.5 inch by the hanging indent.

Default margins: 1"
Double-space throughout — Voice Recognition 16 ← ——— header

References

Ferguson, M. (2004). *Voice recognition systems.* Boston: Garden Printers. ← ——— book—one author

Clooney, I., & Chavez, A. E. (2005). *What's all the talk about?* Chicago: International World ← ——— book—two authors

hanging → Press.
indent

Miller, J. R., Yeung, A. T., & Sanchez, M. M. (November 30, 2003). Perfecting your computer ← ——— journal article—three authors

speaking voice. *PC News,* 32-35.

Phillips, R. (2002, February 9). Talking to your computer. *Boston News,* p. H10. ← ——— newspaper article

Voice recognition systems leading the industry (n.d.). New York: VoiceSystems. Retrieved April ← ——— WWW page

17, 2003, from the World Wide Web: http://www.voicesystems.com/trends.html

Refer to **Reference Manual**

Refer to page R-10D of the Reference Manual for additional guidance.

I. WORKS-CITED PAGES IN MLA STYLE

A works-cited page is an alphabetic listing of all sources of facts or ideas used or cited in a report formatted in MLA style. This reference list is typed on a separate page at the end of a report. For more detailed information on reference list entries, refer to the illustrations in this book or consult a current MLA style guide.

To format a works-cited page:

1. Use the default margins.
2. Double-space the entire page.

3. Insert a header, type the author's last name, insert an automatic page number that continues the page-numbering sequence from the previous page right-aligned inside the header, and close the header.
4. Type Works Cited centered at the top of the page; then press ENTER 1 time.
5. Apply a hanging indent and type the first line at the left margin; the carryover lines will automatically be indented 0.5 inch by the hanging indent.

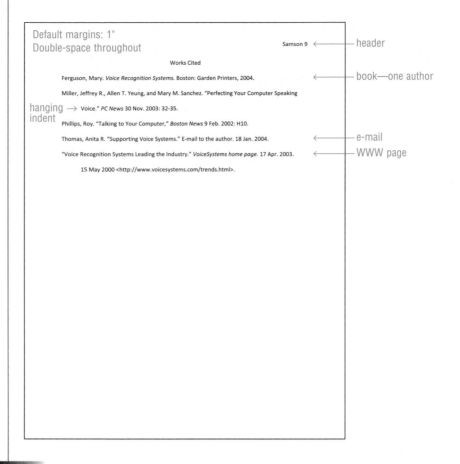

Default margins: 1"
Double-space throughout

Samson 9 ← header

Works Cited

Ferguson, Mary. *Voice Recognition Systems*. Boston: Garden Printers, 2004. ← book—one author

Miller, Jeffrey R., Allen T. Yeung, and Mary M. Sanchez. "Perfecting Your Computer Speaking

hanging → Voice." *PC News* 30 Nov. 2003: 32-35.
indent

Phillips, Roy. "Talking to Your Computer," *Boston News* 9 Feb. 2002: H10.

Thomas, Anita R. "Supporting Voice Systems." E-mail to the author. 18 Jan. 2004. ← e-mail

"Voice Recognition Systems Leading the Industry." *VoiceSystems home page*. 17 Apr. 2003. ← WWW page

15 May 2000 <http://www.voicesystems.com/trends.html>.

Word
Processing
Manual

J. WORD PROCESSING: HANGING INDENT

Study Lesson 44 in your word processing manual. Complete all the shaded steps while
at your computer. Then format the jobs that follow.

DOCUMENT PROCESSING

Report
44-19

Bibliography

Italicize publication titles
rather than underlining
them.

BIBLIOGRAPHY

Bilanski, Charles R., "Corporate Structures in the New Millennium," *Modern Management*, Vol. 43, June 2003, pp. 43-46.

Calhoun, Josten C., *Stockholders' Guide*, Missouri Valley Press, St. Louis, 2003.

Dahlman, Leland, and Joyce C. Mahler, *Trends for Boards of Directors*, Vineyard Press, Boston, 2003.

Hammersmith Institute, *Bold Positions of the New Administration*, Hammersmith Institute Press, Baltimore, Md., 1999.

"Investing in the Corporate World," March 27, 2003, <http://www.efinance.com/invest/today'sworld.htm>, accessed on May 18, 2003.

Polaski, James S., "Summary of Investment Guide," e-mail message, October 10, 2003.

The Economy of America 16

References

Chandler, R. D., & Thompson, A. S. (2002). *The evolution of America's economy in the late 1800's*. Westerville, OH: Glencoe/ McGraw-Hill. ~~Chapter 24, pp. 130-145.~~

Deming, W. H. (2003). Economists' guide to economic indicators. *The Economic Review, XVI*, 42-44.

Fortenberry, J. E., Kingston, A. E., & Worthington, S. O. (2004). *The environment of business*. Los Angeles: The University Press.

Meier, T. D., & Hovey, D. H. (2002). *economics on the world wide web*. Toronto: The Northern Press.

Tetrault, G. M. (2003). A guide for selecting economic indicators for the business entrepreneur. ~~The Southern Economic Forecaster, 23.~~

Zysmanski, R. J. (2004). *American capitalism and its impact on society*. San Francisco: Bay Press Area.

Cleaves 14

Works Cited

Abernathy, Thomas R. "Welcome to the Internet." E-mail to the author. 19 Mar. 2005.

Benson, Lisa, et al. "E-commerce on the Net." *Online Observer*. Vol. 17. Sept. 2004: 144–146.

Cooper, Stanley. *Trends for the New Millennium*. Denver: Mountain Press, 2003.

Lawrence, Donna, and Becky Silversmith. *Surfer's Guide to the Internet*. Atlanta: Southern Publishers, 2005.

"Starting a Business on the Internet." *Entrepreneur*. 19 Dec. 2003. 12 June 2005 <http://www.entrepreneur.com/startups.htm>.

Tidwell, Joel, and Jean Swanson. "Things You Don't Know About the Internet." *New York Ledger*, 13 May 2004: C2.

Preliminary Report Pages

Goals
- Improve speed and accuracy
- Refine language arts skills in proofreading
- Format title pages and tables of contents

A. Type 2 times.

A. WARMUP

```
1      Did Kenny and Hazel see the first Sox ball game? I've    11
2   heard there were 57,268 people there (a new record). Your   23
3   home crowd was quiet when the game ended with a 4-9 loss.   34
    | 1 | 2 | 3 | 4 | 5 | 6 | 7 | 8 | 9 | 10 | 11 | 12
```

SKILLBUILDING

B. PACED PRACTICE

If you are not using the GDP software, turn to page SB-14 and follow the directions for this activity.

C. DIAGNOSTIC PRACTICE: SYMBOLS AND PUNCTUATION

If you are not using the GDP software, turn to page SB-2 and follow the directions for this activity.

LANGUAGE ARTS

D. Study the proofreading techniques at the right.

D. PROOFREADING YOUR DOCUMENTS

Proofreading and correcting errors are essential parts of document processing. To become an expert proofreader:

1. Use the spelling feature of your word processing software to check for spelling errors; then read the copy aloud to see if it makes sense.

2. Proofread for all kinds of errors, especially repeated, missing, or transposed words; grammar and punctuation; and numbers and names.

3. Use the appropriate software command to see an entire page of your document to check for formatting errors such as line spacing, tabs, margins, and bold.

E. Compare this paragraph with the Pretest on page 135. Edit the paragraph to correct any errors.

E. PROOFREADING

```
4      Kim new that her skills at the key board made her a
5   top rivel for the job. About six persons had scene her race
6   home to see if the male showd the company was awarre of it.
```

Refer to **Reference Manual**

Refer to page R-7B of the Reference Manual for additional guidance.

F. TITLE PAGE

Reports may have a title page, which includes information such as the report title, to whom the report is submitted, the writer's name and identification, and the date. To format a title page similar to the one below, follow these steps:

1. Center the page vertically.
2. Center the title in all caps and bold, using a 14-point font.
3. Press ENTER 2 times; then center the subtitle in upper- and lowercase and bold, using a 12-point font.
4. Press ENTER 12 times; then center the words Submitted to.
5. Press ENTER 2 times; then center the recipient's name and identification on separate lines, single-spaced.
6. Press ENTER 12 times; then center Prepared by.
7. Press ENTER 2 times; then center the writer's name and identification on separate lines, single-spaced.
8. Press ENTER 2 times; then center the date.

center page↓

14 pt   **A TECHNOLOGY ASSESSMENT OF THE GRANTLAND CORPORATION**
↓2X

12 pt↓ **The Status of Technology in the New Millenium**
↓12X

Submitted to ↓2X

Marcia Abernathy
Regional Manager
Grantland Corporation ↓12X

Prepared by ↓2X

Timothy R. Rassmussen
District V Manager
Grantland Corporation ↓2X

March 20, 20--

Refer to **Reference Manual**

Refer to page R-7D of the Reference Manual for additional guidance.

G. TABLE OF CONTENTS

A table of contents is usually included in a long report. The table of contents identifies the major and minor sections of a report and includes page numbers preceded by dot leaders. Dot leaders are a series of periods that guide the reader's eye across the page to the page number at the right. To format a table of contents:

1. Press ENTER 5 times to begin the first line 2 inches from the top of the page.
2. Center and type CONTENTS in all-caps, 14-point font, and bold; then press ENTER 2 times.
3. Set a left tab at 0.5 inch; then set a right tab at 6.5 inches with dot leaders.
4. Change to 12-point font and type the main heading in all-caps.

5. Press TAB 1 or 2 times as needed to insert dot leaders and to move to the right margin; then type the page number, and press ENTER 2 times.
6. Type the next main heading in a similar fashion. If the next item is a subheading, press TAB 1 time to indent the subheading 0.5 inch.
7. Type the subheading, and then press TAB to insert dot leaders and to move to the right margin; then type the page number, and press ENTER 1 time to type the next subheading or 2 times to type a new main heading.
8. Continue in like fashion until the table of contents is complete.

Go To **Word Processing Manual**

H. WORD PROCESSING: TAB SET—DOT LEADERS

Study Lesson 45 in your word processing manual. Complete all of the shaded steps while at your computer. Then format the jobs that follow.

Report
45-22
Title Page

↓center page

14 pt **DISTANCE LEARNING CLASSROOMS** ↓2X

12 pt↓ **Using Technology to Reach Students
at a Distance** ↓12X

Prepared by ↓2X

Alicia T. Gonzalez
Technology Coordinator
T-Systems Media, Inc. ↓12X

February 19, 20--

Report
45-23
Table of Contents

Set left tab at 0.5"; right dot-leader tab at 6.5".

↓5X

14 pt **CONTENTS**

↓2X

Create a title page for the report below entitled LOOKING INTO THE 21ST CENTURY and a subtitle that reads Some Predictions for the New Millennium. The report is to be submitted to Alfredo Sanchez, District Manager, Millennium Concepts, Inc. The report is being prepared by Richard P. Morgan, Computer Consultant, Millennium Concepts, Inc. Use a date of May 18, 20--.

CONTENTS

Progress and Proofreading Check

Documents designated as Proofreading Checks serve as a check of your proofreading skill. Your goal is to have zero typographical errors when the GDP software first scores the document.

(!) Do not indent paragraphs in a business report.

LOOKING INTO THE 21ST CENTURY
Some Predictions for the New Millennium
Evelyn Hasagawa

¶ It is predicted that computers will alter almost every activity of our lives in the first ten years of this millennium. There is strong evidence to suggest that this prediction will soon become a reality. This report will summarize the changes we will experience in the areas of artificial intelligence and the Internet.

ARTIFICIAL INTELLIGENCE

¶ Artificial intelligence is generally described as a computer's ability to assume an intelligence similar to that of the human brain—thus, its ability to reason and make decisions based on a preassigned set of facts or data.[1] But many experts predict that the computer's power will not stop there. They predict that the computer will soon become much smarter than humans by a process in which "intelligent" computers create even more intelligent computers. What we learn from these computers will have a far greater impact than the combined discoveries of the microscope, telescope, and X-ray machines.

¶ It is also predicted that the power of computers will double every 18 months through the year 2010.[2] With these enhancements, robots will displace humans from farms and factories; we will travel in cars, planes, and trains that are operated solely by computers; and traveling on the interstate highways will be as safe as watching television at home.

(Continued on next page)

COMPUTERS AND THE INTERNET

¶ The Internet will continue to expand and proliferate around the world. The speed at which information is transmitted on today's Internet will be considered a "snail's pace" on tomorrow's telemetric system. Most computers will transmit information at gigabit speeds and higher.[3] Computer security will be "foolproof," and most business transactions will be conducted on the Net. Fewer people will travel to foreign countries to vacation since "virtual vacations" will be commonplace.

[1] Peter F. Boyd, "Artificial Intelligence," *Journal of Computer Trends*, January 2004, pp. 23–24, 36.

[2] Toshida Doi, "Is Computer Intelligence Better Than the Human Brain?" *Power PC Magazine*, April 2003, pp. 14–17.

[3] Melanie T. Reynolds, "Tomorrow's Brainpower," March 17, 2004, <http://www.businessweek.com/2004/brainpower.htm>, accessed on August 19, 2005.

Strategies for Career Success

Letter of Transmittal

A letter or memo of transmittal introduces a report or proposal. Such letters provide an overview of the report in an informal, conversational writing style.

Let the recipient know what you are sending; for example, "Enclosed is the proposal you requested." If you're submitting an unsolicited report, explain why you've written the report. Include the report topic and identify the person or persons who authorized the report. Recap the main points. Cite any specific information that would help your audience comprehend the material. Is it a draft?

Conclude with a note of appreciation, a willingness to discuss the report, and intended follow-up action. Will you do something? Do you want feedback? If you want the reader to act, explain what you need and provide a deadline; for example, "Please provide your comments by July 15."

YOUR TURN List some ways that a letter of transmittal can promote goodwill between the sender and recipient.

Unit 10

Correspondence

November 30, 20--

Sales Manager
Bachmann's Nursery and Landscaping
6823 Oneta Avenue
Youngstown, OH 44500-2175

Dear Sales Manager:

As you requested on the telephone, I am providing the following list of events relating to my tree problem.

1. On April 15, I purchased at your branch in Warren four silver maples for the atrium outside our Riverdale office. We also purchased four Japanese red maples at your branch in Niles later that afternoon.

2. After about six months, one silver maple and one red maple had died. I phoned both the Warren and Niles branches several times on November 1, but no one returned my messages.

3. On November 8, I phoned your nursery in an attempt to have these trees replaced. Again, there was no response.

As these trees were expensive, I expect that you will either replace them or reimburse me for the cost of the trees. I shall look forward to hearing from you.

Sincerely,

Marvin L. Norgaard
Grounds Manager

January 10, 20--

Mrs. Connie Filstad
4034 Kennedy Lane
Mount Vernon, WA 98274-2340

Dear Mrs. Filstad:

We at Mirror Lake Homes believe that your selection of a SunCity townhouse is just the right choice for you. The SunCity model received three national awards last month. You have selected one of the most popular of our six models. As you requested, a brochure of the SunCity model is enclosed. Fifty-four units in the Creekwood site in Mount Vernon, Washington, have been built since December 2002.

I am certain you will agree that the $500 earnest money you put down was a wise decision on your part, and the 6.5 percent loan you received was the best available through our lending agency.

Thank you, Mrs. Filstad, for the opportunity to work with you these past few days. If you have any questions, please let us know.

Sincerely,

(Mrs.) Maria Martinez
Sales Director

urs
Enclosure

MEMO TO: Charles A. Cornelius, President

FROM: Alfred A. Long, Convention Director

DATE: September 8, 20--

SUBJECT: Convention Locations

As you know, this year's convention will meet in Jacksonville, Florida. It is the Executive Board's decision to rotate the convention site to each of the districts in our region. Our next three conventions will be held in the following locations:

- Mobile, Alabama
- Atlanta, Georgia
- Myrtle Beach, South Carolina

In May the Board will travel to Mobile to visit the location of our next convention site. When we return, we will draft our convention site proposal for you.

urs

Personal Titles and Complimentary Closings in Letters

Goals

- Type at least 37wpm/3'/3e
- Format personal titles in letters
- Format complimentary closings in letters

A. Type 2 times.

A. WARMUP

```
1        B & Z requested 14 boxes at $37/box. The items they      11
2   wanted were #6 and #17. A discount of 20% would bring the     22
3   total to approximately $950. Will you verify that order?      33
    |  1  |  2  |  3  |  4  |  5  |  6  |  7  |  8  |  9  |  10  |  11  |  12
```

SKILLBUILDING

B. DIAGNOSTIC PRACTICE: NUMBERS

If you are not using the GDP software, turn to page SB-5 and follow the directions for this activity.

C. Take three 12-second timed writings on each line. The scale below the last line shows your wpm speed for a 12-second timed writing.

C. 12-SECOND SPEED SPRINTS

```
4   Nine of those new women were on time for the first session.
5   She could see that many of those old memos should be filed.
6   Forty of the men were at the game when that siren went off.
7   The line at the main hall was so long that I did not go in.
    | | | |5| | | |10| | | |15| | | |20| | | |25| | | |30| | | |35| | | |40| | | |45| | | |50| | | |55| | | |60
```

Keyboarding Connection

Evaluating Internet Sources

Are you sure your Internet source has valid information? Because of the broad availability of the Internet and the lack of careful review stages like the ones built into print publishing, you must be cautious about the dependability of information you find on the Internet. Evaluate information on the Internet by the same standards you use to evaluate other sources of information.

The best way to assure that information is valid is to get it from a reputable source. The Internet versions of established, reputable journals in medicine (for example, *Journal of the American Medical Association*), business (for example, *Harvard Business Review*), engineering, computer science, and so forth, warrant the same level of trust as the printed versions.

When you do not use established, reputable Web sites, use caution. Keep in mind that anyone can publish on the Internet. For many sources, there are no editorial review safeguards in place.

YOUR TURN   Search the Web for more assessment methods.

D. Take two 3-minute timed writings. Review your speed and errors.

Goal: At least 37wpm/3'/3e

D. 3-MINUTE TIMED WRITING

```
 8      Now is a great time for you to look for a job. Most    11
 9  employers look for people who have mastered a few office    22
10  skills. For example, if you have acquired good computer    33
11  skills and are capable of working with people around you   45
12  and are steadfast, you can find a good job. There are some 56
13  who will pay top dollar to find and keep good workers.     67
14      Your first impression on a prospective employer will   78
15  be a lasting one. Your resume should list your job skills,  90
16  your experience, and your personal information. Your zeal  102
17  when you interview for a job must come through.            111
    |  1  |  2  |  3  |  4  |  5  |  6  |  7  |  8  |  9  |  10  |  11  |  12
```

FORMATTING

E. PERSONAL TITLES IN CORRESPONDENCE

Inside Addresses
Always use a courtesy title before a person's name in the inside address of a letter; for example, *Mr., Mrs.,* or *Dr.*

Type a person's title on the same line with the name (separated by a comma), if the title is short, or on the line below. The title and business name may be typed on the same line (separated by a comma) if they are both short.

Salutations
When possible, use a person's name in the salutation. The correct form for the salutation is the courtesy title and the last name. If you do not know the name of the person, use a job title or *Ladies and Gentlemen.* A colon is used after the salutation in standard punctuation.

Personal Titles in Inside Addresses
Mr. Frank R. Yashiro, Manager
Landmark Security Systems

Mrs. Joyce Mansfield
Executive Director
Tanner Hospital

Dr. Carlotta Torres
Manager, Duke Oil Co.

Personal Titles in Salutations
Dear Ms. North:

Dear Dr. Chapman:

Dear Mr. Wagner:

Dear Sales Manager:

Ladies and Gentlemen:

F. COMPLIMENTARY CLOSINGS IN CORRESPONDENCE

Every letter should end with a complimentary closing. Some frequently used complimentary closings are *Sincerely, Sincerely yours, Yours truly, Cordially*, and *Respectfully yours*.

In the closing lines, do not use a courtesy title before a man's name. A courtesy title may be included in a woman's typed name or her signature. A comma is used after the complimentary closing in standard punctuation.

Closing Lines

Sincerely yours,

Gretchen Day

Miss Gretchen Day
Account Manager

Cordially,

(Ms.) Juanita Ponce

Juanita Ponce
Marketing Director

Yours truly,

Ben R. Cameron

Ben R. Cameron
Regional Supervisor

DOCUMENT PROCESSING

Correspondence 46-22

Business Letter in Block Style

January 10, 20-- | Mrs. Connie Filstad | 4034 Kennedy Lane | Mount Vernon, WA 98274-2340 | Dear Mrs. Filstad:

¶ We at Mirror Lake Homes believe that your selection of a SunCity townhouse is just the right choice for you. The SunCity model received three national awards last month. You have selected one of the most popular of our six models. As you requested, a brochure of the SunCity model is enclosed. Fifty-four units in the Creekwood site in Mount Vernon, Washington, have been built since December 2002.

¶ I am certain you will agree that the $500 earnest money you put down was a wise decision on your part, and the 6.5 percent loan you received was the best available through our lending agency.

¶ Thank you, Mrs. Filstad, for the opportunity to work with you these past few days. If you have any questions, please let us know.

Sincerely, | (Mrs.) Maria Martinez | Sales Director | urs | Enclosure

Correspondence 46-23

Business Letter in Block Style

May 20, 20-- | Mr. Lawrence S. Alwich | 1800 East Hollywood Avenue | Salt Lake City, UT 84108 | Dear Mr. Alwich:

¶ Our radio station would like you to reply to our editorial about the proposed airport site that aired from Provo, Utah, on May 15. Actually, you are 1 of over 27 listeners who indicated your desire for us to air your rebuttal.

¶ Of the more than 100 request letters for equal time, we selected yours because you touched on most of the relevant points of this topic.

¶ We will contact you further about taping your rebuttal on June 4. Please read the enclosed disclaimer that we would like you to sign before airing the rebuttal.

Yours truly, | Peng T. Lim | General Manager | urs | Enclosure

Personal-Business Letters

Goals

- Improve speed and accuracy
- Refine language arts skills in number expression
- Format personal-business letters

A. Type 2 times.

A. WARMUP

```
1       "Rex analyzed the supply," Margie said. Based on the      11
2  results, a purchase request for 7# @ $140 (23% of what we      22
3  needed) was issued. Was Jackie surprised by this? Vi was!      34
    | 1 | 2 | 3 | 4 | 5 | 6 | 7 | 8 | 9 | 10 | 11 | 12
```

SKILLBUILDING

B. PACED PRACTICE

If you are not using the GDP software, turn to page SB-14 and follow the directions for this activity.

C. PROGRESSIVE PRACTICE: ALPHABET

If you are not using the GDP software, turn to page SB-7 and follow the directions for this activity.

LANGUAGE ARTS

D. Study the rules at the right.

D. NUMBER EXPRESSION

RULE ▶
 # general

In general, spell out numbers zero through ten, and use numerals for numbers above ten.

We rented two movies for tonight.
The decision was reached after 27 precincts sent in their results.

RULE ▶
 # figures

Use numerals for

- **Dates. (Use *st*, *d*, or *th* only if the day comes before the month.)**
  The tax report is due on April 15 (*not* April 15ᵗʰ).
  We will drive to the camp on the 23d (or *23rd* or *23ʳᵈ*) of May.
- **All numbers if two or more *related* numbers both above and below ten are used in the same sentence.**
  Mr. Carter sent in 7 receipts, and Ms. Cantrell sent in 22.
  But: The 13 accountants owned three computers each.
- **Measurements (time, money, distance, weight, and percent).**
  The $500 statue we delivered at 7 a.m. weighed 6 pounds.
- **Mixed numbers.**
  Our sales are up 9½ (or *9 1/2* or *9.5*) percent over last year.

(Continued on next page)

4 On the 3d of June, when she turns 60, 2 of her annuities
5 will have earned an average of 10 3/4 percent.
6 All seven investors were interested in buying 14 condos
7 if they were located within fifteen miles of each other.
8 The credit fee is fifteen dollars, and the interest is set
9 at 8 percent; escrow will close on March 23rd before five p.m.
10 The parcel weighed two pounds. She also mailed three large
11 packages and twelve small packages on June 4.
12 They paid 2.5 points on the loan amount.

FORMATTING

E. PERSONAL-BUSINESS LETTERS

Personal-business letters are prepared by individuals to conduct their personal business. To format a personal-business letter:

1. Type the letter on plain paper or personal stationery, not letterhead.

2. Include the writer's address in the letter directly below the writer's name in the closing lines.

3. Since the writer of the letter usually types the letter, reference initials are not used.

DOCUMENT PROCESSING

Correspondence 47-24

Personal-Business Letter in Block Style

Refer to **Reference Manual**

Refer to page R-3D of the Reference Manual for an illustration of a personal-business letter.

general
figures

general
figures

↓5X

October 1, 20-- ↓4X

Ms. Valarie Bledsoe, Director
City Parks and Recreation Department
7034 Renwick Avenue
Syracuse, NY 13210-0475 ↓2X

Dear Ms. Bledsoe: ↓2X

Thank you for the excellent manner in which your department accommodated our family last summer. About 120 Turners attended the reunion at Rosedale Park on August 21.

I would like to again request that Shelter 5 be reserved for our next year's family reunion on August 20. A confirmation of the date from your office will be appreciated. ↓2X

Sincerely, ↓4X

Blair R. Turner
2410 Farnham Road
Syracuse, NY 13219

This personal-business letter is from Roberto G. Trujillo, who lives at 482 22d Street East, Lawrence, KS 66049. Use July 13, 20--, as the date, and supply the appropriate salutation and closing using standard punctuation. The letter is to be sent to Mr. Robert A. Sotherden, Administrator | Glencrest Nursing Home | 2807 Crossgate Circle | Lawrence, KS 66047.

general

¶ Thanks to you and dozens of other people, the fall crafts sale at Glencrest was highly successful. I am very appreciative of the ways in which you helped. ¶ I particularly wish to thank you for transporting the display tables and chairs to Glencrest and back to the community center. Many people from the community center attended the sale and commented about how nice it was of you and your staff to support such an activity. ¶ Having a parent who is a resident of the home, I am grateful that over 20 people from the Lawrence area volunteer their services to help make life more pleasant for the residents. Please accept my special thanks to you and your staff for supporting the many activities that benefit all Glencrest residents.

June 4, 20-- | Mr. Karl E. Davis | 5270 Rosecrans Avenue | Topeka, KS 67284 | Dear Mr. Davis:

¶ Your presentation at the Sand Hills Country Club was one of the most enjoyable our members have ever observed. It is always a pleasure to have professionals like you speak on ways college graduates can prepare themselves for future employment. I especially enjoyed the question-and-answer session at the conclusion of your wonderful presentation, and I received many favorable comments from other attendees as well.

general

¶ Our professor has suggested that we take the information you gave us and prepare a website that focuses on the key points 6 you mentioned in your speech. That way, many of our classmates can take advantage of your excellent advice when preparing for their job search. We have also found

figure

at least 20 several other sources to use on the world wide web that we plan to include on in our website.

(Continued on next page)

¶ I believe this is one of the most interesting assignments I have ~~ever~~ been assigned, thank(s) to the excellent information you provided. Members of my project team are excited to see the(ir) information on our web site. The project has given other students an incentive to construct their own web sites pertaining to job searches and interviewing techniques.

¶ If you would like to view our Web site, you can do so at the following URL, which will be posted by the 10th of the month: www.tamu.edu/comm/abed3600/interview.html. Again, thank you for all your excellent ideas.

Sincerely, | Tamika Yamemoto | 3421 Carlisle Avenue | Topeka, KS 67209

figure

Memos With Lists

Goals

- Type at least 38 wpm/3'/3e
- Format lists in correspondence

A. Type 2 times.

A. WARMUP

```
1        Three travel agencies (Jepster & Vilani, Quin & Bott,    11
2  and Zeplin & Wexter) sold the most travel tickets for the      23
3  past 12 months. They sold 785, 834, and 960 total tickets.     34
   |  1  |  2  |  3  |  4  |  5  |  6  |  7  |  8  |  9  | 10  | 11  | 12
```

SKILLBUILDING

B. DIAGNOSTIC PRACTICE: SYMBOLS AND PUNCTUATION

If you are not using the GDP software, turn to page SB-2 and follow the directions for this activity.

C. Type each sentence on a separate line by pressing ENTER after each sentence.

C. TECHNIQUE PRACTICE: ENTER KEY

```
4  Debit the accounts. Balance your checkbook. Add the assets.
5  Take the discount. Send the statements. Compute the ratios.
6  Review the accounts. Credit the amounts. Figure the totals.
7  Prepare the statements. Send the catalog. Call the clients.
```

D. Take two 3-minute timed writings. Review your speed and errors.

Goal: At least 38wpm/3'/3e

D. 3-MINUTE TIMED WRITING

```
8         Some of us like to use the Internet for shopping. With  11
9  just a simple click of the mouse, you can shop for almost       23
10 any type of product. You can purchase books, cars, food,        34
11 games, toys, zippers, boxes, and even golf clubs by using       46
12 the computer to shop online.                                    52
13        The advantages of using the Web to shop with such ease   63
14 are many. First, you can shop from any place that has some       75
15 access to the Internet. Second, you can compare all prices       86
16 with other places before you make any purchase. Third, you       98
17 can have your purchases shipped directly to you. All the        110
18 savings mount quickly.                                          114
   |  1  |  2  |  3  |  4  |  5  |  6  |  7  |  8  |  9  | 10  | 11  | 12
```

FORMATTING

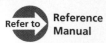

Refer to **Reference Manual**

Refer to pages R-3B, R-3C, and R-5B of the Reference Manual for examples of lists in correspondence. Refer to page R-12C of the Reference Manual for an overview of formatting lists.

E. LISTS IN CORRESPONDENCE

Numbers or bullets may be used in correspondence to call attention to items in a list. If the sequence of the items is important, use numbers rather than bullets.

1. Begin the number or bullet at the left margin for blocked paragraphs.
2. Press ENTER 2 times to insert 1 blank line before and after the list.
3. Within the list, use single spacing as is used in the rest of the document.
4. If all items require no more than 1 line, single-space between the items in the list. If any item requires more than 1 line, single-space each item but press ENTER 2 times to insert 1 blank line between each item.

To format a list in correspondence:

1. Type the list unformatted; then press ENTER 2 times. (**Note:** If you apply the number or bullet feature at the start of the list, any paragraphs that might follow will usually be indented incorrectly.)
2. Select the items in the list.
3. Apply the number or bullet feature.
4. Decrease the indent to move the position of bullets or numbers to the left margin.

DOCUMENT PROCESSING

Correspondence 48-27

Memo

Refer to **Reference Manual**

Refer to page R-12C of the Reference Manual for an overview of formatting lists.

↓5X   → tab

MEMO TO: Charles A. Cornelius, President ↓2X

FROM: Alfred A. Long, Convention Director ↓2X

DATE: September 8, 20-- ↓2X

SUBJECT: Convention Locations ↓2X

As you know, this year's convention will meet in Jacksonville, Florida. It is the Executive Board's decision to rotate the convention site to each of the districts in our region. Our next three conventions will be held in the following locations: ↓2X

- Mobile, Alabama
- Atlanta, Georgia
- Myrtle Beach, South Carolina ↓2X

In May the Board will travel to Mobile to visit the location of our next convention site. When we return, we will draft our convention site proposal for you. ↓2X

urs

Correspondence 48-28

Memo

MEMO TO: Marcia Davis | **FROM:** Alex Pera | **DATE:** April 9, 20-- |
SUBJECT: Program Descriptions

¶As you requested, I have contacted the speakers for our afternoon session discussions. All three speakers have sent me a brief description of their sessions, and they are listed in the order of presentation as follows:

1. Salon A. This session will discuss the advantages of e-commerce and its influence on the economy of the United States.
2. Salon B. This session will introduce several suggestions for enhancing your Web site.
3. Salon C. This session will discuss changes occurring in Internet access and its impact on entrepreneurial ventures.

¶By next Monday I will send you an introduction for each speaker.
urs

Correspondence 48-29

Memo

Open the file for Correspondence 48-27 and make the following changes:

1. Change the three convention sites to Miami, Florida; Raleigh, North Carolina; and Montgomery, Alabama.

2. Change the final paragraph to indicate that the Board will travel to Miami.

Strategies for Career Success

Reducing Bias in Business Communication

Everything we do in business communication attempts to build goodwill. Bias-free language and visuals help maintain the goodwill we work so hard to create.

Bias-free language does not discriminate against people on the basis of sex, physical condition, race, age, or any other characteristic. Do not emphasize gender-specific words in your business vocabulary. Instead, incorporate gender-neutral words (for example, chairman is chairperson) into your business communication.

Organizations that treat people fairly should also use language that treats people fairly. The law is increasingly intolerant of biased documents and hostile work environments. Practice nondiscriminatory behavior by focusing on individual merits, accomplishments, skills, and what you might share in common rather than illustrating differences. Treating every group with respect and understanding is essential to gaining loyalty and future business while cultivating harmonious relationships.

YOUR TURN Review a document that you have recently written. Is the document bias-free?

Letters With Copy Notations

Goals

- Improve speed and accuracy
- Refine language arts skills in spelling
- Format letters with copy notations

A. Type 2 times.

A. WARMUP

```
1    "Look at them! Have you ever seen such large birds?"      11
2  When questioned later on an exam, about 80% to 90% of the   22
3  junior girls were amazed to learn that they were ospreys.   34
   |  1  |  2  |  3  |  4  |  5  |  6  |  7  |  8  |  9  |  10  |  11  |  12
```

SKILLBUILDING

B. MAP

Follow the GDP software directions for this exercise in improving keystroking accuracy.

C. Take a 1-minute timed writing on the first paragraph to establish your base speed. Then take four 1-minute timed writings on the remaining paragraphs. As soon as you equal or exceed your base speed on one paragraph, advance to the next, more difficult paragraph.

C. SUSTAINED PRACTICE: NUMBERS AND SYMBOLS

```
4        The proposed road improvement program was approved      10
5  by the county commissioners at their last meeting. There      22
6  were about ten citizens who spoke on behalf of the project.   34

7        The plan calls for blacktopping a 14-mile stretch on    11
8  County Road #2356. This is the road that is commonly called   23
9  the "roller coaster" because of all the curves and hills.     34

10       There will be 116 miles blacktopped by J & J, Inc.      10
11 (commonly referred to as the Jeremy Brothers*). J & J's       22
12 office is at 1798 30th Avenue past the 22d Street bridge.      33

13       Minor road repair costs range from $10,784 to a high    11
14 of $163,450 (39% of the total program costs). The "county     23
15 inspector" is to hold the project costs to 105% of budget!    34
   |  1  |  2  |  3  |  4  |  5  |  6  |  7  |  8  |  9  |  10  |  11  |  12
```

D. Type this list of frequently misspelled words, paying special attention to any spelling problems in each word.

D. SPELLING

16 per other receipt present provided commission international
17 service position questions following industrial maintenance
18 well absence support proposal mortgage corporate management
19 upon balance approval experience facilities recommendations
20 paid because premium procedure addition directors currently

Edit the sentences to correct any misspellings.

21 The international comission provided a list of proceedures.
22 That industrial maintainance proposal is curently in place.
23 The directers and management supported the recomendations.
24 Those present raised a question about a corperate morgage.
25 Six of the folowing persons have now given their aproval.
26 In adition, Kris has premium experience at the facilitys.

FORMATTING

E. COPY NOTATIONS

Making file copies of all documents you prepare is a good business practice. At times you may also need copies to send to people other than the addressee of the original document.

A copy notation is typed on a document to indicate that someone else besides the addressee is receiving a copy.

1. Type the copy notation on the line below the reference initials or below the attachment or enclosure notation.

2. At the left margin, type a lowercase *c* followed by a colon.
3. Press the SPACE BAR 1 time and type the name of the person receiving the copy.
4. If more than one person is receiving a copy, type the names on one line separated by a comma and space between each name.

Sincerely, ↓4X

Lester A. Fagerlie
Branch Manager ↓2X

jlt
Enclosure
c: Mrs. Coretta D. Rice, Dr. Thomas Moore

Correspondence 49-30 ▶

Business Letter in Block Style

⚠ Highlighted words are spelling words from the language arts activities.

May 11, 20-- | Mr. and Mrs. Richard Belson | 783 Wellcourt Lane | Mount Vernon, WA 98273-4156 | Dear Mr. and Mrs. Belson:

¶ Marian Dickenson has informed me that you have several questions pertaining to the maintenance proposal that was submitted by the directors and approved by management. It is our position, based upon the procedures we provided following last week's meeting, that the proposal was submitted to corporate headquarters prior to your inquiry. Therefore, your questions should be directed to Alfred A. Long in our Seattle office.

¶ It has been our experience that inquiries such as yours will receive an immediate response because of the support you have demonstrated during other maintenance negotiations. I would recommend that you call me if you have not heard from Mr. Long by the 13th of the month. In the absence of Mr. Long's response, I am sending you a copy of other materials related to your inquiry.

¶ Thank you for your interest in this matter.

Sincerely, | Theodore A. Gardner | Sales Director | urs | c: Marian Dickenson

Correspondence 49-31 ▶

Business Letter in Block Style

Open the file for Correspondence 49-30 and make the following changes:

1. Send the letter to Mr. and Mrs. George Tanner | 105 Royal Lane | Commerce, TX 75428
2. Add the following sentence to the end of the second paragraph:

These materials are enclosed for your review.

3. Include an enclosure notation.
4. Send a copy of this letter to Marian Dickenson and also to Carla Orellano.

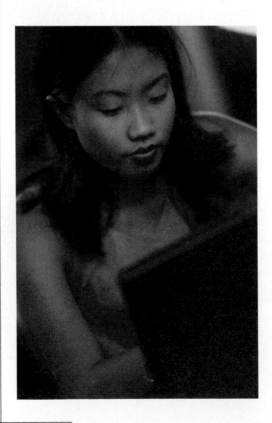

Letters in Modified-Block Style

Goals

- Type at least 38wpm/3'/3e
- Format letters in modified-block style

A. Type 2 times.

A. WARMUP

```
1      Mark Kara's quilts down by 25%: #489, #378, and #460.    11
2  Leave the prices as they are for the remainder of the sizes  23
3  in that section. Eleven adjoining sections will be next.     34
   | 1 | 2 | 3 | 4 | 5 | 6 | 7 | 8 | 9 | 10 | 11 | 12
```

SKILLBUILDING

PPP PRETEST → PRACTICE → POSTTEST

PRETEST
Take a 1-minute timed writing. Review your speed and errors.

B. PRETEST: Alternate- and One-Hand Words

```
4      The chair of the trade committee served notice that    11
5  the endowment grant exceeded the budget. A million dollars  23
6  was the exact amount. The greater part might be deferred.   35
   | 1 | 2 | 3 | 4 | 5 | 6 | 7 | 8 | 9 | 10 | 11 | 12
```

PRACTICE
Speed Emphasis:
If you made 2 or fewer errors on the Pretest, type each *individual* line 2 times.
Accuracy Emphasis:
If you made 3 or more errors, type each *group* of lines (as though it were a paragraph) 2 times.

C. PRACTICE: Alternate-Hand Words

```
7  amendment turndown visible suspend visual height signs maps
8  authentic clemency dormant figment island emblem usual snap
9  shamrocks blandish problem penalty profit thrown chair form
```

D. PRACTICE: One-Hand Words

```
10  pumpkin eastward plumply barrage greater poplin trade holly
11  minikin cassette opinion seaweed created kimono union exact
12  minimum attracts reserve million scatter unhook plump defer
```

POSTTEST
Repeat the Pretest timed writing and compare performance.

E. POSTTEST: Alternate- and One-Hand Words

F. Take two 3-minute timed writings. Review your speed and errors.

Goal: At least 38wpm/3'/3e

F. 3-MINUTE TIMED WRITING

```
13        The Web is a vast source of facts and data on many        10
14   topics. You can view many newspapers, zip through weather       22
15   reports, find a tax form and learn how to complete it, and      34
16   search for a job. You can find answers to health questions      46
17   and learn about world events almost as soon as they occur.      57
18        E-mail is another part of the Internet that people are     69
19   using more often. They use e-mail to keep in touch with         80
20   friends and family in a quick and efficient way that costs      92
21   very little. They can write down their thoughts and send        103
22   messages just as if they were writing a letter or memo.         114
     |  1  |  2  |  3  |  4  |  5  |  6  |  7  |  8  |  9  |  10  |  11  |  12
```

FORMATTING

G. MODIFIED-BLOCK STYLE LETTERS

Modified-block style is a commonly used format for business letters. The date, the complimentary closing, and the writer's identification line(s) are typed at the horizontal centerpoint for each of these lines. Begin the document by first setting a left tab at the centerpoint (at 3.25 inches), and then press TAB 1 time to move to the centerpoint before typing each of these lines. (**Note:** These lines are *not* centered horizontally.)

1. Clear all tabs and set a left tab at the centerpoint (at 3.25 inches).
2. Press ENTER 5 times to begin the letter 2 inches from the top of the page.
3. Press TAB 1 time to move to the centerpoint, and type the date of the letter.
4. Press ENTER 4 times, and type the inside address at the left margin.
5. Press ENTER 2 times, type the salutation at the left margin, and press ENTER 2 times again.
6. Type the paragraphs blocked at the left margin, and press ENTER 2 times after all paragraphs.
7. After typing the final paragraph, press ENTER 2 times and press TAB 1 time to move to the centerpoint.
8. Type the complimentary closing, and then press ENTER 4 times.
9. Press TAB 1 time to move to the centerpoint, and type the writer's identification. If the writer's identification is to be typed on 2 lines, press TAB 1 time again for any additional line.
10. Press ENTER 2 times, and type the reference initials and remaining letter parts at the left margin.

(Continued on next page)

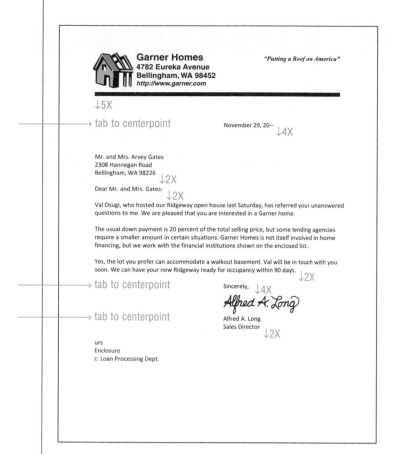

Garner Homes
4782 Eureka Avenue
Bellingham, WA 98452
http://www.garner.com

"Putting a Roof on America"

↓5X

→ tab to centerpoint   November 29, 20-- ↓4X

Mr. and Mrs. Arvey Gates
2308 Hannegan Road
Bellingham, WA 98226 ↓2X

Dear Mr. and Mrs. Gates: ↓2X

Val Osugi, who hosted our Ridgeway open house last Saturday, has referred your unanswered questions to me. We are pleased that you are interested in a Garner home.

The usual down payment is 20 percent of the total selling price, but some lending agencies require a smaller amount in certain situations. Garner Homes is not itself involved in home financing, but we work with the financial institutions shown on the enclosed list.

Yes, the lot you prefer can accommodate a walkout basement. Val will be in touch with you soon. We can have your new Ridgeway ready for occupancy within 90 days. ↓2X

→ tab to centerpoint   Sincerely, ↓4X

Alfred A. Long

→ tab to centerpoint   Alfred A. Long
Sales Director ↓2X

urs
Enclosure
c: Loan Processing Dept.

Word
Processing
Manual

H. WORD PROCESSING: RULER TABS AND TAB SET

Study Lesson 50 in your word processing manual. Complete all of the shaded steps while at your computer. Then format the jobs that follow.

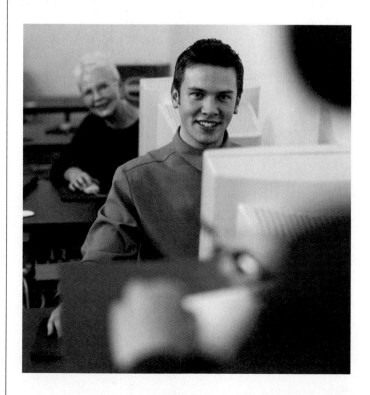

Correspondence ▶
50-32

Business Letter in
Modified-Block Style

**Reference
Manual**

Refer to page R-3B of
the Reference Manual
for additional guidance.

↓5X

————————→ tab to centerpoint November 29, 20--   ↓4X

Mr. and Mrs. Arvey Gates
2308 Hannegan Road
Bellingham, WA 98226   ↓2X

Dear Mr. and Mrs. Gates: ↓2X

Val Osugi, who hosted our Ridgeway open house last Saturday, has referred
your unanswered questions to me. We are pleased that you are interested in a
Garner home.

The usual down payment is 20 percent of the total selling price, but some
lending agencies require a smaller amount in certain situations. Garner Homes
is not itself involved in home financing, but we work with the financial
institutions shown on the enclosed list.

Yes, the lot you prefer can accommodate a walkout basement. Val will be in
touch with you soon. We can have your new Ridgeway ready for occupancy
within 90 days. ↓2X

————————→ tab to centerpoint Sincerely, ↓4X

Alfred A. Long

————————→ tab to centerpoint Alfred A. Long
Sales Director ↓2X

urs
Enclosure
c: Loan Processing Dept.

Correspondence
50-33

Business Letter in
Modified-Block Style

Refer to   **Reference Manual**

Refer to page R-12C of
the Reference Manual for
information on formatting
lists and an illustration.

Use November 30, 20--, as the date as you format this modified-block style letter to be sent to the sales manager at

Bachmann's Nursery and Landscaping | 6823 Oneta Avenue | Youngstown, OH 44500-2175

Dear Sales Manager:

¶ As you requested on the telephone, I am providing the following list of events relating to my tree problem.

1. On April 15, I purchased at your branch in Warren four silver maples for the atrium outside our Riverdale office. We also purchased four Japanese red maples at your branch in Niles later that afternoon.

2. After about six months, one silver maple and one red maple had died. I phoned both the Warren and Niles branches several times on November 1, but no one returned my messages.

3. On November 8, I phoned your nursery in an attempt to have these trees replaced. Again, there was no response.

¶ As these trees were expensive, I expect that you will either replace them or reimburse me for the cost of the trees. I shall look forward to hearing from you.

Sincerely, | Marvin L. Norgaard | Grounds Manager | urs

Correspondence
50-34

Business Letter in
Modified-Block Style

December 10, 20-- | Mr. Marvin L. Norgaard | 4782 Saranac Avenue | Youngstown, OH 44505-6207 | Dear Mr. Norgaard:

¶ This is in response to your recent letter.

¶ Your trees will be replaced without cost to you. We will make sure that the replacement trees will match the others you purchased in both size and color. I am enclosing a warranty for these new trees so that you can feel confident that we stand behind our product.

¶ The survival rate for trees cannot be perfect; however, we are indeed sorry that you have had to have this temporary setback.

¶ The communication breakdown with our two branch offices should not have occurred. We will take steps to ensure that this will not happen in the future. You can be confident that the appearance of your atrium will be restored and that the beauty of the new trees will add to your property's value. Thank you for shopping at Bachmann's.

Sincerely, | Mrs. Alice G. Schmidt | Co-owner | urs | Enclosure | c: Mr. Raul Cornejo, Co-owner

Progress and Proofreading Check

Documents designated as Proofreading Checks serve as a check of your proofreading skill. Your goal is to have zero typographical errors when the GDP software first scores the document.

March 11, 20-- | Ms. Karen Shalicky | Lincoln Travel Center | 2384 Longdale Avenue | Suite 4113 | Boston, MA 02134-3489 | Dear Ms. Shalicky:

¶ I am interested in taking a cruise in one of the following regions:

• Alaska Inland Passageway
• Caribbean Islands
• Greek Isles

¶ Could you please send me some promotional materials for these cruises? My financial resources are such that I would like to limit my cruise package to $5,000 and would prefer a cruise no longer than ten days in length. I will be accompanied by my friend Bonnie Davis, and I assume that any quotes you give me could apply to both of us.

¶ We would like to do sightseeing in some of these locations. Do you have excursions available to passengers? I am enclosing a list of the sites we would like to visit in each of these regions.

¶ The best time for us to travel is between June 1 and June 20, and we would like you to schedule our trip around those dates. I hope to hear from you soon.

Yours truly, | Rita Wright | 678 Ardale Avenue | Milton, MA 02186-2190 | Enclosure | c: Bonnie Davis

Keyboarding Connection

Avoid E-Mail Flame Wars

Don't fan the flames! A flame is an offensive e-mail that expresses anger, criticism, or insults. If flames are transmitted to a mailing list, they can produce a long list of flames and counter flames known as flame wars.

You may be tempted to join in, but this is a waste of everyone's time. Often the initial offense was merely a poorly worded e-mail that a reader interpreted as an insult. There are those who intentionally send inflammatory e-mails called flame bait. Resist the urge to send a cutting response, and consider whether the writer's intent was to provoke you.

If your reader misjudges something you wrote and becomes offended, just apologize. A timely apology can thwart a potential fire. Avoid miscommunication by watching how you word your e-mails.

YOUR TURN Have you ever been insulted by an e-mail? What was your response?

Unit 11

Employment Documents

PATSY R. ROTHEL

2525 Hickory Ridge Drive, Plant City, FL 33567
Phone: 813-555-0704; e-mail: prothel@netmail.com

OBJECTIVE	To continue my career in computer graphics by securing a position related to graphic design.
EDUCATION	Central Florida Business College, Valrico, Florida A.A. degree in graphics design Graduated: May 2005 Plant City High School, Plant City, Florida Graduated: May 2003

EXPERIENCE	*Graphic Designer, NetView, Inc.*
	Orlando, Florida
	October 2005-Present
	    Designed Web pages for Internet
	    Florida. Edited page copy for We
	    based users.
	
	Copy Editor, The Plant City Press
	Plant City, Florida
	May 2003-September 2005
	    Assisted the news editor with ty
	    daily newspaper. Solicited subst
	    Conducted interviews for Citizen

ACTIVITIES	• Member, Phi Beta Lambda, 2004-20 • Newsletter Editor, *CFBC News*, 2004 • President, FBLA Chapter, 2002 • Treasurer, FBLA Chapter, 2001
REFERENCES	References available upon request.

August 10, 20--

Personnel Director
Arlington Communications
2403 Sunset Lane
Arlington, TX 76015-3148

Dear Personnel Director:

Please consider me as an applicant for a position with Arlington Communications. My strengths have always been in the communication arts, as you can see on the enclosed resume, which lists a number of courses in English, speech, and communication technology. The two part-time jobs I held during the summer months at your company convinced me that Arlington Communications is the place where I want to work.

possible openings this summer or fall, please call me
g from you.

April 7, 20--

Ms. Kay Brewer, Personnel Director
Blanchard Computer Systems
2189 Dace Avenue
Sioux City, IA 51107

Dear Ms. Brewer:

Thank you for the opportunity of interviewing yesterday with Blanchard Computer Systems. Please express my appreciation to all of those who were involved.

The interview gave me a good feeling about the company. The positive description that you shared with me convinced me that Blanchard is indeed a company at which I would like to work. I was greatly impressed with the summary of social service programs that are sponsored by Blanchard for citizens throughout the community.

You may recall that I have had experience with all of the equipment that is used. It appears to me that my strengths in computer application software and office systems would blend in well with your company profile.

I look forward to hearing from you soon regarding your decision on the position of data records operator.

Sincerely,

Arlene F. Jefferson
1842 Amber Road
Wayne, NE 68787

Traditional Resumes

Goals

- Improve speed and accuracy
- Refine language arts skills in the use of commas
- Format traditional resumes

A. Type 2 times.

A. WARMUP

```
1      Janice had sales of over $23,000; Kathy's sales were      11
2  only $17,368 for the same quiet period. Craig agreed that     22
3  some inventory sizes were wrong and should be exchanged.      34
   |  1  |  2  |  3  |  4  |  5  |  6  |  7  |  8  |  9  |  10  |  11  |  12
```

SKILLBUILDING

B. MAP

Follow the GDP software directions for this exercise in improving keystroking accuracy.

C. Take a 1-minute timed writing on the first paragraph to establish your base speed. Then take four 1-minute timed writings on the remaining paragraphs. As soon as you equal or exceed your base speed on one paragraph, advance to the next, more difficult paragraph.

C. SUSTAINED PRACTICE: CAPITALIZATION

```
4      There are several different approaches that one can        11
5  take when considering a major purchase. Some people make      22
6  the mistake of simply going to a store and making a choice.   34

7      When one couple decided to buy a chest-type freezer,      11
8  they looked at a consumer magazine in the library. The        22
9  Sears, Amana, and General Electric were shown as best buys.   34

10     That same issue of their magazine compared electric       11
11 ranges. Jonathan and Mary Anne found that the Maytag, Magic   23
12 Chef, Amana, and Gibson were determined to be best buys.      34

13     Best buys for full-size microwave ovens were the Sharp    11
14 Carousel, Panasonic, and GoldStar Multiwave. Good midsize     23
15 models were the Frigidaire, Panasonic, and Sears Kenmore.     34
   |  1  |  2  |  3  |  4  |  5  |  6  |  7  |  8  |  9  |  10  |  11  |  12
```

D. Study the rules at the right.

D. COMMAS

RULE ▶
, date

Use a comma before and after the year in a complete date.

We will arrive on June 2, 2005, for the conference.

But: We will arrive on June 2 for the conference.

But: Work should be submitted between November 2005 and December 2005.

RULE ▶
, place

Use a comma before and after a state or country that follows a city (but not before a ZIP Code).

Joan moved to Vancouver, British Columbia, in May.

Send the package to Douglasville, GA 30135, by Express Mail.

But: Send the package to Georgia by Express Mail

Edit the sentences to correct any errors in the use of commas.

16 The warehouse building will be ready in September, 2004.
17 The attorney told a clerk to use June 30, 2005 as the date.
18 The books were sent to Los Angeles, CA, 90029 on July 13, 2005 and will arrive soon.
19 The move to Toledo, Ohio, was scheduled for November, 2004.

FORMATTING

E. TRADITIONAL RESUMES

When you apply for a job, you may be asked to submit a resume. The purpose of a resume is to convey your qualifications for the position you are seeking. A resume should include the following:

- Personal information (name, address, telephone number, and e-mail address).
- Your career objective (optional).
- A summary of your educational background and special training.
- Previous work experience.
- Any activities or personal achievements that relate to the position for which you are applying.
- References (optional). If an employer requests references, you should have at least three people who can tell a prospective employer what kind of worker you are.

Often, your resume creates the first impression you make on a prospective employer; be sure it is free of errors.

Various styles are acceptable for formatting a resume. Choose a style (or design one) that is attractive and that enables you to get all the needed information on one or two pages. The first page of a resume should start 2 inches from the top of the page.

To format a traditional resume:
1. Press ENTER 5 times.
2. Insert an open table with 2 columns and 1 row for each section of the resume. **Note:** In the example that follows, you would use 6 rows.
3. Merge the cells in Row 1.
4. Change to center alignment.
5. Type your name in all caps in Cambria Bold 14 pt. in Row 1, and press ENTER 2 times.
6. Change to Cambria Bold 12 pt; then type your street address followed by a comma and 1 space; type your city followed by a comma and 1 space; then type your state followed by 1 space and your ZIP Code; press ENTER 1 time.

(Continued on next page)

7. Type `Phone:` followed by 1 space; then type your area code and phone number followed by a semicolon and 1 space.
8. Type `e-mail:` followed by 1 space and your e-mail address.
9. Press ENTER 1 time.
10. Apply a bottom border to Row 1.
11. Move to Row 2, Column A; and press ENTER 1 time.
12. Type the entry in Column A in all caps and bold in Calibri 12 pt., and press TAB to move to Column B.
13. Press ENTER 1 time, and type the information related to the Column A heading in Column B.
14. Press ENTER as needed in each section to insert 1 blank line between sections. **Note:** Type job titles and business names in italics.
15. Continue typing all entries until you are finished. **Note:** For any job descriptions, increase the indent to reposition the information. For any lists, decrease the indent until the list is positioned at the left of the column.
16. Decrease the width of Column A to about 1 inch to accommodate the longest entry and provide a small amount of space after the longest entry.

Insert 2-column open table with 1 row for each section; apply bottom border.

↓5X

Cambria Bold 14 pt → **ANGELICA P. JUAREZ** ↓2X

Cambria Bold 12 pt → **1842 Amber Road, Germantown, TN 38139**
Phone: 901-555-5102; e-mail: ajuarez@netcast.com ↓1X

Calibri Bold 12 pt →

↓1X ↓1X
OBJECTIVE Administrative position in a school setting, preferably in Tennessee. ↓1X ← Calibri 12 pt

EDUCATION B.A. degree in technology support systems, May 2007
Delta State University, Cleveland, Mississippi ↓1X

EXPERIENCE *Office Manager, Germantown Elementary*
Germantown, Tennessee, 2007-Present
indent → Assist teachers in preparing classroom materials. Submit daily cash reports. Prepare, maintain, and update files. Manage department budget. ↓2X   ← Calibri Italic 12 pt

Administrative Assistant, Shaw Industries
Cleveland, Mississippi, 2002-2004
Prepared reports for section supervisor. Maintained budget using Excel software. Planned and prepared itinerary for section supervisor. Supervised area secretaries and office clerks. Dispatched, sorted, and boxed mail. Worked in customer service. Administered bulk mailing transactions. ↓1X

PERSONAL • Competent in Microsoft Office 2007
• Proficient in Internet Explorer and Netscape Communicator
• Olympics volunteer, Atlanta, Georgia, Summer, 1996
• Speak fluent Spanish ↓1X

REFERENCES Available upon request.

Note: The table is shown with "View Gridlines" active.

Manually decrease width of Column A to fit the longest item plus a small amount of space.

Word Processing Manual

F. **WORD PROCESSING: FONTS AND TABLES—CHANGING COLUMN WIDTH**

Study Lesson 51 in your word processing manual. Complete all of the shaded steps while at your computer. Then format the jobs that follow.

Report 51-27

Resume in Traditional Style

Calibri Bold 12 pt

Note: The table is shown with "View Gridlines" active.

Manually decrease width of Column A to fit longest item.

Insert 2-column open table with 1 row for each section; apply top border.

↓5X

Cambria Bold 14 pt → **PATSY R. ROTHEL**

↓2X

Cambria Bold 12 pt → **2525 Hickory Ridge Drive, Plant City, FL 33567**
Phone: 813-555-0704; e-mail: prothel@netmail.com

↓1X

↓1X ↓1X

OBJECTIVE To continue my career in computer graphics by securing a position related to graphic design.

↓1X Calibri 12 pt

EDUCATION Central Florida Business College, Valrico, Florida
A.A. degree in graphics design
Graduated: May 2005

↓2X

Plant City High School, Plant City, Florida
Graduated: May 2003

↓1X

EXPERIENCE *Graphic Designer, NetView, Inc.* ⟵ Calibri Italic 12 pt
Orlando, Florida
October 2005-Present
indent → Designed Web pages for Internet-connected companies in central Florida. Edited page copy for Web sites. Created a database for Web-based users.

↓2X

Copy Editor, The Plant City Press
Plant City, Florida
May 2003-September 2005
Assisted the news editor with typing, proofreading, and editing copy for daily newspaper. Solicited subscriptions from local businesses. Conducted interviews for Citizens of the Week forum.

↓1X

ACTIVITIES
- Member, Phi Beta Lambda, 2004-2005
- Newsletter Editor, *CFBC News,* 2004
- President, FBLA Chapter, 2002
- Treasurer, FBLA Chapter, 2001

↓1X

REFERENCES References available upon request.

Open the file for Report 51-27 and make the following changes:

1. Change the name to JOYCE K. LEE.
2. Change the address to 10234 Wood Sorrell Lane, Burke, VA 22015.
3. Change the phone number to 703-555-4902 and the e-mail address to jklee@netlink.net.
4. Replace the OBJECTIVE entry with the following:

    To gain experience in retail sales as a foundation for a retail management position.

5. Replace both of the EDUCATION entries with the following:

    Central High School, Burke, Virginia | Graduated: May 2003

6. Change the first EXPERIENCE entry to the following:

    Computer Systems Technician, Kramer & Kramer, Inc. | Harrisburg, Virginia | June 2004-Present | Duties include reviewing, installing, and updating software programs used for processing legal documents.

7. Change the second EXPERIENCE entry to the following:

    Salesclerk, Blanchard's Department Store | Richmond, Virginia | May 2002-May 2004 (part-time) | Duties included selling sporting goods and operating Panasonic cash register. Assisted sales manager in completing monthly sales reports.

8. Change the entries for ACTIVITIES to the following:

    Volunteer for Habitat for Humanity, 2000-Present | Member, Computer Technicians Association, 2000-Present | Senior Class President, 2002-2003 | Member, Intramural Soccer Team, 2001-2003 | Member, Beta Club, 2001-2003

Strategies for Career Success

Formatting Your Resume

The format of your resume communicates important skills—neatness and the ability to organize. Make a good first impression by following these guidelines.

Watch the spacing on your resume. A crowded resume implies that you cannot summarize. Leave adequate white space between the section headings of your resume. Use different font sizes, boldface, and italics to separate and emphasize information. Font sizes should be between 10 and 14.

Print your resume on good-quality 8½" × 11" white or off-white bond paper (for example, 20-pound stock). Colored paper doesn't provide enough contrast when your resume is copied or faxed.

Proofread your resume for spelling errors and consistency of format. Ask a few friends to review it and provide feedback.

YOUR TURN Print one copy of your resume on a dark-colored paper and print one copy on white paper. Photocopy each resume. Which provides the better contrast for readability?

Electronic Resumes

Goals

- Type at least 39wpm/5′/5e
- Format an electronic resume

A. Type 2 times.

A. WARMUP

```
1      The new firm, Kulver & Zweidel, will be equipped to    11
2   handle from 1/6 to 1/4 of Martin's tax needs after they    22
3   move to the new location at 1970 Gansby, just east of Main. 34
    |  1  |  2  |  3  |  4  |  5  |  6  |  7  |  8  |  9  |  10  |  11  |  12
```

SKILLBUILDING

B. Take three 12-second timed writings on each line. The scale below the last line shows your wpm speed for a 12-second timed writing.

B. 12-SECOND SPEED SPRINTS

```
4   Pat went back to the store where she had seen the red book.
5   The good girl was sure that she had not seen that old door.
6   There was a huge change when he walked into the same class.
7   Pat was met at the door with one red rose and a giant cake.
    |||||5|||||10|||||15|||||20|||||25|||||30|||||35|||||40|||||45|||||50|||||55|||||60
```

C. PROGRESSIVE PRACTICE: ALPHABET

If you are not using the GDP software, turn to page SB-7 and follow the directions for this activity.

D. Take two 5-minute timed writings. Review your speed and errors.

Goal: At least 39wpm/5′/5e

D. 5-MINUTE TIMED WRITING

```
 8        Have you completed your education when you graduate    11
 9   from high school or finish your college work? Most people    22
10   look forward to reaching milestones, such as graduation or   34
11   completing a course. Have they learned everything they will  46
12   need to know to be successful in the real world? The answer  58
13   is not so simple.                                            62
14        Learning continues to occur long after you leave the    72
15   classroom. No matter what job or career you pursue, you      84
16   will learn something new every day. When you investigate     95
17   new ideas, ask questions, or find a different way to do a    107
18   job, you are continuing to learn. In the process, you gain   118
19   additional experience, develop new skills, and become a      130
20   better worker.                                               133
21        Getting along with your peers, for example, is not      143
22   something that you learn from studying books. You learn to   155
23   be a team player when you listen to your coworkers and       166
24   share your ideas with them. Do not hesitate to acquire new   178
25   skills or to initiate new ideas. Be zealous in your efforts  190
26   to continue your education.                                  195
     | 1 | 2 | 3 | 4 | 5 | 6 | 7 | 8 | 9 | 10 | 11 | 12
```

FORMATTING

E. ELECTRONIC RESUMES

An electronic resume is a resume that has been formatted for display on the Internet and for electronic transmission via e-mail. Format an electronic resume as follows:

1. Use Courier New with a 10-point font size.
2. Use left alignment.
3. Use default margins and word-wrap longer lines.
4. Do not hyphenate words at the end of a line.
5. Begin all lines blocked at the left margin.
6. Do not use any special formatting features (bold, italic, or underline) or graphic features (rules, bullets, pictures, boxes, tables, or columns).
7. Use all-caps as a substitute for bold or underline.
8. Save the resume as a text-only file (one that has a .txt extension).

F. WORD PROCESSING: SAVING IN TEXT-ONLY FORMAT

Study Lesson 52 in your word processing manual. Complete all of the shaded steps while at your computer. Then format the jobs that follow.

DOCUMENT PROCESSING

Report 52-29 ▶

Resume in Electronic Style

Type the electronic resume as shown in the illustration below. Use a 10 pt. Courier

New font; save the resume as a text-only file.

```
BRENDA COTTON
                   ↓2X
1611 Amherst Way
Emporia, KS 66801
Phone: 316-555-1384
E-mail: bcotton@plains.net
Home page: http://www.esc.org/staff/cotton.htm  ↓2X

OBJECTIVE
            ↓2X
Staff-level accounting position in an educational institution or public
accounting firm.  ↓2X

EDUCATION

B.B.A. degree in accounting from Emporia State University, Emporia, Kansas, May
2004

High school diploma from Central High School, Wichita, Kansas, June 2000

EXPERIENCE

STAFF ACCOUNTANT, Gateway Properties
Emporia, Kansas
December 2003-Present
Responsible for budget control. Prepare variance report and annual business
plan. Generate fixed-asset inventory. Prepare consolidated monthly financials.

ACCOUNTS RECEIVABLE CLERK, Aris Corporation
Salina, Kansas
January 2002-December 2003
Posted cash receipts, prepared bank deposits, and processed tax requests.

PERSONAL

Proficient in Microsoft Office desktop tools
Member of AICPA
Graduated summa cum laude from Emporia State

REFERENCES

Available upon request.
```

Type an electronic resume in correct format for ALLEN P. HUNTER, 10234 Wood Sorrell Lane, Burke, VA 22015; Phone: 703-555-4902; E-mail, aphunter@netlink.net.

1. Type this OBJECTIVE entry: Retail management entry-level position with a midsize department store.
2. Type these two EDUCATION entries:
   Central Virginia Business College, Burke, Virginia, December 2004
   High school diploma from Central High School, Burke, Virginia, May 2002
3. Type these EXPERIENCE entries:
   COMPUTER SYSTEMS TECHNICIAN, Kramer & Kramer, Inc. Harrisburg, Virginia June 1999-Present Duties include reviewing, installing, and updating software programs used for processing legal documents and monitoring computer network systems for branch offices.
   SALESCLERK, Blanchard's Department Store Richmond, Virginia May 2000-May 2002 (part-time) Duties included selling sporting goods and operating Panasonic cash register. Assisted sales manager in completing monthly sales reports generated by Word and Excel software programs.
4. Type these three PERSONAL entries:
   Volunteer for Habitat for Humanity, 2000-Present
   Senior Class President, 1999
   Member, Intramural Soccer Team, 1997-1999
5. Type this REFERENCES entry: Available upon request.
6. Save the resume as a text-only file.

```
ALLEN P. HUNTER

10234 Wood Sorrell Lane
Burke, VA 22015
Phone: 703-555-4902
E-mail: aphunter@netlink.net

OBJECTIVE

Retail management entry-level position with a midsize department store.

EDUCATION

Central Virginia Business College, Burke, Virginia, December 2004
High school diploma from Central High School, Burke, Virginia, May 2002

EXPERIENCE

COMPUTER SYSTEMS TECHNICIAN, Kramer & Kramer, Inc.
Harrisburg, Virginia
June 1999-Present
Duties include reviewing, installing, and updating software programs used for
processing legal documents and monitoring computer network systems for branch
offices.

SALESCLERK. Blanchard's Department Store
Richmond, Virginia
May 2000-May 2002 (part-time)
Duties included selling sporting goods and operating Panasonic cash register.
Assisted sales manager in completing monthly sales reports generated by Word and
Excel software programs.

PERSONAL

Volunteer for Habitat for Humanity, 2000-Present
Senior Class President, 1999
Member, Intramural Soccer Team, 1997-1999

REFERENCES

Available upon request.
```

Letters of Application

Goals

- Improve speed and accuracy
- Refine language arts skills in composing paragraphs
- Format letters of application

A. Type 2 times.

A. WARMUP

```
1        Prices were quickly lowered (some by as much as 50%) @   11
2   Julia's garage sale. She could see that extra sales would     24
3   not be over the 9%* she had projected to finance the prize.   36
    |  1  |  2  |  3  |  4  |  5  |  6  |  7  |  8  |  9  |  10  |  11  |  12
```

SKILLBUILDING

PPP PRETEST → PRACTICE → POSTTEST

PRETEST
Take a 1-minute timed writing. Review your speed and errors.

B. PRETEST: Common Letter Combinations

```
4        They formed an action committee to force a motion for    11
5   a ruling on your contract case. This enabled them to comply   24
6   within the lawful time period and convey a common message.    36
    |  1  |  2  |  3  |  4  |  5  |  6  |  7  |  8  |  9  |  10  |  11  |  12
```

PRACTICE
Speed Emphasis:
If you made 2 or fewer errors on the Pretest, type each *individual* line 2 times.
Accuracy Emphasis:
If you made 3 or more errors, type each *group* of lines (as though it were a paragraph) 2 times.

C. PRACTICE: Word Beginnings

```
7   for forget formal format forces forums forked forest formed
8   per perils period perish permit person peruse perked pertly
9   com combat comedy coming commit common compel comply comets
```

D. PRACTICE: Word Endings

```
10  ing acting aiding boring buying ruling saving hiding dating
11  ble bubble dabble double enable feeble fumble tumble usable
12  ion action vision lesion nation bunion lotion motion legion
```

POSTTEST
Repeat the Pretest timed writing and compare performance.

E. POSTTEST: Common Letter Combinations

F. PROGRESSIVE PRACTICE: NUMBERS

If you are not using the GDP software, turn to page SB-11 and follow the directions for this activity.

G. Choose one of the phrases at the right; then compose a paragraph of three to four sentences on that topic.

G. COMPOSING PARAGRAPHS

13 My computer was working fine until it . . .

14 The Internet has helped me complete my class assignments by . . .

15 Several of us decided to take the cruise because . . .

16 I have several skills, but my best skill is . . .

FORMATTING

Reference Manual

Refer to page R-12B of the Reference Manual for additional guidance.

H. LETTERS OF APPLICATION

A letter of application is sent along with a resume to a prospective employer. Together, the letter and the resume serve to introduce a person to the organization.

The letter of application should be no longer than one page and should include (1) the job you are applying for and how you learned of the job, (2) the highlights of your enclosed resume, and (3) a request for an interview.

DOCUMENT PROCESSING

Correspondence 53-36

Personal-Business Letter in Modified-Block Style

September 15, 20-- | Ms. Kay Brewer, Personnel Director | Blanchard Computer Systems | 2189 Dace Ave. | Sioux City, IA 51107 | Dear Ms. Brewer:

¶ Please consider me as an applicant for the position of Data Records Operator advertised in the September 13th edition of the Sioux City Press. *ital*

¶ In May I will graduate with an A.A. degree in Office Systems from West Iowa Business College. My enclosed resume shows that I have completed courses in Excel, Access, and Microsoft Word. I also have considerable experience in working on the Internet. The skills I gained in using these software packages and in accessing the Internet will be extremely useful to your branch office in Sioux City.

¶ The position with your company is very appealing to me. If you wish to interview me for this position, please call me at 402-555-7265. Sincerely, | Arlene F. Jefferson | 1842 Amber Road | Wayne, NE 68787 | Enclosure

August 10, 20-- | Personnel Director | Arlington Communications | 2403 Sunset Lane | Arlington, TX 76015-3148 | Dear Personnel Director:

¶ Please consider me as an applicant for a position with Arlington Communications. My strengths have always been in the communication arts, as you can see on the enclosed resume, which lists a number of courses in English, speech, and communication technology. The two part-time jobs I held during the summer months at your company convinced me that Arlington Communications is the place where I want to work.

¶ If you would like to interview me for any possible openings this summer or fall, please call me at 903-555-2340. I look forward to hearing from you. Sincerely, | Kenneth R. Diaz | 105 Royal Lane | Commerce, TX 75428 | Enclosure

Strategies for Career Success

Writing a Job Application Letter

What's the goal of the letter that accompanies your resume? The goal is to get the interview. No two letters of application are alike.

In the opening paragraph, state your purpose (for example, the position applied for, how you became aware of it).

In the middle section, sell yourself. Convince the reader that you are the best match for the job. If you respond to a job posting, match your qualifications to the job description. If you send an unsolicited letter, specify how the employer will benefit from your qualifications. Also, refer to your resume.

In the closing paragraph, show confidence in your abilities (for example, "I'm certain I can meet your needs for a . . ."). Then state a specific time you will call to schedule an interview.

YOUR TURN   Obtain a job description for which you believe you are qualified. List the job requirements, and then list your qualifications that match.

Follow-Up Letters

Goals

- Type at least 39wpm/5′/5e
- Format follow-up letters

A. Type 2 times.

A. WARMUP

```
1        Quite a night! All sixty senior citizens (including      11
2   the handicapped) really enjoyed that play. Over 3/4 of the    22
3   tickets were sold; most had been sold by Frank's workers.     34
    |  1  |  2  |  3  |  4  |  5  |  6  |  7  |  8  |  9  |  10  |  11  |  12
```

SKILLBUILDING

B. DIAGNOSTIC PRACTICE: SYMBOLS AND PUNCTUATION

If you are not using the GDP software, turn to page SB-2 and follow the directions for this activity.

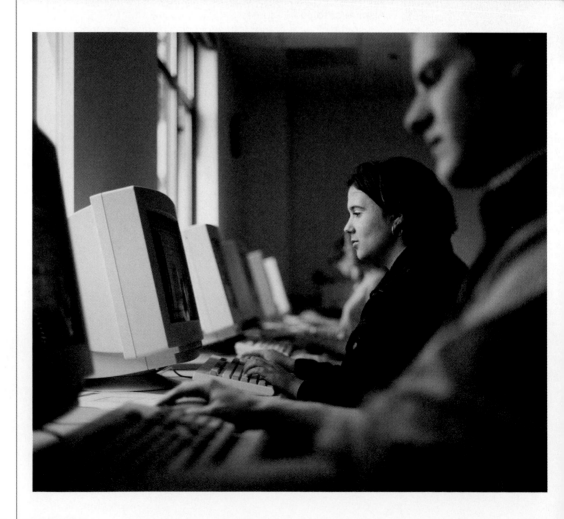

C. Take two 5-minute timed writings. Review your speed and errors.

Goal: At least 39wpm/5'/5e

C. 5-MINUTE TIMED WRITING

```
 4       In the past, typing was a skill that was used only by    11
 5   those who were secretaries, students, and office workers.    23
 6   High school students who were in school with plans for       34
 7   going on took a typing class so that they could type their   45
 8   work with ease and skill. Often students who wanted to be    57
 9   hired for office jobs would make a plan to take advanced      68
10   courses in typing.                                           72
11       As prices drop and as we have more and more advances     83
12   in technology of all types, people are recognizing that      94
13   they need keyboarding skills. From the top executive to the  106
14   customer service representative, everyone needs to be able   118
15   to use a computer keyboard. Workers in almost any kind of    130
16   business use their keyboarding skills to perform their       141
17   daily tasks.                                                 143
18       Employers are looking for skilled workers who type       154
19   with consistent speed and accuracy. People who can type      165
20   documents accurately and enter data quickly are needed for   177
21   many types of careers. Skills in keyboarding are important   188
22   assets for several types of jobs.                            195
     | 1 | 2 | 3 | 4 | 5 | 6 | 7 | 8 | 9 | 10 | 11 | 12
```

FORMATTING

D. FOLLOW-UP LETTERS

As soon as possible after your interview (preferably the next day), you should send a follow-up letter to the person who conducted your interview. In the letter you should:

- Use a positive tone.
- Thank the person who conducted the interview.
- Mention some specific information you learned during the interview.
- Highlight your particular strengths.
- Restate your interest in working for that organization and mention that you look forward to a favorable decision.

Correspondence 54-38

Personal-Business Letter in Block Style

September 12, 20-- | Ms. Carole Rothchild | Personnel Director | Arlington Communications | 2403 Sunset Lane | Arlington, TX 76015-3148 | Dear Ms. Rothchild: ¶ It was a real pleasure meeting with you yesterday and learning of the wonderful career opportunities at Arlington Communications. I enjoyed meeting all the people, especially those working in the Publications Division. Thank you for taking the time to tell me about the interesting start-up history of the company and its location in Arlington.

¶ I believe my experience and job skills match nicely with those you are seeking for a desktop publishing individual, and this position is exactly what I have been looking for. You may recall that I have had experience with all of the equipment and software that are used in your office.

¶ Please let me hear from you when you have made your decision on this position. I am very much interested in joining the professional staff at Arlington Communications.

Sincerely yours, | Kenneth R. Diaz | 105 Royal Lane | Commerce, TX 75428

Correspondence 54-39

Personal-Business Letter in Modified-Block Style

April 7, 20-- | Ms. Kay Brewer, Personnel Director | Blanchard Computer Systems | 2189 Dace Avenue | Sioux City, IA 51107 | Dear Ms. Brewer: ¶ Thanks you for the opportunity of interviewing with Blanchard computer Systems yesterday. Please express my appreciation to all of those who were involved.

¶ The interview gave me a very good feeling about the company. The positive description that you shared me with convinced me that blanchard is indeed a company at which I would like to work. I was greatly impressed with the summary of social service programs for citizens throughout the community that are sponsored by Blanchard

(Continued on next page)

¶ You may recall that I have had experience with all of the equipment that is used. It appears to me that ^my strengths in ~~software~~ ^computer application soft ware ^and office systems would blend in well with your ~~company~~ profile.

¶ I look forward to hearing (you from) soon regarding you ^r decision on the position of data records operator.

Sincerely, | Arlene F. Jefferson | 1842 Amber Road | Wayne, NE 68787

Correspondence 54-40

Personal-Business Letter in Modified-Block Style

Open the file for Correspondence 54-39, and make the following changes:

- Change the date of the letter to August 7, 20--.
- Send the letter to Mr. William E. Takashi | Personnel Director | Hawkeye Computers, Inc. | 5604 Melrose Avenue | Sioux City, IA 51105.
- Replace "Blanchard Computer Systems" with Hawkeye Computers in both the first and the second paragraphs.
- Change "yesterday" in the first paragraph to August 5.
- Change the complimentary closing to Yours truly.
- Change "data records operator" to technology support assistant in the final paragraph.

Strategies for Career Success

Interview Thank-You Letter

Expressing your appreciation is a very important follow-up step in your job search. Send a thank-you letter or e-mail within 24 hours after your interview.

In the opening paragraph, thank the interviewer for taking time to meet with you. Make a positive statement about the company or interview feature (for example, meeting potential coworkers).

In the middle paragraph, close the sale. Address any qualifications you neglected to mention. Turn around an interview weakness (for example, reconsider your statement that you wouldn't travel). Strengthen your relationship with the interviewer (for example, refer the interviewer to a good article on a topic in which he or she expressed interest).

In the closing paragraph, ask to be notified when the decision is made. A thank-you letter ensures that your last impression is a positive one.

YOUR TURN After your next interview, send a thank-you letter that effectively closes the sale.

Integrated Employment Project

Goals

- Improve speed and accuracy
- Refine language arts skills in proofreading
- Format employment documents

A. Type 2 times.

A. WARMUP

```
1    Lex was quite pleased with his travel plans; the trip    11
2  to Bozeman was on Flight #578 on July 30, and the return is  23
3  on August 12 on Flight #643. The ticket will cost $1,090.    34
     | 1 | 2 | 3 | 4 | 5 | 6 | 7 | 8 | 9 | 10 | 11 | 12
```

SKILLBUILDING

B. Type the columns 2 times. Press TAB to move from column to column.

B. TECHNIQUE PRACTICE: TAB

```
4   J. Barnes       P. Varanth      S. Childers     M. Christenson
5   F. Gilsrud      J. Benson       D. Bates        M. Jordan
6   B. Harringer    J. Suksi        J. Lee          P. North
7   V. Hill         A. Budinger     T. Gonyer       S. Kravolec
```

C. PACED PRACTICE

If you are not using the GDP software, turn to page SB-14 and follow the directions for this activity.

LANGUAGE ARTS

D. Edit this paragraph to correct any typing or formatting errors.

D. PROOFREADING

```
8     The Smith were please to learn from their insurance
9   agent that the covrage ona $50,000 life insurance policy
10  policy would be increased by $ 20,000 at no extra cost.

11  The continued to pay the same premum, not knowing that the
12  cash value of there original policy was being taped each
13  month to pay an addition premium for hte new coverage.
```

In this unit you have learned how to prepare a resume, an application letter, and a follow-up letter—all of which are frequently used by job applicants. You will now use these skills in preparing the documents necessary to apply for the job described in the newspaper ad illustrated below.

Desktop Publisher

NetJobs, a worldwide leader in employment and job searches, has an immediate opening for a desktop publisher. This person will work in the ad production and Web page design office.

This is an entry-level position within the Advertising Department in our San Francisco office. Applicant must have experience in using Word, FrontPage, and PageMaker. Creative ability and typing skills are a must. Candidate must be able to work in a fast-paced team environment and be highly self-motivated.

Excellent company benefits are available, and they include a comprehensive medical and dental program, disability insurance, and a credit union.

If interested, send a letter of application and resume to:

Ms. Danielle E. Rose
HRM Department
NetJobs, Inc.
9350 Kramer Avenue
San Francisco, CA 94101

NetJobs Is an Equal Opportunity Employer

Report 55-31 ▶

Resume in Traditional Style

Prepare a resume for yourself as though you are applying for the job described in the ad above. Use actual data in the resume. Assume that you have just graduated from a postsecondary program. Include school-related activities, courses you have completed, and any part-time or full-time work experience you may have acquired. Make the resume as realistic as possible, and provide as much information as you can about your background.

Correspondence 55-41 ▶

Personal-Business Letter in Block Style

Prepare an application letter to apply for the position described in the ad. Date your letter March 10. Emphasize the skills you have acquired during your years in school and while working in any part-time or full-time positions. Use Correspondence 53-37 as a guide for your letter.

Assume that your interview was held on March 25 and that you would very much like to work for NetJobs. It is now the day after your interview. Prepare a follow-up letter expressing your positive thoughts about working for NetJobs. Use Correspondence 54-39 as a guide for your letter.

April 15, 20-- | Mr. Blair N. Scarborough | Wyatt Insurance Agency | 2834 International Blvd. | Fort Worth, TX 76390 | Dear Mr. Scarborough:

¶ My adviser, Dr. Bonnie Allworth, mentioned to me that you have an opening for a computer specialist in your Denton office. I would like to be considered as an applicant for that position.

¶ My extensive training and experience in using various software programs are ideal for the position you have open. As a student at Texas State University, I won two national awards in computer programming competition. Also, as my enclosed resume indicates, I have completed several computer courses that uniquely qualify me for the computer specialist position at Wyatt Insurance Agency.

¶ At Texas State University I took an active leadership role as president of the local chapter of Phi Beta Lambda. In my junior year I was treasurer of my campus fraternity, and during my senior year I was elected class president. These activities have provided me with valuable leadership and teamwork skills that I hope to demonstrate at Wyatt.

¶ I am very interested in working for Wyatt Insurance Company. I will telephone your office later this week to arrange an interview with you at your convenience. If you would like to speak to me prior to that time, please telephone me at my home number, 901-555-3203, after 5 p.m. or e-mail me at pmcclean@stu.edu.

Sincerely, | Pat R. McClean | 894 Cremans Avenue | Fort Worth, TX 76384 | Enclosure

Assume that you have interviewed for the position mentioned in the previous letter and that you would now like to send a follow-up letter dated June 15, 20--, to Mr. Blair N. Scarborough, thanking him for the interview. Use the inside address, salutation, and closing lines shown in Correspondence 55-43 to create the follow-up letter below:

¶ Thank you for the time you spent with me, telling me about the Computer Specialist position with Wyatt. My interview with you reafirmed my interest in working for Wyatt.

¶ I was very impresed with work done in your Information Processing department. The hardware and software you use for writing computer code and the people working in that department are very apealing to me.

¶ I believe my particular background and skills blend perfectly with this position. I hope to hear from you by the end of next week for a positive decision on my employment. Thank you again for bringing me in for the interview.

Strategies for Career Success

Looking for a Job

Don't waste time! Start your job search early. Scan the Help Wanted section in major Sunday newspapers for job descriptions and salaries. The Internet provides electronic access to worldwide job listings. If you are interested in a particular company, access its home page.

Ask a reference librarian for handbooks (for example, *Occupational Outlook Handbook*), government publications (for example, *Federal Career Opportunities*), and journals or magazines in your field. Visit your college placement office. Sign up for interviews with companies that visit your campus.

Talk with people in your field to get advice. Look for an internship or join a professional organization in your field. Attend local chapter meetings to network with people in your chosen profession.

Taking the initiative in your job search will pay off!

YOUR TURN Visit the Internet site for the *National Business Employment Weekly* at http://www.employmentguide.com, which provides more than 45,000 national and international job listings online.

Unit 12

Skillbuilding and In-Basket Review

LESSON 56
In-Basket Review (Insurance)

LESSON 57
In-Basket Review (Hospitality)

LESSON 58
In-Basket Review (Retail)

LESSON 59
In-Basket Review (Nonprofit)

LESSON 60
In-Basket Review (Manufacturing)

MEMO TO: Blanche O. Pruitt

FROM: Kevin Hite

DATE: January 11, 20--

SUBJECT: District Meetings

As you know, each year we rotate the location of our district meetings to one of our regional offices. This year our meeting will be held in your region, preferably in Albuquerque. Would you please contact the hotels in Albuquerque and select a suitable site for this year's meeting, which will be held on March 7 and 8.

We decided at our last meeting that this year's meeting would highlight our [...] want to focus on the following issues:

[...]esign to attract a higher percentage of the market?

[...]e procedures so that our order-processing routine is [...] visitor?

[...]age to encourage visitors to view a greater percentage

[...] arrangements for our meeting site. I look forward to

October 16, 20--

Mr. Brandon T. Wright
District Manager
206 South Rock Road
Wichita, KS 67210

Dear Mr. Wright:

Several of our service representatives have indicated [...] clients are becoming increasingly interested in the cr[...] insurance carriers. All-City has prided itself in years p[...] policyholders, and the service representatives have u[...] prospective customers. However, we want to be cert[...] are also shared with these potential policyholders.

Please be sure that your representatives share the fol[...] potential customers:

- Our claims are handled quickly and with a minim[...]
- Our ratio of number of policies to number of com[...]
- No disciplinary actions have been taken against A[...]

Please share this information with your service repres[...] information on our services is provided on our home [...] policyholders' use.

Sincerely,

Ellen B. Boldt
Executive Vice President

urs

September 15, 20--

Ms. Rolanda L. Farmer
203 Grand Avenue
Bozeman, MT 59715

Dear Ms. Farmer:

Your order for Internet service has been processed, and you can enjoy surfing the Web immediately! As a customer of Global Communications, a subsidiary of Disk Drives, Etc., you will enjoy several benefits:

1. You will receive 24/7 customer service when using our service hotline at 1-800-555-3888.

2. You will be protected by E-Protect, Global's virus protection software. This software is updated weekly, and you can download weekly updates at www.gc.net.

3. You will receive 10 Mbytes of Web page space.

4. You will receive automated credit card billing, as requested.

A complete listing of all our services is enclosed for your perusal.

Thank you for joining Global Communications. Please e-mail us at support@gc.net if you have any questions, or call us on our service hotline. We expect the coming months of providing Internet service to you to be a very enjoyable experience for both of us.

Sincerely,

Nancy Mendez
Sales and Marketing Director

jrt
Enclosure

In-Basket Review (Insurance)

Goals
- Type at least 40wpm/5′/5e
- Format insurance documents

A. Type 2 times.

A. WARMUP

```
1        Kyu Choi jumped at the opportunity to assume 40% of        11
2   the ownership of your restaurant. Alverox & Choi Chinese        22
3   Cuisine will be opening quite soon at 1528 Waysata Street.      34
    |  1  |  2  |  3  |  4  |  5  |  6  |  7  |  8  |  9  |  10  |  11  |  12
```

SKILLBUILDING

B. DIAGNOSTIC PRACTICE: NUMBERS

If you are not using the GDP software, turn to page SB-5 and follow the directions for this activity.

C. Take three 12-second timed writings on each line. The scale below the last line shows your wpm speed for a 12-second timed writing.

C. 12-SECOND SPEED SPRINTS

```
4   Kay Sue is on her way to that new show to take some photos.
5   Most of the ones who go may not be able to make it on time.
6   When they got to their seats, they were glad they had come.
7   Both men and women might take some of their pets with them.
    I I I I 5 I I I I 10 I I I I 15 I I I I 20 I I I I 25 I I I I 30 I I I I 35 I I I I 40 I I I I 45 I I I I 50 I I I I 55 I I I I 60
```

Keyboarding Connection

Creating an E-Mail Signature File

Creating a signature file saves you time and adds a personal touch to your e-mail messages! A signature file is a tag of information at the end of your e-mail. It may include your signature, a small graphic, your address, your phone number, or a quotation. The signature file appears on every e-mail message you send. Use the following guidelines to create a signature file.

Open your e-mail software. Open the menu item that allows you to create a signature file. Type the information you want to include in your signature file. Close the file.

YOUR TURN Create a signature file. Then address an e-mail to yourself. Type "Test" in the Subject box. In the body, type "This is a test of the signature file." Send the e-mail. Open the test e-mail and locate your signature file at the bottom of the e-mail message.

D. Take two 5-minute timed writings. Review your speed and errors.

Goal: At least 40wpm/5'/5e

D. 5-MINUTE TIMED WRITING

8	When you begin to think about a career, you should	10
9	assess your personal abilities and interests. Do you have a	22
10	natural aptitude in a certain area? Do you have special	34
11	interests or hobbies that you would like to develop into a	45
12	career? Do you enjoy working with other people, or do you	57
13	like to work on your own? Would you like to work in a large	69
14	office, or do you prefer to work outdoors? These questions	81
15	are important to consider when you think about your career.	93
16	Your quest to find the perfect career will be more	103
17	successful if you try to maximize the opportunities that	115
18	are available. For example, you might consider working with	127
19	an organization that offers you career counseling. A career	139
20	counselor is trained to help you determine your aptitudes	150
21	and interests. You may contact people who work in a career	162
22	that interests you and ask to shadow them on their jobs and	174
23	ask them questions. You might find an online service to	185
24	help you find a very interesting career that will meet each	197
25	of your goals.	200

| 1 | 2 | 3 | 4 | 5 | 6 | 7 | 8 | 9 | 10 | 11 | 12

DOCUMENT PROCESSING

Correspondence 56-45

Business Letter in Block Style

Situation: You are employed in the office of All-City Insurance of Columbia, Missouri. Their offices are located at 17 North Eighth Street, Columbia, MO 65201-7272. All-City handles auto, home, and life insurance coverage in Iowa, Kansas, and Missouri. You work for Ellen B. Boldt, executive vice president. Ms. Boldt prefers the letter in block style and *Sincerely* as the complimentary closing. Add your reference initials as appropriate.

October 16, 20-- | Mr. Brandon T. Wright | District Manager | 206 South Rock Road | Wichita, KS 67210 | Dear Mr. Wright:

¶ Several of our service representatives have indicated on our Web-site chat room that new clients are becoming increasingly interested in the criteria to consider when evaluating their insurance carriers. All-City has prided itself in years past on its reputable service record with its policyholders, and the service representatives have undoubtedly shared this record with prospective customers. However, we want to be certain that other characteristics about

(Continued on next page)

All-City are also shared with these potential policyholders.

¶ Please be sure that your representatives share the following service characteristics with potential customers:

• Our claims are handled quickly and with a minimum of "red tape."

• Our ratio of number of policies to number of complaints is the highest in the industry.

• No disciplinary actions have been taken against All-City in the past 50 years.

¶ Please share this information with your service representatives and inform them that updated information on our services is provided on our home page for their use or for their policyholders' use.

Reference Manual

Refer to page R-12C of the Reference Manual for information on formatting lists.

Provide suitable closing lines.

Correspondence 56-46

Memo

Ms. Boldt has dictated the following memo for you to transcribe. As you can see, there are several rough-draft changes that you will have to make to the memo.

MEMO TO: Sheila Parsons, Training Director

FROM: Ellen B. Boldt, Executive Vice President

DATE: October 17, 20--

SUBJECT: Training seminar

¶ Our new agent training seminar will be held on December 10, and we plan again this year as we have in the past to conduct separate sessions for auto and life insurance policies. You will be in charge of the auto insurance seminars, and Victor Samuels will conduct the life insurance seminars.

¶ I expect that this year's auto insurance seminars will present our 6 basic coverage areas using the latest presentation demo software for the following:

(Continued on next page)

Reference Manual

Refer to page R-12C of the Reference Manual for information on formatting lists.

- Bodily injury liability
- Medical payments or personal injury protection
- Property damage liability
- Collision
- Comprehensive
- Uninsured Motorist

We are the market leaders in bodily injury liability and property damage liability coverages. Therefore, you should plan to spend at least one-half of your presentation discussing our strengths in these coverages. You might want to include in your presentation the fact that our coverages in these areas have more than surpassed those of our competitors for the past 7 years, or so.

¶ Use Table 1, which is enclosed, to be sure that we explain the variety of discounts offered for Iowa, Kansas, and missouri.

urs | Enclosure

Table 56-17

Boxed Table

Prepare Table 56-17 on a full sheet of paper in correct table format as an enclosure for the memo to Ms. Parsons. Press ENTER to create the 1- and 2-line column headings, as shown, before automatically adjusting the table width.

DISCOUNT PROGRAMS (For Selected States)	
Available Discounts	**Discount Amount (%)**
Air Bag	Up to 8.5
Antitheft Device	Up to 18
Claims Cost Reduction	Up to 1.8
Driving Course	Up to 4.5
Good Driver	20
Good Student	Up to 16
Mature Driver	Up to 1.8
Multipolicy	2 up to 7
Multivehicle	Up to 25
New Driver	Up to 10
Select Professionals Program	4.5 up to 14

In-Basket Review (Hospitality)

Goals

- Improve speed and accuracy
- Refine language arts skills in number expression and in the use of the hyphen
- Format hospitality documents

A. Type 2 times.

A. WARMUP

```
 1        Dexter gave an ultimatum: Quit driving on the lawn or    11
 2   I will call the police. A fine of $100 (or even more) may     23
 3   be levied against Kyle, who lives at 2469 Zaine in Joplin.    34
     |  1  |  2  |  3  |  4  |  5  |  6  |  7  |  8  |  9  |  10  |  11  |  12
```

SKILLBUILDING

B. PROGRESSIVE PRACTICE: ALPHABET

If you are not using the GDP software, turn to page SB-7 and follow the directions for this activity.

C. PACED PRACTICE

If you are not using the GDP software, turn to page SB-14 and follow the directions for this activity.

LANGUAGE ARTS

D. Study the rules at the right.

D. NUMBER EXPRESSION AND HYPHENATION

RULE ▶

word

Spell out

- **A number used as the first word of a sentence.**
  Seventy-five people attended the conference in San Diego.
- **The shorter of two adjacent numbers.**
  We have ordered 3 two-pound cakes and one 5-pound cake for the reception.
- **The words *million* and *billion* in round numbers (do not use decimals with round numbers).**
  Not: A $5.00 ticket can win $28,000,000 in this month's lottery.

  But: A $5 ticket can win $28 million in this month's lottery.
- **Fractions.**
  Almost one-half of the audience responded to the question.

Note: When fractions and the numbers twenty-one through ninety-nine are spelled out, they should be hyphenated.

(Continued on next page)

Hyphenate compound numbers between twenty-one and ninety-nine and fractions that are expressed as words.

Twenty-nine recommendations were approved by at least three-fourths of the members.

Edit the sentences to correct any errors in number expression.

4 Seven investors were interested in buying 2 15-unit condos.
5 The purchase price for the buildings will be $3,000,000.00 each, which is 1/2 the total.
6 The computers were mailed in 5 40-pound boxes for 2/3 of the price paid yesterday.
7 Our food chain sold hamburgers for $3.00 each last year.
8 I can sell nearly one-half of all the tickets at the gate on November 13.
9 59 parking spaces are located within 1/2 mile of the city center.
10 We must place our mailing pieces in 8 twenty-pound bags for the mail clerk.
11 I don't believe more than 1/5 of the drivers have insurance.

DOCUMENT PROCESSING

Situation: Today is August 21, and you are employed in the office of Suite Retreat, a group of vacation resorts in Naples, Florida. Your employer, the general manager, is Mr. Aaron Hynes. Mr. Hynes is attending a meeting in Miami and has left the following jobs for you to complete. Press ENTER to create the 1- and 2-line column headings as displayed before automatically adjusting the table width.

Table
57-18 ▶
Open Table

SUITE RETREAT PROPERTIES
Selected Beach Rentals

Property	Rooms	Rental Rate In Season	Rental Rate Off Season
Carriage House	4	$3,500	$2,400
Naples Hideaway	5	2,750	2,100
Ocean Breeze	5	3,850	2,700
Princeton Palace	4	3,200	2,550
Seville Landings	6	4,250	3,100
The Vanderbilt	5	3,475	2,575
Westover Estates	6	5,250	4,150

August 21, 20-- | Mr. Leland Mott | 243 Worth Street | Raleigh, NC 27603 | Dear Mr. Mott:

¶ We were pleased to hear of your interest in renting one of our prime beach units in Naples, Florida. I have enclosed a listing of all our current properties in the Naples area. We have 14 two-bedroom rentals, 15 three-bedroom rentals, and 11 four-bedroom rentals. Five of our three-bedroom units have already been rented for this season; one-half of the other thirty-four units are still available.

¶ Let me review a few of the particulars of each unit with you. Our Carriage House and Naples Hideaway have Gulf Coast views and garage facilities. The Ocean Breeze and Princeton have lake views and tennis courts. The Seville, Vanderbilt, and Westover have a Gulf Coast view and a private golf course.

¶ If you plan to rent one of our units, please be sure to notify us by writing or by calling our toll-free number at 1-800-555-1348.

Sincerely, | Aaron Hynes | General Manager | urs | Enclosure | c: Theresa McDonald, Celeste Binghamton

Keyboarding Connection

Finding Business Information on the Internet

To begin research on a business-related topic, try one of the following sites:

Business Resources on the Web at www.cio.com/bookmark provides links to Cable News Network (CNN) Business News, the Wall Street Journal Money and Investing Update, and other news sources. It includes information about careers, Electronic Data Interchange (EDI) and the Internet, general business sources, training, marketing, and resources for entrepreneurs.

Business Administration Internet Resources at www.acad.sunytccc.edu/library /busman.htm provides links to news and financial market updates, the Securities and Exchange Commission (SEC), Thomas Register, U.S. Census Bureau, U.S. Economic and Labor Statistics, and World Bank reports.

Selected Business Resources on the Web at www.bls.gov provides information about marketing, finance, small business, business law, international business, stock markets, and a link to the Small Business Administration.

YOUR TURN Access one of the business information sites listed above and explore its offerings.

Mr. Hynes has recently purchased a fishing resort on Lake Okeechobee, Florida, and plans to open it on September 1. Type the following report and send it to the *Naples Press* so that it will appear in this Sunday's special *Travel and Tourism* section. Use a standard business format to prepare the report.

FISHING PARADISE SCHEDULED TO OPEN | Suite Retreat | Naples, Florida

¶ Suite Retreat is celebrating the grand opening of its newest fishing resort, Kamp Kellogg, located on the northwest corner of Lake Okeechobee, on the banks of the Kissimmee River.

GENERAL INFORMATION

¶ The following information will give you an overview of our policies and accommodations:

¶ **Reservations**. The reservation desk will open on September 1 to reserve your cabin at our beautiful resort. You can reach reservations via the Internet by logging on to our Web site at http://www.kampkellogg.com.

¶ **Accommodations.** Whether you're looking for deluxe accommodations or rustic surroundings, Kamp Kellogg has it all. You have a choice of rustic cabins nestled in the woods or large chalets overlooking Lake Okeechobee. If you enjoy an evening of relaxation, each cabin includes a gazebo, out near the water's edge, that is screened in for a perfect evening of comfort.

¶ **Amenities.** Your lodging choice includes full kitchens for those who want to do their own cooking, or you can order a full meal through our catering service. Each unit has a game room with a large-screen television, VCR, videotapes, and computer workstation with Internet connection. Outside the sliding glass door is a covered deck, equipped with a barbecue grill and hot tub.

LAKE OKEECHOBEE

¶ Lake Okeechobee lies geographically in the center of the state of Florida. The name "Okeechobee" was given to the lake by the Seminole Indians, and it means "big water." Lake Okeechobee is the largest freshwater lake in the United States occurring in one state. It is approximately 37 miles long and 30 miles wide, with an average depth of almost 10 feet. The lake produces more bass over 8 pounds than any other lake in the United States. It is famous for bass, crappie, and bluegill fishing. Several species of wildlife also thrive around the lake, such as the bald eagle, blue heron, egret, white ibis, sand hill crane, turkey, vulture, owl, alligator, bobcat, turkey, and panther.

PRICING INFORMATION

¶ We are offering a special introductory rate of $250 through November 1. This rate includes the following:
- Two-night stay for a family of four
- Two half days of fishing
- One USCG-licensed fishing guide
- Tackle and bait

¶ A full refund will be made if the fishing excursion is canceled because of inclement weather or failure of equipment (boat, trailer, or vehicle). If only a partial day of fishing is completed, one-half of the charges will be refunded.

Refer to **Reference Manual**

Refer to page R-12C of the Reference Manual for information on formatting lists.

word

word

word

- number

In-Basket Review (Retail)

Goals

- Type at least 40wpm/5'/5e
- Format retail documents

A. Type 2 times.

A. WARMUP

```
1        Do you think 1/3 of the contents of the five quart-    11
2   sized boxes would be about right? I do! If not, they can    22
3   adjust the portions by adding 6 or 7 gallons of warm water.  34
    | 1 | 2 | 3 | 4 | 5 | 6 | 7 | 8 | 9 | 10 | 11 | 12
```

SKILLBUILDING

B. DIAGNOSTIC PRACTICE: SYMBOLS AND PUNCTUATION

If you are not using the GDP software, turn to page SB-2 and follow the directions for this activity.

C. Type each line 2 times. Change every singular noun to a plural noun, and change every plural noun to a singular noun.

C. TECHNIQUE PRACTICE: CONCENTRATION

```
4   Debit the accounts. Balance your checkbook. Add the assets.
5   Take the discount. Send the statements. Compute the ratios.
6   Review the accounts. Credit the amounts. Figure the totals.
7   Prepare the statements. Send the catalog. Call the clients.
```

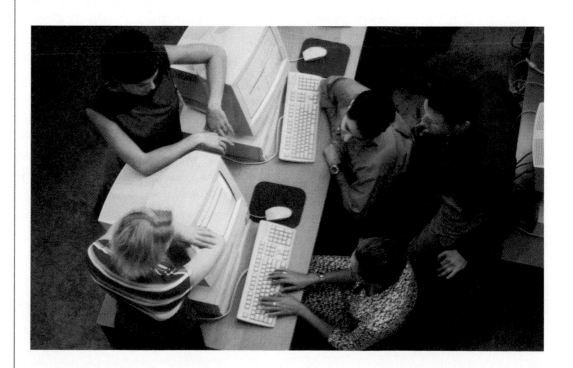

D. Take two 5-minute timed writings. Review your speed and errors.

Goal: At least 40wpm/5'/5e

D. 5-MINUTE TIMED WRITING

```
 8      Most workers will learn about their success on the job    11
 9   at least once a year. The person in charge will be the one    23
10   to conduct these reviews. Even though the job review is        34
11   important, either party might not look forward to such a       46
12   meeting. Frequently, an employee and a boss can view these     57
13   meetings as a time to discuss everything that this person      69
14   has done wrong in the last year. Such a negative approach      81
15   can add a lot of stress and tension between the employee       92
16   and management. In the long run, work performance suffers.    104
17      A good manager must learn a new way to conduct more        114
18   positive job reviews. Such a meeting might start by sizing    126
19   up what the employee has done to help improve things in the   138
20   past year. Positive comments may include coming to work on    150
21   time, working well with others, and being willing to pitch    162
22   in whenever needed. Next, the areas for improvement may be    174
23   discussed. Then the employee should be given the chance to    185
24   ask questions, write a response to the appraisal, and get     197
25   other feedback.                                                200
     | 1  | 2  | 3  | 4  | 5  | 6  | 7  | 8  | 9  | 10 | 11 | 12
```

DOCUMENT PROCESSING

Correspondence 58-48

Business Letter in Block Style

Situation: You are employed as an administrative assistant for Good Sports, a retailer for sports equipment and clothing in Denver, Colorado. Your employer is Mr. Kevin Hite, marketing director for Good Sports. Upon arriving at your office on Monday morning, you notice that Mr. Hite has left several jobs that need to be completed for his signature. He prefers a letter in block style in his correspondence and uses *Sincerely* as the complimentary closing.

January 10, 20-- | Mr. Alex R. Chaney, Principal | Madison Heights High School | 1839 East Colfax Avenue | Denver, CO 80212 | Dear Mr. Chaney: ¶ Thank you for your invitation to advertise on your school's Web site. We were delighted to have the opportunity to sponsor last week's Marathon Mile at Madison Heights High School and hope that all the participants enjoyed the competition and spectator activities.

¶ This week my office staff will be putting together a Web page that we would like to display on the Web space you have so generously provided. It is my understanding that the Web site will remain online throughout this school year. We will be certain to maintain it on a regular basis so that our products and prices always remain current.

(Continued on next page)

Add the closing lines to Mr. Hite's letter. Send copies of this letter to Ardele Stevens, Jennifer Smits, and Randall Campbellton.

¶ The Marathon Mile has certainly become one of the county's most popular school events. We look forward to the opportunity of cosponsoring next year's Marathon Mile at Madison Heights.

Correspondence 58-49 ▶

Memo

MEMO TO: Blanche O. Pruitt | **FROM:** Kevin Hite | **DATE:** January 11, 20-- | **SUBJECT:** District Meetings

¶ As you know, each year we rotate the location of our district meetings to one of our regional offices. This year our meeting will be held in your region, preferably in Albuquerque. Would you please contact the hotels in Albuquerque and select a suitable site for this year's meeting, which will be held on March 7 and 8.

¶ We decided at our last regional managers' meeting that this year's meeting would highlight our Internet sales campaign. Specifically, we want to focus on the following issues:

1. How can we improve our Web page design to attract a higher percentage of the market?
2. How can we improve our e-commerce procedures so that our order-processing routine is easier and faster for the average Web visitor?
3. What links can we add to our home page to encourage visitors to view a greater percentage of our product line?

¶ Please let me know when you have made arrangements for our meeting site. I look forward to meeting with all of you in March. | urs

Refer to Reference Manual

Refer to page R-12C of the Reference Manual for information on formatting lists.

Table 58-19 ▶

Boxed Table

WEEKLY BICYCLE SPECIALS January 13, 20--		
Model	**Price**	**Special Features**
Comanche	$270	15" Y-frame; 18-speed drivetrain; adjustable seat
Cyclone	375	Our lightest bike; preassembled; wired blue color
Duster	480	Front suspension fork; semislick tires; 24-speed
Trail Blazer	725	Titanium frame; aluminum seat post; two bottle mounts

In-Basket Review (Nonprofit)

Goals

- Improve speed and accuracy
- Refine language arts skills in spelling
- Format government documents

A. Type 2 times.

A. WARMUP

```
1      Crowne and Metzner, Inc., employees* joined with 68      11
2  youngsters to repair the brick homes of 13 elderly persons;  23
3  several became very well acquainted with six of the owners.   35
   |  1  |  2  |  3  |  4  |  5  |  6  |  7  |  8  |  9  |  10 |  11 |  12
```

SKILLBUILDING

B. MAP

Follow the GDP software directions for this exercise in improving keystroking accuracy.

C. Take a 1-minute timed writing on the first paragraph to establish your base speed. Then take four 1-minute timed writings on the remaining paragraphs. As soon as you equal or exceed your base speed on one paragraph, advance to the next, more difficult paragraph.

C. SUSTAINED PRACTICE: PUNCTUATION

```
4       The men in the warehouse were having a very difficult    11
5   time keeping track of that inventory. Things began to go     22
6   much more smoothly for them when they got the new computer.  34

7       Whenever something was shipped out, a computer entry     11
8   was made to show the changes. They always knew exactly what  23
9   merchandise was in stock; they also knew what to order.      34

10      Management was pleased with that improvement. "We        10
11  should have made the change years ago," said the supervisor  22
12  to the plant manager, who was in full agreement with him.    34

13      This is just one example (among many) of how the work    11
14  areas can be improved. Workers' suggestions are listened     22
15  to by alert, expert managers. Their jobs are better, too.    34
    |  1  |  2  |  3  |  4  |  5  |  6  |  7  |  8  |  9  |  10 |  11 |  12
```

D. Type this list of frequently misspelled words, paying special attention to any spelling problems in each word.

D. SPELLING

16 development determine enclosed complete members recent site
17 permanent personal facility medical library however purpose
18 representative implementation electrical discussed eligible
19 organization performance minimum discuss expense areas next
20 professional arrangements separate changes reason field pay

Edit the sentences to correct any misspellings.

21 Members of the medicle and profesional group discussed it.
22 The development of the seperate cite will be completed.
23 A recent represenative said the libary facility may be next.
24 A perpose of the electricle organization is to get changes.
25 However, the implimentation of changes will be permenant.
26 Arrangments for the enclosed eligable expenses are listed.

| 1 | 2 | 3 | 4 | 5 | 6 | 7 | 8 | 9 | 10 | 11 | 12

DOCUMENT PROCESSING

Situation: Today is October 10. You work for Quick Trip, a ride-share company located in Windsor, Connecticut.

Your company is a nonprofit commuter company that provides the following services: move people to and from work, conduct parking studies, match people with available rides, and publish a commuter ride-share weekly report.

Your job responsibilities include preparing reports that summarize weekly commuter news, typing correspondence to advertise and promote Quick Trip's services, and communicating with area commuters who subscribe to Quick Trip's services.

Today, you must (1) prepare a report that summarizes services offered by Quick Trip and (2) create a table that lists new additions to the weekly report.

Report 59-33

Business Report

QUICK TRIP
Windsor's Premier Ride- Share

¶ If you're tired of driving that one- to two-hour commute into Connecticut's busy metropolitan areas, then let us take that burden off your shoulders. Quick Trip, the metro's premier ride-share company, is a convenient, economical way to get to & from work. All you have to do is get on board!

(Continued on next page)

Costs of Commuting

¶ A recent article showed that commuting just 15 miles each way can cost a minimum of $1,200 per year; sharing the ride with some one else can cut your commuting expenses in half.[1] In addition to the cost of gas, you must also figure in other costs of transportation such as maintenance on your vehicle, insurance premiums, depreciation, and finance charges.[2] ~~When you consider all these costs, ride-sharing takes on a whole new significance.~~ You should also consider how you are helping the traffic congestion and air pollution problems by ride-sharing. And don't forget about the possibility of being involved in an accident. Finally you can reduce stress by ride-sharing because you can choose to leave the driving to someone else.

RESERVATIONS AND BENEFITS

¶ If you want to reserve a seat on a Quick Trip route, just call one of our professional service representatives at 1-800-555-Trip. Our representatives in the field have information on routes, schedules, rides availability, and other benefits. For example, we have an E-ride available for you if there is an emergency that requires you to get home immediately. Here are some special benefits with Quick Trip:

- A free commute for every 500 commuting miles.
- Separate insurance and medical coverage.
- Flexible payment policies.
- A free commute for every 500 commuting miles.
- Full insurance coverage.
- Flexible payment policies.
- 4 free taxi rides home per year in the event of illness or personal emergency.

SERVICE AREAS

¶ Quick Trip serves the cities of Plainville, Rocky Hill, Manchester, Windsor, New Haven, and Suffield. Next month we will open routes to Avon, Glastonbury,

(Continued on next page)

Refer to **Reference Manual**

Refer to page R-12C of the Reference Manual for information on formatting lists.

Durham, and Middletown. In all, we have over 300 regular routes state wide, and service is expanding monthly. Easy access is guaranteed with all our routes. To view our entire service area, go to our web site, http://www.qt.com, and link to the Quick Trip regional service map area. The map details all our routes, highlights specific pickup points, and identifies our regional service facilities. Visit our site today and become a ride-share enthusiast!

_____

[1] Erica Sommers, "Ride-Sharing for the Environment," *Environmental Planning*, February 21, 2004, p. 18.

[2] Joshua R. Blake, *Cleaning Up America*, New Haven Publishing, Manchester, Connecticut, 2005, p. 138.

Table 59-20
Boxed Table

QUICK TRIP COMMUTER BULLETIN For October			
From	To	Name	Telephone
Manchester	Rocky Hill	S. Baskin	860-555-5581
Manchester	Windsor	E. Lindholm	203-555-4684
Manchester	Suffield	P. Mack	860-555-4322
New Haven	Plainville	I. Thompson	203-555-1249
Rocky Hill	Windsor	J. Kiczuk	860-555-1842
Suffield	Manchester	M. Duprey	203-555-9339
Suffield	New Haven	B. Huehner	203-555-0442
Suffield	New Haven	M. Mac	203-555-1844
Windsor	Manchester	L. Smith	203-555-8893
Windsor	Rocky Hill	R. McCaffrey	203-555-7782

In-Basket Review (Manufacturing)

Goals

- Type at least 40wpm/5'/5e
- Format manufacturing documents

A. Type 2 times.

A. WARMUP

```
1      "Fay's #6 report shows 26 pens @ .49 each and 37 pens   11
2  @ .79 each," the CEO announced. Mrs. Bailey's reaction was   23
3  quite amazing as 80 jobs were validated with checked boxes.  35
   |  1  |  2  |  3  |  4  |  5  |  6  |  7  |  8  |  9  |  10  |  11  |  12
```

SKILLBUILDING

PPP PRETEST → PRACTICE → POSTTEST

PRETEST
Take a 1-minute timed writing. Review your speed and errors.

B. PRETEST: Close Reaches

```
4      Sally took the coins from the pocket of her blouse      10
5  and traded them for seventy different coins. Anyone could   22
6  see that Myrtle looked funny when extra coins were traded.  34
   |  1  |  2  |  3  |  4  |  5  |  6  |  7  |  8  |  9  |  10  |  11  |  12
```

PRACTICE
Speed Emphasis:
If you made 2 or fewer errors on the Pretest, type each *individual* line 2 times.
Accuracy Emphasis:
If you made 3 or more errors, type each *group* of lines (as though it were a paragraph) 2 times.

C. PRACTICE: Adjacent Keys

```
7  as asked asset based basis class least visas ease fast mass
8  we weary wedge weigh towel jewel fewer dwell wear weed week
9  rt birth dirty earth heart north alert worth dart port tort
```

D. PRACTICE: Consecutive Fingers

```
10  sw swamp swift swoop sweet swear swank swirl swap sway swim
11  gr grade grace angry agree group gross gripe grow gram grab
12  ol older olive solid extol spool fools stole bolt cold cool
```

POSTTEST
Repeat the Pretest timed writing and compare performance.

E. POSTTEST: Close Reaches

F. Take two 5-minute timed writings. Review your speed and errors.

Goal: At least 40wpm/5'/5e

F. 5-MINUTE TIMED WRITING

```
13        Information technology is among the fastest-growing      11
14   job fields today and is also one of the fields to change      22
15   the quickest. The goal of many schools is to try to prepare   34
16   students to be specialists in a workplace that continues to   46
17   be challenging and will need to change quickly as advances    58
18   are made in technology.                                       63
19        Those who wish to work in a field that will not stand    74
20   still need to know all about the systems with which they      85
21   labor. Network administrators, for example, will often take   97
22   courses to certify that they have a sound knowledge of any    109
23   of the new hardware. They must also learn about specific      120
24   equipment and have an understanding of how new software       131
25   will function with hardware.                                  137
26        Those who wish to pass certification exams must have     148
27   the zeal, determination, and drive to complete all of the     160
28   requirements. They know that it will not be long before the   172
29   current systems will be upgraded or new software will be      183
30   released. They need to learn the latest systems and review    195
31   their certification again.                                    200

     |  1  |  2  |  3  |  4  |  5  |  6  |  7  |  8  |  9  |  10  |  11  |  12
```

DOCUMENT PROCESSING

Correspondence ▶ 60-50

Business Letter in Block Style

Situation: You are an administrative assistant, and you work for Disk Drives, Etc., in Phoenix, Arizona. Your supervisor is Ms. Nancy Mendez, sales and marketing director. Ms. Mendez has asked you to prepare the following documents for her while she is in a staff meeting this morning. The letter is to be prepared for her signature, the table will be enclosed with the letter, and she will initial the memo before sending it out this afternoon.

September 13, 20-- | Ms. Nancy Luo | 1387 Rim Drive | Flagstaff, AZ 86001-3111 | Dear Ms. Luo:
¶ We were pleased to see that you have used our Web site at www.tosabi.com to inquire about our online catalog. We specialize in computer drives of all types: CD-ROM, DVD, Zip, Jaz, floppy, and hard drives. I have enclosed a listing of our most popular CD-ROM writers that will appear online next week in our catalog. As a new customer, you are invited to visit our catalog and place your order at these special prices.

(Continued on next page)

¶ Our online customers receive the same privileges as our hard-copy catalog shoppers. These online privileges include:

- No shipping charges.
- Toll-free customer support line.
- Discounts on 10 or more purchases.
- Ninety-day warranties (parts and labor) on all purchases.

¶ We look forward to many years of doing business with you. Please e-mail me at nmendez@tosabi.net if you have any questions or would like additional information.

Sincerely, | Nancy Mendez | Sales and Marketing Director | urs | Enclosure | c: S. Choi, W. Matson

Table 60-21

Boxed Table

Your finished table will have different line endings for Column D when you resize the column widths to fit the contents.

CD-ROM WRITERS (Effective Dates September 18-23)			
Model No.	**Part No.**	**Price**	**Specifications**
460RW	841120	$199	4x speed write, 16x speed read, CD recording software
2600E	841111	235	4x speed write, 24x speed read, 4x speed rewrite, stores up to 650 MB per disk
9282E	841415	415	Rewritable. 4x speed write, 8x speed read, Direct CD software
8428S	842013	595	Rewritable. 8x speed write, 24x speed read, 2x speed erase, Direct CD software
93422R	841712	658	Rewritable. 4x speed write, 6x speed read, 2x speed rewrite, Direct CD software, CDR-DJ

Correspondence 60-51

Memo

MEMO TO: Claudia Crenshaw | Publications Department | **FROM:** Nancy Mendez | Sales and Marketing Director | **DATE:** September 13, 20-- | **SUBJECT:** Ad in the *Arizona Daily Sun*

¶ Claudia, please include the following criteria in our ad that will run in the *Arizona Daily Sun* this Sunday:

1. Quarter-page ad
2. Run-time: 2 weeks
3. Location: Business Section as well as Classified Section
4. Contact: Include telephone, fax, and e-mail numbers

¶ This is our first ad piece in the *Sun* since we ran that special promotion last March. Let's add some graphics to make this one an "eye-catcher." | urs

Reference Manual

Refer to page R-12C of
the Reference Manual for
information on formatting
lists.

September 15, 20-- | Ms. Rolanda L. Farmer | 203 Grand Avenue | Bozeman, MT 59715 | Dear Ms. Farmer:

¶ Your order for Internet service has been processed, and you can enjoy surfing the Web immediately! As a customer of Global Communications, a subsidiary of Disk Drives, Etc., you will enjoy several benefits:

1. You will receive 24/7 customer service when using our service hotline at 1-800-555-3888.

2. You will be protected by E-Protect, Global's virus protection software. This software is updated weekly, and you can download weekly updates at www.gc.net.

3. You will receive 10 Mbytes of Web page space.

4. You will receive automated credit card billing, as requested.

¶ A complete listing of all our services is enclosed for your perusal.

¶ Thank you for joining Global Communications. Please e-mail us at support@gc.net if you have any questions, or call us on our service hotline. We expect the coming months of providing Internet service to you to be a very enjoyable experience for both of us. Sincerely, | Nancy Mendez | Sales and Marketing Director | urs | Enclosure

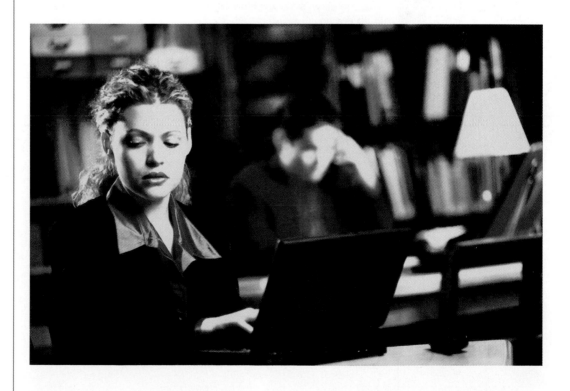

Table
60-22

Boxed Table

Progress and Proofreading Check

Documents designated as Proofreading Checks serve as a check of your proofreading skill. Your goal is to have zero typographical errors when the GDP software first scores the document.

(!) Your finished table will have different line endings for all columns when you resize the column widths to fit the contents.

CUSTOMER SERVICES (Effective October 1, 20--)		
Service	**Description/Comments**	**Representative**
24/7 Service	Call 1-800-555-3888; wait time is usually less than 1 minute.	M. R. Osumi, mrosumi@global.net
Virus-Protection Service	E-Protect software is down-loaded automatically to your computer when service is installed.	W. N. Gauthier, wngauth@global.net
Web Space	10 MB Web page space is standard; an additional 10 MB can be obtained on an as-needed basis.	M. J. Martinez, mjmartinez@global.net
Credit Card Billing	When requested by the customer, we automatically send your monthly bill to a credit card of your choice.	L. T. Matthews, ltmatt@global.net

Strategies for Career Success

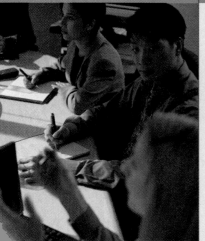

Successful Interviewing Techniques

The interview is a useful tool for researching information. Here are some steps to effective interviewing.

Conduct preliminary research so you can ask intelligent questions and make efficient use of the interview time. Prepare a list of questions (for example, an interview script) to use in the interview. Make sure the questions are open-ended, unbiased, and geared toward gathering insights you can't gain through reading. Be prepared to take notes, listen actively, and ask follow-up questions, as needed.

Greet the interviewee by name and thank him or her for taking time to talk with you. Explain why you are interested in interviewing him or her. Stay within the scheduled time limits. In closing the interview, thank the interviewee again, and ask if you can get in touch if other questions come to mind.

YOUR TURN Prepare a list of questions you might use in interviewing someone concerning the current U.S. immigration policies.

Skills Assessment on Part 3

```
 1        People are often the most prized assets in a business.    11
 2    Excellent firms know that having well-qualified workers is     23
 3    an important step to ensure the success of the company. The    35
 4    people in charge can play a huge part in how much success a    47
 5    firm will have when they provide a workplace that is meant     59
 6    to support teams of people who can work together to achieve    71
 7    a common goal. When people know they are being encouraged      82
 8    to work toward achieving their own goals as well as the        94
 9    goals of the company, they will respond by working to their   106
10    highest potential with ardor and zeal.                        113
11        Managers need to show that they value the hard work       124
12    and long hours that employees put in to ensure the success    136
13    of the business. People thrive on compliments that show       147
14    their work is appreciated. They like to be rewarded in some   159
15    way when they have done an exceptional job. When those in     171
16    charge are successful in motivating the employees to work     182
17    to their full potential, their company will prosper. The      194
18    result is that each person wins.                              200
```

| 1 | 2 | 3 | 4 | 5 | 6 | 7 | 8 | 9 | 10 | 11 | 12

**Correspondence
Test 3-53**

Business Letter in
Block Style

(!) Add an envelope
to the letter, and
omit the return
address.

July 13, 20-- | Mr. Anthony Gillespie | Goddard Properties | 1808 Augusta Court | Lexington, KY 40505-2838 | Dear Mr. Gillespie:

¶ Let me introduce myself. I am committee chair of a group that monitors development projects in Lexington, Kentucky. It was brought to my attention that your proposal to construct 100 three- and four-bedroom homes was approved by the city council last night. As a resident in a neighboring community, I wish to share with you the stipulations

(Continued on next page)

we would like you to incorporate into your development project:

- *The new homes should have no less than 2,700 square feet of living space.*
- *All structures should have brick frontage.*
- *No external, unattached buildings should be constructed.*

¶ Following these stipulations will ensure that your homes adhere to our community building codes. Sincerely, | Dora H. Hayes | Committee Chair | urs | c: S. Benefield, T. Grace

MEMO TO: Ana Pacheco
FROM: Liang Quan
DATE: June 26, 20--
SUBJECT: Desktop Publishing Certificate

¶ Our DTP certificate seminar will be held in St. Louis on August 14. Upon request of last year's participants, we want to be sure to include the following topics:

- Integrated Computer Applications
- Advanced Desktop Publishing
- Introduction to Computer Graphics
- Graphic Design A and B

¶ These were the four most popular topics at last year's seminar. Let's use a brochure design similar to the one we used at the Denver meeting last year. A copy of that brochure is attached for you to review. | urs | Attachment

AIR POLLUTION

¶ When we hear about pollution, we tend to think of smog, traffic congestion, acid rain, and other pollutant-related terms. However, we also need to consider the air we breathe as we work.

AIR QUALITY AND POLLUTANTS

¶ We need to be concerned about indoor air because it can affect the health, comfort, and productivity of workers.[1]

¶ **Strategies to Improve Air Quality.** The three basic approaches to improving air quality include the use of air pressure to keep the pollutants "at bay," the use of ventilation systems to remove the pollutants, and the use of filters to clean the air. The pollutants can appear in various forms but are typically biological contaminants, chemical pollutants, or particles.

¶ **Pollutant Descriptions.** Biological contaminants can include viruses, molds, bacteria, dust mites, pollen, and water spills. These contaminants cause allergic reactions that trigger asthma attacks for an estimated 16 million Americans.[2] Chemical pollutants include tobacco smoke and accidental chemical spills. Particles include such pollutants as dust and dirt from drywall, carpets, copying machines, and printing operations.[3]

MANAGERS' RESPONSIBILITIES

¶ Office managers should help by reviewing records pertaining to air conditioning and ventilation systems. They should also provide training sessions for employees to learn about maintaining clean air. Finally, they should keep a record of reported health complaints related to polluted air and aid in resolving these complaints.

AIR QUALITY IS A TEAM EFFORT

¶ All workers can have a positive impact on improving the quality of the air they breathe. For example, simply making sure that air vents and grilles are not blocked will help improve the quality of air. People who smoke should do so only in areas designated for smoking.

---

[1] Karen Scheid, "Pollution at Work," *Los Angeles Times*, May 4, 2004, p. C8.
[2] "Dirty Air in Today's Offices," March 12, 2004, <http://www.airamerica. com/dirty.htm>, accessed on May 13, 2004.
[3] Carlos Sanchez, *Pollutants in America*, Southwest Press, Albuquerque, 2003.

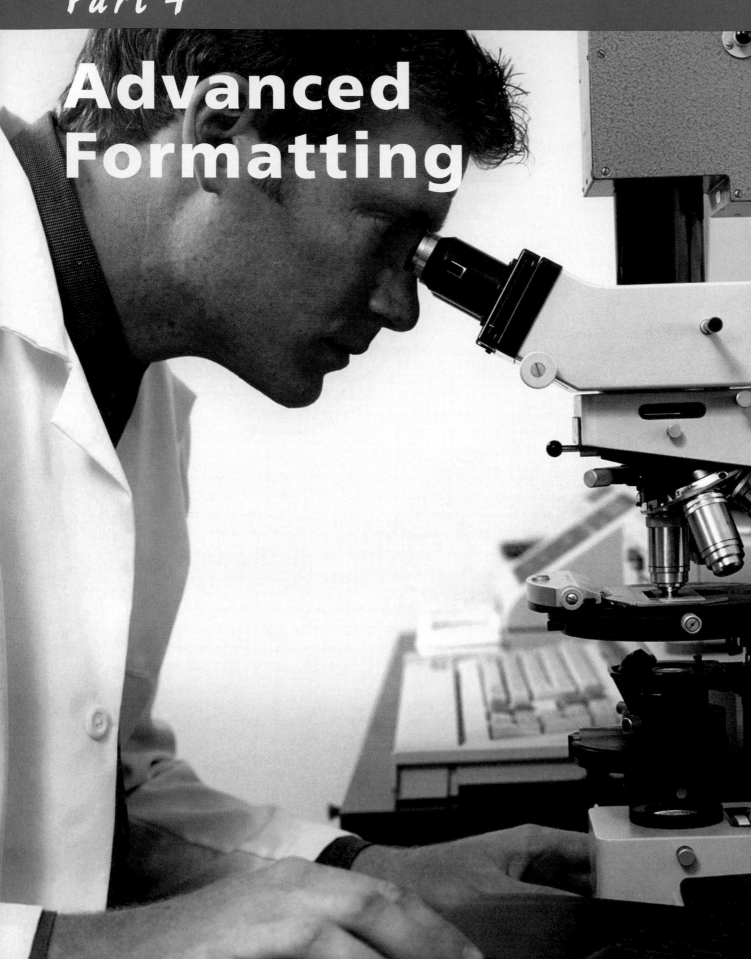

Part 4

Advanced Formatting

Keyboarding in Health Services

Within the health services job cluster, there is an enormous range of job opportunities in the medical and health care industry. Hundreds of different occupations exist in health care practice, including business-oriented positions. In fact, career opportunities within this cluster are among the fastest growing in the national marketplace. The current job outlook is quite positive because the growth in managed care has significantly increased opportunities for doctors and other health professionals, particularly in the area of preventive care. In addition, the aging population requires more highly skilled medical workers.

Opportunities in Health Careers

Consider health care jobs, medical careers, health care management, and medical management. Various job possibilities exist in these areas, and work as a medical transcriber, clinical technician, nurse, medical analyst, surgical technician or surgeon, physical therapist, orderly, pharmacist, or medical researcher can most likely be easily found. Interestingly, keyboarding skill is important for all of these positions.

Objectives

KEYBOARDING

- Type at least 43 words per minute on a 5-minute timed writing with no more than 5 errors.

LANGUAGE ARTS

- Refine proofreading skills and correctly use proofreaders' marks.
- Use capitals, punctuation, and grammar correctly.
- Improve composing and spelling skills.
- Recognize subject/verb agreement.

WORD PROCESSING

- Use the word processing commands necessary to complete the document processing activities.

DOCUMENT PROCESSING

- Format reports, multipage letters, multipage memos, and tables.

TECHNICAL

- Answer at least 90 percent of the questions correctly on an objective test.

Unit 13

Skill Refinement

LESSON 61
Skillbuilding and Report Review

LESSON 62
Skillbuilding and Letter Review

LESSON 63
Skillbuilding, Memo, and E-Mail Review

LESSON 64
Skillbuilding and Table Review

LESSON 65
Skillbuilding and Employment Document Review

2

delegate responsibilities, to be fair with subordinates, and to be consistent.[2] However, Zander also discusses communications, human relations, and a sense of humor as special skills that a leader *should* possess. These skills are often acquired on the job with the assistance of mentors within the firm.

PROBLEM SOLVING

Dealing with problems is a delicate business. On the one hand, leaders do not want to anger anyone, especially union personnel, by being too harsh. On the other hand, they must confront problems head-on. Leaders should first make a special effort to identify clearly the *real* problem. Second, they should pinpoint the individual factors that may be causing the problem. Finally, they should take definite steps to correct the problem.

LEADERSHIP SKILLS NEEDED IN BUSINESS

Sally Rodriguez

Leadership skills are needed now more than ever in business and industry if our nation is to maintain a leading role in the business world of tomorrow. With the advent of a common European community without boundaries, the Asian influence throughout the world, and the development of a common North American business community, we must have leaders with vision and the appropriate skills for meeting the challenges of the new, very technical century.

Each of the new skills that a successful leader needs is discussed in the following pages.

LEADERSHIP

Leadership has been defined in a variety of way individual when he or she is directing the activities of a

A successful leader is one who is committed to services, for improving the firm's market position, and ees. A leader possesses a value system that is ethically

SKILLS THAT A LEADER NEEDS

A good leader must have the prerequisite skills Many textbook and business journal writers have used Zander lists such skills as being critical to success as a l

---

[1] Judith R. Gordon, *A Diagnostic Approach to Organizational Beha* 393.

ed., McGraw-Hill/Irwin, New York, 2002, pp.274-275.

MEMO TO: Frank Janowicz, Ticket Manager

FROM: Sam Steele, Executive Director

DATE: March 1, 20--

SUBJECT: Ticket Sales Campaign

We tentatively have scheduled 114 concerts for Orchestra Hall for the calendar year beginning September 1, 20--. The attached list shows the new season ticket prices for the main floor, mezzanine, balcony, and gallery.

These prices are grouped in 11 different concert categories, which reflect the varied classical tastes of our patrons. These groupings also consider preferences for day of the week, time of day, and season of the year.

Please see me at 3 p.m. on March 10 so that we can review our ticket sales campaign. Last year's season ticket holders have had ample time to renew their subscriptions; we must now concentrate on attracting new season subscribers. I shall look forward to reviewing your plans on the tenth.

lpu
Attachment

Skillbuilding and Report Review

Goals

- Improve speed and accuracy
- Refine language arts skills in the use of commas
- Format reports

A. Type 2 times.

A. WARMUP

```
1        A queen quickly adjusted 12 blinds as the bright sun    11
2    blazed down from the sky; she then paced through the 19     22
3    rooms (all very large) next to the castle for 38 minutes.   33
     |  1  |  2  |  3  |  4  |  5  |  6  |  7  |  8  |  9  |  10  |  11  |  12
```

SKILLBUILDING

B. Take three 12-second timed writings on each line. The scale below the last line shows your wpm speed for a 12-second timed writing.

B. 12-SECOND SPEED SPRINTS

```
4    Most of those autos on the road had only one or two people.
5    Those boys and girls did the right thing by doing the work.
6    Some of the men ran to the gym to work out with their kids.
7    All of the new male workers were given a tour of the plant.
     I I I I 5 I I I 10 I I I 15 I I I 20 I I I 25 I I I 30 I I I 35 I I I 40 I I I 45 I I I 50 I I I 55 I I I 60
```

C. DIAGNOSTIC PRACTICE: SYMBOLS AND PUNCTUATION

If you are not using the GDP software, turn to page SB-2 and follow the directions for this activity.

LANGUAGE ARTS

D. Study the rules at the right.

D. COMMAS

Note: The callout signals in the left margin indicate which language arts rule from this lesson has been applied.

RULE ▶
,series

The underlines call attention to a point in the sentence where a comma might mistakenly be inserted.

Use a comma between each item in a series of three or more.
> We need to order paper, toner, and font cartridges for the printer.
> They saved their work, exited their program, and turned off their computers when they finished.

Note: Do not use a comma after the last item in a series.

RULE ▶
,transitional expression

Use a comma before and after a transitional expression or independent comment.
> It is critical, therefore, that we finish the project on time.
> Our present projections, you must admit, are inadequate.
> *But:* You must admit our present projections are inadequate.

Note: Examples of transitional expressions and independent comments are *in addition to, therefore, however, on the other hand, as a matter of fact*, and *unfortunately*.

Edit the sentences to correct any errors in the use of the comma.

8 The lawyer the bank and the courthouse received copies.
9 The closing was delayed therefore for more than an hour.
10 The abstract deed and contract were all three in order.
11 Ms. Sperry's flight was delayed however for two hours.
12 Happily the drinks snacks and napkins arrived on time.
13 This offer I think will be unacceptable to the board.

DOCUMENT PROCESSING

Report ▶
61-35

Business Report

,transitional expression

The ¶ symbol indicates the start of a new paragraph. In a business report, paragraphs are blocked (not indented).

Word Processing Manual Review:

L. 21–24: *All*
L. 23: Bold
L. 26: Alignment and Font Size

Reference Manual

Review: R-8A: Business Report.

UTI EMPLOYEE TRAINING PROGRAMS

Asako Kudo, Training Coordinator

¶ Various training techniques are used in business and industry to ~~update~~ help employees acquire new skills, ~~and to assist them in acquiring new skills. It should be no surprise, therefore, that conscientious employees are eager to participate in training programs.~~ Some ~~of the various~~ effective techniques that United Transportation Inc. (UTI) uses in its training programs are ~~described below.~~ discussed in this report.

ON-THE-JOB TRAINING AND LECTURES

¶ Two of the most frequently used and highly effective training methods are on-the-job training and lectures.

¶ **On-the-Job Training.** On-the-job training saves time and money by enabling ~~permitting~~ individuals to train at the workplace. ~~This method lets~~ the trainer uses the workstation in place of a classroom. ~~While there are many benefits from this type of experience,~~ on-the-job training does require careful coordination to ensure that learning objectives are achieved.

¶ **Lectures.** Lectures are often used because they are a low-cost method of instruction ~~training.~~ Lectures, which require little action on the part of the trainer, may not be effective when introducing employees to new techniques and work programs.

CONFERENCES

¶ In ~~the~~ a conference, ~~method of instruction,~~ small groups of employees are taught by a ~~conference~~ director, manager, or outside consultant. ~~This method of instruction results in~~ Conferences provide considerable give-and-take, ~~between the director and the employees.~~ For learning to occur, the ~~director~~ trainer must be skilled in the use of interactive techniques.

(Continued on next page)

,series

DISTANCE EDUCATION

¶ A growing segment of UTI's training is now delivered on-line via the internet. Some of these courses, called distance education (DE), are designed and managed by UTI *itself*, but an increasing number are designed and managed ~~form~~ *by* independent vendors, such as educational institutions and management-consulting firms. These on-line courses are not only cost-effective, but also permit the trainee to complete the course at a time that is convenient for *him or her* ~~them~~.

¶ The UTI Training Department estimates that within five years, 80% or more of its training modules will be delivered on-line, at a projected annual cost savings of at least $575,000 ~~dollars~~.

Report 61-36

Academic Report

The ¶ symbol indicates the start of a new paragraph. In an academic report, paragraphs are indented.

Word Processing Manual Review:

L. 27: Page Numbering and Page Break
L. 29: Line Spacing
L. 35: Italic
L. 41: Footnotes

Reference Manual

Review: R-8C and R-8D: Academic Report

,series

,transitional expression

LEADERSHIP SKILLS NEEDED IN BUSINESS
Sally Rodriguez

¶ Leadership skills are needed now more than ever in business and industry if our nation is to maintain a leading role in the business world of tomorrow. With the advent of a common European community without boundaries, the Asian influence throughout the world, and the development of a common North American business community, we must have leaders with vision and the appropriate skills for meeting the challenges of the new, very technical century.

¶ Each of the new skills that a successful leader needs is discussed in the following pages.

LEADERSHIP

¶ Leadership has been defined in a variety of ways. One definition is "the behavior of an individual when he or she is directing the activities of a group toward a shared goal."[1]

¶ A successful leader is one who is committed to ideas—ideas for future products and services, for improving the firm's market position, and for the well-being of his or her employees. A leader possesses a value system that is ethically and morally sound. Leaders who make decisions affecting the firm, employees, and society have a set of beliefs that influence decision-making

SKILLS THAT A LEADER NEEDS

¶ A good leader must have the prerequisite skills if he or she is to be effective in business. Many textbook and business journal writers have used various terms to describe these skills. Zander lists such skills as being critical to success as a leader and identifies them as the ability to delegate responsibilities, to be fair with subordinates, and to be consistent.[2] However, Zander

(Continued on next page)

also discusses communication, human relations, and a sense of humor as special skills that a leader *should* possess. These skills are often acquired on the job with the assistance of mentors within the firm.

PROBLEM SOLVING

¶ Dealing with problems is a delicate business. On the one hand, leaders do not want to anger anyone, especially union personnel, by being too harsh. On the other hand, they must confront problems head-on. Leaders should first make a special effort to identify clearly the *real* problem. Second, they should pinpoint the individual factors that may be causing the problem. Finally, they should take definite steps to correct the problem.

[1] Judith R. Gordon, *A Diagnostic Approach to Organizational Behavior*, 2nd ed., Allyn and Bacon, Boston, 2002, p. 393.
[2] Raymond T. Zander, *Office Management Today*, 3rd ed., McGraw-Hill/Irwin, New York, 2002, pp. 274–275.

Report 61-37

Business Report

Open the file for Report 61-36 and make the following changes.

1. Change the report from academic style to business style.
2. Assume that Aaron Wojak wrote the report, and change the byline accordingly.
3. Delete the third paragraph. Note that this results in the elimination of the first footnote.
4. Add a fourth side heading, THE LEADER AS TEACHER. Then add the following paragraph:

   Those who are in leadership positions often assume that workers learn how to perform a job simply by doing it without guidance. The real leader plans well-structured orientation sessions for new workers and does the same for all workers whenever there is new technology to be learned or when there is a change in policy or procedure.

   (**Note:** If necessary, force a page break to prevent the new side heading from appearing at the bottom of the first page.)

5. Finally, add a footnote at the end of the paragraph you inserted in step 4:

   Ahmed Bazarak, "The Leader as Teacher," *The Manager's Newsletter*, July 18, 2004, pp. 14-17.

Skillbuilding and Letter Review

Goals

- Type at least 40wpm/5'/5e
- Format business letters and personal-business letters

A. Type 2 times.

A. WARMUP

```
1       Quist & Zenk's sales were exactly $247,650; but the    10
2   cost of goods sold was $174,280 (70.37%). The profit made   22
3   was small after other, extensive expenses were subtracted   34
    |  1  |  2  |  3  |  4  |  5  |  6  |  7  |  8  |  9  |  10  |  11  |  12
```

SKILLBUILDING

B. MAP

Follow the GDP software directions for this exercise in improving keystroking accuracy.

Strategies for Career Success

Corrective Feedback

Sometime in your career, you will give someone corrective feedback. You can use positive communication to do this and not appear to criticize the person.

Here are some things you should not do. Do not correct the person in front of others. Avoid giving feedback when you are angry. Stay away from personal comments (for example, "That idea will get us nowhere!"). Do not diminish a person's enthusiasm (for example, "We've never done that before, and we're not starting now.").

Here are some things you should do. Listen to the person's side of the situation. Express yourself in a positive way (for example, "You're getting much closer."). Be specific about what the person can do to correct the situation. Follow up within a short time and identify all progress.

YOUR TURN Think about the last time you received corrective feedback. Did the person giving you feedback use techniques to create a positive outcome?

C. 5-MINUTE TIMED WRITING

C. Take two 5-minute timed writings. Review your speed and errors.

Goal: At least 40wpm/5'/5e

```
 4    Digital photography has revolutionized the way we take   11
 5  pictures. A digital camera puts our photos in a format that  23
 6  makes them easy to print and share with others. Using a     34
 7  digital camera also has the advantage that we can quickly    46
 8  print out our photos and see the results of our efforts. We  58
 9  can also insert our photos into word processing documents,   70
10  send them by e-mail to our friends, or post them on the Web  82
11  where they can be viewed by all. We can even connect our     93
12  camera to a television set and have our images displayed in 105
13  a slide show presentation.                                  111
14    Another advantage of digital photography is that the     121
15  expense of developing your own photos is much less because  133
16  you do not have to buy many rolls of film, nor do you have  145
17  to have your photos developed by others. Also, your photos  157
18  can be edited if you do not like what you see. You can crop 169
19  the photo, adjust its color or contrast, take out red-eye   180
20  imperfections, and even add or delete elements from the     192
21  photo or from other photos you have taken.                  200
    | 1 | 2 | 3 | 4 | 5 | 6 | 7 | 8 | 9 | 10 | 11 | 12
```

DOCUMENT PROCESSING

Correspondence 62-55 ▶

Personal-Business Letter in Modified-Block Style

(!) The ¶ symbol indicates the start of a new paragraph. In a personal-business letter, paragraphs are blocked (not indented).

Refer to **Reference Manual**

Review: R-3D: Personal-Business Letter

October 1, 20-- | Dr. Anthony L. Robbins | 2345 South Main Street | Bowling Green, OH 43402 | Dear Anthony:

¶ Thank you for your letter of September 25, in which you inquired about my trip to New York City. Your letter brought back a lot of memories of those days when I was one of your students.

¶ I plan to leave on October 15 for a two-week business and vacation trip to the city. While at Columbia University, I will be conducting a workshop on the utilization of voice-activated equipment.

¶ My work at Columbia will be completed on October 22, after which I plan to attend a number of plays, visit the Metropolitan Museum of Art, and take one of the sightseeing tours of the city.

¶ If you and your wife would care to join me on October 22, please let me know. I would be most happy to make reservations at the hotel for you and to purchase theater tickets. Why don't you consider joining me in the "Big Apple."

Sincerely, | Bryan Goldberg | 320 South Summit Street | Toledo, OH 43604

Correspondence
62-56

Business Letter in
Modified-Block Style

Go To Word
Processing
Manual
Review:

L. 50: Ruler Tabs and Tab Set

Refer to Reference
Manual

Review: **R-3B:** Business
Letter in Modified-Block
Style

June 3, 20--

Director of Product Development

Hampton Associates, Inc.

830 Market St.

San Francisco, Ca 9410‾3̶-1925

Dear Director of Product Development:

¶ I recently read an article in <u>Business Week</u> *ital* concerning how computer buyers can make standards happen. It was a very interesting article. ¶*The article d* It indicates that if customers demand *standard* products standard when they purchase computers, participate in standard-setting groups, and band together with other customers, they will do better in the long run. Have you had customer groups ~~help~~ *assist* you or provide you with information on the adoption of more standards ~~such~~ ? *computer* *These standards include* as in the areas of industry wide interfaces, a mix and match of computer gear and programs, and building the best system for each application utilized?

¶ I would appreciate any data that you might furnish for me with *regard* ~~relationship~~ to customers and your firm working together to set past or future standards.

Sincerely yours,

Alice Karns

Vice President

urs

Correspondence
62-57

Business Letter
in Block Style

Go To Word
Processing
Manual
Review:

L. 33: Envelopes

Refer to Reference
Manual

Review pages **R-3A** and
R-6A of the Reference
Manual.

Revise Correspondence 62-56, making the following changes:

1. Change the letter to block style.
2. Change the date to June 5, 20--.
3. Send the letter to Ms. Heidi M. Fischer at Gramstad Brothers, Inc., located at 5417 Harbord Drive in Oakland, CA 94618.
4. Change the salutation.
5. Combine the second and third paragraphs into one paragraph.

6. Add the following text as a new third paragraph:

   Some of my colleagues and I would like to get involved with others in an effort to make desired changes. I am confident that there are others around the Bay area who feel the same way.

7. Prepare an envelope for the letter.

Skillbuilding, Memo, and E-Mail Review

Goals

- Improve speed and accuracy
- Refine language arts skills in composing paragraphs
- Format memos and an e-mail message

A. Type 2 times.

A. WARMUP

```
1        "When is the quarterly jury report due?" asked Glenn.      11
2   He had faxed forms* to 64 of the 135 prospective jurors.        22
3   Only about one dozen of 596 citizens could not be located.      34
    | 1 | 2 | 3 | 4 | 5 | 6 | 7 | 8 | 9 | 10 | 11 | 12
```

SKILLBUILDING

 PRETEST ➡ PRACTICE ➡ POSTTEST

PRETEST
Take a 1-minute timed writing. Review your speed and errors.

B. PRETEST: Discrimination Practice

```
4        The entire trip on a large train was better than we       11
5   had hoped. Polite police looked out for both the young and      23
6   old. One unit was outnumbered by herds of frolicking deer.      35
    | 1 | 2 | 3 | 4 | 5 | 6 | 7 | 8 | 9 | 10 | 11 | 12
```

PRACTICE
Speed Emphasis:
If you made no more than 1 error on the Pretest, type each *individual* line 2 times.
Accuracy Emphasis:
If you made 2 or more errors, type each *group* of lines (as though it were a paragraph) 2 times.

C. PRACTICE: Left Hand

```
7   rtr trip trot sport train alert courts assert tragic truest
8   asa mass salt usage cased cease astute dashed masked castle
9   rer rear rest overt rerun older before entire surest better
```

D. PRACTICE: Right Hand

```
10  mnm menu numb hymns unmet manly mental namely manner number
11  pop post coop opera pools opens polite proper police oppose
12  iui unit quit fruit suits built medium guided helium podium
```

POSTTEST
Repeat the Pretest timed writing and compare performance.

E. POSTTEST: Discrimination Practice

F. PACED PRACTICE

If you are not using the GDP software, turn to page SB-14 and follow the directions for this activity.

G. COMPOSING: PARAGRAPH

Read through the paragraphs in the 5-minute timed writing in Lesson 62. Compose a paragraph to include the type of operating system, application software, and utility programs loaded on the computers used in your keyboarding class.

DOCUMENT PROCESSING

Correspondence 63-58

Memo

Refer to Reference Manual

Review: R-4D: Memo

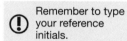

The ¶ symbol indicates the start of a new paragraph. In a memo, paragraphs are blocked (not indented).

Remember to type your reference initials.

MEMO TO: Frank Janowicz, Ticket Manager | **FROM**: Sam Steele, Executive Director | **DATE**: March 1, 20-- | **SUBJECT**: Ticket Sales Campaign

¶We tentatively have scheduled 114 concerts for Orchestra Hall for the calendar year beginning September 1, 20--. The attached list shows the new season ticket prices for the main floor, mezzanine, balcony, and gallery.

¶These prices are grouped in 11 different concert categories, which reflect the varied classical tastes of our patrons. These groupings also consider preferences for day of the week, time of day, and season of the year.

¶Please see me at 3 p.m. on March 10 so that we can review our ticket sales campaign. Last year's season ticket holders have had ample time to renew their subscriptions; we must now concentrate on attracting new season subscribers. I shall look forward to reviewing your plans on the tenth.

urs | Attachment

Correspondence 63-59

E-Mail Message

Refer to Reference Manual

Review: **R-5C**: E-mail Message in Internet Explorer, or **R-5D**: E-mail Message in Hotmail.

Type the e-mail greeting, body, closing, and signature below in correct format.

Greeting: Mr. Phillips:
Body: ¶ Please send information and prices on the security software you recently advertised in *PC Magazine*.
¶ We are interested in implementing a new security program for the personal computers in our main office and would like to study the specifications and features your system provides.
¶ Thank you for your assistance.
Closing: Charles

Signature: C. H. Cox
E-mail address: chcox@mailserver.net
Phone: 770-555-2843

MEMO TO: Edo Dorati, Cabaret pops Conductor
FROM: Sam Steele, Executive Director
DATE: March 2, 20--
Subject: Erving Berlin Concert

Our Patron Advisory Program Committtee recommends in its ~~their~~ attached letter that the Erving Berlin concert begin with some pre-World War I hits, followed by ~~music~~ songs from the '20s and '30s. Favorites from this era are hit songs from Music Box Review, Puttin' on The Ritz, and Follow the ~~the~~ Fleet. After the intermission the committee suggests songs from the '40s and '50s, hits from Annie get Your Gun, Call me Madam, Easter parade. A planning meeting has been scheduled for you, Dolly Carpenter (the Rehearsals Coordinator), and me on Mar. 9 at 10 A.M. at Orchestra Hall. I shall look forward to seeing you then.

urs

Attachment

c: Dolly Carpenter

MEMO TO: Dolly Carpenter, Rehearsals Coordinator
FROM: Sam Steele, Executive Director
DATE: March 3, 20--
SUBJECT: Summer Cabaret Pops Concerts

¶ We are pleased that you will be our rehearsals coordinator for this summer's Cabaret Pops concerts. The five biweekly concerts will run from June 13 through August 8.

¶ As the concert schedule is much lighter during the summer months, I am quite confident that you will be able to use the Orchestra Hall stage for all rehearsals. This is the preference of Edo Dorati, who will be the conductor for this year's Cabaret Pops concerts.

¶ I look forward to seeing you on June 1.

Skillbuilding and Table Review

Goals

- Type at least 40wpm/5'/5e
- Format tables

A. Type 2 times.

A. WARMUP

```
1    There were two big questions: (1) Would both have to      11
2  be present to pick up the license? and (2) Is a blood test  23
3  required? Jeff and Faye were quite dizzy with excitement.   34
   | 1 | 2 | 3 | 4 | 5 | 6 | 7 | 8 | 9 | 10 | 11 | 12
```

SKILLBUILDING

B. Take a 1-minute timed writing on the first paragraph to establish your base speed. Then take four 1-minute timed writings on the remaining paragraphs. As soon as you equal or exceed your base speed on one paragraph, advance to the next, more difficult paragraph.

B. SUSTAINED PRACTICE: ALTERNATE-HAND WORDS

```
4     The town council decided to shape its destiny when a     11
5  rich landowner lent a hand by proposing to chair the audit  23
6  committee. He will be a good chairman, and eight civic      34
7  club members will work to amend some troublesome policies.  46

8     One problem relates to the change in profit for many     11
9  of the firms in the city. As giant property taxes do not    22
10 relate to income, they wish to make those taxes go down.    33
11 The result means increases in their sales or income taxes.  45

12    All eight members of the town council now agree that     11
13 it is time to join with other cities throughout the state   23
14 in lobbying with the state legislature to bring about the   35
15 needed change. The right balance in taxes is the goal.      46

16    The mayor pointed out that it is not only business       10
17 property owners who would be affected. Homeowners should    22
18 see a decrease in property taxes, and renters might see     33
19 lower rents, as taxes on rental property would be lowered.  45
   | 1 | 2 | 3 | 4 | 5 | 6 | 7 | 8 | 9 | 10 | 11 | 12
```

C. Take two 5-minute timed writings. Review your speed and errors.

Goal: At least 40wpm/5'/5e

C. 5-MINUTE TIMED WRITING

20	The computer has changed the way you do things in the
21	office today. Jobs that used to take many hours to complete
22	now can be done in less time. A quick review of ways in
23	which your computer can help you streamline your work may
24	be in order.
25	Most software programs include helpful wizards that
26	can guide you through any project. You can use a stored
27	template, or you can create your own style. You do not need
28	to write your thoughts in longhand on paper before you type
29	them. Composing and revising documents as you type them
30	will save you lots of time.
31	Your computer is valuable for more than just writing
32	letters. Using different software applications, you can
33	create dazzling presentations for all to see. You can also
34	build databases for sorting and storing all types of data,
35	format spreadsheets, create your own calendar and colorful
36	charts, and perform calculations. You can even publish your
37	own newsletter and make business cards. It is exciting to
38	consider the ways you can use a computer.

| 1 | 2 | 3 | 4 | 5 | 6 | 7 | 8 | 9 | 10 | 11 | 12

Word count: 11, 23, 34, 49, 59, 70, 82, 94, 105, 111, 122, 133, 145, 156, 168, 180, 192, 200

DOCUMENT PROCESSING

Table 64-23 ▶

Boxed Table

Go To
Word Processing Manual Review:

L. 36: Table—Insert; Table—AutoFit to Contents
L. 37: Table—Merge Cells
L. 38: Table—Center Horizontally; Table—Center Page
L. 39: Table—Align Text in a Column

Refer to
Reference Manual

Review: R-13A: Boxed Table

$700 COMPOUNDED ANNUALLY FOR 7 YEARS AT 7 PERCENT		
Beginning of Year	**Interest**	**Value**
First	$00.00	$ 700.00
Second	49.00	749.00
Third	52.43	801.43
Fourth	56.10	857.53
Fifth	60.03	917.56
Sixth	64.23	981.79
Seventh	68.72	1,050.51
Eighth	78.68	1,129.19

Table
64-24

Open Table

Word Processing Manual Review:

L. 37: Table—Borders

Reference Manual

Review: R-13B: Open Table

1. Insert a table with 3 columns and 9 rows.
2. Merge the cells in Row 1, and center the title in all-caps, bold, and 14-point font. Press ENTER 1 time.
3. Center the subtitle in upper- and lower-case, bold, and 12-point font. Press ENTER 1 time.
4. Center and bold the column headings.
5. Type the information in the body of the table.
6. Automatically adjust the column widths.
7. Center the table horizontally and vertically.
8. Spell-check, preview, and proofread your table for spelling and formatting errors before printing it.

SALES CONFERENCES
All Sessions at Regional Offices

Date	City	Leader
October 7	Boston	D. G. Gorham
October 17	Baltimore	James B. Brunner
October 24	Miami	Becky Taylor
November 3	Dallas	Rodney R. Nordstein
November 10	Minneapolis	Joanne Miles-Tyrell
November 17	Denver	Becky Taylor
November 26	Los Angeles	Rodney R. Nordstein

Table
64-25

Ruled Table

Reference Manual

Review: R-13C: Ruled Table

SECOND HALF-YEAR SALES
Ending December 31, 20--

Month	Sales Quotas ($)	Actual Sales ($)
July	335,400	350,620
August	370,750	296,230
September	374,510	425,110
October	390,270	390,110
November	375,890	368,290
December	360,470	378,690
TOTAL	2,207,290	2,209,050

Skillbuilding and Employment Document Review

Goals

- Improve speed and accuracy
- Refine language arts skills in proofreading
- Format employment documents

A. Type 2 times.

A. WARMUP

```
1      Only 6 of the 18 competitors weighed more than 149#.     11
2   All Big Five matches were scheduled in Gym #3. Amazingly,   23
3   about 1/3 of the #1 Jaguars were picked to acquire titles.  35
    | 1 | 2 | 3 | 4 | 5 | 6 | 7 | 8 | 9 | 10 | 11 | 12
```

SKILLBUILDING

B. PROGRESSIVE PRACTICE: NUMBERS

If you are not using the GDP software, turn to page SB-11 and follow the directions for this activity.

C. TECHNIQUE PRACTICE: BACKSPACE KEY

Type each word as shown until you reach the backspace sign (←). Then backspace 1 time and replace the previously typed character with the one shown.

First Letter
Middle Letter
Last Letter

```
4   h←fall s←dash h←lead k←heel p←cage b←rare d←bark l←date t←sold
5   has←lf far←te mak←de roo←am do←ive fas←ce war←ve wee←ak yok←1k
6   sale←t they←m helm←d wall←k pals←e milk←d told←1 quip←t main←1
```

D. PROGRESSIVE PRACTICE: ALPHABET

If you are not using the GDP software, turn to page SB-7 and follow the directions for this activity.

LANGUAGE ARTS

E. Compare this paragraph with the fourth paragraph of Report 61-36 on page 217. Edit the paragraph to correct any errors.

E. PROOFREADING

```
7       A successful leader is one who is commited to ideas-
8    ideas for future product and services for improving the
9    firms market position, and for the wellbeing of his or her
10   employes. A leeder possesses a value system that is
11   ethicly and morally sound. leaders who make decisions
12   effecting the firm, employees, and society, have set of
13   beliefs that influence decision making.
```

Report 65-38

Traditional Resume

Word Processing Manual Review:

L. 51: Fonts

Reference Manual

Review: R-12A: Resume

Note: The table is shown with "View Gridlines" active.

1. Press ENTER 5 times.
2. Insert an open table with 2 columns and 5 rows.
3. Merge the cells in Row 1.
4. Change to center alignment.
5. Type the individual's name in Cambria Bold, all-caps, and 14-point font. Press ENTER 2 times.
6. Change to 12-point Cambria Bold, and type the street address, city, state, and ZIP Code. Press ENTER 1 time.
7. Type the phone number and e-mail address. Press ENTER 1 time.
8. Apply a bottom border to Row 1.
9. Move to Row 2, Column A. Press ENTER 1 time; then type the section heading in 12-point Calibri Bold, all-caps.
10. Move to Column B, press ENTER 1 time, and type the information pertaining to the section. Press ENTER 1 time after the final line in Row 2, Column B.
11. Move to Row 3, Column A, and type the second section heading. Then move to Column B, and type the corresponding information for this section. Press ENTER 1 time after the final line in Row 3, Column B.
12. Move to Row 4, and repeat steps 9 and 10 until all remaining sections have been completed. (Do not insert a hard return at the end of the references section information.)
13. Manually adjust the column widths as needed.

TIMOTHY J. ROBINSON

5816 Foxfire Road, Lawton, OK 73501
Phone: 405-555-3039; e-mail: trobinso@lcc.edu

EDUCATION	Lawton Community College, Lawton, Oklahoma Associate in Business degree, Office Systems, June 2003 Specialization in computer applications software (Microsoft Word, Excel, Access), business communication, and office systems management. Frederick High School, Frederick, Oklahoma Graduated: May 2001

EXPERIENCE	*Computer Systems Technician*, September 2001-Present
	Selkirk & Associates, Lawton, Oklahoma
	    Duties include installing and updating computer software programs throughout the firm.
	
	Secretary II, July 1999-August 2001 (part-time)
	Kittredge Insurance Agency, Frederick, Oklahoma
	    Duties included typing and word processing while reporting to the administrative assistant to the owner.

ACTIVITIES	College Choir, 2001-2003 Business Students Club, 2001-2003 (Secretary, 2002-2003) Varsity Basketball, 2001-2003 Intramural Soccer, 2001-2003
REFERENCES	Available upon request.

Correspondence 65-62 ▶

Application Letter
in Block Style

Reference
Manual

Review: R-12B:
Application Letter

March 10, 20-- | Mrs. Denise F. Klenzman | Director of Human Resources | Cole Enterprises | 3714 Crestmont Avenue | Norman, OK 73069 | Dear Mrs. Klenzman:

¶ Please consider me an applicant for the position of Computer Systems Coordinator with your firm. I became aware of the new position through a friend who is an employee at Cole Enterprises. I have been employed at Selkirk & Associates since graduating from high school in 2001. During this time I have also earned an assoc. in business degree at Lawton Community College. The resume enclosed shows that I have had several courses in computer application soft ware and office systems. I am confident that my educational background experience and my computer systems experience make me highly qualified for the position with your firm. You may call me for an interview at 405-555-3039 4572.

Sincerely yours, | Timothy J. Robinson | 5816 Foxfire Road | Lawton, OK 73501 | Enclosure

Progress and Proofreading Check ✓

Documents designated as Proofreading Checks serve as a check of your proofreading skill. Your goal is to have zero typographical errors when the GDP software first scores the document.

March 19, 20-- | Mrs. Denise F. Klenzman | Director of Human Resources | Cole Enterprises | 3714 Crestmont Avenue | Norman, OK 73069

Dear Mrs. Klenzman:

¶ Thank you for the opportunity to meet with you yesterday and to learn of the exciting career opportunities at Cole Enterprises. It was inspiring for me to learn about future plans for your forward-looking company.

¶ I am confident that my education and my experience qualify me in a special way for your position of computer systems coordinator. I am familiar with all of your present equipment and software.

¶ I would very much like to join the professional staff at Cole Enterprises. Please let me know when you have made your decision.

Sincerely yours, | Timothy J. Robinson | 5816 Foxfire Road | Lawton, OK 73501

Unit 14

Reports

LESSON 66
Itineraries

LESSON 67
Agendas and Minutes of Meetings

LESSON 68
Procedures Manual

LESSON 69
Reports Formatted in Columns

LESSON 70
Report Review

Presentation Software Guide   Cartwright Services, Page 2

FORMATTING SLIDES

Once you have written your presentation, you can place your key points on slides using presentation software. Follow these steps to prepare your presentation slides.

- Select a template or background that is appropriate for every slide.
- Select a layout such as text copy or bulleted or numbered lists.
- Use the edit, copy, and paste commands to add text to your presentation slides.

FORMATTING THE PRESENTATION

After you finish preparing the slides for your presentation, you may want to change the method by which each slide appears on the screen or the way individual points are displayed on the screen. In presentation software, moving from one slide to another is known as transition. Transition is accomplished by following these steps:

- Select the slides you want to control by the transition method.
- Select a transition method such as Cover Right or Wipe Left.
- Run through the slide show to determine whether or not you are satisfied with the transition.

Slide presentations can also be formatted so that each point you make on an individual slide appears individually on the screen. To structure your slides this way, follow these steps:

by a build effect.
Fly From Left.
to determine whether or not you are satisfied with the

CALIFORNIA PLANNING MEETING

Itinerary for Nancy Perkins

July 8-10, 20--

MONDAY, JULY 8

2:45 p.m.-4:05 p.m.   Flight from Houston to Los Angeles; United Flight 834; Seat 10C; nonstop

Marriott (310-555-1014) K late arrival guaranteed (Re

TUESDAY, JULY 9

10 a.m.-11:15 a.m.   Flight from Los Angeles to Seat 4A; nonstop

WEDNESDAY, JULY 10

7 p.m.-11:15 p.m.   Flight from Sacramento to nonstop; dinner

---

PERFORMING SUCCESSFULLY

Ginger Nichols

We have been involved in giving performances since our very early years. The most terrifying part of each performance was probably the fear that we would "freeze" when it came our turn to perform. Whenever we find ourselves in this predicament, the best thing to do is to accept that fear and to learn to let it work for us, not against us. We need to recognize that nervousness or fear may set in during our performance. Then, when it does happen (if it does), we will be ready to cope with it and overcome it.

If you forget some of your lines in a recitation, try to remember other lines and recite them. Doing so may help those forgotten lines to "pop back" into your memory so that you put them in at a later time, if possible.

You always want to leave your audience with the idea that you have given them something worthwhile that they can use or apply to their own lives. For maximum impact on your audience and to make sure that they remember what you say, use audiovisual aids to reinforce your message. Remember, however, that audiovisual aids are nothing more than aids. The real message should come in the words you choose when giving your presentation.

Study your speech well; even rehearse it if necessary. However, do not practice it to the extent that it appears that you are merely reading what is written down on the paper in front of you. Much of your personality should be exhibited while you are giving your speech. If you are an enthusiastic, friendly person who converses well with people face-to-face, then that same persona should be evident during your speech. A good piece of advice is to just go out there and be yourself—you will be much more comfortable by doing so, and your audience will relate to you better than if you try to exhibit a different personality when at the podium.

No matter how rapidly you speak in general, slow down when you are in front of a group. The fact that you are nervous can cause your speech rate to increase. The best way to slow down your speaking is to breathe deeply. Doing so also causes your nervous system to relax, allowing you to proceed with your speech calmly.

Finally, possibly the best advice for giving a successful speech is to be prepared. You will be more confident if you are thoroughly prepared. Do your research, rehearse your speech, and make notes about where you want to give emphasis or use an audiovisual aid.

Itineraries

Goals

- Type at least 41wpm/5′/5e
- Format itineraries

A. Type 2 times.

A. WARMUP

```
1      Had Phil been given a quiz on a subject that had been    11
2  reviewed by Max and Kay? Frank scored 89 on that quiz; Sue   23
3  scored 93 (*math only). Both tests were taken on 10/25/04.   35
   |  1  |  2  |  3  |  4  |  5  |  6  |  7  |  8  |  9  |  10  |  11  |  12
```

SKILLBUILDING

B. Take three 12-second timed writings on each line. The scale below the last line shows your wpm speed for a 12-second timed writing.

B. 12-SECOND SPEED SPRINTS

```
4  This is not the person who is my first choice for this job.
5  The day was bright as the sun shone on the clear blue lake.
6  All of you should take a long walk when the sun sets today.
7  This line has many easy words in it to type your very best.
   ' ' ' ' 5 ' ' ' 10 ' ' ' 15 ' ' ' 20 ' ' ' 25 ' ' ' 30 ' ' ' 35 ' ' ' 40 ' ' ' 45 ' ' ' 50 ' ' ' 55 ' ' ' 60
```

Keyboarding Connection

Observing Netiquette

Netiquette is proper conduct for e-mail users. It shows courtesy and professionalism and conveys a good impression of you and your company. Since e-mail is close to speech, it is the most informal of business documents.

Check your e-mail daily. Try to answer it the same day it arrives. Don't let it accumulate in your mailbox; you risk offending the sender. Use regular capitalization. All-caps indicate SHOUTING; all-lowercase letters convey immaturity. Most readers tolerate an infrequent typo, but if your message is filled with errors, you appear unprofessional. Use your spell-checker, and don't overwhelm people with unnecessary e-mails. Use discretion. Make sure the information is relevant to each e-mail recipient.

Be considerate. Be professional. Anything you write can wind up in your personnel file. E-mail that criticizes another person can be forwarded to him or her without your knowledge.

YOUR TURN   Review your next e-mail message for the use of netiquette.

C. PROGRESSIVE PRACTICE: ALPHABET

If you are not using the GDP software, turn to page SB-7 and follow the directions for this activity.

If you are not using the GDP software, turn to page SB-7 and follow the directions for this activity.

D. 5-MINUTE TIMED WRITING

D. Take two 5-minute timed writings. Review your speed and errors.

Goal: At least 41wpm/5'/5e

```
 8      Making a successful presentation to an audience is a      11
 9   skill that is absolutely essential in your career. The art   23
10   of speaking before a group requires planning and hard work.  35
11   Although different speakers prepare in much different ways,   47
12   a speaker should try to adhere to certain rules.             56
13      As the speaker, you are quite visible to people in the    68
14   audience. Therefore, you should always try to make a good    79
15   first impression. When you walk to the podium to speak, you  91
16   give the audience a chance to notice your neat appearance,   103
17   good posture, and confident manner. You will improve the    114
18   quality of your voice if you stand up straight and hold     126
19   your shoulders back and stomach in.                         133
20      As you talk, use your eyes, face, and hands to help      143
21   you connect with your listeners. Maintain eye contact by    155
22   just moving your eyes over the group without focusing on    166
23   any one person. Use hand movements and facial expressions   177
24   to convey meanings to your audience. By utilizing these     189
25   techniques, you will improve your speaking skills, and your 201
26   effort will be noted.                                       205
   | 1 | 2 | 3 | 4 | 5 | 6 | 7 | 8 | 9 | 10 | 11 | 12
```

FORMATTING

E. ITINERARIES

An itinerary is a proposed outline of a trip that provides a traveler with information such as flight times and numbers, meeting times, travel dates, and room reservations. An itinerary may also include notes of special interest to the traveler.

Report 66-39

Itinerary

Refer to **Reference Manual**

Review R-11C: Itinerary

1. Press ENTER 5 times to leave a 2-inch top margin.
2. Insert an open table with 2 columns and 10 rows.
3. Merge the cells in Row 1, and center the title in all-caps, bold, and 14-point font. Press ENTER 2 times.
4. Center the subtitle in upper- and lower-case, bold, and 12-point font. Press ENTER 2 times.
5. Center and bold the date. Press ENTER 1 time.
6. Move to Row 2, Column A, and type the date in all-caps; then press ENTER 1 time.
7. Move to Row 3, Column A, and type the time. Then move to Column B and type the corresponding information for this time. Press ENTER 1 time after the final line in Column B.
8. Move to Row 4 and repeat steps 6 and 7 until all dates, times, and entries have been completed. (Do not insert a hard return at the end of the final itinerary entry.)
9. Manually adjust the column widths as needed.

 Note: The table is shown with "View Gridlines" active.

↓5X

14 pt **PORTLAND SALES MEETING** ↓2X 12 pt **Itinerary for Arlene Gilsdorf** ↓2X **March 12-18, 20--** ↓1X	
THURSDAY, MARCH 12 ↓1X	
5:10 p.m.-5:55 p.m.	Flight from Detroit to Minneapolis; Northwest 83 (Phone: 800-555-1222); e-ticket; Seat 8D; nonstop ↓1X
6:30 p.m.-8:06 p.m.	Flight from Minneapolis to Portland; Northwest 2363; e-ticket; Seat 15C; nonstop; dinner ↓1X
SUNDAY, MARCH 15	
10:35 a.m.-12:22 p.m.	Flight from Portland to Los Angeles; United Airlines 360; e-ticket; Seat 15F; nonstop; breakfast
TUESDAY, MARCH 17	
8 a.m.-9:22 a.m.	Flight from San Francisco to Los Angeles; United Airlines 748; e-ticket; Seat 10D; nonstop; snack
WEDNESDAY, MARCH 18	
3:40 p.m.-5:50 p.m.	Flight from Los Angeles to Detroit; Southwest 327; e-ticket; Seat 17D; nonstop; snack

INTERCO SEMINAR
Itinerary for Mrs. Helen Kyslowsky
September 25-29, 20--

WEDNESDAY, SEPTEMBER 25

6:50 p.m. - 9:10 p.m.   *Flight from Columbus to Boston;*
America West 2053;
Seat 13 F; nonstop

FRIDAY, SEPTEMBER 27

9 a.m. - 10:17 a.m.   *Flight from Boston to New York City;*
US Airways 454; Seat 10 D; nonstop

SUNDAY, SEPTEMBER 29

2:07 p.m. - 4:18 p.m.   *Flight from New York City to Columbus;*
US Airways 324; Seat 9A; nonstop

CALIFORNIA PLANNING MEETING | **Itinerary for Nancy Perkins** | **July 8-10, 20--** | **MONDAY, JULY 8** | Leave at 2:45 p.m. and arrive at 4:05 p.m. Houston to Los Angeles; United Flight 834; Seat 10C; nonstop | Marriott (310-555-1014) King-sized bed; nonsmoking room; late arrival guaranteed (Reservation No. 45STX78) | **TUESDAY, JULY 9** | Leave at 10 a.m. and arrive at 11:15 a.m. Los Angeles to Sacramento; American Flight 206; Seat 4A; nonstop | **WEDNESDAY, JULY 10** | Leave at 7 p.m. and arrive at 11:15 p.m. Sacramento to Houston; United Flight 307; Seat 7B; nonstop; dinner

Agendas and Minutes of Meetings

Goals

- Improve speed and accuracy
- Refine language arts skills in the use of hyphens, abbreviations, and agreement
- Format agendas and minutes of meetings

A. Type 2 times.

A. WARMUP

```
1        Rex Yantz was calm before quitting his job at the zoo    11
2   on 7/10/03. On 8/23/03 he applied for a job at Vance &        22
3   Walton, "specialists" in corporate law and bankruptcies.      33
    |  1  |  2  |  3  |  4  |  5  |  6  |  7  |  8  |  9  |  10  |  11  |  12
```

SKILLBUILDING

B. DIAGNOSTIC PRACTICE: SYMBOLS AND PUNCTUATION

If you are not using the GDP software, turn to page SB-2 and follow the directions for this activity.

C. DIAGNOSTIC PRACTICE: NUMBERS

If you are not using the GDP software, turn to page SB-5 and follow the directions for this activity.

D. Type 2 times!

D. TECHNIQUE PRACTICE: SHIFT/CAPS LOCK

```
4        RHONDA KORDICH was promoted on APRIL 1 to SENIOR
5   SECRETARY. The SOLD sign replaced the FOR SALE sign at
6   1904 ELM DRIVE. The trip to DULUTH was on INTERSTATE 35.
```

LANGUAGE ARTS

E. Study the rules at the right.

E. HYPHENS

Note: The callout signals in the left margin indicate which language arts rule from this lesson has been applied.

RULE ▶

-compound adjective

The underline calls attention to a point in the sentence where a hyphen might mistakenly be inserted.

Hyphenate compound adjectives that come before a noun (unless the first word is an adverb ending in *-ly*).

We reviewed an up-to-date report on Wednesday.

But: The report was up to date.

But: We reviewed the highly rated report.

Note: A compound adjective is two or more words that function as a unit to describe a noun.

F. AGREEMENT

RULE ▶

agreement singular
agreement plural

Use singular verbs and pronouns with singular subjects; use plural verbs and pronouns with plural subjects.

I <u>was</u> happy with <u>my</u> performance.

<u>Janet and Phoenix</u> <u>were</u> happy with <u>their</u> performance.

Among the items discussed <u>were</u> our <u>raises and benefits</u>.

G. ABBREVIATIONS

RULE ▶

abbreviate none

In general business writing, do not abbreviate common words (such as *dept.* or *pkg.*), compass points, units of measure, or the names of months, days of the week, cities, or states (except in addresses).

Almost one-half of the audience indicated they were at least 5 feet 8 inches tall.

Note: Do not insert a comma between the parts of a single measurement.

Edit the sentences to correct any errors in grammar and mechanics.

7 The Queens visited Hickory to look at four bedroom homes.
8 Cindy Wallace has a part time job after school.
9 The accountants was extremely busy from March through April.
10 Lydia and Margaret were invited to present their report.
11 The portfolio include several technology stocks.
12 The planning committee will meet on Tue., Sept. 26.
13 Please credit the acct. for the amt. of $55.48.
14 The mgr. said the org. will move its headquarters to NC.

FORMATTING

H. AGENDAS

An agenda is a list of topics to be discussed at a meeting. It may also include a formal program of a meeting and consist of times, rooms, speakers, and other related information. Follow these steps to format an agenda:

1. Press ENTER 5 times to leave a 2-inch top margin.

2. Center and type the name of the company or committee in all-caps, bold, and 14-point font.

3. Press ENTER 2 times, and then center and type Meeting Agenda in upper- and lowercase, bold, and 12-point font.

4. Press ENTER 2 times, and then center and type the date in upper- and lowercase, bold, and 12-point font.

5. Press ENTER 2 times, change the line spacing to double, and turn off bold.

6. Type all the items in the agenda, and then highlight the items and apply a number format to them.

Remember to position the numbers at the left margin.

↓5X
14 pt **ALLIANCE CORPORATION STAFF MEETING** ↓2X

12 pt↓ **Meeting Agenda** ↓2X

November 17, 20-- ↓2X

1. Approval of minutes of October 15 meeting ↓2X

2. Progress reports of new district offices

3. Discussion of attendance at the National Hardware Association's meeting

4. Multimedia installation update: B. Harris

5. Annual fund drive: T. Henderson

I.   MINUTES OF MEETINGS

Minutes of a meeting are a record of items discussed during a meeting. To format meeting minutes, follow these steps:

1. Press ENTER 5 times to leave a 2-inch top margin.
2. Insert an open table with 2 columns and 6 rows.
3. Merge the cells in Row 1, and center the title in all-caps, bold, and 14-point font. Press ENTER 2 times.
4. Center Minutes of the Meeting in upper- and lowercase, bold, and 12-point font. Press ENTER 2 times.
5. Center the date; then press ENTER 1 time.
6. Move to Row 2, Column A; then type the first section heading, ATTENDANCE, in bold, all-caps.
7. Move to Column B, and type the information pertaining to the section. Press ENTER 1 time after the final line in all Column B entries.
8. Move to Row 3, Column A, and type the second section heading. Then move to Column B and type the corresponding information for this section. Press ENTER 1 time after the final line in Row 3, Column B.
9. Move to Row 4 and repeat steps 6 and 7 until all remaining sections have been completed.
10. Type the closing and signature lines in Column B of the final row. Remember to press ENTER 4 times to allow room for the signature. Do not press ENTER after typing the signature line.
11. Manually adjust the column widths as needed.

Note: The table is shown with "View Gridlines" active.

Word
Go To Processing
Manual

J.   WORD PROCESSING: HYPHENATION

Study Lesson 67 in your word processing manual. Complete all of the shaded steps while at your computer. Then format the jobs that follow.

Report 67-42
Agenda

Word Processing Manual Review:

Review: L. 28: Bullets and Numbering

Reference Manual

Review: R-11A: Meeting Agenda

↓5X

14 pt **ALLIANCE CORPORATION STAFF MEETING** ↓2X

12 pt↓ **Meeting Agenda** ↓2X

November 17, 20-- ↓2X

1. Approval of minutes of October 15 meeting ↓2X

2. Progress reports of new district offices

3. Discussion of attendance at the National Hardware Association's annual meeting

4. Multimedia installation update: B. Harris

5. Annual fund drive: T. Henderson

Report 67-43
Agenda

APEX MULTIMEDIA CORPORATION
Meeting Agenda
October 13, 20--

1. Call to order
2. Approval of minutes of September 10 meeting
3. Progress reports on Sherman contract
   (Julia Adams)
4. Upgrading of 8.0 presentation media
5. CD-ROM development program (Ray Sanchez)
6. Internet configuration (JoAnn Hubbard)
7. Adjournment

↓5X
14 pt **PLANNING COMMITTEE** ↓2X

12 pt↓ **Minutes of the Meeting** ↓2X

February 10, 20-- ↓1X

ATTENDANCE	The Planning Committee meeting was called to order at 1 p.m. on February 10, 20--, by Michelle North, chairperson. Members present were Cal Anderson, L. T. Braddock, Lisa Samson, Sharon Owens, and J. R. Stern. ↓1X
OLD BUSINESS	The committee reviewed bids for the purchase of a new computer for the Cheyenne office. We will accept the lower of two bids that have been submitted.
NEW BUSINESS	The committee reviewed a proposal for a new complex in Helena. After much discussion, the committee agreed to contact the Helena county clerk's office to get information on zoning ordinances.
ADJOURNMENT	The meeting was adjourned at 2:45 p.m. The next meeting is scheduled for March 22 in Room 16. ↓1X
	Respectfully submitted, ↓4X
	L. T. Braddock, Secretary

N
PERSONEL COMMITTEE
∧

Minutes of the Meeting

May 14, 20--

A
        special   on May 14, 20--,
ATTENDENCE   ∧meeting of the Personnel Committee was held∧in
                         All
the office of Mr. Cameron.∧Members (present) were

(Continued on next page)

except Richard Dixon, who was represented by Monica Zick man. The meeting was called to order at 2 p. m.

Old Business

A copy of the survey is attached. Eighty-eight employees participated in a survey that had been completed by Andrea Fields. The minutes of the last monthly meeting were read.

NEW BUSINESS

Ms. ~~Samuels~~ Daniels discussed the need for planning a campaign for job applicants, letting about vacancies, know that occur within the company. Frank Lundquist will draft a flyer to be sent to the Park view sentinel *ital*. Programs for the N P A convention to be held in Des Moines were distributed to all members. Each committee member ~~were~~ was asked to distribute copies to all employees in his or her department.

ADJOURN^MENT

The meeting was adjourned at 3:25 p.m. The next meeting has been scheduled for July 10 in the conference center.

Respectfully submitted,

Brandon Stinson, Secretary

Procedures Manual

Goals

- Type at least 41wpm/5'/5e
- Format a procedures manual

A. Type 2 times.

A. WARMUP

```
1      Zach sharpened the ax for Quinn just to help him win    10
2   the $100 tree-cutting event to be held in Kildeer on May 8   23
3   (if it doesn't rain). The prize will be $250--fantastic!    34
    |  1  |  2  |  3  |  4  |  5  |  6  |  7  |  8  |  9  |  10  |  11  |  12
```

SKILLBUILDING

B. MAP

Follow the GDP software directions for this exercise in improving keystroking accuracy.

C. Take two 5-minute timed writings. Review your speed and errors.

Goal: At least 41wpm/5'/5e

C. 5-MINUTE TIMED WRITING

```
 4       Taking photos with a digital camera is a process that    11
 5   is quite unique and very different from taking photos with    23
 6   film. Most digital cameras store images on a device such as   35
 7   a memory card or a memory stick. The number of photos you     46
 8   can store on a card or stick depends on how many megabytes    58
 9   it can hold. Once you reach the limit of the memory device,   70
10   you can store no new images until you either transfer or      82
11   delete the old ones to make room for new ones.                91
12       The advantages of using a memory device are many. For    102
13   example, the card or stick can be used over and over; or,    114
14   when the device is full, just simply remove it and put in a  126
15   new device. You can also move the images to the computer,    137
16   where they can reside on your hard drive for as long as you  149
17   want. If the memory card or stick you have does not have     161
18   enough memory, you can upgrade the megabyte size. Finally,   172
19   you can see instantly any images you have taken with the     184
20   camera. If you decide not to keep an image in the camera,    195
21   you can delete it to make room for other images.             205
     |  1  |  2  |  3  |  4  |  5  |  6  |  7  |  8  |  9  |  10  |  11  |  12
```

D. PROCEDURES MANUAL

Organizations often prepare procedures manuals to assist employees in identifying the steps or methods they must follow to accomplish particular tasks. To format a procedures manual:

1. Type the manual as a single-spaced report.
2. Place a header on every page except the first page. The header may include such items as the title of the manual (at the left margin) and the company name and page number (at the right margin).
3. Place a footer on every page including the first page. The footer should be in italics and may include the same information as the header, or it may identify the content of that page (for example, "Training Program").

Employees' Manual   Chandler Industries, Page 7

The purpose of this procedures manual is to assist managers who are responsible for developing training programs for new employees who have been hired in any of the seven regional branches of Chandler Industries. The basic content of this training program is outlined in the following paragraphs. ↓2X

INTRODUCTION ↓2X

This section identifies specific ways the manual should be used at Chandler Industries as well as the content of the manual. Answers are provided to the following questions: ↓2X

1. Where does the training manual fit within the training program?
2. For whom is the manual designed, and what does it contain?
3. How should the manual be used?
4. Can the manual be used in a classroom setting?
5. Can the manual be used as self-paced instructional material?
6. Can study guides accompany the manual? ↓2X

PROGRAM PHILOSOPHY AND GOALS ↓2X

This section describes the nature of the training program. The statements below provide the context for all courses within Chandler Industries. The focus of the section is as follows: ↓2X

• Why does this program exist, and who benefits from it?
• What company needs are satisfied by this program?
• What goals, tasks, and competencies are satisfied by this program?
• What specific skills does this training program develop?

Training Program

Report 68-46

Procedures Manual

Word Processing Manual Review:

L. 27: Page Numbering
L. 42: Headers and Footers

1. In page numbering, change the page number to start at page 7, and then create a header as follows: Type `Employees' Manual` at the left margin. Type `Chandler Industries, Page 7` aligned at the right margin.

2. Create a footer by typing *Training Program* in italic and aligned at the left margin.

3. Type the following portion of a procedures manual.

Employees' Manual   Chandler Industries, Page 7

¶ The purpose of this procedures manual is to assist managers who are responsible for developing training programs for new employees who have been hired in any of the seven regional branches of Chandler Industries. The basic content of this training program is outlined in the following paragraphs.

(Continued on next page)

INTRODUCTION

¶ This section identifies specific ways the manual should be used at Chandler Industries as well as the content of the manual. Answers are provided to the following questions:

1. Where does the training manual fit within the training program?
2. For whom is the manual designed, and what does it contain?
3. How should the manual be used?
4. Can the manual be used in a classroom setting?
5. Can the manual be used as self-paced instructional material?
6. Can study guides accompany the manual?

PROGRAM PHILOSOPHY AND GOALS

¶ This section describes the nature of the training program. The statements below provide the context for all courses within Chandler Industries. The focus of the section is as follows:

- Why does this program exist, and who benefits from it?
- What company needs are satisfied by this program?
- What goals, tasks, and competencies are satisfied by this program?
- What specific skills does this training program develop?

Training Program

Report 68-47 ▶

Procedures Manual

1. In page numbering, change the page number to start at page 2.
2. Create a header as follows: Type `Presentation Software Guide` at the left margin. Type `Cartwright Services, Page 2` aligned at the right margin.
3. Type *Formatting* as a footer at the left margin and in italic.

Presentation Software Guide   Cartwright Services, Page 2

FORMATTING SLIDES

¶ Once you have written your presentation, you can place your key points on slides using presentation software. Follow these steps to prepare your presentation slides.

- Select a template or background that is appropriate for every slide.
- Select a layout such as text copy or bulleted or numbered lists.
- Use the edit, copy, and paste commands to add text to your presentation slides.

FORMATTING THE PRESENTATION

¶ After you finish preparing the slides for your presentation, you may want to change the method by which each slide appears on the screen or the way individual points are displayed on the screen. In presentation software, moving from one slide to another is known as transition. Transition is accomplished by following these steps:

- Select the slides you want to control by the transition method.
- Select a transition method such as Cover Right or Wipe Left.
- Run through the slide show to determine whether or not you are satisfied with the transition.

(Continued on next page)

Remember to single-space the entire list if all items in the list are 1 line long.

Remember to insert a blank line between items in a multiline list in a single-spaced document.

¶ Slide presentations can also be formatted so that each point you make on an individual slide appears individually on the screen. To structure your slides this way, follow these steps:
- Select the slides to be controlled by a build effect.
- Select a build effect style such as Fly From Left.
- Run through the slide show again to determine whether or not you are satisfied with the build effect.

Formatting

Report 68-48

Procedures Manual

1. Open the file for Report 68-47.
2. Remove the third bulleted item under the FORMATTING SLIDES heading.
3. Add the following sections to the end of the report.

ADDING CLIP ART

¶ Clipart enhances the appearance of a slide, and it can be easily added to selected slides or to every other slide in your presentation. Several clip art images are included in this presentation package, and any one of them can be used in slides that you prepare. If you choose, however, you can insert clip art images from other packages. To insert a clip art image from your presentation package, follow these steps:

- Select the slide on which you want the clip art to appear.

- Click the icon for adding a clip art image. This icon is found on the menu bar.

- Select the image from the software clip art library. The slide can come and size and move it to its new location from the presentation package or you can retrieve it from another clip art package.

- Size and move the image to its correct location on the presentation slide.

- Copy the image to the master slide if it is to appear on all slides.

¶ You can also change the appearance of the clip art image by (1) changing the colors used in the image; (2) flipping the image so that its horizontal or vertical position is reversed (mirror image); (3) changing the contrast or brightness of the image; and (4) cropping the image so that unwanted sections are eliminated from view.

Reports Formatted in Columns

Goals

- Improve speed and accuracy
- Refine language arts skills in spelling
- Format magazine articles

A. Type 2 times.

A. WARMUP

```
1        On 12/30/02 Jim gave Alex and Pam a quiz--it was quite   11
2   difficult! Neither scored higher than 82%; their average      22
3   was 79. They should retake the quiz by the 4th or 5th.        32
    |  1  |  2  |  3  |  4  |  5  |  6  |  7  |  8  |  9  |  10  |  11  |  12
```

SKILLBUILDING

B. PACED PRACTICE

If you are not using the GDP software, turn to page SB-14 and follow the directions for this activity.

PPP PRETEST → PRACTICE → POSTTEST

PRETEST
Take a 1-minute timed writing. Review your speed and errors.

C. PRETEST: Horizontal Reaches

```
4        Four famous adults gazed at a wren on our farm gate.    11
5   A group of gawking writers wrote facts about an additional    23
6   upward gain in wildlife numbers on their supply of pads.      34
    |  1  |  2  |  3  |  4  |  5  |  6  |  7  |  8  |  9  |  10  |  11  |  12
```

PRACTICE
Speed Emphasis:
If you made no more than 1 error on the Pretest, type each *individual* line 2 times.
Accuracy Emphasis:
If you made 2 or more errors, type each *group* of lines (as though it were a paragraph) 2 times.

D. PRACTICE: In Reaches

```
7   wr wrap wren wreak wrist wrote writer unwrap writhe wreaths
8   ou pout ours ounce cough fouls output detour ousted coupons
9   ad adds dead adult ready blade advice fading admits adheres
```

E. PRACTICE: Out Reaches

```
10  fa fact farm faith sofas fakes faulty unfair famous defames
11  up upon soup upset group upper upturn supply uplift upsurge
12  ga gate gave cigar gains legal gazing legacy gawked garbage
```

POSTTEST
Repeat the Pretest timed writing and compare performance.

F. POSTTEST: Horizontal Reaches

G. Type this list of frequently misspelled words, paying special attention to any spelling problems in each word.

G. SPELLING

13 personnel information its procedures their committee system
14 receive employees which education services opportunity area
15 financial appropriate interest received production contract
16 important through necessary customer employee further there
17 property account approximately general control division our

Edit the sentences to correct any misspellings.

18 The revised systom was adopted by the finantial division.
19 Four employes want to serve on the new property commitee.
20 Approximatly ten proceedures were included in the contract.
21 Further informasion will be recieved from the customers.
22 Their was much interest shown by the production personal.
23 The services in that aria are necesary for needed control.

FORMATTING

H. MAGAZINE ARTICLES

Magazine articles can be formatted as two-column reports. Follow these steps:

1. Press ENTER 5 times to leave a 2-inch top margin on page 1.
2. Center and type the article title in all-caps, bold, and 14-point.
3. Press ENTER 2 times; then center and type the byline in upper- and lower-case, bold, and 12-point.
4. Press ENTER 2 times and change to left alignment.
5. Turn hyphenation on.

6. Format the document for a 2-column layout; then change to justified alignment.
7. Type the article single-spaced; insert 1 blank line before and after all side headings.
8. Create a header to print on all pages except page 1 to identify the author's name and the page number at the top right of every page. Usc only the author's last name and the page number in the header (for example, Davis 2).

The preview document (two pages shown at top) contains:

Page 1:

↓5X

14 pt **MEMBER BUYING SERVICES**

↓2X

12 pt↓ Brenda T. Mysweski

↓2X

Policyholders of AICA (and their dependents) are eligible for a wide range of discount services. These services provide you with a variety of items you can purchase, from automobiles to computers to jewelry. Here are some examples of the merchandise and services that are available to all AICA members.

↓2X
AUTO PRICING

↓2X

You can order the most sophisticated auto information guide on the market. The guide will give you information on retail prices, vehicle specifications, safety equipment, and factory-option packages.

↓2X

When you are ready to place your order for an automobile, a team of company experts will work with you and with the prospective dealer to ensure that you are getting the best possible price through a network of nationwide dealers. You are guaranteed to get the best price for the automobile you have chosen.

Once you have purchased your automobile, AICA will provide all your insurance needs. Discounts on policy rates are provided for completion of a driver-training program, for installed antitheft devices, and for installed passive restraint systems such as air bags.

Finally, we can make your purchase decision an easy one by always providing a low-rate finance plan for you. You can be certain that you are getting the most competitive interest rate for the purchase of your automobile when you finance with AICA.

CAR RENTAL DISCOUNTS

When you need to rent an automobile while traveling, special rates are available to you from five of the largest car rental agencies.

ROAD AND TRAVEL SERVICES

You can enjoy the security of emergency road service through the AICA Road and Travel Plan. This plan also includes discounts on hotels and motels.

As an AICA traveler, you can take advantage of our exclusive discounts and bonuses on cruises and tours. Our travel plan provides daily and weekend trips to over 100 destinations. Take advantage of this wonderful opportunity to let AICA serve all your travel needs.

MERCHANDISE BUYING

Each quarter a buying services catalog will be sent to you. This catalog includes a variety of items that can be purchased

Page 2:

Mysweski 2

through AICA—and you'll never find better prices! Through the catalog you can purchase jewelry, furniture, sports equipment, electronics, appliances, and computers. To place an order, all you have to do is call AICA toll-free at 1-800-555-3838. Your order will arrive within 10 to 15 days.

Word
Go To Processing
Manual

I. WORD PROCESSING: COLUMNS

Study Lesson 69 in your word processing manual. Complete all of the shaded steps while at your computer. Then format the jobs that follow.

DOCUMENT PROCESSING

Report 69-49

Magazine Article in Two Columns

MEMBER BUYING SERVICES | Brenda T. Mysweski

¶ Policyholders of AICA (and their dependents) are eligible for a wide range of discount services. These services provide you with a variety of items you can purchase, from automobiles to computers to jewelry. Here are some examples of the merchandise and services that are available to all AICA members.

AUTO PRICING

¶ You can order the most sophisticated auto information guide on the market. The guide will give you information on retail prices, vehicle specifications, safety equipment, and factory-option packages.

¶ When you are ready to place your order for an automobile, a team of company experts will work with you and with the prospective dealer to ensure that you are getting the best possible price through a network of nationwide dealers. You are guaranteed to get the best price for the automobile you have chosen.

(Continued on next page)

¶ Once you have purchased your automobile, AICA will provide all your insurance needs. Discounts on policy rates are provided for completion of a driver-training program, for installed antitheft devices, and for installed passive restraint systems such as air bags.

¶ Finally, we can make your purchase decision an easy one by always providing a low-rate finance plan for you. You can be certain that you are getting the most competitive interest rate for the purchase of your automobile when you finance with AICA.

CAR RENTAL DISCOUNTS

¶ When you need to rent an automobile while traveling, special rates are available to you from five of the largest car rental agencies.

ROAD AND TRAVEL SERVICES

¶ You can enjoy the security of emergency road service through the AICA Road and Travel Plan. This plan also includes discounts on hotels and motels.

¶ As an AICA traveler, you can take advantage of our exclusive discounts and bonuses on cruises and tours. Our travel plan provides daily and weekend trips to over 100 destinations. Take advantage of this wonderful opportunity to let AICA serve all your travel needs.

MERCHANDISE BUYING

¶ Each quarter a buying services catalog will be sent to you. This catalog includes a variety of items that can be purchased through AICA—and you'll never find better prices! Through the catalog you can purchase jewelry, furniture, sports equipment, electronics, appliances, and computers. To place an order, all you have to do is call AICA toll-free at 1-800-555-3838. Your order will arrive within 10 to 15 days.

Report 69-50 ▶

Magazine Article in Two Columns

INTERVIEW TECHNIQUES | By Paul Sanford

The interview process ~~allows~~ enables a company to gather information about you that ~~has~~ was not ~~been~~ provided on your resume or application form. This information includes may ~~such~~ items as your career goals, appearance, personality, poise, and ability to express yourself verbally.

APPEARANCE

There are ~~several~~ things you should keep in mind when going ~~for~~ to an interview. You should plan your wardrobe ~~well~~ carefully because first impressions are lasting ones when you walk into the interviewer's office. If you are not quite certain ~~as to~~ about what you should wear, dress conservatively. Whatever you ~~select~~ choose, be sure that your clothing is clean, neat, and comfortable. You should

(Continued on next page)

also pay attention to ^(important) details such as clean hair, shined shoes, well-groomed nails, and appropriate jewelry and other accessories.

MEETING THE INTERVIEWER

Be sure to arrive at the interview site a few minutes early. Stand when you meet the interviewer ~~for the first time.~~ If ~~a handshake is~~ the interviewer offered~~,~~ s to shake hands, shake hands in a confident, firm manner. It is also a good idea not to smoke or chew gum during the interview.

THE INTERVIEW PROCESS

Maintain ~~good~~ direct eye contact with the interviewer when you respond to his or her questions. Listen intently to everything that is said. Be aware of ~~the~~ any movements you make with your eyes, your hands, and other parts of your body during the interview. Too much movement may be a signal to the interviewer that you are nervous, that you lack confidence, or that you are not certain of your answers.

¶ During the interview ~~process,~~ the interviewer will judge not only what you say but also how you say it. As you ~~speak,~~ answer questions, you will be judged on grammar, articulation, vocabulary, and tone of voice. The nonverbal skills that may ~~be~~ the interviewer judged are your attitude, enthusiasm, listening abilit~~ies~~y, and promptness in responding to questions.

ENDING THE INTERVIEW

Let the interviewer determine when it is time to close the interview. When this time arrives, ask the interviewer when he or she expects to make a decision on hiring for this position and when you ~~can~~ may expect to hear about the job. Thank the interviewer for taking the time to meet with you.

¶ After the interview, send a follow-up letter to remind the interviewer of your name and your ~~continued~~ interest in the company. Let that person know how to contact you by providing a telephone number where you can be reached, either at home or at your current work location.

Report 69-51

Magazine Article
in Two Columns

Word
Go To Processing
Manual
Review:

L. 30:
Cut/Copy/Paste

Open the file for Report 69-49 and make the following changes:

1. Make Maria Sanchez the author of the article.
2. Make the MERCHANDISE BUYING section the second paragraph in the article.
3. Add the following section to the end of the article:

MISCELLANEOUS SERVICES | In addition to the above services, AICA provides permanent life insurance, pension plan funding, cash

management, and credit card programs. At your request, detailed catalogs will be sent to you that explain each of these services. Or, you can view all of our programs on our Web site and print out selected information you wish to review.

Report Review

Goals

- Type at least 41wpm/5′/5e
- Improve speed and accuracy
- Review report formats

A. Type 2 times.

A. WARMUP

1   Felix Quayle sat in Seat #14 when he won the jackpot; 11
2 Van Gill sat in Seat #23 but did not win a prize. Do you 22
3 think Row 19 (Seats #1560 and #1782) will be lucky for me? 34

| 1 | 2 | 3 | 4 | 5 | 6 | 7 | 8 | 9 | 10 | 11 | 12

SKILLBUILDING

B. Take a 1-minute timed writing on the first paragraph to establish your base speed. Then take four 1-minute timed writings on the remaining paragraphs. As soon as you equal or exceed your base speed on one paragraph, advance to the next, more difficult paragraph.

B. SUSTAINED PRACTICE: ROUGH DRAFT

4   The possibility of aging and not being able to live as 11
5 independently as we want to is a prospect that no one wants 23
6 to recognize. One resource designed to counter some of the 35
7 negative realities of aging is called the Handyman Project. 47

8   This type of ~~project~~ *program* helps support elders and disabled 12
9 residents in their efforts to maintain the*ir* homes. As the 24
10 name implies, "handy" volunt*e*ers per for*m* minor home repairs 36
11 such as tight*e*ning leaky faucets and fixing broken windows. 48

12 *H*Other type*s* of work include: (painting, (plumbing), yard 11
13 work, and carpent*e*ry. The volunteers are all as divers*i*fied 23
14 as the wor*k* itself. You may find a retire*e* working next to*o* 35
15 an executive or a student ~~helping~~ *assisting* a li*c*ensed electrician. 47

(Continued on next page)

16 Their back grounds may vary, but that they share is the 11
    desire
17 ~~hope~~ to put their capabilities to good use. Volunteers ~~take~~ 23
                                                           find
                                                      finishing
18 a high level of personal satisfaction after ~~doing~~ a job 35
    and
19 ~~but~~ spending time with *an elder who really needs the* help. 47

    | 1 | 2 | 3 | 4 | 5 | 6 | 7 | 8 | 9 | 10 | 11 | 12

C. Take two 5-minute timed writings. Review your speed and errors.

C. 5-MINUTE TIMED WRITING

20   In most offices, many products that are used each day 11
21 are made of materials that can now be recycled. Amazingly, 23
22 items made of glass, steel, aluminum, plastics, and paper 34
23 can be recycled to make many products that we need. Also, 46
24 the recycling process can help the environment. 56
25   Some unique examples of the process of recycling the 66
26 items we often throw away are listed here. Those old coffee 78
27 filters can be used to make soles for new shoes. Pieces of 90
28 paper that are thrown away each day can be used to make 101
29 tissue paper and paper towels. Most plastics that are used 113
30 in soda bottles can be recycled for insulation for jackets 125
31 and car interiors. Used lightbulbs and some glass products 137
32 can also be used to replace the surface on our streets. 148
33   Look around the room in which you are working. If you 159
34 are not already taking part in a recycling program, you may 171
35 want to recycle some items that you no longer need. Items 183
36 such as used paper, file folders, and aluminum cans can be 194
37 collected very quickly. What other items can you add? 205

    | 1 | 2 | 3 | 4 | 5 | 6 | 7 | 8 | 9 | 10 | 11 | 12

UNIT 14   Lesson 70   253

Report 70-52 ▶
Agenda

Crandall First National Bank | Meeting Agenda | May 15, 20--

1. Call to Order
2. Approval of minutes of April 17 [16] meeting
3. (Mortgage loans (J. William Hokes)
4. Installment loans (Lorraine Hagen))
5. Series EE bonds (Joni Ellickson)
6. Club memberships (Louise Abbey)
7. Certificates of deposit (~~Louise Abbey~~) Robert Hunt
8. Closing remarks
9. Adjournment

Report 70-53 ▶
Minutes of a Meeting

LITTLETON WATERCOLOUR SOCIETY
Minutes of the Meeting
October 23, 20--

CALL TO ORDER   The meeting was called to order by Sandra Garvy at 8 p.m. in the Littleton library conference room.

OLD BUSINESS   Susan Firtz furnished each member with a list of artists and the names of the watercolor paintings each artist is entering in the Fall Arts Fair.

NEW BUSINESS   John Champion informed members that a new supply of canvas and oil paint arrived. Members can check out any items ~~they need~~ to begin their winter projects. He reminded everyone that Winter Fair will be held December 14 at the Expo.

ADJOURNMENT   The meeting was adjourned at 9:45 p.m. The next meeting ~~is~~ will be held November 12.

Respectfully submitted,

Catherine Argetes

**Magazine Article
in Two Columns**

Type the article in two columns and balance the columns.

PERFORMING SUCCESSFULLY
Ginger Nichols

¶ We have been involved in giving performances since our very early years. The most terrifying part of each performance was probably the fear that we would "freeze" when it came our turn to perform. Whenever we find ourselves in this predicament, the best thing to do is to accept that fear and to learn to let it work for us, not against us. We need to recognize that nervousness or fear may set in during our performance. Then, when it does happen (if it does), we will be ready to cope with it and overcome it.

¶ If you forget some of your lines in a recitation, try to remember other lines and recite them. Doing so may help those forgotten lines to "pop back" into your memory so that you put them in at a later time, if possible.

¶ You always want to leave your audience with the idea that you have given them something worthwhile that they can use or apply to their own lives. For maximum impact on your audience and to make sure that they remember what you say, use audiovisual aids to reinforce your message. Remember, however, that audiovisual aids are nothing more than aids. The real message should come in the words you choose when giving your presentation.

¶ Study your speech well; even rehearse it if necessary. However, do not practice it to the extent that it appears that you are merely reading what is written down on the paper in front of you. Much of your personality should be exhibited while you are giving your speech. If you are an enthusiastic, friendly person who converses well with people face-to-face, then that same persona should be evident during your speech. A good piece of advice is to just go out there and be yourself—you will be much more comfortable by doing so, and your audience will relate to you better than if you try to exhibit a different personality when at the podium.

¶ No matter how rapidly you speak in general, slow down when you are in front of a group. The fact that you are nervous can cause your speech rate to increase. The best way to slow down your speaking is to breathe deeply. Doing so also causes your nervous system to relax, allowing you to proceed with your speech calmly.

¶ Finally, possibly the best advice for giving a successful speech is to be prepared. You will be more confident if you are thoroughly prepared. Do your research, rehearse your speech, and make notes about where you want to give emphasis or use an audiovisual aid.

Unit 15

Correspondence

LESSON 71
Multipage Letters

LESSON 72
Special Letter Features

LESSON 73
More Special Letter Features

LESSON 74
Multipage Memos With Tables

LESSON 75
Memo Reports

November 8, 20--

CONFIDENTIAL

Mrs. Katie Hollister
11426 Prairie View Road
Kearney, NE 68847

Dear Mrs. Hollister:

Subject: Site for New Elementary School

As you are aware, your 160-acre farm, located in th
township, is a part of Independent School District
occupies 2 acres and is adjoined by an 8-acre park.
a fourth elementary school. As your farm is central
me to initiate discussions with you for the purchase

Please call me at your convenience to arrange a me
me. I look forward to our discussions.

Yours truly,

Irvin J. Hagg
Superintendent

az
c: District 17 Board

March 1, 20--

Mr. Rodney Graae
Thompson Corporation
42 Harris Court
Trenton, NJ 08648

Dear Mr. Graae:

We are indeed interested in designing a new corporate logo and the corresponding stationery
for your fine corporation. As I indicated in our recent telephone conversation, we have a design
staff that has won many national awards for letterhead form design, and we consider it an
honor to be contacted by you.

Within a month, we will submit several basic designs to you and your board of directors. At that
time, please feel free to make any comments and suggestions that will help us finalize a design.
Here is a modified price list for the printed stationery:

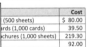

	Cost
(500 sheets)	$ 80.00
ards (1,000 cards)	39.50
chures (1,000 sheets)	219.30
	92.00

can be of further service.

MEMO TO: All Employees

FROM: Adrienne Barzan

DATE: March 2, 20--

SUBJECT: New Building Site

We have consulted with several architects and have finalized plans to build a new
administrative center at 6400 Easton Plaza. This memo provides general information about
plans for the center's exterior and interior development.

EXTERIOR PLANS

Exterior plans will maintain the historical integrity and beauty of the surrounding area and
reflect the architecture of other buildings in the office park. Landscaping plans include a
parklike area, a picnic area, and a small pond.

INTERIOR PLANS FOR STAFF

Staff will be located within the new facility as follows:

1. Accounting will be located on the first floor in the west wing.

2. Sales and marketing will be located on the first floor in the east wing. All staff will be
    grouped according to product line.

3. All other staff will be located on the second floor. Exact locations will be determined at a
    later date.

INTERIOR PLANS FOR SPECIAL FACILITIES

Conference rooms will be located in the center of the building on the first floor to provide easy
access for everyone. All rooms will be equipped with state-of-the-art technology. Our new
center will also include a full-service cafeteria, a copy center, a library, an athletic center, and
an on-site day care center. Construction of the new center will begin when we obtain the
necessary permits.

az

Multipage Letters

Goals

- Improve speed and accuracy
- Refine language arts skills in the use of commas
- Format multipage letters

A. Type 2 times.

A. WARMUP

```
1        We were quite dazzled when the plumber drove up in a      11
2    C-150 pickup truck! She was joined by 26 young people (all     23
3    students) who gazed intently as she welded six of the rods.    35
     |  1  |  2  |  3  |  4  |  5  |  6  |  7  |  8  |  9  |  10  |  11  |  12
```

SKILLBUILDING

B. Take three 12-second timed writings on each line. The scale below the last line shows your wpm speed for a 12-second timed writing.

B. 12-SECOND SPEED SPRINTS

```
4    Pam knew that five girls in the other car were on the team.
5    The women drove eight blue autos when they made some trips.
6    All the girls in four other autos may go on the same trips.
7    Spring is the time of the year when they have a lot of pep.
     ' ' ' '5' ' ' '10' ' ' '15' ' ' '20' ' ' '25' ' ' '30' ' ' '35' ' ' '40' ' ' '45' ' ' '50' ' ' '55' ' ' '60
```

C. DIAGNOSTIC PRACTICE: SYMBOLS AND PUNCTUATION

If you are not using the GDP software, turn to page SB-2 and follow the directions for this activity.

LANGUAGE ARTS

D. Study the rules at the right.

D. COMMAS

Note: The callout signals in the left margin indicate which language arts rule from this lesson has been applied.

RULE ▶

,nonessential expression

The underline calls attention to a point in the sentence where a comma might mistakenly be inserted.

Use a comma before and after a nonessential expression.

Andre, who was there, can verify the statement.

But: Anyone_who was there_can verify the statement.

Van's first book, *Crisis of Management*, was not discussed.

Van's boo_k Crisis of Management_was not discussed.

Note: A nonessential expression is a group of words that may be omitted without changing the basic meaning of the sentence. Always examine the noun or pronoun that comes before the expression to determine whether the noun needs the expression to complete its meaning. If it does, the expression is *essential* and does *not* take a comma.

Use a comma between two adjacent adjectives that modify the same noun.

We need an intelligent, enthusiastic individual for this job.

But: Please order a new bulletin board for our main conference room.

Note: Do not use a comma after the second adjective. Also, do not use a comma if the first adjective modifies the combined idea of the second adjective and the noun (for example, *bulletin board* and *conference room* in the second example).

Edit the sentences by inserting any needed punctuation.

8 The school president Mr. Roberts will address the students.

9 The fall planning meeting which is held in Charlotte has been canceled.

10 Students planning to take the certification test must register for the orientation class.

11 The sleek luxury car is scheduled for delivery next week.

12 Margaret brought her fast reliable laptop to the meeting.

13 A stamped addressed envelope should be included with the survey.

FORMATTING

E. MULTIPAGE LETTERS

To format a multipage letter:

1. Type the first page on letterhead stationery, and type continuation pages on plain paper that matches the letterhead.

2. Insert a page number in the top right-hand corner of the page header of all continuing pages, and remove the page number from the first page.

> 2
>
> I have never been involved with anything like this before. Any help that you give me will be appreciated. I shall look forward to working with you.
>
> Sincerely,
>
> Ms. Jeanne M. Hoover
> Attorney-at-Law
>
> az
> Enclosure

DOCUMENT PROCESSING

Correspondence ▶
71-64

Business Letter in
Modified-Block Style

Refer to   **Reference
Manual**

Review: R-5A and R-5B:
Multipage Business Letter

October 16, 20-- | Miss Florence B. Glashan | Attorney-at-Law | 2406 Shadows Glade | Dayton, OH 45426-0348 | Dear Miss Glashan: |
¶ It was good to meet you at the convention for trial attorneys in Detroit last week. In addition to the interesting program highlights of the regular sessions, I find that the informal discussions with people like you are an added plus at these meetings. Your contribution to the program was very beneficial to me.
¶ You may recall that I told you I had just been appointed by the court to defend a woman here in Dayton who has been charged with embezzling large sums of money from her previous employer. The defendant had been employed at a large department store for more than 25 years. Because of her valuable years of experience in accounting with the store, she was in charge of accounts receivable at the store. Her previous employer, the plaintiff in the case, claims that she embezzled $18,634 in 2000, $39,072 in 2001, and $27,045 in 2002.

(Continued on next page)

¶ I feel that it is my responsibility to represent my client and to provide the best defense possible. I recall that you mentioned that you had represented defendants in similar cases in previous years. As I prepare for this defense, perhaps you might help me in the following ways:

1. Please send me the appropriate citations for all similar trials in which you participated.
2. Also, please provide me with any other case citations that you think might be helpful to me in this case.
3. Arrange to meet with me soon so that I can benefit from your experience as I prepare for the trial.

¶ A copy of the formal complaint is enclosed for your review. I shall call you in about a week to arrange a time and place for our meeting. Please let me know if there is additional information that would be helpful in preparing for this case.

¶ I have never been involved with anything like this before. Any help that you give me will be appreciated. I shall look forward to working with you. Sincerely, | Ms. Jeanne M. Hoover | Attorney-at-Law | urs | Enclosure

Correspondence 71-65

Business Letter in Block Style

April 3, 20-- | Mr. Michael McGinty | District Manager | Starr & Morgan Company | One DuPont circle | Washington, DC 20063-2133 |

Dear Mike:

¶ It was good to see you at our sales conference in Reston, Virginia, last week. Your winning the "golden apple" award for the most sales for the year was well deserved. When you first became part of our sales team, you showed great enthusiasm for your job immediately. There is no doubt in my mind that Starr & Morgan Company is very well represented in the metro Washington area. We particularly want to commend you for obtaining the Westminster Account. Acquiring this account has been a major objective for a number of years. None of our company's other sales representatives have been able to accomplish this feat. Just the idea of a new account of over $500,000 is quite mind-boggling. How did you do it? Did you:

1. spend considerable time with the President, Mr. Arch Davis, or the Director of Purchasing, Ms. Betsy Martin?
2. Conduct a series of hands-on workshops for the employees and managers?
3. Develop a special marketing campaign for Westminster and customize it for Westminster or use a regular campaign model?
4. Combine various strategies in your efforts to obtain this account?

(Continued on next page)

¶ Please let me know what approaches you used to make this sale?

Successes of this nature do not happen without a lot of hard work. You are to be commended for putting forth your best efforts to sign the account.

¶ If we can arrange time, we would like to have you make a presentation to our annual sales meeting, we. The other sales representatives would benefit greatly from having you share your success story. Our annual meeting will be held in late September in Richmond, Virginia. Congratulations on receiving this prestigious award.

All of us here in the home office are greatly pleased with the performance of our entire sales team. Indications are that this will be a year when our sales records will be broken and we will again be in the media spotlight.

Sincerely yours, | Robert D. Miley (Pres) | urs | c: R. Olson, Director of Sales

Correspondence 71-66

Business Letter in Modified-Block Style

Open the file for Correspondence 71-64 and make the following changes:

1. Change the addressee to Ms. Cynthia Barnes, Attorney-at-Law.
2. Change the office address to:
   4066 Quarry Estates
   Dayton, OH 45429-1362.
3. Change the salutation and header as needed.
4. Add this sentence at the end of the second paragraph:
   The defendant is also being accused of embezzling $35,680 in 2003.

Special Letter Features

Goals

- Type at least 42wpm/5'/5e
- Format special letter features

A. Type 2 times.

A. WARMUP

```
1        Six citizens from 14th Avenue East joined 83 other      10
2    residents to discuss the #794 proposal* for a new swimming  22
3    pool. Barry Kelm quoted numbers about current pool usage.    34
     |  1  |  2  |  3  |  4  |  5  |  6  |  7  |  8  |  9  |  10  |  11  |  12
```

SKILLBUILDING

B. MAP

Follow the GDP software directions for this exercise in improving keystroking accuracy.

Strategies for Career Success

Audience Analysis

Knowing your audience is fundamental to the success of any message. Ask the following questions to help identify your audience.

What is your relationship to your audience? Are they familiar—people with whom you work—or people unknown to you? The latter will prompt you to conduct some research to better communicate your purpose. What is the attitude of your audience? Are they hostile or receptive to your message? How will your message benefit them? What is your anticipated response? Asking these questions first can help prevent message mishap later.

When writing to a diverse audience, direct your message to the primary audience. These key decision makers will make a decision or act on the basis of your message. Determine the level of detail, organization, formality, and use of technical terms and theory.

YOUR TURN Compose a thank-you e-mail to a friend. How would it differ from an interview thank-you letter?

C. Take two 5-minute timed writings. Review your speed and errors.

Goal: At least
42wpm/5'/5e

C. 5-MINUTE TIMED WRITING

4	Whether you are searching for your first job or are	11
5	looking to change jobs, your networking skills may play a	22
6	crucial role in how successful you are in that endeavor.	34
7	Networking can be defined in some respects as a group of	45
8	people who are linked closely together for the purpose of	56
9	achieving some sort of end result. In this case, the end	68
10	result will be to establish new contacts who might be able	80
11	to assist you in your job search.	86
12	Your network is made up of dozens of people you have	97
13	met. You can never be sure who has the potential of helping	109
14	you the most in your job search. Therefore, it is important	121
15	that you consider all acquaintances. You should certainly	133
16	network with business associates, and especially those you	145
17	have met at various meetings and conferences. And don't	156
18	forget former teachers in whose classes you were enrolled.	168
19	Former classmates provide an excellent base on which to	179
20	build your network, and friends and family should also be	190
21	included. Finally, use the Internet to nurture any online	202
22	contacts you have made over the years.	210

| 1 | 2 | 3 | 4 | 5 | 6 | 7 | 8 | 9 | 10 | 11 | 12 |

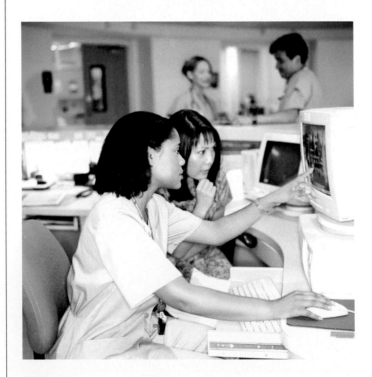

D. MULTIPLE ADDRESSES

Often a letter may be sent to two or more people at the same address or to different addresses:

1. If a letter is addressed to two people at the same address, type each name on a separate line above the same inside address.

2. If a letter is addressed to two people at different addresses, type each name and address, one under the other. Press ENTER 2 times between the addresses.

3. If a letter is addressed to three or more people, type the names and addresses side by side, with one at the left margin and another beginning at the center-point. Insert 1 blank line before typing the third name and address at the left margin.

November 19, 20-- ↓4X

Dr. Albert Russell, Professor
Department of English
Appalachian State University
Boone, NC 28608 ↓2X

Dr. Kay Smith, Professor
Director of Business
Grove City College
Grove City, PA 16127 ↓2X

Dear Dr. Russell and Dr. Smith: ↓2X

It is with great pleasure that I announce the scholarship winners for this year's awards banquet to be held in the next month. The awardees' names are listed below.

E. ON-ARRIVAL NOTATIONS

On-arrival notations (such as *CONFIDENTIAL*) should be typed on the second line below the date, at the left margin. Type the notation in all-caps. Press ENTER 2 times to begin the inside address.

November 19, 20-- ↓2X

CONFIDENTIAL ↓2X

Mr. and Mrs. Earl Walters
3408 Washington Boulevard
New Tripoli, PA 18066 ↓2X

Dear Mr. and Mrs. Walters: ↓2X

We are very pleased to tell you that your daughter will be the recipient of a very prestigious scholarship this semester. She will be recognized at a banquet to be held next month.

F. SUBJECT LINES

A *subject line* indicates what a letter is about. Type the subject line below the salutation at the left margin, preceded and followed by 1 blank line. (The term *Re* or *In re* may be used in place of *Subject*.)

November 19, 20-- ↓4X

Mr. and Mrs. Earl Walters
3408 Washington Boulevard
New Tripoli, PA 18066 ↓2X

Dear Mr. and Mrs. Walters: ↓2X

Subject: Scholarship Awarded ↓2X

We are very pleased to tell you that your daughter will be the recipient of a very prestigious scholarship this semester. She will be recognized at a banquet to be held next month.

Word Processing Manual

G. WORD PROCESSING: SORT

Study Lesson 72 in your word processing manual. Complete all of the shaded steps while at your computer. Then format the jobs that follow.

DOCUMENT PROCESSING

Correspondence 72-67

Business Letter in Block Style

November 8, 20--

CONFIDENTIAL

Mrs. Katie Hollister

11426 Prairie View Rd.

Kearney, NE 68847

Dear Mrs. Hollister:

Subject: Site for New ~~Elementary~~ School

¶ As you are aware, your 160-acre farm, located in the northeast quarter ~~northeast~~ of Section 25 in Tyro township, is a part of independent School District 17. Each of our three elementary schools occupies ~~two~~ 2 acres and is adjoined by an 8-acre park. We are now in the early planning stages for a ~~third~~ fourth elementary school. As your large farm is centrally located, the District 17 Board has directed me to initiate discussions with you for the purchase of 10 acres of land.

(Continued on next page)

¶ (I look forward to our discussions.) Please call me at your convenience to arrange a meeting with you and/or your attorney and me.

Yours truly,

Irvin J. Hagg

Superintendent

urs

c: District 17 Board

Correspondence 72-68

Business Letter in Block Style

Sort each bulleted list in the letter in ascending order.

October 4, 20-- | Ms. Deborah Campbell Wallace | 7835 Virginia Avenue Northwest | Washington, DC 20037 | Mr. Thomas E. Campbell | 3725 Stevens Road Southeast | Washington, DC 20020 | Dear Ms. Wallace and Mr. Campbell:

¶ We received your letter requesting instructions for transferring stock. The most common stock transfer situations are provided below. Determine which type of transfer you require and select the instructions that apply to your stock transfer.

- Name change
- Transferring shares to another individual(s)
- Transfers involving a deceased shareholder (individual ownership)
- Transfers involving a deceased shareholder (multiple owners)
- Transfers involving a minor
- Transfers involving a power of attorney
- Transfers involving a trust

¶ Every transfer requires a letter of instruction specifying how you want your shares transferred. The following items are required for all types of transfers:

- Name and address of new owner(s)
- Social security number or tax payer identification number
- Preferred form of ownership (that is, joint tenants or tenants in common)
- Indicate total shares that are being transferred
- Sign and date the form

¶ Please be sure to submit all required documentation and note that all documents submitted become part of the permanent record of transfer and will not be returned.

(Continued on next page)

¶ All transfers must have your signature(s) guaranteed by a financial institution participating in the Medallion Signature Guarantee Program.

¶ If you need additional information, you may visit our Web site for step-by-step instructions or you may call one of our customer service representatives at our toll-free number.

Sincerely, | William J. Shawley | Shareholder Services | urs

Correspondence 72-69

Personal-Business Letter in Block Style

(!) Format book titles in italic instead of underlining.

November 17, 20--

Dr. Arif Gureshi
8726 East Ridge Drive
Morehead, KY 40351-7268
Dear Dr. Gureshi:
Subject: The Middle East in the Year 2005 Discussion
¶ Your new book, The Middle East in the Year 2005, has gotten excellent reviews. The citizens of Morehead are pleased that a respected member of one of our local colleges is receiving national attention.
¶ Our book discussion group in Morehead, composed of members of the AAUW (American Association of University Women), has selected your book for discussion at our May meeting. We would very much like you to be a participant; your attendance at the meeting would be a real highlight.
¶ I shall call you next week. Our members are hoping that you will be able to attend and that an acceptable date can be arranged.
Sincerely,

Theresa A. Gorski
2901 Garfield Court
Morehead, KY 40351-2687

More Special Letter Features

Goals

- Improve speed and accuracy
- Refine language arts skills in composing paragraphs
- Format letters with special features

A. Type 2 times.

A. WARMUP

```
1      The 83 Lions Club members raised $6,690 (95% of the      11
2   requested sum) to resurface the tennis courts. Gayle was     22
3   amazed when sixteen jolly members picked up over 10% more.   34
    |  1  |  2  |  3  |  4  |  5  |  6  |  7  |  8  |  9  |  10  |  11  |  12
```

SKILLBUILDING

B. PACED PRACTICE

If you are not using the GDP software, turn to page SB-14 and follow the directions for this activity.

PPP PRETEST → PRACTICE → POSTTEST

PRETEST
Take a 1-minute timed writing. Review your speed and errors.

C. PRETEST: Vertical Reaches

```
4      The scents in the trunk scared the rest of the drama     11
5   class. One judge drank juice and ate pecans as the cranky    23
6   coach scolded the best junior and bought the pink dresses.   35
    |  1  |  2  |  3  |  4  |  5  |  6  |  7  |  8  |  9  |  10  |  11  |  12
```

PRACTICE
Speed Emphasis:
If you made no more than 1 error on the Pretest, type each *individual* line 2 times.
Accuracy Emphasis:
If you made 2 or more errors, type each *group* of lines (as though it were a paragraph) 2 times.

D. PRACTICE: Up Reaches

```
7   dr draft drank dryer drain drama dread dream drag drew drug
8   ju judge juice jumpy junks juror julep jumbo judo jump just
9   es essay nests tests less dress acres makes uses best rest
```

E. PRACTICE: Down Reaches

```
10  ca cable caddy cargo scare decay yucca pecan cage calm case
11  nk ankle blank crank blink think trunk brink bank junk sink
12  sc scale scalp scene scent scold scoop scope scan scar disc
```

POSTTEST
Repeat the Pretest timed writing and compare performance.

F. POSTTEST: Vertical Reaches

G. COMPOSING: PARAGRAPH

Compose a paragraph expressing your opinion on whether or not it is safe to make purchases online. Include precautions and potential dangers.

FORMATTING

H. TABLES WITHIN DOCUMENTS

To format a table that is part of a letter, memo, or report:

1. In a single-spaced document, press ENTER 2 times before and 1 time after the table. Be sure you are outside the table structure before pressing ENTER 1 time.
2. In a double-spaced document, press ENTER 1 time before and after the table.
3. Single-space the body of the table.
4. Adjust the column widths, and center the table within the margins of the document.
5. Never split a table between two pages if it will fit on one page. If a table will not fit at the bottom of the page on which it is first mentioned, place it at the top of the next page.

MEMO TO:	Leo Guthrie
FROM:	Paul Forester
DATE:	January 10, 20--
SUBJECT:	Sales Comparison

Listed below are the sales totals for the last two quarters. Please review the information before our staff meeting on Friday. ↓2X

SALES SUMMARY December 31, 20-- ↓1X		
↓1X Region	Third Quarter	Fourth Quarter
Northeast	456,321	512,980
Southeast	335,765	375,112
Northwest	425,666	457,034
Southwest	388,546	410,478

↓1X

Come to the meeting prepared to discuss plans for the upcoming sales promotions that will take place in our district.

I. COMPANY NAME IN CLOSING LINES

Some business firms show the company name in the closing lines of a letter. Type the company name in all-caps on the second line below the complimentary closing. Then press ENTER 4 times and type the writer's name.

Thank you for inviting me to participate in the discussion concerning this issue. It has been very informative and helpful. ↓2X

Sincerely, ↓2X

HENDERSON AND SONS, INC. ↓4X

Mark Henderson, President ↓2X

mjd

J. BLIND COPY NOTATION

A *blind copy (bc:) notation* is used when the addressee is not intended to know that one or more other persons are being sent a copy of the letter. Type the *bc* notation on the file copy at the left margin on the second line after the last item in the letter.

When preparing a letter with a blind copy, print one copy of the letter; then add the blind copy notation and print another.

> Thank you for inviting me to participate in the discussion concerning this issue. It has been very informative and helpful.
>
> Sincerely, ↓4X
>
> Mark Henderson
> President ↓2X
>
> mjd ↓2X
> bc: Mary Stevenson

K. DELIVERY NOTATION

Type a delivery notation (such as *By fax*) on the line below the enclosure notation (if used) or on the line below the reference initials. A delivery notation comes before a copy notation.

> Thank you for inviting me to participate in the discussion concerning this issue. It has been very informative and helpful.
>
> Sincerely, ↓4X
>
> Mark Henderson
> President ↓2X
>
> az
> Enclosure
> By fax
> c: Mary Stevenson

L. POSTSCRIPT

If a postscript *(PS)* is added to a letter, it is typed as the last item in the letter, preceded by 1 blank line. If a blind copy notation and postscript are used, the bc: notation follows the postscript.

> smr
> Enclosure ↓2X
> PS: You will be reimbursed for all expenses. Complete an expense report and submit it to your supervisor. ↓2X
> bc: Mary Stevenson

Word
Processing
Manual

M. WORD PROCESSING: SHADING

Study Lesson 73 in your word processing manual. Complete all of the shaded steps while at your computer. Then format the jobs that follow.

Correspondence 73-70

Business Letter in Block Style

March 1, 20-- | Ms. Maureen Testa | Austin Communications | 37 Pittsburgh Road | Franklin, PA 16323 | Dear Ms. Testa:

¶ We are indeed interested in designing a new corporate logo and the corresponding stationery for your fine company. As I indicated in our recent telephone conversation, we have a design staff that has won many national awards for letterhead form design, and we consider it an honor to be contacted by you.

¶ Within a couple of weeks, we will submit to you and your committee several basic designs. Based on your evaluation and suggestions, we can go from there. Here is a modified price list for the printed stationery:

Automatically adjust the column widths and center the table horizontally.

Stationery	Cost
Letterhead (500 sheets)	$ 80.00
Business cards (1,000 cards)	39.50
Coated brochures (1,000 sheets)	219.30
Envelopes	92.00

¶ In the meantime, please call me if we can be of further service. Sincerely yours, | Samantha A. Steele | General Manager | urs | By fax | bc: Design Department

Correspondence 73-71

Business Letter in Block Style

Open the file for Correspondence 73-70 from Ms. Steele and make the following changes:

1. Send the letter to Mr. Rodney Graae | Thompson Corporation | 42 Harris Court | Trenton, NJ 08648
2. Change the word "company" in the first paragraph to corporation.
3. Revise the first two sentences of the second paragraph to say:

Within a month, we will submit several basic designs to you and your board of directors. At that time, please feel free to make any comments and suggestions that will help us finalize a design.

4. Change the table to a boxed table.
5. Apply 25 percent shading to the first row of the table.

Correspondence 73-72

Business Letter in Modified-Block Style

November 5, 20-- | Master Gyms, Inc. | 4201 Castine Court | Raleigh, NC 27613-5981 | Ladies and Gentlemen:

¶We have 494 apartments at Fountain Ridge. As the recreation coordinator, I have concerns not only about the leisure-time activities of our residents but also about the health and physical fitness of the more than 1,100 people who call Fountain Ridge home.

(Continued on next page)

¶ Our recreation facilities are excellent. In addition to our two outdoor tennis courts and swimming pool, we have the following indoor facilities: two racquetball courts, swimming pool, whirlpool bath, sauna, steam room, and two billiard tables. However, we have no workout equipment.

¶ During the next few months we will be equipping a new gymnasium. The dimensions of the gym are shown on the enclosed sketch. There will be exercise bicycles, treadmills, and rowing machines. In addition, we would like to install a muscle-toning machine that includes features such as the following: leg press, chest press, shoulder press, arm pull, leg pull, arm lift, leg lift, and sit-up board.

¶ The needs and interests of our residents are varied. Some residents will take full advantage of the equipment we have suggested for the gymnasium. However, many of our residents have expressed interests in an indoor track for walking; others would like to add a track for running. We hope to accommodate as many of the suggestions as we feel are feasible.

¶ The population of the residents in the Fountain Ridge complex consists of a mixture of young and middle-age adult couples as well as single residents. Some of the couples have children who would be old enough to enjoy the facilities. Therefore, safety and durability of the equipment are very important considerations. In addition, we would like to continue to develop our complex in a way that would invite family participation in our recreational activities.

¶ Do you have a sales representative serving this area who could meet with me within a week or ten days? As an alternative, perhaps you have some brochures, including prices, that could be sent to me. We are very eager to begin our research into all of this and hope that you will be eager to contact us also.

Sincerely yours, | FOUNTAIN RIDGE | Rosa Bailey-Judd | Recreation Coordinator | urs | Enclosure | By fax | PS: Please send a current catalog and price list immediately so that we can prepare for our meeting with the sales representative.

Multipage Memos With Tables

Goals

- Type at least 42wpm/5′/5e
- Format multipage memos with tables

A. Type 2 times.

A. WARMUP

```
1        Over 270 cars were backed up near the Baxter & Meintz    11
2    building after an 18-wheeler jackknifed at an icy junction.   23
3    About 1/3 to 1/2 of the cars were required to use a detour.   35
     |  1  |  2  |  3  |  4  |  5  |  6  |  7  |  8  |  9  |  10  |  11  |  12
```

SKILLBUILDING

B. PROGRESSIVE PRACTICE: ALPHABET

If you are not using the GDP software, turn to page SB-7 and follow the directions for this activity.

C. PROGRESSIVE PRACTICE: NUMBERS

If you are not using the GDP software, turn to page SB-11 and follow the directions for this activity.

Keyboarding Connection

Virus and Spam Prevention

Use caution when opening e-mail attachments or downloading files from the Internet. Download files only from reliable Web sites. Do not open files attached to an e-mail from an unknown source. Also question files attached to a known source. Some viruses replicate themselves and are sent through e-mail without users' knowledge.

Delete any e-mail with an odd subject, a chain e-mail, or electronic junk mail, commonly known as spam. If you're given the opportunity to unsubscribe from a spammer's list, think twice. Your reply will stop the messages on a reputable mailing list but may incite disreputable list marketers.

To protect against lost data, back up your files on a regular basis. Then you will be prepared if a virus infects your computer. New viruses are discovered daily, so update your antivirus software regularly.

YOUR TURN How do you handle junk mail via post? Do you notice similarities when dealing with spam?

D. Take two 5-minute timed writings. Review your speed and errors.

Goal: At least 42wpm/5'/5e

D. 5-MINUTE TIMED WRITING

```
 4      Have you ever given any thought to starting your own      11
 5   business? Obviously, there is some risk in starting out in    23
 6   a venture such as this. However, if you realize there are    34
 7   some issues to starting up a business, it may not seem to    46
 8   be such a daunting undertaking. Let's quickly look at just    58
 9   some of the issues that are involved in this task.           64
10      First of all, you need to think about whether you want    75
11   to do so badly enough to work long hours without knowing if   87
12   you will make any money at the end of the month. It would    99
13   be advantageous if you had worked previously for another    110
14   company as a manager or have managerial experience.         121
15      You have to have some sense for just how much money      131
16   you will need to start your business. It will take some     143
17   working capital to get you started. If you have put money    154
18   aside to invest in the company, there is a good possibility 166
19   you will succeed. If you don't have enough put aside, can    178
20   you get credit from a lending institution to assist you     189
21   through the first few months of operation? And, of course,  201
22   you'll also need to get credit from suppliers.              210
     | 1 | 2 | 3 | 4 | 5 | 6 | 7 | 8 | 9 | 10 | 11 | 12
```

FORMATTING

Word Processing Manual

E.   WORD PROCESSING: FIND AND REPLACE

Study Lesson 74 in your word processing manual. Complete all of the shaded steps while at your computer. Then format the jobs that follow.

DOCUMENT PROCESSING

Correspondence
74-73

Memo

MEMO TO: L. B. Chinn, Station Manager | **FROM**: Mitzi Grenell, News Director | **DATE**: May 5, 20-- | **SUBJECT**: FCC European Trip

¶ As you requested, this memo is being sent to you as one in a series to keep you informed about my upcoming trip to Europe. I have been invited by the Federal Communications Commission to participate in a study of television news in European countries. The invitation came from Jill Andrews, FCC vice-chair; and I am, of course, delighted to take part in this challenging project.

(Continued on next page)

¶ One function of this study will be to compare the news in countries that have a long history of free-access broadcasting with the programming in newly democratic countries. I have been assigned to lead a study group to six European countries to gather firsthand information on this topic. We will be visiting England, France, Germany, Poland, Romania, and Latvia from August 24 through September 3. In addition to me, our group will consist of the following members:

Arkady Gromov	Executive Editor *Miami Herald*	Miami, Florida
Manuel Cruz	News Director National Public Radio	Boise, Idaho
Katherine Grant	Station Manager WLBZ-TV	Bangor, Maine
Richard Logan	Operations Manager Cable News System	Provo, Utah

¶ Our initial plans are to spend at least one full day in each of the countries, meeting with the news staff of one or two of the major networks, touring their facilities, viewing recent broadcasts, and becoming familiar with their general operations.

¶ If you need to contact me during my absence, Barbara Brooks, our liaison at the Federal Communications Commission (1919 M Street, NW, Washington, DC 20554; phone: 202-555-3894), will be able to provide a location and phone number.

¶ Arrangements will be made with several different staff members in the News Department to handle my responsibilities here at Channel 5 while I am gone. Dave Gislason will be the contact person for the department. As you can imagine, this is an exciting time for me. Thank you for supporting the project.

| urs | PS: Thanks also for suggesting that this trip be combined with a vacation. My husband and I have discussed the possibility of his joining me for a two-week tour of the Scandinavian countries after the FCC trip has been completed. I shall let you know what our plans are by the end of May.

Correspondence 74-74

Memo

Open the file for Correspondence 74-73 and make the following changes:

1. Jill Andrews has just been promoted to FCC chair.
2. Finland has been added as a seventh country.
3. The trip has been extended through September 5.
4. Each occurrence of the word "news" (lowercase) has to be changed to news programming. (Do not replace News.)
5. Reggie Jordan, Staff Assistant, FCC, Washington, DC, will replace Manuel Cruz on the trip.
6. Gil Friesen will replace Dave Gislason as contact person.

MEMO TO: Terri Hackworth, Manager

FROM: Rosa Bailey, Judd, Recreation Coordinator

DATE: April 14, 20--

SUBJECT: Fitness room

The new Fitness Room will be ready for use in about ① month. Your leadership in bringing this about is sincerely appreciated. After ~~much~~ extensive investigation (much reading and several interviews), I likely will be requesting approval soon to purchase the following equipment:

No.	Type
4	exercise bicycles
2	treadmills
1	muscle-toning machine

Three other types of equipment were considered seriously, but those listed above enable users to reach objectives with out excessive cost. I am not quite ready to recommend the specific brands or the suppliers for these machines. As we expect that there will be very heavy usage, we are concerned with durability, warranties, and the availability of dependable service personnel. Thanks again for your full support and cooperation with this project.

urs

Strategies for Career Success

Developing Confidence as a Presenter

Public speaking anxiety is quite common. As many as 77 percent of experienced speakers admit to having some anxiety on each speaking occasion. Normally, stage fright decreases with experience.

Even if there are no physical expressions of anxiety, speakers often assume others can see through their smiles to their fears. However, listeners are actually poor judges of the amount of anxiety that speakers experience.

A little anxiety can actually stimulate a better presentation. The best way to control your anxiety is to be well prepared for the presentation. Carefully analyze your audience, research your topic, organize the speech, practice its delivery, and believe in its ideas. Being well prepared puts you in an excellent position to control your anxiety.

YOUR TURN   "I'm glad I'm here. I'm glad you're here. I know that I know." What are the benefits of repeating this to yourself before each presentation?

Memo Reports

Goals

- Improve speed and accuracy
- Format memo reports

A. Type 2 times.

A. WARMUP

```
1    The sizable judge asked three questions: "What's the      11
2  best time of the day for you to be in court? Can you leave   23
3  your job at exactly 4 p.m.? If not, 5 p.m. or 7 p.m.?"       34
   |  1  |  2  |  3  |  4  |  5  |  6  |  7  |  8  |  9  |  10 |  11 |  12
```

SKILLBUILDING

B. Take a 1-minute timed writing on the first paragraph to establish your base speed. Then take four 1-minute timed writings on the remaining paragraphs. As soon as you equal or exceed your base speed on one paragraph, advance to the next, more difficult paragraph.

B. SUSTAINED PRACTICE: SYLLABIC INTENSITY

```
4      Each of us has several bills to be paid on a monthly    11
5  basis. For most of us, a checkbook is the tool that we use   23
6  to take care of this chore. However, in this electronic      34
7  age, other ways of doing this have received rave reviews.    45

8      You will likely be surprised to learn that the most     11
9  basic way and the cheapest way to pay bills electronically   23
10 involves the use of a Touch-Tone phone. The time required    35
11 is approximately a third of that used when writing checks.   47

12     Several banking institutions offer or plan to offer     11
13 screen phones as a method for paying bills. It is possible   22
14 to buy securities, make transfers, and determine account     34
15 balances. You will save time by using a Touch-Tone phone.    45

16     A third type of electronic bill processing involves     10
17 using a microcomputer and a modem. Software programs have    21
18 on-screen checkbooks linked to bill-paying applications.      34
19 Other microcomputers use online services through a modem.    46
   |  1  |  2  |  3  |  4  |  5  |  6  |  7  |  8  |  9  |  10 |  11 |  12
```

C. TECHNIQUE PRACTICE: SPACE BAR

```
20     We will all go to the race if I win my event today.
21 Do you think that I will be able to finish the race at the
22 front of the pack, or do you think there are lots of very
23 fast runners out there who surely can finish ahead of me?
```

D. Edit this paragraph to correct any typing or formatting errors.

D. PROOFREADING: EDITING

24   Many home computer user like the challenge of haveing
25 the latest in both hardware and software technology. Their
26 are those however, who's needs likely can be satisfied at
27 a very low costs. A used 486-chip personnel computer with
28 color monitor and keyboard might be your's for under $ 300.
29 Check out th Yellow Page, or visit a used-computer store.

FORMATTING

E. REPORT HEADINGS IN MEMOS

There are times when a memo report is used rather than a cover memo to accompany a report. The memo and the report are combined into one, and headings are formatted as they are in a report.

DOCUMENT PROCESSING

Report 75-55

Memo Report

Refer to Reference Manual

Review:
R-9C: Memo Report

MEMO TO: All Employees | **FROM:** Franklin Coates, Director | **DATE:** February 24, 20-- | **SUBJECT:** Security System

¶ Beginning March 1, we will install a new security access system. Complete installation should occur by the end of March. The system will include new magnetic card readers at all entrances. It will also provide a more secure working environment, especially in the evenings and on weekends. Entrances will lock and unlock automatically each day during working hours. Please carefully read and follow the detailed instructions for using the new system.

RECEIVING A NEW ACCESS CARD

¶ Once the new system is installed, you will need a new access identification card to enter the building during nonworking hours. Human Resources will begin taking pictures for new cards during the week of March 20. When you are called, report immediately. The cards will be issued as soon as they are ready. To receive your new card, you must turn in your old one.

(Continued on next page)

ENTERING THE BUILDING

¶ Entrances will automatically unlock each working day at 8 a.m and lock at 5 p.m. To enter the building during nonworking hours, slide your access identification card (with the magnetic strip facing left) through the card reader at the right of the entrance door. When the green light comes on, open the door. Do not hold the door open longer than 30 seconds.

¶ Once you enter the building during nonworking hours, please proceed immediately to the front desk and sign in. Record in the logbook your name, department, extension number, and arrival time.

LEAVING THE BUILDING

¶ Before leaving the building, you must sign out. Please record your departure time beside your name. Do not use the special latch handle to open the door, or the alarm will sound. Instead, use the push bar. Once you have opened the door, do not let it remain open longer than 30 seconds, or the alarm will sound. If you accidentally set off the alarm, return to the front desk and call the security company (the telephone number is at the top of the logbook). Be prepared to provide the security personnel with your name, extension number, and access card number.

¶ At times you may need to have the door held open for extended periods of time during nonbusiness hours. In these situations, please make arrangements with Building Maintenance by calling extension 4444.

¶ If you have questions about our new security access system and procedures, please contact me.

urs

Report 75-56 ▶

Memo Report

Mr. Coates has asked you to revise Report 75-55 as follows:

1. Use February 25 as the date.
2. Change "nonworking" to nonbusiness throughout the report.

3. Add the following sentence at the end of the second paragraph:

   New employees will be asked for a special form, to be provided by their supervisors.

4. Change "Building Maintenance" to Building Security in the next-to-last paragraph.

MEMO TO: All Employees
FROM: Adrienne Barzan
DATE: March 2, 20--
SUBJECT: New Building Site

¶ We have consulted with several architects and have finalized plans to build a new administrative center at 6400 Easton Plaza. This memo provides general information about plans for the center's exterior and interior development.

EXTERIOR PLANS

¶ Exterior plans will maintain the historical integrity and beauty of the surrounding area and reflect the architecture of other buildings in the office park. Landscaping plans include a parklike area, a picnic area, and a small pond.

INTERIOR PLANS FOR STAFF

¶ Staff will be located within the new facility as follows:

1. Accounting will be located on the first floor in the west wing.
2. Sales and marketing will be located on the first floor in the east wing. All staff will be grouped according to product line.
3. All other staff will be located on the second floor. Exact locations will be determined at a later date.

INTERIOR PLANS FOR SPECIAL FACILITIES

¶ Conference rooms will be located in the center of the building on the first floor to provide easy access for everyone. All rooms will be equipped with state-of-the-art technology. Our new center will also include a full-service cafeteria, a copy center, a library, an athletic center, and an on-site day care center. Construction of the new center will begin when we obtain the necessary permits.

urs

Unit 16

Tables

CITY BANK
Interest Rates Schedule
Effective Date: November 11, 20--

	Rate	APY
Value Checking	0.00%	0.00%
City Checking	1.25%	1.27%
Prestige Checking	1.25%	1.27%
Golden Checking	1.50%	1.55%
Regular Savings	1.75%	1.90%
Young Savers	1.75%	1.90%
Christmas Club	1.75%	1.90%
Money Market—Tier I	2.25%	2.30%
Money Market—Tier II	2.50%	2.60%
Money Market—Tier III	2.75%	2.80%
Money Market—Tier IV	3.00%	3.10%
CD—6 month	2.25%	2.50%

CITY BANK
Interest Rates Schedule
Effective Date: November 11, 20--

	Rate	APY*
Value Checking	0.00%	0.00%
City Checking	1.25%	1.27%
Prestige Checking	1.25%	1.27%
Golden Checking	1.50%	1.55%
Regular Savings	1.75%	1.90%
Young Savers	1.75%	1.90%
Christmas Club	1.75%	1.90%
Money Market—Tier I	2.25%	2.30%
Money Market—Tier II	2.50%	2.60%
Money Market—Tier III	2.75%	2.80%
Money Market—Tier IV	3.00%	3.10%
CD—6 month	2.25%	2.50%
CD—1 year	2.35%	2.65%
CD—2 year	2.45%	2.70%
CD—3 year	2.50%	2.75%
*APY=Annual Percentage Yield		

CUSTOMER DATABASE INFORMATION
(Ohio District)
August 31, 20--

Customer	Address	City	ZIP	Telephone No.	Item	Stock No.
Westphal, Darlene	3309 Aaron Place Street	Kenton	44426	419-555-2384	Pentium Computer	4-238-CW
Roanne, Dennis	20604 Lucile Road South	Columbus	43230	614-555-2074	Laser Printer	3-895-LP
Byrnes, Carl	322 West Lyons Road	Mansfield	44902	216-555-2002	Laser Printer	3-895-LP
Dawson, Cynthia	5914 Bay Oaks Place	Chillicothe	45601	614-555-1399	Color Ink-Jet Printer	2-550-CIJ
Graupmann, Meg	10386 Power Drive	Steubenville	43952	614-555-7821	Pentium Computer	4-238-CW
Neusome, Jo	Box 365	Youngstown	44502	216-555-3885	Pentium Computer	4-238-CW
Shapiro, Tony	6823 Creekwood Drive	Columbus	43085	614-555-2934	Pentium Computer	4-238-CW
Garand, Lisa	26044 Manzano Court	Youngstown	44505	216-555-1777	Flatbed Color Scanner	6-882-CSC
Parker, Tom	936 Eastwind Drive	Cleveland	44121	216-555-2839	Laser Printer	3-895-LP

Tables With Footnotes or Source Notes

Goals

- Type at least 43wpm/5′/5e
- Change text direction
- Insert or delete rows or columns

A. Type 2 times.

A. WARMUP

```
1        Order #Z391 must be processed "quickly" and exactly    11
2   as specified! In January several orders were sent out by     22
3   mistake; regrettably, one order worth $5,680 was canceled.   34
    |  1  |  2  |  3  |  4  |  5  |  6  |  7  |  8  |  9  |  10 |  11 |  12
```

SKILLBUILDING

B. Take three 12-second timed writings on each line. The scale below the last line shows your wpm speed for a 12-second timed writing.

B. 12-SECOND SPEED SPRINTS

```
4   You paid for the ruby that she owned when he was just five.
5   Toby wishes to thank all eight of the girls for their time.
6   Yale is a very fine place to learn about the world of work.
7   She has a theory that the icy roads will cause a bad wreck.
    | | | |5| | | |10| | | |15| | | |20| | | |25| | | |30| | | |35| | | |40| | | |45| | | |50| | | |55| | | |60
```

C. DIAGNOSTIC PRACTICE: SYMBOLS AND PUNCTUATION

If you are not using the GDP software, turn to page SB-2 and follow the directions for this activity.

Strategies for Career Success

Cell Phone Manners Matter

Mind your cell phone manners! Although the cell phone allows you to keep in touch with your boss, coworkers, and clients, it also requires you to consider your communication etiquette. One of the worst violations of etiquette and safety is driving and talking at the same time; and in some states such as New Jersey, cell phone use while driving is restricted to hands-free devices. It is much safer to pull off the road to make a call.

Consider others when you use a cell phone in a public place (for example, a restaurant). If you use the phone in public, talk quietly and watch what you say. Cell phones in meetings can distract others; some companies prohibit them in business meetings.

When you call a cell phone user, keep your message brief.

YOUR TURN Observe cell phone users in a public place. Are they mindful of others when they use their phones?

D. Take two 5-minute timed writings. Review your speed and errors.

Goal: At least 43wpm/5′/5e

D. 5-MINUTE TIMED WRITING

8	Starting up your own business may mean that you are	11
9	thinking about acquiring an existing business. If so, is	22
10	that business doing well in the community? If you are going	34
11	to buy out an established business, you need to know the	45
12	reason the current owner wishes to sell the company. If	57
13	there are other businesses in the area, you should first	68
14	find out what reputation that business has built up in the	80
15	community. Do other businesses think highly of the company?	92
16	You must also consider what type of advertising you	103
17	plan to use to get your business off to a good start. You	114
18	might use ads in newspapers, on television, in magazines,	126
19	or on the Internet. When you start your ad campaign, you	137
20	should consider hiring an ad agency to put out the best	149
21	message for your company and its products. You should also	160
22	consider the types of ads being used by your competitors to	172
23	determine what has worked well for them.	181
24	Yes, there are major issues that need to be addressed	192
25	when starting up your own business; and all of the issues	203
26	should be dealt with before you decide to take such a step.	215

| 1 | 2 | 3 | 4 | 5 | 6 | 7 | 8 | 9 | 10 | 11 | 12

FORMATTING

Reference Manual

Refer to pages R-8B and R-13A of the Reference Manual.

E. TABLES WITH FOOTNOTES OR SOURCE NOTES

To format tables with footnotes or source notes:

1. When you insert a table, include an additional row at the bottom of the table for the footnote or source note.
2. Merge the cells in the bottom row.
3. In the bottom row, type the word Note: or Source: if there is a note or source for the table. Then type the information for the note or source.
4. If there is a footnote, type an asterisk (or another symbol) at the appropriate point within the table. Then type the information for the footnote.

Word Processing Manual

F. WORD PROCESSING: TABLE—TEXT DIRECTION, AND TABLE—INSERT OR DELETE ROWS OR COLUMNS

Study Lesson 76 in your word processing manual. Complete all of the shaded steps while at your computer. Then format the jobs that follow.

DOCUMENT PROCESSING

Table 76-26

Boxed Table

Your completed table will look different from the one shown.

1. Insert a boxed table with 7 columns and 6 rows.
2. Select Row 1, and change the text direction to display vertically bottom to top.
3. Drag down on the bottom border of Row 1 until the column headings display as shown on page 283.
4. Type the information in the body of the table.

(Continued on next page)

5. Right-align the text in the number columns. **Note:** Do not change the left alignment of the column headings.
6. Merge the cells in the bottom row, and then type the table note.

7. Automatically adjust the column widths.
8. Center the table horizontally and vertically.

Always automatically adjust column widths and center tables horizontally and vertically.

Account Number	Blue Sierra Letterhead	Italian Renaissance Letterhead	Sonoma Desert Letterhead	Watercolor Wash Letterhead	Sandstone Marble Letterhead	Greek Acropolis Letterhead
GV-11	3,500	500	750	1,000	250	1,250
GV-29	2,500	250	250	500	500	250
GV-37	750	1,000	500	2,500	250	2,500
GV-10	250	500	1,000	250	1,500	250
Note: This information is subject to change.						

Table 76-27

Boxed Table

Open the file for Table 76-26 and make the following changes:

1. Delete the table note row.
2. Delete Column G, and insert a column to the left of Column B.
3. Insert a row above Row 3. Type: GV-72 | 1,250 | 500 | 1,000 | 250 | 750 | 2,000
4. In Column B, type: French Patina Letterhead | 750 | 1,250 | 250 | 1,000 | 500
5. Right-align the text in the numbers columns as needed.
6. Apply 25 percent shading to Row 1.

Table 76-28

Boxed Table

Your completed table will look different from the one shown.

1. Insert a boxed table with 5 columns and 6 rows.
2. Select Row 1, and change the text direction to display vertically bottom to top.
3. Drag down on the bottom border of Row 1 until the column headings display in one continuous line without wrapping.
4. Type the information in the body of the table.
5. Right-align the text in the number columns. **Note:** Do not change the left alignment of the column headings.
6. Merge the cells in the bottom row, and then type the source note.
7. Automatically adjust the column widths.
8. Center the table horizontally and vertically.

Office Supply Account	LED Laser Printer	Internal Fax Modem	Cash Management System	Plain-Paper Laser Fax
OE-9	$405	$181	$199	$249
DD-7	395	150	205	234
US-2	410	125	183	252
OB-1	420	167	179	245
Source: March invoices				

Tables With Braced Column Headings

Goals

- Improve speed and accuracy
- Refine language arts skills in capitalization
- Format braced headings in tables

A. Type 2 times.

A. WARMUP

```
1        Six citizens from 14th Avenue East joined 83 other      10
2   residents to discuss the #794 proposal* for a new swimming   22
3   pool. Barry Kelm quoted numbers about current pool usage.     33
    |  1  |  2  |  3  |  4  |  5  |  6  |  7  |  8  |  9  |  10  |  11  |  12
```

SKILLBUILDING

B. DIAGNOSTIC PRACTICE: NUMBERS

If you are not using the GDP software, turn to page SB-5 and follow the directions for this activity.

C. MAP

Follow the GDP software directions for this exercise in improving keystroking accuracy.

LANGUAGE ARTS

D. Study the rules at the right.

D. CAPITALIZATION

RULE ▶

≡ noun #

Capitalize nouns followed by a number or letter (except for the nouns *line*, *note*, *page*, *paragraph*, and *size*).
Please read Chapter 5, which begins on page 94.

RULE ▶

≡ compass point

Capitalize compass points (such as *north*, *south*, or *northeast*) only when they designate definite regions.
From Montana we drove south to reach the Southwest.

Edit the sentences to correct any errors in capitalization.

```
4   The marketing manager had a reservation on flight 505 to Atlanta
5   Please order two model 6M printers.
6   The desktop publishing seminar will be held in Room 101.
7   Study pages 120-230 for the unit test.
8   Please contact all representatives in the northern states.
9   Have you visited the city of Pittsburgh?
10  The population of the south continues to increase.
```

FORMATTING

E. BRACED COLUMN HEADINGS

A braced column heading is a heading that applies to more than one column (for example, *Retirement Account* in the table shown below):

1. To create a braced column heading, position the insertion point where you want the braced heading to appear.

2. Merge the cells over which the braced heading will appear.
3. Center the braced column heading over the appropriate columns.

DOCUMENT PROCESSING

Table 77-29

Boxed Table

1. Insert a boxed table with 6 columns and 6 rows.
2. Center and type the braced column headings in upper- and lowercase and bold.
3. Type the regular column headings in bold; right-align the number columns.
4. Follow the standard table format.
5. Merge cells as necessary.
6. Center the table horizontally and vertically.

INSURED ACCOUNT DEPOSITS For Melanie and Frank Bush					
First World Savings		**Individual Account**		**Retirement Account**	
Month	**Branch**	**M. Bush**	**F. Bush**	**M. Bush**	**F. Bush**
January	Reseda	$5,500	$2,350	$2,000	$10,000
February	Valencia	7,950	5,700	5,500	4,300
March	Van Nuys	2,400	7,300	9,300	2,550

Table 77-30

Boxed Table

1. Insert a boxed table with 4 columns and 6 rows.
2. Center and type the braced column headings in upper- and lowercase and bold.
3. Type the regular column headings in bold; right-align the number columns.
4. Follow the standard table format.
5. Merge cells as necessary.
6. Center the table horizontally and vertically.

CINEPLEX VIDEOS Sales Trends			
Western Region		**Total Sales**	
State	**Manager**	**Last Year**	**This Year**
California	George Lucas	$1,956,250	$2,135,433
Nevada	Marjorie Matheson	859,435	1,231,332
Washington	Valerie Harper	737,498	831,352

Table
77-31

Boxed Table

Open the file for Table 77-30 and make the following changes.

1. Change the column heading "Western Region" to Eastern Region.
2. Change the state names to New York | New Jersey | Delaware.
3. Change the managers' names to Robert DeLuca | Doris Lynch | Megan Bennett.

4. Change last year's amounts to $2,052,659 | 534,958 | 894,211.
5. Change this year's amounts to $3,345,312 | 2,311,478 | 925,138.

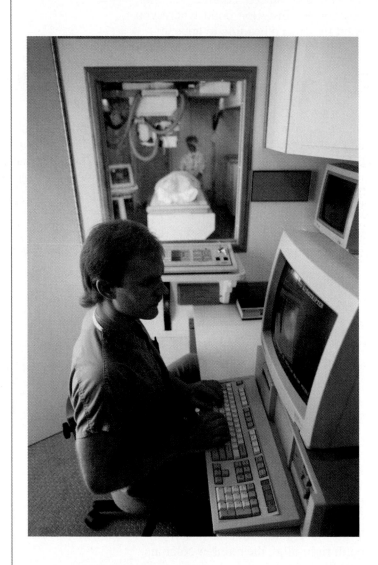

Tables Formatted Sideways

Goals

- Type at least 43wpm/5'/5e
- Format tables in landscape orientation

A. Type 2 times.

A. WARMUP

```
1        This week order a monitor with a resolution of 1280 x    11
2   1024 that supports an optimal refresh rate from V & Q Inc.    23
3   It will cost $573* (*a 9% savings) if ordered before July!    35
    |  1  |  2  |  3  |  4  |  5  |  6  |  7  |  8  |  9  |  10 |  11 |  12
```

SKILLBUILDING

B. PACED PRACTICE

If you are not using the GDP software, turn to page SB-14 and follow the directions for this activity.

Keyboarding Connection

Finding People on the Internet

Remember that long-lost friend from high school? Well, he or she may not be lost for long if you use the Internet's assistance. It is easy to search for a person on the Net by following a few simple steps.

Access a search engine. Click hyperlinks pertaining to finding people such as People Finder or People Search. Enter the information requested about the person, and press the Search button.

Conduct a search for Web sites where you can also find e-mail addresses. Enter the information about the person you are seeking. Click the Search button. Your search should list any names and e-mail addresses that match the name you entered.

YOUR TURN   Access a search engine and try to locate the address of a high school friend.

C. Take two 5-minute timed writings. Review your speed and errors.

Goal: At least 43wpm/5′/5e

C. 5-MINUTE TIMED WRITING

```
 4        This is the third in a series of timed writings on    10
 5   starting up a new business. In this presentation, you will  22
 6   consider some expense and merchandise issues as well as     33
 7   some thoughts on the building you will move into or build.   45
 8        There are several expenses that you will have to look   57
 9   at for your new business. For example, do you realize how    69
10   much construction costs will be, or, if you are going to     80
11   rent a building, how much that expense will amount to? You   92
12   must also project expenses for insurance on the building    103
13   and its contents, utilities costs for running the business, 115
14   interest expense on any loans you secure to purchase or     126
15   renovate the building, and any advertising expenses.        137
16        You must also consider the amount of merchandise you   148
17   will have on hand when you first open your store. If you     159
18   have several lines of merchandise, you need to determine    171
19   how many products and how much of each product you will     182
20   keep on the shelves and how much you will keep in inventory 194
21   in your warehouse. To acquire this merchandise, you must    205
22   locate suppliers who will sell you what you need.           215
     |  1  |  2  |  3  |  4  |  5  |  6  |  7  |  8  |  9  |  10  |  11  |  12
```

FORMATTING

Word Processing Manual

D.   WORD PROCESSING: PAGE ORIENTATION

Study Lesson 78 in your word processing manual. Complete all of the shaded steps while at your computer. Then format the jobs that follow.

DOCUMENT PROCESSING

Table 78-32

Boxed Table

1. Format the table in landscape orientation.
2. Set 0.5-inch side margins for the page.
3. Insert a boxed table with 7 columns and 11 rows.
4. Type the following column headings in bold:

Customer | Address | City | ZIP | Telephone No. | Item | Stock No.

5. In Column A, type the customer's last name followed by a comma; then type the first name.

(Continued on next page)

CUSTOMER DATABASE INFORMATION

(Ohio District)

August 31, 20--

~~Maria~~ Darlene Westphal | 3309 aaron Place ~~Avenue~~ Street | Kenton | 44426 | 419-555-2384 | Pentium computer | 4-238-cw

Dennis Roanne | 20604 Lucile Rd. South | Columbus | 43230 | 614-555-2074 | laser printer | 3-895-LP

Carl Byrnes | 322 W. Lyons Road | Mansfield | 44902 | 216-555-2002 | ~~Color~~ Laser Printer | 3-895-LP

Cynthia Dawson | 5914 Bay Oaks Place | Chilicothe | 456l0 | 614-555-1399 | Color Ink-Jet Printer | 2-550-cij

Meg Graupmann | 10386 power Dr. | Steubenville | 43952 | 614-555-7821 | Pentium Computer | 4-238-CW

Jo Neusome | Box 365 | Youngstown | 44502 | 216-555-3885 | Pentium computer | 4-238-CW

Tony Shapiro | 6823 Creekwood ~~Lane~~ Drive | Columbus | 43085 | 614-555-2934 | Pentium Computer | ~~5-987 PC~~ 4-238-CW

Lisa Garand | 26044 Manzano Court | Youngstown | 44505 | 216-555-1777 | FlatBed Color Scanner | 6-8820-CSC

Tom Parker | 936 East wind Drive | Cleveland | 44121 | 216-555-2839 | Lasser Printer | 3-895-LP

Table 78-33 ▶

Boxed Table

Open the file for Table 78-32, and make the following changes:
1. Change the date to August 19, 20--.
2. Sort the table alphabetically by the customers' last names.
3. Shade the headings with a 25 percent fill.

Table
78-34

Boxed Table

1. Change the page orientation to landscape.
2. Insert a boxed table with 7 columns and 6 rows.
3. Use standard table format to type the headings and body of the table.
4. Bold and center-align the column headings.
5. Merge the cells in the bottom row; then type the table footnote.

REGIONAL SALES OFFICES
General Information*

Region	Street Address	City	State	ZIP	Telephone	Fax
East	8787 Orion Place	Columbus	OH	43240	614-555-4951	614-555-4999
Mid-Continent	1415 Elbridge Payne Road	Chesterfield	MO	63017	636-555-9940	636-555-9034
Southeast	3100 Breckinridge Boulevard	Duluth	GA	30096	770-555-7007	770-555-7422
West	21600 Oxnard Street	Woodland Hills	CA	91367	818-555-2675	818-555-2697
*Information on all regional offices is updated each year on July 1.						

Multipage Tables

Goals

- Improve speed and accuracy
- Refine language arts skills in spelling
- Format multipage tables

A. Type 2 times.

A. WARMUP

```
1        Please request this key item by June: an XYZ 2000      10
2   motherboard with 512-MB RAM. I don't expect delivery until  22
3   7/5; I realize this is a "great" investment for the money!   34
    |  1  |  2  |  3  |  4  |  5  |  6  |  7  |  8  |  9  |  10  |  11  |  12
```

SKILLBUILDING

PPP PRETEST → PRACTICE → POSTTEST

PRETEST
Take a 1-minute timed writing. Review your speed and errors.

B. PRETEST: Alternate- and One-Hand Words

```
4        They both blame the fight on the visitor. The girl      10
5   had no right to imply that the proxy was brave enough to     21
6   draw you into the unholy case. The union will reward you.    32
    |  1  |  2  |  3  |  4  |  5  |  6  |  7  |  8  |  9  |  10  |  11  |  12
```

PRACTICE
Speed Emphasis:
If you made no more than 1 error on the Pretest, type each *individual* line 2 times.
Accuracy Emphasis:
If you made 2 or more errors, type each *group* of lines (as though it were a paragraph) 2 times.

C. PRACTICE: Alternate-Hand Words

```
7   also angle field bushel ancient emblem panel sight fish big
8   both blame fight formal element handle proxy signs girl and
9   city chair giant island visitor profit right their laid cut
```

D. PRACTICE: One-Hand Words

```
10  acts hilly award uphill average poplin refer jolly adds him
11  area jumpy based homily baggage you'll serve union beat ink
12  case brave extra limply greater unholy wages imply draw you
```

POSTTEST
Repeat the Pretest timed writing and compare performance.

E. POSTTEST: Alternate- and One-Hand Words

F. PROGRESSIVE PRACTICE: ALPHABET

If you are not using the GDP software, turn to page SB-7 and follow the directions for this activity.

G. TECHNIQUE PRACTICE: ENTER KEY

G. Type each sentence on a separate line by pressing ENTER after each sentence.

```
13      Start a business. See the banker. Rent a building.
14   Check state codes. Check city codes. Get needed licenses.
15   Contact suppliers. Call utility companies. Buy furniture.
16   Hire the employees. Open the doors. Hope for customers.
```

LANGUAGE ARTS

H. SPELLING

H. Type this list of frequently misspelled words, paying special attention to any spelling problems in each word.

```
17   assistance compliance initial limited corporation technical
18   operating sufficient operation incorporated writing current
19   advice together prepared recommend appreciated cannot based
20   benefit completing analysis probably projects before annual
21   issue attention location association participation proposed
```

Edit the sentences to correct any misspellings.

```
22   The complience by the corporation was sufficient to pass.
23   I cannot reccomend the project based on the expert advise.
24   The location of the proposed annual meeting was an issue.
25   Your assistance in completeing the project is appreciated.
26   Together we prepared an analysis of their current operation.
27   The writing was incorporated in the initial asociation bid.
```

FORMATTING

I. MULTIPAGE TABLES

Tables should generally be formatted to fit on one page. However, if a table extends to another page, follow these formatting rules:

1. Repeat the column headings at the top of each new page.
2. Number all pages in the upper right-hand corner.

Word
Processing
Manual

J. WORD PROCESSING: TABLE—REPEATING TABLE HEADING ROWS

Study Lesson 79 in your word processing manual. Complete all of the shaded steps while at your computer. Then format the jobs that follow.

DOCUMENT PROCESSING

Table 79-35

Boxed Table

Note: Your completed table may look different from the table shown.

Follow these steps to create a multipage table:

1. Insert a boxed table with 3 columns and 52 rows.
2. Type the information in the table as shown below.
3. Apply 25 percent shading to the column headings row.
4. Repeat the table heading rows on page 2.
5. Number the pages in the upper right-hand corner.

50 LONGEST RIVERS OF THE WORLD (Miles rounded to nearest 10)		
River	**Outflow**	**Miles**
Nile	Mediterranean	4,160
Amazon	Atlantic Ocean	4,000
Chang	East China Sea	3,960
Huang	Yellow Sea	3,400
Ob-Irtysh	Gulf of Ob	3,360
Amur	Tatar Strait	2,740
Lena	Laptev Sea	2,730
Congo	Atlantic Ocean	2,720
Mekong	South China Sea	2,600
Niger	Gulf of Guinea	2,590
Yenisey	Kara Sea	2,540
Parana	Rio de la Plata	2,490
Mississippi	Gulf of Mexico	2,340
Missouri	Mississippi River	2,320
Murray-Darling	Indian Ocean	2,310
Volga	Caspian Sea	2,290
Purus	Amazon River	2,100
Medeira	Amazon River	2,010
Sao Francisco	Atlantic Ocean	1,990
Yukon	Bering Sea	1,980
Rio Grande	Gulf of Mexico	1,900
Brahmaputra	Bay of Bengal	1,800
Indus	Arabian Sea	1,800
Danube	Black Sea	1,780
Japura	Amazon River	1,750
Euphrates	Shatt al Arab	1,700
Zambezi	Indian Ocean	1,700
Tocantins	Para River	1,680
Orinoco	Atlantic Ocean	1,600
Amu	Aral Sea	1,580

50 LONGEST RIVERS OF THE WORLD (Miles rounded to nearest 10)		
River	**Outflow**	**Miles**
Paraguay	Parana River	1,580
Ural	Caspian Sea	1,580
Ganges	Bay of Bengal	1,560
Salween	Andaman Sea	1,500
Arkansas	Mississippi River	1,460
Colorado	Gulf of California	1,450
Dnieper	Black Sea	1,420
Negro	Amazon	1,400
Syr	Aral Sea	1,370
Irrawaddy	Bay of Bengal	1,340
Orange	Atlantic Ocean	1,300
Red	Atchafalaya River	1,290
Columbia	Pacific Ocean	1,240
Don	Sea of Azov	1,220
Peace	Slave River	1,210
Xi	South China Sea	1,200
Tigris	Shatt al Arab	1,180
Angara	Yenisey River	1,150
Songhua	Amur River	1,150
Snake	Columbia River	1,040

Table
79-36

Boxed Table

Open the file for Table 79-35, and make the following changes:

1. Sort the table alphabetically by river in ascending order.

2. Apply a double border at the bottom of Row 2.

Table
79-37

Boxed Table

Follow these steps to create a boxed table.

1. Change the page orientation to landscape.
2. Insert a boxed table with 5 columns and 7 rows.
3. Type the table as shown.
4. Apply 100 percent shading (black) to the title row.
5. Apply 25 percent shading to the column heading row.
6. Merge the cells in the bottom row; then type the table footnote.

INVESTMENT SUMMARY				
Limited Partnership	Date of Issue	Initial Cost	Dividend*	Owner
HS Properties	January 2001	$ 50,000	$ 6,066	Alpha Association
Northern Lumber	May 2001	50,000	4,750	CXT Corporation
ST1	February 2001	50,000	7,500	Smith & Sons, Incorporated
ST2	December 2001	100,000	12,250	Q and S Company
*Annual dividends based on current market analysis.				

Using Predesigned Table Formats

Goals

- Type at least 43wpm/5′/5e
- Format tables using Table AutoFormat

A. Type 2 times.

A. WARMUP

```
 1      "Just when can we expect to realize a profit of 5% or    11
 2   more?" This kind of question will be important to 2/3 of     22
 3   the shareholders; they own over 89% of the prime holdings.   34
     | 1 | 2 | 3 | 4 | 5 | 6 | 7 | 8 | 9 | 10 | 11 | 12
```

SKILLBUILDING

B. Take a 1-minute timed writing on the first paragraph to establish your base speed. Then take four 1-minute timed writings on the remaining paragraphs. As soon as you equal or exceed your base speed on one paragraph, advance to the next, more difficult paragraph.

B. SUSTAINED PRACTICE: NUMBERS AND SYMBOLS

```
 4      There is a need at this time to communicate our new      11
 5   pricing guidelines to our franchise outlets. In addition,   23
 6   they must be made aware of inventory implications. They      34
 7   will then be in a position to have a successful operation.   46

 8      Franchise operators could be requested to use either     11
 9   a 20% or a 30% markup. A $50 item would be marked to sell    23
10   for either $60 or $65. Depending on future prospects for    34
11   sales, half of the articles would be priced at each level.  46

12      Ms. Aagard's suggestion is to assign items in Groups     11
13   #1470, #2830, and #4560 to the 20% category. The Series 77  23
14   items* would be in the 30% markup category except for the   35
15   items with a base rate under $100. What is your reaction?    46

16      Mr. Chavez's recommendation is to assign a 30% markup    11
17   to Groups #3890, #5290, #6480, and #7180. About 1/4 of the  22
18   remainder (except for soft goods) would also be in the 30%  34
19   category. Groups #8340 and #9560 would have a 20% markup.    46
     | 1 | 2 | 3 | 4 | 5 | 6 | 7 | 8 | 9 | 10 | 11 | 12
```

C. Take two 5-minute timed writings. Review your speed and errors.

Goal: At least 43wpm/5'/5e

C. 5-MINUTE TIMED WRITING

```
20        Finding a job is a challenge in today's job market,      11
21   but there are some steps you can take to remain competitive   23
22   in the job market. First of all, be sure you know something   35
23   about the company. Do they have offices in a location to      46
24   which you would move, and is the position in that company      58
25   one in which you would like to spend the next five to ten      69
26   years?                                                         71
27        To be successful during your interview, you need to      81
28   know yourself. What are your strengths, and what are your      93
29   weaknesses, if any? Be sure to emphasize your unique skills   105
30   both in your resume and during the interview. Let others      116
31   know what makes you the best candidate for the job. Some      128
32   excellent traits to emphasize would be enthusiasm, a high     139
33   motivation level, and an excellent work ethic.                149
34        When you go for your interview, take into account how    160
35   you dress. Choose your wardrobe as you would for your first   172
36   day on the job. If you are uncertain as to the particular     183
37   dress code, always err on the side of conservatism. Also,     195
38   be watchful of your personal grooming. Make certain your      206
39   hair is trimmed and your shoes are polished.                  215
     |  1  |  2  |  3  |  4  |  5  |  6  |  7  |  8  |  9  |  10  |  11  |  12
```

FORMATTING

Go To Word Processing Manual

D. WORD PROCESSING: TABLE—STYLES

Study Lesson 80 in your word processing manual. Complete all the shaded steps while at your computer. Then format the jobs that follow.

Table 80-38

Predesigned Table

 Note: Your completed table may look different from the table shown.

1. Use a landscape page orientation.
2. Insert a table with 3 columns and 17 rows.
3. Type the table contents, and then automatically adjust the column widths.
4. Apply a table style of your choice.
5. Center the table horizontally and vertically.

CITY BANK Interest Rates Schedule Effective Date: November 11, 2008		
	Rate	APY
Value Checking	0.00%	0.00%
City Checking	1.25%	1.27%
Prestige Checking	1.25%	1.27%
Golden Checking	1.50%	1.55%
Regular Savings	1.75%	1.90%
Young Savers	1.75%	1.90%
Christmas Club	1.75%	1.90%
Money Market—Tier I	2.25%	2.30%
Money Market—Tier II	2.50%	2.60%
Money Market—Tier III	2.75%	2.80%
Money Market—Tier IV	3.00%	3.10%
CD6 month	2.25%	2.50%
CD—1 year	2.35%	2.65%
CD—2 year	2.45%	2.70%
Average	2.06%	2.19%

Table 80-39

Predesigned Table

Open the file for Table 80-38 and make the following changes:

1. Use a portrait page orientation.
2. Add 1 blank row between Christmas Club and Money Market—Tier 1.
3. Add 1 blank row between Money Market—Tier IV and CD—6 month.
4. Merge the cells in the inserted rows.
5. Type an asterisk (*) after "APY" in Column C.
6. Insert 1 blank row at the bottom of the table, merge the cells, and type *APY=Annual Percentage Yield.
7. Apply a different table style.
8. Center the table horizontally and vertically.

Progress and Proofreading Check

Documents designated as Proofreading Checks serve as a check of your proofreading skill. Your goal is to have zero typographical errors when the GDP software first scores the document.

Follow these steps to insert a table using Table AutoFormat.

1. Insert the following table in default format.

2. Apply a table style of your choice.
3. Center the table horizontally and vertically.

No.	Room Name	Seating	Square Feet
BUILDING DIRECTORY Paulding Meeting Facility			
102	Alabama	35	400
104	Colorado	150	1,600
106	Delaware	25	350
108	Georgia	50	600
202	Montana	35	400
204	Nevada	50	600
206	New Jersey	300	3,200
208	Pennsylvania	350	3,600

Skills Assessment on Part 4

5-Minute Timed Writing

```
 1      Many business firms create their own special documents  11
 2  today by using software packages that are designed to do    23
 3  the job. These packages help people with limited design     34
 4  skills create pages with very little effort. The challenge, 46
 5  though, is for the person to design the pages effectively    57
 6  so that the reader will read them. After all, the reason     69
 7  for putting in all that time and money is to get people to   81
 8  read the articles.                                           84
 9      Designing pages that are easy to read is not quite as   95
10  easy as it seems. For example, a reader may be confused if  107
11  a page has too many headlines. Instead, a reader may want   119
12  to read fewer headlines that are printed in larger type.    130
13      Desktop publishers require just a few good tools to     141
14  interest the reader. A good plan to use is to be sure to     152
15  put the most important article at the top of the first page  164
16  and the less important articles on the inside pages. The    176
17  use of bullets and side headings are also helpful guides to  188
18  help a reader zip through pages. A final suggestion is to    199
19  use pictures and graphics that can make the text much more   211
20  interesting to read.                                         215
```

| 1 | 2 | 3 | 4 | 5 | 6 | 7 | 8 | 9 | 10 | 11 | 12

Correspondence Test 4-76

Memo Report

MEMO

TO: All employees

FROM: Paula Sullivan

Date: January 15, 20--

SUBJECT: Capital Communication Co.

Capital Communication Co. (CCC) operates the fourth-largest network in the U.S. In addition, CCC owns 8 television stations, 3 radio stations, and 4 newspapers.

HISTORY

CCC was started in 1962 by a subsidiary of Heartland Publications as a public service network. It began with three radio stations and added both radio and television stations until it went public in 1956. In 1987 it merged with Pacific

(Continued on next page)

Media Company and added ④ newspapers. CCCs largest news paper, *The San Antonio Times*, won a pulitzer Prize for feature writing last year.

¶ **EARNINGS** With sales of $4.9 billion dollars for the most recent 12-month period and a net income of $486 million, CCC continues to lead the "buy" list of most stock brokers. The following table shows a break down of CCC s earnings.

CAPITAL COMMUNICATION COMPANY			
Company	Last Year	This Year	Next Year*
Radio	$ #1.3	$1.4	$1.4
Television	$1.8	$2.10	$2.2
Newspapers	$1.4	$1.5	$2.0
*Projected			

— Sales (in Billions)

urs

Correspondence Test 4-77 ▶

Business Letter in Block Style

January 10, 20-- | Mr. Owen F. Austin | 1734 Perry Street | Flint, MI 48504 | Dear Mr. Austin:

¶ I am sorry that time constraints shortened our telephone conversation yesterday. Given the circumstances as you presented them, you would be wise to consider drafting a general durable power of attorney as described in Section 495 of the new act.

¶ A power of attorney, under the old law, is effective only up to the time that a person is disabled or incompetent. Now the general durable power of attorney, under the new statute, will remain in effect until a person either revokes it or passes away.

¶ The new law will be very helpful to many elderly and infirm people. Sincerely yours, | C. F. Storden | Attorney-at-Law | urs | PS: You may want to discuss this matter with your children before calling my office for an appointment. | bc: Peggy Austin, Walter Austin

Boxed Table

Add 25 percent shading to the title row, column headings row, and total row.

AMERICAN TRADE (As a Percentage of Total)			
Exports		**Imports**	
Canada	22	Japan	20
Japan	12	Canada	19
Mexico	7	Mexico	6
United Kingdom	6	Germany	5
Germany	5	Taiwan	5
South Korea	4	South Korea	4
Other countries	44	Other countries	41
TOTAL	**100**	**TOTAL**	**100**

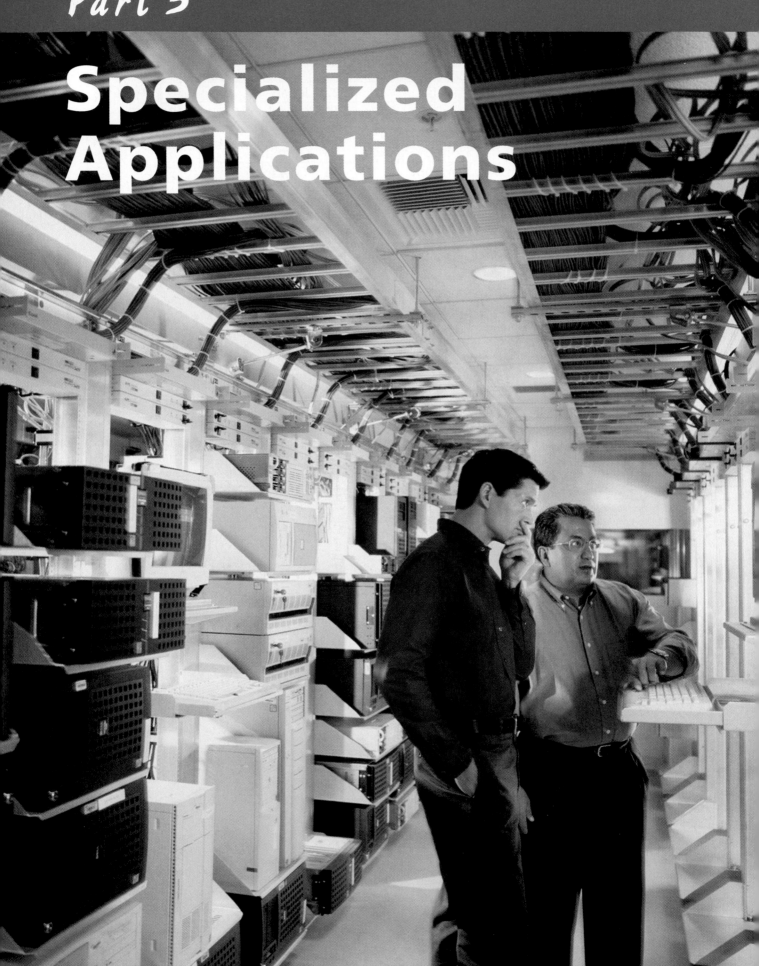

Part 5

Specialized
Applications

Keyboarding in Information Technology (IT) Services

Work in the IT services cluster involves designing, developing, managing, and operating communication and IT systems, networks, and related hardware and software for telecommunications and computing services.

Opportunities in IT Services

People working in telecommunications design and maintain telephone, satellite, and laser communication systems. Among the numerous IT jobs are programmer, software engineer, technical support representative, information systems operator/analyst, and network administrator. Satellites above the earth receive and send signals, thus speeding up communications. Skilled engineers design systems that enhance the ways by which people communicate.

We are all globally connected by technology, and IT services support those necessary connections. Technology is spreading at an ever-increasing rate and affecting every aspect of our daily lives. This industry is full of opportunity for individuals with superior technical and mathematical skills. The ability to communicate complex ideas clearly, handle many details, and solve problems is an asset. Of course, keyboarding proficiency is critical.

Objectives

KEYBOARDING

- Type at least 47 words per minute on a 5-minute timed writing with no more than 5 errors.

LANGUAGE ARTS

- Refine proofreading skills and correctly use proofreaders' marks.
- Use abbreviations, capitals, and punctuation correctly.
- Improve composing and spelling skills.
- Recognize subject/verb agreement.

WORD PROCESSING

- Use the word processing commands necessary to complete the document processing activities.

DOCUMENT PROCESSING

- Format formal report projects, international business documents, medical office documents, and legal office documents.

TECHNICAL

- Answer at least 90 percent of the questions correctly on an objective test.

Unit 17

Formal Report Project

LESSON 81
Formal Report Project

LESSON 82
Formal Report Project

LESSON 83
Formal Report Project

LESSON 84
Formal Report Project

LESSON 85
Formal Report Project

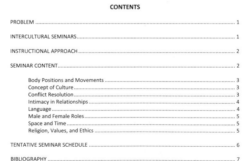

INTERCULTURAL SEMINARS
Jordan D. Sylvester, Director
Human Resources Department
February 12, 20--

The Marketing Department has been conducting surveys of our worldwide offices, foreign customers, and prospective foreign customers over the last several months. Information received through the use of mailed questionnaires has made us aware of an urgent need to improve our communication skills at the international level.

PROBLEM
Some incidents have been reported to us in which we have failed to negotiate contracts with foreign customers and prospective foreign customers because of serious breakdowns in communication. Some of these setbacks have been the result of conscious negative acts on the part of our employees. However, the main culprit seems to ... differences and lack of appreciation for the nuances that re... Indeed, there are almost unlimited possibilities for misund... avenues for people of good intent to miscommunicate.

INTERCULTURAL SEMINARS
Three-day seminars designed to improve intercultural comm... regional sites in the United States and in foreign cities whe...

- Beijing
- Hamburg
- Madrid
- Melbourne
- Oslo
- Rio de Janeiro
- Tokyo
- Warsaw

It will be our intent that all employees who have direct cont... countries will participate in these seminars over a four-mon...

INTERCULTURAL SEMINARS

Submitted to

Jordan D. Sylvester, Director
Human Resources Department

...red by

...rketing Manager
... Healthcare

... 12, 20--

CONTENTS

Formal Report Project

Goals

- Improve speed and accuracy
- Refine language arts skills in grammar
- Format a formal report

A. Type 2 times.

A. WARMUP

```
1      The jalopy quivered as it crossed over the 1/5-mile-    11
2   long bridge on Route 267 about 14 miles south @ Granite    22
3   Falls. The axle on Richard's truck broke as he whizzed by. 34
    | 1 | 2 | 3 | 4 | 5 | 6 | 7 | 8 | 9 | 10 | 11 | 12
```

SKILLBUILDING

B. MAP

Follow the GDP software directions for this exercise in improving keystroking accuracy.

C. Take a 1-minute timed writing on the first paragraph to establish your base speed. Then take four 1-minute timed writings on the remaining paragraphs. As soon as you equal or exceed your base speed on one paragraph, advance to the next, more difficult paragraph.

C. SUSTAINED PRACTICE: CAPITALIZATION

```
4       A visit to Europe is a vacation that many people dream   11
5   of doing. There are many countries to visit and hundreds of 23
6   sites to see if you can spend at least four weeks on the     34
7   continent. A trip to Europe is one you will never forget.    46

8       If you decide to visit Europe, the months of June and    11
9   July would probably be the prettiest, but they would also    23
10  be the busiest. England, France, and Germany are popular     34
11  countries to visit; Spain is popular for Americans as well.  46

12      In England you will want to visit St. Paul's Cathedral   11
13  and Big Ben. And, of course, when you are in England, you    23
14  do not want to pass up the opportunity to see Buckingham     34
15  Palace. Plan on staying a few days to see all the sites.     45

16      France certainly is a highlight of any European visit.   11
17  Paris offers many sites such as the Arc de Triomphe, the     22
18  Louvre, the Eiffel Tower, and the Gothic Cathedral of Notre  34
19  Dame. Other cities to visit are Nice, Lyon, and Versailles.  46
    | 1 | 2 | 3 | 4 | 5 | 6 | 7 | 8 | 9 | 10 | 11 | 12
```

D. Study the rules at the right.

D. AGREEMENT

RULE ▶
agreement pronouns

Some pronouns (*anybody, each, either, everybody, everyone, much, neither, no one, nobody,* and *one*) **are always singular and take a singular verb. Other pronouns** (*all, any, more, most, none,* and *some*) **may be singular or plural, depending on the noun to which they refer.**

<u>Each</u> of the employees <u>has</u> finished <u>his or her</u> task.
<u>Much</u> <u>remains</u> to be done.
<u>Most</u> of the pie <u>was</u> eaten, but <u>most</u> of the cookies <u>were</u> left.

RULE ▶
agreement intervening words

Disregard any intervening words that come between the subject and verb when establishing agreement.

The <u>box</u> containing the books and pencils <u>has</u> not been found.
<u>Alex</u>, accompanied by Tricia, <u>is</u> attending the conference and taking <u>his</u> computer.

Edit the sentences to correct any errors in grammar.

20 Everybody who signed up for the trip are to be at Building 16.
21 All the tourists are sending cards to us from their hotels.
22 Everyone on the trip, including spouses, have been having fun.
23 Some of the postcards from their vacations are not arriving.
24 Two of the sales reps from Region 4 were given cash bonuses.
25 The fastest runner from all five teams are receiving a trophy.

FORMATTING

Word Processing Manual

E. WORD PROCESSING: STYLES

Study Lesson 81 in your word processing manual. Complete all of the shaded steps while at your computer. Then format the job that follows.

DOCUMENT PROCESSING

Report 81-58 ▶

Business Report

Reference Manual

Refer to Reference Manual pages R-8A and R-8B to review the correct format for business reports. Refer to Reference Manual page R-12C for a review of list formatting.

Report 81-58 begins in this lesson and is continued through Lesson 85. You will be applying styles throughout this report that automatically effect formatting changes to fonts, paragraph spacing, bold, and so on. You will therefore notice some differences from standard business report format. Such changes will be called out in directions and illustrations. Use the following guidelines to format the report.

1. Press ENTER 5 times.
2. Type the title in all-caps, and press ENTER 1 time. **Note:** Do not apply any styles until you have typed the entire report for a given lesson.
3. Type the byline information and the date in upper- and lowercase, and press ENTER 1 time between each line.

4. Press ENTER 2 times after the date and continue typing the remainder of the report in the same way. Press ENTER only 1 time before and after all side headings.
5. Create a header that will display on all pages except the first page. Type the header in 10-point Cambria italic. Type Human Resources Department at the left margin. Press TAB until you reach the right margin, type Page followed by 1 space, and insert an automatic page number. Add a bottom border and close the header.

After you have finished typing the entire document for a particular lesson, go back and make these changes:

1. Apply the Title style to the report title.
2. Apply the Subtitle style to the subtitle, byline, and date.
3. Apply the Heading 2 style to the side headings. **Note:** The Heading 2 style includes italic.
4. Apply the Heading 3 style to the paragraph headings, including the period at the end.
5. Type the table titles in 14-point Calibri Bold. Type the table column headings in 12-point Calibri Bold. Type the table body in 12-point Calibri.
6. Apply 12-point Calibri font to the body of the report as needed.
7. Use the default formatting for the footnotes at the bottom of the page.

↓5X

INTERCULTURAL SEMINARS ↓1X

Apply the Title style.

Jordan D. Sylvester, Director ↓1X

Apply the Subtitle style.

Human Resources Department ↓1X

February 12, 20-- ↓2X

Calibri 12 pt

agreement intervening words

¶ The marketing department has been ~~doing~~ *conducting* surveys of our world wide offices, foreign customers, and prospective foreign customers over the last several months. Information received through the use of *mailed* questionnaires has made us aware of an urgent need to improve our communication skills at the international level. ↓1X

Apply the Heading 2 style.

agreement pronouns

PROBLEM ↓1X

¶ Some incidents have been reported to us in which we have failed to negotiate contract*s* with foreign customers and prospective foreign customers because of serious break downs in com*m*unication. ~~Very few~~ *Some* of these setbacks have been the result of conscious negative acts on the part of our employees. *However,* The main culprit seems to be lack of awareness of cultural differences and a lack of appreciation for the nuances that reflect these cultural differences. Indeed, there almost are unlimited possibilities for misunderstandings, insults, miscues, and avenues for people of good intent to miscommunicate. ↓1X

(Continued on next page)

Apply the Heading 2 style.

agreement intervening words

Reference Manual

Refer to page R-12C of the Reference Manual for a review of list formatting.

agreement intervening words

agreement pronouns

agreement pronouns

Save this unfinished report. You will resume work on it in Lesson 82.

INTERCULTURAL SEMINARS ↓1X

¶ Three-day seminars designed to improve intercultural communication skills will be held at regional sites in the U. S. and in foreign cities where we have offices: ↓2X

- Beijing
- Hamburg
- Madrid
- Melbourne
- Oslo
- Rio de Janeiro
- Tokyo
- Warsaw ↓2X

¶ It will be our intent that all employees who have direct contact with people from other countries will participate in these seminars over a four-month period.

¶ It would be unreasonable to assume that a small team of people from our company would have the breadth of knowledge needed to conduct these seminars in 8 foreign countries. However, Angela Demirchyan, William Hamilton, and Chang Ho Han have agreed to work together as the coordinating team for this effort.

¶ Each of these individuals has worked over the past 2 months with the managers of our international offices as well as natives in specific countries to formulate a preliminary plan for these in-service programs. Their plan will utilize the expertise of our employees who have had negotiating experience in each country and who have knowledge of local customs as demonstrated by natives. We are confident that through this team approach, everyone will gain an understanding of problems only not from the position of our company but also from the perspective of those with whom they conduct business.

Formal Report Project

Goals

- Type at least 44wpm/5'/5e
- Format a formal report

A. Type 2 times.

A. WARMUP

```
1        The path will be covered by approximately 30 pieces     11
2   of slate from Quarry #19. Schreiner & Zimmer (the general     23
3   contractor) took the joint bid of $638, including delivery.  35
    | 1 | 2 | 3 | 4 | 5 | 6 | 7 | 8 | 9 | 10 | 11 | 12
```

SKILLBUILDING

B. Take three 12-second timed writings on each line. The scale below the last line shows your wpm speed for a 12-second timed writing.

B. 12-SECOND SPEED SPRINTS

```
4   There are many things to think about if you buy a used car.
5   Two of the main things are its age and the number of miles.
6   Take the car for a test drive in town and on the open road.
7   Pay a fee to an auto expert who will check it over for you.
    I I I 5 I I I 10 I I I 15 I I I 20 I I I 25 I I I 30 I I I 35 I I I 40 I I I 45 I I I 50 I I I 55 I I I 60
```

C. PROGRESSIVE PRACTICE: ALPHABET

If you are not using the GDP software, turn to page SB-7 and follow the directions for this activity.

Strategies for Career Success

Letter of Complaint

Is poor product or bad service getting you down? By writing a concise, rational letter of complaint, you have the possibility of the reader honoring your request.

In the first paragraph, give a precise description of the product or service (for example, model, serial number). Include a general statement of the problem (for example, "It is not working properly."). In the middle section, provide the details of what went wrong (for example, when it happened, what failed). Refer to copies of invoices, checks, and so on. Describe how you were inconvenienced, with details about time and money lost. State what you want (for example, refund, repair, replace). In the closing paragraph, ask for a timely response to the complaint (for example, "Please resolve this problem within the next two weeks.").

YOUR TURN Think about the last time that you experienced poor product or service. Did you write a letter of complaint?

D. Take two 5-minute timed writings. Review your speed and errors.

Goal: At least 44wpm/5'/5e

D. 5-MINUTE TIMED WRITING

8   Critical thinking is a skill that can be learned and   11
9 applied to more than a few situations. There are many ways   23
10 to describe critical thinking skill. The common theme that   34
11 runs through each of these descriptions is related to the   46
12 use of cognitive skill. With this skill, the person thinks   58
13 with a purpose in mind and likely directs some of the focus 70
14 toward goals. The person looks at a situation and decides   81
15 rationally what to believe or not to believe. In critical   93
16 thinking, the goal is to achieve understanding, judge more 105
17 than one viewpoint, and then solve problems. After a person 117
18 thinks through all the elements of the problem, a decision 129
19 is made based on all of the facts and exact findings. Bias, 141
20 prejudice, and feelings should not sway the final outcome. 152
21   Critical thinking is useful in reading, listening, 163
22 speaking, and writing. A critical thinker will ask great   174
23 questions. He or she listens carefully to others and gives 186
24 feedback. A critical thinker seeks the truth with zeal and 198
25 then willingly accepts change when new facts are presented. 210
26 Critical thinking is important for problem solving.   220

| 1 | 2 | 3 | 4 | 5 | 6 | 7 | 8 | 9 | 10 | 11 | 12

DOCUMENT PROCESSING

Report 81-58 ▶

(Continued)

Continue working on Multipage Business Report 81-58.

Refer to   **Reference Manual**

Refer to page R-12C of the Reference Manual for a review of list formatting.

INSTRUCTIONAL APPROACH

¶ Alvarez and Hwang suggest a framework of instruction with the following: *three components*

1. The cognitive component includes information about communicating with people *of other cultures*

2. The effective (a) component is the area in which attention is given to attitudes, emotions, and resulting behaviors as they are effected (a) by human interaction in a multicultural environment.

(Continued on next page)

3. The experiential component is the "hands-on" element ~~which~~ *that* suggests different possibilities. Others have found that the use of simulations is a natural for this type of experience. The writing of letters, memos, and reports to persons in other cultures also provides beneficial learning experiences. In addition, the use of tutors can be very helpful to workers unfamiliar with a particular culture.[1]

SEMINAR CONTENT

¶ The cognitive, affective, and experiential ~~frames~~ *components* would be applied as appropriate for each of the topics included. The coordinating team members have utilized the resources available to them at our ③ local universities.

¶ Most colleges and universities now provide instruction in international communication. While the content at times is integrated into several business administration courses, there has been a trend in recent years to provide a course ~~or courses~~ specifically designed for business interaction in an intercultural setting. The very nature of this type of study makes it very difficult to segment the broad topical areas, as all elements are so closely intertwined. However, the tentative seminar plan is to cover the content as described in Table 1.

¶ The seminars must reflect the broad involvement of our international operations. There is a need for many workers in our domestic offices to develop an appreciation of the intercultural challenge. This is true not only for those in the marketing and sales areas. Those in our Finance Department and our Legal Department are *increasingly* involved not only with foreign companies but also with huge multinational corporations that, at times, are as large as or larger than the biggest companies in the ~~entire~~ United States.

¶ Demirchyan, Hamilton, and Han suggest the following list of tentative instructional topics:[2]

---

[1] Ana Maria Alvarez and Allen Hwang, "Communication Across Cultures," *International Business World,* April 2006, pp. 39-42.

[2] Angela Demirchyan, William Hamilton, and Chang Ho Han, *The Dynamics of Intercultural Seminars*, Gateway Publishing, Boston, 2005.

(Continued on next page)

Reference Manual

Review the format for placing a table in a report on page R-8B of the Reference Manual.

↓2X

TABLE 1. SEMINAR TOPICS		← Calibri Bold 14 pt
Instructional Topic	**Time**	← Calibri Bold 12 pt
Body ^Positions and^ Movements	2 hours	
Concept of Culture	~~4~~ 3 hours	
(Language)	3 hours	
Conflict Resolution	2 hours	← Calibri 12 pt
Intimacy in Relationships	3 hours	
Male and female Roles	~~2~~ 3 hours	
Space and Time	2 hours	
Religion, Values, and ethics	4 hours	

↓1X

Apply the Heading 3 style to the paragraph heading.

¶ **Body Positions and Movements.** Body language, that is, facial expressions, gestures, and body movements, conveys messages about attitude and may be interpreted differently by people in *different* cultures. For example, firm handshakes are the norm in the U.S.; loose handshakes are the custom in some other countries. The way we stand, sit, and hold our arms may convey different messages in different cultural settings.

Apply the Heading 3 style to the paragraph heading.

¶ **Concept of culture.** This session will be an overview of the various cultures in which we conduct business, including e-commerce. Clooney identifies the need for varied marketing strategies within the different economic, political, and cultural environments:

> International Web use and access are growing exponentially,
> and many businesses are wanting to capitalize on this trend
> and grab their fair share of this global market. English-speaking
> audiences are not expected to continue to dominate this
> market. Certainly, more than a literal translation will be required
> to reach this culturally diverse audience.[3]

Reference Manual

Refer to page R-8B in the Reference Manual or to Lesson 41-F for a review of long quotations.

Case studies will be reviewed that are considered classics in the field of international communication. *In addition,* Summaries of some of our own successes and failures will be reported.

Save this unfinished report. You will resume work on it in Lesson 83.

---

[3] Arlene D. Clooney, "Cultural Comparisons in E-Commerce," December 19, 2005, <http://www.ecommerce.com/news.htm>, accessed on January 18, 2006.

Formal Report Project

Goals

- Improve speed and accuracy
- Refine language arts skills in composing
- Format a formal report

A. Type 2 times.

A. WARMUP

```
1        The 16 young farmers (only 50% over 30 years of age)     11
2   gathered in Room 209 to begin discussing the earthquake       22
3   threat; an extra door prize was given as a "joke present."     34
    | 1 | 2 | 3 | 4 | 5 | 6 | 7 | 8 | 9 | 10 | 11 | 12
```

SKILLBUILDING

PPP PRETEST → PRACTICE → POSTTEST

PRETEST
Take a 1-minute timed writing. Review your speed and errors.

B. PRETEST: Common Letter Combinations

```
4        The insurance agent read the report before giving it      11
5   to your deputy director. This weekly action showed that        22
6   the agent really knew the actual input on a daily basis.       33
    | 1 | 2 | 3 | 4 | 5 | 6 | 7 | 8 | 9 | 10 | 11 | 12
```

PRACTICE
Speed Emphasis:
 If you made no more than 1 error on the Pretest, type each *individual* line 2 times.
Accuracy Emphasis:
 If you made 2 or more errors, type each *group* of lines (as though it were a paragraph) 2 times.

C. PRACTICE: Word Beginnings

```
7   re- repel renew remit relax refer ready react really reveal
8   in- inept inert inset input infer index incur inches insert
9   be- bears beams beach below being began befit beauty beside
```

D. PRACTICE: Word Endings

```
10  -ly truly madly lowly early daily apply hilly simply weekly
11  -ed sized hired dated cited based acted added opened showed
12  -nt plant meant giant front event count agent amount fluent
```

POSTTEST
Repeat the Pretest timed writing and compare performance.

E. POSTTEST: Common Letter Combinations

F. PROGRESSIVE PRACTICE: NUMBERS

If you are not using the GDP software, turn to page SB-11 and follow the directions for this activity.

G. COMPOSING A DOCUMENT

Compose a 1-page document in which you describe how you can use the Styles feature in a resume you are preparing for a job search. You might include features such as fonts, font sizes, indentations, and spacing to control the appearance of your resume. Use default margins, double spacing, and two paragraphs in your document. Provide a title, and type your name at the top of the document.

In paragraph 1, you could include information on using styles for those items you want to highlight in your resume such as (1) your name and address at the top of the resume, (2) the section headings that often run down the left side of the resume, and (3) any bullets you want to include for items that contain multiple entries.

In paragraph 2, you could include a brief discussion on (1) the margins to use for your resume, (2) line spacing to use for individual entries, and (3) line spacing to use between entries.

Include a brief summary statement to emphasize the importance of proofreading your document and the need for accuracy in a resume.

FORMATTING

Word Processing Manual

H. WORD PROCESSING: INSERT CLIP ART AND FILES

Study Lesson 83 in your word processing manual. Complete all of the shaded steps while at your computer. Then format the job that follows.

DOCUMENT PROCESSING

Report 81-58

(Continued)

Continue working on Report 81-58.

Insert clip art that is related to communication and similar to this example.

Set the clip art at a size of 1-inch square, and place it at the right margin even with the first line of the Language paragraph.

¶ **Conflict Resolution**. Whether people are involved in negotiating a contract, working together to remedy product quality issues, or resolving contract interpretations, the need for tact and skill is particularly important in the foreign setting. Many of the seminar topics have implications in the area of conflict resolution. While every effort should be made to prevent conflict, there is a need for guidance in resolving disagreements in foreign cultures.

¶ **Intimacy in Relationships**. The degree of physical contact that is acceptable varies considerably. Hugs and kisses are the standard, even in the business office, in some countries. By contrast, the act of touching a person is considered an extreme invasion of privacy in other places. The use of first names may or may not be acceptable. To ask a personal question is extremely offensive in some cultures. While socializing with business clients is to be expected in some countries, it would be highly inappropriate in others. These are only a few of the relationship concerns that will be explored.

¶ **Language**. It is obvious that language differences play a major part in business miscommunication. Whenever there is an interpreter or a written translation involved, the chances for error are increased. There are over 3,000 languages used on the earth. Just as with English, there are not only

(Continued on next page)

grammar rules but also varied meanings as words are both spoken and written. Even with the English language, there are differences in usage between the English used in the United States and that used in England.

¶ Although English is the language usually used in international communication, the topics identified in Table 1 illustrate the complexity of communicating accurately; and the problem continues to grow. For example, literal translations of American advertising and labeling have sometimes resulted in negative feelings toward products. As world trade increases, so does the need for American businesses to understand the complexities of cultural differences. Gregorian offers this example:

> A businessperson must change his or her expectations and assumptions away from what is customary and acceptable in the United States in terms of personal and social conduct to what is customary and acceptable within the culture of the country where they are conducting business. Any other assumption can have serious consequences and undesirable results. In the other person's mind, you are the foreigner and therefore you will be the one who might look out of place or act in a way that is considered socially unacceptable.[4]

¶ A good sense of humor is an asset not only in our personal lives but also in the business environment. However, it probably should be avoided in multicultural settings because the possibilities for misinterpretation are compounded. Do not use humor that makes fun of a particular individual, group, or culture. Remember that what may appear to be humorous to you may have a negative connotation in another culture.

¶ **Male and Female Roles.** There are major contrasts in the ways male and female roles are perceived in different cultures. The right to vote is still withheld from women in countries all over the world. Opportunities for female employment in the business environment vary considerably. Pay differentials for men and women continue to exist even when they are performing the same tasks. Opportunities for advancement for men and women often are not the same.

¶ **Space and Time.** The distance one stands from someone when engaged in conversation is very important. If a person stands farther away than usual, this may signal a feeling of indifference or even a negative feeling. Standing too close is a sign of inappropriate familiarity. However, it should be recognized that different cultures require a variety of space for business exchanges to take place. In the United States, that space is typically from three to five feet, but in the Middle East and in Latin American countries, this distance is considered too far.

¶ There is also the element of time--a meeting that is scheduled for 9 a.m. likely will start on time in the United States, but in some other cultures the meeting may not start until 9:30 or even 10 o'clock. Punctuality and time concepts vary with the customs and practices of each country. Patience really can be a virtue.

Insert clip art that is related to time and similar to this example. The style should be similar to the first clip art you inserted.

Set the clip art at a size of 1-inch square, and place it at the right margin even with the first line in the second paragraph of the Space and Time paragraph.

Save this unfinished report. You will resume work on it in Lesson 84.

---

[4] Gerald Gregorian, *Comparing Cultural Differences*, Dana Publishing Company, Los Angeles, 2003, p. 49.

Formal Report Project

Goals

- Type at least 44wpm/5'/5e
- Format a formal report

A. Type 2 times.

A. WARMUP

```
1        The new schedule* has the Lynx at their home park on      11
2   July 27 with the zany Waverley Blackhawks. The Lynx scored     23
3   five fourth-quarter goals in their last game to win 8 to 4!    34
    | 1 | 2 | 3 | 4 | 5 | 6 | 7 | 8 | 9 | 10 | 11 | 12
```

SKILLBUILDING

B. DIAGNOSTIC PRACTICE: SYMBOLS AND PUNCTUATION

If you are not using the GDP software, turn to page SB-2 and follow the directions for this activity.

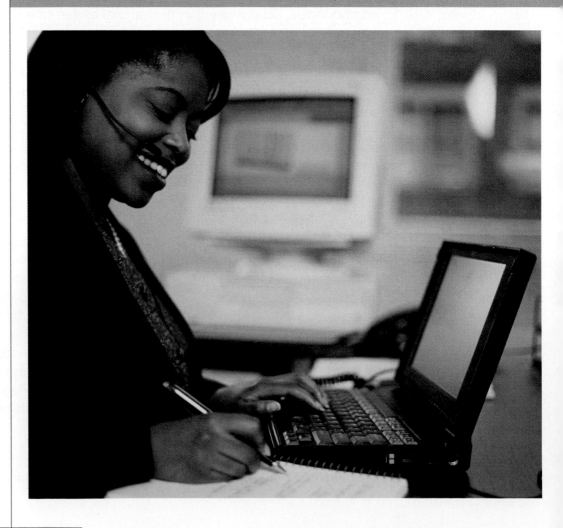

C. Take two 5-minute timed writings. Review your speed and errors.

Goal: At least 44wpm/5′/5e.

C. 5-MINUTE TIMED WRITING

```
 4        Proofreading skill is developed with practice. You may   11
 5   want to master several techniques that will help develop      23
 6   and improve your proofreading skills.                         30
 7        In order to be a successful proofreader, you will want    41
 8   to schedule time to read through the completed job several     53
 9   times. At the first reading, check your work to see if the    65
10   margins are correct and the page numbers are in the right     77
11   places. Determine if the spacing and the font styles are      80
12   correct. With each reading, zoom in on a specific type of     100
13   error. If possible, read your work out loud and read only     111
14   one word at a time. You may find that placing a ruler under   123
15   each line as you read it will give your eyes a manageable     135
16   amount of text to read.                                       140
17        At the next reading, be sure that the content of the     150
18   document follows a logical order. If any cited works are      162
19   included, be sure the citations are in the proper format      173
20   with complete and accurate data. Check to be sure that all    185
21   the basic rules of grammar, spelling, and punctuation have    197
22   been followed. Proofread your document when you are fresh      208
23   and alert. Remember, proofreading takes time and patience.    220
     |  1  |  2  |  3  |  4  |  5  |  6  |  7  |  8  |  9  |  10  |  11  |  12
```

Keyboarding Connection

Sending E-Mail Attachments

Your e-mail program will tell you if an attachment has been sent, but the attachment may arrive in unusable or partially usable form. Often the sender and recipient need to use the same or compatible software to open and use each other's documents, especially if the files contain visuals, records, or spreadsheets.

Send a test e-mail by attaching a test document and ask your receiver to send you one in return. If the test fails with a word processing document, open your word processor, and save the document again as a text file. You may lose some formatting (indents, bold, bullets), but any e-mail program, as well as any word processor, can usually read the file.

YOUR TURN Open a word processing file. Save it as a text file. Open the text file in your word processor. What formatting has changed? Send both files to yourself as e-mail attachments. Open them and note any changes.

Table 84-42

Boxed Table

TABLE 2. FOREIGN-CITY SEMINARS		
City	**First Seminar**	**Second Seminar**
Melbourne	May 2-4	July 5-7
Rio de Janeiro	May 9-11	July 11-13
Beijing	May 16-18	July 18-20
Hamburg	May 23-25	July 25-27
Tokyo	June 6-8	August 1-3
Warsaw	June 13-15	August 8-10
Oslo	June 20-22	August 15-17
Madrid	June 27-29	August 22-24

Calibri Bold 14 pt
Calibri Bold 12 pt
Calibri 12 pt

Report 81-58

(Continued)

Continue working on Report 81-58.

¶ **Religion, Values, and Ethics**. While we can recognize the difficult challenge presented by language differences, this category (religion, values, and ethics) is in some ways the area that can bring about the most serious breakdowns in relations with those from other cultures.

• The very nature of religious beliefs suggests that this is a delicate area for those involved in business transactions in foreign countries. Also, religious beliefs affect the consumption of certain products throughout the world. Examples are tobacco, liquor, pork, and coffee.

• Values are a reflection of religious beliefs for most people. We often hear references to right and wrong as applied to the ideals and customs of a society. Values relate to a range of topics, and they may pertain to areas such as cleanliness, education, health care, and criminal justice. Such values are often very personal and as such can have a variety of interpretations. The more interpretations there are, the more likely it is that miscommunication will occur.

• Ethics can be considered as standards of conduct that reflect moral beliefs as applied to both one's personal life and one's business life.

¶ Huntington suggests that now more than ever, a code of ethics is essential within the business environment. When this code of ethics is missing or if it is not enforced, chaos and financial ruin for everyone associated is often the result.

A code of ethics is increasingly being recognized as an intrinsic and critical component in any business environment. Newspapers are filled with reports of scandalous, unconscionable, nonethical behavior that has led to the downfall of otherwise successful businesses. The lack of ethics in business conduct has led to disastrous effects for both the businesses in question and the consumers and their investments in these companies.[5]

[5] Marilyn C. Huntington, *Business Ethics and Workplace Compliance*, Horizon Publishing Company, New York, 2005, p. 53.

TENTATIVE SEMINAR SCHEDULE

Insert clip art that is related to world travel and similar to this example. The style should be similar to that of the earlier clip art you inserted.

Set the clip art at a size of 1-inch square, and place it at the right margin even with the first line of the first paragraph.

¶ As indicated earlier, it is our intent that all employees who have direct contact with people in other cultures will participate in these seminars. For that reason there will be two identical three-day seminars scheduled at each foreign site. Only selected employees in our regional sites in the United States will participate. These people have been tentatively identified on the basis of the extent of their involvement with persons from other countries. ¶ As all employees in our foreign offices will participate, a decision has been made to schedule these seminars through the summer. A tentative schedule for these seminars is shown in Table 2.

↓2X
(Insert Table 84–42 here)
↓1X

The Marketing Department is to be commended for calling our attention to the seriousness of our international communication problem. Angela Demirchyan, William Hamilton, and Chang Ho Han also deserve our sincere thanks for their planning efforts for our intercultural communication seminars. As can be seen, special attention is being given to the seminar topics for these in-service programs. Efforts are also being made to identify instructors and resource persons who will develop instructional strategies that will be effective, interesting, and well received by the participants. These seminars will help significantly in increasing our market share in the international market.

Save this unfinished report. You will resume work on it in Lesson 85.

Formal Report Project

Goals

- Improve speed and accuracy
- Refine language arts skills in proofreading
- Format a formal report

A. Type 2 times.

A. WARMUP

```
1        Bev ordered the following: 24 #794 napkin boxes, 48     11
2  #265B quarts of ketchup, and 72 reams of 20-1b white print   22
3  paper. Did you receive the prize jalapeno peppers we sent?   34
   | 1 | 2 | 3 | 4 | 5 | 6 | 7 | 8 | 9 | 10 | 11 | 12
```

SKILLBUILDING

B. Type the columns 2 times. Press TAB to move from column to column.

B. TECHNIQUE PRACTICE: TAB

```
4  M. A. Barnes    Julie Herden    Lynn Masica    Don Trueblood
5  Nathan Favor    Brett Irvin     Lisa O'Keefe   Matthew Utbert
6  Lee Chinn       Rick Kenwood    J. E. Perry    Jill Voss-Walin
7  Xavier Saxon    Lance King      Chad Quinn     Robin Yager
```

C. PACED PRACTICE

If you are not using the GDP software, turn to page SB-14 and follow the directions for this activity.

LANGUAGE ARTS

D. Compare this paragraph with lines 4-7 on page 305.

D. PROOFREADING

```
8         A visitt to Europe is a vacation that many people dreem
9  of doing. There are many countrys to visit and hundreds
10 of sights to see if you can spend at least for weeks on the
11 continent. A trip too Europe is one you will never forget.
```

Report 85-59 ►

Title Page

Reference Manual

Refer to page R-7B of the Reference Manual or to Lesson 45-F to format the title page.

Create a title page for Report 81-58 as a separate document using standard format and making these changes:

1. Change to 12-point Calibri before typing any part of the title page.
2. Type INTERCULTURAL SEMINARS as the title.
3. The report is to be submitted to Jordan D. Sylvester, Director, Human Resources Department. Type Jordan D. Sylvester, Director on one line followed by the department name on the next line.
4. The report is being prepared by Lydia Reyes, Marketing Manager, Gold Coast Healthcare.
5. The date is February 12, 20--.
6. When you are finished typing the title page, apply the Title style to the title.

Report 85-60 ►

Table of Contents

Reference Manual

Refer to page R-7D of the Reference Manual or to Lesson 45-G to format the table of contents.

Create a table of contents for Report 81-58 as a separate document using standard format. The table of contents shown is incomplete. Refer to your report to compose and complete the table of contents. Make these changes:

1. Change to 12-point Calibri before typing any part of the table of contents page.
2. Refer to the finished report to compose and type the table of contents. The entries should include all side headings and paragraph headings from the report. Refer to the finished report for the page numbers.
3. Type the side headings in all-caps at the left margin.
4. Type the paragraph headings in upper- and lowercase indented 0.5 inch from the left margin.
5. Do not include the report header.

(Continued on next page)

↓5X

Title style **CONTENTS** ↓2X

Calibri 12 pt

Report 85-61

Bibliography

Refer to **Reference Manual**

Refer to page R-9B of the Reference Manual to format the bibliography page.   Calibri 12 pt

Spell-check your report for errors. Proofread it for omitted or repeated words, errors that form a new word, and formatting errors.

Type the bibliography for Report 81-58, shown here as a separate document using standard format. Follow these steps:

1. Change to 12-point Calibri.
2. Type the bibliography in standard format.

3. When you are finished with all entries, apply the Title style to "BIBLIOGRA-PHY."
4. Do not include the report header.

Title style **BIBLIOGRAPHY**

Alvarez, Ana Maria, and Allen Hwang, "Communication Across Cultures," *International Business World*, April 2006, pp. 39-42.

Clooney, Arlene D., "Cultural Comparisons in E-Commerce," December 19, 2005, <http://www.ecommerce.com/news.htm> accessed on January 18, 2006.

Demirchyan, Angela, William Hamilton, and Chang Ho Han, *The Dynamics of Intercultural Seminars*, Gateway Publishing, Boston, 2005.

Gregorian, Gerald, *Comparing Cultural Differences*, Dana Publishing Company, Los Angeles, 2003.

Huntington, Marilyn C., *Business Ethics and Workplace Compliance*, Horizon Publishing Company, New York, 2005.

Report 81-58

(Continued)

Progress and Proofreading Check

Documents designated as Proofreading Checks serve as a check of your proofreading skill. Your goal is to have zero typographical errors when the GDP software first scores the document.

Finalize the report project:

• Proofread all the pages for format and typing errors.
• Assemble the pages in this order: title page, table of contents, body, bibliography, and a blank page for a back cover sheet.
• Staple the report pages together.

Unit 18

International Formatting

16 April 20--

Mr. Henry R. Defforey
Human Resources Director
Gemey Techtronics
Avenue Raymond Poincore
75116 Paris
FRANCE

Dear Mr. Defforey:

... an employee exchange this coming year. As we ... 26 production employees will benefit both

... ough the various units of our production process, ... and continuing right on through our shipping ... rotation plan for you to review. Included in the plan ... ussed at our last meeting. Please review the plan and ... wish to make. You can e-mail me at ... wish to speak to me directly, you can call

... coming year. As soon as we have agreed on the ... all affected employees. I know that everyone from ... aborative effort.

MEXICO TRAVEL DESTINATIONS

Most Popular Attrac...

April 15, 20--

Since the mid-1990s, national parks in Mexico have be... from the Americas, Europe, and Asia. As a result, an i... been made for travel brochures and maps from our Vi... few weeks, we will be publishing several new brochur... requests.

BROCHURES

The brochures will include a detailed description of th... beginning and ending visitation schedules, highlights ... locations. Brochures will be prepared on the sites and ... The fourth column indicates how many years each site... most popular sites in Mexico.

Area	Site
Northern	Cumbres de Majalca
Northern	Cumbres de Monterrey
Northern	Sierra del Pinacate
Central	El Tepozteco
Central	Iztaccihuatl y Popocatepetl
Central	Malinche
Southern	Bonampak/Yaxchilan Monume...
Southern	Chichén Itzá
Southern	Dzibilchaltun
Southern	Sian Káan Biosphere Reserve...

MAPS

Maps will be supplied for the locations listed above, ... from the nearest cities to the tourist attractions. Walk... highlighted, and approximate walking times will be n... be prepared for each area (northern, central, and sou... all three visitor areas will also be available. Please ser... promote to Señor Garcia, Public Relations Director.

---

18 April 20--

Ms. Sharla D. Enterline
Project Coordinator
Carroll Technology
8723 Hill Avenue
Bowling Green, KY 42823

Dear Ms. Enterline:

The following information is being sent to assist you with Japanese mailing rules. As a service to your employees, I am providing the following summary of these rules.

A Japanese mailing address consists of the name, street address, town, city, prefecture, postal code, and country. The illustration below shows how an address should appear on an envelope going to Japan.

Address Items	Address Example
Name	Mr. Yoshifumi Uda
Street Address, Town (first address)	1-17, Akai-cho
City, Prefecture (second address), Postal Code	Minato-ku, Tokyo 108-8005
JAPAN	JAPAN

Please e-mail me if you have questions about mailing rules in Japan. You can reach me at shiroshi@tadashi.jp.com.

Very sincerely,

S. Hiroshi
Shipping Department

hk
c: K. Tachikawa

International Formatting (Canada)

Goals

- Type at least 45wpm/5′/5e
- Format international documents

A. Type 2 times.

A. WARMUP

```
1        The lynx at the zoo fought wildly and had to be moved   11
2    quickly to a new cage (#248-I or #357-II). These adjoining   23
3    cages place the lynx (all of them) into individual areas.    34
     |  1  |  2  |  3  |  4  |  5  |  6  |  7  |  8  |  9  |  10  |  11  |  12
```

SKILLBUILDING

B. DIAGNOSTIC PRACTICE: NUMBERS

If you are not using the GDP software, turn to page SB-5 and follow the directions for this activity.

C. Take three 12-second timed writings on each line. The scale below the last line shows your wpm speed for a 12-second timed writing.

C. 12-SECOND SPEED SPRINTS

```
4    The car will now have to turn off on the lane to the lake.
5    Mark must type these lines fast and press for a high speed.
6    We had a lunch at the lake and went for a walk in the park.
7    Take this disk to have it fixed by the end of your workday.
     | | | |5| | | |10| | | |15| | | |20| | | |25| | | |30| | | |35| | | |40| | | |45| | | |50| | | |55| | | |60
```

D. Take two 5-minute timed writings. Review your speed and errors.

Goal: At least 45wpm/5'/5e

D. 5-MINUTE TIMED WRITING

```
 8        During good economic times, businesses have trouble      11
 9   finding and keeping their skilled workers. As a result,       22
10   some places may offer great benefits to their workers. This   34
11   could include such things as sick leave, life insurance,      45
12   profit sharing, paid time off each year, and flextime.        56
13        The concept of flextime was introduced to the work       67
14   force quite a few years ago. Companies adopted the concept     78
15   for a lot of reasons. Among the top reasons for flexible       90
16   work schedules at that time were to reduce the number of      101
17   cars on the road, to help workers to meet their families'     113
18   needs and demands, and also to attract more women back to     124
19   the work force.                                               128
20        Businesses can manage such a schedule in a few ways.     138
21   Employees may have a chance to choose when to arrive and      150
22   leave for the day. This policy allows people who like to      161
23   work early in the day to start early and end early and vice   173
24   versa. Other companies may allow their employees to work      185
25   extended hours for four days and then enjoy three days off.   197
26   This type of benefit has helped both workers and companies.   209
27   Companies recognize that their workers are more productive    220
28   and absences are lower.                                       225
```

| 1 | 2 | 3 | 4 | 5 | 6 | 7 | 8 | 9 | 10 | 11 | 12 |

Keyboarding Connection

Effective Teleconferencing for Meetings

Teleconferencing is a useful way to conduct meetings with businesspersons across the globe. To make the best use of teleconference meetings, follow these guidelines.

Since sound quality varies greatly, use the best equipment available. Allow individual participants enough time to use their technology. Participants should select a conference leader and alternate that leadership. Distribute agendas to everyone in advance, possibly via e-mail.

Be sensitive to time zone differences. Since it is possible someone will experience an inconvenient time, consider rotating the times of the meetings. Assign someone to prepare and e-mail to the participants a brief summary covering the main discussion topics and action items of the teleconference.

YOUR TURN List what you think are the advantages and disadvantages of conducting meetings via teleconference.

E. METRIC PAPER SIZE

Paper size for correspondence in the United States is typically 8.5 × 11 inches. However, correspondence in many foreign countries is often formatted on metric-sized paper. The most popular of these is called A4 paper, and it measures 210 × 297 millimeters—approximately 8.25 × 11.75 inches.

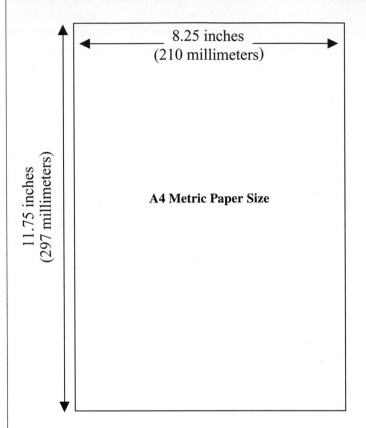

8.25 inches
(210 millimeters)

11.75 inches
(297 millimeters)

A4 Metric Paper Size

F. METRIC ENVELOPE SIZE

A standard large envelope (No. 10) measures 9.5 × 4.125 inches. A large envelope for metric size paper is called DL, and it measures 110 × 220 millimeters—approximately 4.33 × 8.67 inches. The No. 10 envelope is not as deep as the metric envelope, but it is slightly wider.

8.67 inches
(220 millimeters)

4.33 inches
(110 millimeters)

DL Metric Envelope

G. INTERNATIONAL ADDRESSES IN LETTERS

International addressing is becoming more common with the increased popularity of the Internet and frequently requires changes to the address lines, such as the addition of special codes, abbreviations, and capitalization. Individual organizational preferences for international address formatting will vary. Therefore, the most technologically efficient formats for international addresses will be used, including the use of all caps and the name of the country spelled out as the last entry of the address, as shown in the examples below.

Canada Address Example:

8437 Dixie Road ◄——————— Street Address [street number followed by street name]

Brampton, ON L6T 5P6 ◄——— City/Province/Postal Code [2 spaces after the province; 1 space between first 3 and last 3 characters]

CANADA ◄————————— Country Name [typed in all-capitals]

Mexico Address Example:

Av. Chapultepec 28 ◄——— Street Address [street name followed by street number]

06724 Mexico D.F. ◄——— Postal Code/City [postal code and city name; "Mexico D.F." denotes Mexico City]

MEXICO ◄——————— Country Name [typed in all-capitals]

France Address Example:

14, Rue Royale ◄——— Street Address [street number followed by a comma and then street name]

75008 Paris ◄——— Postal Code/City

FRANCE ◄——————— Country Name [typed in all-capitals]

Germany Address Example:

Mannesmannufer 2 ◄——— Street Address [street name followed by street number]

D-40213 Duesseldorf ◄——— Postal Code/City [international sorting code followed by postal code and city name]

GERMANY ◄——————— Country Name [typed in all-capitals]

Japan Address Example:

10-1, Toranomon 2-chome ◄——— Division of the City [lot and building number, followed by neighborhood name, followed by area number]

Minato-ku Tokyo 105-8436 ◄——— City, District/City Name/Postal Code

JAPAN ◄——————— Country Name [typed in all-capitals]

H. DAY/MONTH/YEAR FORMAT

In international correspondence, the date line is often formatted in this sequence: day, month, year. Thus, the first line of a letter to a foreign recipient may appear as shown in the illustration.

12 April 20--

Mr. James E. Burillon
Sales Director
Avian Industries
14, Rue Royale
75008 Paris
FRANCE

Dear Mr. Burillon:

Word Processing Manual

I. WORD PROCESSING: PAPER SIZE

Study Lesson 86 in your word processing manual. Complete all of the shaded steps while at your computer. Then format the jobs that follow.

Situation: You work for World-Tech Industries, an international computer manufacturer located in Vancouver, Canada. World-Tech Industries has a client base in both the United States and Canada. For the purposes of this simulation, your name will be Hiroki Kayano. Your e-mail address is hkayano@worldtech.com and your phone number is +1.702.555.1839.

For the next five days, you will prepare documents for several World-Tech executives. Your firm follows formatting guidelines for metric paper and envelope size and international addresses, dates, phone numbers, and measurements. You will use A4 metric paper and DL metric envelopes for all documents.

Today is April 14, and you will spend your first day preparing documents, which appear in your in-basket. Proofread your work carefully and check for spelling, punctuation, grammar, and formatting errors so that your documents are mailable.

Correspondence 86-78

Business Letter in Modified-Block Style

(!) This letter is typed on A4 paper, which has a slightly different midpoint at which to start typing the date and closing lines. However, use a left tab of 3.25 to type these lines, as you do on a standard 8½- × 11-inch sheet of paper.

(!) Type *hk* as the reference initials for this simulation.

14 April 20-- | Mr. Alec R. Cousins | Manager, Computer Services | Columbia Enterprises, Ltd. | 338 Dunsmuir Street | Vancouver, BC V4B 5R9 | CANADA | Dear Mr. Cousins:

¶ Thank you for your recent computer order. As you requested, we have added the DVD drives to the 50 computers. There will be no extra charge for exchanging the DVD drives for the ZIP drives that come standard with the C-420 model you ordered.

¶ Your order will be shipped ten business days from the date of your order. Our order processing and shipping departments are online, and you can check the progress of your order by going to www.worldtech.com and clicking on Customer Orders.

¶ We look forward to the opportunity to serve your computer needs for many years to come.

Sincerely, | Sharon T. Yates | Sales Manager | hk | c: Terry Mourieux, Pamela Phillips | PS: The special software you ordered with your computers will be installed at our factory, ready for your use when your computers arrive.

Table 86-43

Boxed Table

Prepare Table 86-43 on A4 paper, in landscape orientation. **Note:** Entries are arranged in ascending order by kilometers from Vancouver, British Columbia.

CUSTOMER SHIPPING ADDRESSES AND DISTANCE				
Name	**Address**	**City/Province**	**Postal Code**	**Kilometers**
Francis Stevens	17820 Attwood Road	Prince George, BC	V2N 653	520
Helene Abrams	269 Acadia Drive, SE	Calgary, AB	T2J 0A6	673
Connie Visocki	39 Blackburn Drive, SW	Edmonton, AB	T6W 1C5	817
Clarence Brewer	157 Caribou Street, E.	Moose Jaw, SK	S6H 0R4	1,266
Christine Osborn	P.O. Box 613	The Pas, MB	R9A 1K7	1,597
Andrew Svenson	14 Island Drive	Flin Flon, MB	R8A 058	1,850
Gary Fitzpatrick	635 Agnes Street	Winnipeg, MB	R3E 1X8	1,869
Lazo Aida	P.O. Box 1016	Churchill, MB	R0B 0E0	2,152
Note: Distance is measured in kilometers from Vancouver.				

Table 86-44

Boxed Table

Open the file for Table 86-43 and make the following changes:

1. Rearrange the entries in Column A so that the last name is given first, followed by a comma, followed by the first name.

2. Rearrange the entries in the table by placing the last names of the customers in alphabetic order.

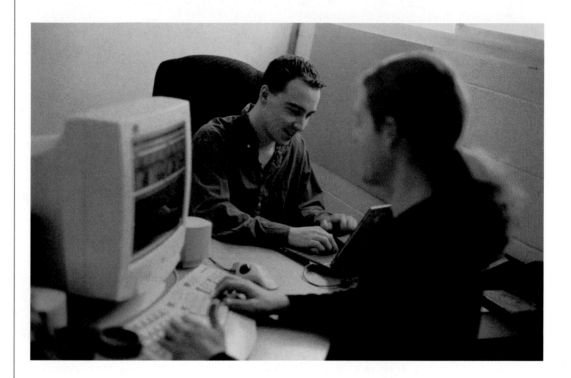

International Formatting (Mexico)

Goals

- Improve speed and accuracy
- Refine language arts skills in the use of abbreviations
- Format international documents

A. Type 2 times.

A. WARMUP

```
1        On 4/25/05 Jamie exercised by "power walking" on the      11
2   athletic tracks. She also zipped along the city's favorite     23
3   route (Polk Street & Bell Avenue). It was a quick walk!        34
    | 1 | 2 | 3 | 4 | 5 | 6 | 7 | 8 | 9 | 10 | 11 | 12
```

SKILLBUILDING

B. PROGRESSIVE PRACTICE: ALPHABET

If you are not using the GDP software, turn to page SB-7 and follow the directions for this activity.

C. Type the paragraph 2 times, concentrating on each letter typed.

C. TECHNIQUE PRACTICE: CONCENTRATION

```
4        El uso de la bicicleta es muy popular en Barranquilla.
5   Cuando el tiempo es bueno a toda la gente joven le gusta ir
6   a pasear en bicicletas. Me gusta ir a montar en bicicleta,
7   especialmente cuando hace sol y el tiempo es agradable.
```

LANGUAGE ARTS

D. Study the rules at the right.

D. ABBREVIATIONS

RULE ▶
abbreviate measure

In technical writing, on forms, and in tables, abbreviate units of measure when they occur frequently. Do not use periods.

    14 oz   5 ft 10 in   50 mph   2 yrs 10 mo

RULE ▶
abbreviate lowercase

In most lowercase abbreviations made up of single initials, use a period after each initial but no internal spaces.

a.m.	p.m.	i.e.	e.g.	e.o.m.
Exceptions:	mph	mpg	wpm	

RULE ▶
abbreviate ≡

In most all-capital abbreviations made up of single initials, do not use periods or internal spaces.

OSHA	PBS	NBEA	WWW	VCR	MBA
Exceptions:	U.S.A.	A.A.	B.S.	Ph.D.	P.O.
	B.C.	A.D.			

Edit the sentences to correct any errors in the use of abbreviations.

8 A mixture of 25 lb of cement and 100 lb of gravel was used.
9 The desk height must be reduced from 2 ft. 6 in. to 2 ft 4 in.
10 The 11 a. m. meeting was changed to 1 p. m. because of a
11 conflict.
12 The eom statement was published over the Internet on the W.W.W.
13 She enlisted in the U.S.M.C. after she received her MBA degree.
14 His Ph. D. dissertation deals with the early history of NATO.

FORMATTING

E. INTERNATIONAL URLs

Uniform resource locators (URLs) identify a site on the World Wide Web where specific information can be found. In international URLs, an abbreviation for a country is often included in the URL, as shown in red below.

Country	Uniform Resource Locator (URL)
Canada	http://www.pearlson.animate.chap2.ca
France	http://www.education.grad.up.fr
Germany	http://www.mercedes.de
Japan	http://www.sushi.co.jp
Mexico	http://www.reloj.baja.mx

F. WORD PROCESSING: INSERT SYMBOL

Accents and other marks are used in many languages to indicate how words should be pronounced. Some examples of accents used in Mexico, where Spanish is spoken, are shown below.

Symbol	Spanish Word	English Translation
ñ	Señor, Señorita	Mr., Mrs.
í	el río	river
ó	adiós	good-bye

DOCUMENT PROCESSING

Correspondence 87-79

E-Mail Message

 Reference Manual

Refer to pages R-5C and R-5D: E-Mail Message.

abbreviate lowercase

 Reference Manual

Refer to page R-12C of the Reference Manual for a review of list formatting.

abbreviate ≡

Today is April 15, your second day, and you will prepare an e-mail message and a business report with a table. Begin with the e-mail. Type the e-mail greeting, Hi, Mr. Noriega:, and the body shown below in correct format. Type Hiroki as the closing, and type this signature: Hiroki Kayano | E-Mail: hkayano@ worldtech.com | Phone: +1.702. 555.1839. Save the e-mail message, but do not send it.

¶ As you know, sales in our international divisions have been accelerating since the advent of our new Jefe automobile. As a result, several new manufacturing plants will open in the next eight years. The first five of these plants will open in France and Germany.

¶ To market our new manufacturing plants and promote the Jefe, our Marketing Division is planning to open new Web sites on the Jefe home page. The following links will be added to advertise our plant expansion:

- Bordeaux, France: http://www.bordeaux.fr.jefe.new.html
- Toulouse, France: http://www.toulouse.fr.jefe.new.html
- Grenoble, France: http://www.grenoble.fr.jefe.new.html
- Hamburg, Germany: http://www.hamburg.de.jefe.new.html
- Stuttgart, Germany: http://www.stuttgart.de.jefe.new.html

¶ You will be notified when the Web sites go online. Until then, plan to work with your Marketing Division personnel to implement the marketing plan we discussed at our meeting last month (the Henderson Proposal). When the sites go online, we hope to maximize our exposure on the WWW. If they are as successful as we believe they will be, our promotional campaign may also be implemented at our plants in Piedras Negras, Morelia, and Cancún.

Type the report on A4-size paper.

MEXICO TRAVEL DESTINATIONS
Most Popular Attractions
April 15, 20--

¶ Since the mid-1990s, national parks in Mexico have become popular tourist sites for visitors from the Americas, Europe, and Asia. As a result, an increasing number of requests have been made for travel brochures and maps from our Visitors' Bureau. Therefore, in the next few weeks, we will be publishing several new brochures and maps to accommodate these requests.

BROCHURES

¶ The brochures will include a detailed description of the site, providing information on beginning and ending visitation schedules, highlights of the site, and popular photography locations. Brochures will be prepared on the sites and locations shown in the table below. The fourth column indicates how many years each site has been ranked among the top ten most popular sites in Mexico.

Type the copy at the right in boxed table format, inserting the table into the report.

abbreviate measure

Accent used in Chichén Itzá

Accent used in Sian Káan

Area	Site	State	Top 10
Northern	Cumbres de Majalca	Chihuahua	2 yrs
Northern	Cumbres de Monterrey	Nuevo Leon	2 yrs
Northern	Sierra del Pinacate	Mexicali	4 yrs
Central	El Tepozteco	Morelos	10 yrs
Central	Iztaccihuatl y Popocatepetl	Morelos	10 yrs
Central	Malinche	Puebla	3 yrs
Southern	Bonampak/Yaxchilan Monuments	Chiapas	7 yrs
Southern	Chichén Itzá	Merida	15 yrs
Southern	Dzibilchaltun	Yucatán	5 yrs
Southern	Sian Káan Biosphere Reserve	Quintana Roo	4 yrs

(Continued on next page)

MAPS

¶ Maps will be supplied for the locations listed above, with detailed insets to guide visitors from the nearest cities to the tourist attractions. Walking trails and resting stations will be highlighted, and approximate walking times will be noted on the maps. Individual maps will be prepared for each area (northern, middle, and southern), and a comprehensive map for all three visitor areas will also be available. Please send any advertising pieces you wish to promote to Señor Garcia, Public Relations Director.

ñ used in Señor

International Formatting (France)

Goals

- Type at least 45wpm/5′/5e
- Format international documents

A. Type 2 times.

A. WARMUP

```
1      On May 4, 2004, Kaye gave a dazzling talk on graphics;   11
2  it was quite fantastic! She is also writing an excellent      23
3  book about graphics with text. It might sell for $23.85.      34
   | 1 | 2 | 3 | 4 | 5 | 6 | 7 | 8 | 9 | 10 | 11 | 12
```

SKILLBUILDING

B. DIAGNOSTIC PRACTICE: SYMBOLS AND PUNCTUATION

If you are not using the GDP software, turn to page SB-2 and follow the directions for this activity.

C. PACED PRACTICE

If you are not using the GDP software, turn to page SB-14 and follow the directions for this activity.

Keyboarding Connection

Protecting Your Files With Antivirus Programs

A virus is a computer program intentionally written to contaminate your computer system. Viruses can enter your system from files downloaded from the Internet or can be acquired from infected files sent to you via e-mail, diskette, or other storage media.

You can protect your computer by purchasing an antivirus program. These programs periodically scan your computer system for viruses. They also scan files that you bring into the system. Some antivirus manufacturers allow you to download a trial copy of their software from their Web site. You can try the software for a few days before you decide if you want to buy it.

YOUR TURN If you want to visit antivirus sites to find out what they have to offer, search for *antivirus software* on your search engine.

D. Take two 5-minute timed writings. Review your speed and errors.

Goal: At least 45wpm/5'/5e

D. 5-MINUTE TIMED WRITING

```
 4        Technology surrounds us. It is everywhere you look.    11
 5  People use cellular phones to speak to one another just      22
 6  about anywhere. They carry their pagers so that they can be  34
 7  reached at any time. Everyone, from the busy executive to    45
 8  the college student, is now quite used to being available    57
 9  at all hours of the day or night.                            64
10        In recent years, busy travelers have become used to    74
11  using their laptops everywhere. They use computer ports in   86
12  airports, hotel rooms and lobbies, and even taxis. This      97
13  technology allows the busy traveler to have access to the   109
14  Internet while on the go. Using the laptop, the user can    120
15  access the latest weather report, sports scores, and news,  132
16  almost as soon as they happen.                              138
17        Using the latest technology, you can keep up with your 150
18  work and maintain contact with your office. You can even    161
19  access your bank accounts and pay bills while waiting in    172
20  traffic. Also, if you are in a new place, you can find a    184
21  restaurant or call for directions as needed. The technology 196
22  options that have become available to almost everyone are   207
23  quite amazing. We are living in a small world that seems to 219
24  be getting smaller each day.                                225
    | 1 | 2 | 3 | 4 | 5 | 6 | 7 | 8 | 9 | 10 | 11 | 12
```

FORMATTING

E. DOT-STYLE TELEPHONE NUMBERS

In the United States, hyphens are used in telephone numbers. A hyphen is used after the 3-digit area code and after the first 3 digits of the telephone number; for example, 701-555-1234. Another format, used in many countries, is to replace the hyphens with periods; for example, 701.555.4832 or 818.555.3424.

F. INTERNATIONAL TELEPHONE ACCESS CODES

Special access codes are needed to make a phone call from one country to another. To make an international call, dial the IDD (International Direct Dialing) code first. Then dial the country code for the country you are calling, next the area code (if any), and finally the phone number. The IDD code in many countries changes periodically.

The United States and Canada have the same IDD (011) and country code (1). When you provide a United States (or Canadian) telephone number in a document being sent to an international address, use a plus sign (+) in front of the area code, instead of the IDD code, followed by 1 (the country code for the United States). For example, if you are writing a letter to an international address and you are giving your own phone number in Los Angeles, you would express your number as +1.323.555.8923. Some of the more common access codes are listed below.

Country	From U.S. to Foreign Country		From Foreign Country to U.S.	
	IDD Code	Country Code	IDD Code	Country Code
Canada	011	1	011	1
France	011	33	00	1
Germany	011	49	00	1
Italy	011	39	00	1
Japan	011	81	001	1
Mexico	011	52	98	1
Taiwan	011	886	002	1
United Kingdom	011	44	00	1
Note: The United States and Canada have the same IDD (011) and country code (1).				

DOCUMENT PROCESSING

Today is April 16, your third day, and you will prepare a letter, a table, and an e-mail message. Begin with the letter.

Correspondence 88-80
_____

Business Letter in Block Style

Type the letter on A4-size paper.

16 April 20-- | Mr. Henry R. Defforey | Human Resources Director | Gemey Techtronics | Avenue Raymond Poincore | 75116 Paris | FRANCE | Dear Mr. Defforey:

¶ I am pleased that we will be involved in an employee exchange this coming year. As we discussed earlier, the exchange of our 26 production employees will benefit both companies.

¶ We plan to rotate all 26 employees through the various units of our production process, starting from the raw materials division and continuing right on through our shipping operations. I have enclosed a projected rotation plan for you to review. Included in the plan are all the employee rotations we discussed at our last meeting. Please review the plan and e-mail me if there are any changes you wish to make. You can e-mail me at ssouthern@worldtech.com, or, if you wish to speak to me directly, you can call +1.214.555.9090.

(Continued on next page)

¶ I look forward to working with you this coming year. As soon as we have agreed on the rotation plan, we can make copies for all affected employees. I know that everyone from our end is eagerly anticipating this collaborative effort.

Sincerely, | Sheila T. Southern | Human Resources Manager | hk | Enclosure | c: Ted Lambeer, Shirley Gouet

Table 88-45

Boxed Table

Type the table on A4-size paper.

Apply 25 percent shading to the column headings.

| ROTATION PLAN |||
| Tech-Group Inc. and Gemey Techtronics |||
Department	**Rotation Start Date**	**Rotation End Date**
Raw Materials	3 July 20--	August 11 20--
Board assembly	14 August 20--	22 September 20--
Drive ~~and~~ Assembly	25 Sept 20--	3 November 20--
Power Unit	6 November 20--	15 December 20--
Testing & Evaluation	18 December 20--	2 February 20--

Correspondence 88-81

E-Mail Message

Type the e-mail greeting, Hi, Mr. Deforey:, and the body shown below in correct format. Type Hiroki as the closing, and type this signature: Hiroki Kayano | E-Mail: hkayano@worldtech.com | Phone: +1.702.555.1839 Save the e-mail message, but do not send it.

¶ I am sending you this e-mail to alert you to a change we must make in the rotation plan I sent you last week. We will have to refit several of our board assembly production unit relay systems during the week of 14 August through 18 August. To avoid significantly altering the remaining rotation plan, I would like to suggest that we use one-half of the drive assembly rotation period to complete the board assembly rotation. ¶ Please respond to my e-mail as soon as possible so that we can make whatever changes are necessary.

International Formatting (Germany)

Goals

- Improve speed and accuracy
- Refine language arts skills in spelling
- Format international documents

A. Type 2 times.

A. WARMUP

```
1      Did Jacqueline get 62% of the vote in the election on   11
2  9/04/00? I think Buzz* (*Kelly) voted for her at 7:35 p.m.  23
3  that evening, and she was really excited when Jackie won.   34
    | 1 | 2 | 3 | 4 | 5 | 6 | 7 | 8 | 9 | 10 | 11 | 12
```

SKILLBUILDING

B. MAP

Follow the GDP software directions for this exercise in improving keystroking accuracy.

C. Take a 1-minute timed writing on the first paragraph to establish your base speed. Then take four 1-minute timed writings on the remaining paragraphs. As soon as you equal or exceed your base speed on one paragraph, advance to the next, more difficult paragraph.

C. SUSTAINED PRACTICE: PUNCTUATION

```
4      One of the strengths you must have if you are going to  11
5  be a success in business is good writing skills. You must   23
6  practice your writing skills every day if you want them to  35
7  improve. Perfection of writing skills takes much practice.  46

8      You must always strive to write clearly, concisely,     11
9  and accurately. Remember always that your writing can be    22
10 examined by more people than just the one to whom you have  34
11 written. It's often looked at by other readers as well.     45

12     You want to be sure that your letters always convey a   11
13 positive, helpful attitude. Don't forget, you represent     22
14 more than yourself when you write--you also represent your   34
15 company! This is an important, useful rule to remember.     45

16     Try to stay away from negative words like "can't" or    11
17 "won't." Readers also do not like phrases such as "because  23
18 of company policies" or "due to unforeseen circumstances."  34
19 Using these words and phrases never helps resolve problems. 46
    | 1 | 2 | 3 | 4 | 5 | 6 | 7 | 8 | 9 | 10 | 11 | 12
```

D. Type this list of frequently misspelled words, paying special attention to any spelling problems in each word.

D. SPELLING

20   means valve entry patient officer similar expenses industry
21   quality judgment academic provisions previously cooperation
22   foreign closing indicated secretary especially construction
23   monitoring assessment continuing registration manufacturing
24   products policies capacity presently accordance implemented

Edit the sentences to correct any misspellings.

25   Every company offiser will have simaler expenses next week.
26   In my judgement, we must insist on co-operation from all.
27   My secretery said that she traveled to a foriegn country.
28   We must continue monitering the progress for assesment.
29   The new policeis must be implimented for all products.

FORMATTING

E. METRIC UNITS OF MEASUREMENT

The metric system of measurement was devised in 1670. It is based on units of 10 and is used by almost every nation in the world. The five common measurements in the metric system are length, area, volume, capacity, and weight and mass. The table below gives the basic units of measure used in the metric and U.S. systems.

Quantity	Metric Units of Measure	U.S. Units of Measure
Length	millimeter, centimeter, meter, kilometer	inch, foot, yard, mile
Area	square centimeter, square meter, hectare	square inch, square foot, square yard
Volume	cubic centimeter, cubic decimeter, cubic meter, liter, hectoliter	cubic inch, cubic foot, fluid ounce, pint, gallon
Weight	milligram, gram, kilogram, tonne	ounce, pound, ton

Correspondence 89-82

E-Mail Message

Highlighted words are spelling words from the language arts activities.

Today is April 17, your fourth day, and you will prepare an e-mail message, a business letter, and a multipage business report with tables. Begin with the e-mail. Type the e-mail greeting, Hi, Mr. Neubuerger:, and the body shown below in correct format. Type Hiroki as the closing, and type this signature: Hiroki Kayano | E-Mail: hkayano@worldtech.com | Phone: +1.702.555.1839. Save the e-mail message, but do not send it.

¶ The total conversion of our manufacturing plant in Wiesbaden to a metric system, which was discussed previously, is six months away. Ms. Schneider has asked for your continuing support and cooperation as you prepare employees who are presently transferring to the Wiesbaden plant in accordance with the provisions of our policies. Please send me the summary report used when you were monitoring the conversion last year.

¶ The metric system will be quite foreign to many employees, especially the younger ones, who were not involved in the planning stages. The summary report will give them a head start on metrication as indicated in the assessment.

¶ Call Ms. Schneider Thursday morning (+1.702.555.2354) to discuss the Frankfurt plant closing. Plant operations will be transferred to Wiesbaden in July. She has asked that you use your judgment to monitor the quality of the operation closely until the transfer has been fully implemented.

Correspondence 89-83

Business Letter in Block Style

Type the letter on A4-size paper.

17 April 20-- | Ms. Geraldine Sommer | Marketing Department | Deutsch Lebensmittel, Inc. | Mannesmannufer 2 | D-40213 Dusseldorf | GERMANY | Dear Ms. Sommer:

¶ Amalia Rios has asked that I send a copy of the summary report on metrics that we completed last year. As you recall, I sent you that report previously to share with the new employees at our Stuttgart plant.

¶ If you wish, you can e-mail me the copy that accompanied the report, and my secretary will distribute it as needed.

Sincerely, | Klaus Neubuerger | Human Resources Manager | hk

Type the report on
A4-size paper.

Insert clip art that is
related to measurements
and similar to this example.

Set the clip art at a size
of about 1-inch square,
and place it at the right
margin even with the first
line of the paragraph.

(!) Insert 1 blank line
between the two
tables.

METRIC SUMMARY REPORT

April 17, 20--

¶ The metric system was devised by Gabriel Mouton, a French man, in 1607. It is a system based on units of 10 and is considered by ~~some~~ many to be more accurate and easier to use than the imperial system of measure used in the United States. When it was first defined, a meter was considered to be 1/10,000,000 of the distance from the Pole to the Equator.

¶ The most common metric measurements are for length, area, volume, capacity, and weight and mass. For our wiesbaden plant, the most crucial measurements for new employees from the U.S. will be volume and weight. Comparisons between these two measures appear in Table 1 and Table 2.

Table 1. METRIC/U.S. COMPARISONS FOR VOLUME		
Metric Unit	**Metric Example**	**U.S. Equivalent**
Cubic centimeter	1 cubic centimeter	0.061 cubic inch
Cubic decimeter	1,000 cubic centimeters	0.053 cubic ft
Cubic meter	1,000 cubic decimeters	1.31 cubic yards
Liter	1 cubic decimeter	1.76 pints
Hectoliter	100 Liters	21.99 ~~gal~~ gallons

Table 2. METRIC/U.S. COMPARISONS FOR WEIGHT		
Metric Unit	**Metric Example**	**U.S. Equivalent**
Milligram	1 milligram	0.015 grain
gram	1,000 milligrams	0.035 ounce
Kilogram	1,000 grams	2.205 ~~lbs~~ pounds
Tonne	1,000 kilograms	0.984 ton

(Continued on next page)

¶ Employees will quickly adapt to the metric system when they use it daily. ^on a basis^ Although we encourage all employees to make calculations in the metric system, it may be helpful for the first few days if they are aware of the conversion factors involved in comparing the ② measurement systems. The following conversions may therefore be helpful to them:

- Multiply inches by 2.45 to get centimeters
- Multiply feet by 0.305 to get meters
- Multiply miles by 1.6 to get kilometers
- Divide lbs by 2.2 to get kilograms
- Multiply ounces by 28 to get grams
- Multiply fluid ounces by 30 to get milliliters
- Multiply gallons by 3.8 to get liters

¶ More ~~detailed~~ conversions and metric information can be obtained by visiting the web site for the U.S. metric association at http://lamar.colostate.edu/~hillger/.

Reference Manual

Refer to page R-12C of the Reference Manual for a review of list formatting.

The tilde (~) is usually found next to the 1 on the top row of the keyboard.

International Formatting (Japan)

Goals
- Type at least 45wpm/5'/5e
- Format international documents

A. Type 2 times.

A. WARMUP

```
1     James used a dozen of Harold's power trucks to quickly   11
2     move over 17 large boxes on 11/30/00. I think these trucks  23
3     (just the diesels) may need maintenance work on 3/24/01.    34
      |  1  |  2  |  3  |  4  |  5  |  6  |  7  |  8  |  9  |  10  |  11  |  12
```

SKILLBUILDING

PPP PRETEST → PRACTICE → POSTTEST

PRETEST
Take a 1-minute timed writing. Review your speed and errors.

B. PRETEST: Close Reaches

```
4     Uncle Bert chased a fast, weary fox into the weeds of     11
5     the swamp. He hoped to grab the old gray fox under the     22
6     bridge with a rope as he darted swiftly from his cold lair.  34
      |  1  |  2  |  3  |  4  |  5  |  6  |  7  |  8  |  9  |  10  |  11  |  12
```

PRACTICE
Speed Emphasis:
If you made no more than 1 error on the Pretest, type each *individual* line 2 times.
Accuracy Emphasis:
If you made 2 or more errors, type each *group* of lines (as though it were a paragraph) 2 times.

C. PRACTICE: Adjacent Keys

```
7     as asked asset based basis class least visas ease fast mass
8     op opera roped topaz adopt scope troop shops open hope drop
9     we weary wedge weigh towed jewel fewer dwell wear weed week
```

D. PRACTICE: Consecutive Fingers

```
10    sw swamp swift swoop sweet swear swank swirl swap sway swim
11    un uncle under undue unfit bunch begun funny unit aunt junk
12    gr grade grace angry agree group gross gripe grow gram grab
```

POSTTEST
Repeat the Pretest timed writing and compare performance.

E. POSTTEST: Close Reaches

F. Take two 5-minute timed writings. Review your speed and errors.

Goal: At least 45wpm/5'/5e

F. 5-MINUTE TIMED WRITING

```
13        Anyone with a supervisory position will occasionally     11
14   have to deal with a problem employee. If you learn to deal    23
15   with this type of worker in a good way, it will benefit       34
16   everyone within the organization. As a manager, you should    46
17   address the problem as soon as you are made aware of it.       57
18   However, if you are extremely upset, it may be best to wait   69
19   until you calm down and have time to plan what you will       80
20   say. Avoid using an approach based on reaction, which can     86
21   often be ineffective and too emotional. Speaking up too       92
22   quickly might bring you unwanted results.                     103
23        When you talk to an employee, be sure you get to the    111
24   real issue. Present the facts and tell the employee exactly  122
25   what he or she is doing wrong on the job. Do not express     134
26   your own personal opinion. You need to present a positive    146
27   and mutually fair solution to the employee in question to    157
28   solve a problem. At the end of the meeting, ask the person   169
29   to explain his or her problem to you and the changes that    181
30   are necessary. By following this procedure, you know that    192
31   everyone understands what is happening. Set up a time to     204
32   meet in a few days to follow up with this person.            215
                                                                  225

   |  1  |  2  |  3  |  4  |  5  |  6  |  7  |  8  |  9  |  10  |  11  |  12
```

DOCUMENT PROCESSING

Correspondence 90-84

Business Letter in Block Style

Type the letter on A4-size paper.

Today is April 18, your fifth day, and you will prepare several letters, an e-mail message, and a table. Begin with the letter.

18 April 20-- | Mr. Kouji Tachikawa | Chief Technology Officer | Tadashi Corporation | 7-1, Shiba 5-chome | Minato-ku, Tokyo 108-8001 | JAPAN | Dear Mr. Tachikawa:

¶ It is a distinct pleasure to learn that we will be working together to develop the training manual to be used in our joint venture. Your company has long been known for its excellence in developing instructional materials, and Carroll Technology is pleased to play a collaborative part with you in this venture.

¶ Our development teams have been working with their counterparts in Tadashi over the past several weeks. Your suggestion that we pool our personnel resources was indeed an excellent one that will give us a head start in the development stage.

(Continued on next page)

¶ If I may make one suggestion, I believe it would be helpful for the personnel in our mailing and shipping department to have a better understanding of the labeling procedures used in Japan for distributing the training manuals. Could you please send me some information that might be helpful in this regard? I will do the same for you by sending you the labeling procedures used at Carroll Technology.

Sincerely | Sharla D. Enterline | Project Coordinator | hk | c: Roberta Akiyama, Samuel Hiroshi, Charlene Brandenburger

Correspondence ▶
90-85

E-Mail Message

Type the e-mail greeting, Hi, Ms. Enterline:, and the body shown below in correct format. Type Hiroki as the closing, and type this signature: Hiroki Kayano | E-mail: hkayano@worldtech.com | Phone: +1.702.555.1839. Save the e-mail message, but do not send it.

¶ It is my pleasure to inform you that Samuel Hiroshi will be forwarding to your office a summary of the package labeling procedures used at Tadashi Inc. Employees from many different foreign countries have used these procedures to help them understand mailing requirements in Japan.

¶ After receiving the procedures, feel free to e-mail Mr. Hiroshi with any questions you may have. You can reach him at shiroshi@tadashi.jp.com. If you prefer, you can call Mr. Hiroshi at +81.3.34543113.

Correspondence ▶
90-86

Business Letter
in Block Style

Type the letter on A4-size paper.

18 April 20-- | Ms. Sharla D. Enterline | Project Coordinator | Carroll Technology | 8723 Hill Avenue | Bowling Green, KY 42823 | Dear Ms. Enterline:

¶ The following information is being sent to assist you with Japanese mailing rules. As a service to your employees, I am providing the following summary of these rules.

¶ A Japanese mailing address consists mainly of the name, street address, town, city, prefecture, postal code, and country. The illustration below shows how an address should appear on an envelope going to Japan.

(Continued on next page)

Address Items	Address Example
Name ~~St.~~ *Street* Address, Town (1st) address) City, Prefecture (2d) address), *Postal* ⌃ Code JAPAN	Mr. Yoshifumi Uda 1-17, Akai-cho Minato-ku, Tokyo 108-8005 JAPAN

¶ Please ~~E~~-mail me if you have questions about mailing rules in japan. You can reach me at shiroshi@tadashi.jp.com.

Very sincerely, | S. Hiroshi | Shipping (Dept.) | hk | c: K. Tachikawa

Table 90-46 ▶

Boxed Table

Your line endings will be different from those shown here.

JAPANESE POSTAL CODE REGULATIONS Prepared by Hiroki Kayano	
Postal Code Rule	**Example**
The first line of a Japanese address is used for the addressee's name.	Mr. Takashi Imaizumi Mr. Kazuki Terada
The second line provides a street name or building number.	Kifune 3-402 (this represents building 402 on the 3rd street within the Kifune neighborhood)
The third line gives the city, prefecture (a district within the city), and postal code.	Meito-ku, Nagoya 112-3844 Minato-ku, Tokyo 105-8436
The fourth line gives the name of the country to which the document or package is being mailed.	JAPAN

Correspondence 90-87 ▶

Business Letter in Block Style

Type the letter on A4-size paper.

Progress and Proofreading Check

Documents designated as Proofreading Checks serve as a check of your proofreading skill. Your goal is to have zero typographical errors when the GDP software first scores the document.

18 April 20-- | Mr. Fujio Okuda | Sales Manager | Naruto Publishing Company | 7-35, Kitashinagawa 6-chome | Shinagawa-ku, Tokyo 141-0001 | JAPAN | Dear Mr. Okuda:

¶ We are pleased to have this opportunity for two of our computer textbooks to be translated into Japanese and for you to do the same for two of your textbooks in the computer area. As we agreed at our meeting in Takasaki last week, sales for both of our book companies should improve substantially with these translations.

¶ I am enclosing with this letter the first three units of *Computer Essentials* so that your editors can begin the translation process. We will do the same here at Globe Publishing when your first three units from *Global Computers* arrive in Chicago.

¶ Should your editorial staff have any questions during the translation, they can e-mail me at shaddock@worldtech.com or call me at +1.402.555.3848. Sincerely, | Shannon Haddock | Editorial Director | hk | Enclosure

LESSON 91
Medical Office Documents

LESSON 92
Medical Office Documents

LESSON 93
Medical Office Documents

LESSON 94
Medical Office Documents

LESSON 95
Medical Office Documents

RECOVERING FROM KNEE SURGERY

Dr. Alec Pera, M.D.

November 5, 20--

Specific procedures should be followed by patients who are recovering from knee surgery. Depending on the particular surgery that was performed, the recovery period for knee replacements vary greatly. Healthy, young individuals may need only a few therapy sessions to recover from their surgery completely. Older patients who have no one to help them at home may need special assistance or a longer recovery period. Some patients may benefit from a short stay in a rehabilitation facility. To ensure full recovery, patients should identify and address any potential obstacles to recovery before their operation.

To promote full recovery, Lakewood Hospital has developed physical therapy and occupational therapy for patients' use. Patients' physicians and Lakewood Hospital have collaborated on recommended procedures to follow.

Prior to your surgery, we recommend that you:

1. Determine any special equipment that will be needed at home.

2. Learn correct techniques for performing day-to-day activities such as getting in and out of bed, driving your automobile, taking showers, and going up and down stairs.

3. Learn what exercises will help facilitate your recovery.

After surgery, patients must participate in physical therapy to:

- Extend their knee straight or bend it past 90 degrees.

- Place weight on their knee to ensure that they can bear full weight.

- Use the knee without discomfort (this may take several months).

On Friday I visited with Mr. Bryan Owensby to discuss his options relative to the muscle transfer we plan to complete following radiation treatment. Mr. Owensby is a 53-year-old male who recently had multiple lesions excised.

Mr. Owensby is aware that our goal is to provide healthy tissue that could tolerate the radiation treatment he would need to destroy the malignant cells on his upper thigh. At this time, we plan to complete a skin graft from the contralateral thigh to provide the healthy tissue for radiation treatment. I believe this will give Mr. Owensby the best opportunity for early healing.

[...] and this may be an option if the contralateral graft is [...] the risks and complications of either method.

[...] offices. Thank you for this opportunity to participate

[...] a, Dr. Monica Stevens

DESCRIPTIONS AND TREATMENTS OF ADULT BRAIN TUMORS	
Types of Tumors	**Description and Treatment**
Astrocytomas	Tumors that start in brain cells. Treatment includes surgery, chemotherapy, and radiation.
Brain stem gliomas	Tumors located in the bottom part of the brain, which connects to the spinal cord. Treatment includes radiation and biological therapy.
Cerebellar astrocytomas	Tumors that occur in the area of the brain called the cerebellum. Treatment is similar to that for astrocytomas.
Craniopharyngiomas	Tumors that occur near the pituitary gland. Treatment includes surgery and radiation.
Oligodendrogliomas	Tumors that begin in brain cells that provide support and nourishment for the cells that transmit nerve impulses. Treatment includes surgery, chemotherapy, and radiation.

Medical Office Documents

Goals

- Improve speed and accuracy
- Refine language arts skills in punctuation
- Format medical office documents

A. Type 2 times.

A. WARMUP

```
 1        The taxes* were quickly adjusted upward by 20 percent    11
 2   because of the improvements to her house (built in 1901).     23
 3   A proposed law might not penalize good homeowners like her.   34
     |  1  |  2  |  3  |  4  |  5  |  6  |  7  |  8  |  9  |  10  |  11  |  12
```

SKILLBUILDING

B. MAP

Follow the GDP software directions for this exercise in improving keystroking accuracy.

C. Take a 1-minute timed writing on the first paragraph to establish your base speed. Then take four 1-minute timed writings on the remaining paragraphs. As soon as you equal or exceed your base speed on one paragraph, advance to the next, more difficult paragraph.

C. SUSTAINED PRACTICE: ALTERNATE-HAND WORDS

```
 4        A downturn in world fuel prices signals a lower profit   11
 5   for giant oil firms. In fact, most downtown firms might       22
 6   see the usual sign of tight credit and other problems. The    34
 7   city must get down to business and make plans in the fall.    46

 8        The hungry turkeys ate eight bushels of corn that were   11
 9   given to them by our next-door neighbors. They also drank     22
10   the eight bowls of water that were left in the yard. All in   34
11   all, the birds caused quite a bit of chaos early that day.    46

12        A debate on what to do about that extra acreage in the   11
13   desert dragged on for four hours. One problem is what the     23
14   effect may be of moving the ancient ruins to a much safer     34
15   place. City officials must always protect our environment.    46

16        Molly was dressed in a plain pink dress at the annual    11
17   meeting that was taking place at the hotel in Tempe later     23
18   that last week in September. The agenda included four very    34
19   controversial topics that have often generated much debate.   46
     |  1  |  2  |  3  |  4  |  5  |  6  |  7  |  8  |  9  |  10  |  11  |  12
```

D. Study the rules at the right.

D. PUNCTUATION

RULE ▶

: explanatory material

Use a colon to introduce explanatory material that follows an independent clause.

> The computer satisfies three criteria: speed, cost, and power.
> *But:* The computer satisfies the three criteria of_speed, cost, and power.
> Remember this: <u>o</u>nly one coupon is allowed per customer.

Note: An independent clause can stand alone as a complete sentence. Do not capitalize the word following the colon.

RULE ▶

. polite request

Use a period to end a sentence that is a polite request.

> Will you please call me if I can be of further assistance.

Note: Consider a sentence a polite request if you expect the reader to respond by doing as you ask rather than by giving a yes-or-no answer.

Edit the sentences to correct any errors in punctuation.

```
20  We need the following items, pens, pencils, and paper.
21  May I suggest that you send the report by Tuesday?
22  These are some of your colleagues: Bill, Mary, and Ann.
23  Would you please pay my bills when I am on vacation?
24  Our flag is these three colors; red, white, and blue.
25  Would you please start my car to warm it up for me.
```

DOCUMENT PROCESSING

Situation: You work for Lakewood Hospital in Springfield, Oregon. For the purposes of this simulation, your name will be Lucille R. Medford. Your e-mail address is lmedford@lakewood.com.

For the next five days, you will prepare documents for several units within the hospital—Admissions, Billing, Dermatology, Oncology, and Surgery. You will also format various documents including correspondence and medical reports for these units.

Today is November 1. You will spend your first day working in the Admissions Office preparing the documents that appear in your in-basket for today. Proofread your work carefully and check for spelling, punctuation, grammar, and formatting errors so that your documents are mailable.

Correspondence 91-88 ▶

Business Letter in Block Style

: explanatory material

November 1, 20-- | Ms. Nancy J. Dodson | 3727 Harris Street | Eugene, OR 97405-4246 | Dear Ms. Dodson:

¶ Thank you for contacting us and considering us as your primary care provider. We are confident that you will be pleased with our services and our patient care, and we look forward to many years of serving your health needs. ¶ Now that you have made your final selection, we would like you to complete the enclosed Patient Information Form and send it back to us at your earliest convenience. As you can see, the form asks mostly for personal information so that we can contact you or your employer if necessary. In addition, the form requests the following information: the name, address, and telephone number of your insurance company and your insurance policy number.

(Continued on next page)

¶ Again, welcome to Lakewood Hospital! If there is any additional information we can provide about our services, do not hesitate to call us at 555-2300 or e-mail me at lmedford@lakewood.com.

Sincerely, | Lucille R. Medford | Office Manager | ap | Enclosure

Table 91-47

Table

Create a patient information form using the illustration below and these steps:

1. Insert a table with 1 column and 15 rows.
2. Split cells as shown to provide room for individual entries.
3. Type the information as shown.
4. Bold the information in Rows 1, 7, and 11.
5. Insert blank lines above and below the centered section headings, and type the headings in 14-point Cambria.
6. Insert 1 blank line above the information in Rows 2 to 6, 8 to 10, and 12 to 15.
7. Apply 25 percent shading to Rows 1, 7, 11, and 15.

Cambria 14 pt ↓1X **PATIENT INFORMATION** ↓1X

↓1X Date:	
Name (last, first):	Birth Date:
Street Address:	Phone:
City:	State:	ZIP:
E-Mail:	
EMPLOYER INFORMATION	
Employer:	
Street Address:	Phone:
City:	State:	ZIP:
INSURANCE INFORMATION	
Name of Company:	
Address:	
Phone:	Policy Number:
Signature:	Date:

: explanatory material

. polite request

MEMO TO: Dr. Abraham Kramer
FROM: Paula Campbell
DATE: November 1, 20--
SUBJECT: Radiology Lab Closing

¶ Next week the Radiology Lab in Building D will be closed for repairs. I realize that this is the week you were going to take a group of interns to see our new equipment.

¶ I have arranged to have the Radiology Lab in Building C open for you to use so that you do not have to postpone the meeting with the interns. I am sending over a passkey for the lab. The passkey will open three doors: main entry, hall entry, lab door.

¶ Would you please give me a call on Ext. 75 if this lab substitution is not satisfactory with you.

ap

c: Dr. Arnold, Dr. Kazinofski

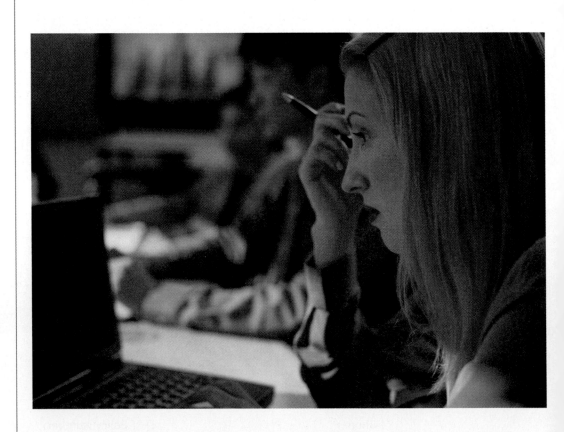

Medical Office Documents

Goals

- Type at least 46wpm/5′/5e
- Format medical office documents

A. Type 2 times.

A. WARMUP

```
1        Missy examined these items: the #4261 oil painting, a    11
2   Bowes & Elkjer porcelain vase, and the 86-piece collection    23
3   of glazed antique pitchers. There were 337 people present.    34
        |  1  |  2  |  3  |  4  |  5  |  6  |  7  |  8  |  9  |  10  |  11  |  12
```

SKILLBUILDING

B. Take three 12-second timed writings on each line. The scale below the last line shows your wpm speed for a 12-second timed writing.

B. 12-SECOND SPEED SPRINTS

```
4   Their home is on a lake that is right south of the prairie.
5   They have a boat and motor and spend a lot of time fishing.
6   Kay caught so many fish that she gave some to the old lady.
7   She was so pleased that a young girl would do this for her.
    I I I I 5 I I I I 10 I I I I 15 I I I I 20 I I I I 25 I I I I 30 I I I I 35 I I I I 40 I I I I 45 I I I I 50 I I I I 55 I I I I 60
```

C. PROGRESSIVE PRACTICE: ALPHABET

If you are not using the GDP software, turn to page SB-7 and follow the directions for this activity.

Strategies for Career Success

Business Communication

There are five components to the communication process, whether written or oral.

The sender is the person who initiates the communication process. The message is the information that needs to be communicated (for example, "There will be a meeting at . . ."). The channel is the method for transmitting the message (for example, e-mail, letter, memo, orally). The audience is the person(s) who receives the message. Feedback is the response given to the sender by the audience that enables the sender to determine if the message was received as intended.

The most effective communication within companies must flow not only downward but also upward.

YOUR TURN Suppose you send an e-mail to 20 people in your department announcing a meeting to discuss your company's new policy on flextime. Who is the sender? What is the message? What is the channel you use to transmit the message? Who is the audience? What is the ultimate feedback?

D. Take two 5-minute timed writings. Review your speed and errors.

Goal: At least 46wpm/5'/5e

D. 5-MINUTE TIMED WRITING

8	The first impression you make on a job interview will	11
9	be a lasting one, and you will want it to be favorable. A	23
10	safe choice is to dress conservatively. If you have time,	34
11	find out what people who are currently employed at this	45
12	company wear to work. You can acquire this information by	57
13	simply calling the human resources office. Or, you could	68
14	observe what the current employees are wearing when you	80
15	pick up a job application from a company.	88
16	As you plan the details of your appearance before your	99
17	job interview, be cognizant of all the details. You will	111
18	want to present a neat and clean appearance. Your clothing	122
19	should be clean and very neatly pressed. Your hair and your	134
20	nails should be neatly groomed, and your shoes should be	146
21	clean and polished. You should use only a small amount of	157
22	perfume or cologne and wear only basic jewelry. Plan to	169
23	arrive for the appointment in time to make a final check of	181
24	your appearance before the interview.	188
25	Your appearance may not be the sole factor that will	199
26	secure the job, but it will help you make a positive first	211
27	impression. Remember to dress for the position you would	222
28	like rather than the position you have.	230

| 1 | 2 | 3 | 4 | 5 | 6 | 7 | 8 | 9 | 10 | 11 | 12 |

DOCUMENT PROCESSING

This is November 2, the second day of your assignment at Lakewood Hospital. Today you are assigned to the Billing Office, where you will complete documents related to the activities in that office. Your first assignment is to prepare a report describing the billing process at Lakewood Hospital.

LAKEWOOD BILLING PROCESS
November 2, 20--

¶ The billing process at Lakewood Hospital will be undergoing review soon. This report will explain how fees are determined, how transactions are recorded, how payments are made, and how overdue accounts are collected.

Determining Fees

¶ Fees that a physician charges for services should be fair both to the patients that are under his or her care and to the medical profession. A doctor's fees should be based on the following criteria:

(Continued on next page)

Refer to Reference Manual

Refer to page R-12C of the Reference Manual for a review of list formatting.

- the amount of time involved in providing ~~the~~ service
- the level of skill required in providing the service
- the degree of expertise required to interpret the results of the service provided

¶ Fees should be identified in a fee schedule that lists procedures performed and the charges assessed for those procedures. The fee schedule should be made available to patients if (it's) requested. If patients inquire ~~as to~~ about the amount of the fee, an estimate should be given to the patient. In all instances, this estimate should be made available to the patient before treatment begins.

RECORDING TRANSACTIONS

¶ A record of all patient visits must be maintained. A charge slip should be used to record all procedures. The charge slip includes information such as a checklist of all procedures; a checklist of all diagnoses; space for additional information; and an area for all previous charges, payments, and balances. As the doctor performs procedures, annotations and changes are made to the charge slip so that it is ~~always~~ kept current. The charge slip should be attached to the patient's chart. When all procedures have been completed, a copy of the charge slip is sent to the patient to indicate the charges incurred during the patient's visit.

MAKING PAYMENT ARRANGEMENTS

¶ A patient's bill can be paid by one of the following methods:

- A patient can pay the bill by cash or check at the conclusion of the visit.
- A patient can pay fixed amounts of the bill at ~~any~~ designated times, weekly or monthly.
- A bill (statement) can be sent to the patient at the conclusion of the visit.
- A bill can be sent to the Health Insurance Carrier.

COLLECTING OVERDUE ACCOUNTS

¶ There are a number of reasons why a patient might not pay a bill. Whatever the reason, however, steps must be taken to collect delinquent accounts. Depending on the number of days the account has been overdue, here are some suggestions for steps that can be taken to collect payment:

(Continued on next page)

1. Attach a reminder when the bill is sent if payment is over ~~thirty~~ 30 days overdue (this is the usual grace period given to accounts).

2. If payment is not received after the reminder is sent, it may be necessary to call the patient to request payment.

3. The next step would be to attach a personal note to a statement that is over due, possibly as long as 60 days.

4. Make one further attempt to telephone the patient for payment.

5. Send a collection letter for payment. The letter should be friendly but firm. Remind the patient that the account is overdue. Offer to assist the patient in making payments on a fixed schedule by establishing a payment plan. Leave your telephone number so the patient can call you if there are any questions that need to be answered regarding the bill.

6. The final alternative in collecting an unpaid bill is to turn over the account to a collection agency or go to court for legal action. This is a costly step for both caregivers and patients and it should be used only as a last resort.

Table 92-48

Boxed Table

Press the SPACE BAR 10 times between the phone number and the e-mail address.

Set a right tab to align the Total Due amount at the right.

↓1X

STATEMENT
↓2X

WENDY NEWMAN, M.D.
Lakewood Hospital
970 Kruse Way
Springfield, OR 97477
Phone: 541-555-2300   E-Mail: billing@lakewood.com
↓1X

Patient:	Marion W. Fleming
Address:	1654 Franklin Boulevard
City/State/ZIP:	Eugene, OR 97403

Date	Description	Charge	Payment	Balance
3/18/06	EKG	185.00	50.00	135.00
3/18/06	Laboratory work	125.00	25.00	100.00
3/19/06	X-ray	85.00	0.00	85.00
3/21/06	Cholesterol check	75.00	25.00	50.00
3/21/06	Laboratory work	80.00	25.00	55.00
Total Due				**425.00**

Medical Office Documents

Goals

- Improve speed and accuracy
- Refine language arts skills in composing
- Format medical office documents

A. Type 2 times.

A. WARMUP

```
1        Did you hear the excellent quartet of junior cadets?    11
2   Everybody in that crowd (estimated at over 500) applauded    23
3   "with gusto." The sizable crowd filled the 3/4-acre park.    35
    | 1 | 2 | 3 | 4 | 5 | 6 | 7 | 8 | 9 | 10 | 11 | 12
```

SKILLBUILDING

PPP PRETEST → PRACTICE → POSTTEST

PRETEST
Take a 1-minute timed writing. Review your speed and errors.

B. PRETEST: Discrimination Practice

```
4        Did the new clerk join the golf team? James indicated    11
5   to me that Patricia invited her prior to last Wednesday. He   23
6   believes she must give you a verbal commitment at once.       34
    | 1 | 2 | 3 | 4 | 5 | 6 | 7 | 8 | 9 | 10 | 11 | 12
```

PRACTICE
Speed Emphasis:
If you made no more than 1 error on the Pretest, type each *individual* line 2 times.
Accuracy Emphasis:
If you made 2 or more errors, type each *group* of lines (as though it were a paragraph) 2 times.

C. PRACTICE: Left Hand

```
7   vbv bevy verb bevel vibes breve viable braves verbal beaver
8   wew went week weans weigh weave wedges thawed weaker beware
9   ded dent need deals moved ceded heeded debate edging define
```

D. PRACTICE: Right Hand

```
10  klk kale look kilts lakes knoll likely kettle kernel lacked
11  uyu buys your gummy dusty young unduly tryout uneasy jaunty
12  oio oils roil toils onion point oriole soiled ration joined
```

POSTTEST
Repeat the Pretest timed writing and compare performance.

E. POSTTEST: Discrimination Practice

F. PROGRESSIVE PRACTICE: NUMBERS

If you are not using the GDP software, turn to page SB-11 and follow the directions for this activity.

G. COMPOSING AN E-MAIL MESSAGE

Compose an e-mail message to your employer, Dr. Natalie Benson, whose e-mail address is nbenson@lakewood.com, informing Dr. Benson of the appointments you have scheduled for Tuesday, April 17, 20--. The first appointment is with James Mitchell, who is coming for his annual physical—make this appointment at 9 a.m. The second appointment is with Karen McDaniels, who is going to have her blood pressure and cholesterol checked. She will see Dr. Benson at 10 a.m. The final appointment is with Mary Ann Bradley, who will see the doctor about flu symptoms. Be sure you use an appropriate greeting, closing, and signature. Save but do not send this e-mail message.

DOCUMENT PROCESSING

Correspondence 93-90

Business Letter in Modified-Block Style

This is November 3, the third day of your assignment. You will work in a specialty area—the Dermatology Unit. Dermatology is a branch of science dealing with the skin and its structure, functions, and diseases.

November 3, 20-- | Dr. Stanley G. Streisand | Professor of Medical Science | Hillside Medical College | 110 Sunset Drive | Eugene, OR 97403-2120 | Dear Dr. Streisand:

¶ Thank you for the invitation to address the students in your medical science class on the topic of dermatology. As you know, this is my specialty; I am particularly interested in the topic of skin rashes and their causes and treatments.

¶ I recognize that your students are beginning medical school students, so my presentation will focus on a very general talk about dermatology. I am enclosing a copy of a paper I presented at the AMA meeting in San Francisco last week that I think would be appropriate for your students. The audience at my AMA presentation was primarily first-year nursing students who were interested in a general background of the more common types of skin rashes.

¶ Please send me a copy of your program with directions on how to reach your classroom on the day of my presentation. I look forward to meeting with your students.

Sincerely yours, | Angela Miller, M.D. | ap | Enclosure | PS: Please let me know how many students you have in your class so I can prepare an adequate number of handouts for them.

(Continued on next page)

COMMON SKIN RASHES
Their Causes and Cures
Dr. Stanley G. Streisand

¶ Skin rashes are caused by many different things. They are often recognized by symptoms of reddening, itching, blistering, dryness, or scabbing of the skin. Some of the more common ailments that fall into the category of skin rashes are dermatitis, eczema, and psoriasis. This paper will discuss these three common types of skin rashes.

DERMATITIS

¶ Dermatitis is often referred to as _contact dermatitis_. Some of the more common substances that cause dermatitis are soaps, rubber, jewelry, plants, household and industrial chemicals, cosmetics, and perfumes. Contact dermatitis is further classified as either _allergic contact dermatitis_ or _irritant contact dermatitis_.

¶ Allergic Contact Dermatitis. This skin rash occurs after contact is made with certain substances, called allergens. The rash occurs as a reaction of the body's immune system to expel the allergen from your skin. Some common allergens are metals in jewelry, cosmetics, and rubber boots.

¶ Irritant Contact Dermatitis. This skin rash does not require exposure to an allergen but can develop when you come in contact with certain substances—skin cleansers, detergents, solvents, and oils.

(Continued on next page)

ECZEMA

¶ Eczema, also known as atopic dermatitis, causes the skin to appear red and blotchy all over. The disease occurs at any age but mainly from infancy to childhood. It affects about 3 percent of the United States population. There are two types of eczema—atopic eczema and hand eczema.

¶ Atopic Eczema. This form of eczema is caused by the house dust mite, by heat, by contact with woolen clothing, by detergents, and by stress.

¶ Hand Eczema. Hand eczema is caused by sensitive skin, too much exposure to wet work, detergents, oils, and greases.

PSORIASIS

¶ Psoriasis is a chronic skin disease characterized by inflammation and skin scaling. This disease affects about 5.5 million people in the United States. It occurs in all age groups and affects both men and women. When psoriasis develops, patches of skin redden and become covered with scales. The skin then cracks and may cause severe irritation in places like the elbows, knees, face, scalp, and lower back.

¶ It is believed that psoriasis is a disorder of the immune system in which there are not enough white blood cells to help protect the body against infection and diseases of this type.

Medical Office Documents

Goals

- Type at least 46wpm/5'/5e
- Format a formal report

A. Type 2 times.

A. WARMUP

```
1       Mr. Baxter will move to 1749 Larkin Street; his old      11
2   home is in Gray's Woods, just east of the corner of Parson   22
3   and 167th Avenue. The house sizes are quite different!       33
    |  1  |  2  |  3  |  4  |  5  |  6  |  7  |  8  |  9  |  10  |  11  |  12
```

SKILLBUILDING

B. DIAGNOSTIC PRACTICE: SYMBOLS AND PUNCTUATION

If you are not using the GDP software, turn to page SB-2 and follow the directions for this activity.

C. Take two 5-minute timed writings. Review your speed and errors.

Goal: At least 46wpm/5'/5e

C. 5-MINUTE TIMED WRITING

```
 4        Innovative technology may bring new problems for our    11
 5   homes and businesses. A rising shift to use a cell phone is  23
 6   causing many people to look at the etiquette of cell phone   35
 7   usage. Are there times and places where a cell phone should  47
 8   not be used?                                                 49
 9        People want to be able to stay in touch, no matter      60
10   where they are or what they are doing. However, in some      71
11   places cell phone usage is inappropriate or not allowed.     82
12   For example, you would not want a ringing cell phone to      93
13   disrupt an entire production if you are enjoying a concert   105
14   or play. As a consideration to everyone in the audience,    117
15   the management may make an announcement asking audience      128
16   members to turn off their cell phones or pagers before the  140
17   production begins. Making this request gives everyone the   151
18   chance to enjoy the show.                                   156
19        Often you see someone driving a car while talking on a 168
20   cell phone. Talking on the phone while you are driving is   179
21   not a good idea. When you are talking on the phone and not  191
22   concentrating on driving, you may cause an accident. If you 203
23   are driving a vehicle in traffic, your full focus should be 215
24   on the road. Be cognizant of this. Do not use your cell     226
25   phone when driving.                                         230
```
| 1 | 2 | 3 | 4 | 5 | 6 | 7 | 8 | 9 | 10 | 11 | 12

DOCUMENT PROCESSING

Table 94-49

Boxed Table

This is November 4, the fourth day of your assignment. Today you are working in the Oncology Unit. Oncology is a branch of science dealing with the study of tumors.

You will begin by typing this boxed table. Insert 1 blank line after the information in each row.

DESCRIPTIONS AND TREATMENTS OF ADULT BRAIN TUMORS	
Types of Tumors	**Description and Treatment**
Astrocytomas	Tumors that start in brain cells. Treatment includes surgery, chemotherapy, and radiation.
Brain stem gliomas	Tumors located in the bottom part of the brain, which connects to the spinal cord. Treatment includes radiation and biological therapy.

(Continued on next page)

Cerebellar astrocytomas	Tumors that occur in the area of the brain called the cerebellum. Treatment is similar to that for astrocytomas.
Craniopharyngiomas	Tumors that occur near the pituitary gland. Treatment includes surgery and radiation.
Oligodendrogliomas	Tumors that begin in brain cells that provide support and nourishment for the cells that transmit nerve impulses. Treatment includes surgery, chemotherapy, and radiation.

Correspondence 94-91

Business Letter in Block Style

November 4, 20-- | Dr. Samuel Abbott | Sacred Heart Medical Center | 267 Ferry Street | Eugene, OR 97401-2409 | Dear Sam: | Subject: Paul R. Williams.

¶ On September 3 I examined Mr. Williams and discovered a Stage 1A, Cleaved B cell follicular lymphoma in the left inguinal region. I conducted a surgical excision and recommended radiation therapy. Mr. Williams completed his radiation therapy four weeks ago and feels well at this time. He has no complaints, his appetite and energy are normal, and he looks good. His weight is down five pounds upon my recommendation four weeks ago that he lose some excess weight.

¶ There are no abdominal or inguinal lymph nodes to his scrotal sac exam. There are, however, three- to four-millimeter nodes in the right inguinal region that appear totally unchanged from his original exam on September 3. His lungs are clear, his heartbeat is regular, the liver and spleen are not enlarged, and there are no palpable masses.

¶ It appears to me that Mr. Williams has recovered satisfactorily from his radiation therapy. He has requested a second opinion, and I am therefore recommending that he make an appointment with you at his earliest convenience. We will prepare a referral for Mr. Williams and forward it to your office in a day or two.

Sincerely, | Donna Stensland, M.D. | ap

Table 94-50

Boxed Table

Open the file for Table 94-49 and make the following changes:

1. Press ENTER 2 times after the title, change to 12-point Calibri, and type the subtitle November 4, 20-- in bold.
2. Add this entry to the table so that it will appear in alphabetical order:

   Gliomas
   The general name for tumors that come from the supportive tissue of the brain; for example, astrocytomas or oligodendrogliomas. They may be benign or malignant.

3. Apply a table style of your choice. Select one with distinctive borders and shading that will make the table easier to read.

Medical Office Documents

Goals

- Improve speed and accuracy
- Refine language arts skills in proofreading
- Format medical office documents

A. Type 2 times.

A. WARMUP

```
1      The extra black vacuum cleaners with the large-sized    11
2   grips were just lowered to $160 from $240 (a 33 1/3% mark-  23
3   down). Jay's #57 quilts were marked down to $98 from $108.  34
    |  1  |  2  |  3  |  4  |  5  |  6  |  7  |  8  |  9  |  10  |  11  |  12
```

SKILLBUILDING

B. Type each word as shown until you reach the backspace sign (←). Then backspace 1 time and replace the previously typed character with the character shown. For example, if you see "hi←at," type "hi," backspace 1 time, and then type "at," resulting in the word "hat."
Technique Tip: Press the BACKSPACE key with the Sem finger, without looking at your keyboard.

B. TECHNIQUE PRACTICE: BACKSPACE KEY

```
4   p←cat c←tab b←peg p←but p←tie m←say t←car s←tea s←mad f←car
5   di←ye be←ag ge←um ri←ob mu←ad pa←it ca←ut fa←it fa←in pa←od
6   ham←d any←t new←t was←r sea←t mad←t gag←p tab←r tax←p ant←d
7   cheat←p scalp←e charm←t peace←h chart←m trace←k hub←t bib←t
```

C. PACED PRACTICE

If you are not using the GDP software, turn to page SB-14 and follow the directions for this activity.

LANGUAGE ARTS

D. Edit this paragraph to correct any keyboarding or formatting errors.

D. PROOFREADING

```
8       Suprising as it may seem, their has been a good deal
9   of interest in comunicating with a computer thruogh the
10  human voice for about fourty years. Researchers haev spent
11  millions ofdollars in hteir efforts to improve voice input
12  tecknology. It is likly that in the next decade we will
13  see many use ful applications in busness and in education.
```

Table 95-51 ▶

Boxed Table

This is November 5, the final day of your assignment, and today you are working in the Surgery Unit. The specialty within this unit is knee surgery. Your first assignment is to create a table listing various medical terms and their definitions. Insert 1 blank line after the information in each row.

MEDICAL TERMS AND THEIR DEFINITIONS November 5, 20--	
Adenopathy	Swelling or morbid enlargement of the lymph nodes
Auscultation	The act of listening to sounds made by the various body structures as a diagnostic method
Cholecystectomy	Surgical removal of the gall bladder
Enterostomy	An incision into the intestines that produces a small hole in the abdomen which through the intestines are emptied
Femur	The long bone of the thigh
Fibroperitoneal	Related to the tissue that lines the abdominal cavity which and covers most of the viscera
Laparoscopy	A minimally invasive surgical technique using a fiber optic instrument
Hemostasis	The arrest of bleeding
Laparotomy	incision into the abdominal wall
Trocar	An instrument for withdrawing fluid from a cavity

RECOVERING FROM KNEE SURGERY

Dr. Alec Pera, M.D.

November 5, 20--

¶ Specific procedures should be followed by patients who are recovering from knee surgery. Depending on the particular surgery that was performed, postoperative needs of patients with knee replacements vary greatly. Healthy, young individuals may require only a few therapy sessions to recover from their surgery completely. Older individuals with no family or friends to help them at home may need special assistance or equipment to aid their mobility. Some patients may benefit from a short stay in a rehabilitation facility. To enhance the rate of recovery, patients should identify and address any special needs that may require attention before their operation.

Refer to page R-12C of the Reference Manual for a review of list formatting.

¶ To promote full recovery, Lakewood Hospital has developed a coordinated pathway of physical and occupational therapy for patients' use. Patient Rehabilitation and Therapy Service (PRTS) and Lakewood Hospital have collaborated on recommending a specific sequence of procedures to follow.
¶ Prior to your surgery, we recommend that you:
1. Determine any special equipment that will be required to promote your recovery.
2. Learn correct techniques for performing day-to-day activities such as getting in and out of bed, driving your automobile, taking showers, getting up from a seat, and going up and down stairs.
3. Learn what exercises will help facilitate your recovery.
¶ After surgery, patients must participate in physical therapy to ensure that they can:
•   Extend their knee straight or bend it past 90 degrees.
•   Place weight on their knee to ensure that they have the strength and stability to hold their weight.
•   Use the knee without discomfort (this may take several months).

Prepare this e-mail message. Type the e-mail greeting, Hi, Dr. Lockhart:, and the body shown below in correct format. Type Anna as the closing, and type this signature: Anna Padilla | E-Mail: apadilla@lakewood.com | Phone: 541-555-2303. Save the e-mail message, but do not send it.

Mr. Walden came in today with a crusted lesion in his back. Lesion was removed using 1% Xylocaine with epinephrine loc. Wound was closed with 4.0 nylon sutures. Stitches should be removed in approximately 10 days. Sutures should be kept dry for 3 days. Mr. Walden is to call if he has questions or if problems arise.

Dr. Charlene T. Gutierrez, Director of Plastic Surgery, was asked to assist Dr. Alec Pera with surgery on Bryan Owensby. After an office visit with Mr. Owensby, Dr. Gutierrez dictated the following memo to Dr. Pera. Use November 5, 20--, as the date and type the subject Mr. Owensby's Surgery. Type Dr. Gutierrez's title on the same line as her name, and use a comma and space between them.

Progress and Proofreading Check

Documents designated as Proofreading Checks serve as a check of your proofreading skill. Your goal is to have zero typographical errors when the GDP software first scores the document.

On Friday I visited with Mr. Bryan Owensby to discuss his options relative to the muscle transfer we plan to complete following radiation treatment. Mr. Owensby is a 53-year-old male who recently had multiple lesions excised. ¶ Mr. Owensby is aware that our goal is to provide healthy tissue that could tolerate the radiation treatment he would need to destroy the malignant cells on his upper thigh. At this time, we plan to complete a skin graft from the contralateral thigh to provide the healthy tissue for radiation treatment. I believe this will give Mr. Owensby the best opportunity for early healing. ¶ A free tissue transfer was also discussed, and this may be an option if the contralateral graft is unsuccessful. Mr. Owensby understands the risks and complications of either method. Scheduling is pending jointly through our offices. Thank you for this opportunity to participate in Mr. Owensby's care. ap | c: Dr. Taiwo Owakoniro, Dr. Lewis Sethna, Dr. Monica Stevens

Legal Office Documents

Article (except motor vehicles) to my children who survive me, to be divided among them as they shall agree, or in the absence of such agreement, as my Personal Representative shall determine, which determination shall be conclusive.

ARTICLE VI

If any beneficiary named or described in this Will fails to survive me for 120 hours, all the provisions in this Will for the benefit of such deceased beneficiary shall lapse, and this Will shall be construed as though the fact were that he or she predeceased me.

ARTICLE VII

All estate, inheritance, transfer, succession, and any other taxes plus interest and penalties thereon (death taxes) that become payable by reason of my death upon property passing under this instrument shall be paid out of the residue of my estate without reimbursement from the recipient and without apportionment. All death taxes upon property not passing under this instrument shall be apportioned in the manner provided by law.

IN WITNESS WHEREOF, I have hereunto affixed my hand and seal this _____ day of _____, 20--. ↓2X

IRMA J. GOMEZ   Testator ↓2X

The foregoing instrument, consisting of TWO (2) pages (this page included), was on this _____ day of _____, 20--, subscribed on each page and at the end thereof by Irma J. Gomez, the above-named Testator and by her signed, sealed, published and declared to be her Last Will, in the presence of us, and each of us, who thereupon, at her _____ ce of each other, have hereunto subscribed our

_____ residing at _____

_____ residing at _____

2

STATE OF KANSAS → 6.5" right tab **IN DISTRICT COURT** ↓2X

COUNTY OF DOUGLAS **NORTHEAST JUDICIAL DISTRICT** ↓2X

PEOPLE'S BANK → 3.25" tab → 6.5" right tab **NO.** _20 underscores_
607 New Hampshire Street)
Lawrence, KS 66044-2243)
→3.25" tab)
→1" tab Plaintiff, →3.25" tab)
)
→1" tab vs. →3.25" tab) → 6.5" right tab **SUMMONS**
)
JOHN COUZINS)
)
Defendant.)↓2X

THE STATE OF KANSAS TO THE ABOVE-NAMED DEFENDANT: ↓2X

You are hereby summoned and required to appear and defend against the Complaint in this action, which is hereby served upon you by serving upon the undersigned an Answer or other proper response within twenty (20) d Complaint upon you, exclusive of the day of service.

If you fail to do so, judgment by default demanded in the Complaint.

SIGNED this _____ day of December 20
5 underscores →3.25" tab
Ann B
806 K
Lawre
Telep
Attorr

LAST WILL AND TESTAMENT
OF
IRMA J. GOMEZ ↓2X

→1" tab I, IRMA J. GOMEZ, residing in Corvallis, Oregon, do hereby make and declare this to be my Last Will and Testament, hereby revoking any and all former Wills and Codicils by me at any time heretofore made. ↓2X

ARTICLE I ↓2X

This will is made in Oregon and shall be governed, construed, and administered according to Oregon law, even though subject to probate or administered elsewhere. The Oregon laws applied shall not include any principles or laws relating to conflicts or choice of laws.

ARTICLE II

Whenever used herein, words importing the singular shall include the plural and words importing the masculine shall include the feminine and neuter, and vice versa, unless the context otherwise requires.

ARTICLE III

I am married and my husband's name is Ricardo E. Gomez. All references hereinafter made to "husband" or "spouse" shall refer to him and no other; and if he is not my legal husband at the time of my death, then he shall be deemed for the purpose of this, my last Will and Testament, to have predeceased me. I was formerly married to Henry Woo, who is now deceased. There were three (3) children born of my marriage to Henry Woo. The names of those children are as follows: Judy Parsons, Henry Wayne, and Randy Woo.

ARTICLE IV

If My Spouse Survives. Except as may otherwise be provided hereunder in this Article IV, if my spouse survives me, I devise to my spouse all my interest in household furniture and furnishings, books, apparel, art objects, collections, jewelry, and similar personal effects; sporting and recreational equipment; all other tangible property for personal use; all other like contents of my home and any vacation property that I may own or reside in on the date of my death; all animals; any motor vehicles that I may own on the date of my death; and any unexpired insurance on all such property.

ARTICLE V

If My Spouse Does Not Survive. Except as may be otherwise provided in this Article IV, if my spouse does not survive me, I devise the property described above in this

1

Legal Office Documents

Goals
- Type at least 47wpm/5'/5e
- Format legal office documents

A. Type 2 times.

A. WARMUP

```
1       Marshal bought five chances for the contest. He won    11
2  six prizes and was given a check for $2,350--these prizes   22
3  are equal to 1/4th of Jill's winnings for all of last year. 34
   |  1  |  2  |  3  |  4  |  5  |  6  |  7  |  8  |  9  | 10  | 11  | 12
```

SKILLBUILDING

B. DIAGNOSTIC PRACTICE: NUMBERS

If you are not using the GDP software, turn to page SB-5 and follow the directions for this activity.

C. Take three 12-second timed writings on each line. The scale below the last line shows your wpm speed for a 12-second timed writing.

C. 12-SECOND SPEED SPRINTS

```
4  They saw the sun shine through after days and days of rain.
5  She hopes to get a much higher math score on the next test.
6  Jo did not study for the math exam she took late last week.
7  This time he spent at least ten days studying for the test.
   | | | |5| | | |10| | | |15| | | |20| | | |25| | | |30| | | |35| | | |40| | | |45| | | |50| | | |55| | | |60
```

Keyboarding Connection

Capturing an Image From the Internet

Would you like to copy an image or graphic from the Internet? It's easy!

Point to the image or graphic and press the right mouse button. When the shortcut menu appears, choose Save Picture As (or Save Image As). The Save Picture dialog box appears. Select the appropriate drive and name the file if necessary. Click Save. The image is usually saved with a .gif, .jpg, or .bmp file extension. To insert the image into a Word document, select the Insert tab, choose Picture, locate the file, and click Insert. You could also right-click the image, choose Copy, and then click the Paste button in Word.

YOUR TURN Conduct a Web search and locate an image or graphic to save. Right-click the image, choose Save Picture As, name the file, and save the image. Insert the image into a word processing document.

D. Take two 5-minute timed writings. Review your speed and errors.

Goal: At least 47wpm/5'/5e

D. 5-MINUTE TIMED WRITING

```
 8      Many businesses across the country are adopting a new    11
 9   dress code called business casual. Depending on the type of  23
10   place for which you work, business casual can have various   35
11   meanings. Most places allow their workers to dress down a    46
12   notch from what was expected in the past. If people wore     58
13   suits and ties in the past, then the business casual code    69
14   would allow them to stop wearing ties and suit jackets. It   81
15   is quite necessary for a business to formulate dress code    93
16   guidelines for workers to follow when business casual goes  105
17   into effect.                                                107
18      Surveys of various companies show mixed results when     118
19   employees were given a choice of dressing more casually.    129
20   Some companies feel business casual is a perk that works    141
21   for employees. However, other companies report that job     152
22   productivity rates zoom down when workers are allowed to     163
23   dress down. More research is needed.                        171
24      When you feel good about the way you look, you will      181
25   show this attitude in your performance. If your company has 193
26   adopted a business casual dress code, you must keep in mind 205
27   that business casual does not mean that you can dress in a   217
28   sloppy manner. A neat appearance and good grooming always   229
29   enhance a business casual look.                             235
```

| 1 | 2 | 3 | 4 | 5 | 6 | 7 | 8 | 9 | 10 | 11 | 12 |

FORMATTING

E. LEGAL DOCUMENTS

Court rules (federal, state, appellate, and so on) and law office preferences determine the format of legal documents including margins, line numbering, line spacing, line lengths, page numbering, indents, alignment, and bolding. Therefore, the legal documents and guidelines in this unit have been designed to serve as simplified examples of acceptable legal formats.

Legal documents are typed on either 8.5- × 14-inch legal paper or 8.5- × 11-inch paper. Court documents often include numbered lines for easy reference in a court of law. *Legal cap* is the name given to the vertical rules that appear at the left and right margins. In legal documents, the *venue* states the name and location of the court and county. The *caption* states the court, the names of the parties, the docket (case) number, the title of the document, and sometimes the name of the judge.

Follow these general formatting guidelines for legal documents in this unit. Refer to the summons shown in the illustration.

- Use default margins all around, single spacing, left alignment, and no bold.
- Set a 1-inch tab, and indent paragraphs 1 inch; press ENTER 2 times between paragraphs.
- Set a 6.5-inch right tab, and type 20 underscores for the case number.
- Single-space court documents (such as an affidavit of possession, a summons, a complaint, and a judgment), and number all lines. Restart line numbers on each page.

(Continued on next page)

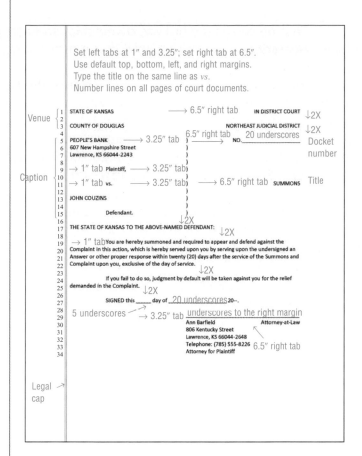

Set left tabs at 1" and 3.25"; set right tab at 6.5".
Use default top, bottom, left, and right margins.
Type the title on the same line as *vs.*
Number lines on all pages of court documents.

- Single-space noncourt documents (such as a warranty deed and last will and testament), and do not number lines.
- For multipage documents, insert a centered page number at the bottom of each page.
- Set a 3.25-inch tab, and type the closing parentheses at 3.25 inches; for signature lines, type continuous underscores from this 3.25-inch tab setting to the right margin.
- Type 20 underscores for months and case numbers and 5 underscores for dates; insert spaces before and after underscores when the underscores appear in the middle of a sentence.
- Insert a space after "NO." before typing the 20 underscores for case numbers.

Word Processing Manual

F. WORD PROCESSING: LINE NUMBERING

Study Lesson 96 in your word processing manual. Complete all of the shaded steps while at your computer. Then format the jobs that follow.

DOCUMENT PROCESSING

An affidavit is a sworn written statement made under oath.

Report 96-67

Affidavit of Possession

Add line numbering for all lines in this document. When this document is actually typed, the line numbers will vary from those shown here.

1   AFFIDAVIT OF POSSESSION ↓2X

2

3 STATE OF VERMONT ↓2X

4

5 COUNTY OF WINDSOR ↓2X

6

7 → 1" tab   Eric Wesley, being first duly sworn, deposes and says: ↓2X

8

9   That he is an adult person and is a resident of Windsor County,

10 Vermont, and that his mailing address is P.O. Box 801, Ludlow, VT 05149. ↓2X

11

(Continued on next page)

12 That he knows the history, ownership, and occupancy of the
13 following-described property situated in Windsor County, Vermont, to wit:
14
15 All that part of the Southeast Quarter of the Northeast Quarter of
16 Section Nine (9), Township Seventy-two (72), further described as follows:
17 Beginning at the Northeast corner of said Southeast Quarter of the Northeast
18 Quarter; thence South along the East line of said quarter 1000.00 feet;
19 thence West 575.00 feet; thence North 200.00 feet; thence West 204.00 feet;
20 thence North 800.00 feet; thence East 979.00 feet.
21
22 That the record title holder in fee simple of the above property is
23 Eric Wesley, a single person; that he is presently in possession of the above-
24 described premises;
25
26 That ownership of the aforesaid property is based upon an
27 unbroken chain of title through immediate and remote grantors by deed of
28 conveyance which has been recorded for a period of more than twenty-one
29 (21) years, to wit: Since August 21, 1943, at 2 a.m.;
30
31 That the purpose of this Affidavit of Possession is to show proof of
32 ownership by providing and recording evidence of possession for
33 marketable title as required by the Marketable Record Title Act of the State
34 of Vermont.
35   ↓2X
36   5 underscores
                DATED this _____ day of May 2006, at Ludlow, Vermont.
37   ↓2X
38   underscores to the right margin
                                    _____
39   ⟶ 3.25" tab   Blake Crawford   6.5" right tab⟶   Attorney-at-Law
40   ↓2X
41   Subscribed and sworn to before me this ____ day of May 2006.
42
43   _____
44   Shirley Blakely   Notary Public
45   Windsor County, Vermont
46   My Commission Expires July 17, 2012

Underscore is 5
characters wide.

Underscore starts at
3.25-inch left tab and
ends at the right margin.

Signature title ends at
6.5-inch right tab.

Underscore starts at
3.25-inch left tab and
ends at the right margin.

Correspondence▶
96-94

Business Letter
in Block Style

August 30, 20-- | Mr. Eric Wesley | P.O. Box 801 | Ludlow, VT 05149 | Dear
Mr. Wesley:
¶ Enclosed is your copy of the Affidavit of Possession that was filed on your
behalf with the Windsor County Courthouse.
¶ As you can see, only the Southeast Quarter of your property was included
in the affidavit. We will have to file an additional affidavit if you want to add
the Northwest Quarter as well as your Franklin County properties. All
affidavits must be completed prior to your property being advertised in the
Windsor News.
¶ I will be out of the office all of next week. If you have questions, please
call my associate, Betty Yu.
Sincerely, | Blake Crawford | urs | Enclosure | c: Marvin Steele, Beverley
Perez

Legal Office Documents

Goals

- Improve speed and accuracy
- Refine language arts skills in the use of punctuation
- Format legal office documents

A. Type 2 times.

A. WARMUP

```
1      Jacqueline kept prize #2490 instead of #3761 because    11
2   it was worth 58.5% more value. That was a great prize! Last  23
3   year the law firm of Adams & Day donated all grand prizes.   34
     |  1  |  2  |  3  |  4  |  5  |  6  |  7  |  8  |  9  |  10  |  11  |  12
```

SKILLBUILDING

B. PROGRESSIVE PRACTICE: ALPHABET

If you are not using the GDP software, turn to page SB-7 and follow the directions for this activity.

C. PACED PRACTICE

If you are not using the GDP software, turn to page SB-14 and follow the directions for this activity.

LANGUAGE ARTS

D. Study the rules at the right.

D. SEMICOLONS

RULE ▶
; no conjunction

Use a semicolon to separate two closely related independent clauses that are not connected by a conjunction (such as *and, but*, or *nor*).

Management favored the vote; stockholders did not.
But: Management favored the vote, but stockholders did not.

RULE ▶
; series

Use a semicolon to separate three or more items in a series if any of the items already contain commas.

Staff meetings were held on Thursday, May 7; Monday, June 7; and Friday, June 12.
Note: Be sure to insert the semicolon between (not within) the items in a series.

Edit the sentences to correct any errors in the use of semicolons.

```
4   Paul will travel to Madrid, Spain; Lisbon, Portugal, and
5   Nice, France.
6   Mary's gift arrived yesterday, Margie's did not.
7   Bring your textbook to class; I'll return it tomorrow.
8   The best days for the visit are Monday, May 10, Tuesday,
9   May 18, and Wednesday, May 26.
10  Jan is the president; Peter is the vice president.
```

Report 97-68

Warranty Deed

A seller who provides a warranty deed warrants (or guarantees) that he or she has full ownership of a property and has the right to sell it. The seller also guarantees all rights of the property to the buyer.

WARRANTY DEED ↓2X

→ 1" tab   THIS INDENTURE, made this ⁵ underscores _____ day of October, 2006, between Maria J. Lopez, Grantor, whether one or more, and Barbara Denman, Grantee, whether one or more, whose post office address is 315 Clark Avenue, Ames, IA 50010-3314. ↓2X

WITNESSETH, for and in consideration of the sum of SEVENTY-FIVE THOUSAND and 00/100 DOLLARS ($75,000), Grantor does hereby GRANT to Grantee, all of the following real property lying in the County of Story, State of Iowa, and described as follows, to-wit:

Lots Seventeen (17) and Eighteen (18), Block Seventy-three (73), Original Townsite of Ames, Iowa, SUBJECT TO easements, special or improvement taxes and assessments, mineral conveyances, rights-of-way and reservations of record.

(THIS DEED IS IN FULFILLMENT OF THAT CERTAIN CONTRACT FOR DEED ENTERED INTO BY AND BETWEEN THE SAME PARTIES ON THE DATE HEREOF.)

And the said Grantor for herself, her heirs, executors and administrators, does covenant with the Grantee that she is well seized in fee of the land and premises aforesaid and has good right to sell and convey the same in manner and form aforesaid: that the same are free from all encumbrances, except installments of special assessments or assessments for special improvements which have not been certified to the County Treasurer for collection, and the above granted lands and premises in the possession of said Grantee, against all persons lawfully claiming or to claim the whole or any part thereof, the said Grantor will warrant and defend.

WITNESS, the hand of the Grantor.

→ 3.25" tab _____ underscores to the right margin _____
Maria J. Lopez

(Continued on next page)

STATE OF IOWA

County of Story

On this _____ day of October, 2006, before me, a notary public within and for said County and State, personally appeared Maria J. Lopez, to me known to be the person described in and who executed the within and foregoing instrument and acknowledged to me that she executed the same as her free act and deed.

_____

Boyd H. Fraser   6.5" right tab →   Notary Public
Story County, Iowa
My Commission Expires June 15, 2012

Table 97-52 ▶

Boxed Table

Your finished table will have different line endings for column B when you resize the column widths to fit the contents.

WARRANTY DEED TERMINOLOGY *State of Iowa*	
Term	*Definition*
Appurtenance	Something attached to the land
Consideration	The value of the property
Escrow	A system of document transfer in which the document is given to a third party to hold until the conditions of the agreement have been met
Grantee	The person who is buying the property
Grantor	The person who owns the property
Mortgage	The pledge of property as security for a loan
Tenement	Something that can be possessed, such as land or a building
Warranty deed	A deed in which the seller forever guarantees clear title to the land

Refer to — **Reference Manual**

Refer to pages R-5C and R-5D: E-Mail Message.

; no conjunction

; series

; no conjunction

Type the e-mail greeting, body, closing, and signature as indicated below in correct format:

1. Type Hi, David: as the greeting, type the body shown below, and type Yen as the closing.

2. Type this signature: Yen Nguyen | E-Mail: ynguyen@webmail.net | Phone: 712-555-3435

3. Save the e-mail message in GDP, but do not send it.

¶ You might recall last week that I indicated there might be some foreclosure property available and that it would be auctioned at the Story county Courthouse. On September 9, 3 properties in southern Story county will be auctioned as foreclosures. These properties are located adjacent to the lots you purchased last year. I know that you would be interested in expanding your lot size with this purchase. Specifically, they are located in Spring Township, Lot 23; Aiken Township, Lot 17; and Andrews Township, Lot 9.

¶ I expect these properties will sell for around $36,000 each; their excellent or $50,000 location may force the bidding into the $40,000 range. If you cannot be present for the auction but would like to place a bid on the properties, please let me know so that I can act on your behalf as your agent. If you elect want to do this, send me the bidding range you wish to present for each of the properties or for all 3 as one combined property. I need confirmation from you no later than September 7 so that I can register as your agent to present your bid.

Legal Office Documents

Goals

- Type at least 47wpm/5′/5e
- Format legal office documents

A. Type 2 times.

A. WARMUP

```
1        Janet bought dozens of disks (5 or 6) to store her      10
2   article, "The Internet Sanctions." She quickly sent it to    23
3   her editor, Max Pavlow, on the 18th or 19th of September.     34
    |  1  |  2  |  3  |  4  |  5  |  6  |  7  |  8  |  9  |  10  |  11  |  12
```

SKILLBUILDING

B. DIAGNOSTIC PRACTICE: SYMBOLS AND PUNCTUATION

If you are not using the GDP software, turn to page SB-2 and follow the directions for this activity.

C. Type the paragraph 2 times, concentrating on each letter typed.

C. TECHNIQUE PRACTICE: SHIFT/CAPS LOCK

```
4        Raymond and Karen must travel through TENNESSEE and
5   KENTUCKY on TUESDAY and WEDNESDAY. Raymond will speak in
6   NASHVILLE on the topic of COMPUTER AWARENESS; Karen will
7   speak in LOUISVILLE, and her talk is on INTERNET ACCESS.
```

Strategies for Career Success

Enhance Your Presentation With Visual Aids

Visual aids capture people's attention while increasing their retention. Use visual aids to present an outline of your presentation, explain detailed technical or numerical information, and summarize your key points.

Be selective. Don't bombard your audience with visuals. Your visual aids should support and clarify your verbal presentation. Consider the size of your audience and the size of the room before selecting your visuals. Audiences have little patience for visuals that are too small to read. Types of visual aids are overhead transparencies, slides, photographs, flip charts, maps, flowcharts, posters, handouts, and computer graphics including tables, graphs, and charts.

Limit the amount of information on a visual. Use simple graphics. Continue displaying the current visual until you are ready to discuss the next one. Always keep the projector or overhead on.

YOUR TURN In what ways would your visual aids differ if your audience had 10 people or 110?

D. Take two 5-minute
timed writings. Review
your speed and errors.

Goal: At least
47wpm/5'/5e

D. 5-MINUTE TIMED WRITING

8	From the time you start attending school, you begin to	11
9	develop new skills in making friends and getting along with	23
10	people. These skills are used throughout your life journey.	35
11	If you want to be successful in any business or career, you	47
12	can't be a loner. You must learn skills for working with	59
13	people from all cultures.	64
14	In a corporation, people use their unique skills to	74
15	work as a team in order to accomplish their goals. Like a	86
16	finely tuned orchestra or a football team, all members must	98
17	work together to achieve a desired objective. If a person	110
18	does not work efficiently within the group, then other team	122
19	members may have to work harder to compensate so that the	133
20	effort of the team will not fall short.	141
21	Working with others allows you the chance to learn	152
22	from other people. You may also learn some things about	163
23	yourself. To get along with your coworkers, you may have to	175
24	overlook the personal faults of others. Everyone has some	186
25	faults, and your faults may be just as disconcerting to	198
26	other people as their faults are to you. Your ability to	209
27	work with people will also enhance your quest for career	220
28	advancement. You can expect amazing results when you work	232
29	with your team.	235

| 1 | 2 | 3 | 4 | 5 | 6 | 7 | 8 | 9 | 10 | 11 | 12

Report 98-69 ▶

Summons

Add line numbers for all lines in this court document. When this document is actually typed, the line numbers will vary from those shown here.

Type the title on the same line as *vs.*

A summons is a document that notifies a defendant that a lawsuit has been filed and an appearance must be made before the court, at a specified time, to answer the charges.

1 STATE OF KANSAS   ⟶ 6.5" right tab   IN DISTRICT COURT
2   ↓2X

3 COUNTY OF DOUGLAS   NORTHEAST JUDICIAL DISTRICT
4   ↓2X

5 PEOPLE'S BANK   ⟶ 3.25" tab)   6.5" right tab   NO. _____ 20 underscores _____
6 607 New Hampshire Street   )
7 Lawrence, KS 66044-2243   )
8   ⟶ 3.25" tab)
9 ⟶ 1" tab   Plaintiff,   ⟶ 3.25" tab)
10   )
11 ⟶ 1" tab   vs.   ⟶ 3.25" tab)   ⟶ 6.5" right tab   SUMMONS
12   )
13 JOHN COUZINS   )
14   )
15   Defendant.   )
16   ↓2X

17 THE STATE OF KANSAS TO THE ABOVE-NAMED DEFENDANT:
18   ↓2X

19 ⟶ 1" tab   You are hereby summoned and required to appear and defend
20 against the Complaint in this action, which is hereby served upon you by
21 serving upon the undersigned an Answer or other proper response within
22 twenty (20) days after the service of the Summons and Complaint upon
23 you, exclusive of the day of service.   ↓2X
24

25   If you fail to do so, judgment by default will be taken against you
26 for the relief demanded in the Complaint.
27

28   SIGNED this _____ day of December 20--.
29   5 underscores
30   ⟶ 3.25" tab _____ underscores to the right margin _____
31   Ann Barfield   6.5" right tab⟶   Attorney-at-Law
32   806 Kentucky Street
33   Lawrence, KS 66044-2648
34   Telephone: (785) 555-8226
35   Attorney for Plaintiff
36

MEMO TO: Raymond Ruiz

FROM: Charlotte Libretto

DATE: December 28, 20--

SUBJECT: Client listing

¶ As you requested, I am ~~now~~ enclosing an up-to-date new client list for our Atlanta area clients. This list is cur**r**ent as of ~~last~~ *this* week, and it includes clients in the counties of Carroll, Cobb, Douglas, Fulton, and paulding. Please note that the *total* billing hours are *also* shown in this list.

¶ Douglas and ~~Cobb~~ *Fulton* counties represent the greatest number of clients over all, although this list doesn't # *not* reveal the total number of clients per county. Just in the past quarter, these two counties represented nearly ~~eighty~~ *80* (%) of our client base. Cobb County clients do not represent a sizable percentage of our client base, but the opening of ~~three~~ *two* new law offices in that county will most certainly generate considerable *new* business in the coming months.

¶ We will send you an updated list biweekly. The ~~next~~ list will most certainly show substantial gains in Cobb County, and we expect business in Douglas and Fulton counties to continue growing because of the *tremendous* growth in the area West of Atlanta. If you have any questions about any of our new clients, please call our main office at 770-555-1843.

urs | Enclosure | c: Blair Kiplan

Table▸
98-53

Boxed Table

⚠ Press ENTER to create the 2-line column heading as displayed before automatically adjusting column widths.

CLIENT LIST
December 28, 20--

Name	Address	County	Billing Hours
Jose Azteca	128 Holly St.	Douglas	25
Carroll Bryan	323 Newnan St.	Carroll	28
Margie Coulon	301 Bradley St.	Paulding	15
Thomas Henry	2900 Shady Grove	Cobb	22
Debra Johnson	215 Griffin Dr.	Cobb	34
Maria Mateo	156 Cypress Circle	Fulton	10
Luther Nicholson	6703 Burns Rd.	Paulding	12
Pearl Nix	106 Alice Lane	Douglas	18
James Presley	622 North Ave.	Carroll	23
Janie Ramey	1202 Park St.	Fulton	32
Heather Sanders	248 Lakeshore Dr.	Cobb	12
Thomas Tarpley	2950 Chapel Hill Rd.	Douglas	29
Vickie Thomas	4821 Hope Rd.	Carroll	9
Kim Wong	111 Pierce St.	Fulton	18
Ray Young	108 Waverly Way	Douglas	30
Tong Zhen	286 Laurel Terrace	Paulding	35

Keyboarding Connection

Coping With Spam

Have you received heaps of unsolicited e-mail, commonly known as spam? Everyone wants to get rid of those irritating online sales pitches. Contrary to popular advice, however, there is not much you can do about them. You can make use of various filters, but they aren't foolproof.

If you end up on a spammer's list and receive a courteous e-mail asking you to reply if you wish to be removed from the list, *do not reply*. The spammer may interpret your reply to mean that you read e-mail, and you may be put on the hot list. The best action is to try to avoid divulging your e-mail address to spammers. Most important, use an alternate account if posting to any kind of online forum.

YOUR TURN How do you deal with postal "junk mail" that you receive? Are there similarities in dealing with spam?

Legal Office Documents

Goals

- Improve speed and accuracy
- Refine language arts skills in spelling
- Format legal office documents

A. Type 2 times.

A. WARMUP

```
1     Zeke sharpened his ax so that he could quite easily      11
2   saw through 15 very large pine trees. Each load will sell   23
3   for $175 (to Blake & James Inc.) at next Friday's auction.  35
    | 1 | 2 | 3 | 4 | 5 | 6 | 7 | 8 | 9 | 10 | 11 | 12
```

SKILLBUILDING

B. MAP

Follow the GDP software directions for this exercise in improving keystroking accuracy.

C. Take a 1-minute timed writing on the first paragraph to establish your base speed. Then take four 1-minute timed writings on the remaining paragraphs. As soon as you equal or exceed your base speed on one paragraph, advance to the next, more difficult paragraph.

C. SUSTAINED PRACTICE: ROUGH DRAFT

```
4      The pattern of employment in our country is undergoing   11
5   some major changes. Companies are slowly decreasing their    23
6   permanent staff to just a core group of managers and other   35
7   high-powered people and are using temporaries for the rest.  47

8      This trend is creating an acordion aftermath in many      11
9   firms: the ability to expand and contract as the time or     23
                                                    and
10  the balance sheets dictate. Have this range of flexibility   35
                               Having
11  would be a key ingredient in the competative fight to come.  47
    will                                        i

12     All of these changes would make it tough for all unions   11
                            will                    the
13  to stay a float. They do not have a satisfactory method of   23
                                                  o
14  organizing such employes. Unions can try to change in to     35
                          e        could
15  social agenceis, providing aid to members outside of work.   47
             fl

16     Such services as elder or child care, counseling, debt    11
17  managment, and even health care maybe of great asistance     23
        e                              #            s
18  as employers find it more and more dificult to offer these   35
                                        f
19  benfits. unions may find their niche by filling this gap.    47
       e
    | 1 | 2 | 3 | 4 | 5 | 6 | 7 | 8 | 9 | 10 | 11 | 12
```

D. Type this list of frequently misspelled words, paying special attention to any spelling problems in each word.

D. SPELLING

20 distribution executive extension requested specific carried
21 recommended alternative programs access budget issued seize
22 objectives indicated calendar family could these until your
23 administrative accommodate possibility students fiscal past
24 transportation employee's categories summary offered estate

Edit the sentences to correct any misspellings.

25 The execitive requested an extention on spicific programs.
26 I have recomended alternitive programs for early next week.
27 These objectives were indacated for the new calender year.
28 These passed administrative goals will accomodate the team.
29 These categories could be included in the employee summery.

DOCUMENT PROCESSING

Report 99-70

Last Will and Testament

Insert a centered page number at the bottom of each page.

A last will and testament is a legal document stating how a person wants his or her property distributed after death.

LAST WILL AND TESTAMENT
OF
IRMA J. GOMEZ ↓2X

⟶ 1" tab I, IRMA J. GOMEZ, residing in Corvallis, Oregon, do hereby make and declare this to be my Last Will and Testament, hereby revoking any and all former Wills and Codicils by me at any time heretofore made. ↓2X

ARTICLE I ↓2X

This will is made in Oregon and shall be governed, construed, and administered according to Oregon law, even though subject to probate or administered elsewhere. The Oregon laws applied shall not include any principles or laws relating to conflicts or choice of laws.

ARTICLE II

Whenever used herein, words importing the singular shall include the plural and words importing the masculine shall include the feminine and neuter, and vice versa, unless the context otherwise requires.

(Continued on next page)

ARTICLE III

I am married and my husband's name is Ricardo E. Gomez. All references hereinafter made to "husband" or "spouse" shall refer to him and no other; and if he is not my legal husband at the time of my death, then he shall be deemed for the purpose of this, my last Will and Testament, to have predeceased me. I was formerly married to Henry Woo, who is now deceased. There were three (3) children born of my marriage to Henry Woo. The names of those children are as follows: Judy Parsons, Henry Wayne, and Randy Woo.

ARTICLE IV

If My Spouse Survives. Except as may otherwise be provided hereunder in this Article IV, if my spouse survives me, I devise to my spouse all my interest in household furniture and furnishings, books, apparel, art objects, collections, jewelry, and similar personal effects; sporting and recreational equipment; all other tangible property for personal use; all other like contents of my home and any vacation property that I may own or reside in on the date of my death; all animals; any motor vehicles that I may own on the date of my death; and any unexpired insurance on all such property.

ARTICLE V

If My Spouse Does Not Survive. Except as may be otherwise provided in this Article IV, if my spouse does not survive me, I devise the property described above in this Article (except motor vehicles) to my children who survive me, to be divided among them as they shall agree, or in the absence of such agreement, as my Personal Representative shall determine, which determination shall be conclusive.

ARTICLE VI

If any beneficiary named or described in this Will fails to survive me for 120 hours, all the provisions in this Will for the benefit of such deceased beneficiary shall lapse, and this Will shall be construed as though the fact were that he or she predeceased me.

ARTICLE VII

All estate, inheritance, transfer, succession, and any other taxes plus interest and penalties thereon (death taxes) that become payable by reason of my death upon property passing under this instrument shall be paid out of the residue of my estate without reimbursement from the recipient and without apportionment. All death taxes upon property not passing under this instrument shall be apportioned in the manner provided by law.

↓2X

(Continued on next page)

IN WITNESS WHEREOF, I have hereunto affixed my hand and seal this _____ day of ___20-character underscore___, 20--. ↓2X

↖ 5-character underscore

⟶ 3.25" tab ___underscores to the right margin___

IRMA J. GOMEZ → 6.5" right tab Testator
↓2X

The foregoing instrument, consisting of TWO (2) pages (this page included), was on this _____ day of _____, 20--, subscribed on each page and at the end thereof by Irma J. Gomez, the above-named Testator and by her signed, sealed, published and declared to be her Last Will, in the presence of us, and each of us, who thereupon, at her request, in her presence, and in the presence of each other, have hereunto subscribed our names as attesting witnesses thereto. ↓2X

Center the last 2 lines.

___34-character underscore___ residing at _____

_____ residing at _____

Correspondence 99-97

Business Letter in Block Style

Reference Manual

Refer to page R-12C of the Reference Manual for an overview of formatting lists.

July 1, 20-- | Mrs. Irma J. Gomez | 768 Southwest Adams Avenue | Corvallis, OR 97333-4523 | Dear Mrs. Gomez: | Subject: Will Provisions ¶ Your last will and testament has been drafted and is enclosed for your review. Please review it carefully for any specific omissions or deletions. ¶ Although your will has been drafted as you indicated, there are still a couple of alternative inclusions that I would recommend.

• Do you wish to include a fiduciary powers summary in the will?

• What division of estate do you wish to include for your family?

¶ These inclusions could be rather comprehensive. Therefore, could we schedule a meeting for next Tuesday to accommodate these changes? Please call my administrative assistant so she can put you on my calendar. Sincerely, | Andrea L. Grainger | Attorney-at-Law | urs | Enclosure | c: T. Carter, S. Rohrer, A. Winchester

Legal Office Documents

Goals

- Type at least 47wpm/5′/5e
- Format legal office documents

A. Type 2 times.

A. WARMUP

1   Val Lopez and Jack Drew quickly bought six tickets for   11
2 Sam's $24,600 collector's auto (a 1957 Chevrolet). Over the   23
3 past month, its value increased by 1.5%. That is fantastic!   35
  | 1 | 2 | 3 | 4 | 5 | 6 | 7 | 8 | 9 | 10 | 11 | 12

SKILLBUILDING

PPP   PRETEST → PRACTICE → POSTTEST

PRETEST
Take a 1-minute timed writing. Review your speed and errors.

B. PRETEST: Horizontal Reaches

4   Bart enjoyed his royal blue race car. He bragged about   11
5 how he learned to push for those speed spurts that helped   23
6 him win those races. The car had a lot of get-up-and-go.   34
  | 1 | 2 | 3 | 4 | 5 | 6 | 7 | 8 | 9 | 10 | 11 | 12

PRACTICE
Speed Emphasis:
If you made no more than 1 error on the Pretest, type each *individual* line 2 times.
Accuracy Emphasis:
If you made 2 or more errors, type each *group* of lines (as though it were a paragraph) 2 times.

C. PRACTICE: In Reaches

7 oy toy ahoy ploy loyal coyly royal enjoy decoy annoy deploy
8 ar fare arch mart march farms scars spear barns learn radar
9 pu pull push puts pulse spurt purge spuds pushy spurs pupil

D. PRACTICE: Out Reaches

10 ge gear gets ages getup raged geese lunge pages cagey forge
11 da dare date data dance adage dazed sedan daubs cedar daily
12 hi high hick hill hinge chief hires ethic hiked chili hitch

POSTTEST
Repeat the Pretest timed writing and compare performance.

E. POSTTEST: Horizontal Reaches

F. Take two 5-minute timed writings. Review your speed and errors.

Goal: At least 47 wpm/5'/5e

F.   5-MINUTE TIMED WRITINGS

```
13        Company loyalty may be a thing of the past. A worker    11
14   who stayed and worked in one place for thirty or more years   23
15   is rare these days. People are moving to different jobs at    35
16   a faster pace than in the past. Changing jobs many times      46
17   over a career no longer carries the stigma of the past.       57
18   People are looking for new challenges.                        65
19        Those who change jobs are able to market their skills    76
20   and to get salary increases. Hopping from job to job can      87
21   pay amazing returns for some careers. Businesses are quite    99
22   willing to offer higher pay and more perks to attract the    111
23   best and most skilled people. People who change jobs a lot   123
24   have the experience and knowledge that other companies are   134
25   willing to retain.                                           138
26        The opportunity to change jobs is there not only for    149
27   younger workers but also for older workers who are well      160
28   into their careers. For example, computer technology has     172
29   been experiencing a boom. The Internet industry has a big    183
30   demand for computer programmers. People with knowledge in    195
31   this field can request higher salaries. A company may even   207
32   offer additional benefits in order to attract experienced    208
33   workers with great credentials. It is really up to each      229
34   person to decide what to do.                                 235
   |  1  |  2  |  3  |  4  |  5  |  6  |  7  |  8  |  9  |  10 |  11 |  12
```

Strategies for Career Success

Letter of Resignation

When you plan to leave a job, you should write a resignation letter, memo, or e-mail to your supervisor and send a copy to Human Resources. Follow these guidelines to write an effective resignation.

Start a resignation letter positively, regardless of why you are leaving. Include how you benefited from working for the company, or compliment your coworkers.

In the middle section, state why you are leaving. Provide an objective, factual explanation and avoid accusations. Your resignation becomes part of your permanent company record. If it is hostile, it could backfire on you when you need references. Stipulate the date your resignation becomes effective (provide at least a two-week notice).

End the letter of resignation with a closing of goodwill (for example, "I wish all of you the best in the future.").

YOUR TURN   List the benefits of *not* "burning your bridges" (showing anger or bitterness) in your letter of resignation.

Report 100-71 ▶

Complaint

A complaint uses the same format as a summons, as shown in Report 98-69.

Add line numbers for all lines in this court document, and restart line numbers on each page. When this document is typed, the line numbers will vary from those shown here.

Type the title on the same line as *vs.*

Press ENTER 2 times before each Roman numeral.

All Roman numerals are centered between the margins.

A complaint is the initial document filed with a court by a plaintiff to begin an adversarial or action at law proceeding. A judgment is the decision of the court.

```
1  STATE OF NORTH DAKOTA                        IN DISTRICT COURT
2
3  COUNTY OF WALSH                       NORTHEAST JUDICIAL DISTRICT
4
5  WALSH COUNTY BANK            )           NO. _____
6  170 Main Street             )
7  Adams, ND 58210             )
8                              )
9        Plaintiff,            )
10                             )
11       vs.                   )              COMPLAINT
12                             )
13 KENNEDY FARMERS, INC.       )
14 JAMES D. KENNEDY and        )
15 CAROL KENNEDY,              )
16                             )
17       Defendants.           )
18
19 PLAINTIFF FOR ITS CAUSE OF ACTION AND COMPLAINT
20 AGAINST THE DEFENDANTS, COMPLAINS, ALLEGES AND SHOWS
21 TO THE COURT:
22
23                              I.
24       That defendants owe plaintiff $5,685.00, plus interest and charges,
25 under the terms of a promissory note executed April 10, 20--, a copy of
26 which is attached hereto and incorporated by reference as "Exhibit A."
27
28                             II.
29       That defendants have not, upon due demand, satisfied their
30 obligation under the terms of the promissory note.
31
32                             III.
33       That Kennedy Farmers, Inc., is a North Dakota for-profit
34 corporation duly organized under the corporate laws of the State of North
35 Dakota.
36
37                             IV.
38       That the registered agent of Kennedy Farmers, Inc., is James D.
39 Kennedy.
```

(Continued on next page)

1   V.

2   That James D. Kennedy executed a Commercial Guaranty for the

3 note dated April 10, 20--, a copy of which is attached hereto and

4 incorporated herein as "Exhibit B."

5

6   VI.

7   That Carol Kennedy executed a Commercial Guaranty on the

8 prior promissory note No. 7249, and the Commercial Guaranty provides

9 that the guaranty extends to ". . . all renewals of, extensions of,

10 modifications of, refinancings of, consolidations of, and substitutions for

11 the promissory note or agreement." A copy of that Commercial Guaranty is

12 attached hereto and incorporated hereby by reference as "Exhibit D."

13

14   VII.

15   That the indebtedness was the renewal of a prior promissory note

16 executed by Kennedy Farmers, Inc., to Walsh County Bank on June 17, 20--,

17 which was in the original principal amount of $6,685.00, a copy of which is

18 attached hereto and incorporated by reference as "Exhibit C."

19

20   VIII.

21   That James D. Kennedy and Carol Kennedy are personally liable

22 for the amount of the debt, as is the corporation, Kennedy Farmers, Inc.

23

24   WHEREFORE, PLAINTIFF DEMANDS JUDGMENT AGAINST

25 THE DEFENDANTS, AND EACH OF THEM, AS FOLLOWS:

26

27   1. For the amount of $3,585.00, plus interest on that amount from

28   and after April 10, 20--, at the rate of 10.75% per annum; and

29   for its costs, late charges, and disbursements in this action;

30

31   2. For such other and further relief as the Court may deem

32   appropriate.

33

34   SIGNED this _____ day of December, 20--.

35

36   _____

37   Harold E. Jensen   Attorney-at-Law

38   405 1st Street

39   Adams, ND 58210

40   Telephone: (701) 555-4832

41   Attorney for Plaintiff

Reference Manual

Refer to page R-12C of the Reference Manual for an overview of formatting lists.

Judgment

A judgment uses the same format as a summons, as shown in Report 98-69.

Add line numbers in this court document.

1 STATE OF ARIZONA   IN DISTRICT COURT
2
3 COUNTY OF MARICOPA   CENTRAL JUDICIAL DISTRICT
4
5 Timothy Barnes d/b/a Barnes Computers)   CIVIL NO. 43-89-D-00145
6 1651 West Baseline Road   )
7 Tempe, AZ 85283   )
8   )
9   Plaintiff,   )
10   )
11   vs.   )   JUDGMENT
12   )
13 Maricopa Hospital Association   )
14 d/b/a Maricopa Nursing Care   )
15   )
16   Defendant.   )
17
18 ¶ The defendant, Maricopa Hospital Association,
19 d/b/a Maricopa Nursing Care, having been
20 regularly served with process, and having failed
21 to appear and answer the plaintiff's Complaint filed
22 herein, and the default of said defendant having
23 been duly entered, and it appearing that said
24 defendant is not an infant or an incompetent
25 person, and an affidavit of nonmilitary service
26 having been filed herein, and it appearing by the
27 affidavits of plaintiff that plaintiff is entitled to
28 judgment herein,
29 ¶ IT IS THEREFORE ORDERED AND ADJUDGED, that
30 the plaintiff have and recover from the
31 defendant, Maricopa Hospital Association d/b/a
32 Maricopa Nursing Care, the sum of $8,000.00
33 plus interest thereon from and after August 10,
34 20--, until paid, together with costs in the sum
35 of $252.75.
36 ¶ SIGNED this _____ day of _____, 20 -- .
37
                                    _____
                                    Clerk of the District Court

Use the same format as in the affidavit shown in Report 96-67.

Add line numbers for all lines in this court document.

Progress and Proofreading Check ✓

Documents designated as Proofreading Checks serve as a check of your proofreading skill. Your goal is to have zero typographical errors when the GDP software first scores the document.

AFFIDAVIT OF POSSESSION

1
2
3 STATE OF OREGON
4
5 COUNTY OF LINN
6
7   I, MARILYN T. HUGGINS, being first duly sworn, depose and say:
8
9   That I am the petitioner in the above-entitled suit.
10
11   That the respondent, RICHARD M. HUGGINS, and I are the
12 parents of BENJAMIN T. HUGGINS. That BENJAMIN T. HUGGINS is
13 currently residing exclusively with me. Respondent is currently residing
14 away from the home at 1529 South Oak Street, Albany, Oregon. That I am a
15 fit and proper person to have immediate and temporary custody of
16 BENJAMIN T. HUGGINS.
17
18   I believe that these pending dissolution proceedings will aggravate
19 this situation; therefore, I believe that it is necessary and appropriate for
20 the Court to issue an Order restraining and enjoining respondent from
21 physically or verbally abusing or harassing me or our child in any way.
22
23   _____
24
25   Subscribed and sworn to before me this _____ day of
26 _____, 20--.
27
28   _____
29   Notary Public for Oregon
30   My commission expires January 7, 2012

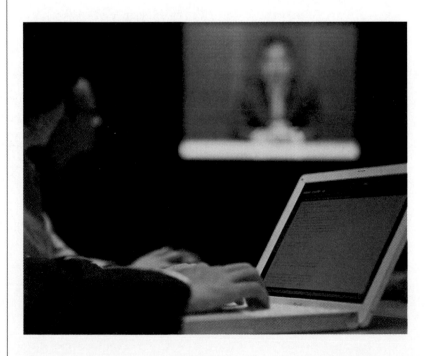

Skills Assessment on Part 5

1	When you submit your resume to apply for a job, you	11
2	want your resume to be noticed. Here are some things you	22
3	might do to make certain your resume receives the time and	34
4	focus it deserves.	38
5	First, be neat. Review each page to make sure that it	49
6	is free of typos and spelling errors. Check each page for	60
7	correct grammar. Remember that this document will make the	72
8	first impression with a potential employer. You want the	83
9	document to represent you in the best way. Use white paper	95
10	of good quality to print your resume.	103
11	Second, try to be creative. Make your resume unique. A	114
12	future employer may be looking for specific things when he	126
13	or she scans the pages of your resume. Be sure to provide	137
14	facts that explain exactly what skills you have acquired in	149
15	positions you have held in the past. Avoid using the same	161
16	buzzwords that everyone else uses.	168
17	Finally, state a career objective on your resume. Some	179
18	experts suggest that by stating a career objective, you are	191
19	showing a career path. Others think that stating a career	203
20	objective may limit many job possibilities. If you state a	215
21	career objective, make sure the objective is in line with	226
22	the specific job for which you are applying.	235

| 1 | 2 | 3 | 4 | 5 | 6 | 7 | 8 | 9 | 10 | 11 | 12

13 July 20-- | Mr. Antoine Lauvergeon | Marketing Director | Alatel Inc. |
54, Rue la Boetie | 75382 Paris | France | Dear Mr. Lauvergeon:

¶ As we predicted, our jefe effort marketing was a tremendous success in the 5 new plants opened last Spring in France and Germany. In fact, sales at those two plants have surpassed our Switzerland and Italy sales over the same period. Much of this sucess is due to your timely marketing campaign that was conducted during the first quarter. Congratulations to you and your staff on this fine effort.

Because of this positive experience, we have decided to expand our promotional campaign at our plants in Negras Piedras, Morelia, and Puebla. Would you please put together a proposal for these plants and send it to me by the end of next week. We are excited about this opportunity and look forward to recieving your proposal.

¶ Again, nice work on the France and Germany effort.

Sincerely, | Harold Deforey | V.P. Marketing | c: Mari Lynn Somnolet, James Lafforgue | urs

Manually adjust the column widths similar to those in the illustration at the right.

HEMATOLOGY REPORT			
Patient Name:		**Date:**	
	WBC		Glucose
	Hemoglobin		Cholesterol
	PMN		BUN
	Bands		Calcium
	Lymphs		Phosphorous
	Mono		Bilirubin
	Eos		Uric acid
	Baso		Alkaline phosphate
	Platelets		Albumin
	Thyroid		Protein, total

When this document is typed, the line numbers will vary from those shown here.

1 STATE OF NEBRASKA   IN DISTRICT COURT
2
3 COUNTY OF WAYNE   NORTHEAST JUDICIAL DISTRICT
4
5 PAUL C. CREWS   )   NO. _____
6 601 Thorman Street   )
7 Wayne, NE 66787-2243   )
8   )
9   Plaintiff,   )
10   )
11   vs.   )   SUMMONS
12   )
13 ANGELINA WASHINGTON   )
14   )
15   Defendant.   )
16
17 THE STATE OF NEBRASKA TO THE ABOVE-NAMED DEFENDANTS:
18
19   You are hereby summoned and required to appear and defend
20 against the Complaint in this action, which is hereby served upon you by
21 serving upon the undersigned an Answer or other proper response within
22 twenty (20) days after the service of the Summons and Complaint upon
23 you, exclusive of the day of service.
24
25   If you fail to do so, judgment by default will be taken against you
26 for the relief demanded in the Complaint.
27
28   SIGNED this _____ day of May, 20--.
29
30   _____
31   Jeremy Richfield   Attorney-at-Law
32   Box 148
33   Wayne, NE 67878-2648
34   Telephone: (402) 555-1205
35   Attorney for Plaintiff

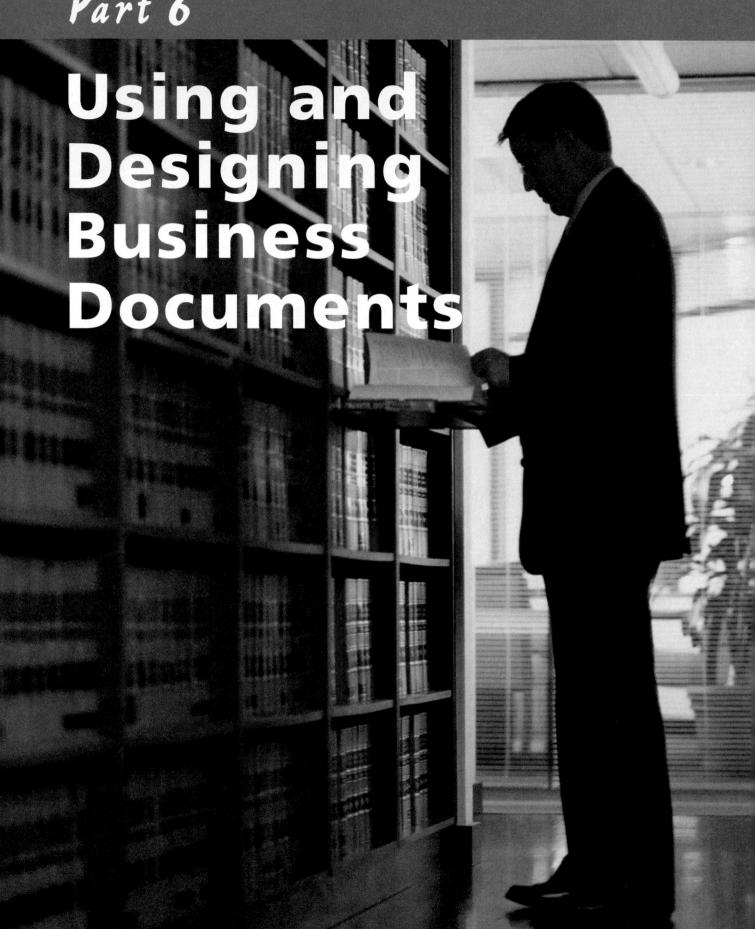

Part 6

Using and Designing Business Documents

Keyboarding in Legal Services Careers

A career in legal services can take many forms. Lawyers, of course, are responsible for legal work, but a number of other positions in the legal services field are available. Often, lawyers assign tasks to paralegals. Paralegals—also referred to as legal assistants—have taken on a larger percentage of responsibilities in recent years. Another profession in the law field, that of court reporter, requires excellent communication skills. Court reporters are responsible for taking exact notes in court, in meetings, and at any other event where an accurate account of the proceedings is needed. Keyboarding skills are important for many job functions in legal services careers, and they can prove to give a job candidate an advantage.

Paralegals can work in many different business settings, but they are found most commonly in law firms and government offices. Court reporters are responsible for providing an accurate and detailed legal record of any proceeding. For individuals working in the legal services field, strong communication skills, written and spoken, are very important, but being able to convey ideas in a typed report in a timely manner is even more important.

Objectives

KEYBOARDING

- Type at least 50 words per minute on a 5-minute timed writing with no more than 5 errors.

LANGUAGE ARTS

- Refine proofreading skills and correctly use proofreaders' marks.
- Use capitals, punctuation, and grammar correctly.
- Improve composing and spelling skills.
- Recognize subject/verb agreement.

WORD PROCESSING

- Use the word processing commands necessary to complete the document processing activities.

DOCUMENT PROCESSING

- Design office forms, office publications, and Web pages.

TECHNICAL

- Answer at least 90 percent of the questions correctly on an objective test.

Unit 21

Using and Designing Office Forms

LESSON 101
Using Correspondence Templates

LESSON 102
Using Report Templates

LESSON 103
Designing Letterheads

LESSON 104
Designing Notepads

LESSON 105
Designing Miscellaneous Office Forms

 From the Desk of Amber Bristol

 From the Desk of Amber Bristol

☐ Urgent
☐ Do Today
☐ Follow-Up

☐ Urgent
☐ Do Today
☐ Follow-Up

 From the Desk of Amber Bristol

 From the Desk of Amber Bristol

☐ Urgent
☐ Do Today
☐ Follow-Up

☐ Urgent
☐ Do Today
☐ Follow-Up

Memorandum

To:	Naoe Okubo, Senior Graphics Artist
CC:	Roy Phillips, Marketing Manager
From:	Gloria Hernandez, Vice President
Date:	June 17, 20--
Re:	Web Site Redesign

Our Web site needs a complete reorganization and redesign. I know this assignment will be a major challenge, and I have full confidence in your experience and ability. Within the next week, please contact five Web design firms and make arrangements for a formal presentation to you and your staff. Invite Roy Phillips and his staff in marketing as well. When you have chosen the two best candidates, submit your findings to our key executives in a formal presentation. The better of the two will then be chosen.

Because our Web site is critical to our sales and marketing efforts, you must make this assignment a top priority. If you need temporary help to support you in your efforts, let me know.

Thank you for your continued good work, Naoe. I look forward to the presentation and your recommendations.

sz

1

Winter Sports

2820 Cerillos Road ♦ Santa Fe, NM 87505 ♦ 505-555-3496
www.wintersports.com

Using Correspondence Templates

Goals

- Improve speed and accuracy
- Refine language arts skills in grammar
- Format correspondence using a template

A. Type 2 times.

A. WARMUP

```
1        The secretary made a reservation on Flight #847; it      11
2     departs at exactly 3:05 on July 6. A sizable number of      22
3     key executives (about 1/2) requested seats in Rows G to M.   33
   |  1  |  2  |  3  |  4  |  5  |  6  |  7  |  8  |  9  |  10  |  11  |  12
```

SKILLBUILDING

B. Take three 12-second timed writings on each line. The scale below the last line shows your wpm speed for a 12-second timed writing.

B. 12-SECOND SPEED SPRINTS

```
4   Bob will lend all the keys to you if you will fix the leak.
5   Ruth wanted to thank you for all of the work you did today.
6   Both of the books will have to be sent to her by next week.
7   Dick paid her half of the money when she signed the papers.
    I I I I 5 I I I 10 I I I I 15 I I I I 20 I I I 25 I I I 30 I I I 35 I I I 40 I I I 45 I I I 50 I I I 55 I I I 60
```

C. PROGRESSIVE PRACTICE: ALPHABET

If you are not using the GDP software, turn to page SB-7 and follow the directions for this activity.

D. PROGRESSIVE PRACTICE: NUMBERS

If you are not using the GDP software, turn to page SB-11 and follow the directions for this activity.

LANGUAGE ARTS

E. Study the rules at the right.

E. ADJECTIVES AND ADVERBS AND AGREEMENT

RULE ▶
adjective/adverb

Use comparative adjectives and adverbs (-er, more, and less) when referring to two nouns or pronouns; use superlative adjectives and adverbs (-est, most, and least) when referring to more than two.

The shorter of the two training sessions is the more helpful one.

The longest of the three training sessions is the least helpful one.

RULE ▶

agreement nearer noun

If two subjects are joined by *or, either/or, neither/nor,* or *not only/but also,* make the verb agree with the subject nearer to the verb.

Neither the coach nor the <u>players</u> <u>are</u> at home.

Not only the coach but also the <u>referee</u> <u>is</u> at home.

But: <u>Both</u> the coach and the referee <u>are</u> at home.

Edit the sentences to correct any errors in grammar.

8 Of the three printers, the faster one was the most expensive.
9 Of the two phones purchased, the first one is the better model.
10 The quietest of the five printers is also the less expensive.
11 Not only the manager but also the employees wants to attend.
12 Neither the printer nor the monitors is in working order.
13 Either Mr. Cortez or his assistants have to sign the order.
14 Coffee or soft drinks is available for the afternoon session.
15 Not only the manual but also the software were mailed.

FORMATTING

F.   FILLING IN FORMS

Many business forms can be created by using templates that are provided within word processing software. When a template is opened, a generic form is displayed on the screen. Specific information that is appropriate for that form may then be added.

Template forms contain data fields that correspond to blank sections on printed forms. For example, a memo template may include the guide words *To:, CC:, From:, Date:,* and *Re:* for the subject. Templates are usually designed so that you can replace data in fields easily by clicking in the field and typing or by selecting the information you want to replace and typing. Built-in styles are also readily available.

You can customize a generic template by filling in repetitive information (such as the company name and telephone number) and save it as a new template. Then each time you open that newly created template, the customized information appears automatically.

Word Processing Manual

G.   WORD PROCESSING: CORRESPONDENCE TEMPLATES

Study Lesson 101 in your word processing manual. Complete all of the shaded steps while at your computer. Then format the jobs that follow.

DOCUMENT PROCESSING

Form ▶
101-1

Memo Template

Note: You may want to print the information in the template before deleting it.

1. Type this memo using the preselected blank memo template that has opened automatically.
2. Review the steps in Lesson 101 in your word processing manual to use this template.

3. Use the month/day/year format for the date.
4. Type the information for the memo from the copy shown on the next page.

To: Naoe Okubo, Senior Graphics Artist

CC: ~~Mr.~~ Roy Phillips, Marketing Manager

From: Gloria Hernandez, Vice President

Date: June 17, 20--

Re: Website Redesign

¶ Our web site needs a complete (redesign and reorganization). I know this assignment ~~is~~ *will be* a major challenge, and I have full confidence in your ~~skill~~ *experience* and ability. Within the next week, ~~you should~~ *please* contact 5 web design firms and make arrangements for a formal presentation to you and your staff. ~~Please~~ invite Roy Phillips and his staff in Marketing as well. When you have chosen the two best candidates, submit your findings to *our* key executives in a *formal* presentation. The better of the two will then be chosen.

¶ Because our web site is ~~crucial~~ *critical* to our sales and marketing efforts, you must make this assignment a top priority. If you need temporary help to support you in your efforts, let me know. Thank you for your continued good work, Naoe. I look forward to ~~your~~ *the* presentation and your recommendations.

urs

Form 101-2 ▶

Letter Template

adjective/adverb

adjective/adverb

1. Type this letter using the preselected blank letter template that has opened automatically.
2. Review the steps in Lesson 101 in your word processing manual to use this template.
3. The company name is Global Web Resources.
4. Type each line of the return address on a separate line. (The setup of the return address should be similar to the arrangement you use for the inside address.)

The return address is as follows:
   575 Eighth Avenue, Suite 1104
   New York, NY 10018
   212-555-3495
   www.globalwebresources.com

5. Use the default spacing provided by the template between the date and the inside address.
6. Type the rest of the information into the template, as indicated in the copy below, using standard business letter format for a block-style letter.

agreement nearer noun

June 23, 20-- | Naoe Okubo | Contempo Fashions | 22802 Soledad Canyon | Santa Clarita, CA 91355 | Dear Ms. Okubo:

¶ Thank you for your request for more information on Web page design, layout, and graphics. I have enclosed some brochures that address some of your questions.

¶ Ms. Ina Phillips is our senior account manager in your area. Either her staff members or Ms. Phillips is going to schedule an appointment with you and your staff for a formal presentation of our design portfolios this week. The best way to answer your questions and to help you reach a decision is to

(Continued on next page)

have you see examples of some of the Web sites we have developed for other clients in the fashion industry. I know you will be impressed by the creativity and innovative concepts that Global Web Resources is known for in this business.

¶If you would like a preview now, please go to www.globalwebresources.com and click the link entitled Professional Images to see some of our best designs. Again, thank you for your interest in our services.

Sincerely, | Linda Vigil | Vice President | urs | Enclosures

adjective/adverb

 If necessary, press SHIFT + ENTER 2 times after typing "Vice President" to position your reference initials correctly at the left margin.

Form 101-3 ▶

Memo Template

agreement nearer noun

 1. Type this memo using the preselected blank memo template that has opened automatically.
2. Review the steps in Lesson 101 in your word processing manual to use this template.

To: Roy Phillips, Marketing Manager | **CC:** Gloria Hernandez, Vice President | **From:** Naoe Okubo, Senior Graphics Artist | **Date:** August 7, 20-- | **Re:** Web Site Redesign

¶I have contacted five Web design firms for formal presentations in our executive boardroom. A schedule of the meeting dates and times is attached. Because Ms. Hernandez has indicated that this assignment is to take top priority, not only current projects but also future work is to be put on hold. If you need any temporary help with any projects in progress, let me know.

¶The Web design firms that have been scheduled are very innovative and creative. The presentations should be exciting. Ask your staff to prepare for the meeting by visiting the Web sites and doing some research on each company. Please forward this memo to the members of your staff.

urs | Attachment

Keyboarding Connection

Transferring Text From a Web Page

Have you ever wished you could copy the text from a Web page? You can!

To select the desired text to copy, click in front of the text and drag to the end of it. (If the text won't highlight, try to click at the end of the desired text and drag backward.) To copy the Web text, from the Edit menu, select Copy. Open your word processing document. Position the cursor where you want to paste the text. From the Edit menu of the word processor, select Paste. The text will appear in the word processing document.

When you copy text information from the Web, you must cite the source in your word processing document by giving information such as the URL (Web page address), Web page name, and author, if given.

YOUR TURN Open a Web page. Copy some text and paste it in a word processing document.

Using Report Templates

Goals

- Type at least 48wpm/5'/5e
- Format reports using a template

A. Type 2 times.

A. WARMUP

```
1       I am glad the office measures just 15 X 23* (*feet)      11
2  because the carpet is quite expensive! At $64/yard, we        22
3  can't afford any mistakes; contact v&zcarpets@mail.com.       33
   | 1 | 2 | 3 | 4 | 5 | 6 | 7 | 8 | 9 | 10 | 11 | 12
```

SKILLBUILDING

B. PACED PRACTICE

If you are not using the GDP software, turn to page SB-14 and follow the directions for this activity.

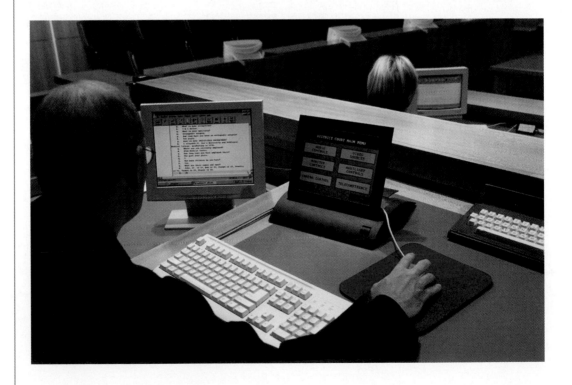

C. Take two 5-minute timed writings. Review your speed and errors.

Goal: At least 48wpm/5'/5e

C. 5-MINUTE TIMED WRITING

```
4        Job stress is not that uncommon in today's workplace.     11
5   There may be many causes of job stress; but the most likely   23
6   reasons it occurs are overwork, possible layoffs, conflicts   35
7   with people at work, or just simply working in a job that     47
8   is no longer to your liking.                                   52
9        Symptoms of job stress are common to many people, and    63
10  they include changes in sleeping patterns, short temper,      75
11  upset stomach, headache, and low morale. Although many of     86
12  us suffer from one or more of the above symptoms, we should   98
13  take them seriously if the symptoms continue or if we tend    110
14  to experience three or four of the symptoms at the same       121
15  time continuously.                                             125
16       Sometimes it is possible to reduce the stress in your    136
17  work by taking a commonsense approach to the situation. If    148
18  you think that you are being overworked, take a vacation or   160
19  avoid taking work home with you. If you are concerned about   172
20  layoffs, then be certain that you are prepared to make a      183
21  career change if it is required. If you have conflicts with   195
22  your boss or with others at the office, try to work them      207
23  out by discussing the issues with the people involved to be   219
24  certain they understand all aspects of the conflict. Then,    231
25  work together to minimize any future conflicts.               240
    |  1  |  2  |  3  |  4  |  5  |  6  |  7  |  8  |  9  |  10  |  11  |  12
```

FORMATTING

Word Processing Manual

D. WORD PROCESSING: REPORT TEMPLATES

Study Lesson 102 in your word processing manual. Complete all of the shaded steps while at your computer. Then format the jobs that follow.

Form 102-4 ▶

Report Template

Note: You may want to read and print the information in the template before deleting it.

1. Type this report using the preselected blank report template that has opened automatically.
2. Review the steps in Lesson 102 in your word processing manual to use this template.
3. On the title page, type the following address:

       575 Eighth Avenue, Suite 1104
       New York, NY 10018
       212-555-3495
       www.globalwebresources.com.

4. The company name is Global Web Resources.
5. The title is Web Design Proposal.
6. The subtitle is Strategies for the Online Presence of Contempo Fashions.
7. Use the same title and subtitle on the second page of the report.
8. Type the rest of the information into the template, as indicated in the copy below.

Introduction

¶ Two major issues need to be addressed in terms of the web site design for Contempo Fashions. The site's most obvious weakness is its lack of unity. The content seems to be out of sync with the design. This division is definitely noticeable to the casual observer.

¶ Often those in charge of content don't have any background in html or coding of any kind, and feel locked into the current design because they simply don't know what their options are. Those in charge of the design can get caught up in trying to create an attractive page that doesn't really work effectively with the content. Global Web Resources is in the business of providing workable solutions to address both these needs.

Content Issues

¶ The content is the first and most important element in a web site. If the content is not effective, it doesn't matter how attractive the design is because no one will bother to read beyond the first page or even the first line. Spelling and grammar must be checked with meticulous care. The credibility of your company is at stake. The readability of the web site can be dramatically improved. Headings, subheadings, bullets, and numbers are critical in making your pages readable. Visitors to your site scan for major headings and want to move quickly and efficiently to any items of interest. Visual separation between paragraphs is also critical for readability. The use of

(Continued on next page)

whitespace created by inserting blank lines between paragraphs is generally more effective than indenting paragraphs. Short lines and short pages make readers want to look at your site pages rather than avoid them.

Design Issues

¶ The design of the web site is done well overall. Appropriate fonts, colors, and art were used in a manner that complements the image of Contempo Fashions. The site navigation is intuitive and easy to use. However, the design is dated and needs a new look.

¶ The 2 groups that are now managing the site must be given guidance in working together to produce a unified site that is both attractive and effective. The goals of the design group and those in charge of content must be brought into alignment in order to make the content work within the context of the current design. Global Web Resources has a web design solution that will bring the needs of both groups into alignment. Your redesigned site will be visually appealing, informative, and intuitive to the visitor. We look forward to our meeting this week.

Form 102-5 ▶

Report Template

Open the file for Form 102-4 and make the following changes:

1. On the title page, change the address as follows:

    8502 North Ashley Street
    Tampa, FL 33604
    813-555-1205
    www.CTI.com

2. The company name is CompuTek International.
3. Change the report title both on the title page and on the first page of the report to Web Site Proposal.
4. Change the report subtitle both on the title page and on the first page of the report to Content and Design Recommendations for Contempo Fashions.
5. Delete the second paragraph under the heading "Introduction."
6. Delete the second paragraph under the heading "Content Issues."
7. Delete the last paragraph of the report.

8. Move the insertion point to the end of the first paragraph under the heading "Design Issues," and press ENTER 1 time.
9. Use the Heading 1 style to add the heading Solutions.
10. Move to the end of the report, and add the following paragraphs.
    Paragraph 1:

    Your Web site should always have new and updated content so that your visitors will have good reason to return. If you continue with your current Web site plan, the maintenance of your site will become a major responsibility. Hundreds of files will need to be maintained whenever you want to make a fundamental change to your site.

(Continued on next page)

The best approach is to let your writers post new content themselves without having to worry about design issues. This is accomplished through a database-driven Web site.

Paragraph 2:
Building a database-driven Web site requires a great deal of technical expertise and tools such as scripting languages and relational database software. Your operating system must be compatible with these languages and databases. Server-side programming is also critical here. CompuTek International would build a database-driven site design and host the site to minimize technical troubleshooting issues. We look forward to our meeting this week.

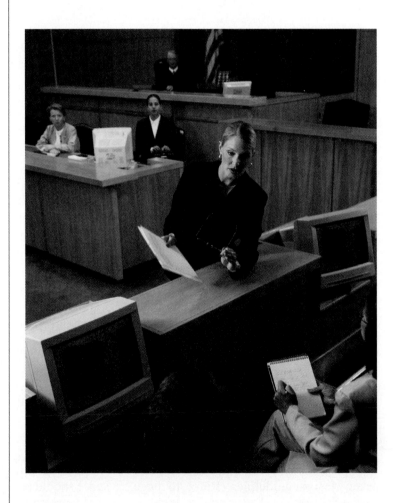

Designing Letterheads

Goals

- Improve speed and accuracy
- Refine language arts skills in composing
- Design letterheads

A. Type 2 times.

A. WARMUP

```
1        Does Quentin know if 1/2 of the January order will be    11
2    ready? At 5:30 about 46% of the orders still hadn't been     22
3    mailed! Mr. Gray expects a very sizable loss this month.     34
     |  1  |  2  |  3  |  4  |  5  |  6  |  7  |  8  |  9  |  10  |  11  |  12
```

SKILLBUILDING

B. DIAGNOSTIC PRACTICE: SYMBOLS AND PUNCTUATION

If you are not using the GDP software, turn to page SB-2 and follow the directions for this activity.

C. These paragraphs are made up of very short words, requiring the frequent use of the SPACE BAR. Do not pause before or after pressing the SPACE BAR. Type the paragraph 2 times.

C. TECHNIQUE PRACTICE: SPACE BAR

```
4        He had the car in the shop and knew that the cost for
5    the work might be high. If the bill for the work was to be
6    more than he could pay, he knew that he would skip it. It
7    did not make any sense to put more money into the old car.
8        If you are near the old shop, come in to see if you can
9    pay the bill at that time. If you are not able to pay it at
10   that time, you can come back to see us when you are able.
```

LANGUAGE ARTS

D. COMPOSING A MEMO

Compose the body of a memo to explain basic design guidelines. Refer to page 409—Section E, Designing a Form—frequently. Use the following suggestions for composing each paragraph:

Paragraph 1. Explain that a simple, balanced design is essential and that typefaces (fonts), attributes, and sizes should be limited.

Paragraph 2. Explain that white space should be used to make text easier to read and graphics easier to see.

Paragraph 3. Explain that word processing software is a powerful tool that makes experimenting easy.

E. DESIGNING A FORM

Use the following guidelines to design an attractive, effective form:

1. Keep all elements of your design simple and balanced.
2. Limit the number of typefaces, attributes (bold, italics, and so on), and sizes. Using two typefaces is a good rule of thumb.
3. Use white space liberally to separate and open up text and graphics.
4. Use different alignments (left, center, right, and full) to add interest and emphasis.
5. Experiment and change—word processing software makes both easy to do.

Word Processing Manual

F. WORD PROCESSING: SMALL CAPS AND TEXT BOXES

Study Lesson 103 in your word processing manual. Complete all of the shaded steps while at your computer. Then format the jobs that follow.

Form 103-6

Letterhead Form

Note: When creating, sizing, or positioning a text box, switch to a whole-page view. When typing text, switch to a page-width view or larger as desired. As you add information to the text box, adjust the size of the text box as needed.

1. Change the left and right margins to 0.25 inch, and press ENTER 2 times.
2. Apply a border to the bottom of the second blank line.
3. Insert a picture related to school or school work.
4. Drag and size the picture so that it looks similar to the one in the illustration at the left and on page 410.
5. Create a text box next to the picture, about the size and in the same position as the one in the illustration, to hold the business name.
6. Remove the line around the text box, and change the fill to none.

7. Change to Calibri 18-point small caps, and center and type Tutor Time.
8. Change the font color as desired to coordinate with the picture.
9. Create a text box, about the size and in the same position as the one in the illustration, to hold the address of the business.
10. Remove the line around the text box, and change the fill to none.
11. Change the font to Calibri 10 point, and right-align and type the lines of the address:

    4219 Richmond Avenue,
    Suite 205
    Houston, TX 77027
    713-555-7337
    www.tutortime.com

(Continued on next page)

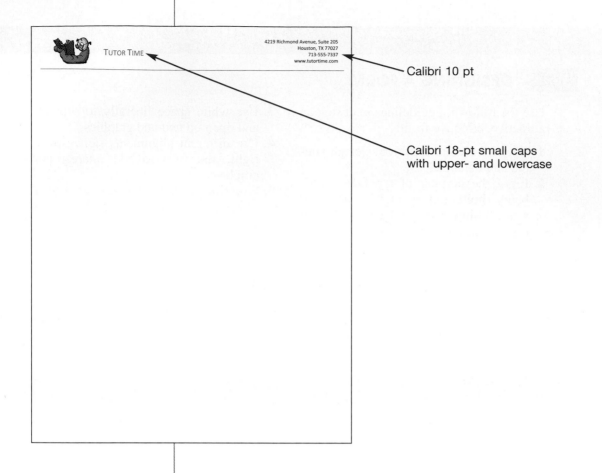

Calibri 10 pt

Calibri 18-pt small caps
with upper- and lowercase

Form 103-7 ▶

Letterhead Form

1. Press ENTER 2 times, and insert a picture of your favorite winter sport.
2. Drag and size the picture so that it looks like the one in the illustration on the left and on page 411.
3. Create a text box, about the size and in the same position as the one in the illustration, to hold the name of the business.
4. Remove the line around the text box, and change the fill to none.
5. Change to Cambria Italic 24-point small caps, and type `Winter Sports` centered and bolded with upper- and lowercase.
6. Change the font color of the business name to coordinate with one of the colors in the picture.
7. Create a text box, about the size and in the same position as the one in the

illustration, to hold the address of the business.
8. Change the font to Cambria 16 point and center and type the lines of the address, all on one continuous line.

    `2820 Cerillos Road`
    `Santa Fe, NM 87505`
    `505-555-3496`

9. Insert a diamond-shaped symbol between each item in the address block as shown in the illustration. Insert 1 space before and after the symbol.
10. Press ENTER and type www.wintersports.com.
11. Add a fill to the text box to coordinate with the colors in the picture.

(Continued on next page)

WINTER SPORTS

2820 Cerillos Road ◆ Santa Fe, NM 87505 ◆ 505-555-3496
www.wintersports.com

Cambria Italic 24-pt small caps
with upper- and lowercase

Cambria 16 pt

**Form
103-8**

Letterhead Form

1. Create a letterhead design of your own—for you personally, for your school, or for a business.
2. Insert at least one picture that enhances the theme of the letterhead.
3. Remember to include complete information in the address block.
4. Try using fonts that you have not yet applied—experiment with point sizes and attributes.

Strategies for Career Success

Designing the Page for Readability

A well-designed document is appealing to the eye, is easy to read, and shows you are professional and competent. Follow these simple guidelines to increase the readability of your documents.

Use white space (that is, empty space) to make material easier to read by separating it from other text. Side margins should be equal. Create white space by varying paragraph length. The first and last paragraphs should be short—three to five typed lines.

Use bulleted or numbered lists to emphasize material. Make sure all the items in the list are grammatically parallel in structure. Use headings to introduce new material. Use full caps sparingly. Consider desktop publishing software to visually enhance your document. Remember to balance graphics, lists, and text.

YOUR TURN Review a document you have recently written. What page design and format techniques did you use to make the document more readable?

Designing Notepads

Goals

- Type at least 48wpm/5′/5e
- Design notepads

A. Type 2 times.

A. WARMUP

```
1      This series* (*2 films, 9 minutes) by J. Zeller goes      11
2  beyond the "basics" of computers. Viewers keep requesting     22
3  an extension on the dates; this includes 3/2, 5/5, and 8/9.   34
   |  1  |  2  |  3  |  4  |  5  |  6  |  7  |  8  |  9  |  10  |  11  |  12
```

SKILLBUILDING

B. MAP

Follow the GDP software directions for this exercise in improving keystroking accuracy.

C. Take two 5-minute timed writings. Review your speed and errors.

Goal: At least 48wpm/5'/5e

C. 5-MINUTE TIMED WRITING

4	Employers are always searching for people who have	10
5	salable skills. Having salable skills makes you unique and	22
6	desirable as an employee. Developing skills and qualities	34
7	such as a pleasing personality, a good sense of humor, a	45
8	positive attitude, an ability to get along with people, and	57
9	the ability to manage your time and prioritize your work	69
10	may help you find a job.	74
11	A tenacious person is persistent and maintains strong	85
12	work habits. He or she does not give up on a task easily	96
13	and always expects to finish the assigned task.	106
14	A good sense of humor and a positive attitude are two	117
15	traits that can help a person advance on the job. Although	128
16	there are times to be serious at work, sometimes you have	140
17	to look at things humorously. If you maintain a positive	151
18	attitude, other workers will like to work with you.	162
19	When you acquire the skills to manage your time and	172
20	prioritize your work, you will be successful in anything	184
21	you try to do. When you are given an assignment, ask for	195
22	guidelines so that you will know what needs to be done and	207
23	in what order. Then try to complete the assignment in a	218
24	timely fashion. The skills may be difficult to learn, but	230
25	you will be glad you can manage your time and work.	240

| 1 | 2 | 3 | 4 | 5 | 6 | 7 | 8 | 9 | 10 | 11 | 12

FORMATTING

Word Processing Manual

D. WORD PROCESSING: PRINT OPTIONS

Study Lesson 104 in your word processing manual. Complete all of the shaded steps while at your computer. Then format the jobs that follow.

Many ink-jet printers do not print beyond the bottom half inch on a sheet of paper. Keep this in mind when positioning objects at the bottom of a page.

1. Press ENTER 2 times, and insert a picture of an office desk or a picture related to an office notepad.
2. Drag and size the picture so that it looks similar to the one in the illustration on this page.
3. Create a text box, about the size and in the same position as the one in the illustration, to hold the words "From the Desk of Amber Bristol."
4. Remove the line around the text box, and change the fill to none.
5. Change to Calibri Bold 36 point, and center and type From the Desk of Amber Bristol inside the text box.
6. Create a text box, about the size and in the same position as the one in the illustration, to hold the check box list at the bottom of the notepad.
7. Remove the line around the text box, and change the fill to none.
8. Insert a check box using Wingdings Italic 28 point. Space 1 time.
9. Change to Calibri Italic 28 point, type Urgent inside the text box, and press ENTER 1 time.
10. Repeat steps 8 and 9 for the remaining lines in the check box list, adding the words Do Today and Follow-Up. Anchor all objects to the first blank line at the top of the page.
Note: You should display formatting marks to complete this step and the remaining steps.
11. Change to a whole-page view, and select and copy the entire document.
12. Move to the end of the document and insert three manual page breaks to create three additional blank pages.
13. Paste the copied document into each of the three newly created pages by moving the insertion point just before each manual page break and then pasting.
14. Use the print option to print four pages per sheet on 8.5- × 11-inch paper.

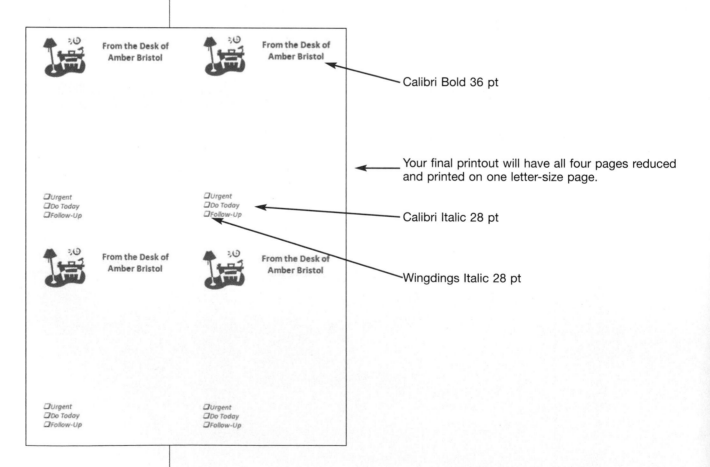

Calibri Bold 36 pt

Your final printout will have all four pages reduced and printed on one letter-size page.

Calibri Italic 28 pt

Wingdings Italic 28 pt

1. Press ENTER 2 times, and insert a picture of an office desk or a picture related to a musical note or a personalized office note.
2. Drag and size the picture so that it looks similar to the one in the illustration on this page.
3. Create a text box, about the size and in the same position as the one in the illustration, to hold the words "Just a Note to Say . . ."
4. Remove the line around the text box, and change the fill to none.
5. Change to a script font of your choice in 48-point bold and italic.
6. Center and type Just a Note to Say followed by 1 space and 3 periods with 1 space after each period.
7. Create a text box, about the size and in the same position as the one in the illustration, to hold the words at the bottom of the notepad.
8. Change to the same script font used in the first text box, also in 36-point size, and center and type From the Desk of Darin Diaz inside the text box.
9. Change to a whole-page view, and select and copy the entire document.
10. Move to the end of the document, and insert three manual page breaks to create three additional blank pages.
11. Paste the copied document into each of the three newly created pages just before the page break marks.
12. Use the print option to print four pages per sheet on 8.5- × 11-inch paper.

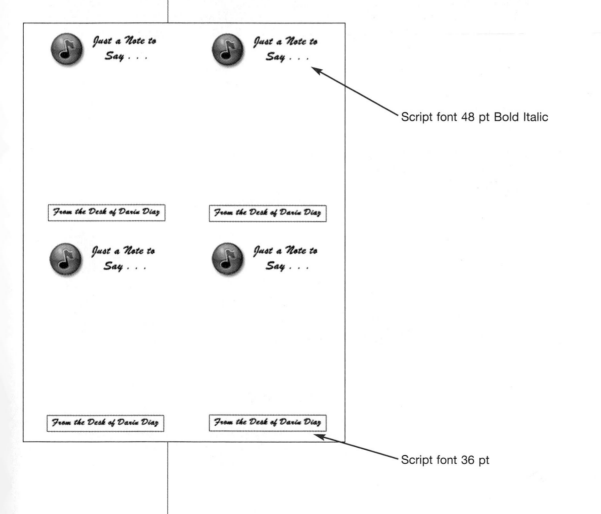

Script font 48 pt Bold Italic

Script font 36 pt

1. Create a notepad design of your own—for you personally, for your school, or for a business.
2. Insert at least one picture that enhances the theme of the notepad.

3. Insert at least one text box with a fill.
4. Try using fonts that you have not yet applied. Experiment with point sizes and attributes.

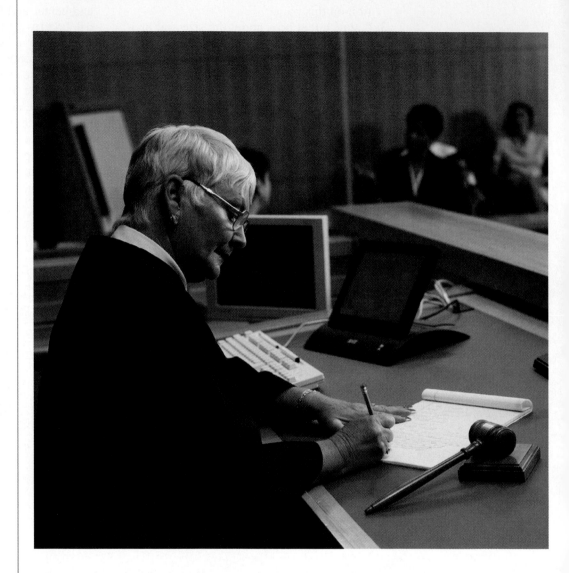

Lesson 105

Designing Miscellaneous Office Forms

Goals
- Improve speed and accuracy
- Refine language arts skills in proofreading
- Design miscellaneous office forms

A. Type 2 times.

A. WARMUP

```
1       Item #876 won't be ordered until 9/10. Did you gather   11
2  all requests and input them exactly as they appeared? Zack   23
3  will never be satisfied until he contacts jack@orders.com.   34
   | 1 | 2 | 3 | 4 | 5 | 6 | 7 | 8 | 9 | 10 | 11 | 12
```

SKILLBUILDING

PPP PRETEST → PRACTICE → POSTTEST

PRETEST
Take a 1-minute timed writing. Review your speed and errors.

B. PRETEST: Vertical Reaches

```
4       The man knelt on the lawn and used a knife with skill   11
5  to raise the valve away from the brace. His back ached in   23
6  vain as he crawled over the knoll to fix the flawed valve.   34
   | 1 | 2 | 3 | 4 | 5 | 6 | 7 | 8 | 9 | 10 | 11 | 12
```

PRACTICE
Speed Emphasis:
If you made no more than 1 error on the Pretest, type each *individual* line 2 times.
Accuracy Emphasis:
If you made 2 or more errors, type each *group* of lines (as though it were a paragraph) 2 times.

C. PRACTICE: Up Reaches

```
7  aw away award crawl straw drawn sawed drawl await flaw lawn
8  se self sense raise these prose abuse users serve send seem
9  ki kind kites skill skier skims skips skits kilts king skid
```

D. PRACTICE: Down Reaches

```
10  ac ache track paced brace races facts crack acute back aces
11  kn knob knife kneel knows knack knelt known knoll knot knew
12  va vain vague value valve evade naval rival avail vats vase
```

POSTTEST
Repeat the Pretest timed writing and compare performance.

E. POSTTEST: Discrimination Practice

F. Take a 1-minute timed writing on the first paragraph to establish your base speed. Then take four 1-minute timed writings on the remaining paragraphs. As soon as you equal or exceed your base speed on one paragraph, advance to the next, more difficult paragraph.

F. SUSTAINED PRACTICE: SYLLABIC INTENSITY

```
13      People continue to rent autos for personal use or for    11
14  their work, and the car-rental business continues to grow.    23
15  When you rent a car, look carefully at the insurance cost.    35
16  You might also have to pay a mileage charge for the car.      46

17      It is likely that a good deal of insurance coverage is    11
18  part of the standard rental cost. But you might be urged      23
19  to procure extra medical, property, and collision coverage.   35
20  If you accept, be ready to see your rental charge increase.   46

21      Perhaps this is not necessary, as you may already have    11
22  the kind of protection you want in a policy that you have     23
23  at the present time. By reviewing your own auto insurance     34
24  policy, you may easily save a significant amount of money.    46

25      Paying mileage charges could result in a really large     11
26  bill. This is especially evident when the trips planned       22
27  involve destinations that are many miles apart. Complete a    34
28  total review of traveling plans before making a decision.     43
```

LANGUAGE ARTS

G. Compare these lines with lines 25-28 in the Sustained Practice drill above. Edit the lines to correct any errors.

G. PROOFREADING

```
29      Paying milage charges could result in a very large
30  bill. This is especially evident when the trips planned
31  involve destinations that are manymiles apart. complete a
32  total review of traveling plans before making a decsion.
```

DOCUMENT PROCESSING

Form 105-12 ▶

Directory Form

1. Change the page orientation to landscape.
2. Change the top margin to 2.3 inches and the other margins to 0.75 inch.
3. Press ENTER 1 time.
4. Create a boxed table with 4 columns and 17 rows.
5. Select the entire table and change the font to Calibri Bold 18 point.
6. Type these column headings in Row 1: Name | Department | Phone Number | E-Mail Address. Change the alignment in the row to center.
7. Move to the top of the document, and insert a picture, associated with a directory, in the same position and about the same size as the one in the illustration on the left and on page 419.
8. Insert a text box, about the size and in the same position as the one in the illustration, to hold the heading.
9. Change to Calibri 48 point, and center and type Directory at a Glance inside the text box. Change the font color as desired.
10. Remove the line around the text box, and change the fill to none.
11. Add shading to the cells in Row 1 of the boxed table, using a color that complements the picture.

(Continued on next page)

Directory at a Glance

← Calibri 48 pt

Name	Department	Phone Number	E-Mail Address

← Calibri Bold 18 pt

Form 105-13 ▶

Sign-In Form

Facey Medical Group

1. Change the top margin to 2 inches and the other margins to 0.75 inch.
2. Create a boxed table with 4 columns and 30 rows.
3. Select Row 1 and change the font to Calibri Bold 18 point.
4. Type these column headings in Row 1: Name | Time In | Doctor's Name | Purpose. Change the alignment in the row to center.
5. Adjust the column widths manually so they appear similar to the column widths in the illustration on the left and on page 420.
6. Select Rows 2-29 and change the font to Calibri Bold 16 point.
7. Insert a picture of an office desk or clip art related to an office notepad as shown, and size it to about 1.5 inches on each side.
8. Move the insertion point outside the table below the bottom row, then insert a text box, about the size and in the same position as the one in the illustration, to hold the name of the medical group.
9. Change to Cambria 48 point, and center and type Facey Medical Group.
10. Remove the line around the text box, and change the fill to none.
11. Create a text box, about the size and in the same position as the one in the illustration, to hold the date line.
12. Change to Calibri Bold 12 point, and type Date: followed by a series of underlines to form a date line similar to the one in the illustration.
13. Remove the fill and the lines around the text box.
14. Create a text box, about the size and in the same position as the one in the illustration, to hold the names of the doctors.
15. Change to Cambria Italic 12 point, and type the following doctors' names in a bulleted list:
    Dr. Mary Chavez
    Dr. Irving K. Levine
    Dr. Evelyn Jones
16. Remove the line around the text box, and change the fill to none.
17. Change the font color of the words on the form as desired to coordinate with the picture.

(Continued on next page)

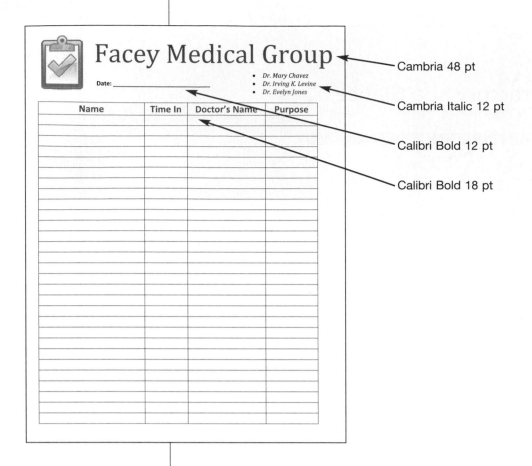

Facey Medical Group

Cambria 48 pt

Date: _____

- *Dr. Mary Chavez*
- *Dr. Irving K. Levine*
- *Dr. Evelyn Jones*

Cambria Italic 12 pt

Calibri Bold 12 pt

Calibri Bold 18 pt

Name	Time In	Doctor's Name	Purpose

Form 105-14

Memo Template

1. Type this memo using the preselected blank memo template that has opened automatically.
2. Review the steps in Lesson 101 in your word processing manual to use this template.

Progress and Proofreading Check

Documents designated as Proofreading Checks serve as a check of your proofreading skill. Your goal is to have zero typographical errors when the GDP software first scores the document.

To: Gloria Hernandez, Vice President | **CC:** Roy Phillips, Marketing Manager | **From:** Naoe Okubo, Senior Graphics Artist | **Date:** September 3, 20-- | **Re:** Web Site Redesign

¶ I have finished evaluating the five Web design firms that made formal presentations to our Web site team last week. The two finalists are Global Web Resources and CompuTek International. Their portfolios and presentations were very impressive. I believe either firm would be an excellent choice. Mr. Phillips agrees with this assessment.

¶ I have arranged for a formal presentation to our key executives for Wednesday afternoon of next week in our corporate dining room. We will have a luncheon first followed by the presentations. I have attached key information from the portfolios of both firms as well as details of Wednesday's meeting. Please let me know if you need any further information. urs | Attachment

Unit 22

Designing Office Publications

The Traveler's Connection

A Newsletter From E-Travel.com

Volume 9, Issue No. 5   Spring 20--

In This Issue:
Tips for the Frequent Air Traveler, Page 1
Planning Your Travel Online, Page 1
Focus on Dallas-Fort Worth, Page 2
Texas Tidbits, Page 2
Thistle Hill, Page 2

Tips for the Frequent Air Traveler

We all have visions of the perfect vacation. They usually include a beautiful hotel, a comfortable room, great food, and wonderful entertainment. Unfortunately, sometimes our vision doesn't exactly align itself with reality, and our dream has suddenly turned into a nightmare. You can avoid this situation if you do some smart advance planning.

Here are some smart travel tips that can turn your dream vacation into a reality:

- Do your homework. Your best bet is to find out all you can about your destination before you do anything else. Find a good travel agent, do your own research on the Internet, and buy some good travel books on your destination in your favorite bookstore.

- Carry medications and other essentials with you. To avoid a disaster, carry everything you can't function without on the plane with you in case your luggage is lost.

- Buy travel insurance. If you are taking an expensive vacation and are not completely sure you can make it, buying travel insurance is a wise expenditure. Many people today have children and aging parents whose needs are unpredictable, so travel insurance may be a good value.

- Confirm all reservations. Be sure that all your reservations, including hotels, cars, and entertainment, are confirmed and written down. Nothing can ruin a trip faster than finding out that you don't have a place to sleep or transportation.

Planning Your Travel Online

The Internet has opened up a wealth of information that used to be the sole

Page 1

domain of individual travel agencies. If you have a computer and Internet access, you can make reservations, buy tickets, book entertainment packages, and do any number of other things.

Save hours of time and lots of money by using the Internet wisely when you plan your travel. You can shop for the best airline rates and even name your own price if you are flexible in your travel plans.

Focus on Dallas-Fort Worth

this is the world's second busiest airport, it is surprisingly easy to use. However, the transportation between terminals is slow.

LOVE FIELD

Love Field is a $15 to $20 taxi ride from downtown Dallas. The phone number is 214-555-6073.

Love Field is the hub of Western Airlines, which offers service within Texas, to many cities in the surrounding states, and, with stops, to destinations as far away as Chicago.

BETWEEN THE AIRPORT AND TOWN

It costs around $35 to get

Texas Tidbits

- To receive mail while traveling in Dallas, have it sent c/o General Delivery at the city's main post office.
- Most businesses open between 8 a.m. and 10 a.m. and close around 6 p.m. Many are also open on weekends.
- Banks operate weekdays from 9 a.m. until 2 or 3 p.m., and some are also open on Saturday mornings.
- Post offices are open

Global Savings & Loan

Your Guide to Online Banking

Account	ATM Card	Check Writing	Monthly Fee
Regular Checking	None	Unlimited	$ 9.00
Interest Checking	Express Card	Unlimited	10.00
Basic Checking	Express Card	Unlimited	4.50
Student Checking	Express Card	Unlimited	3.00
Note: Fees may apply to telephone banking calls and the use of the ATM Express Card.			

Designing Cover Pages

Goals

- Type at least 49wpm/5'/5e
- Design cover pages

A. Type 2 times.

A. WARMUP

```
1      Buzz told us that Flight #7864 got into Phoenix just    11
2   3 minutes before Vick's! This is quite remarkable when     22
3   you realize that we never planned for such a "coincidence." 34
    | 1 | 2 | 3 | 4 | 5 | 6 | 7 | 8 | 9 | 10 | 11 | 12
```

SKILLBUILDING

B. PROGRESSIVE PRACTICE: ALPHABET

If you are not using the GDP software, turn to page SB-7 and follow the directions for this activity.

C. DIAGNOSTIC PRACTICE: NUMBERS

If you are not using the GDP software, turn to page SB-5 and follow the directions for this activity.

Keyboarding Connection

Searching the Yellow Pages

Do you find the Yellow Pages of your phone directory handy? Try the Internet as an alternate source. Many of the Web's search engines have a Yellow Pages feature that is quite useful.

You can use the Yellow Pages feature to search for mailing addresses and phone numbers of businesses and organizations. The Yellow Pages link appears in most leading Internet search engines. These search engines may also provide a map of the location of the business or organization.

The Yellow Pages feature of a search engine is like having all the phone directories in the United States at your fingertips.

YOUR TURN Click the Yellow Pages feature on one of your favorite search engines. Search for a business in your city by name and then by category. Did you retrieve the address and phone number of the business using both search methods?

D. Take two 5-minute timed writings. Review your speed and errors.

Goal: At least 49wpm/5'/5e

D. 5-MINUTE TIMED WRITING

```
 4        Why do people choose a particular career? Your first    11
 5   instinct might likely be to say that people work to make     22
 6   money. That may be true, but extensive research has shown    34
 7   that many other factors are considered just as important     45
 8   and that these factors should be carefully considered when   57
 9   you are about to accept a new position.                      65
10        There are many rewards that a job can provide such as   76
11   a chance to be creative, or the chance to spend time with    88
12   people whose company you enjoy, or the feeling that you are 100
13   doing something useful for yourself or for your employer.   111
14   The quality of the work environment is also an important    123
15   consideration in choosing a career, as is the chance to     134
16   work closely with people on a daily basis.                  142
17        Obviously, your career should allow you to advance in  153
18   your field and to be competitive for promotions. You should 165
19   be able to see a clear line for advancement in your job and 177
20   be given a chance to demonstrate your abilities so that     189
21   your coworkers and supervisors recognize your strengths.    200
22   Parallel to these factors is the need for your job to give  212
23   you adequate challenges on a daily, continuing basis. If    223
24   your work is not challenging, boredom will set in, and you  235
25   might soon be looking for a change in your career.          245
    | 1 | 2 | 3 | 4 | 5 | 6 | 7 | 8 | 9 | 10 | 11 | 12
```

FORMATTING

Word Processing Manual

E. WORD PROCESSING: WORD ART

Study Lesson 106 in your word processing manual. Complete all of the shaded steps while at your computer. Then format the jobs that follow.

DOCUMENT PROCESSING

Report 106-75

Cover Page

To ensure that your document is scored properly, insert 2 spaces at the beginning of the document.

1. Press the SPACE BAR 2 times and insert a picture related to vision or reading.
2. Drag and size the picture so that it looks similar to the one in the illustration on page 424.
3. Insert word art, about the size and in the same position as the one at the top of the illustration, with the words Preferred Optical Vision Plan in 2 lines as shown. Use the default font.

(Continued on next page)

4. Choose a style and color to coordinate with the picture.
5. Create a text box, about the size and in the same position as the one at the bottom of the illustration, to hold the directory information.
6. Remove the line around the text box, and change the fill to none.
7. Change to Cambria Bold 20 point, center and type `Directory of Participating Vision Care Specialists` in 2 lines as shown in the illustration, and press ENTER 2 times.

8. Change to Cambria 16 point, center, and type for all salaried employees of the San Francisco Community College District in 2 lines as shown in the illustration, and press ENTER 2 times.
9. Change to Cambria 18 point, center, and type `September 20--`.
10. Change any of the font colors to coordinate with the picture as desired.

Preferred Optical
Vision Plan

Directory of
Participating Vision Care Specialists ← Cambria Bold 20 pt

for all salaried employees of the
San Francisco Community College District ← Cambria 16 pt

September 20-- ← Cambria 18 pt

Report 106-76
Cover Page

1. Press the SPACE BAR 2 times, and insert a picture related to dining.
2. Drag and size the picture so that it looks similar to the one in the illustration on page 425.
3. Insert word art, about the size and in the same position as the one at the top of the illustration, with the words `Sonoma County's Dining Guide` in 2 lines as shown.
4. Choose a style and color for the word art to coordinate with the picture, and use the default font.

5. Create a text box, about the size and in the same position as the one at the bottom of the illustration, to hold the bulleted list.
6. Remove the line around the text box, and change the fill to none.
7. Change to Cambria Bold 24 point, and type the following list unformatted (without bullets):

    Fine Dining
    Midrange
    Bargain

8. Apply bullets to the list.

(Continued on next page)

9. Create a text box, about the size and in the same position as the one at the bottom of the illustration, to hold the date.
10. Add a line around the text box, and change the fill to a color that coordinates with the picture.

11. Change to Cambria Bold Italic 26 point, and type Summer 20--.
12. Change any of the font colors to coordinate with the picture as desired.

Sonoma County's Dining Guide

• **Fine Dining** ⟵ Cambria Bold 24 pt
• **Midrange**
• **Bargain**

Summer 20-- ⟵ Cambria Bold Italic 26 pt

Report 106-77 ▶

Cover Page

1. Create a cover page design of your own to be used as the insert for a view binder that holds information for one of your courses.
2. Insert at least one picture related to the subject of the course.

3. Insert at least one text box with a fill.
4. Insert some word art.
5. Change any of the font colors to coordinate with the picture or word art as desired.

Designing Announcements and Flyers

Goals

- Improve speed and accuracy
- Refine language arts skills in grammar
- Design announcements and flyers

A. Type 2 times.

A. WARMUP

```
1        Does Quentin know if 1/2 of the January order will be    11
2   ready? At 5:30 about 46% of the orders still hadn't been      22
3   mailed! Mr. Gray expects a very sizable loss this month.      34
    |  1  |  2  |  3  |  4  |  5  |  6  |  7  |  8  |  9  |  10  |  11  |  12
```

SKILLBUILDING

B. Take three 12-second timed writings on each line. The scale below the last line shows your wpm speed for a 12-second timed writing.

B. 12-SECOND SPEED SPRINTS

```
4   Rico will rush to tidy the big room that held the supplies.
5   Yale is a very fine school that has some very strict rules.
6   Helen will audit the books of one civic leader in the city.
7   The man had a name that was hard for the small girl to say.
    I I I 5 I I I 10 I I I 15 I I I 20 I I I 25 I I I 30 I I I 35 I I I 40 I I I 45 I I I 50 I I I 55 I I I 60
```

C. Type each sentence on a separate line by pressing ENTER after each sentence. Type 2 times.

C. TECHNIQUE PRACTICE: ENTER

```
8    Decorate the room. Attend the seminar. Go to the theater.
9    Watch the inauguration. Go to the rally. See the recital.
10   Run in the marathon. Bake the bread. Vacuum the bedrooms.
11   Visit the nursing home. Sell the ticket. Drive the truck.
```

D. DIAGNOSTIC PRACTICE: SYMBOLS AND PUNCTUATION

If you are not using the GDP software, turn to page SB-2 and follow the directions for this activity.

LANGUAGE ARTS

E. Study the rules at the right.

E. PRONOUNS

RULE ▶

nominative pronoun

Use nominative pronouns (such as *I, he, she, we, they*, and *who*) as subjects of a sentence or clause.

The programmer and <u>he</u> are reviewing the code.
Barb is a person <u>who</u> can do the job.

(Continued on next page)

RULE ▶

objective pronoun

Use objective pronouns (such as *me, him, her, us, them*, and *whom*) as objects of a verb, preposition, or infinitive.

The code was reviewed by the programmer and <u>him</u>.

Barb is the type of person <u>whom</u> we can trust.

Edit the sentences to correct any errors in the use of pronouns.

12 We hope they will take all of them to the concert tomorrow.
13 John gave the gift to she on Monday; her was very pleased.
14 If them do not hurry, Mary will not finish her work on time.
15 The book was proofread by her; the changes were made by he.
16 It is up to them to give us all the pages they read today.
17 Me cannot assure they that it will not rain for the picnic.

FORMATTING

Word Processing Manual

F. WORD PROCESSING: TABLE—MOVE

Study Lesson 107 in your word processing manual. Complete all of the shaded steps while at your computer. Then format the jobs that follow.

DOCUMENT PROCESSING

Report 107-78 ▶

Announcement

1. Change the left and right margins to 0.5 inch.
2. Press the SPACE BAR 2 times, and insert a picture associated with a large city.
3. Drag and size the picture so that it looks similar to the one in the illustration at the left and on page 428.
4. Create a text box, about the size and in the same position as the one at the top of the illustration, to hold the welcoming message.
5. Remove the line around the text box, and change the fill to none.
6. Change to Cambria 28 point, center, and type The Hotel Cosmopolitan in 2 lines as shown in the illustration, and press ENTER 1 time.
7. Change to Cambria 22 point, and center and type welcomes.
8. Insert word art, about the size and in the same position as the one at the top of the illustration, with the words NBEA Conference Attendees.
9. Drag and size the word art so that it looks similar to the word art shown in the illustration.
10. Change the word art font for readability if desired.
11. Choose a style and color for the word art to coordinate with the picture.
12. Insert a boxed table with 3 columns and 7 rows, and drag it into position as shown in the illustration.
13. Change to Calibri Bold 20 point, and type the centered column headings.
14. Change to Calibri 20 point, and type the left-aligned column entries.
15. Type the information in Column C in 2 lines as shown.
16. Merge the cells in Row 7, change to Calibri 16 point, and type the information as shown.
17. Automatically adjust the column width for all entries, and drag the table into position again.
18. Add a shading color to the first and last rows to coordinate with the word art and picture.

(Continued on next page)

Event	Time	Location
President's Welcome	8:30-9:30 a.m.	Mezzanine Ballroom B
Internet Training	10-11:30 a.m.	First Floor Cityscape Room
NBEA Luncheon	12-1 p.m.	Mezzanine Grand Ballroom
Computer Workshops	1-3 p.m.	First Floor Rooms A, B, and D
Research Sessions*	3-5:30 p.m.	Third Floor Rooms 1, 3, and 5

nominative pronoun
nominative pronoun
objective pronoun
nominative and objective pronouns

*President's Note: I encourage anyone who is interested to attend our research sessions this afternoon. Dr. Roy Phillips, who will be the facilitator, is excellent. Both of us are available to answer group questions during the session, or you may direct individual questions to either him or me after the session.

Cambria 28 pt

Cambria 22 pt

Calibri Bold 20 pt

Calibri 20 pt

Calibri 16 pt

Report 107-79

Flyer

1. Press the SPACE BAR 2 times, and insert a picture associated with the summer season.
2. Drag and size the picture so that it looks similar to the one shown in the illustration on page 429.
3. Insert word art, about the size and in the same position as the one at the top of the illustration, with the words Summerset Homes.
4. Choose a style and color for the word art to coordinate with the picture.

(Continued on next page)

5. Create a text box, about the size and in the same position as the one in the middle of the illustration, to hold the message.
6. Remove the line around the text box, and change the fill to none.
7. Change to Cambria 20 point; center and type Summerset Homes proudly invites you to the grand opening of our newest group of single-family homes! as shown in the illustration.
8. Create a text box, about the size and in the same position as the one at the bottom of the illustration, to hold the address information.
9. Remove the line around the text box, and add a fill using a color to coordinate with the word art and the fill.
10. Change to Cambria 12 point; center and type as shown in the illustration:

```
Summerset Homes
520 Southwest Harbor Way
Portland, OR 97201
800-555-2649
www.Summerset.com
```

11. Insert a star-shaped symbol (Wingdings font, character code 171) between each item in the address block as shown in the illustration.
12. Insert 2 spaces before and after the star-shaped symbol.
13. Insert a boxed table with 3 columns and 5 rows, and drag it into position as shown in the illustration.
14. Change to Calibri 16 point, and type the column entries.
15. Automatically adjust the column width for all entries, and drag the table into position again.

Shadow Pines	1,235 sq. ft.	$209,990
Ocean View	1,495 sq. ft.	223,990
Country Meadow	1,759 sq. ft.	265,990
Desert Breeze	2,042 sq. ft.	295,990
Valley Oasis	2,537 sq. ft.	322,990

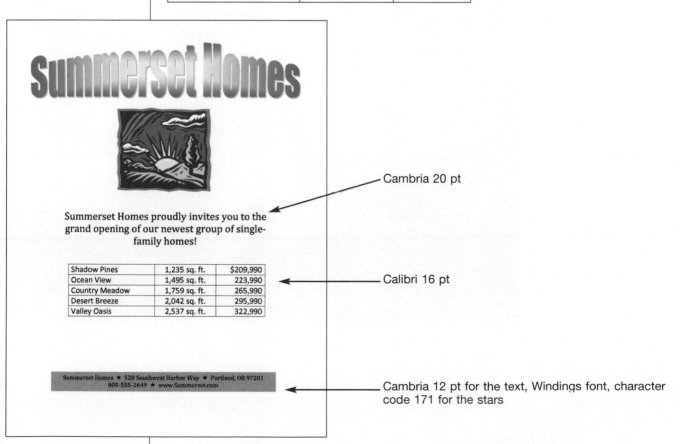

Cambria 20 pt

Calibri 16 pt

Cambria 12 pt for the text, Windings font, character code 171 for the stars

1. Create an announcement or flyer design of your own for an upcoming event at work or on campus.
2. Press the SPACE BAR 2 times and insert at least one picture related to the topic of the announcement or flyer.
3. Insert at least one text box with a fill.
4. Insert some word art.
5. Apply color to your fonts to coordinate with the picture or word art.
6. Insert a table that contains information related to the topic of the flyer or announcement.

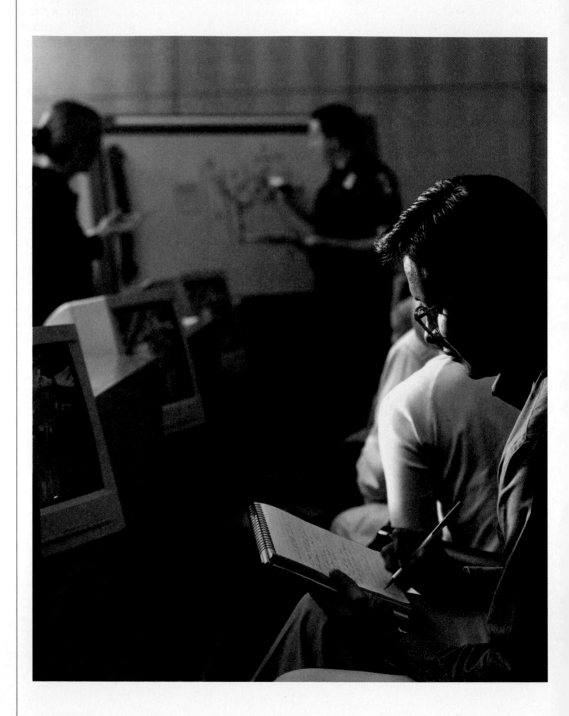

Designing Newsletters: A

Goals

- Type at least 49wpm/5'/5e
- Design newsletters

A. Type 2 times.

A. WARMUP

```
1      Does Pamela know if Region 29* (*Ventura) has met the   11
2 sales quota? Their exact target zone is just not clear;      22
3 they don't have to submit their totals until 4:30 on 5/7.    34
   |  1  |  2  |  3  |  4  |  5  |  6  |  7  |  8  |  9  |  10  |  11  |  12
```

SKILLBUILDING

B. PACED PRACTICE

If you are not using the GDP software, turn to page SB-14 and follow the directions for this activity.

Strategies for Career Success

Managing Business Phone Time

The average American spends an hour a day on the phone. Phone calls can be extremely distracting. Time is spent taking the call and following up after the call. You can take steps to reduce wasted time on the phone.

When you make an outgoing call, organize the topics you want to discuss. Have all the materials you need: pencils, paper, order forms, and so on. When you take an incoming call, answer it promptly. Identify yourself. It is common to answer the phone with your first and last name (for example, "Mary Smith speaking" or "Mary Smith").

Limit social conversation; it wastes time. Give concise answers to questions. At the end of the call, summarize the points made. End the conversation politely.

YOUR TURN Keep a log of your time on the phone for one day. What is your average conversation time? What can you do to reduce your average phone conversation time?

C. Take two 5-minute timed writings. Review your speed and errors.

Goal: At least 49wpm/5'/5e

C. 5-MINUTE TIMED WRITING

4	Purchasing a home is probably one of the most critical	11
5	financial decisions you will make in your lifetime. Dozens	23
6	of questions need to be answered when buying a home. For	34
7	example, how much of a down payment will you make and how	46
8	much of a monthly payment on your mortgage will you be able	58
9	to afford?	60
10	In addition to your mortgage payment, there are other	71
11	costs associated with buying a new home. The mortgage will	83
12	cover the principal and interest for your loan, but you	94
13	will also have homeowner's insurance and utilities to pay	106
14	such as water, sewer, electricity, and gas.	115
15	You may want to purchase a home through a real estate	126
16	agent, and it is important that you find out how much of a	137
17	commission will be charged for that service. When working	149
18	with a real estate agent, you need to let that person know	161
19	about the kind of community in which you would prefer to	172
20	live. Do you want to be close to schools, shopping centers,	184
21	and restaurants, or would you rather purchase a home in a	195
22	secluded neighborhood away from the noise and congestion of	207
23	a metropolitan city?	211
24	When you find a home that you like, look at it very	222
25	carefully to see if it is structurally well built, if you	234
26	like the floor plan, and if it is large enough for you.	245

| 1 | 2 | 3 | 4 | 5 | 6 | 7 | 8 | 9 | 10 | 11 | 12

FORMATTING

D. NEWSLETTER DESIGN

Newsletters are an excellent forum for communicating information on a wide range of subjects. A well-planned newsletter will employ all the basic principles of good design. However, because newsletters usually include information on a wide variety of topics, they are generally complex in their layout.

Most newsletters have the following elements in common: mastheads, main headings and subheadings, text arranged in flowing newspaper-column format using various column widths to add interest, text boxes to emphasize and summarize, pictures to draw readers' attention and interest to a topic, and a variety of borders and fills.

The design of a multipage newsletter must look consistent from one page to the next. This consistency provides unity to the newsletter design and is often achieved through the use of headers and footers.

Report 108-81

Newsletter

Reminder: You will finish the newsletter in Lessons 109 and 110.

Follow these steps to create the masthead and footer for the first page of the newsletter shown below.

1. Set all margins at 0.75 inch.
2. Create an open table with 2 columns and 2 rows. Drag the middle column border to the left so the first column is about 1.75 inches wide.
3. Right-align Column B.
4. In Column B, Row 1, change to Calibri Bold 48 point and type The Traveler's Connection on two lines.
5. Press ENTER 1 time, change to Cambria Bold 14 point, and type A Newsletter From E-Travel.com.
6. Move to Column A, Row 2, and type Volume 9, Issue No. 5.

7. Move to Column B, Row 2, and type Spring 20--.
8. Apply borders to the top and bottom of Row 2.
9. In Column A, Row 1, insert a picture associated with world travel.
10. Drag and size the picture so that it looks similar to the one shown in the illustration.
11. Select the newsletter title and change the font color to coordinate with the picture in Column 1.
12. Insert a blank footer, and center and type Page followed by 1 space.
13. Insert a page number field and close the footer.

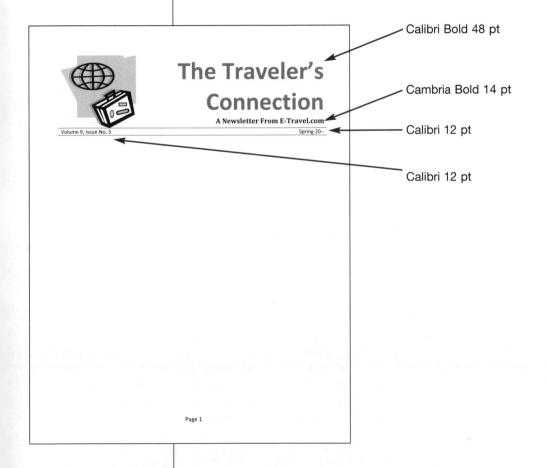

Calibri Bold 48 pt

Cambria Bold 14 pt

Calibri 12 pt

Calibri 12 pt

Report 108-82

Newsletter

1. Create a newsletter masthead of your own related to travel and similar to the one in Report 108-81.

2. Use any picture that enhances the purpose of your travel newsletter.

Designing Newsletters: B

Goals

- Improve speed and accuracy
- Refine language arts skills in spelling
- Design newsletters

A. Type 2 times.

A. WARMUP

```
1        Approximately 90% of the weekly budget was just used    11
2   to buy equipment. A very sizable amount totaling $12,654      22
3   was spent on "necessities" as requested by the department!    34
    |  1  |  2  |  3  |  4  |  5  |  6  |  7  |  8  |  9  |  10  |  11  |  12
```

SKILLBUILDING

PPP PRETEST ➞ PRACTICE ➞ POSTTEST

PRETEST
Take a 1-minute timed writing. Review your speed and errors.

B. PRETEST: Alternate- and One-Hand Words

```
4        A great auditor is eager to spend a minimum of eighty    11
5   hours to amend a problem. If he assessed a penalty that       22
6   exceeded the usual fee, I reserve the right to correct it.    34
    |  1  |  2  |  3  |  4  |  5  |  6  |  7  |  8  |  9  |  10  |  11  |  12
```

PRACTICE
Speed Emphasis:
If you made no more than 1 error on the Pretest, type each *individual* line 2 times.
Accuracy Emphasis:
If you made 2 or more errors, type each *group* of lines (as though it were a paragraph) 2 times.

C. PRACTICE: Alternate-Hand Words

```
7   also amend maps thrown blame city problem panel formal down
8   snap rigid lens social visit with penalty right height half
9   chap usual such enrich shape dish auditor spend eighty kept
```

D. PRACTICE: One-Hand Words

```
10  was only great pupil regret uphill scatter homonym assessed
11  bed join water nylon target pompon savages minimum exceeded
12  age hook eager union teased limply reserve opinion attracts
```

POSTTEST
Repeat the Pretest timed writing and compare performance.

E. POSTTEST: Alternate- and One-Hand Words

F. SUSTAINED PRACTICE: NUMBERS AND SYMBOLS

13	Shopping in the comfort and convenience of your own	11
14	living room has never been more popular than it is right	22
15	now. Shopping clubs abound on cable channels. You could	33
16	buy anything from exotic pets to computers by mail order.	45
17	Sometimes you can find discounts as high as 20% off	11
18	the retail price; for example, a printer that sells for	22
19	$565 might be discounted 20% and be sold for $452. You	33
20	should always investigate quality before buying anything.	44
21	Sometimes hidden charges are involved; for example,	11
22	a printer costing $475.50 that promises a discount of 12%	22
23	($57.06) has a net price of $418.44. However, if charges	34
24	for shipping range from 12% to 15%, you did not save money.	45
25	You must also check for errors. Several errors have	11
26	been noted so far: Invoice #223, #789, #273, and #904 had	22
27	errors totaling $21.35, $43.44, $79.23, and $91.23 for a	34
28	grand total of $235.25. As always, let the buyer beware.	45

LANGUAGE ARTS

G. SPELLING

29	operations health individual considered expenditures vendor
30	beginning internal pursuant president union written develop
31	hours enclosing situation function including standard shown
32	engineering payable suggested participants providing orders
33	toward nays total without paragraph meetings different vice

34	The participents in the different meetings voted for hours.
35	The presdent of the union is working toward a resolution.
36	The health of each individal must be seriously considered.
37	Engineering has suggested providing orders for the vendor.
38	One expanditure has been written off as part of oparations.
39	He is inclosing the accounts payible record as shown today.

Report 109-83 ▶

Newsletter
(continued)

⚠ Reminder: You will finish the newsletter in Lesson 110.

Open the file for Report 108-81 shown on page 433. Follow these steps to continue the newsletter as shown on page 437.

1. Move outside the table below Column A and press ENTER 2 times.
2. Insert File 109, and turn on automatic hyphenation.
3. Carefully place your insertion point in front of the second blank line under the masthead, and select all the newly inserted text including 1 blank line below the last line of text.
4. Create 3 columns with a line between columns.
5. Select the following headings in the newsletter, and change the font to Cambria 24 point:

   ```
   Tips for the Smart Traveler
   Planning Your Travel Online
   Focus on Dallas-Fort Worth
   ```
6. Select the following subheadings in the newsletter and bold them:

   ```
   THE AIRPORT
   LOVE FIELD
   BETWEEN THE AIRPORT AND TOWN
   ```
7. Place your insertion point in front of the second blank line under the masthead.
8. Insert a table with 1 column and 1 row.
9. Change to Cambria 12 point, and type In This Issue:. Press ENTER 1 time.

10. Change to Calibri Italic 12 point, and type the following lines:

    ```
    Tips for the Smart
      Traveler, Page 1
    Planning Your Travel
      Online, Page 1
    Focus on Dallas-Fort
      Worth, Page 2
    Texas Tidbits, Page 2
    Thistle Hill, Page 2
    ```
11. Add a shading color to the table to coordinate with the picture in the masthead.
12. Insert a picture in the space above each of the bulleted items in the first article on the first page of the newsletter. The pictures should be associated in some way with the topic in each of the bulleted items.
13. Drag and size the pictures so that they look similar to the ones shown in the illustration. If necessary, adjust the number of blank lines to accommodate the picture.
14. Place your insertion point in the blank line above the heading "Planning Your Online Travel," and apply a top border.
15. Place your insertion point in the blank line above the heading "Focus on Dallas-Fort Worth," and apply a top border.

(Continued on next page)

The Traveler's Connection

A Newsletter From E-Travel.com

Volume 9, Issue No. 5   Spring 20–

Tips for the Frequent Air Traveler

We all have visions of the perfect vacation. They usually include a beautiful hotel, a comfortable room, great food, and wonderful entertainment. Unfortunately, sometimes our vision doesn't exactly align itself with reality, and our dream has suddenly turned into a nightmare. You can avoid this situation if you do some smart advance planning.

Here are some smart travel tips that can turn your dream vacation into a reality:

- Do your homework. Your best bet is to find out all you can about your destination before you do anything else. Find a good travel agent, do your own research on the Internet, and buy some good travel books on your destination in your favorite bookstore.

- Carry medications and other essentials with you. To avoid a disaster, carry everything you can't function without on the plane with you in case your luggage is lost.

- Buy travel insurance. If you are taking an expensive vacation and are not completely sure you can make it, buying travel insurance is a wise expenditure. Many people today have children and aging parents whose needs are unpredictable, so travel insurance may be a good value.

- Confirm all reservations. Be sure that all your reservations, including hotels, cars, and entertainment, are confirmed and written down. Nothing can ruin a trip faster than finding out that you don't have a place to sleep or transportation.

Planning Your Travel Online

The Internet has opened up a wealth of information that used to be the sole

Page 1

---

domain of individual travel agencies. If you have a computer and Internet access, you can make reservations, buy tickets, book entertainment packages, and do any number of other things.

Save hours of time and lots of money by using the Internet wisely when you plan your travel. You can shop for the best airline rates and even name your own price if you are flexible in your travel plans.

Focus on Dallas-Fort Worth

This month's focus is on Dallas-Fort Worth and the surrounding areas of our state.

THE AIRPORT

The Dallas-Fort Worth International Airport is 17 miles from the business districts of each city. Although this is the world's second busiest airport, it is surprisingly easy to use. However, the transportation between terminals is slow.

LOVE FIELD

Love Field is a $15 to $20 taxi ride from downtown Dallas. The phone number is 214-555-6073.

Love Field is the hub of Western Airlines, which offers service within Texas, to many cities in the surrounding states, and, with stops, to destinations as far away as Chicago.

BETWEEN THE AIRPORT AND TOWN

It costs around $35 to get to downtown Dallas by taxi from the Dallas-Fort Worth International Airport. It is about $30 to downtown Fort Worth.

Cheaper bus and van service is also available. Check our Web site at www.ttc.com for details, as well as for monthly specials.

Page 2

Report 109-84

Newsletter (continued)

1. Open the file for Report 108-81 with the newsletter masthead you created.
2. Follow the steps for Report 109-83, and then delete everything on the second page of the newsletter.
3. Change the information in the contents text box at the top of the first column, insert a picture at the end of the last column of the newsletter to balance the page, and move any pictures around as needed.

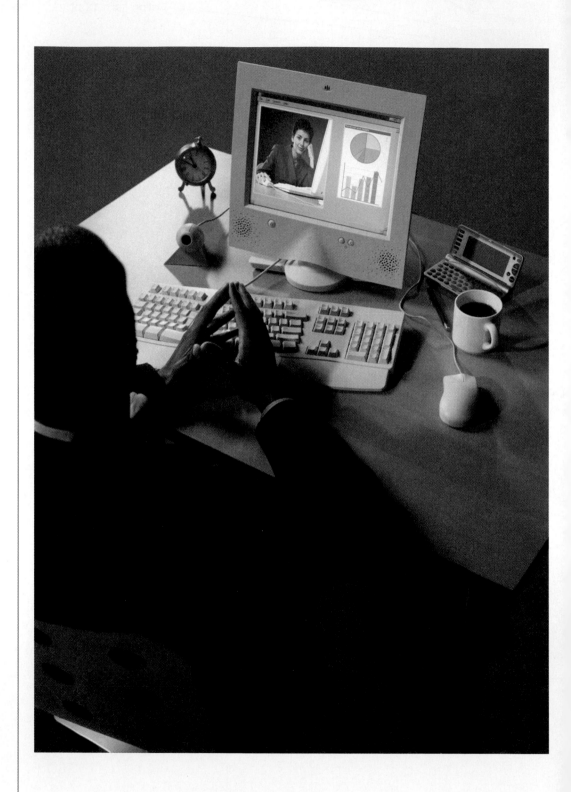

Designing Newsletters: C

Goals

- Type at least 49wpm/5′/5e
- Design newsletters

A. Type 2 times.

A. WARMUP

```
 1        At exactly 8:30 a.m., Quigley & Co. will host a wide    11
 2   variety of chat room meetings; send e-mail to chat@QC.com.    23
 3   Organizational skills will be the topics in Rooms K5 or J6.   34
     |  1  |  2  |  3  |  4  |  5  |  6  |  7  |  8  |  9  |  10  |  11  |  12
```

SKILLBUILDING

B. MAP

Follow the GDP software directions for this exercise in improving keystroking accuracy.

Keyboarding Connection

Effective E-Mail Management

Are you bombarded with e-mail? Take a few simple steps to manage e-mail more efficiently and reduce wasted time.

Create separate accounts for receiving messages that require your direct attention. Keep your mailbox clean by deleting messages you no longer need. Create folders to organize messages you need to keep (for example, set up folders for separate projects).

If you receive numerous e-mail messages, consider purchasing an e-mail manager. E-mail manager programs help you manage multiple e-mail accounts, find messages using powerful search functions, and notify you when you receive a message from a specified person.

Keep backups of important files. Be cautious of e-mail from people you do not know. Check your e-mail on a regular basis to avoid buildup of messages.

YOUR TURN Review the current organization of your e-mail. List ways you can improve the management of your e-mail.

C. Take two 5-minute timed writings. Review your speed and errors.

Goal: At least 49wpm/5'/5e

C. 5-MINUTE TIMED WRITINGS

4	When the rate of unemployment is very low, jobs are	11
5	easier to find. Although you may find a job easily, what	22
6	can you do to make sure your job is one you will enjoy?	33
7	Here are some suggestions to assist you.	41
8	First, be certain you receive a job description when	52
9	you are hired. The job description should list all of the	64
10	requirements of the job and the details of what you will be	76
11	expected to do.	79
12	Second, you should receive some type of orientation to	90
13	your job and the company. During orientation, you will fill	102
14	out various tax forms, benefit forms, and insurance papers.	114
15	You may view a video that will help you learn more about	126
16	the company and available benefits.	133
17	Third, when you start your training, you should take	144
18	notes, pay attention, and ask questions. You should also	155
19	have your trainer check your work for a period of time to	167
20	be sure you are performing your duties correctly. If your	178
21	tasks are complex, you can break them down into smaller	189
22	parts so you can remember all aspects of your job.	200
23	Finally, when you know your job requirements, chart	210
24	your work each day. Concentrate on being part of the team.	222
25	Be zealous in striving to work beyond the expectations of	234
26	your supervisor. Then, you will achieve job satisfaction.	245

| 1 | 2 | 3 | 4 | 5 | 6 | 7 | 8 | 9 | 10 | 11 | 12

DOCUMENT PROCESSING

Report 110-85

Newsletter (continued)

Open the file for Report 109-83, shown on page 437. Follow these steps to finish creating the newsletter shown on pages 441 and 442.

1. Place your insertion point directly in front of the first blank line underneath the last line of text in Column 3.
2. Insert File 110A.
3. Insert a picture in the space to the right of the heading "Focus on Dallas-Fort Worth" on the second page of the newsletter. The pictures should be associated with the concept of focusing on a subject or associated with Texas.
4. Drag and size the picture so that it looks similar to the one shown in the illustration on page 442.
5. Insert word art, about the size and in the same position as the word art at the top of the bulleted list on the second page of the newsletter, with the words Texas Tidbits.
6. Choose a style and color for the word art to coordinate with the newsletter.
7. Create a simple text box, about the size and in the same position as the one at the bottom of the newsletter, to hold the information about Thistle Hill.
8. Delete the text in the text box, insert File 110B, and adjust the size of the text box as needed.
9. Delete the outside borders and add a fill color or fill effect to the text box to coordinate with the picture to the left of the text box.

(Continued on next page)

10. Insert a picture at the bottom of the second page in the space to the left of the information on "Thistle Hill." The picture should be associated with the information about Thistle Hill or with Texas.

11. Drag and size the picture so that it looks similar to the one shown in the illustration.

12. Select the title "Thistle Hill" and change to Calibri Bold 18 point.

13. Create a simple text box, about the size and in the same position as the one at the bottom of the newsletter, to hold the information about tours.

14. Delete the text in the text box, change to Calibri Bold 12 point, and center and type For tour informa-tion, call 817-555-2663.

15. Remove the lines around the text box, and change the fill to none.

16. Make whatever adjustments are needed to make your newsletter look attractive.

The first page of the newsletter should look like the illustration below. The second page of the newsletter should look like the illustration on page 442.

(Continued on next page)

domain of individual travel agencies. If you have a computer and Internet access, you can make reservations, buy tickets, book entertainment packages, and do any number of other things.

Save hours of time and lots of money by using the Internet wisely when you plan your travel. You can shop for the best airline rates and even name your own price if you are flexible in your travel plans.

Focus on Dallas-Fort Worth

This month's focus is on Dallas-Fort Worth and the surrounding area of our state.

THE AIRPORT

The Dallas-Fort Worth International Airport is 17 miles from the business districts of each city. Although

For tour information, call 817-555-2663.

this is the world's second busiest airport, it is surprisingly easy to use. However, the transportation between terminals is slow.

LOVE FIELD

Love Field is a $15 to $20 taxi ride from downtown Dallas. The phone number is 214-555-6073.

Love Field is the hub of Western Airlines, which offers service within Texas, to many cities in the surrounding states, and, with stops, to destinations as far away as Chicago.

BETWEEN THE AIRPORT AND TOWN

It costs around $35 to get to downtown Dallas by taxi from the Dallas-Fort Worth International Airport. It is about $30 to downtown Fort Worth.

Cheaper bus and van service is also available. Check our Web site at www.ttc.com for details, as well as for monthly specials.

Texas Tidbits

- To receive mail while traveling in Dallas, have it sent c/o General Delivery at the city's main post office.
- Most businesses open between 8 a.m. and 10 a.m. and close around 6 p.m. Many are also open on weekends.
- Banks operate weekdays from 9 a.m. until 2 or 3 p.m., and some are also open on Saturday mornings.
- Post offices are open weekdays from 8 a.m. to 5 p.m.
- At traffic lights, it's legal to make a right turn on a red light except when there is a sign at the intersection stating that such a turn is *not* permitted. Of course, come to a full stop first and make sure no traffic is coming.

Thistle Hill

In 1903, cattle baron William T. Waggoner built his daughter a three-story mansion as a wedding present. The Georgian Revival-style mansion has been restored to its 1912 condition and is listed in the National Register. It is located today on Pennsylvania Avenue near the hospital district. It cost around $38,000 when the nearly 11,000-square-foot, red-brick structure was built in 1903. The house was used for lavish dinners and parties to entertain many of Fort Worth's powerful and elite.

Page 2

Calibri Bold 12 pt

Report 110-86

Flyer

Progress and Proofreading Check

Documents designated as Proofreading Checks serve as a check of your proofreading skill. Your goal is to have zero typographical errors when the GDP software first scores the document.

1. Press the SPACE BAR 2 times, and insert a picture related to a globe.
2. Drag and size the picture so that it looks similar to the one shown in the illustration on page 443.
3. Insert word art, about the size and in the same position as the one at the top of the illustration, with the words Global Savings & Loan.
4. Choose a style and color for the word art to coordinate with the picture.
5. Create a text box with no lines or fill and about the size and in the same position as the one shown at the middle of the illustration.
6. Change to Calibri 48 point, and center and type Your Guide to Online Banking in 2 lines as shown.
7. Insert a boxed table with 4 columns and 6 rows, and drag it into position as shown in the illustration.
8. Change to Cambria Bold 18 point, and type the one- and two-column headings in Row 1 aligned as shown.
9. Move to Row 2, change to Calibri 20 point, and type the left-aligned column entries as shown.
10. Right-align the information in Column D, and add spaces after the dollar sign to align the dollar sign just to the left of the widest entry below it.
11. Merge the cells in Row 6, change to Calibri 14 point, and type the information as shown.
12. Adjust the column widths manually as shown.
13. Add a shading color to the first and last rows to coordinate with the word art and picture.

(Continued on next page)

↓1X Account	↓1X ATM Card	Check Writing	Monthly Fee
Regular Checking	None	Unlimited	$ 9.00
Interest Checking	Express Card	Unlimited	10.00
Basic Checking	Express Card	Unlimited	4.50
Student Checking	Express Card	Unlimited	3.00
Note: Fees may apply to telephone banking calls and the use of the ATM Express Card.			

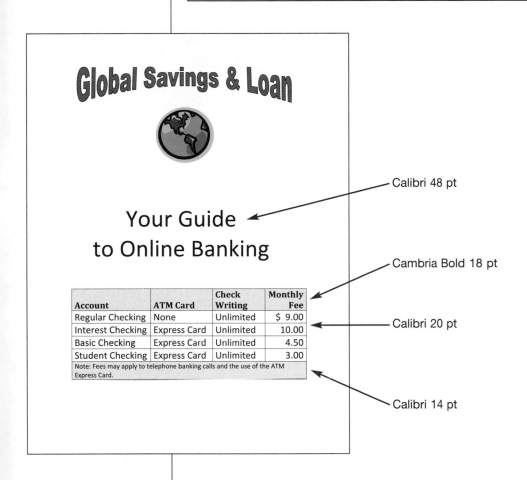

Calibri 48 pt

Cambria Bold 18 pt

Calibri 20 pt

Calibri 14 pt

Unit 23

Designing Web Pages

In The Game

5779 Del Monte Drive
Santa Rosa, CA 95409
888-555-7897
email@InTheGame.com

Home | Contact Us

If there is any sporting good item or apparel item related to baseball and softball, soccer, track and field, or gymnastics that you can't find on our site, we want to hear from you.

E-Mail
Send us an e-mail message now at email@InTheGame.com.

Call Us
Call us toll free at 888-555-7897.

Snail Mail
If you prefer good old snail mail, write to us at the address below:

In the Game
5779 Del Monte Drive
Santa Rosa, CA 95409

In The Game

5779 Del Monte Drive
Santa Rosa, CA 95409
888-555-7897
email@InTheGame.com

Home | Contact Us

Welcome to In The Game, your online supplier specializing in sporting goods for baseball and softball, soccer, track and field, and gymnastics. We can offer you quality products at low prices delivered to you fast!

Baseball and Softball
If you can't wait to play ball, you'll love what we h
automated batting cages, pitching machines, battin
such as caps, jerseys, and t-shirts.

Soccer
If scoring goals is on the top of your list, you've c
soccer equipment and clothing.

Track and Field
Is running your game? We have batons, cross bar
starting pistols, stop watches, and more.

Gymnastics
You'll flip for our line of clothing, fan wear, and u
first quality.

The Virtual Assistant

901 S. Rainbow, Suite 1
Las Vegas, Nevada 89145
888-555-3499
email@TVA.com

Home | Services | Fees | References

Do you need a skilled assistant who works tirelessly on your documents, doesn't need any office space, and gives your work that personal touch? The Virtual Assistant is a professional document processing and design service that will help create the professional image your business demands.

You don't get a second chance at a first impression. The graphics experts in our word processing and desktop publishing departments will make sure your documents look gorgeous. Our editors, who have completed a series of rigorous courses in business English and business communications, will make sure they are letter perfect. Please browse around our site for details.

Word Processing
- Correspondence
- Reports
- Proposals
- Manuals

Desktop Publishing
- Newsletters
- Brochures
- Letterheads
- Resumes

Layout Editing
- In-house Styles
- Custom Styles
- Master Documents
- Table of Contents
- Indexes

Copy Editing
- Proofreading
- Technical Editing
- Grammar Checking
- Writing Style

Creating, Saving, and Viewing Web Pages

Goals

- Improve speed and accuracy
- Refine language arts skills in capitalization
- Create, save, and view Web pages

A. Type 2 times.

A. WARMUP

```
1      The taxes* were quickly adjusted upward by 20 percent    11
2  because of the improvements to her house (built in 1901).    23
3  A proposed law will not penalize good homeowners like this.   34
   |  1  |  2  |  3  |  4  |  5  |  6  |  7  |  8  |  9  |  10  |  11  |  12
```

SKILLBUILDING

B. Take three 12-second timed writings on each line. The scale below the last line shows your wpm speed for a 12-second timed writing.

B. 12-SECOND SPEED SPRINTS

```
4  Their home is on a lake that is just east of her old house.
5  He has an old boat that is in bad need of a good paint job.
6  He got so many fish that she gave some to the nice old man.
7  She was so nice that it was easy for him to help her drive.
   | | | |5| | | |10| | | |15| | | |20| | | |25| | | |30| | | |35| | | |40| | | |45| | | |50| | | |55| | | |60
```

C. PROGRESSIVE PRACTICE: ALPHABET

If you are not using the GDP software, turn to page SB-7 and follow the directions for this activity.

D. PACED PRACTICE

If you are not using the GDP software, turn to page SB-14 and follow the directions for this activity.

E. BASIC PARTS OF A WEB PAGE

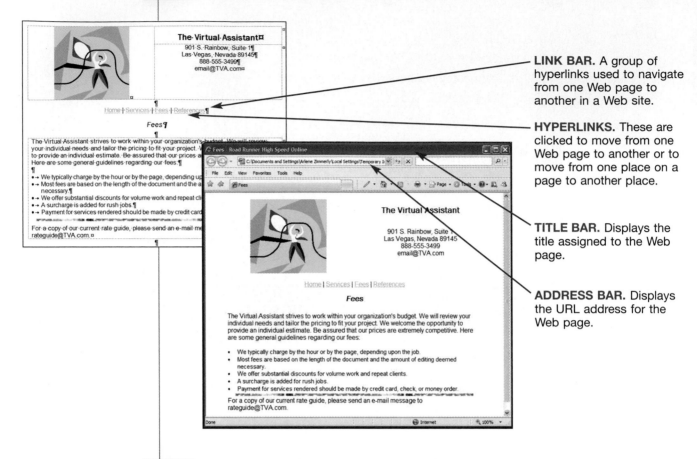

LINK BAR. A group of hyperlinks used to navigate from one Web page to another in a Web site.

HYPERLINKS. These are clicked to move from one Web page to another or to move from one place on a page to another place.

TITLE BAR. Displays the title assigned to the Web page.

ADDRESS BAR. Displays the URL address for the Web page.

F. WEB SITE DESIGN GUIDELINES

Follow these guidelines to design effective Web sites:

- Plan appropriate, specific content first. Define the purpose of the site, and make a list of what visitors need to know.
- Organize the content into logical groups and subgroups, the way you would set up an outline in a report.
- Plan the main page (usually called a home page), which should identify the business and its services.
- Plan and test the site navigation. Hyperlinks help visitors jump from one spot or page to another.

- Plan the content and design details of specific pages, and use tables to position information.
- Design an appropriate, attractive visual theme with consistent design elements on each page to unify your site. Many programs come with a gallery of attractive themes with unified design elements and eye-catching color schemes.
- Use graphics to enhance your page, but use them sparingly because they increase download times.
- Use color to create a mood, attract attention, and categorize information.

Word Processing Manual

G. WORD PROCESSING: WEB PAGE—CREATING, SAVING, AND VIEWING

Study Lesson 111 in your word processing manual. Complete all of the shaded steps while at your computer. Then format the jobs that follow.

Report ▶ 111-87

Web Site

> The projects in this unit must be completed in sequence in order for the steps to work correctly!

> The file names assigned to the Web pages in this text are not typical. Most home pages are named either index.htm or default.html. The commercial server hosting a Web site should be contacted for any specific requirements for file names and extensions.

The Virtual Assistant Web site that starts in this lesson is continued through Lesson 115. Because each Web page builds upon a previous one, make certain that each Web page is correct before continuing to the next one. Follow these steps to create Report 111-87.mht, the home page of the Web site. Refer to the Web layout view of the home page on page 448 as needed. Note that hyphens are used in place of spaces in Web page file names so that the pages will display properly in a browser.

1. Save Report-111-87.doc as a Web page named Report-111-87.mht, and change the title to The Virtual Assistant.
2. Insert a centered, open table with 2 columns and 2 rows.
3. In Column B, Row 1, center and type The Virtual Assistant.
4. In Column B, Row 2, center and type these lines:

   901 S. Rainbow, Suite 1
   Las Vegas, Nevada 89145
   888-555-3499
   email@TVA.com

5. Merge the cells in Column A, and insert a picture related to an office or business.
6. Resize the picture proportionally until it is about 2 inches wide, and center the picture.
7. Move the insertion point under the table, and press ENTER 1 time,
8. Type the following line centered, using the pipe symbol with 1 space before and after it as shown here. This line will be referred to as the link bar from now on.

   Home | Services | Fees | References

   Note: The pipe symbol is above the backslash symbol on most keyboards.
9. Press ENTER 2 times, and insert a centered, open table with 2 columns and 7 rows.
10. Merge the cells in Row 1, and type the information shown on page 448 in Row 1.
11. Move to Row 3, and continue typing the rest of the table as arranged on page 448, leaving Row 2 and Row 5 empty.
12. Save the page, view the Web page in a browser, and compare the browser view with the layout view in your word processor.

Do you need a skilled assistant who works tirelessly on your documents, doesn't need any office space, and gives your work that personal touch? The Virtual Assistant is a professional document processing and design service that will help create the professional image your business demands.

You don't get a second chance at a first impression. The graphics experts in our word processing and desktop publishing departments will make sure your documents look gorgeous. Our editors, who have completed a series of rigorous courses in business English and business communications, will make sure your documents are letter perfect. Please browse around our site for details.

≡ organization

≡ course

Word Processing	Desktop Publishing
Correspondence	Newsletters
Reports	Brochures
Proposals	Letterheads
Manuals	Resumes
Layout Editing	Copy Editing
In-house Styles	Proofreading
Custom Styles	Technical Editing
Master Documents	Grammar Checking
Table of Contents	Writing Style
Indexes	

> Reminder: You will finish building the Web site in Lessons 112 through 115.

(Continued on next page)

The·Virtual·Assistant¤ ¤
901·S.·Rainbow,·Suite·1¶ ¤
Las·Vegas,·Nevada·89145¶
888-555-3499¶
email@TVA.com¤

¶
Home·|·Services·|·Fees·|·References¶
¶

Do·you·need·a·skilled·assistant·who·works·tirelessly·on·your·documents,·doesn't·need·any·office- ¤
space,·and·gives·your·work·that·personal·touch?·The·Virtual·Assistant·is·a·professional·document-
processing·and·design·service·that·will·help·create·the·professional·image·your·business·
demands.¶
¶
You·don't·get·a·second·chance·at·a·first·impression.·The·graphics·experts·in·our·word·processing-
and·desktop·publishing·departments·will·make·sure·your·documents·look·gorgeous.·Our·editors,·
who·have·completed·a·series·of·rigorous·courses·in·business·English·and·business·
communications,·will·make·sure·they·are·letter·perfect.·Please·browse·around·our·site·for·details.¤

¤	¤	¤
Word·Processing¤	Desktop·Publishing¤	¤
Correspondence¶	Newsletters¶	¤
Reports¶	Brochures¶	
Proposals¶	Letterheads¶	
Manuals¤	Resumes¤	
¤	¤	¤
Layout·Editing¤	Copy·Editing¤	¤
In-house·Styles¶	Proofreading¶	¤
Custom·Styles¶	Technical·Editing¶	
Master·Documents¶	Grammar·Checking¶	
Table·of·Contents¶	Writing·Style¤	
Indexes¤		

¶

Web layout view of home page.

Report 111-88

Your Web Site

Plan and write the content for a Web site for a business of your own to include a home page and three related pages very similar to the Web pages in this unit. You may want to look ahead to the finished Web site on pages 465–466 for ideas. The Web site that starts in this lesson is continued through Lesson 114.

1. Save Report-111-88.doc as a Web page named Report-111-88.mht, and change the title to the name of the business.
2. Insert a centered, open table with 2 rows and 2 columns.
3. In Column B, Row 1, center and type the name of the Web site.
4. In Column B, Row 2, center and type the mailing address and e-mail address of the business.
5. Merge the cells in Column A, and insert a picture related to the business.
6. Resize and align the picture proportionally as needed.
7. Move the insertion point under the table, and press ENTER 1 time.

8. Type the following line centered using the pipe symbol with 1 space before and after it as shown here. This line will be referred to as the link bar from now on.

    Home | Services | Fees | References

    Note: The pipe symbol is above the backslash symbol on most keyboards.

9. Press ENTER 2 times, and insert a centered, open table with 2 columns and 7 rows.
10. Merge the cells in Row 1, and type the desired introductory information in the first row.
11. Move to Row 3, and continue typing the rest of the headings and information, as is done in Report 111-87, leaving Row 2 and Row 5 empty.
12. Save the page, view the Web page in a browser, and compare the browser view with the layout view in your word processor.

Creating More Web Pages

Goals

- Type at least 50wpm/5'/5e
- Create more Web pages

A. Type 2 times.

A. WARMUP

```
1       Missy examined these items: the #426 oil painting, a      11
2   Bowes & Elkjer porcelain vase, and the 86-piece collection    23
3   of glazed antique pitchers. There were 337 people present.    34
    | 1 | 2 | 3 | 4 | 5 | 6 | 7 | 8 | 9 | 10 | 11 | 12
```

SKILLBUILDING

B. PROGRESSIVE PRACTICE: NUMBERS

If you are not using the GDP software, turn to page SB-11 and follow the directions for this activity.

LANGUAGE ARTS

C. Study the rules at the right.

C. CAPITALIZATION

RULE ▶
≡ organization

Capitalize common organizational terms (such as *advertising department* and *finance committee*) only when they are the actual names of the units in the writer's own organization and when they are preceded by the word *the*.

The report from the Advertising Department is due today.

But: Our advertising department will submit its report today.

RULE ▶
≡ course

Capitalize the names of specific course titles but not the names of subjects or areas of study.

I have enrolled in Accounting 201 and will also take the marketing course.

Edit the sentences to correct any errors in capitalization.

```
4   The advertising department at their firm is excellent.
5   The Finance Committee here at Irwin will meet today.
6   I think I am going to pass keyboarding 1 with flying colors.
7   Their marketing department must approve the proposal first.
8   A class in Business Communications would be very helpful.
9   To take Math 102, you must have taken a beginning math course.
```

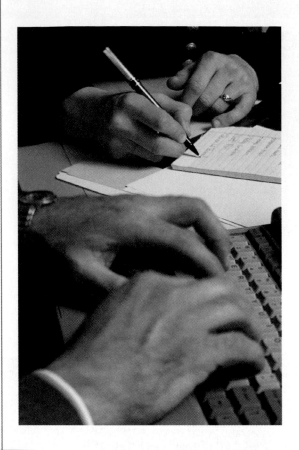

D. Take two 5-minute timed writings. Review your speed and errors.

Goal: At least 50wpm/5′/5e

D. | **5-MINUTE TIMED WRITING**

10	Employers want the people who work for them to have	11
11	many qualities of good character. Character is defined as a	23
12	distinctive feature of a person or thing. Character may be	34
13	what you are known for and may be why you remember someone	46
14	else. What are some of the traits you think of that are	57
15	linked with good character? A few traits might be respect,	69
16	honesty, trust, caring, leadership, attitude, tolerance,	81
17	fairness, and patience.	85
18	All people should have respect for themselves and for	96
19	others. If you respect people, you have a high regard for	108
20	the way they conduct themselves in all aspects of life.	119
21	However, before you can respect others, you need to have	131
22	respect for yourself.	135
23	Honesty and trustworthiness are similar traits. In	145
24	business dealings, people expect honesty and will admire	157
25	people who have this quality. They like to build business	168
26	relationships with companies whose employees are honest,	180
27	just, and trustworthy.	184
28	Your attitude is reflected in the way you act toward	195
29	other people or in the way you speak to them. You can make	207
30	great strides in advancing your career by taking a look at	219
31	the way you interact with people. You may want to take a	230
32	closer look at some character traits you want to improve.	242
33	Such improvements in life will amaze you.	250

| 1 | 2 | 3 | 4 | 5 | 6 | 7 | 8 | 9 | 10 | 11 | 12

Follow these steps to create a new services page for the Web site named Report-112-89.mht. Refer to the Web layout view of the services page on page 452 as needed. Make the following changes:

1. Change the title to Services.
2. Select and delete the table below the link bar.

3. Type Services centered on the second blank line below the link bar, and press ENTER 2 times.
4. Insert a centered open table with 1 cell.
5. Type the information below inside the table as shown in the Web layout view of the services page.
6. Save the page, and view the Web page in a browser.

Word Processing¶

We prepare documents with a professional look for correspondence of all types as well as reports, proposals, manuals, and so on.¶

Desktop Publishing¶

Our professional design specialists will create newsletters, brochures, letterheads, and other documents that are sure to capture your imagination.¶

Layout Editing¶

Our layout editors will transform your documents using in-house styles or custom styles. For your longer projects, they are experts at building master documents that include a cover page, table of contents, and index.¶

Copy Editing¶

Our copy editors will make sure that your document content is perfect. Proofreading, grammar, and writing style will all be checked so that your ideas are expressed clearly and effectively.

(Continued on next page)

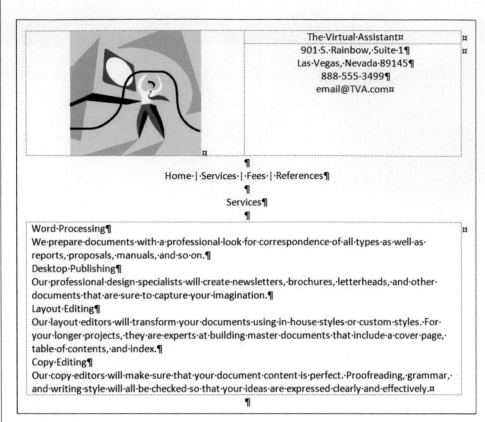

The·Virtual·Assistant¤
901·S.·Rainbow,·Suite·1¶
Las·Vegas,·Nevada·89145¶
888-555-3499¶
email@TVA.com¤

¶
Home·|·Services·|·Fees·|·References¶
¶
Services¶
¶

Word·Processing¶
We·prepare·documents·with·a·professional·look·for·correspondence·of·all·types·as·well·as·
reports,·proposals,·manuals,·and·so·on.¶
Desktop·Publishing¶
Our·professional·design·specialists·will·create·newsletters,·brochures,·letterheads,·and·other·
documents·that·are·sure·to·capture·your·imagination.¶
Layout·Editing¶
Our·layout·editors·will·transform·your·documents·using·in-house·styles·or·custom·styles.·For·
your·longer·projects,·they·are·experts·at·building·master·documents·that·include·a·cover·page,·
table·of·contents,·and·index.¶
Copy·Editing¶
Our·copy·editors·will·make·sure·that·your·document·content·is·perfect.·Proofreading,·grammar,·
and·writing·style·will·all·be·checked·so·that·your·ideas·are·expressed·clearly·and·effectively.¤
¶

Web layout view of services page.

Report 112-90

Your Web Site (continued)

Follow these steps to create a new services page for your Web site named Report 112-90.mht similar to the Web layout view of the services page on this page. Make the following changes:

1. Change the title to Services.
2. Select and delete the table below the link bar.
3. Type Services centered on the second blank line below the link bar, and press ENTER 2 times.
4. Create a centered open table with 1 cell.
5. Inside the table, type four headings followed by one or two sentences, each describing the services of your business.
6. Save the page, and view the Web page in a browser.

Creating Web Pages With Hyperlinks

Goals

- Improve speed and accuracy
- Refine language arts skills in composing
- Create Web pages with hyperlinks

A. Type 2 times.

A. WARMUP

```
1        Did you hear the excellent quartet of junior cadets?    11
2   Everybody in the crowd (estimated at over 500) applauded    22
3   "with gusto." The sizable crowd filled the 3/4-acre park.   34
    |  1  |  2  |  3  |  4  |  5  |  6  |  7  |  8  |  9  |  10  |  11  |  12
```

SKILLBUILDING

B. DIAGNOSTIC PRACTICE: SYMBOLS AND PUNCTUATION

If you are not using the GDP software, turn to page SB-2 and follow the directions for this activity.

C. Type the columns 2 times. Press TAB to move from column to column.

C. TECHNIQUE PRACTICE: TAB KEY

```
4   T. Waters     L. Vigil      S. Zimmerly   D. Colwell   C. Foster
5   M. Goldbach   R. Hempker    G. Beckert    M. Kinsey    A. Lucero
6   C. Maclean    J. Nichols    I. Ohlsen     R. Parlee    S. Quale
7   J. Rondeau    G. Snowden    Y. Tokita     C. Upton     C. Vaughn
```

LANGUAGE ARTS

D. COMPOSING A PERSONAL-BUSINESS LETTER

Compose a two-paragraph personal-business letter that summarizes the content of the Web site design guidelines on page 446. Address the letter to your instructor; provide a suitable inside address and salutation for your letter. Also, provide a complimentary closing and sign the letter yourself.

In the letter, discuss the following:
Paragraph 1. Describe how to plan an effective Web site.
Paragraph 2. Describe how to design an effective Web site.

E. HYPERLINKS

Hyperlinks are powerful navigational tools that are critical to the overall plan and design of a Web site. When clicked, they move a visitor from one page or one location on a page to another.

When you create a hyperlink, you must indicate the target. The hyperlink can point to the same page, to a different page, to another site, or perhaps to an e-mail address. You can assign a hyperlink to a word, a group of words, or a picture.

The presence of a text hyperlink is usually indicated by text that is underlined in a color different from that used on the rest of the words on the page. Also, the mouse pointer changes to a hand shape when hovering over a hyperlink.

Word Processing Manual

F. WORD PROCESSING: WEB PAGE—HYPERLINKS

Study Lesson 113 in your word processing manual. Complete all of the shaded steps while at your computer. Then format the jobs that follow.

DOCUMENT PROCESSING

Report 113-91

Web Site (continued)

Follow these steps to create a new fees page for the Web site named Report-113-91.mht. Refer to the Web layout view of the fees page on page 455 as needed. Make the following changes:

1. Change the title to Fees.
2. Change Services to Fees on the second blank line below the link bar.
3. Move inside the table below "Services," and select and delete the information inside the table.
4. Type the information below inside the table as shown in the Web layout view of the fees page.
5. Save the page, and view the Web page in a browser.

The Virtual Assistant strives to work within your organization's budget. We will review your individual needs and tailor the pricing to fit your project. We welcome the opportunity to provide an individual estimate. Be assured that our prices are extremely competitive. Here are some general guidelines regarding our fees:
¶
We typically charge by the hour or by the page, depending upon the job. ¶
Most fees are based on the length of the document and the amount of editing deemed necessary. ¶
We offer substantial discounts for volume work and repeat clients. ¶
A surcharge is added for rush jobs. ¶
Payment for services rendered should be made by credit card, check, or money order. ¶
¶
For a copy of our current rate guide, please send an e-mail message to rateguide@TVA.com. ¶

(Continued on next page)

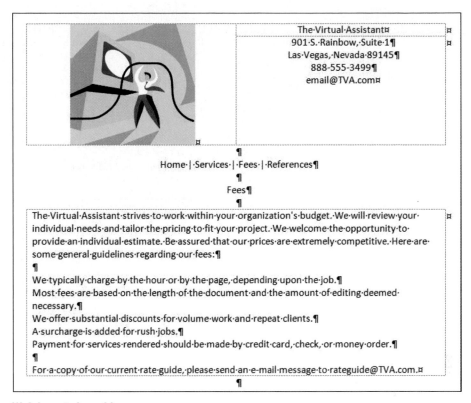

The Virtual Assistant¤

901 S. Rainbow, Suite 1¶
Las Vegas, Nevada 89145¶
888-555-3499¶
email@TVA.com¤

¶
Home | Services | Fees | References¶
¶
Fees¶
¶

The Virtual Assistant strives to work within your organization's budget. We will review your individual needs and tailor the pricing to fit your project. We welcome the opportunity to provide an individual estimate. Be assured that our prices are extremely competitive. Here are some general guidelines regarding our fees:¶
¶
We typically charge by the hour or by the page, depending upon the job.¶
Most fees are based on the length of the document and the amount of editing deemed necessary.¶
We offer substantial discounts for volume work and repeat clients.¶
A surcharge is added for rush jobs.¶
Payment for services rendered should be made by credit card, check, or money order.¶
¶
For a copy of our current rate guide, please send an e-mail message to rateguide@TVA.com.¤
¶

Web layout view of fees page.

Report 113-92

Web Site (continued)

Follow these steps to insert hyperlinks on the link bar for the fees page. Make the following changes:

1. Insert three text hyperlinks for the first three words on the link bar as follows:

   Home links to Report-111-87a.mht
   Services links to Report-112-89a.mht
   Fees links to Report-113-92.mht

2. Navigate to Report-111-87a.mht (the home page) and Report-112-89a.mht (the services page).

3. Insert three text hyperlinks for the first three words on the link bar for each page just as you did in step 1.

4. On Report-111-87a.mht (the home page), insert four more text hyperlinks for each of the four headings on the home page ("Word Processing," "Desktop Publishing," "Layout Editing," and "Copy Editing") to link to the services page, Report-112-89a.mht.

5. Save all pages, test all the hyperlinks, and edit any hyperlinks as needed.

(Continued on next page)

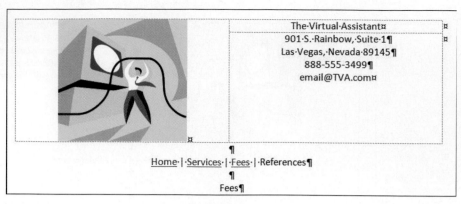

The·Virtual·Assistant¤

901·S.·Rainbow,·Suite·1¶

Las·Vegas,·Nevada·89145¶

888-555-3499¶

email@TVA.com¤

¤

Home·|·Services·|·Fees·|·References¶

¶

Fees¶

Web layout view of fees page with hyperlinks.

¤		¤		¤
Word·Processing¤		Desktop·Publishing¤		¤
Correspondence¶		Newsletters¶		¤
Reports¶		Brochures¶		
Proposals¶		Letterheads¶		
Manuals¤		Resumes¤		
¤		¤		¤
Layout·Editing¤		Copy·Editing¤		¤
In-house·Styles¶		Proofreading¶		¤
Custom·Styles¶		Technical·Editing¶		
Master·Documents¶		Grammar·Checking¶		
Table·of·Contents¶		Writing·Style¤		
Indexes¤				

Web layout view of home page with hyperlinks.

Report 113-93

Your Web Site (continued)

Follow these steps to create a new page for your Web site named Report-113-93.mht similar to the Web layout view of the fees page on this page. Make the following changes:

1. Change the title to Fees.
2. Change Services to Fees on the second blank line below the link bar.

3. Move inside the table below "Services," and select and delete the information inside the table.
4. Type content similar to the fees page on page 455.
5. Save the page, and view the Web page in a browser.

Report 113-94

Your Web Site (continued)

Follow these steps to insert hyperlinks on the link bar for the fees page. Make the following changes:

1. Insert three text hyperlinks for the first three words on the link bar as follows:

   Home links to Report-111-88.mht
   Services links to Report-112-90.mht
   Fees links to Report-113-94.mht

2. Navigate to Report-111-88.mht (the home page) and Report-112-90.mht (the services page).

3. Insert three text hyperlinks for the first three words on the link bar for each page just as you did in step 2.
4. On Report-111-88.mht (the home page), insert four more text hyperlinks for each of the four headings on your home page to link to the services page, Report-112-90.mht.
5. Save all pages, test all the hyperlinks, and edit any hyperlinks as needed.

Creating More Web Pages With Hyperlinks

Goals

- Type at least 50wpm/5'/5e
- Create more Web pages with hyperlinks

A. Type 2 times.

A. WARMUP

```
1        This series* (*6 films, 28 minutes) by J. Zeller goes   11
2   beyond the "basics" of computers. Viewers keep requesting    23
3   an extension on the dates; this includes 3/2, 5/5, and 8/9.  34
    |  1  |  2  |  3  |  4  |  5  |  6  |  7  |  8  |  9  |  10  |  11  |  12
```

SKILLBUILDING

B. MAP

Follow the GDP software directions for this exercise in improving keystroking accuracy.

Keyboarding Connection

Using Hypertext

Do you know how to surf the Web? It's easy! The Web contains pages, which are blocks of text, visuals, sound, or animation. Hypertext is a format in which certain words in the text of a Web page are highlighted, underlined, or colored differently from the other words. These colored or highlighted words link to other pages on the Web.

When you point to a hyperlink and click the mouse button, the page connected to that word is displayed. Therefore, one page on the Web can link to many other pages. Hypertext pages do not have to be read in any specific order.

Hypertext enables you to connect and retrieve Web pages from computer networks worldwide. With hypertext, you can point and click or surf your way all over the Web.

YOUR TURN Open a page on the Web. Surf the Web using the hyperlinks displayed on the page.

C. Take two 5-minute timed writings. Review your speed and errors.

Goal: At least 50wpm/5'/5e

C. 5-MINUTE TIMED WRITING

4	Before you apply for jobs, you will want to do some	11
5	detective work. First, choose a business for which you want	23
6	to work and then use the Internet to find out about the	34
7	company. If you find a Web site for the business, then you	46
8	can learn all about the company, its hiring policies, the	57
9	job listings, and how to apply for a job opening.	67
10	When you are researching a company, you want to learn	78
11	about the history of the company. You may be able to find	90
12	out how stock analysts expect the company stock to perform	102
13	in the coming months if the company is publicly held.	112
14	When you find a job opening for which you know that	123
15	you want to apply, read carefully to see what type of work	135
16	experience and education the company requires for the job.	147
17	When you prepare your resume, emphasize your qualifications	159
18	based on the requirements listed for the job. If the person	171
19	who should receive job inquiries is not listed, contact the	183
20	company by phone or e-mail to get a name. Personalize your	194
21	cover letter and resume, if possible, for the company.	205
22	The information you find in your research will be	217
23	very helpful during the interview with a representative of	228
24	the company. Ask good questions and speak confidently about	240
25	the job. Emphasize how your skills would be valuable.	250

| 1 | 2 | 3 | 4 | 5 | 6 | 7 | 8 | 9 | 10 | 11 | 12

Report 114-95

Web Site (continued)

Follow these steps to create a new references page for the Web site named Report-114-95.mht. Refer to the Web layout view of the references page on page 460 as needed. Make the following changes:

1. Change the title to References.
2. Change Fees to References on the second blank line below the link bar.

3. Move inside the table below "References," and select and delete the information inside the table.
4. Type the information below inside the table as shown in the Web layout view of the references page.
5. Save the page, and view the Web page in a browser.

↓2X

I've been in a highly successful business for over 10 years and attribute much of that success to the skilled professionals at The Virtual Assistant. I am always confident that my work will go out error-free. They are top-notch professionals and can work for my team anytime! ↓2X

Mike Rashid
Network Engineer
Denver, Colorado ↓4X

The documents produced by The Virtual Assistant are impeccable! I can count on professional, reliable, competent, and efficient service without question. It is so easy to send documents back and forth via the Internet, and we all know that time is money. I highly recommend TVA for any of your word processing needs. ↓2X

Nancy Shipley
Attorney-at-Law
Chicago, Illinois ↓2X

(Continued on next page)

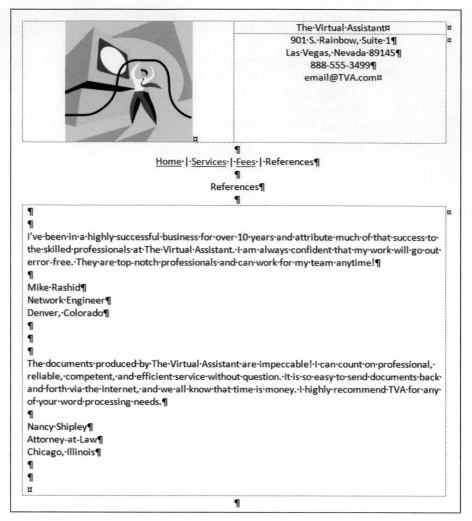

The·Virtual·Assistant¤
901·S.·Rainbow,·Suite·1¶
Las·Vegas,·Nevada·89145¶
888-555-3499¶
email@TVA.com¤

Home·|·Services·|·Fees·|·References¶
References¶

I've·been·in·a·highly·successful·business·for·over·10·years·and·attribute·much·of·that·success·to·the·skilled·professionals·at·The·Virtual·Assistant.·I·am·always·confident·that·my·work·will·go·out·error-free.·They·are·top-notch·professionals·and·can·work·for·my·team·anytime!¶

Mike·Rashid¶
Network·Engineer¶
Denver,·Colorado¶

The·documents·produced·by·The·Virtual·Assistant·are·impeccable!·I·can·count·on·professional,·reliable,·competent,·and·efficient·service·without·question.·It·is·so·easy·to·send·documents·back·and·forth·via·the·Internet,·and·we·all·know·that·time·is·money.·I·highly·recommend·TVA·for·any·of·your·word·processing·needs.¶

Nancy·Shipley¶
Attorney-at-Law¶
Chicago,·Illinois¶

Web layout view of references page.

Report 114-96

Web Site (continued)

Follow these steps to insert any missing hyperlinks on the link bar for all pages. Make the following changes:

1. Insert a text hyperlink for the last word on the link bar as follows:
   References links to Report-114-96.mht.

2. Navigate to Report-111-87b.mht (the home page), Report-112-89b.mht (the services page), and Report-113-92a.mht (the fees page).

3. Insert any missing text hyperlinks on the link bar for each page as needed.

4. Save all pages, test all the hyperlinks, and edit any hyperlinks as needed.

Report
114-97

Your Web Site
(continued)

Follow these steps to create a new references page for your Web site named Report-114-97.mht similar to the Web layout view of the references page on page 460. Make the following changes:

1. Change the title to References.
2. Change Fees to References on the second blank line below the link bar.

3. Move inside the table below "References," and select and delete the information inside the table.
4. Type the information for two references; follow the setup for the references page on page 460.
5. Save the page, and view the Web page in a browser.

Report
114-98

Your Web Site
(continued)

Follow these steps to insert any missing hyperlinks on the link bar for all pages of your Web site. Make the following changes:

1. Insert a text hyperlink for the last word on the link bar as follows:
   References links to Report-114-98.mht.

2. Navigate to Report-111-88.mht (the home page), Report-112-90.mht (the services page), and Report-113-94.mht (the fees page).
3. Insert any missing text hyperlinks on the link bar for each page as needed.
4. Save all pages. To test these hyperlinks, point to each hyperlink and read the screen tip. Edit any hyperlinks as needed.

Formatting Web Pages

Goals

- Improve speed and accuracy
- Refine language arts skills in proofreading
- Format Web pages

A. Type 2 times.

A. WARMUP

```
1        Contact bxvacuum@clean.com to order the large-sized      11
2   grips. They were just lowered to $160 from $240 (a 33 1/3%    22
3   markdown). Jay's #55 quilts were reduced to $88 from $99.     34
   |  1  |  2  |  3  |  4  |  5  |  6  |  7  |  8  |  9  |  10  |  11  |  12
```

SKILLBUILDING

PPP PRETEST → PRACTICE → POSTTEST

PRETEST
Take a 1-minute timed writing. Review your speed and errors.

B. PRETEST: Common Letter Combinations

```
4        He did mention that they are sending a lawful taping     11
5   of the comedy format to a performing combo. A motion to       22
6   commit a useful option forced a fusion of forty persons.      33
   |  1  |  2  |  3  |  4  |  5  |  6  |  7  |  8  |  9  |  10  |  11  |  12
```

PRACTICE
Speed Emphasis:
If you made no more than 1 error on the Pretest, type each *individual* line twice.
Accuracy Emphasis:
If you made 3 or more errors, type each *group* of lines (as though it were a paragraph) 2 times.

C. PRACTICE: Word Beginnings

```
7   for forty forth format former forget forest forearm forbear
8   per peril perky period permit person peruse perform persist
9   com combo comic combat commit common combed compose complex
```

D. PRACTICE: Word Endings

```
10  ing doing mixing living filing taping sending biking hiding
11  ion onion nation lotion motion option mention fusion legion
12  ful awful useful joyful earful lawful helpful sinful armful
```

POSTTEST
Repeat the Pretest timed writing and compare performance.

E. POSTTEST: Common Letter Combinations

F. SUSTAINED PRACTICE: CAPITALIZATION

F. Take a 1-minute timed writing on the first paragraph to establish your base speed. Then take four 1-minute timed writings on the remaining paragraphs. As soon as you equal or exceed your base speed on one paragraph, advance to the next, more difficult paragraph.

```
13   Even though he was only about thirty years old, Jason    11
14   knew that it was not too soon to begin thinking about his   23
15   retirement. He soon found out that there were many things   34
16   involved in his plans for an early and long retirement.     45

17   Even without considering the uncertainty of social        10
18   security, Jason knew that he should plan his career moves   22
19   so that he would have a strong company retirement plan. He  34
20   realized that he should have an Individual Retirement Plan. 45

21   When he became aware that The Longman Company, the        10
22   firm that employed him, would match his contributions to a  22
23   supplemental retirement account, he began saving even more. 34
24   He used the Payroll Department funds from the Goplin Group. 46

25   He also learned that The Longman Company retirement       11
26   plan, his Individual Retirement Plan, and his supplemental  22
27   retirement account are all deferred savings. With those    33
28   tax-dollar savings, Jason bought New Venture Group mutuals. 45
```

LANGUAGE ARTS

G. Edit this paragraph to correct any typing or formatting errors.

G. PROOFREADING

```
29   The idea and practise of sharing risk originated in
30   antiquetry. Many years ago, Chinese merchants deviced an
31   injenious way of protecting themselves against the chance
32   of a financialy ruinous accadent in the dangerous river
33   along the trade routtes when they were delivring goods.
```

FORMATTING

H. MORE WEB SITE DESIGN GUIDELINES

Follow these guidelines to design effective Web sites:

- Experiment with the themes that come with most programs.
- If you use a theme, experiment with the embedded styles that can be applied to titles, headings, subheadings, and so on, for design consistency.

- Choose a consistent look for headings and subheadings, including font size, color, and alignment, for design unity.
- Use color to establish moods: black is somber; white is clean, organized, or sterile; bright colors are energetic but may be hard to read. Experiment and use your judgment.

I. WORD PROCESSING: WEB PAGE—DESIGN THEMES

Study Lesson 115 in your word processing manual. Complete all of the shaded steps while at your computer. Then format the jobs that follow.

DOCUMENT PROCESSING

Report 115-99

Web Site (continued)

Follow these steps to format the Web site.

1. Navigate to Report-111-87c.mht (the home page), Report-112-89c.mht (the services page), Report-113-92b.mht (the fees page), and Report-114-96a.mht (the references page).
2. Apply a design theme, page background, and font colors to each page that coordinate with the picture at the top of each page. Remove any table borders as needed or if desired.
3. Move to each page, and apply a Heading 1 style to "The Virtual Assistant." Align the text and adjust the table as needed to position the picture and text attractively. Copy and paste the table from one page to the next if desired.
4. Move to the home page, and add a bullet to each item under each heading beginning with the heading "Word Processing."
5. Apply a Heading 3 style to each heading beginning with the heading "Word Processing."
6. Move to the services page, apply a Heading 2 style to "Services," center the line, and delete the blank line above the link bar.
7. Add a bullet to each sentence under each heading.
8. Apply a Heading 3 style to each heading beginning with "Word Processing."
9. Move to the fees page, apply a Heading 2 style to "Fees," center the line, and delete the blank line above the link bar.
10. Add a bullet to each sentence under the first paragraph except for the last sentence on the page.
11. Insert a horizontal line in the blank line after the last bulleted item.
12. Move to the references page, apply a Heading 2 style to "References," center the line, and delete the blank line above the link bar.
13. Place the insertion point in front of the first blank line in the table, and insert a horizontal line.
14. Place the insertion point in front of the second blank line between the references, and insert a horizontal line.
15. Place the insertion point in front of the second blank line under the last reference, and insert a horizontal line.
16. Decrease any indents on lists and change any themes, page backgrounds, styles, font colors, borders, or colors as desired.
17. Test all the hyperlinks, edit any hyperlinks as needed, and save all pages.
18. View your finished Web site in a browser.

Note: If you would like to format the Web site you created for your own business in Lessons 111–114, follow steps similar to those in Report 115-99.

Keyboarding Connection

Choosing a Different Home Page

You don't have to start at the same home page every time you use your browser. You can change the browser's home page to start at one of your favorite Web pages. Here's how to do it.

In Netscape, go to the chosen page and select Preferences from the Edit menu. Click the Navigator category in the Preferences dialog box. Click the Use Current Page button in the "home page" area. Choose Home Page in the "Navigator starts with" area. Click OK.

In Internet Explorer, from the chosen page select Internet Options from the Tools menu. Click the General tab, and then click the Use Current button in the "home page" area. Click OK.

YOUR TURN Using your browser, access a favorite Web page. Make it your browser's home page.

The Virtual Assistant

901 S. Rainbow, Suite 1
Las Vegas, Nevada 89145
888-555-3499
email@TVA.com

Home | Services | Fees | References

Do you need a skilled assistant who works tirelessly on your documents, doesn't need any office space, and gives your work that personal touch? The Virtual Assistant is a professional document processing and design service that will help create the professional image your business demands.

You don't get a second chance at a first impression. The graphics experts in our word processing and desktop publishing departments will make sure your documents look gorgeous. Our editors, who have completed a series of rigorous courses in business English and business communications, will make sure they are letter perfect. Please browse around our site for details.

Word Processing
- Correspondence
- Reports
- Proposals
- Manuals

Desktop Publishing
- Newsletters
- Brochures
- Letterheads
- Resumes

Layout Editing
- In-house Styles
- Custom
- Master
- Table of
- Indexes

Copy Editing
- Proofreading

The Virtual Assistant

901 S. Rainbow, Suite 1
Las Vegas, Nevada 89145
888-555-3499
email@TVA.com

Home | Services | Fees | References

Services

Word Processing
- We prepare documents with a professional look for correspondence of all types as well as reports, proposals, manuals, and so on.

Desktop Publishing
- Our professional design specialists will create newsletters, brochures, letterheads, and other documents that are sure to capture your imagination.

Layout Editing
- Our layout editors will transform your documents using in-house styles or custom styles. For your longer projects, they are experts at building master documents that include a cover page, table of contents, and index.

Copy Editing
- Our copy editors will make sure that your document content is perfect. Proofreading, grammar, and writing style will all be checked so that your ideas are expressed clearly and effectively.

(Continued on next page)

The Virtual Assistant

901 S. Rainbow, Suite 1
Las Vegas, Nevada 89145
888-555-3499
email@TVA.com

Home | Services | Fees | References

Fees

The Virtual Assistant strives to work within your organization's budget. We will review your individual needs and tailor the pricing to fit your project. We welcome the opportunity to provide an individual estimate. Be assured that our prices are extremely competitive. Here are some general guidelines regarding our fees:

- We typically charge by the hour or by the page, depending upon the job.
- Most fees are based on the length of the document and the amount of editing deemed necessary.
- We offer substantial discounts for volume work and repeat clients.
- A surcharge is added for rush jobs.
- Payment for services rendered should be made by credit card, check, or money order.

For a copy of our current rate guide, please send an e-mail message to rateguide@TVA.com.

The Virtual Assistant

901 S. Rainbow, Suite 1
Las Vegas, Nevada 89145
888-555-3499
email@TVA.com

Home | Services | Fees | References

References

I've been in a highly successful business for over 10 years and attribute much of that success to the skilled professionals at The Virtual Assistant. I am always confident that my work will go out error-free. They are top-notch professionals and can work for my team anytime!

Mike Rashid
Network Engineer
Denver, Colorado

The documents produced by The Virtual Assistant are impeccable! I can count on professional, reliable, competent, and efficient service without question. It is so easy to send documents back and forth via the Internet, and we all know that time is money. I highly recommend TVA for any of your word processing needs.

Nancy Shipley
Attorney-at-Law
Chicago, Illinois

Follow these steps to create the home page and Contact Us page for this Web site:

1. Change the title of Report-115-100.mht to In The Game, Home.
2. Press ENTER 1 time, and insert home-115a.mht into the home page (Report-115-100A.mht).
3. Leave Report-115-100.mht open, and create an additional new Web page named Report-115-100B; change the title to In The Game, Contact Us.
4. Insert the file contactus-115b.mht into Report-115-100B.mht.
5. Insert a picture related to sports in the open cell in Column A on the Contact Us page (Report-115-100B.mht).
6. Resize the picture proportionally until it is about 1 inch wide, and center the picture in the open cell in Column A on the Contact Us page.
7. Apply a design theme, page background, and font colors to the Contact Us page that coordinate with the picture.
8. Apply a Heading 1 style to "In The Game," and center the line on the Contact Us page.
9. Apply a Heading 3 style to the headings "E-Mail," "Call Us," and "Snail Mail" on the Contact Us page.
10. Select the table and the link bar at the top of the Contact Us page, copy it, move to the top of the home page, and paste it.
11. Apply the same design theme to the home page that you used on the Contact Us page.
12. Apply a Heading 3 style to the headings "Baseball and Softball," "Soccer, Track and Field," and "Gymnastics" on the home page.
13. Change any styles, fonts, borders, or colors as desired on both pages.
14. Insert text hyperlinks on the link bar of each page as follows:
    Home links to Report-115-100.mht
    Contact Us links to Report-115-100B.mht
15. Test all the hyperlinks, edit any hyperlinks as needed, and save all pages.
16. View your finished Web site in a browser.

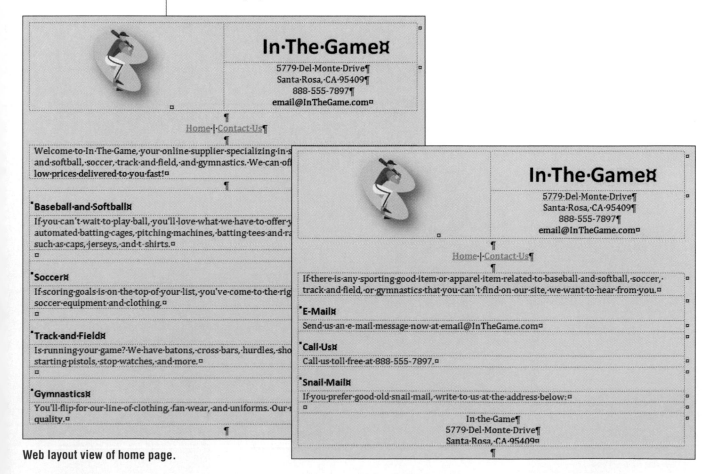

Web layout view of home page.

Web layout view of contact us page.

Unit 24

Skillbuilding and In-Basket Review

Suite Retreat

3539 Shell Basket Lane
Sanibel Island, Florida 33957
941-555-3422
email@SuiteRetreat.com

Home | Rates

Are you ready to experience a private beach retreat with warm waters, ~~~kies?~~ The personnel at Suite Retreat are at ~~~~~ your stay is a pleasurable one.

~~~~ a private beach on the Gulf of Mexico at the ~~~~ You will feel the soothing effects of our ~~~~ charming cottage suites the moment you ~~~~uite is beautifully decorated and appointed ~~~~ whirlpools for your personal use. Click here for

~~~~ recreation during your stay, we have a variety ~~~~operty:

~~~~ennis courts

~~~~g, you will find a small golf course and ~~~~valking distance about a half mile farther

All-City, Inc.
17 North Eighth Street   Columbia, MO 65201   800-555-9981   www.ACI.com

Insuring you at home

SRU Sunwear

Sports 'R Us
3939 Townsgate Drive
San Diego, CA 92130
www.SRU.com

In-Basket Review (Insurance)

Goals

- Type at least 50wpm/5′/5e
- Format documents used in the insurance industry

A. Type 2 times.

A. WARMUP

```
1      He realized that exactly 10% of the budget ($62,475)    11
2  was questionable. Several key people reviewed it; most of    22
3  them wanted to reject about 1/3 of the proposed line items!  34
   | 1 | 2 | 3 | 4 | 5 | 6 | 7 | 8 | 9 | 10 | 11 | 12
```

SKILLBUILDING

B. PROGRESSIVE PRACTICE: ALPHABET

If you are not using the GDP software, turn to page SB-7 and follow the directions for this activity.

Strategies for Career Success

Managing Group Conflict

Not all team members have the same opinion or approach to solving a problem. Before a group can reach an agreement, conflicts must be addressed and expressed openly. Follow these steps to manage group conflict.

Take everyone's feelings and opinions seriously. Don't be afraid to disagree. Offer and accept constructive criticism. Find points of agreement. When the group makes a decision, support it fully.

Be a good listener. Take notes, maintain eye contact, restate what you hear, and listen for the emotions behind the words. Try to view the situation through the other person's eyes. Don't jump to conclusions. Ask nonthreatening questions to clarify meaning, and listen without interrupting. Most group conflicts don't get resolved until everyone feels he or she has had a chance to be heard.

YOUR TURN When is the last time you had a conflict with a coworker? What did you do about it? What was the result?

C. Take two 5-minute timed writings. Review your speed and errors.

Goal: At least 50wpm/5'/5e

C. 5-MINUTE TIMED WRITING

```
 4        Several factors should be considered before you buy a     11
 5  new printer for your computer. First, decide how you will       23
 6  use the new printer. If you plan to use the printer for         34
 7  composing letters or reports, you may want to shop for an       45
 8  ink jet printer that is reasonably priced and capable of        57
 9  doing general tasks. If you are purchasing the printer for      69
10  office use, you may wish to shop for a printer that prints      80
11  documents more quickly and of exceptional quality. Finally,    92
12  if you plan to use a digital camera with the printer, you      104
13  will want a printer that is designed to print documents of     116
14  photo quality.                                                 119
15        Resolution, speed, and paper handling are some other     130
16  factors you should consider when you purchase a printer.       141
17  Resolution refers to how sharp the image appears on the        152
18  paper. With printers producing a higher resolution, the        163
19  imaging gives you higher-quality output. You will see this     175
20  amazing difference in imaging when you compare some samples    187
21  of print from the other kinds of printers.                     196
22        If you expect to print long documents, then you will     207
23  want to look for a reliable printer with a feed tray that      218
24  holds large amounts of paper. The more expensive printers     230
25  are usually faster printers. After assessing your printer     241
26  needs, you are ready to make your purchase.                    250
```

| 1 | 2 | 3 | 4 | 5 | 6 | 7 | 8 | 9 | 10 | 11 | 12

DOCUMENT PROCESSING

Form 116-15

Letter Template

Use the first letter template in your word processing software.

Situation: Today is December 27, 20--. You are employed in the office of All-City, Inc., an insurance company in Columbia, Missouri. Offices are located at 17 North Eighth Street, Columbia, MO 65201, and their phone number is 800-555-9981. All City, Inc., handles auto, home, and life insurance coverage. The Web site address is www.ACI.com.

Mr. Greg Scher, executive vice president, has written the letter shown on page 471. You are to type it using a correspondence template. He prefers block-style letters with *Sincerely* as his complimentary closing and uses his title in the writer's identification. The letter should be addressed to Ms. Rosa Nunez, 731 Broad Street, Newark, NJ 07102, and you should use standard punctuation. This letter includes two enclosures. The company slogan is "Insuring you at home and around the world."

¶ Your recent letter was filled with excellent questions, Ms. Nunez, and I am more than happy to answer them for you.

¶ All City, Inc., handles auto, home, and life insurance coverage for you and your family. However, since you are primarily interested in auto insurance, I have enclosed a brochure with the details and a table with required minimum coverage for the states you mentioned.

¶ ACI's automobile policy combines both mandatory and optional coverages in one package. This policy can be tailored to meet your individual needs so that you end up with a policy that provides comprehensive protection. However, the best way for you to understand fully what we can offer you is to schedule a meeting at your convenience.

¶ Ms. Elena Ortega will be calling you in the next day or two to arrange an appointment after you have had a chance to review the enclosed materials. We also have an excellent Web site at ACI.com filled with helpful information. Again, thank you for your inquiry, Ms. Nunez.

Table
116-55

Boxed Table

The boxed table below is to be enclosed with the letter when it is sent to Ms. Nunez.

STATE MINIMUM COVERAGE REQUIREMENTS		
Minimum Limits	**State**	**Required Coverage**
25/50/10	NY	Bodily Injury and Property Damage Liability, Personal Injury Protection, Uninsured Motorist
15/30/5	NJ	Bodily Injury and Property Damage Liability, Personal Injury Protection, Uninsured Motorist
15/30/5	PA	Bodily Injury and Property Damage Liability, Medical Payments
20/40/10	CT	Bodily Injury and Property Damage Liability, Uninsured and Underinsured Motorist

Mr. Scher has sketched out a letterhead form, and he would like you to design the finished letterhead for All-City, Inc.

Insert a decorative image.

Identify our company, including our Web site.

Insert our company slogan with a border above it.

In-Basket Review (Hospitality)

Goals

- Improve speed and accuracy
- Refine language arts skills in word usage
- Format documents used in the hospitality industry

A. Type 2 times.

A. WARMUP

```
1        The executive meeting won't begin until 8:15; please      11
2   contact just the key people at zfnet@mail.com. Did Kay say      23
3   that quite a group* (*234) is expected by 9 o'clock today?      34
    |  1  |  2  |  3  |  4  |  5  |  6  |  7  |  8  |  9  | 10  | 11  | 12
```

SKILLBUILDING

B. Take three 12-second timed writings on each line. The scale below the last line shows your wpm speed for a 12-second timed writing.

B. 12-SECOND SPEED SPRINTS

```
4   Half of the space was going to be used for seven new desks.
5   She will soon know if all their goals have been met or not.
6   You must learn to focus on each one of your jobs every day.
7   The group will meet in the new suite that is down the hall.
    | | | |5| | | |10| | | |15| | | |20| | | |25| | | |30| | | |35| | | |40| | | |45| | | |50| | | |55| | | |60
```

C. Type line 8. Then type lines 9–11 (as a paragraph), reading the words from right to left. Type 2 times.

C. TECHNIQUE PRACTICE: CONCENTRATION

```
8        When typing, always strive for complete concentration.
9   concentration. complete for strive always typing, When
10  errors. your on down cut may rate typing your in decrease A
11  errors. of number the reduce to rate reading your down Slow
```

D. DIAGNOSTIC PRACTICE: SYMBOLS AND PUNCTUATION

If you are not using the GDP software, turn to page SB-2 and follow the directions for this activity.

E. Study the rules at the right.

E. WORD USAGE

RULE ▶
accept/except

Accept means "to agree to"; *except* means "to leave out."
All employees <u>except</u> the maintenance staff should <u>accept</u> the agreement.

RULE ▶
affect/effect

Affect is most often used as a verb meaning "to influence"; *effect* is most often used as a noun meaning "result."
The ruling will <u>affect</u> our domestic operations but will have no <u>effect</u> on Asian operations.

RULE ▶
farther/further

Farther refers to distance; *further* refers to extent or degree.
The <u>farther</u> we drove, the <u>further</u> agitated he became.

RULE ▶
personal/personnel

Personal means "private"; *personnel* means "employees."
All <u>personnel</u> agreed not to use e-mail for <u>personal</u> business.

RULE ▶
principal/principle

Principal means "primary"; *principle* means "rule."
The <u>principle</u> of fairness is our <u>principal</u> means of dealing with customers.

Edit the sentences to correct any errors in word usage.

12 The company cannot accept any collect calls, except for his.
13 The affect of the speech was dramatic; everyone was affected.
14 Further discussion by office personal was not appropriate.
15 Comments made during any meeting should never be personal.
16 If the meeting is held any further away, no one will attend.
17 The principle reason for the decision was to save money.
18 Office ethics is a basic principle that should be practiced.
19 He cannot except the fact that the job was delegated to Jack.
20 Any further effects on office personnel will be evaluated.

DOCUMENT PROCESSING

Situation: You are employed at the office of Suite Retreat, a group of vacation cottage-style suites in Sanibel, Florida. The office and suites are located at 3539 Shell Basket Lane, Sanibel Island, FL 33957. The phone number is 941-555-3422, and the e-mail address is email@SuiteRetreat.com.

Ms. Maxwell, your boss, has asked you to redesign the Web site for Suite Retreat. She has written a description of

Suite Retreat that she wants you to use in the home page. You should also include identifying information and a picture that will capture the feeling of a carefree beach vacation spot. The theme and styles you choose for the Web site should reflect the same image.

Begin by creating the home page as shown on page 476. Add the title Suite Retreat Home.

Report
117-101 ▶

Web Site
personal/personnel

affect/effect

personal/personnel

farther/further

¶ Are you ready to experience a private beach retreat with warm waters, endless white sand, and blue skies? The personnel at Suite Retreat are at your service and will make sure your stay is a pleasurable one.

¶ Suite Retreat is hidden away on a private beach on the Gulf of Mexico at the end of a secluded country road. You will feel the soothing effects of our lush, tropical surroundings and charming cottage suites the moment you enter our winding drive. Each suite is beautifully decorated and appointed with marble baths and private whirlpools for your personal use. Click here for further details on our suites.

¶ If you are interested in a little recreation during your stay, we have a variety of activities available on the property:

- Shuffleboard courts and tennis courts
- Bicycles and kayaks
- Swimming and shelling

¶ If you enjoy golf and fine dining, you will find a small golf course and excellent seafood within easy walking distance about a half mile farther down the beach.

Refer to **Reference Manual**

Refer to page R-12C of the Reference Manual for a review of list formatting.

farther/further

Strategies for Career Success

What to Exclude From Your Resume

What items should you omit from your resume? Don't list salary demands. If the job posting requires a salary history, create a separate page listing the salaries for each position you've held. If the job posting wants your salary requirements, in the application letter state, "Salary expectation is in the range . . . ," and provide a range (usually a $5,000 range).

Exclude personal information such as race, gender, health status, age, marital status, religious preference, political preference, national origin, and physical characteristics (for example, height, weight). Do not provide your Social Security number or your photograph.

Exceptions to listing personal information do exist. For example, if you are applying for a job at a political party's headquarters and you are a member of that party, listing your party affiliation might be important to your potential employer.

YOUR TURN Review your resume. Have you included any personal information? If your answer is yes, does it serve a purpose for being in your resume?

Ms. Maxwell has asked you to continue building the Web site by making the following changes: Change the title to "Suite Retreat Rates." Add two hyperlinks on the rates page to the link bar on both pages. The Home hyperlink should point to Report-117-101.htm, and the Rates hyperlink should point to Report-117-102.htm.

Also add a hyperlink on the home page to the word *here* in the last sentence of the second paragraph to link to the Rates page. Apply the same theme and styles as used on the home page to the Rates page, and type the information as shown in the illustration below.

Home page.

Rates page.

In-Basket Review (Retail)

Goals

- Type at least 50wpm/5′/5e
- To format documents used in the retail industry

A. Type 2 times.

A. WARMUP

```
1       Does Pamela know if Region 29* (*Ventura) has met the     11
2   sales quota? Their exact target zone is just not clear;       22
3   they don't have to submit their totals until 4:30 on 5/7.     34
    | 1 | 2 | 3 | 4 | 5 | 6 | 7 | 8 | 9 | 10 | 11 | 12
```

SKILLBUILDING

B. PACED PRACTICE

If you are not using the GDP software, turn to page SB-14 and follow the directions for this activity.

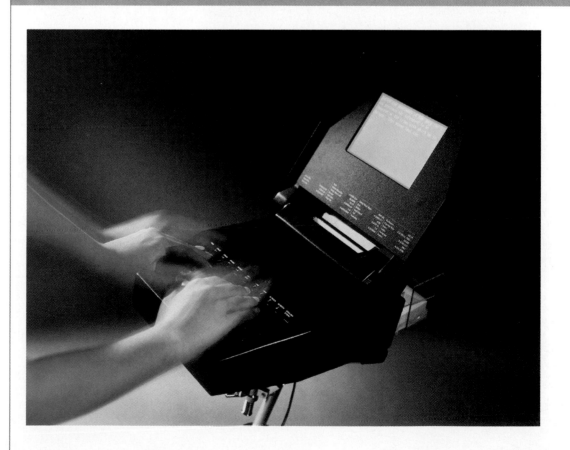

C. Take two 5-minute timed writings. Review your speed and errors.

Goal: At least 50wpm/5'/5e

C. 5-MINUTE TIMED WRITING

```
 4        Job sharing is a current concept that many places are   11
 5   using to keep valued workers. People are finding a wide       22
 6   range of reasons for not wanting to work full time. Here      34
 7   are some tips on how to approach your boss if you would       45
 8   like to try job sharing.                                      50
 9        First, check your company handbook for an authorized     61
10   policy regarding this concept. If there is no rule that       72
11   prohibits the concept, then try to enlist a coworker who      83
12   would like to job share and help you in writing a proposal    95
13   for job sharing where you work.                              101
14        Next, define your needs and your goals. Develop a work  113
15   schedule that will meet all of your personal and monetary    124
16   needs. Be sure that you include enough time to get the work  136
17   done. If you want to work at your home on occasion, be sure  148
18   to state your desires. You might find it is often quite      159
19   helpful to maintain a journal of your job duties, noting     171
20   how much time is devoted to each task. Your plan should      182
21   also include details about the logistics of your proposal.   194
22   Decide how to cope with unexpected crisis situations.        205
23        Finally, time your presentation so there will be no     215
24   unnecessary interruptions. Be organized, persistent, and     227
25   professional in your presentation. Prepare to be successful  239
26   by compiling clearly defined ideas to support your plans.    250
```
| 1 | 2 | 3 | 4 | 5 | 6 | 7 | 8 | 9 | 10 | 11 | 12

DOCUMENT PROCESSING

Form 118-17

Memo Template

Use the first memo template in your word processing software.

Situation: Today is January 5, 20--. You are employed as an administrative assistant to Kelley O'Brian. Ms. O'Brian is vice president of marketing for Sports 'R Us, a retailer for sports equipment and clothing in San Diego, California, at 3939 Townsgate Drive, San Diego, CA 92130. The Web site is www.SRU.com.

The company is in the midst of launching a brand-new line of women's sportswear for the beach. Ms. O'Brian has written the memo below to Hitochi Morimoto, president of Sports 'R Us, with a copy to Barbara Warrick, vice president of sales. You are to type the memo, using a memo template. The subject of the memo is SRU Sunwear Ad Campaign.

(Continued on next page)

¶ I am pleased to tell you that we are in the final stages of our ad campaign to launch our newest line of women's beach sportswear named SRU Sunwear. We are just about to sign Cindy Bloom to serve as our spokesperson and featured model in our magazine ad campaign.

¶ I have scheduled a meeting for next week so that you can meet Cindy and see a representative sampling of our exciting new sportswear line. My staff members will also be ready with a presentation for our ad campaign, which will focus on the practicality and smart good looks of our newest beachwear. I have attached an agenda for your review.

¶ Our company has always been known for the value and quality of our sportswear. This line is based on a smaller emerging brand that will save our customers money while still maintaining the high quality they have come to expect. I look forward to our meeting next week.

Report 118-103

Agenda

Prepare the meeting agenda shown below. The agenda should be attached to the memo when it is sent to Mr. Morimoto. It should be titled SRU SUNWEAR AD CAMPAIGN. The meeting will be held on January 12, 20--, at 11 a.m.

Call to order
Approval of minutes of December 20 meeting
Introduction of Cindy Bloom
Progress report on the status of the ad campaign
Presentation of the ad campaign
Presentation of some samples from the new sportswear line
Announcements
Miscellaneous
Adjournment

Ms. O'Brian has sketched out a cover page for the ad campaign report and would like you to design the finished cover page for the SRU Sunwear line of beach apparel. The report will be distributed at the meeting.

---

*Insert some word art
with the name of our
sportswear line.*

*Insert a picture
related to our new
line of beach
sportswear.*

*Identify our company and our
address, including our Web site.*

In-Basket Review (Government)

Goals

- Improve speed and accuracy
- Refine language arts skills in spelling
- Format documents used in government work

A. Type 2 times.

A. WARMUP

```
1        Turner & Finch will charge us $10,234 to complete the    11
2   job. Do they realize that they quoted us an initial fee of    23
3   exactly $9,876? Kelly will call them very soon to verify.     34
    |  1  |  2  |  3  |  4  |  5  |  6  |  7  |  8  |  9  |  10  |  11  |  12
```

SKILLBUILDING

PPP PRETEST → PRACTICE → POSTTEST

PRETEST
Take a 1-minute timed writing. Review your speed and errors.

B. PRETEST: Close Reaches

```
4        Sadly, the same essay was used to oppose and deny the    11
5   phony felony charge. After the weapon was located in his      22
6   pocket, the jury was left to cast the joint ballot anyway.    34
    |  1  |  2  |  3  |  4  |  5  |  6  |  7  |  8  |  9  |  10  |  11  |  12
```

PRACTICE
Speed Emphasis:
If you made no more than 1 error on the Pretest, type each *individual* line 2 times.
Accuracy Emphasis:
If you made 2 or more errors, type each *group* of lines (as though it were a paragraph) 2 times.

C. PRACTICE: Adjacent Keys

```
7   po post spot pours vapor poker powder oppose weapon pockets
8   sa sash same usage essay sadly safety dosage sample sailing
9   oi oily join point voice doing choice boiled egoist loiters
```

D. PRACTICE: Conscecutive Fingers

```
10  ft left soft often after shift gifted crafts thrift uplifts
11  ny onyx deny nylon vinyl phony anyway skinny felony canyons
12  lo loss solo loser flood color locate floral ballot loaders
```

POSTTEST
Repeat the Pretest timed writing and compare performance.

E. POSTTEST: Close Reaches

F. Take a 1-minute timed writing on the first paragraph to establish your base speed. Then take four 1-minute timed writings on the remaining paragraphs. As soon as you equal or exceed your base speed on one paragraph, advance to the next, more difficult paragraph.

13	Have you ever noticed that a good laugh every now and	11
14	then really makes you feel better? Research has shown that	23
15	laughter can have a very healing effect on our bodies. It	34
16	is an excellent way to relieve tension and stress all over.	46

17	When you laugh, your heart beats faster, you breathe	11
18	deeper, and you exercise your lungs. When you laugh, your	22
19	body produces endorphins--a natural painkiller that gives	34
20	you a sense of euphoria that is very powerful and pleasant.	46

21	Someone said, "Laugh in the face of adversity." As it	11
22	happens, this is first-rate advice. It's a great way to	22
23	cope with life's trials and tribulations; it's also a good	34
24	way to raise other people's spirits and relieve tension.	45

25	Finding "humor" in any situation takes practice--try	11
26	to make it a full-time habit. We're all looking for ways	22
27	to relieve stress. Any exercise--jogging, tennis, biking,	34
28	swimming, or golfing--is a proven remedy for "the blues."	45

LANGUAGE ARTS

G. Type these frequently misspelled words, paying special attention to any spelling problems in each word.

G. SPELLING

29	practice continue regular entitled course resolution assist
30	weeks preparation purposes referred communication potential
31	environmental specifications original contractor associated
32	principal systems client excellent estimated administration
33	responsibility mentioned utilized materials criteria campus

Edit the sentences to correct any misspellings.

34	It is the responsability of the administration to assist.
35	The principle client prepared the excellent specifications.
36	He mentioned that the critiria for the decision were clear.
37	The contractor associated with the project referred them.
38	He estamated that the potential for resolution was great.
39	I was told that weeks of reguler practice were required.

**Correspondence
119-99**

Business Letter
in Block Style

Highlighted words are
spelling words from the
language arts activities.

Situation: Today is November 4, 20--. Use this date in all documents as needed. You work as an administrative assistant for Ruth McBride. She is research director for Ride Share, a free government-funded commuter service in Chicago that informs people about commuting alternatives. For the purposes of this simulation, your name will be Roberto Duran. Your e-mail address is rduran@rideshare.net.

Ms. McBride has left the letter below in your in-basket to be sent to Mr. Jason Davis, executive director for Canadian CarShare, which is located at 1233 West Third Avenue, Vancouver, BC V6J 1K1 in Canada. When communicating with Cana-dian firms, use A4 metric-size paper and adhere to Canadian mailing guidelines.

Ms. McBride prefers a block-style letter with standard punctuation, uses *Sincerely* as the complimentary close, and likes her business title typed below her name in a letter closing. Add this post-script notation at the end of the letter:

```
Any statistics you might
choose to include on the
environmental impact
associated with car sharing
in your Web site at
http://www.carshare.ca
would be very helpful.
```

¶ Ride Share is a government-funded commuter service whose mission is to inform our citizens about commuting alternatives in the Chicago area. My responsibility is to gather as many facts as possible regarding the regular practice of car sharing in Canada.

¶ As I understand this concept, a car share client could conceivably mix and match alternative modes of transportation and also have exclusive use of a reserved car for a fixed period of time. For example, a commuter could arrive at work on a train, pick up a reserved car at a nearby parking lot to run errands at lunch, return the car an hour later, and then continue home perhaps using a van pool or bus. The commuter would pay about 20 to 40 cents a kilometer along with some monthly membership fees.

¶ If you can tell me which cities have successfully utilized car sharing in Canada since it was first introduced and why, I can begin preparation for a proposal for a car sharing pilot project as a potential commuter alternative here in the Chicago area.

Correspondence ▶ 119-100

Business Letter
in Block Style

Open the file for Correspondence 119-99. Ms. McBride would like you to send the same letter to Mr. Frans Zimmerly, executive director of Europa CarShare at Siesmayerstrasse 23, 60323 Frankfurt, GERMANY. When communicating with German firms, use A4 metric-size paper and adhere to German mailing guidelines.

Find and replace all instances of "Canada" with "Germany." Add this postscript at the end of the letter:

```
Any statistics you might
choose to fax to me at
+1.800.555.5553 regarding
the environmental impact
associated with car sharing
in Germany would be very
helpful.
```

Correspondence ▶ 119-101

E-Mail Message

Prepare this e-mail message to be sent to Ms. McBride. Type the e-mail greeting, Hi, Ms. McBride:, and the body shown below in correct format. Type Roberto as the clos-ing and type this signature: Roberto Duran | E-Mail: rduran@rideshare. net | Phone: 773-555-0107. Save the e-mail message, but do not send it.

¶ I sent the two letters to the executive directors of CarShare as you requested. I will follow up in a week with phone calls and e-mail messages as follows:

¶ Mr. Jason Davis

+1.604.877.5555

jdavis@carshare.ubc.ca

¶ Mr. Frans Zimmerly

+49.30.20304-0

fzimmerly@carshare.de

¶ I found some statistics about car sharing that might be useful. Car sharing was first introduced in Quebec City in 1994 and now has about 1,200 users in six Canadian cities. About 90,000 car share commuters are located worldwide, with about half of them in Europe.

Keyboarding Connection

E-Mail Privacy

How private are your e-mail messages? Although there has been a lot of discussion about hacking and Internet security, e-mail may be more secure than your phone or postal mail. In fact, most new-generation e-mail programs have some kind of encryption built in.

It is not hackers who are the most likely to read your e-mail. It is anyone with access to your incoming mail server or your computer. If your computer and incoming server are at work, then you can assume that your supervisor can read your e-mail. In some companies, it is a normal practice to monitor employees' e-mail. Therefore, you should not send e-mail from work that you wouldn't want anyone there to read.

If you are serious about e-mail privacy, you may want to examine other encryption methods. Different products are available to ensure that your e-mail is read only by the intended recipient(s).

| YOUR TURN | Perform a keyword search, using a search engine (for example, www.altavista.com), for information on different products that are available to protect your e-mail privacy. |

In-Basket Review (Manufacturing)

Goals

- Type at least 50wpm/5'/5e
- Format documents used in the manufacturing industry

A. Type 2 times.

A. WARMUP

```
1        Order extra color cartridges very soon! G & K Supply      11
2  just announced a 15% discount on orders for the following       22
3  cartridges: QB728 and ZM 436* (*for the ink-jet printers).      34
   |  1  |  2  |  3  |  4  |  5  |  6  |  7  |  8  |  9  | 10 | 11 | 12
```

SKILLBUILDING

B. DIAGNOSTIC PRACTICE: NUMBERS

If you are not using the GDP software, turn to page SB-5 and follow the directions for this activity.

C. MAP

Follow the GDP software directions for this exercise in improving keystroking accuracy.

D. Take two 5-minute timed writings. Review your speed and errors.

Goal: At least 50wpm/5'/5e

D. 5-MINUTE TIMED WRITING

4	With modern technology, it is possible to work at a	11
5	job full time and never leave your house. You can set up a	22
6	home office with a phone line, a facsimile, and a computer	34
7	system. Before choosing to work at home, however, you will	46
8	want to examine carefully your reasons for working at home.	58
9	Some people think about working at home so they can	69
10	have more time to spend with their families. Other people	80
11	like to have more flexibility in their work schedule. They	92
12	are looking for the opportunity to enjoy a better quality	104
13	of life or to participate in other activities.	113
14	There are some factors to consider before you make	124
15	the decision to work at home. You will want to consider the	135
16	ultimate cost of benefits that you could give up if you	147
17	change your place of work. You will want to check with your	159
18	employer to see if you are entitled to paid vacation days	170
19	and health insurance or if you can make contributions to	182
20	your retirement plan. Another factor to consider is the	193
21	limited contact with peers.	198
22	Before making the ultimate decision to work at home,	209
23	develop some realistic expectations of how you will spend	221
24	each day. Although you can organize your work to fit your	232
25	schedule, you will find the real challenge is to determine	244
26	a routine that works for you.	250

| 1 | 2 | 3 | 4 | 5 | 6 | 7 | 8 | 9 | 10 | 11 | 12

DOCUMENT PROCESSING

Situation: Today is November 5, 20--. Use this date on all documents as needed. You work as an administrative assistant for Melanie Stone at MedPro Manufacturing, one of the largest medical diagnostic equipment manufacturers in the world. The home office is located in Arden, North Carolina, with branch offices located worldwide.

Your boss has left a business report in your in-basket for you to format and type. The title of the report is MedPro Manufacturing. The subtitle of the report is Vision, Innovation, and Partnership. Use the date after the subtitle.

(Continued on next page)

¶ Med Pro Manufacturing is ① of the largest medical diagnostic equipment manufacturers in the world. We have been in business for almost ~~eighty~~ 80 years, and our company has a solid reputation for quality and reliability in all our manufacturing processes. We take great pride in our ~~current~~ state-of-the-art manufacturing facilities because we realize that doctors' reputations and patients' lives depend on the quality and reliability of our products and medical supplies.

VISION

¶ MedPro's vision for the New Millennium is to continue the manufacturing of circuit boards, light sources, fiber-optic light guides, and scanning engines. We have in place a stringent quality management process so that our customers are guaranteed a superior product at a competitive price. Because of these high standards, ~~we have~~ our company has attained the most current ISO Certification. We have reduced/consistently our manufacturing cycles without sacrificing quality.

INNOVATION.

¶ Everyone at MedPro, from those on the manufacturing floor to those in the president's office, ~~are~~ is committed to the continuation of the research and development of innovative products and ~~state-of-the-art~~ high-tech manufacturing processes.

¶ Products. Our electronic stethoscope system combined a revolutionary acoustic technology and teamed it with the power of a computer to produce extraordinary results in doctors' offices. We specialize in innovative products for ~~kids~~ children. Our autorefractor has allowed optometrists and ophthalmologists to perform objective refraction on children ~~that is~~ more quickly and easily than ever before. We are committed to the continuous development of innovative products like these.

Manufacturing processes. Our fiber-optic light guides and scanning engines are ② more examples of how MedPro is committed to innovation in the manufacturing process, ~~as well.~~ Our computer controlled manufacturing

(Continued on next page)

and CAD/ECAD equipment helps us to control ^precisely the manufacturing of all our medical equipment. These same innovative processes have helped us reduce our costs and reduce our manufacturing cycle.

PARTNERSHIP

¶ One of the most effective ways to ensure success is to develop partnerships with other innovative business^es that have the same commitment to high standards and are leaders in ~~there~~ their respective fields. Our team work and collaboration with our partners have helped us to establish an international presence and reputation. Our website ~~is~~ can be found at http://medpro.com, and it is filled with a wealth of ~~excellent~~ information. All details of our products, services, employees, contact information, and so on, can be found there. We look forward to your business.

Correspondence 120-102

Business Letter in Block Style

A letter that includes a table has also been left in your in-basket to be typed. The letter is to be sent to Mrs. Carmen Tamashiro, associate director for Medical Relief International, which is located at 3-5-1 Kanda Jinbo-cho, Chiyoda-ku Tokyo 101, JAPAN. The subject line is `Relief Medical Supplies`. When communicating with Japanese firms, use A4 metric-size paper and adhere to Japanese mailing guidelines.

Ms. Stone, public relations director, prefers a block-style letter with standard punctuation and likes to use a predesigned format for tables. She prefers *Sincerely* as the complimentary close, uses the company name in the closing, and likes her business title typed below her name in the closing. She does not use a courtesy title.

¶ Med Pro Manufacturing is happy to send our tenth shipment of relief medical supplies to be distributed as needed to the people of Japan who have been devastated by recent earthquakes and other natural disasters.

(Continued on next page)

¶ Our previous shipments to Japan have amounted to well over $1 million worth of medical supplies such as antibiotics, surgical supplies, catheters, packs, crutches, splints, braces, and slings. MedPro Manufacturing usually sends medical goods and equipment exclusively; however, some of the earlier shipments have also included basic survival supplies. Our employees have helped us in our efforts to gather hundreds of tents, sleeping bags, blankets, flashlights, coats, socks, gloves, and all-weather apparel. ¶ Several international branches of our company would also like to offer their help if you need it. The table below includes all the pertinent information:

Address	E-Mail	Telephone
Marie Desaulnier 27, rue Pasteur 14390 Cabaurg FRANCE	medpro.com@email.fr	+33.1.64531515
Frank Liberman Mittlerer Pfad 9 D-70499 Stuttgart GERMANY	medpro.com@email.de	+49.711.8871624
Manny Yamamoto 16-13, 2-chome Hongo Tokyo 113-0033 JAPAN	medpro.com@email.jp	+81.3.38138841

¶ If I can offer you any further assistance or information, please don't hesitate to contact me at +1.704.555.8945.

Skills Assessment on Part 6

5-Minute
Timed Writing

1	The potential to reach your career goals has never	10
2	been better. The person who will move forward in a career	22
3	is the one who will make the bold moves to follow his or	33
4	her dreams. He or she will have the required attributes of	45
5	initiative and motivation to put forth maximum efforts in	57
6	order to realize a fulfilling career.	64
7	If you want to get ahead in the highly competitive	75
8	business world today, you need a personal coach or mentor	86
9	who is experienced in motivating people who want to reach	98
10	their potential. You may be afraid to go after your dream	110
11	career because you are afraid of failure. Your personal	121
12	mentor will help you to minimize any problems you incur. He	133
13	or she will encourage you to strive for more.	142
14	When you decide to work with a qualified coach, you	153
15	are investing in yourself. You can trust your coach to help	165
16	you through this joyful process of expanding your horizons	176
17	until you reach your goal. When you think you have reached	188
18	your limit, your coach will make suggestions for additional	200
19	improvement. He or she will present the strategies you can	212
20	use to be successful. Your coach will guide you in making	224
21	the critical decisions for advancing your career. The final	236
22	decision to improve your skills and become successful is	247
23	yours, however.	250

| 1 | 2 | 3 | 4 | 5 | 6 | 7 | 8 | 9 | 10 | 11 | 12

Form
Test 6-18

Memo Template

Type this memo using the preselected blank memo template that has opened automatically.

To: Michael Lani, Human Resources Director | **CC:** Armando Lopez, President | **From:** Charlene Morimoto, Committee Chairperson | **Date:** October 18, 20-- | **Re:** Turkey Trot Fun Run Fund-Raiser

¶ It's time once again for our annual Turkey Trot Fun Run, in which all proceeds are donated to the Read-2-Learn literacy program for inner-city youth. Since 1980, our Read-2-Learn Committee has donated over $200,000 to this very worthy cause, and we have every intention of raising at least $8,000 in this Fun Run on Thanksgiving Day, but we need your help.

¶ As our director of human resources, you are in a unique position to help us raise funds. If you could encourage each of our employees to donate $20 to sponsor one runner in this event, we would easily meet our goals this year. Last year we had over 400 sponsored runners.

(Continued on next page)

¶ The Read-2-Learn program is specifically targeted at the inner-city elementary students in our neighborhood in their quest for basic literacy skills. Our business is located in a rich, multicultural urban neighborhood that is in desperate need of this type of program. I have attached a brochure that explains all details of this reading program and an event flyer. If you need additional copies, please let me know. Also, please visit our Web site at http://www.turkeytrot.org for further details.

¶ urs | Attachments

Report Test 6-106 ▶

Web Page

1. Change the title of Report-Test-6-106.mht to Read-2-Learn.
2. Insert a centered, boxed table with 2 columns and 4 rows.
3. Type the information on page 492 and arrange it as shown below.
4. Insert a picture related to reading and size it approximately as shown. Apply a coordinated design theme.
5. Insert horizontal lines in Rows 2 and 4. Change any styles, fonts, or colors as desired.

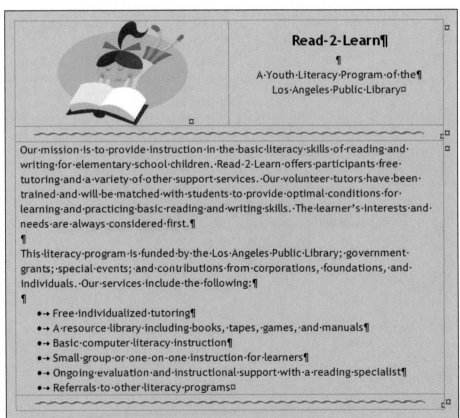

(Continued on next page)

Read-2-Learn

A Youth Literacy Program of the
Los Angeles Public Library

Our mission is to provide instruction in the basic literacy skills of reading and writing for elementary school children. Read-2-Learn offers participants free tutoring and a variety of other support services. Our volunteer tutors have been trained and will be matched with students to provide optimal conditions for learning and practicing basic reading and writing skills. The learner's interests and needs are always considered first.

This literacy program is funded by the Los Angeles Public Library; government grants; special events; and contributions from corporations, foundations, and individuals. Our services include the following:

- Free individualized tutoring
- A resource library including books, tapes, games, and manuals
- Basic computer literacy instruction
- Small group or one-on-one instruction for learners
- Ongoing evaluation and instructional support with a reading specialist
- Referrals to other literacy programs

Report
Test 6-107

Flyer

Press the SPACE BAR 2 times, and create the flyer as shown in the illustration.

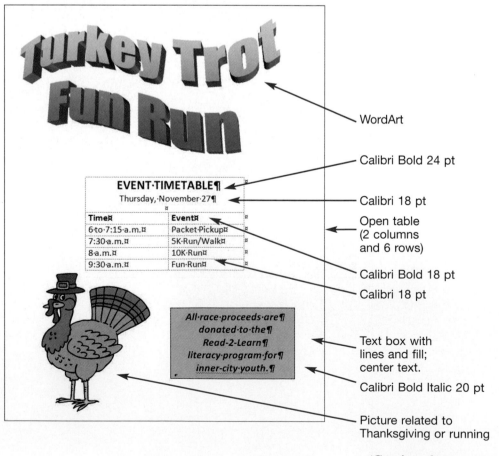

WordArt

Calibri Bold 24 pt

Calibri 18 pt

Open table
(2 columns
and 6 rows)

Calibri Bold 18 pt

Calibri 18 pt

Text box with
lines and fill;
center text.

Calibri Bold Italic 20 pt

Picture related to
Thanksgiving or running

(Continued on next page)

Type this information in the open table and text box as shown in the flyer illustration on page 492.

EVENT TIMETABLE
Thursday, November 27

Time	Event
6 to 7:15 a.m.	Packet Pickup
7:30 a.m.	5K Run/Walk
8 a.m.	10K Run
9:30 a.m.	Fun Run

All race proceeds are donated to the Read-2-Learn literacy program for inner-city youth.

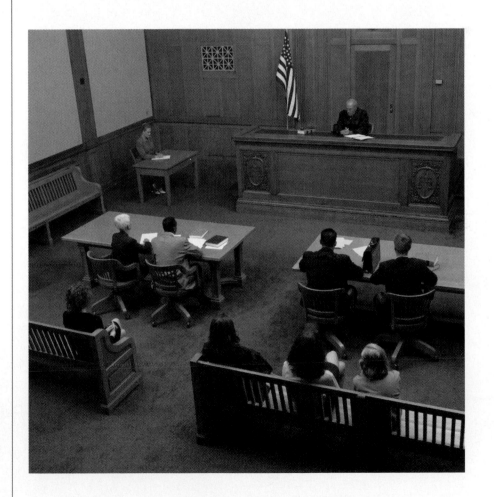

SKILLBUILDING

Diagnostic Practice: Symbols and Punctuation

The Diagnostic Practice: Symbols and Punctuation program is designed to diagnose and then correct your keystroking errors. You may use this program at any time throughout the course after completing Lesson 19.

Directions

1. Type one of the three Pretest/Posttest paragraphs 1 time, pushing *moderately* for speed. Review your errors.
2. Note your results—the number of errors you made on each symbol or punctuation key. For example, if you typed *75&* for *75%*, you would count 1 error on the % key.
3. For any symbol or punctuation key on which you made 2 or more errors, type the corresponding drill lines 2 times. If you made only 1 error, type the drill line 1 time.
4. If you made no errors on the Pretest/Posttest paragraph, type one set of the Practice: Symbols and Punctuation lines on page SB-4.
5. Finally, retype the same Pretest/Posttest, and compare your performance with your Pretest.

PRETEST/POSTTEST

Paragraph 1

Price & Joy stock closed @ 5 1/8 yesterday; it was up 13% from yesterday. If we had sold our "high-demand" shares* (*300 of them) before 3:30 p.m., we'd have made $15,000, wouldn't we? Oh, well! I'll be in my office (#13C) crying.

Paragraph 2

The Time/CNN poll had the slate of Myers & Bassey ahead by just 5%. Weren't you surprised? I was; after all, "they"* (*meaning the crew) had ordered 60# of food @ $9.50 a pound for a victory party at 3:30 p.m. today. What a sad mix-up!

Paragraph 3

Didn't my colleague* (*Elsa Jones-Salizar) send in $50 as a 10% deposit for reserving Room #5B on Friday and/or Monday? Attached to her deposit was a note that said, "Call Tibby, & me @ 10:30 a.m."; I was surprised. She sounded desperate!

PRACTICE: Individual Reaches

Ampersand

juj ju7j j7j j7&j j&&j j&&j juj ju7j j7j j7&j j&&j j&&j &&&
Alma & Bill & Carr & Dern & Epps & Farr & Gary & Horn & Ing
Jack & Kyle & Mann & Nash & Okum & Parr & Rand & Star & Tua
Uber & Vern & Will & Xang & Year & Zack & Sons & Bros & Inc

Apostrophe

;;; ;'; ;'; ';' ';' ''' Al's Bo's Di's it's Jo's Li's Moe's
you'd he'll she'd it'll she'll they'd aren't you're they're
we're we've we'll can't you've you'll hasn't didn't they've
she's don't isn't won't hadn't wasn't here's that's what'll

Asterisk	kik ki8k k8*k k8*k k**k k**k ki8k k8*k k8*k k**k k**k Note* Ames* Beck* Carr* Dern* Epps* Farr* Gary* Horn* Iago* Jack* Kyle* Mann* Nash* Okum* Parr* Rand* Star* Teri* Uber* Vern* Will* Xang* Year* Zack* Note* Star* Also* List* Text* Cite*
At Sign	sws sw2s s2@s s2@s s@s s@@s and sws sw2s s2@s s2@s s@s s@@s 138 @ 34 and 89 @ 104 and 18 @ 458 and 89 @ 10 and 18 @ 340 162 & 31 and 48 & 606 and 81 @ 923 and 69 @ 42 and 54 @ 128 277 @ 89 and 57 & 369 and 70 @ 434 and 50 @ 15 and 37 @ 512
Colon	;;; ;;; ;;; :;: ::: and :/: and :?: and :p: and :-: and ::: From: Name: City: Madam: 4:30 Bill to: Address: To: cc: PS: Date: Rank: Time: Dept.: 27:1 Subject: Time in: Hi: Re: Cf: Sirs: Ext.: Apt.: State: 1:00 Ship to: Acts 4:2 FY: ID: OS:
Comma	kkk k,k k,k and ,k, and ,i, and ,8, and I,I and K,K and ,,, Ava, ebb, lac, had, foe, elf, hug, ugh, poi, raj, ink, gal, bum, Ben, ago, cop, req, far, has, dot, tau, env, wow, sax, I am, you are, he is, we are, they are, Al, Ty, Hy, Jo, Ann
Diagonal	;;; ;/; /// and p/p and /p/ and 0/0 ;;; ;/; /// and p/p /// a/c c/o B/L ft/s ac/dc and/or he/she cad/cam due/dew 1/2005 I/O n/a B/S n/30 AM/FM ob/gyn on/off lay/lie fir/fur 2/2006 p/e m/f w/o km/h d/b/a ad/add to/too set/sit him/her 3/2007
Dollar Sign	frf fr4 f4f f$f f$f f$f $40 $44 $44 f$f f4f $ff $45 $54 $$$ $40 and $82 and $90 and $13 and $33 and $56 and $86 and $25 $214 plus $882 plus $900 plus $718 plus $910 plus $112 plus $1,937.53 plus $337.89 tax $3,985.43 minus $150.75 discount
Exclamation Mark	aqa aqla aq!a a!!a a!!a aqa aqla aq!a a!!a a!!a Go! Hi! Lo! Oh! Wow! Gas! Dig! Yes! Sit! Rats! Darn! Well! Drat! Shoot! So! Eat! Air! Out! Not! Aim! Whoa! Wait! Whee! Oops! Yahoo! No! Yea! Eek! Run! Boo! Buy! Look! Help! Duck! Alas! There!
Hyphen	;;; ;p; ;-; -;- --- and -;- and -;- and -/- and -:- and -P- add-on be-all F-stop H-bomb A-frame age-old all-day boo-boo how-to in-out jam-up log-in come-on cop-out end-all fade-in mix-up no-win say-so tie-up one-act pig-out rip-off T-shirt
Number/Pound	de3d de3#d d3#d d3#d d##d d##d #33 #33 #333 de3d de3#d d3#d 45# of #245 and 837# of #013 and 31# of #981 and 2# of #013 12# of #883 and 345# of #328 and 67# of #112 and 8# of #109 54# of #542 and 378# of #310 and 13# of #189 and 6# of #657
Parentheses	lo91 lo91 lo(1 lo(1 1((1 1((1 ;p0; ;p0; ;p); ;p); ;)); ;)); (a) (b) (c) (d) (e) (f) (g) (h) (i) (j) (k) (l) (m) (n) (o) (p) (q) (r) (s) (t) (u) (v) (w) (x) (y) (z) (1) (2) (3) (4) (5) (6) (7) (8) (9) (0) (@) (#) ($) (&) (*) (-) (;) (,) (:)

Percent

```
ftf ft5f f5f f5%f f%%f f%%f ftf ft5f f5f f5%f f%%f f%%f %%%
40% and 82% and 90% and 13% and 33% and 56% and 86% and 25%
21% and 48% and 82% and 90% and 70% and 18% and 91% and 10%
34.5% off 89% increase 12% credit 67% finished 10% discount
```

Period

```
1.1 ... and .1. and .o. and .9. and .(. and .O. and L.L ...
Jan. Feb. Mar. Apr. Jun. Jul. Aug. Sep. Oct. Nov. Dec. a.m.
Sun. Mon. Tue. Wed. Thu. Fri. Sat. Mrs. Esq. Mex. Can. D.C.
I am. I see. We do. He is. I can. Do not. Help me. Go slow.
```

Question Mark

```
;;; ;/; ;?; ??? ?;? and p?p and ?O? and ?)? and ?-? and ???
So? Who? What? Can I? Why not? Who does? Stop here? Is she?
Me? How? When? May I? Who, me? Says who? Do it now? For me?
Oh? Why? Am I? Do we? Am I up? How much? Who knows? Will I?
```

Quotation Mark

```
;'; ;"; ;"; ";" """ and ;'; ;"; ;"; ";" """ and ;"; ";" """
"Eat" "Sit" "Rest" "Stay" "Roll" "Hello" "Look" "Pet" "Dry"
"Yes" "Lie" "Halt" "Next" "Move" "Write" "Type" "Ink" "Sew"
"Beg" "See" "Walk" "Wave" "Stop" "Speak" "File" "Run" "Cry"
```

Semicolon

```
;;; ;;; and ;'; and ;"; and ;p; and ;-; and ;/; and ;?; ;;;
tea; ebb; Mac; mid; lie; arf; hug; nth; obi; Taj; ark; Hal;
dim; man; bio; hop; seq; our; Gus; let; you; Bev; row; lax;
do not cry; that is Liz; see to it; I am sad; we do; I can;
```

PRACTICE: SYMBOLS AND PUNCTUATION

```
Doe & Fry sued May & Ito; Ho & Fox sued Doe & Lee for M&Ms.
Ann's dad said he's happy she's out of school; she'd agree.
Yesterday* (*April 9), the rock star said **** right on TV.
E-mail them at glyden@sales.com to buy 3 @ $89 or 9 @ $250.

Hi, Ross: Place odds of 3:1 on the game at 10:30 and 11:15.
Tom gave Ava, Jo, Al, and Tyson a red, white, and blue car.
On 3/1/2008, he will receive a pension and/or a big buyout.
The $80 skirt was cut to $70 and then $55 for a $25 saving.

What! No ice! I'm mortified! Run, order some more. Quickly!
Jones-Lynch built an all-season add-on to her A-frame home.
Please order 500# of #684, 100# of #133, and 200# of #1341.
The answer is (a) 1, (b) 4, (c) 7, or (d) all of the above.

The car was cut 15% and then 25% for a final saving of 40%.
Mr. R. J. Dix ordered from L. L. Bean on Dec. 23 at 11 a.m.
Who? Me? Why me? Because I can type? Is that a good reason?
"Look," he said, "see that sign?" It says, "Beware of Dog."
Stop here; get out of your car; walk a foot; begin digging.
```

Diagnostic Practice: Numbers

The Diagnostic Practice: Numbers program is designed to diagnose and then correct your keystroking errors. You may use this program at any time throughout the course after completing Lesson 14.

Directions

1. Type one of the three Pretest/Posttest paragraphs 1 time, pushing *moderately* for speed. Review your errors.
2. Note your results—the number of errors you made on each key and your total number of errors. For example, if you type *24* for *25*, you would count 1 error on the number *5*.
3. For any number on which you made 2 or more errors, select the corresponding drill lines and type the drills 2 times. If you made only 1 error, type the drill 1 time.
4. If you made no errors on the Pretest/Posttest paragraph, type 1 set of the drills that contain all numbers on page SB-6.
5. Finally, retype the same Pretest/Posttest, and compare your performance with your Pretest.

PRETEST/POSTTEST

Paragraph 1

    The statement dated May 24, 2004, listed 56 clamps; 15 batteries; 169 hammers; 358 screwdrivers; 1,298 pliers; and 1,475 files. The invoice numbered 379 showed 387 hoes, 406 rakes, 92 lawn mowers, 63 tillers, and 807 more lawn items.

Paragraph 2

    My inventory records dated May 31, 2004, revealed that we had 458 pints; 1,069 quarts; and 8,774 gallons of paint. We had 2,953 brushes; 568 scrapers; 12,963 wallpaper rolls; 897 knives; 5,692 mixers; 480 ladders; and 371 step stools.

Paragraph 3

    Almost 179 hot meals were delivered to the 35 shut-ins in April, 169 in May, and 389 in June. Several workers had volunteered 7,564 hours in 2004; 9,348 hours in 2003; 5,468 in 2002; and 6,577 in 2001. About 80 people were involved.

PRACTICE: INDIVIDUAL REACHES

```
1 aq aql aqlqa 111 ants 101 aunts 131 apples 171 animals al
They got 11 answers correct for the 11 questions in BE 121.
Those 11 adults loaded the 711 animals between 1 and 2 p.m.
All 111 agreed that 21 of those 31 are worthy of the honor.

2 sw sw2 sw2ws 222 sets 242 steps 226 salads 252 saddles s2
The 272 summer tourists saw the 22 soldiers and 32 sailors.
Your September 2 date was all right for 292 of 322 persons.
The 22 surgeons said 221 of those 225 operations went well.

3 de de3 de3ed 333 dots 303 drops 313 demons 393 dollars d3
Bus 333 departed at 3 p.m. with the 43 dentists and 5 boys.
She left 33 dolls and 73 decoys at 353 West Addison Street.
The 13 doctors helped some of the 33 druggists in Room 336.
```

```
4 fr fr4 fr4rf 444 fans 844 farms 444 fishes 644 fiddles f4
My 44 friends bought 84 farms and sold over 144 franchises.
She sold 44 fish and 440 beef dinners for $9.40 per dinner.
The 1954 Ford had only 40,434 fairly smooth miles by May 4.

5 fr fr5 fr5rf 555 furs 655 foxes 555 flares 455 fingers f5
They now own 155 restaurants, 45 food stores, and 55 farms.
They ordered 45, 55, 65, and 75 yards of that new material.
Flight 855 flew over Farmington at 5:50 p.m. on December 5.

6 jy jy6 jy6yj 666 jets 266 jeeps 666 jewels 866 jaguars j6
Purchase orders numbered 6667 and 6668 were sent yesterday.
Those 66 jazz players played for 46 juveniles in Room 6966.
The 6 judges reviewed the 66 journals on November 16 or 26.

7 ju ju7 ju7uj 777 jays 377 jokes 777 joists 577 juniors j7
The 17 jets carried 977 jocular passengers above 77 cities.
Those 277 jumping beans went to 77 junior scouts on May 17.
The 7 jockeys rode 77 jumpy horses between March 17 and 27.

8 ki ki8 ki8ik 888 keys 488 kites 888 knives 788 kittens k8
My 8 kennels housed 83 dogs, 28 kids, and 88 other animals.
The 18 kind ladies tied 88 knots in the 880 pieces of rope.
The 8 men saw 88 kelp bass, 38 kingfish, and 98 king crabs.

9 lo lo9 lo9ol 999 lads 599 larks 999 ladies 699 leaders 19
All 999 leaves fell from the 9 large oaks at 389 Largemont.
The 99 linemen put 399 large rolls of tape on for 19 games.
Those 99 lawyers put 899 legal-size sheets in the 19 limos.

0 ;p ;p0 ;p0p; 100 pens 900 pages 200 pandas 800 pencils ;0
There were 1,000 people who lived in the 300 private homes.
The 10 party stores are open from 1:00 p.m. until 9:00 p.m.
They edited 500 pages in 1 book and 1,000 pages in 2 books.
```

All numbers

```
ala s2s d3d f4f f5f j6j j7j k8k 191 ;0; Add 6 and 8 and 29.
That 349-page script called for 10 actors and 18 actresses.
The check for $50 was sent to 705 Garfield Street, not 507.
The 14 researchers asked the 469 Californians 23 questions.
```

All numbers

```
ala s2s d3d f4f f5f j6j j7j k8k 191 ;0; Add 3 and 4 and 70.
They built 1,299 houses on the 345-acre site by the canyon.
Her research showed that gold was at 397 in September 2004.
For $868 extra, they bought 15 new books and 61 used books.
```

All numbers

```
ala s2s d3d f4f f5f j6j j7j k8k 191 ;0; Add 5 and 7 and 68.
A bank auditor arrived on May 26, 2004, and left on May 27.
The 4 owners open the stores from 9:30 a.m. until 6:00 p.m.
After 1,374 miles on the bus, she must then drive 185 more.
```

Progressive Practice: Alphabet

This skillbuilding routine contains a series of 30-second timed writings that range from 16wpm to 104wpm. The first time you use these timed writings, take a 1-minute timed writing with three or fewer errors on the Entry Timed Writing paragraph. Note your speed.

Select a passage that is 2wpm higher than your current speed. Then take six 30-second timed writings on the passage.

Your goal each time is to complete the passage within 30 seconds with no errors. When you have achieved your goal, move on to the next passage and repeat the procedure.

Entry Timed Writing

Bev was very lucky when she found extra quality in the home she was buying. She quietly told the builder that she was extremely satisfied with the work done on her new home. The builder said she can move into her new house next week.

11
23
35
47

| 1 | 2 | 3 | 4 | 5 | 6 | 7 | 8 | 9 | 10 | 11 | 12

16wpm
The author is the creator of a document.

18wpm
Open means to access a previously saved file.

20wpm
A byte represents one character to every computer.

22wpm
A mouse may be used when running Windows on a computer.

24wpm
Soft copy is text that is displayed on your computer screen.

26wpm
Memory is the part of the word processor that stores information.

28wpm
A menu is a list of choices to direct the operator through a function.

30wpm
A sheet feeder is a device that will insert sheets of paper into a printer.

32wpm
An icon is a small picture that illustrates a function or an object in software.

34wpm
A window is a rectangular area with borders that displays the contents of open files.

36wpm
To execute means to perform an action specified by an operator or by the computer program.

38wpm
Output is the result of a word processing operation. It can be either printed or magnetic form.

40wpm
Format refers to the physical features which affect the appearance and arrangement of your document.

42wpm

A font is a style of type of one size or kind which includes all letters, numbers, and punctuation marks.

44wpm

Ergonomics is the science of adapting working conditions or equipment to meet the physical needs of employees.

46wpm

Home position is the starting position of a document; it is typically the upper left corner of the display monitor.

48wpm

The mouse may be used to change the size of a window and to move a window to a different location on the display screen.

50wpm

An optical scanner is a device that can read text and enter it into a word processor without the need to type the data again.

52wpm

Hardware refers to the physical equipment used, such as the central processing unit, display screen, keyboard, printer, or drives.

54wpm

A peripheral device is any piece of equipment that will extend the capabilities of a computer system but is not required for operation.

56wpm

A split screen displays two or more different images at the same time; it can, for example, display two different pages of a legal document.

58wpm

When using Windows, it's possible to place several programs on a screen and to change the size of a window or to change its position on a screen.

60wpm

With the click of a mouse, one can use a button bar or a toolbar for fast access to features that are frequently applied when using a Windows program.

62wpm

An active window can be reduced to an icon when you use Windows, enabling you to double-click another icon to open a new window for formatting and editing.

64wpm

Turnaround time is the length of time needed for a document to be keyboarded, edited, proofread, corrected if required, printed, and returned to the originator.

66wpm

A local area network is a system that uses cable or another means to allow high-speed communication among many kinds of electronic equipment within particular areas.

68wpm

To search and replace means to direct the word processor to locate a character, word, or group of words wherever it occurs in the document and replace it with newer text.

70wpm

Indexing is the ability of a word processor to accumulate a list of words that appear in a document, including page numbers, and then print a revised list in alphabetic order.

72wpm

When a program needs information from you, a dialog box will appear on the desktop. Once the dialog box appears, you must identify the option you desire and then choose that option.

74wpm

A facsimile is an exact copy of a document, and it is also a process by which images, such as typed letters, graphs, and signatures, are scanned, transmitted, and then printed on paper.

76wpm

Compatibility refers to the ability of a computer to share information with another computer or to communicate with some other apparatus. It can be accomplished by using hardware or software.

78wpm

Some operators like to personalize their desktops when they use Windows by making various changes. For example, they can change their screen colors and the pointer so that they will have more fun.

80wpm

Wraparound is the ability of a word processor to move words from one line to another line and from one page to the next page as a result of inserting and deleting text or changing the size of margins.

82wpm

It is possible when using Windows to evaluate the contents of different directories on the screen at the very same time. You can then choose to copy or move a particular file from one directory to another.

84wpm

List processing is a capability of a word processor to keep lists of data that can be updated and sorted in alphabetic or numeric order. A list can also be added to any document that is stored in one's computer.

86wpm

A computer is a wondrous device, which accepts data that are input and then processes the data and produces output. The computer performs its work by using one or more stored programs, which provide the instructions.

88wpm

The configuration is the components that make up your word processing system. Most systems include the keyboard that is used for entering data, a central processing unit, at least one disk drive, a monitor, and a printer.

90wpm

Help for Windows can be used whenever you see a Help button in a dialog box or on a menu bar. Once you finish reading about a topic that you have selected, you will see a list of some related topics from which you can choose.

92wpm

When you want to look at the contents of two windows when using Windows, you will want to reduce the window size. Do this by pointing to a border or a corner of a window and dragging it until the window is the size that you want.

94wpm

Scrolling means to display a large quantity of text by rolling it horizontally or vertically past the display screen. As the text disappears from the top section of the monitor, new text will appear at the bottom section of the monitor.

96wpm

The Windows Print Manager is used to install and configure printers, join network printers, and monitor the printing of documents. Windows requires that a default printer be identified, but you can change the designation of it at any point.

98wpm

A stop code is a command that makes a printer pause while it is printing to permit an operator to insert text, change the font style, or change the kind of paper in the printer. To resume printing, the operator must use a special key or command.

100wpm

A computerized message system is a class of electronic mail that enables any operator to key a message on any computer terminal and have the message stored for later retrieval by the recipient, who can then display the message on his or her terminal.

102wpm

Many different graphics software programs have been brought on the market in recent years. These programs can be very powerful in helping with a business presentation. If there is any need to share data, using one of these programs could be quite helpful.

104wpm

Voice mail has become an essential service that many people in the business world use. This enables anyone who places a call to your phone to leave a message if you cannot answer it at that time. This special feature helps lots of workers to be more productive.

Progressive Practice: Numbers

This skillbuilding routine contains a series of 30-second timed writings that range from 16wpm to 80wpm. The first time you use these timed writings, take a 1-minute timed writing with three or fewer errors on the Entry Timed Writing paragraph. Note your speed.

Select a passage that is 4 to 6wpm *lower* than your current alphabetic speed.

(The reason for selecting a lower speed goal is that sentences with numbers are more difficult to type.) Take six 30-second timed writings on the passage.

Your goal each time is to complete the passage within 30 seconds with no errors. When you have achieved your goal, move on to the next passage and repeat the procedure.

Entry Timed Writing

Their bags were filled with 10 sets of jars, 23 cookie cutters, 4 baking pans, 6 coffee mugs, 25 plates, 9 dessert plates, 7 soup bowls, 125 recipe cards, and 8 recipe boxes. They delivered these 217 items to 20487 Mountain Boulevard.

11
23
35
47

| 1 | 2 | 3 | 4 | 5 | 6 | 7 | 8 | 9 | 10 | 11 | 12

16wpm

There were now 21 children in Room 2110.

18wpm

Fewer than 12 of the 121 boxes arrived today.

20wpm

Maybe 12 of the 21 applicants met all 15 criteria.

22wpm

There were 34 letters addressed to 434 West Cranbrooke.

24wpm

Jane reported that there were 434 freshmen and 43 transfers.

26wpm

The principal assigned 3 of those 4 students to Room 343 at noon.

28wpm

Only 1 or 2 of the 34 latest invoices were more than 1 page in length.

30wpm

They met 11 of the 12 players who received awards from 3 of the 4 trainers.

32wpm

Those 5 vans carried 46 passengers on the first trip and 65 on the next 3 trips.

34wpm

We first saw 3 and then 4 beautiful eagles on Route 65 at 5 a.m. on Tuesday, June 12.

36wpm

The 16 companies produced 51 of the 62 records that received awards for 3 of 4 categories.

38wpm

The 12 trucks hauled the 87 cows and 65 horses to the farm, which was about 21 miles northeast.

40wpm

She moved from 87 Bayview Drive to 657 Cole Street and then 3 blocks south to 412 Gulbranson Avenue.

42wpm

My 7 or 8 buyers ordered 7 dozen in sizes 5 and 6 after the 14 to 32 percent discounts had been bestowed.

44wpm

There were 34 men and 121 women waiting in line at the gates for the 65 to 87 tickets to the Cape Cod concert.

46wpm

Steve had listed 5 or 6 items on Purchase Order 241 when he saw that Purchase Requisition 87 contained 3 or 4 more.

48wpm

Your items numbered 278 will sell for about 90 percent of the value of the 16 items that have code numbers shown as 435.

50wpm

The managers stated that 98 of those 750 randomly selected new valves had about 264 defects, far exceeding the usual 31 norm.

52wpm

Half of the 625 volunteers received over 90 percent of the charity pledges. Approximately 83 of the 147 agencies will have funds.

54wpm

Merico hired 94 part-time workers to help the 378 full-time employees during the 62-day period when sales go up by 150 percent or more.

56wpm

Kaye only hit 1 for 4 in the first 29 games after an 8-game streak in which she batted 3 for 4. She then hit at a .570 average for 6 games.

58wpm

The mail carrier delivered 98 letters during the week to 734 Oak Street and also took 52 letters to 610 Faulkner Road as he returned on Route 58.

60wpm

Pat said that about 1 in 5 of the 379 swimmers had a chance of being among the top 20. The best 6 of those 48 divers will receive the 16 best awards.

62wpm

It rained from 3 to 6 inches, and 18 of those 20 farmers were fearful that 4 to 7 inches more would flood about 95 acres along 3 miles of the new Route 78.

SKILLBUILDING

64wpm

Those 7 sacks weighed 48 pounds, more than the 30 pounds that I had thought. All 24 believe the 92-pound bag is at least 15 or 16 pounds above its true weight.

66wpm

They bought 7 of the 8 options for 54 of the 63 vehicles last month. They now own over 120 dump trucks for use in 9 of the 15 new regions in the big 20-county area.

68wpm

Andy was 8 or 9 years old when they moved to 632 Glendale Street away from the 1700 block of Horseshoe Lane, which is about 45 miles directly west of Boca Raton, FL 33434.

70wpm

Doug had read 575 pages in the 760-page book by March 30; Darlene had read only 468 pages. Darlene has read 29 of those optional books since October 19, and Doug has read 18.

72wpm

That school district has 985 elementary students, 507 middle school students, and 463 high school students; the total of 1,955 is 54, or 2.84 percent, over last year's grand total.

74wpm

Attendance at last year's meeting was 10,835. The goal for this year is to have 11,764 people. This will enable us to plan for an increase of 929 participants, a rise of 8.57 percent.

76wpm

John's firm has 158 stores, located in 109 cities in the West. The company employs 3,540 males and 2,624 females, a total of 6,164 employees. About 4,750 of those employees work part-time.

78wpm

Memberships were as follows: 98 members in the Drama Guild, 90 members in Zeta Tau, 82 members in Theta Phi, 75 in the Bowling Club, and 136 in the Ski Club. This meant that 481 joined a group.

80wpm

The association had 684 members from the South, 830 members from the North, 1,023 members from the East, and 751 from the West. The total membership was 3,288; these numbers increased by 9.8 percent.

Paced Practice

The Paced Practice skillbuilding routine builds speed and accuracy in short, easy steps by using individualized goals and immediate feedback. You may use this program at any time after completing Lesson 9.

This section contains a series of 2-minute timed writings for speeds ranging from 16wpm to 96wpm. The first time you use these timed writings, take the 1-minute Entry Timed Writing with two or fewer errors.

Select a passage that is 2wpm higher than your current typing speed. Then use this two-stage practice pattern to achieve each speed goal: (1) concentrate on speed, and (2) work on accuracy.

Speed Goal. To determine your speed goal, take three 2-minute timed writings in total. Your goal each time is to complete the passage in 2 minutes without regard to errors. When you have achieved your speed goal, work on accuracy.

Accuracy Goal. To type accurately, you need to slow down—just a bit. Therefore, to reach your accuracy goal, drop back 2wpm from the previous passage. Take consecutive timed writings on this passage until you can complete the passage in 2 minutes with no more than 2 errors.

For example, if you achieved a speed goal of 54wpm, you should then work on an accuracy goal of 52wpm. When you have achieved 52wpm for accuracy, move up 4wpm (for example, to the 56-wpm passage) and work for speed again.

Entry Timed Writing

If you can dream it, you can live it. Follow your	10
heart. There are many careers, from the mundane to the	21
exotic to the sublime. Start your career planning now.	32
Prepare for the future by exploring your talents, skills,	44
and interests.	47

| 1 | 2 | 3 | 4 | 5 | 6 | 7 | 8 | 9 | 10 | 11 | 12

16wpm

Your future is now. Seize each day. After you have explored your personal interests, study the sixteen career clusters for a broad range of job possibilities.

18wpm

While exploring various job options, think about what a job means to you. A job can mean something you do simply to earn money or something you find more rewarding and challenging.

20wpm

If you have a job you enjoy, work means more than just receiving wages. It means using your talents, being among people with like interests, making a contribution, and gaining a sense of satisfaction.

22wpm

What is the difference between a job and a career? Think carefully. A job is work that people do for money. A career is a sequence of related jobs built on a foundation of interests, knowledge, training, and experiences.

24wpm

Learn more about the world of work by looking at the sixteen career clusters. Most jobs are included in one of the clusters that have been organized by the government. During your exploration of careers, list the clusters that interest you.

26wpm

Once you identify your career clusters of interest, look at the jobs within each cluster. Find out what skills and aptitudes are needed, what education and training are required, what the work environment is like, and what is the possibility for advancements.

28wpm

Use your career center and school or public libraries to research career choices. Search the Internet. Consult with professionals for another perspective of a specific career. As you gather information about career options, you may discover other interesting career possibilities.

30wpm

Gain insights into a career by becoming a volunteer, participating in an internship, or working a part-time or temporary job within a chosen field. You will become more familiar with a specific job while developing your skills. You'll gain valuable experience, whether you choose that career or not.

32wpm

Whichever path you choose, strive for a high level of pride in yourself and your work. Your image is affected by what you believe other people think of you as well as by how you view yourself. Evaluate your level of confidence in yourself. If you have self-doubts, begin to build up your self-confidence and self-esteem.

34wpm

Self-esteem is essential for a positive attitude, and a positive attitude is essential for success in the world of work. While you cannot control everything that happens at work, you can control how you react. Your attitude matters. Becoming more confident and cultivating positive thoughts can bring you power in your life and on the job.

36wpm

Several factors lead to success on the job. People who have studied the factors say that it is the personal traits that often determine who is promoted or who is not. One of the finest traits a person can possess is the trait of being likable. Being likable means a person is honest, courteous, loyal, thoughtful, pleasant, kind, and most assuredly, positive.

38wpm

If you are likable, probably you relate well with others. Your kindness serves you well in the workplace. Developing good interpersonal relationships with coworkers will make work more enjoyable. After all, think of all the hours you will spend together. By showing that you are willing to collaborate with your coworkers, most likely you will receive their cooperation in return.

40wpm

Cooperation begins on the first day of your new job. When you work for a company, you become part of the team. Meeting people and learning new skills can be exciting. For some people, however, any new situation can trigger anxiety. The best advice is to remain calm, do your job to the best of your ability, learn the workplace policies, be flexible, avoid being too critical, and always be positive.

42wpm

When you begin a new job, even if you have recently received your college diploma, chances are you will start at the bottom of the organizational chart. Each of us has to start somewhere. But don't despair. With hard work and determination, soon you will be climbing up the corporate ladder. If you are clever, you will embrace even the most tedious tasks, take everything in stride, and use every opportunity to learn.

44wpm

If you think learning is restricted to the confines of an academic institution, think again. You have plenty to learn on the job, even if it is a job for which you have been trained. As a new worker, you won't be expected to know everything. When necessary, do not hesitate to ask your employer questions. Learn all you can about your job and the company. Use the new information to enhance your job performance and to prepare for success.

46wpm

Begin every valuable workday by prioritizing all your tasks. Decide which tasks must be done immediately and which can wait. List the most important tasks first; then determine the order in which each task must be done. After you complete a task, triumphantly cross it off your priority list. Do not procrastinate; that is, don't put off work you should do. If a task needs to be done, do it. You will be on top of your task list if you use your time wisely.

48wpm

Prevent the telephone from controlling your time by learning to manage your business phone calls. Phone calls can be extremely distracting from necessary tasks. When making an outgoing call, organize the topics you want to discuss. Gather needed materials such as pencils, papers, and files. Set a time limit, and stick to business. Give concise answers, summarize the points discussed, and end the conversation politely. Efficient telephone usage will help you manage your time.

50wpm

As with anything, practice makes perfect, but along the way, we all make mistakes. The difference between the successful people and those who are less successful is not that the successful people make fewer mistakes. It's that they don't give up. Instead of letting mistakes bring them down, they use their mistakes as opportunities to grow. If you make a mistake, be patient with yourself. You might be able to fix your mistake. Look for more opportunities for success to be just around the corner.

52wpm

Be patient with yourself when handling problems and accepting criticism. Handling criticism gracefully and maturely may be a challenge. Still, it is vital in the workplace. Criticism presented in a way that can help you learn and grow is constructive criticism . When you see criticism as helpful, it's easier to handle. Believe it or not, there are some employees who welcome criticism. It teaches them better ways to succeed on the job. Strive to improve how you accept constructive criticism, and embrace your growth.

54wpm

People experience continuous growth during a career. Goal setting is a helpful tool along any career path. Some people believe that goals provide the motivation needed to get to the place they want to be. Setting goals encourages greater achievements. The higher we set our goals, the greater the effort we will need to reach these goals. Each time we reach a target or come closer to a goal, we see an increase in our confidence and our performance, leading to greater accomplishments. And the cycle continues to spiral onward and upward.

56wpm

One goal we should all strive for is punctuality. When employees are tardy or absent from the workplace, it costs the company money. If you are frequently tardy or absent, others have to do their own work and cover for you. If you are absent often, your peers will begin to resent you, causing everyone stress in the department. Being late and missing work can damage the relationship with your manager and have a negative effect on your career. To avoid these potential problems, develop a personal plan to assure that you arrive every day on time or early.

58wpm

Holding a job is a major part of being an adult. Some people begin their work careers as adolescents. From the beginning, various work habits are developed that are as crucial to success as the actual job skills and knowledge that a person brings to the job. What traits are expected of workers? What do employers look for when they evaluate their employees? Important personal traits include being confident, cooperative, positive, and dependable. If you are organized, enthusiastic, and understanding, you have many of the qualities that employers value most in their employees.

60wpm

Being dependable is a desirable trait. When a project must be completed by a specific time, a manager will be reassured to know that reliable workers are going to meet the deadline. Workers who are dependable learn to utilize their time to achieve maximum results. Dependable workers can always be counted on, have good attendance records, are well prepared, and arrive on time ready to work. If a company wants to meet its goals, it must have a team of responsible and dependable workers. You, your coworkers, your supervisors, and your managers are all team members, working to reach common goals.

62wpm

The ability to organize is an important quality for the employee who wishes to display good work habits. The worker should have the ability to plan the work that needs to be completed and then be able to execute the plan in a timely manner. An employer requires a competent worker to be well organized. If an office worker is efficient, he or she handles requests swiftly and deals with correspondence without delay. The organized worker does not allow work to accumulate on the desk. Also, the organized office worker returns all phone calls immediately and makes lists of the activities that need to be done each day.

64wpm

Efficiency is another work habit that is desired. An efficient worker completes a task quickly and begins work on the next project eagerly. He or she thinks about ways to save steps and time. For example, an efficient worker may plan a single trip to the copier with several copying jobs rather than multiple trips to do each separate job. Being efficient also means having the required supplies to successfully complete each job. An efficient employee zips along on each project, uses time wisely, and stays focused on the present task. With careful and thorough planning, a worker who is efficient can accomplish more tasks in less time.

66wpm

Cooperation is another ideal work habit. As previously mentioned, cooperation begins on the first day on the job. Cooperation is thinking of all team members when making a decision. A person who cooperates is willing to do what is necessary for the good of the whole group. For you to be a team player, it is essential that you take extra steps to cooperate. Cooperation may mean being a good sport if you are asked to do something you would rather not do. It may mean you have to correct a mistake made by another person in the office. If every employee has the interests of the company at heart and works well as a team player, then cooperation is at work.

68wpm

Enthusiasm is still another work trait that is eagerly sought after by employers. Being enthusiastic means that a person has lots of positive energy. This is reflected in actions toward your work, coworkers, and employer. It has been noted that eagerness can be catching. If workers show they are eager to attempt any project, they will not only achieve the highest praise but will also be considered for career advancement. How much enthusiasm do you show at the workplace? Do you encourage people or complain to people? There will always be plenty of good jobs for employees who are known to have a wealth of zeal and a positive approach to the projects that they are assigned.

70wpm

Understanding is also a preferred work habit for every excellent worker. In today's world, virtually all business includes both men and women of different religions, races, cultures, work ethic, abilities, aptitudes, and attitudes. You'll interact with various types of people as customers, coworkers, and owners. Treat everyone fairly, openly, and honestly. Any type of prejudice is hurtful, offensive, and unacceptable. Prejudice cannot be tolerated in the office. Each employee must try to understand and accept everyone's differences. Because so many diverse groups of people work side by side in the workplace, it is essential that all coworkers maintain a high degree of mutual understanding.

72wpm

It can be concluded that certain work habits or traits can play a major role in determining the success of an employee. Most managers would be quick to agree on the importance of these traits. It is most probable that these habits would be evaluated on performance appraisal forms. Promotions, pay increases, new responsibilities, and your future with the company may be based on these evaluations. You should request regular job performance evaluations even if your company does not conduct them. This feedback will improve your job performance and career development by helping you grow. If you continually look for ways to improve your work habits and skills, then you will enjoy success in the workplace and beyond.

74wpm

You can be certain that no matter where you work, you will use some form of computer technology. Almost every business is dependent upon computers. Companies use such devices as voice mail, fax machines, cellular phones, and electronic schedules. Technology helps to accomplish work quickly and efficiently. A result of this rapidly changing technology is globalization, which is the establishment of worldwide communication links between people. Our world is becoming a smaller, global village. We must expand our thinking beyond the office walls. We must become aware of what happens in other parts of the world. Those events may directly affect you and your workplace. The more you know, the more valuable you will become to the company.

76wpm

Technological advancements are affecting every aspect of our lives. For example, the advent of the Internet has changed how we receive and send information. It is the world's largest information network. The Internet is often called the information superhighway because it is a vast network of computers that connect people and resources worldwide. It is an exciting medium to help you access the latest information. You can even learn about companies by visiting their Web sites. Without any doubt, we are all globally connected, and information technology services support those necessary connections. This industry offers many different employment opportunities. Keep in mind that proficiency in keyboarding is beneficial in this field and in other fields.

78wpm

It is amazing to discover the many careers in which keyboarding skill is necessary today, and the use of the computer keyboard by executive chefs is a prime example. The chefs in major restaurants must prepare parts or all of the meals served while directing the work of a staff of chefs, cooks, and other kitchen staff. The computer has become a necessary tool for a variety of tasks, including tracking inventories of food supplies. By observing which items are favorites and which items are not requested, the chef can calculate food requirements, order food, and supervise the food purchases. Additionally, the computer has proven to be a very practical tool for such tasks as planning budgets, preparing purchase orders for vendors, creating menus, and printing out reports.

80wpm

Advanced technology has opened the doors to a wider variety of amazing new products and services to sell. It seems the more complex the products, the higher the price of the products, or the greater the sales commission, the stiffer the competition. Selling these technical products requires detailed product knowledge, good verbal skills, smooth sales rapport, and proficient keyboarding skills. Business favors people with special training. For example, a pharmacy company may prefer a person with knowledge in chemistry to sell its products. Selling is for people who thrive on challenges and changes in products and services. Sales is appealing to people who enjoy using their powers of persuasion to make the sales. The potential for good earnings is very high for the well-trained salesperson.

82wpm

As you travel about in your sales job or type a report at the office or create Friday night's pasta special for your five-star restaurant, always remember to put safety first. Accidents happen, but they don't have to happen regularly or to have such serious consequences. Accidents cost businesses billions of dollars annually in medical expenses, lost wages, and insurance claims. A part of your job is to make certain you're not one of the millions of people injured on the job every year. You may believe you work in a safe place, but accidents occur in all types of businesses. A few careless people cause most accidents, so ensure your safety on the job. Safety doesn't just happen. Safety is the result of the careful awareness of many people who plan and put into action a safety program that benefits everyone.

84wpm

In today's market, you need more than the necessary skill or the personal qualities described above to succeed in the workplace. Employers also expect their employees to have ethics. Ethics are the principles of conduct governing an individual or a group. Employees who work ethically do not lie, cheat, or steal. They are honest and fair in their dealings with others. Employees who act ethically build a good reputation for themselves and their company. They are known to be dependable and trustworthy. Unethical behavior can have a spiraling effect. A single act can do a lot of damage. Even if you haven't held a job yet, you have had experience with ethical problems. Life is full of many opportunities to behave ethically. Do the right thing when faced with a decision. The ethics you practice today will carry over to your workplace.

86wpm

Now that you know what is expected of you on the job, how do you make sure you will get the job? Almost everyone has experienced the interview process for a job. For some, the interview is a traumatic event, but it doesn't have to be stressful. Preparation is the key. Research the company with whom you are seeking employment. Formulate a list of questions. Your interview provides you the opportunity to interview the organization. Don't go empty-handed. Take a portfolio of items with you. Include copies of your resume with a list of three or more professional references, your academic transcript, and your certificates and licenses. Be sure to wear appropriate business attire. The outcome of the interview will be positive if you have enthusiasm for the job, match your qualifications to the company's needs, ask relevant questions, and listen clearly.

88wpm

How can you be the strongest candidate for the job? Be sure that your skills in reading, writing, mathematics, speaking, and listening are solid. These basic skills will help you listen well and communicate clearly, not only during a job interview, but also at your workplace. The exchange of information between senders and receivers is called communication. It doesn't matter which occupation you choose; you will spend most of your career using these basic skills to communicate with others. You will use the basic skills as tools to gain information, solve problems, and share ideas. You will use these skills to meet the needs of your customers. The majority of jobs available during the next decades will be in the industries that will require direct customer contacts. Your success will be based upon your ability to communicate effectively with customers and coworkers.

90wpm

Writing effectively can help you gain a competitive edge in your job search and throughout your career. Most of us have had occasion to write business letters whether to apply for a job, to comment on a product or service, or to place an order. Often it seems easy to sit and let our thoughts flow freely. In other cases, we seem to struggle to find the proper wording while trying to express our thoughts in exactly the right way. Writing skill can improve with practice. Implement the following principles to develop your writing skill. Try to use language that you would be comfortable using in person. Use words that are simple, direct, kind, confident, and professional. When possible, use words that emphasize the positive side. Remember to proofread your work. Well-organized thoughts and proper grammar, spelling, and punctuation show the reader that you care about the quality of your work.

92wpm

Listening is an essential skill of the communication process. It is crucial for learning, getting along, and forming relationships. Do you think you are an active or passive listener? Listening is not a passive activity. Conversely, active listening is hearing what is being said and interpreting its meaning. Active listening makes you a more effective communicator because you react to what you have heard. Study the following steps to increase your listening skills. Do not cut people off; let them develop their ideas before you speak. If a message is vague, write down your questions or comments, and wait for the entire presentation or discussion to be finished. Reduce personal and environmental distractions by focusing on the message. Keep an open mind. Be attentive and maintain eye contact whenever possible. By developing these basic communication skills, you will become more confident and more effective.

94wpm

Speaking is also a form of communication. In the world of work, speaking is an important way in which to share information. Regardless of whether you are speaking to an audience of one or one hundred, you will want to make sure that your listeners get your message. Be clear about your purpose, your audience, and your subject. A purpose is the overall goal or reason for speaking. An audience is anyone who receives information. The subject is the main topic or key idea. Research your subject. Using specific facts and examples will give you credibility. As you speak, be brief and direct. Progress logically from point to point. Speak slowly and pronounce clearly all your words. Do people understand what you say or ask you to repeat what you've said? Is the sound of your voice friendly and pleasant or shrill and off-putting? These factors influence how your message is received. A good idea is worthless if you can't communicate it.

96wpm

Developing a career is a process. You have looked at your interests, values, skills, aptitudes, and attitudes. Your exploration into the world of work has begun. The journey doesn't stop here, for the present is the perfect place to start thinking about the future. It's where you begin to take steps toward your goals. It's where you can really make a difference. As you set personal and career goals, remember the importance of small steps. Each step toward a personal goal or career goal is a small victory. That feeling of success encourages you to take other small steps. Each step builds onto the next. Continue exploring your personal world as well as the world you share with others. Expect the best as you go forward. Expect a happy life. Expect loving relationships. Expect success in life. Expect fulfilling and satisfying work in a job you truly love. Last but not least, expect that you have something special to offer the world, because you do.

Supplementary Timed Writings

All problem solving, whether personal or academic, 10
involves decision making. You make decisions in order to 21
solve problems. On occasion, problems occur as a result of 33
decisions you have made. For example, you may decide to 44
smoke, but later in life, you face the problem of nicotine 56
addiction. You may decide not to study mathematics and 67
science because you think that they are too difficult. 78
Because of this choice, many career opportunities will be 90
closed to you. There is a consequence for every action. Do 102
you see that events in your life do not just happen, but 113
that they are the result of your choices and decisions? 124

How can you prepare your mind for problem solving? A 135
positive attitude is a great start. Indeed, your attitude 147
affects the way in which you solve a problem or make a 158
decision. Approach your studies, such as science and math 170
courses, with a positive and inquisitive attitude. Try to 182
perceive academic problems as puzzles to solve rather than 192
homework to avoid. 198

Critical thinking is a method of problem solving that 209
involves decoding, analyzing, reasoning, evaluating, and 220
processing information. It is fundamental for successful 231
problem solving. Critical thinking is a willingness to 242
explore, probe, question, and search for answers. Problems 254
may not always be solved on the first try. Don't give up. 266
Try, try again. Finding a solution takes sustained effort. 278
Use critical thinking skills to achieve success in today's 290
fast-paced and highly competitive world of business. 300

| 1 | 2 | 3 | 4 | 5 | 6 | 7 | 8 | 9 | 10 | 11 | 12

For many, the Internet is an important resource in 10
their private and professional lives. The Internet provides 22
quick access to countless Web sites that contain news, 33
products, games, entertainment, and many other types of 44
information. The Web pages on these sites can be designed, 56
authored, and posted by anyone, anywhere around the world. 68
Utilize critical thinking when reviewing all Web sites. 79

Just because something is stated on the radio, printed 90
in the newspaper, or shown on television doesn't mean that 102
it's true, real, accurate, or correct. This applies to 113
information found on the Internet as well. Don't fall into 125
the trap of believing that if it's on the Net, it must be 137
true. A wise user of the Internet thinks critically about 149
data found on the Net and evaluates this material before 160
using it. 162

When evaluating a new Web site, think about who, what, 173
how, when, and where. Who refers to the author of the Web 185
site. The author may be a business, an organization, or a 197
person. What refers to the validity of the data. Can this 209
data be verified by a reputable source? How refers to the 221
viewpoint of the author. Is the data presented without 232
prejudice? When refers to the time frame of the data. Is 244
this recent data? Where refers to the source of the data. 256
Is this data from an accurate source? By answering these 267
critical questions, you will learn more about the accuracy 279
and dependability of a Web site. As you surf the Net, be 290
very cautious. Anyone can publish on the Internet. 300

| 1 | 2 | 3 | 4 | 5 | 6 | 7 | 8 | 9 | 10 | 11 | 12

**Supplementary
Timed Writing 3**

Office employees perform a variety of tasks during 10
their workday. These tasks vary from handling telephone 21
calls to forwarding personal messages, from sending short 33
e-mail messages to compiling complex office reports, and 44
from writing simple letters to assembling detailed letters 56
with tables, graphics, and imported data. Office workers 67
are a fundamental part of a company's structure. 77

The office worker uses critical thinking in order to 88
accomplish a wide array of daily tasks. Some of the tasks 100
are more urgent than other tasks and should be completed 111
first. Some tasks take only a short time, while others take 123
a lot more time. Some tasks demand a quick response, while 135
others may be taken up as time permits or even postponed 147
until the future. Some of the tasks require input from 158
coworkers or managers. Whether a job is simple or complex, 170
big or small, the office worker must decide what is to be 182
tackled first by determining the priority of each task. 193

When setting priorities, critical thinking skills are 204
essential. The office worker evaluates each aspect of the 216
task. It is a good idea to identify the size of the task, 228
determine its complexity, estimate its effort, judge its 239
importance, and set its deadline. Once the office worker 250
assesses each task that is to be finished within a certain 262
period of time, then the priority for completing all tasks 274
can be set. Critical thinking skills, if applied well, 285
can save the employer money or, if executed poorly, can 296
cost the employer. 300

| 1 | 2 | 3 | 4 | 5 | 6 | 7 | 8 | 9 | 10 | 11 | 12

SKILLBUILDING

Each day business managers make choices that keep 10
businesses running smoothly, skillfully, and profitably. 21
Each decision regarding staff, finances, operations, and 32
resources often needs to be quick and precise. To develop 44
sound decisions, managers must use critical thinking. They 56
gather all the essential facts so that they can make good, 68
well-informed choices. After making a decision, skilled 79
managers review their thinking process. Over time, they 90
refine their critical thinking skills. When they encounter 102
similar problems, they use their prior experiences to help 114
them solve problems with ease and in less time. 124

What type of decisions do you think managers make that 135
involve critical thinking? Human resources managers decide 147
whom to employ, what to pay a new employee, and where to 158
place a new worker. In addition, human resources managers 170
should be unbiased negotiators, resolving conflict between 182
other employees. Office managers purchase copy machines, 194
computers, software, and office supplies. Finance officers 206
prepare precise, timely financial statements. Top managers 218
control business policies, appoint mid-level managers, and 230
assess the success of the business. Plant supervisors set 242
schedules, gauge work quality, and evaluate workers. Sales 254
managers study all of the new sales trends, as well as 265
provide sales training and promotion materials. 275

Most managers use critical thinking to make wise, well- 286
thought-out decisions. They carefully check their facts, 297
analyze these facts, and make a final judgment based upon 309
these facts. They should also be able to clearly discern 320
fact from fiction. Through trial and error, managers learn 332
their own ways of solving problems and finding the most 343
effective and creative solutions. 350

| 1 | 2 | 3 | 4 | 5 | 6 | 7 | 8 | 9 | 10 | 11 | 12

In most classes, teachers want students to analyze 10
situations, draw conclusions, and solve problems. Each 21
of these tasks requires students to use thinking skills. 32
How do students acquire these skills? What is the process 44
students follow to develop thinking skills? 53

During the early years of life, children learn words 63
and then combine these words into sentences. From there, 74
they learn to declare ideas, share thoughts, and express 85
feelings. Students learn numbers and simple math concepts. 97
They may learn to read musical notes, to keep rhythm, to 108
sing songs, and to recognize many popular and classical 119
pieces of music. Students learn colors, identify shapes, 130
and begin drawing. During the early years, students learn 142
the basic problem-solving models. 149

One way to solve problems and apply thinking skills 159
is to use the scientific approach. This approach requires 171
the student to state the problem to be solved, gather all 183
the facts about the problem, analyze the problem, and pose 195
viable solutions. Throughout this process, teachers ask 206
questions that force students to expand their thinking 217
skills. Teachers may ask questions such as these: Did you 229
clearly state the problem? Did you get all the facts? Did 241
you get the facts from the right place? Did you assume 252
anything? Did you pose other possible solutions? Did you 263
keep an open mind to all solutions? Did you let your bias 275
come into play? Did you listen to others who might have 286
insights? Did you dig deep enough? Does the solution make 298
sense to you? 301

This simple four-step process for solving problems 311
gives students a model to use for school, for work, and 322
for life. While the process may not be used to solve every 334
problem, it does provide a starting point to begin using 345
critical thinking skills. 350

| 1 | 2 | 3 | 4 | 5 | 6 | 7 | 8 | 9 | 10 | 11 | 12

SKILLBUILDING

A major goal for nearly all educators is to teach 10
critical thinking skills to a class. Critical thinking, 21
which is the process of reasonably or logically deciding 32
what to do or believe, involves the ability to compare and 44
contrast, resolve problems, make decisions, analyze and 55
evaluate, and combine and transfer knowledge. These skills 67
benefit the student who eventually becomes a part of the 78
workforce. Whether someone is in a corporate setting, is 89
in a small business, or is self-employed, the environment 101
of today is highly competitive and skilled employees are in 113
great demand. 116

One factor in achieving success in the workforce is 127
having the ability to deal with the varied demands of the 139
fast-paced business world. Required skills are insightful 150
decision making, creative problem solving, and earnest 162
communication among diverse groups. These groups could be 174
employees, management, employers, investors, customers, 185
or clients. 187

In school, we learn the details of critical thinking. 198
This knowledge extends far beyond the boundaries of the 209
classroom. It lasts a lifetime. We use critical thinking 220
throughout our daily lives. We constantly analyze and 231
evaluate music, movies, conversations, fashion, magazine 242
or newspaper articles, and television programs. We all had 254
experience using critical thinking skills before we even 265
knew what they were. So keep on learning, growing, and 276
experimenting. The classroom is the perfect setting for 287
exploration. Take this opportunity to see how others solve 299
problems, give each other feedback, and try out new ideas 311
in a safe environment. 316

A person who has learned critical thinking skills is 327
equipped with the essential skills for achieving success 338
in today's workforce. There are always new goals to reach. 350

| 1 | 2 | 3 | 4 | 5 | 6 | 7 | 8 | 9 | 10 | 11 | 12

**Supplementary
Timed Writing 7**

Use your unique creativity when applying critical   10
thinking skills. One of the first steps in unlocking your   22
creativity is to realize that you have control over your   33
thinking; it doesn't control you. Creativity is using new   45
or different methods to solve problems. Many inventions   56
involved a breakthrough in traditional thinking, and the   67
result was an amazing experience. For example, Einstein   78
broke with tradition by trying lots of obscure formulas   89
that changed scientific thought. Your attitude can form   100
mental blocks that keep you from being creative. When you   112
free your mind, the rest will follow.   120

Do your best to unleash your mind's innate creativity.   131
Turn problems into puzzles. When you think of a task as a   143
puzzle, a challenge, or a game instead of a difficult   154
problem, you open your mind and encourage your creative   165
side to operate. Creative ideas often come when you are   176
having fun and are involved in an unrelated activity.   187
You will find that when your defenses are down, your brain   199
is relaxed and your subconscious is alive; then creative   210
thoughts can flow.   214

Habit often restricts you from trying new approaches   225
to problem solving. Remember, there is usually more than   237
one solution. Empty your mind of the idea of only one way   249
of looking at a problem and strive to see situations in a   261
fresh, new way. How many times have you told yourself that   273
you must follow the rules and perform tasks in a certain   284
way? If you want to be creative, look at things in a new   295
way, break the pattern, explore new options, and challenge   307
the rules. If you are facing a difficult problem and can't   319
seem to find a solution, take a quick walk or relax for   330
a few minutes; then go back to the problem renewed. When   341
working on homework or taking a test, always work the   352
easiest problems first. Success builds success.   362

A sense of humor is key to being creative. Silly and   373
irrelevant ideas can lead to inventive solutions. Humor   384
generates ideas, puts you in a creative state of mind,   395
and makes work exciting!   400

| 1 | 2 | 3 | 4 | 5 | 6 | 7 | 8 | 9 | 10 | 11 | 12

SKILLBUILDING

Keyboarding is a popular business course for many 10
students. The major objectives of a keyboarding course are 22
to develop touch control of the keyboard and proper typing 34
techniques, build basic speed and accuracy, and provide 45
practice in applying those basic skills to the formatting 57
of letters, reports, tables, memos, and other kinds of 68
personal and business communications. In the early part of 80
a keyboarding course, students learn to stroke by touch 91
using specific techniques. They learn to hit the keys in a 103
quick and accurate way. After the keys are learned and 114
practiced, students move into producing documents of all 125
sizes and types for personal and vocational use. 135

When you first learn keyboarding, there are certain 145
parameters, guidelines, and exercises to follow. There are 157
rules intended to help you learn and eventually master the 169
keyboard. Creating documents requires students to apply 180
critical thinking. What format or layout should be used? 191
What font and font size would be best? Are all the words 202
spelled correctly? Does the document look neat? Are the 213
figures accurate? Are punctuation and grammar correct? 224

There is a lot to learn in the world of keyboarding. 235
Be persistent, patient, and gentle with yourself. Allow 246
failure in class and on the job; that's how we learn. It's 258
okay to admit mistakes. Mistakes are stepping-stones for 269
growth and creativity. Being creative has a lot to do with 281
risk taking and courage. It takes courage to explore new 292
ways of thinking and to risk looking different, being 303
silly and impractical, and even being wrong. Your path to 315
creativity is such a vital component of your critical 326
thinking skills. Allow your creative thoughts to flow 337
freely when producing each of your keyboarding tasks. 348

Keyboarding skill and personal creativity are valuable 359
attributes for life and on the job. The worker who can see 371
situations and problems in a fresh way, reason logically, 383
explore options, and come up with inventive ideas is sure 395
to be a valuable employee. 400

| 1 | 2 | 3 | 4 | 5 | 6 | 7 | 8 | 9 | 10 | 11 | 12

**Supplementary
Timed Writing 9**

One of the most important decisions we all have to | 10
face is choosing a career. The possibilities can appear | 21
overwhelming. Fear not! Your critical thinking skills will | 33
save you! Start your career planning today. Begin with | 44
self-assessment. What are your interests? Do you enjoy | 55
working indoors or outdoors? Do you prefer working with | 66
numbers or with words? Are you the independent type or | 77
would you rather work with a group? What are your favorite | 89
academic studies? Think about these questions and then | 100
create a list of your interests, skills, aptitudes, and | 111
values. What you discover about yourself will help you in | 123
finding the career that is right for you. | 131

After you have explored your personal interests, look | 142
at the sixteen career clusters for a wide range of job | 153
prospects. Most jobs are included in one of these clusters | 165
that have been organized by the government. During your | 176
exploration, make a note of the clusters that interest you | 188
and investigate these clusters. | 194

Gather as much information as possible by using all | 205
available resources. Scan the Help Wanted section in the | 216
major Sunday newspapers for job descriptions and salaries. | 228
Search the Net. The Internet provides electronic access to | 240
worldwide job listings. If you want to know more about a | 251
specific company, access its home page. Go to your college | 263
placement office. Sign up for interviews with companies | 274
that visit your campus. Visit your local school or county | 286
library and ask the reference librarian for occupational | 297
handbooks. Talk with people in your field of interest to | 308
ask questions and get advice. Attend chapter meetings of | 319
professional organizations to network with people working | 331
in your chosen profession. Volunteer, intern, or work a | 342
part-time or temporary job within your career choice for | 353
valuable, first-hand insight. Taking an initiative in your | 365
job search will pay off. | 370

A career search requires the use of critical thinking | 381
skills. These skills will help you to choose the career | 392
that will match your skills and talents. | 400

| 1 | 2 | 3 | 4 | 5 | 6 | 7 | 8 | 9 | 10 | 11 | 12

Appendix

Ten-Key Numeric Keypad

Goal

- To control the ten-key numeric keypad keys.

Some computer keyboards have a separate ten-key numeric keypad located to the right of the alphanumeric keyboard. The arrangement of the keypad enables you to type numbers more rapidly than you can when using the top row of the alphanumeric keyboard.

To input numbers using the ten-key numeric keypad, you must activate the Num Lock (Numeric Lock) key. Usually, an indicator light signals that the Num Lock is activated.

On the keypad, 4, 5, and 6 are the home keys. Place your fingers on the keypad home row as follows:

- First finger (J finger) on 4
- Second finger (K finger) on 5
- Third finger (L finger) on 6

The keypad keys are controlled as follows:

- First finger controls 1, 4, and 7
- Second finger controls 2, 5, and 8
- Third finger controls 3, 6, 9, and decimal point

- Right thumb controls 0
- Fourth finger controls ENTER

Since different computers have different arrangements of ten-key numeric keypads, study the arrangement of your keypad. The illustration shows the most common arrangement. If your keypad is arranged differently from the one shown in the illustration, check with your instructor for the correct placement of your fingers on the keypad.

NEW KEYS

A. THE 4, 5, AND 6 KEYS

A. Use the first finger to control the 4 key, the second finger to control the 5 key, and the third finger to control the 6 key.

Keep your eyes on the copy.

Before beginning, check to be sure the Num Lock key is activated.

Type the first column from top to bottom. Next, type the second column; then type the third column. Press ENTER after typing the final digit of each number.

444	456	454
555	654	464
666	445	546
455	446	564
466	554	654
544	556	645
566	664	666
644	665	555
655	456	444
456	654	456

B. Use the 4 finger to control the 7 key, the 5 finger to control the 8 key, and the 6 finger to control the 9 key.

Keep your eyes on the copy.

Press ENTER after typing the final digit of each number.

B. THE 7, 8, AND 9 KEYS

474	585	696
747	858	969
774	885	996
447	558	669
744	855	966
477	588	699
444	555	666
747	858	969
774	885	996
747	858	969

C. Use the 4 finger to control the 1 key, the 5 finger to control the 2 key, and the 6 finger to control the 3 key.

Keep your eyes on the copy.

Press ENTER after typing the final digit of each number.

C. THE 1, 2, AND 3 KEYS

444	555	666
111	222	333
144	225	336
441	552	663
144	255	366
411	522	633
444	555	666
414	525	636
141	252	363
411	525	636

D. Use the right thumb to control the 0 key.

D. THE *0* KEY

Keep your eyes on the copy.

Press ENTER after typing the final digit of each number.

404	470	502
505	580	603
606	690	140
707	410	250
808	520	360
909	630	701
101	407	802
202	508	903
303	609	405
505	401	506

E. Use the 6 finger to control the decimal key.

E. THE . KEY

Keep your eyes on the copy.

Press ENTER after typing the final digit of each number.

4.5	7.8	1.2
6.5	9.8	3.2
4.4	7.7	1.1
4.4	7.7	1.1
5.5	8.8	2.2
5.5	8.8	2.2
6.6	9.9	3.3
6.5	9.9	3.3
4.5	7.8	1.2
6.5	8.9	1.3

INDEX

NOTE: Page numbers preceded by A- indicate material in Appendix; page numbers preceded by R- indicate material in Reference Manual; page numbers preceded by SB- indicate material in Skillbuilding supplement.